APPLIED HUMAN RELATIONS

AN ORGANIZATIONAL AND SKILL DEVELOPMENT APPROACH

Sixth Edition

Douglas A. Benton
with the assistance of Mary L. Tucker
both of Colorado State University

Prentice Hall, Upper Saddle River, New Jersey 07458

Library of Congress Cataloging-in-Publication data

Benton, Douglas,
    Applied human relations: an organizational and skill development approach/Douglas A.
  Benton.—6th ed.
     p. cm.
    Includes bibliographical references and index
    ISBN 0-13-755919-4
    1. Organizational behavior.   2. Management.   3. Personnel
management. I. Title
  HD58.7.B463 1998
  658.3—dc21

Acquisition editor: Elizabeth Sugg
Editorial/production supervision: Lori Harvey
Managing editor: Mary Carnis
Director of production and manufacturing: Bruce Johnson
Marketing manager: Danny Hoyt
Interior design: Carlisle Communications, Ltd.
Electronic page make-up: Carlisle Communications, Ltd.
Cover design: Marianne Frasco
Manufacturing buyer: Ed O'Dougherty
Editorial assistant: Emily Jones

Chapter 5 and Chapter 15 opening photographs used with the permission of:
Robert A. Isaacs/Photo Researchers and Jeffrey Blackman/The Stock Market.

 ©1998, 1995, 1991, 1987, 1983, 1978 by Prentice-Hall, Inc.
Simon & Schuster/A Viacom Company
Upper Saddle River, New Jersey 07458

Printed in the United States of America

10 9 8 7 6 5 4 3 2

ISBN 0-13-755919-4

Prentice-Hall International (UK) Limited, *London*
Prentice-Hall of Australia Pty. Limited, *Sydney*
Prentice-Hall Canada Inc., *Toronto*
Prentice-Hall Hispanoamericana, S.A., *Mexico*
Prentice-Hall of India Private Limited, *New Delhi*
Prentice-Hall of Japan, Inc., *Tokyo*
Simon & Schuster Asia Pte. Ltd., *Singapore*
Editora Prentice-Hall do Brasil, Ltda., *Rio de Janeiro*

CONTENTS

4   PERSONAL PROBLEMS AND COUNSELING: ALCOHOL, DRUGS, AND SEX   95

5   HUMAN MOTIVATION   127

6   JOB PERFORMANCE AND MORALE   159

PART THREE: GROUP CHALLENGES: GETTING TO KNOW AND INTERACTING WITH OTHERS   191

7   INTERPERSONAL AND INFORMAL COMMUNICATION   192

8   ORGANIZATIONAL DESIGN AND FORMAL COMMUNICATION   221

12 ORIENTATION, TRAINING, AND DISCIPLINE   339

13 APPRAISALS, PROMOTIONS, AND DISMISSALS   371

14 CREATIVITY AND INNOVATION IN DECISION MAKING   406

**PART FIVE: ORGANIZATIONAL DYNAMICS AND CULTURE: WE CHANGE AND GET
TO KNOW OUR ORGANIZATIONS, SOCIETIES, AND CULTURE   443**

15   MANAGING CHANGE THROUGH TEAMWORK   444

16   JOB AND PAY DISCRIMINATION   475

PREFACE

The sixth edition of this book reflects the changes in the current and future trends of human relations within organizations. The emphasis on *applied* human and organizational behavior continues, and there is additional concentration on *skill development* as reflected in the book's subtitle.

As in previous editions, the book is designed to meet the needs of popular courses taught in junior colleges, four-year colleges, universities, adult education and extension programs, and management training seminars. The direct, straightforward language used attempts to emphasize the person in the organization rather than traditional theories of management philosophy. It is not a book on organizational theory, office management, or supervision. Rather, it is about the daily interactions between leaders/managers and other employees.

NEW AND REVISED TOPICS

Major parts of the sixth edition include new and updated information. The user-friendly, logical flow of chapters is unchanged. New and expanded material includes major additions on communications and management in virtual organizations, conflict management, and expanded discussions on quality management, service orientation, selective teamwork, diversity, values, and leadership.

Specifically, this edition incorporates new and increased emphasis on the following topics:

- Personal performance and organizational productivity
- Teamwork and "people skills"
- Personal values including attitude, humor, courtesy, compassion, and dependability
- Organizational values including equity/fairness, teamwork and cooperation, entrepreneurship, and risk-taking
- Combined personal and organizational values including business and work ethics, honesty and integrity, and mutual trust and respect
- Career planning and development
- Positive stress and stress management
- Anger control and burnout avoidance
- Time management
- Alcoholism and drug abuses
- Sexual harassment and its prevention
- Employee assistance programs
- Approaches to motivation and job design
- Approaches to performance appraisal and measurement
- Job performance and rewarding results
- Improved communication techniques
- Improving listening and understanding
- How to diminish communication barriers

- Communications in cyberspace: electronic communications and virtual organizations
- How to obtain group consensus
- Conflict management
- Sources and types of power
- Office politics
- Catalytic leadership
- Delegation do's and don'ts
- Job orientation, positive discipline, and commitment
- 360-degree feedback
- Decision making, mistakes, and risk-taking
- Change management
- Sociometry and sociograms
- Women in the workforce
- Prejudices, antidiscrimination measures, and diversity
- Employee relations in both nonunion and union organizations including alternative dispute resolution, employee involvement programs, and grievance handling
- Arbitration, mediation, and conciliation in both nonunion and union organizations
- Individuals working in the "shrinking world" of global organizations
- Models of comparative, cross-cultural management
- What organizations and individuals can do to improve their effectiveness in global settings

NEW AND EXPANDED FEATURES

The material was written to develop the types of skills and thinking that lead to a more effective organization. To this end, each chapter is introduced with To *Start* You Thinking questions and Learning Goals, followed by Self-Appraisals, Express Your Opinion, other experiential exercises, and Action Projects. Because human relations means self-discovery and interchange among persons, the more participative the class can become, the more the students can learn from each experience.

Each chapter closes with summaries, endnotes, and recommended readings, as well as case studies that can be used during class or as outside assignments. All the case studies are based on real-life experiences. Marginal notes identify important information within the paragraphs. They are ideal for reviewing the chapter or finding necessary material.

Each chapter contains relevant examples and illustrative anecdotes. Specific features in this edition include the incorporation of the Action Projects into the text, highlighting and definition of key terms and concepts as they occur in the text (as well as in the end-of-text glossary), and an expanded feature—Profiles of Human Behavior. These profiles are real-world examples of individuals at various organizational levels, and their human behaviors that relate to concepts presented in the chapter. Discussion and study questions—To *Keep* You Thinking—are included at the end of each chapter.

Almost half of the profiles of human behavior, action projects, cases, and other exercises are new or substantially modified in this edition. An Instructor's Manual and Test Item File are available with classroom-tested questions, other learning aids, and transparency masters.

In summary, the chapters contain

1. To *Start* You Thinking questions
2. Learning Goals
3. Key Terms and Concepts
4. Express Your Opinion and/or Self-Appraisal exercises
5. Marginal notes
6. Profiles of Human Behavior
7. Action Projects
8. Summary
9. Case Studies
10. Discussion and Study Questions—To *Keep* You Thinking
11. Endnotes
12. Recommended Reading

ACKNOWLEDGMENTS AND DEDICATION

One of the main sources of assistance for this edition was provided by Mary L. Tucker, professor of communication and organization management. Mary brought new life and perspective to the book. Specifically, she added material on conflict management, communication, and management in cyberspace and virtual organizations. In addition, she is co-authoring the Instructor's Manual.

I still have *fun* writing and interacting with end users—teachers, organization leaders and managers, their students and employees, and other clientele. The book continues to be classroom- and workplace-tested, and well received by readers at all levels. I have benefited from and acted on constructive criticism from diverse publics noted below.

My colleagues and students at Colorado State University and many other educational institutions have been very helpful and supportive. Specifically, College of Business Deans Steve Bolander and Dan Costello and President Al Yates (profiled in Chapter 11) have been sources of encouragement and moral support. Carol Bemus, Todd Cirelli, Burt Deines, and other graduate students have made great suggestions and have been hard workers in this effort.

Editors and other staff at Prentice Hall have been forthright and understanding during this revision. In alphabetical order, I am particularly indebted to Mary Carnis, Dave Garza, Danny Hoyt, Emily Jones, Elizabeth Sugg, and Patrick Walsh. I want to single out Lori Harvey as a very professional and well-organized project editor at Carlisle Publishers Services; Veronica Burnett of Carlisle Communications, who contributed to the design; and Lorretta Palagi, an outstanding copyeditor.

This edition is dedicated with love to *all* learners—faculty and students, young and mature, personal and professional. Specifically, I respect my colleagues and students, and want them to learn and self-actualize to the greatest extent possible. Likewise, I encourage my personal family to continue their learning. By mentioning some, I risk omitting others who are very special to me but let me single out Dorothy, Sheryl, Bill, Gary, Mitchell, Matthew, Braiden, and other family members as well as business associates like Howard Smith and Jim Sprout, men I admire greatly for their values and friendship. Finally, it is my hope that I too have learned to be more considerate of all people.

Comments from readers are always welcome. Please let me hear from you in care of Prentice Hall or contact me directly at Colorado State University in Fort Collins, Colorado.

Doug Benton

PART 1
INTRODUCTION

PEOPLE ARE HUMAN

1

FUNDAMENTALS OF HUMAN BEHAVIOR

Before each chapter in the book, we have provided a set of questions that is designed to stimulate your thinking. Some of the answers will be found in the readings; others will depend on your own personal opinion or experiences. Such open-ended questions are written to generate discussions and an exchange of ideas.

- What is your definition of human relations? Is it different from organizational behavior?
- What are some common misconceptions about human relations?
- Why should we study human relations?
- Why would the study of human relations be more important to the supervisor than to the average worker?
- Has *scientific management* helped or hindered human relations?
- How do you explain that responsibility is a two-way street between the employer and the employee?
- Are the skills required of managers changing?
- How are Deming's and others' principles helping to transform organizations?

LEARNING GOALS

After studying this chapter, you should be able to:

1. Dispel some myths about human relations.
2. Explain why there is a need for an interdisciplinary approach to human relations in business.
3. Define human relations as it is used in business and its importance to the individual.
4. Discuss both the goals and results of scientific management today in light of almost a century of experience with the concept.
5. Explain recent developments in human relations, including quality management, employee empowerment, excellence, and organizational transformation.
6. Describe recurrent trends in human relations.
7. Describe the technical, human relations, and conceptual skills of management.
8. Distinguish among leadership, management, administration, and supervision.

9. Define and apply the following terms and concepts (in order of first occurrence):

- human relations
- organizational behavior
- management
- human goals
- scientific management
- Hawthorne studies
- informal organization
- quality circles

- total quality management
- zero-defects management
- employee empowerment
- organizational transformation
- empathy
- individual differences
- whole person

DEFINITIONS AND PURPOSES

 Human relations is the study of interaction among people.

As every book must do at the beginning, we define the subject matter—what it is, and what it is not. **Human relations,** in its most general sense, refers to all interactions that occur among people, whether organizational or personal, conflicting or cooperating. The main focus of this book is human relations at work in organizations or **organizational behavior,** the study of how people, groups, and organizations behave. Because organizations are the sum of their parts, we focus on personal behavior and relationships.

COMMON GROUND

By the time most people reach college age, they have developed a system of human relations in their social and personal exchanges that satisfies most of their needs. Frequently, however, people who feel confident and secure in their personal relationships lack confidence and are insecure in their business relationships.

Human relationships at work involve what is commonly referred to as management. **Management** can be defined as an integrated hierarchy and team of people whose activities must be coordinated to achieve specific objectives. *Hierarchy* implies leadership in an organizational structure. *Team* implies working together to accomplish goals and objectives. Emphasis should be on teamwork rather than the hierarchical structure of boss–subordinate relationships. Nevertheless, we all have bosses and at the very least coworkers, if not subordinates, so it is in our best interests to learn as much about these work relationships as possible.

COMMON MISCONCEPTIONS

Someone observed that "it ain't what people don't know that hurts, it's the things they know that ain't so." Another anonymous saying is "Strange how much you've got to know before you know how little you know."

Human relations is not common sense.

Human relations is not just making people feel good at work. It is not manipulation of others to get your way. Rather, it is being direct, honest, and positive in dealing with others. Finally, human relations is not "common sense." What is usually described as common sense is really *un*common. Poor interpersonal relationships and communication are all too common, so coping with them is not common sense.

Managers don't have to "manage" all the time.

Another understandable misconception is that managers should manage all the time. Managers should be human (and humane!) all the time but, more importantly, they should be leaders—setting good examples, being facilitators and standard setters, but not necessarily always bosses, order-givers, or directors. The author held the title of "director" in an organization once, but the job was more that of a leader/facilitator who was working *with* others, not having others work *for* him.

NEED FOR HUMAN RELATIONS SKILLS

When people work together in groups to achieve a common objective, there is a strong possibility that the differences among their individual viewpoints will cause conflicts. In this edition, we have added a new discussion of conflict management in Chapter 9.

Many people do not know how to resolve business conflicts in a constructive manner. But, clearly, the person who does know how to work harmoniously even with those who hold different views or are motivated by different goals has found an important clue to successful human relations in the world of work.

Human relations is a discipline within business.

Most employers agree that the majority of those who fail in managerial positions do so because they lack human relations skills, even though they may be competent in technical matters. The need to find new solutions to the day-to-day problems associated with modern job responsibilities has led to the development of human relations as a separate field of study, a discipline within the business curriculum.

A key to success in business is satisfying company objectives and personal goals.

From both the managerial and workers' points of view, good human relations are necessary if people are to achieve economic, social, and psychological satisfaction from the work they do. *The study of human relations in business and industry is the study of how people can work effectively in groups to satisfy both (1) organizational objectives and (2) personal goals.* We prefer the terms *objectives* for organizations and *goals* for people.

ACTION PROJECT 1–1   DISTINGUISHING YOUR INDIVIDUAL GOALS FROM ORGANIZATIONAL OBJECTIVES (PRIMARILY AN INDIVIDUAL EXERCISE)

This exercise will help distinguish between individual goals and organizational objectives, and also help you prioritize them.

Use the following rating scale (1 = primary, 2 = secondary):*

INDIVIDUAL GOAL	ORGANIZATIONAL OBJECTIVE	ELEMENT TO BE RATED
_____	_____	Pass the course
_____	_____	Acquire a basic understanding of human relations concepts
_____	_____	Start class on time
_____	_____	Create classroom environment for learning
_____	_____	Maximize grade opportunities
_____	_____	Learn from text readings, action projects, cases, and the instructor
_____	_____	Apply knowledge gained from readings and classroom activities
_____	_____	Learn to work with others in group settings
_____	_____	Learn expectations of group (team) leaders and followers
_____	_____	Other individual goal 1: _____
_____	_____	Other individual goal 2: _____
_____	_____	Other organizational objective 1: _____
_____	_____	Other organizational objective 2: _____

*You may rate each element as both a goal and an objective or as either, but you should rate one as primary. Compare your ratings with those of other members in the class or as the instructor advises.

ORGANIZATION AND RATIONALE OF THIS BOOK

One of the tests of a good manager is the ability to meet organizational objectives and to fulfill workers' personal needs at the same time. Another test is how well a manager balances efficiency and effectiveness. These relationships are a major thrust of the book.

The book is arranged so that we take on the challenges of human relations and management as we come to them as individuals, groups, organizations, and systems. *We cannot communicate effectively with others until we know our own values and confront our individual challenges of career development, personal problems, motivation, and job performance.* Therefore, unlike other books that take a piecemeal approach, we take a logical approach to applying human relations—getting one's own act together before trying to manage or lead others.

Human goals such as job satisfaction, recognition, and career advancement are influenced by many different kinds of social and psychological factors as well as by the organizational condition of the work environment. Consequently, because human goals are affected by so many more variables than are organizational objectives, they are far more complex to deal with and more difficult to satisfy.

> **Short-term solutions do not solve long-term human relations problems.**

The work of the past several years has demonstrated conclusively that short-term solutions, no matter how popular they may be, do not solve complex human relations problems. Such problems demand carefully thought-out measures that must be given enough time in actual practice to prove or disprove their worth.

How people manage or lead in the world of work is the study of practical attempts to achieve two separate goals: (1) greater productivity at work and (2) greater human satisfaction within the organization (Figure 1–1). Patterns of be-

FIGURE 1–1 Human Relations is a Study of How People Relate and Work Together to Achieve Satisfaction Within an Organization.

havior develop within groups of all kinds. For instance, parents and children interact in a special kind of group called the family; people jammed together at a football game are interacting in still another kind of human group. The focus of this book is on the patterns of human behavior at work within organizations.

THE INTERDISCIPLINARY ASPECT OF HUMAN RELATIONS

Human relations is an interdisciplinary field because the study of human behavior in an industrial or business setting must include the research of several social and physical sciences if it is to be coherent. This interdisciplinary approach requires an understanding of the separate contributions made by other disciplines and then the integration of that information into a unified whole.

Psychologists and sociologists have contributed to human relations.

For example, psychologists have done extensive research and experimentation on the relation of the individual to the work environment. They have conducted many valuable studies on job satisfaction, job placement, incentives, testing, training, counseling, and various other work-related areas.

Sociologists, anthropologists, and social psychologists have made major contributions to human relations with their studies of group behavior and group dynamics. Their concepts of role behavior, status effects, and the influence of informal groupings have proved invaluable in understanding behavior in work environments.

Political science has contributed useful information about the relationships between organizational structure, power struggles, and the processes of leadership, management, administration, and supervision. The continuing evolution of business and of government organizations is an example of political processes and bureaucratic organizations at work. A goal of political and other organizational scientists should be to minimize the negative impact on humans *in* and *served by* those organizations.

These fields and others have added separate elements to our knowledge of human relations. Consequently, following a brief history of the human relations movement, we will consider aspects of communication, motivation, leadership, and decision making, among others, keeping in mind that they are important not only in and of themselves but also as parts, or elements, of an integrated, interdisciplinary field of study.

A BRIEF HISTORY OF HUMAN RELATIONS

It is impossible to specify the exact date on which the human relations movement came into being, but it is fair to say that it was not until the second half of the nineteenth century that much attention was paid to workers' needs, nor was there much understanding of how those needs affected total productivity. Prior to that time, most managers and employers viewed the labor force as a commodity that could be bought and sold like any other commodity. Long hours, low wages, and miserable working conditions were the commonplace realities of the average worker's life. Labor unions were still struggling for existence and had not yet won the right to represent the labor force.

SCIENTIFIC MANAGEMENT

Frederick Taylor developed the theory of scientific management.

Then, at about the turn of the century, Frederick Taylor and his contemporaries introduced and developed the theory and practice of **scientific management.** This approach held that greater productivity could be achieved by breaking down work into isolated, specific, specialized tasks. Not too surprisingly, this theory became popular at approximately the same time mass production became feasible, and it helped pave the way for the assembly line.

Scientific management has often been described as a series of techniques for increasing production rates through the means of better cost accounting procedures, premium and incentive payments, time and motion studies, and so on. But Taylor himself lodged a vigorous protest against this interpretation. In his view, utilizing these techniques did not in itself constitute scientific management, because, as he put it, the main objective of scientific management was "to remove the causes for antagonism between the boss and the men who were under him."[1] Ironically, at times during his experimentation, Taylor achieved the opposite effect by creating antagonism. In fact, conditions became so bad that it was necessary for Pinkerton guards to escort him home.

Taylor and followers like Frank and Lillian Gilbreth, authors of *Cheaper By the Dozen*, were criticized on the grounds that scientific management tended to exploit workers more than it benefited them. Critics said that scientific management paid no attention to the complex social networks created by workers within the work environment. These critics held that it was precisely those complex social networks that had the greatest influence on production rates.

A NEW VIEW OF SCIENTIFIC MANAGEMENT INCLUDING TESTING

The new view of scientific management held that all workers were complex, unique beings whose individual skills and abilities could be measured, tested, and applied. The individual worker came to be seen as a combination of various traits that could be measured accurately and improved by appropriate training. During the 1980s, many managers came to believe that testing could solve most if not all of the problems related to job selection, placement, and promotion.

Scientific management has come under even further attack. Figure 1–2 is a revealing and slashing indictment of the concept.

A 1989 study by leaders at the Massachusetts Institute of Technology (MIT) also faults outdated strategies of mass production, parochialism, and

FIGURE 1–2 "A Secret Is Shared." Source: "A Secret Is Shared," *Manufacturing Engineering*, February 1988, p. 15.

Konosuke Matsushita, founder of and executive advisor for Matsushita Electric Industrial Co. (Osaka, Japan), is certain that his country will win the manufacturing war. Not only that, but he thinks he knows just why that will be. "We will win and you will lose," he says. "You cannot do anything about it because your failure is an internal disease. Your companies are based on Taylor's principles. Worse, your heads are Taylorized too. You firmly believe that sound management means executives on one side and workers on the other, on one side men who think and on the other side men who can only work. For you, management is the art of smoothly transferring the executives' ideas to the workers' hands.

"We have passed the Taylor stage. We are aware that business has become terribly complex. Survival is very uncertain in an environment increasingly filled with risk, the unexpected, and competition. Therefore, a company must have the constant commitment of the minds of all of its employees to survive. For us, management is the entire work force's intellectual commitment at the service of the company . . . without self-imposed functional or class barriers."

"We have measured—better than you—the new technological and economic challenges. We know that the intelligence of a few technocrats—even very bright ones—has become totally inadequate to face these challenges. Only the intellects of all employees can permit a company to live with the ups and downs and the requirements of its new environment. Yes, we will win and you will lose. For you are not able to rid your minds of the obsolete Taylorisms that we never had."

neglect of human resources in U.S. manufacturing. They are very specific in faulting educational institutions for productivity problems:

> Have Americans lost the work ethic? What has happened to the energy, mechanical genius, inventiveness, and willingness to work hard that drove American economic progress in the past? The idea that workers and managers are to blame for the trends in U.S. productivity is widespread today. Many people believe that America produces less well than the Japanese or the West Germans because American workers have become too affluent, lazy, and secure.
>
> Our research on productivity and the quality of the work force suggests a very different explanation. We think the origins of the problem lie not in the disappearance or weakening of basic American values and capabilities but in the institutions that educate Americans for work. We have concluded that without major changes in the ways schools and firms train workers over the course of a lifetime, no amount of macroeconomic fine-tuning or technological innovation will be able to produce significantly improved economic performance and a rising standard of living.[2]

The authors of the MIT study suggest several imperatives for a more productive America:

1. Focus on new fundamentals of manufacturing.
   a. Put products and manufacturing processes ahead of finance.
   b. Establish new measures of productive performance.
   c. Focus on effective use of technology in manufacturing.
   d. Embrace product customization and production flexibility.
   e. Innovate in production processes.
2. Cultivate a new economic citizenship in the work force.
   a. Learn for work and at work.
   b. Increase employee breadth, responsibility, and involvement.
   c. Provide greater employment stability and new rewards.
3. Blend cooperation and individualism.
   a. Organize for both cooperation and individualism.
   b. Promote better intra- and interfirm relations.
   c. Expand partnerships.
   d. Strengthen cooperation between labor and management.
4. Learn to live in the world economy.
   a. Understand foreign languages, cultures, and practices.
   b. Shop internationally.
   c. Enhance distribution and service.
   d. Develop internationally conscious policies.
5. Provide for the future.
   a. Invest in basic education and technical literacy.
   b. Develop long-term business strategies.
   c. Establish policies that stimulate productive investment.
   d. Invest in infrastructure for productive performance.[3]

W. Edwards Deming, best known for his work that created a revolution in quality and economic production, has long been a critic of American manufacturing and productivity. His criticisms stemmed from the spurning he suffered at the hands of American business and the almost universal acceptance in Japan of his postulated 14 principles for the transformation of management. Included in his principles are "drive out fear, so that everyone may work effectively for the company," "create constancy of purpose toward improvement of production and service," "institute a vigorous program of education and self-improvement," "break down the barriers between departments," and "put everybody in the company to work in teams."[4]

THE DEVELOPMENT OF UNIONS

Membership in unions increased at the start of the twentieth century.

At the same time that the new image of the worker was gaining popularity among employers, unions were becoming an increasingly powerful force in industrial affairs. During the years from 1897 to 1904, membership in trade unions grew from 400,000 to 2 million—and unions kept on growing. By 1920 trade unions throughout the nation had received a large measure of recognition from the owners and managers of industry. Now, membership in trade unions is in decline, but much of their impact remains. Chapter 17, Organized Employee Relations, explores the role of unions.

Thus three developments—the emergence of scientific management techniques, the struggles of the trade unionists, and testing—all led to increased acceptance of the idea of the worker as a person with multiple needs. The same developments also led large numbers of managers to reexamine their own image. They took a fresh look at themselves and began to question the wisdom of their traditional views of hard-line management and decision making. But it has taken fifty years or more for much of the new-found knowledge of human behavior to be recognized. Much of the good advice is still largely unheeded despite some excellent efforts by Deming, Peter Drucker, Tom Peters, and other management experts, as well as research by Elton Mayo and other psychologists.

ELTON MAYO'S HAWTHORNE EXPERIMENT

Elton Mayo's famous Hawthorne experiment was the focus of human research.

In the mid-1920s the focal point for the human relations approach in business and industry was the famous **Hawthorne studies** conducted by Elton Mayo and his colleagues. Mayo's group began its work by studying the effects of illumination, ventilation, and fatigue on workers at the Hawthorne plant of Western Electric.

In one area of study, two groups of employees working under similar conditions and doing similar types of work were selected and output records were kept for each group. The intensity of the light under which one group worked was varied systematically; the light was held constant for the second group. When the intensity of the light of the first group was increased, the general result was the productivity of the group increased. This fact was anticipated. However, decreasing the intensity of the light under which employees worked also increased productivity. In fact, the productivity of the group continued to increase as the level of illumination was lowered and one of the highest levels of productivity was recorded during an extremely low level of illumination. Obviously some other variables were contaminating the effects of the experiment.

The employees themselves provided a clue to the changes in the output. They stated that it was easier to work faster because work in the test room was fun and there was little regular supervisory control. In effect, the employees were saying that their productivity increases were attributable to greater freedom and a feeling of importance.

After a few years of experimentation, it became clear to the researchers that group morale and personal motivation factors were so important that they completely obscured the effects of the illumination, ventilation, and fatigue factors under investigation. Another important finding of the Hawthorne studies was that sociability is a key factor that influences the power of the informal group.

THE INFORMAL ORGANIZATION

The informal group can have as much influence as the formal organization.

The Hawthorne studies showed conclusively, by quantitative measurements, that the normal interactions of workers at work always create a social network called the **informal organization,** which exerts tremendous influence over workers' behavior patterns. These particular studies also showed that the informal organization frequently countermanded official orders passed down through the formal organization and consequently played a determining role in setting production rates.

From that point on, it was no longer possible for management to view workers as mere economic tools or as isolated units in the production process. They had to be seen as complex human beings whose normal human interactions were bound to affect total production output, no matter how sophisticated the technological processes employed were. Mayo's findings developed the image of workers as whole persons, creatures of sentiment, whose basic human desires often resulted in complex outcomes, outcomes that cannot be predicted in a purely technological framework.

A classic, contemporary example of these phenomena can be found in Ben Hamper's *Rivethead: Tales from the Assembly Line.*[5] This anthology of blue-collar stories of employer–employee relations at General Motors reveals that some conditions still have not changed.

MORE INFLUENCES FOR HUMAN RELATIONS DURING THE FOLLOWING DECADES

Interest in human relations diminished in the 1930s during the early part of the Great Depression. With the passage of the Wagner Act in 1935, however, and the reemergence of militant unionism, business leaders turned again toward meeting workers' needs—particularly as those needs influenced total productivity. The industrial and business expansion during World War II and the prosperous postwar period stimulated and encouraged a deeper understanding of the relationship between productivity and worker satisfaction.

Countless studies were published by business theorists and social scientists. Three of the most important were Douglas McGregor's paper on traditional theory, which he called Theory X, as opposed to his humanistic approach to management called Theory Y; Abraham Maslow's studies on the hierarchy of human needs; and Frederick Herzberg's motivation–hygiene theory. All of these were milestones in human relations studies and still exert considerable influence, as discussed in later chapters.

THE INFLUENCES OF JAPAN AND OTHER COUNTRIES

Japanese management characteristics.

By the beginning of 1980, we were observing management theories and human relations concepts in other countries. Theory Z, originated by William Ouchi, focuses on Japan's work philosophy, which includes a belief in lifetime employment, strong company loyalty, and group consensus. Japan's loyalty, high productivity, group decision making, and efficient production have been based on long-term planning, not on short-term plans designed to head off a crisis.

One measure of loyalty to an organization is the number of years that a person stays on the job. That number is decreasing steadily, indicating that there may be unrest in the workforce. Further, at times it seems that we live in an absenteeism culture.

In contrast, some progressive firms in Japan, unable to convince their employees to go on vacation, have shut down factories for a week or two to force the workers to take a holiday. Is it little wonder then that a steelworker in Japan might produce three times more product than his counterpart in the United States?

Note that how we treat our employees, customers, and others is no longer a management prerogative subject to unilateral or even a national decision. These human relations decisions affect us all. *The actual decision-making process in Japan is less efficient than that of the United States, but it produces a companywide consensus on the best course of action.*

There are significant exceptions to the Japanese trends: Hewlett-Packard, Microsoft Corporation, Saturn Corporation—at least in the short run—and the productivity of small steel mills in the United States are just a few examples. All of these organizations have considerable employee participation and positive human interaction. Human relations has become a body of knowledge that no student of business or other organizations can afford to ignore.

NEW DEVELOPMENTS IN HUMAN RELATIONS

"But what have you done for me lately?" may be an appropriate question for employees to ask today. Surely great advances have been made in scientific management, use of psychological and other behavioral science techniques, and the influences of Japanese management. The Japanese have been very helpful in inspiring quality circles, total quality management, and other quality management programs. But are these programs a fad?

QUALITY MANAGEMENT

QUALITY CIRCLES.   **Quality circles** (QCs) are voluntary groups of employees engaged in decision making at the lowest practical level of the organization. They show concern for the individual's lifestyle and aid problem solving in work-related areas. Quality circles have been in existence in the United States since the early 1970s and continue to be used under various names.

People want to be part of the solution. They want to use their minds. A good manager asks his or her staff "How can we do this better?" and "How can we achieve this goal?" Workers are being asked to help make decisions about their jobs through a process often called *industrial democracy*, which is also leading to basic changes in the worker–boss relationship. During the 1970s, several European countries adopted laws mandating worker participation plans that ranged from worker representatives on corporate boards of directors to shop-floor workers' councils to help make daily decisions.

American workers do not want to be treated like children or, even worse, like machines. Figure 1–3 is a poem from the auto workers' underground and illustrates the approach of some businesses.

FIGURE 1–3 The Immaturity of the American Management Approach. Source: Thomas J. Peters and Robert H. Waterman, Jr., *In Search of Excellence* (New York: Harper & Row, 1982), pp. 235–236.

Are these men and women
Workers of the world?
or is it an overgrown nursery
with children—goosing, slapping, boys
giggling, snotty girls?
What is it about that entrance way,
those gates to the plant? Is it the
guard, the showing of your badge—the smell?
is there some invisible eye
that pierces you through and
transforms your being? Some aura
or ether, that brain and spirit washes you
and commands, "For eight hours
you shall be different."
What is it that instantaneously makes
a child out of a man?
Moments before he was a father, a husband,
an owner of property,
a voter, a lover, an adult.
When he spoke at least some listened.
Salesmen courted his favor.
Insurance men appealed to his family responsibility
and by chance the church sought his help. . . .
But that was before he shuffled past the guard,
climbed the step,
hung up his coat and
took his place along the line.

The use of small problem-solving groups of workers at GM is typical of the revolutionary changes taking place between workers and managers across the nation. Ford, like GM, is fully committed to what Ford calls *employee involvement*, with worker–management committees jointly considering decisions at every level of the corporation from the highest executive suite to the shop floor.

Whether they are still called quality circles or some other name, QCs or other decision-making groups are used frequently in industry today. The input of many employees is invaluable in making more intelligent, rational decisions. Of course, these voluntary teams are not appropriate for all decision making. They ought to be used selectively for problems that can be solved within a relatively short time, and give positive reinforcement to the group.

Sadly, there is some thought and support from the National Labor Relations Board that only organized labor and trade unions can represent workers to management.[6] Of course, unions can serve that role, but so can quality circles—or other participation groups—and there is plenty of room for improvement to go around!

TOTAL QUALITY MANAGEMENT. Similarly, total quality management (TQM) has enjoyed a very successful reputation and adoption in American industry. **Total quality management** is a comprehensive approach to quality that encourages everyone in the organization to provide customers with reliable products and services. The successes of TQM as a program may have waned, but the underlying principles and purposes of improved quality remain.

One of the pitfalls of TQM programs is reliance on the process instead of on people. There is a tendency to require a lock-step approach dictated by a TQM consultant rather than allowing employees—the real experts—to solve their own problems.

Figure 1–4 shows a comparison of organizations of the past and the future. Notice particularly the differences in the people and quality variables. We need

FIGURE 1–4 Organizations of the Past and Future. Source: David S. Bushnell and Michael B. Halus, "TQM in the Public Sector: Strategies for Quality Service," *National Productivity Review*, Summer 1992, p. 368. Reprinted with permission from National Productivity Review, VIIN3, Summer 1992. Copyright 1992 by Executive Enterprises, Inc., 22 West 21st Street, New York, NY 10010-6990. 212-645-7880. All rights reserved.

OLD	NEW
Hierarchical	Flatter and smaller
Centralized planning and decision making	Centralized planning process and decentralized decision making
Separate data systems	Strategic thinking at all levels
Internal focus	Integrated data systems
Little interest in retooling workers	Strong customer orientation
People as variable cost	Continuous retraining
Quality control through inspection	Job security for core staff
	Built-in quality through process control

to keep the overall objective of quality in mind—that is, we must not lose sight of the forest (quality) because of the trees (programs or fads). The point is not whether TQM makes sense, but how it is implemented.

Oakley and Krug recommend that people be part of a TQM solution and that businesses strive to accomplish the following:

- Constantly look for small successes you are achieving.
- Research extensively what you are doing to generate these successes.
- Continually reclarify the specific objectives.
- Clarify the benefits to all parties (customers, shareholders, team, each person) of achieving those objectives.
- Continually search for what you could do more of, do better, or do differently to move closer to the objectives.[7]

ZERO-DEFECTS MANAGEMENT.   If we are to be successful in quality management, we need new strategies for the new realities of the twenty-first century. Peter Drucker makes the point that leadership throughout the developed world no longer rests on financial control or traditional cost advantages but on control of brain power. He asserts that effective companies "are moving from total quality management toward zero-defects management based on drastically different principles and methods."[8] **Zero-defects management** is a type of quality management that emphasizes products and services adhering to exact standards.

Drucker cites an example that illustrates quality management by quoting a Toyota official:

> We can't use TQM. . . . At its very best—and no one has reached that yet—it cuts defects to 10%. But we turn out four million cars, and a 10% defect rate means that 400,000 Toyota buyers get a 100% defective car. But zero-defects management is now possible and actually not too difficult.[9]

Not all quality management is a Japanese phenomenon nor a one-way street from Japan. In fact, when Disneyland went to Japan, the Japanese believed that it would take several years to work the bugs out of this huge undertaking. "Instead it ran with zero-defects the day it opened. Every single operation had been engineered all the way through and simulated on the computer."[10] In a sense, zero defects is a return to Frederick Taylor's scientific management—seeking perfection not through the use of the stopwatch and other industrial engineering techniques but through computer simulation.

Emphasis on quality is not a fad. Effective businesses and other organizations offering good products and services were providing quality long before it became fashionable to talk about QC or TQM, or even zero defects. Thus, although the individual programs leading up to quality products and services may be fads, the ultimate purpose is long enduring. We will examine the value of quality products and services in Chapter 2.

EMPLOYEE EMPOWERMENT

Employee empowerment increases power and effectiveness.

In recent years there have been many names for the concept of empowering employees: "liberation management" from Tom Peters,[11] "emancipation capitalism" from John Case in *Inc.* magazine,[12] and many other synonyms for employee empowerment. **Employee empowerment** means to give power or authority, to give ability, to enable or enfranchise employees to do their jobs. Both effectiveness and efficiency must be considered when doing a job. If employees are to do their jobs effectively, they need tools including training to do them efficiently. Once they have the objectives, goals, and tools in mind, they are empowered, emancipated, and liberated. Get out of their way and let them do their jobs!

Tom Peters is noted for his movement to empower people. In fact, his guiding premises for empowerment are to "involve everyone in everything" and "use self-managing teams."[13] Of course, there may be limitations on the use of teams and they should be used selectively, but Peters goes so far as to say that *"the power of the team is so great that it is often wise to violate apparent common sense and force a team structure on almost everything."*[14]

Supporting and inhibiting prescriptions for empowerment are shown in Figure 1–5. Notice the admonitions regarding listening to and training people and simplifying structures.

EXCELLENCE

All these admonitions follow on the heels of Peters's earlier work with Robert Waterman, *In Search of Excellence.* They outline eight characteristics of successful, innovative companies as shown in the accompanying box. Peters and Waterman have since disavowed the universality of these characteristics of excellence, but these concepts remain applicable to many organizations. At the heart of the empowerment and excellence issues are the relationships between boss and subordinate, between the company and the union, in short between "us" and "them." But John Case says:

> . . . the marketplace has changed dramatically in the last 20 years, and now the old thinking no longer works. You can see its failure in the sorry state of so many American companies—and in managers' frenzy to try out Employee Empowerment and Total Quality and all the other hot-off-the-presses managerial techniques.
>
> Meanwhile, a growing number of pathbreaking managers, in large companies and small, are ignoring both the old ideas and the latest fads. Instead, they're creating a wholly different mind-set about business and a different way of organizing work—one in which there's no room for *us* and *them.*
>
> Whatever their differences—and there are many—each of those innovators is creating not a company of employees and managers but a company of businesspeople.[15]

FIGURE 1–5 Supports and Inhibitors for Empowering People.[16]	
Five Supports (Add Them)	**Three Inhibitors (Take Them Away)**
• Listen/celebrate/recognize	• Simplify/reduce structure
• Spend time lavishly on recruiting	• Reconceive the middle manager's
• Train and retrain	role
• Provide incentive pay for everyone	• Eliminate bureaucratic rules and
• Provide an employment guarantee	humiliating conditions

THE EXCELLENCE CHARACTERISTICS

1. *Bias for Action*—A preference for doing something—anything—rather than sending an idea through endless cycles of analyses and committee reports.

2. *Staying Close to the Customer*—Learning customer preferences and catering to them.

3. *Autonomy and Entrepreneurship*—Breaking the corporation into small companies and encouraging them to think independently and competitively.

4. *Productivity through People*—Creating in all employees the awareness that their best efforts are essential and that they will share in the rewards of the company's success.

5. *Hands-on, Value-Driven*—Insisting that executives keep in touch with the firm's essential business and promote a strong corporate culture.

6. *Stick to the Knitting*—Remaining with the businesses the company knows best.

7. *Simple Form, Lean Staff*—Few administrative layers, few people at the upper levels.

8. *Simultaneous Loose–Tight Properties*—Fostering a climate where there is dedication to the central values of the company combined with tolerance for all employees who accept those values.

SOURCE: Thomas J. Peters and Robert H. Waterman, Jr., *In Search of Excellence: Lessons from America's Best-Run Companies* (New York: Harper & Row, 1982).

ORGANIZATIONAL TRANSFORMATION

Empowerment is a way of doing business—a way of thinking about business that is dramatically different from everyone else's philosophy or style, and one that requires commitment. Indeed, it requires an organizational transformation.

An **organizational transformation** is a way of thinking and action—not so many techniques or gimmicks but a commitment to change—and is required to create a new type of employee relationship. See Figure 1–6 for one view of the emancipation transformation necessary to create a company of business-people. This kind of commitment requires rethinking employee mentality. We can no longer afford to "use" people as factors of production; we need to transform our organizations and the way people think of themselves as employees and managers who must *work together* rather than as "us" and "them."

Common qualities noted include the dignity of humans, communication, leadership, and teamwork. We will examine these recurrent themes in human relations in the next section. A number of common values continue to occur in these discussions of human relations: entrepreneurship, positive attitudes, learning as well as quality itself, among many others. We will devote Chapter 2 to a discussion of these values.

FIGURE 1–6 Four Steps in Creating a Company of Businesspeople.[17]

First, people at all levels have to be able to make decisions, and the company must be structured to encourage it. That doesn't mean democracy, let alone anarchy; decisions obviously have to be coordinated, and some will require an OK from top management.

Second, people need the information necessary to make intelligent decisions. That is a truism, and any company that sets up quality teams of any other modification of the traditional systems makes sure its employees have some data to work with.

Third, employees need training. Few Americans outside of accounting classes are taught to understand the financial information that governs a business.

Fourth, people need a stake in the outcome of their decisions—and in the company itself. A stake cuts through cynicism ("Why should I bust my butt just so someone else can make more money?") and adds to the intrinsic satisfaction of helping to create a successful company.

RECURRENT THEMES IN HUMAN RELATIONS

There are many fundamentals of human relations that help define and can help reduce human relations problems. Foremost among these fundamentals are human dignity, empathy, individual differences and diversity, communications, motivation, leadership, teamwork, responsible job behavior, and the whole person.

HUMAN DIGNITY

The basic premise of all human relations is the dignity and worth of humans. People are not like other factors of production. *We are born, learn, love, live, retire, and die.* These activities form a challenging cycle for humans and especially for managers.

Managers and other employees must balance individual concerns in their private lives with the demands of their jobs. There are both personal and professional management responsibilities associated with each phase of the cycle. Human dignity applies to personal human relations as well as the workplace. No person should be someone else's slave. Marian Wright Edelman, founder and president of the Children's Defense Fund and prolific writer on personal human relationships, makes the point that in family relationships, your spouse is not your maid, but your partner.[18] A similar approach to work relationships could create greater work harmony as well.

Certainly there are boss–subordinate relationships and times when both boss and subordinates must do very unpleasant jobs. Terminating a worthwhile employee because of economic conditions is every bit as difficult for the boss to do as pumping out a septic tank or other labor-type job—the author knows because he has done both! But day-to-day work is best accomplished by recognizing the inherent worth of the human beings on whom we are dependent regardless of status or place in a hierarchy (see Figure 1–7). Again, flatter and smaller organizations make this objective easier to accomplish.

EMPATHY

To achieve the spirit of human dignity, empathy is required. **Empathy** is the ability to put yourself in someone else's place and to understand that person's motives, point of view, needs, and reasons for his or her actions. Lack of empathy is a primary cause of conflict in organizations. Empathy is the chief quality that mediators of labor disputes must have, and successful salespersons are usually empathic to a very high degree. Empathy is an important element in leadership, and its absence can create insurmountable barriers to communication.

An example of how difficult it is to empathize is that of the chief executive officer (CEO) who does not understand work–family conflicts. *The Wall Street Journal* asked CEOs from various sized organizations and various industries about child care arrangements. The survey showed "that the overwhelming majority of chief executives have never experienced the work–family pressures that burden so many of their employees."[19] That does not mean that they are insensitive or unaware, but it limits their abilities to appreciate the child care frustrations that have become common for many of their subordinates. In short, it inhibits their ability to empathize.

FIGURE 1–7 The "Sweat Shop" or Intense Pressure Does Little to Recognize Human Dignity.

The theme of empathy, in the form of understanding and making allowances for other people's needs and desires, is the integrating and unifying theme of this book. It is stressed particularly in the chapter on interpersonal communication, and it is basic to the discussions in the chapters on creativity, unions, discrimination, and intercultural relations.

INDIVIDUAL DIFFERENCES AND DIVERSITY

The concept of individual differences.

The psychological concept of **individual differences** states that for any given variable, such as mental ability, there are marked differences among people. These differences have an important impact on organizations in the selection of applicants for employment and in their motivation in various jobs. Individual differences need to be considered in three contexts: (1) differences among individuals in terms of job potential (e.g., abilities to learn a job), (2) the effects of training on individuals, and (3) differences in job performance after training. All are the concern of managers who are responsible for others' job performances.

Each person is different, but most are also the same in many ways, including the need for respect, recognition, socialization, and trust. It is the individual differences that really make the management of human relationships a challenge. Some people have more need for recognition; others want more respect; still others want more promotion opportunities.

The workforce is diverse.

People in general and the workforce in particular are more ethnically, gender, and educationally diverse than ever before. The average age of the workforce is also increasing. By the year 2000, the U.S. Department of Labor predicts that 49 percent of the workforce will be between the ages of 35 and 54, up from 40 percent in 1988 and 36 percent in 1976. These are strikingly dramatic shifts that have great impact on management and leadership styles. They introduce the art as well as the scientific aspects of managing human relationships.

PROFILE OF HUMAN BEHAVIOR

ELAINE KING MILLER

Elaine King Miller has experienced a highly productive and successful career that has taken her on a fascinating journey from her early years of development in the "wheat belt" to higher education administration and teaching. She grew up in an agricultural area of western Michigan where she learned early that such things as taking pride in one's work, giving the best effort possible when called on, and being both independent of and dependent on others are key factors in an individual's goal attainment, growth, and productivity.

She remembers learning from her parents that farmers must pull together collectively in order to survive economically. Meeting with other farmers and coming to a collective consensus about whether to enter into a soil bank or other cooperative agreement required considering what was best for the group as well as individuals. Her early development experiences were broadened during her years at the University of Michigan where her undergraduate studies included philosophy and biological sciences. She has a master's in counseling and a Ph.D. in higher education management.

Dr. Miller drew heavily on her knowledge of human behavior as dean of student services divisions at a major metropolitan educational institution. As manager and leader, she was respected by students, institutional CEOs, and division head counterparts in the organization. This respect was earned through the establishment of mutual trust with all "customers" within the campus. A display of honesty and collaboration with all concerned led to the realization that "our effectiveness was dependent upon operating as a team, serving our constituents, and knowing strengths and weaknesses were a necessity." Elaine continues to teach organizational behavior and human resource management subjects.

Elaine says that being independent means "having a sense of responsibility, making decisions about what must come first, knowing what one must do in the next job or task ahead, and knowing when to ask for assistance and support. Sometimes individuals must delay their own desires and needs for those of the entire organization—whether that is a family unit, an agricultural co-op, community, or business. At the same time, one must learn to be dependent in a positive sense—knowing that few if any of the achievements we realize in our personal and work lives are ever totally achieved alone without benefit of other people's knowledge, experience, or perspective."

What is so striking about Elaine is the degree to which she continues to have a desire to learn, explore, and work in challenging environments. She is currently series editor for the American College of Physicians' multivolume book series on managed health care, which is designed to inform and prepare physicians for changes occurring in interactions with insurance companies, medical care intermediaries, and the customer/patient.

Finally, Elaine notes that "the emerging work environment calls for us to rethink the historically vertical and universal application of career paths and career development. A symbolic–analytic job may be done by a trained physician, lawyer, engineer, business manager, account executive and others. The concept of there being 'one best way' to accomplish a project or task as handed down by Taylor's scientific management has to be revisited within the context of the twenty-first-century worker and economy."

THE WHOLE PERSON

As much as business might like to hire only a person's physical or mental skills, it must "take the bitter with the sweet" and employ the whole person. As much as a company might like to hire only Joe's brawn or Jill's brain, it gets both their brawn and brain, and all the infirmities associated with each. If something at home is bothering the employee, it might be desirable from the organization's viewpoint to have them leave that concern at home, but it is just not possible to separate people from their problems that easily. We bring with us our family problems, frustrations, and perhaps bad tempers. The **whole person** refers to the interrelationships of the mind and the body and their total effect on the individual.

In a prophetic article, "More than Just a Paycheck," which predicts work-place behavior for the remainder of this decade and the next century, Carol Clurman writes: "Essentially, employers are being forced to have a stake in the professional *and* personal well-being of their employees, realizing single parents and dual-income duos must be able to juggle things at home in order to hack it at work."[20] Pat Aburdene, coauthor with John Naisbitt of *Megatrends 2000,* adds: "This most certainly is the new model of the corporate form that we will see created in the 1990s and into the 21st century."[21]

COMMUNICATIONS

In modern organizations, all other functions depend on communication. It is the way in which information and understanding are transmitted, it unifies group behavior, and it provides the basis for group cooperation. Without effective communication procedures, no business can survive, much less prosper. If managers cannot communicate effectively with employees, neither can they motivate them nor exercise the functions of leadership. If workers cannot communicate well with management, neither can they perform their jobs properly nor receive adequate recognition for their work. If communication in an organization is not good, then there is no way in which the human relations in that organization can satisfy the people who work there.

Chapters 7 and 8 deal exclusively with communication principles and processes, first on the interpersonal, face-to-face level and then on the organizational level. Chapter 7 presents a number of principles and communication behavior patterns, the mastery of which will lead to more effective communication. Chapter 8 describes the interlocking relationships that exist between an organization's structural forms and its communication procedures. The importance of effective communication is implicit throughout this text.

MOTIVATION

Although human relations is a vast and complicated subject composed of and influenced by many variables, it can be described simply as the total response of individuals to various motivating forces. In other words, people in organizations relate to each other in the ways that they do because they are driven by psychological, social, and economic forces that have the power to motivate them to behave in particular ways. The way in which people behave when they experience conflicting motives within and among themselves is a major source of organizational strife. It is well established that in most circumstances proper motivation on the part of leadership can increase overall productivity.

All performance is a function of motivation and ability. When someone's abilities and ambitions match the demands of a particular job, the job will be done well if the person has the motivation to do the job. If the demands of the job exceed a person's abilities or ambitions, the job will not be done well and personal frustration will result no matter how hard the individual tries. If the drives and abilities of the person far outdistance the job demands, he or she may experience boredom and the job may be done carelessly.

Chapter 5, Human Motivation, introduces some of the theoretical and experimental approaches to motivation that have been influential in the human relations movement. As with communication, motivation is a pervasive theme in this book, most notably in the chapters on job performance and morale, change, status, appraisals, and creativity.

LEADERSHIP

In a very real sense, the history of the human relations movement is the history of modern leadership. A leader's fundamental responsibility in any kind of organization is to get work done through the combined cooperative efforts of others.

A leader must communicate with and motivate his or her subordinates in a just and satisfactory manner or the work will not get done. The human relations function is not, of course, the only responsibility a leader must discharge. Planning, coordinating, and controlling the organization's affairs from finances to work flow are also important. But good human relations with subordinates is necessary if leaders are to handle these other functions well. In the next two sections on guiding an organization and management skills, leadership is put in perspective with other tasks and skills.

Chapter 11 is devoted entirely to the leadership function. There, we will discuss the points that the best managers do not always manage—leading and facilitating others' work. The leader's job is to set the example and enable others to "shine" or stand out in accomplishing organizational objectives.

TEAMWORK

If individuals and groups are to be effective, they must learn to work and communicate as a team. If leader-managers are to work effectively with subordinate-associates, they must learn to work and be evaluated as a team. Americans prize our independence and individuality. We fought for our independence as a nation and continue to place a high value on individuality as discussed earlier.

But just because we become a member of a team does not mean we give up our individuality—quite the contrary. Any team athlete or musician who performs in a band or orchestra knows that the individual can continue to excel but must work as a team player if the performance is to be excellent or better. We will revisit teamwork in Chapters 2 and 15.

RESPONSIBLE JOB BEHAVIOR

The exercise of responsibility is discussed from the managerial point of view in the chapters on job performance, leadership, change, and making decisions. The focus of the theme shifts to the worker's point of view in the chapter on morale.

Patricia Levi talked with teenagers in various jobs and cites several do's and don'ts at work. They apply to any job—for teenagers now and others in the future:

- Try to work with people who will help you learn.
- Get work done on time.

- Be on time.
- Be polite.
- Don't sleep on the job.
- Don't talk to your friends all day.[22]

These admonitions may sound trite but they are so true. We are primarily responsible for our own actions. Surely, there are environmental factors in our heritage and family upbringing that influence our willingness to take responsibility for everything that we do. But basically, we make our own decisions and take action based on what we want to do. Someone else does not "make us" commit a positive or negative act. We do it ourselves.

A good example is individual responsibility for career development or job placement. Our schools or employers can help us obtain better jobs, but the decision to act on information provided by other agencies is an individual responsibility. We will explore this concept further in the career development section of Chapter 3.

We are all only as responsible as our upbringing and character allow us to be. If we have been or are too dependent on others, then we are not as responsible as we could be. On the other hand, we owe gratitude and some allegiance or, at least, respect to our benefactors. How we express that gratitude and allegiance may vary appreciably from one person to another, but pay it we must if we are to be responsible. It is probably best shown by deed and example, like most aspects of responsibility.

In Chapter 4, Personal Problems and Counseling, the theme of individual responsibility is expressed in terms of the reciprocal responsibilities that workers practice with each other to achieve good human relations. And, as with the themes of communication and motivation, the notion of responsibility underlies many of the concepts and practices discussed elsewhere in the text.

CONSTANT CHANGE

Change is constantly accelerating.

A final major theme of human relations is constant change. Leadership, management, and organizational human relationships are always changing. No longer can organizations conduct business as usual. People's economic, social, and psychological needs are changing. The goal is to balance the organization's interests with its people's interests.[23] We will put these changes into perspective throughout the book.

The qualities of initiative, teamwork, creativity, and all the others noted in this section are themselves part of the change process. These qualities are basic skills that all managers and other employees must have to be successful. We will look at the change process further in Chapter 15. The abilities of analysis, judgment, and problem solving in an age of high technology are necessary skills that will be explored more fully in Chapter 14, Creativity and Innovation in Decision Making.

Additional emphasis is also being placed on cross-cultural management skills and global opportunities for employee betterment. These will be explored in Chapters 17 and 18.

Should all people:

1. Experience human dignity?
2. Experience empathy?
3. Recognize individual differences?
4. Be motivated, developed, and communicated with in different ways?
5. Exercise responsibility within the constraints of the whole person concept?
6. Be subjected to or capable of adapting to change?

WHAT IS REQUIRED TO GUIDE OUR ORGANIZATIONS?

Figure 1–8 shows a hierarchy of skills required to conduct operations within organizations. Notice that the top echelon must provide the greater part of organizational leadership, but there is also room for administrators and middle managers and supervisors to provide leadership. Similarly, supervisors are charged primarily with running day-to-day operations, but the top leaders must be willing to get their "hands on" their organizations without micromanaging.

Our economy is increasingly run by professional managers. How successful are they? What is really required of the people who run our organizations? Are they managers? leaders? caretakers? administrators? automatons?

One view asserts that the best managers don't manage. The best managers lead, sponsor, and facilitate rather than order, direct, or tell others what to do. Good leaders and managers set good examples. Next, let us examine other management skills.

MANAGEMENT SKILLS

Management has three broad aspects: technical, human relations, and conceptual. The technical aspect is the easiest to understand. Most people obtain their jobs because of their ability to do certain tasks. Their first promotion may be based on how much they know about the department and the technical aspects related to their particular positions. However, as a person is promoted up the ranks, the technical aspects become less important, and the ability to work with people and to handle abstract ideas becomes more important. Figure 1–9 illustrates the varying mix of these three types of abilities.

FIGURE 1–8 Hierarchy of Skills Required to Guide Organizations.

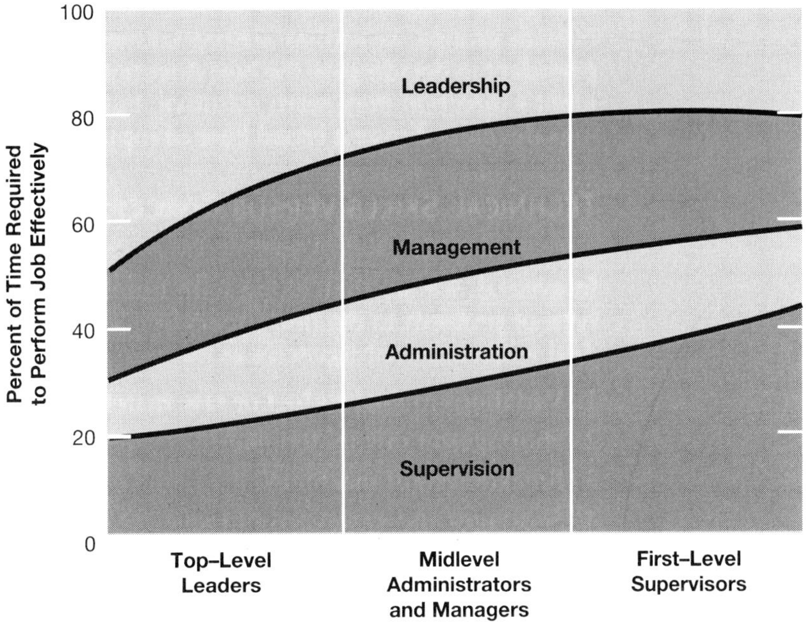

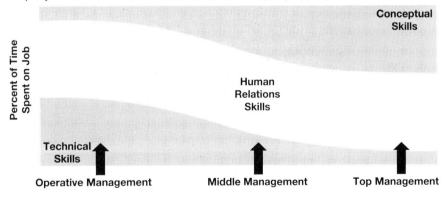

Y-axis: Percent of Time Required to Perform Job Effectively — 0, 20, 40, 60, 80, 100

Leadership

Management

Administration

Supervision

Top–Level Leaders | Midlevel Administrators and Managers | First–Level Supervisors

FIGURE 1–9 Three Skills Are Necessary in Management. Technical Skills Are More Important to the First-Line Supervisor. Conceptual Skills Are More Important to the Company President. Human Relations Skills Are Equally Important to All Levels.

Y-axis: Percent of Time Spent on Job

Conceptual Skills

Human Relations Skills

Technical Skills

Operative Management | Middle Management | Top Management

HUMAN RELATIONS SKILLS

Human relations skills are important at all levels.

The human relations aspect, or the ability to work well with people, will be important at any level, regardless of how many promotions one receives. More important at the upper levels is the conceptual skill—the ability to take many unrelated ideas and combine them to form new approaches to operating a department or a company. A company president spends time studying not only the firm's problems but also new laws, lobbying groups, the community reaction to the company, and, of course, the competition. Information on all these outside groups, as well as actions taking place inside the firm, is used by the president in deciding on the best direction for the company to travel. The president's direction may seem intuitive, but it is based on information and feelings developed over a broad base of input.

TECHNICAL SKILLS VERSUS CONCEPTUAL SKILLS

In general, we see that, along with human relations problems, the important type of problem to the line supervisor is the technical one. A supervisor may deal with such contingencies as these:

1. Variations in the product or raw material
2. Shortages of raw materials
3. Breakdowns of machines
4. Shortages and variations of tools and equipment
5. Shortages of space

Top management, on the other hand, might have to deal with more broadly conceptual problems, such as the following:

1. Failure of a bank to grant a needed loan
2. Community objections to a new plant
3. Failure to receive a large sales contract that was expected
4. An unexpected wildcat strike

A supplementary view of the middle manager's role is presented in Figure 1–10, an adaptation of an advertisement by Dun & Bradstreet Software.

Human skills are important now and will become even more so as technical and conceptual skills develop. Our major emphasis, of course, will be on the human relations skills.

SELF-APPRAISAL

Of the basic themes mentioned in this chapter, which one do you feel most adept at performing? (1) Do you feel that you can communicate your ideas, feelings, and thoughts to others well? (2) Or do you feel that you are best at giving "pep talks" and encouraging people to pursue their personal goals? Do you have a strong sense of direction and goal in life? (3) Perhaps responsibility and the desire for leadership are some of your strongest characteristics. Do you feel that you could, with a little time, lead a group of five students in a group discussion? (4) Finally, is the ability to empathize one of your assets? Do you feel that you really know how others feel and can place yourself in their shoes? Do people come to you for counsel and help on personal matters?

It is always exciting to see how you feel about the attitudes you expressed at the beginning of a course. At the end of the course look back and see if your feelings about certain ideas have changed. These questions will be hard to answer, but put the first ideas that come to mind down on paper. This will be a study of value clarifications that will have you thinking about these questions long after you have answered them.

1. Which are your strongest and weakest areas in the human relations discipline?
   a. Ability to communicate _____
   b. Ability to motivate yourself and others _____
   c. Ability to accept responsibility and lead others _____
   d. Ability to empathize with others and understand their problems _____
      _____
   e. Commitment to task _____
   f. Commitment to people (boss, coworkers, customers, subordinates, etc.)
      _____

2. Which is more important, team spirit or individual achievement?
   _____

3. Is today's fun more important than future accomplishments?
   _____

4. What do you regard as your greatest personal achievement to date?
   _____

5. What do you regard as your greatest personal failure to date?
   _____

6. What two things would you most like to be said of you if you died today?
   _____ and _____

FIGURE 1–10 "Is There a Middle Manager in the House?" Source: Adapted from an advertisement by Dun & Bradstreet Software. Used with permission.

If an accident happened and you YELLED,
"Is there a middle manager in the house?,"
would anyone come to the rescue?
What is a middle manager, anyway?
Valuable decision-maker, or paper pusher?
How do you measure?
Sales per employee? Memo count?
Meetings per hour (MPH)?
And now that we're all trying to
re-invent the corporation,
what do we do with them?
Try asking *them* to re-invent their jobs.
From the ground up.
Maybe you can eliminate waste and inefficiency.
(Instead of people.)
Take advantage of the knowledge,
experience and ideas of your managers.
They'll probably surprise you.
(They can't wait to be asked.)

SUMMARY

Human relations refers to all the interactions that can occur among people, including organizational and personal, and conflicting or cooperative relationships. Organizational behavior is a larger study of how people, groups, and organizations behave. How you and others interact determines the quality of your work and personal lives.

Some common misconceptions about human relations are that it just makes people feel good at work, that it is common sense, and that managers manage all the time. There is a strong need to learn how people work together cooperatively—and sometimes in conflict—in organizations.

The approach that this book follows is a logical, applied approach to life and work: The study of human relations begins with you, the individual. Included in this study are the study of values, personal management and problems, motivation, and job performance. Next comes the study of group challenges, including communications, group behavior, and conflict management. Then comes how we lead, develop, and make decisions in organizations. Finally, we need to study the "big picture"—how we change through teamwork and diversity, through organized employee relations, and intercultural relations. That's the map for your trip through this book. Please enjoy the journey!

The history of human relations is colorful because of the ironies and personalities of individuals involved. Frederick Taylor, the father of scientific management, and his followers were responsible for structuring management and allowing it to be studied as a science. Surprisingly, he antagonized many of the people he was trying to help. Elton Mayo, one of the principals responsible for the Hawthorne experiment, learned that the social aspects of the job were as important, if not more so, than the technical aspects.

All the changes that have been taking place in management and employee human relations have been accelerated in recent years. Major contributing factors to this knowledge are quality management, people empowerment, excellence, and intercultural relations. Americans have learned much about management from the Japanese and others, and vice versa.

Fundamental concepts of human relations include the concepts of human dignity, empathy, individual differences, communications, motivation, leadership, teamwork, and responsibility. How we relate to one another as human beings, how we put ourselves in others' places, and how we recognize individual needs make the management of human relations truly challenging.

People are hired primarily because of their technical and human relations skills. As a person is promoted to higher levels of management, the conceptual ability to handle abstract ideas becomes more important. Human relations skills are equally applicable to all levels of work and life.

There are major opportunities for leadership and management available today. We are more diverse as a culture and a workforce than ever before—a position that creates both opportunities and challenges. Managing in this dynamic environment will be fun. Enjoy it and your life!

JOE RILEY

Joe Riley is a charge nurse for the emergency room (ER) at Endo Valley Community Hospital. He is a good technical nurse whose initial training as an emergency medical technician (EMT) took place during Desert Storm. After separation from the army, Joe completed his bachelor of science in nursing at a well-accredited university. He has maintained and expanded his proficiencies in nursing by taking advantage of continuing education in nursing offered through Endo Valley and local colleges and universities.

Joe is recognized by medical doctors, nursing peers, and those that he supervises as a good diagnostician. He is quick to spot life-threatening situations and to assist other members of the emergency room staff in alleviating physical pain and suffering of patients.

Joe's technical competence and expertise in providing nursing care is in sharp contrast to his people skills. He has managed to offend many patients, coworkers, doctors, and other members of the emergency room team. Some have complained bitterly to hospital administration about his arrogance, impatience with, and rudeness to others—both patients and coworkers.

But the chief of ER medicine, Dr. Jake Banowetz, says that "there is no way we can terminate Joe. He has saved way too many lives by his quick actions to trade off some hurt, ruffled, or sensitive feelings." His subordinates resent his "holier-than-thou" attitude and turnover is high among personnel in the ER. Turnover is sometimes higher in all emergency rooms because of the highly stressful environment but much of the turnover here can be attributed to Joe's actions.

1. What is the problem? What "facts" do we need to know that we don't know? What courses of action are available to Joe and the administration/leadership of Endo Valley Community Hospital?
2. What do you recommend, that is, what would you do about Joe? Is this a problem with which you can identify in a different setting?
3. Can Joe and others like him learn people skills?
4. Is rudeness ever justified?

THE AEROBICS INSTRUCTOR

Jill Greenwood is the head aerobics instructor for the HealthCare Club. Jill and several other instructors conduct both high- and low-impact aerobics classes for men and women of different age groups. Jill recognizes that there are differences in the abilities of the various groups and even differences within the groups.

All the participants have a different reason for attending the aerobics classes: Most want to attain and maintain a level of physical fitness; others enjoy a socialization process within the classes. Within any given class, some individuals desire autonomy—to be left alone to perform their exercises; others want continual praise, recognition, and feedback; still others increase their self-esteem.

Similarly, Jill finds that all the instructors are different in their abilities to communicate with, motivate, and lead their classes. Jill wants to know how to help her instructors better meet the needs of the participants. One of the instructors working with high-impact groups is Fred Billingsley. Fred likes to get the group "pumped up" and energized. He is a dynamic performer. The people in his class expect a tough workout, but they also expect a fun, entertaining time and they don't want to have to think. Fred attracts such a large following that it is difficult for him to pay attention to newcomers' and other individuals' aerobic needs.

Another instructor who desires recognition from her classes is Jan Grossman. Sometimes Jan has a great class, but other times it is a drag. Jan feeds off the mood of the class; if they are down, she is down. She takes her cues from the class instead of the other way around.

Jan is not as confident in her own aerobic and leadership skills as she would like to be. Jack Helmsley is very popular with students, but he is not keeping abreast of changes in the fitness industry. Some of his biomechanical moves are not as safe as they should be. HealthCare offers quarterly in-house training opportunities at no cost to all its aerobics instructors, but Jack very seldom takes advantage of the training.

1. What can Jill do to help her instructors better meet the needs of the participants?
2. Would you recommend training? If so, what specifically would you include in the training and how long would you recommend the training last? How would you structure any training?
3. Empathize with Jill—put yourself in her place—and try to communicate with Fred, Jan, and Jack in helping them perform their jobs better.

DISCUSSION AND STUDY QUESTIONS—TO KEEP YOU THINKING . . . _____

1. What is your definition of human relations? Why would the study of human relations be more important to the supervisor than the average worker?
2. Can you name misconceptions about human relations that reading and studying this chapter may have helped clarify?
3. What are the various disciplines involved in human relations that require an interdisciplinary approach?
4. What is meant by the term *scientific management*? Has it been a help or a hindrance to human relations?
5. What were major findings of the Hawthorne studies?
6. What are the newest developments in human relations?
7. What are recurrent themes in human relations?
8. What are the three basic skills required of all managers? Which set of skills is most important to the middle manager?
9. Distinguish among leadership, management, administration, and supervision.

NOTES

1. Frederick Taylor, *Scientific Management* (New York: Harper, 1947), pp. 128–129.

2. Michael L. Dertouzos et al., *Made in America: Regaining the Productive Edge* (Cambridge, Mass.: The MIT Press, 1989), p. 81.

3. Ibid., pp. 132–146.

4. W. Edwards Deming, *Out of the Crisis* (Cambridge, Mass.: Massachusetts Institute of Technology, 1986), pp. 23–24.

5. Ben Hamper, *Rivethead: Tales from the Assembly Line* (New York: Warner Books, 1991).

6. "Quality Circle Busters," *The Wall Street Journal,* June 6, 1993, p. A14.

7. Ed Oakley and Doug Krug, *Enlightened Leadership* (New York: Simon & Schuster, 1993), p. 116.

8. Peter F. Drucker, "Japan: New Strategies for a New Reality," *The Wall Street Journal,* October 2, 1991, p. A12.

9. Ibid.

10. Ibid.

11. Tom Peters, *Liberation Management* (New York: Alfred A. Knopf, 1992).

12. John Case, "A Company of Businesspeople," *Inc.,* April 1993, pp. 79–93.

13. Tom Peters, *Thriving on Chaos: Handbook for a Management Revolution* (New York: Alfred A. Knopf, 1988), p. 283.

14. Ibid., p. 302 (italics in original).

15. Case, "A Company of Businesspeople," p. 79.

16. Adapted from Peters, *Thriving on Chaos,* p. 283.

17. Adapted from ibid., pp. 89–90.

18. Marian Wright Edelman, *The Measure of Our Success: A Letter to My Children and Yours* (Boston: Beacon Press, 1992), p. 46.

19. Frank Edward Allen, "What Problem?" *The Wall Street Journal,* June 21, 1993, p. R7.

20. Carol Clurman, "More than Just a Paycheck," *USA Weekend,* January 19–21, 1990, p. 4.

21. Ibid.

22. Adapted from Patricia Levi, "On the Job: Real-Life Advice for Doing Well on the Job," *Scholastic Update,* November 6, 1992, pp. 10–11.

23. Denise Rousseau, "Corporate Culture Isn't Easy to Change," *The Wall Street Journal,* August 12, 1996, p. A12.

RECOMMENDED READING

Belasco, James A., and Ralph C. Stayer. *Flight of the Buffalo: Soaring to Excellence, Learning to Let Employees Lead.* New York: Warner Books, 1993.

Berry, Leonard L. *On Great Service: A Framework for Action.* New York: Free Press, 1995.

Cohen, Allan R., and David L. Bradford. *Influence without Authority.* New York: John Wiley, 1990.

Deming, W. Edwards. *Out of the Crisis.* Cambridge, Mass.: Massachusetts Institute of Technology, Center for Advanced Engineering Study, 1986.

Dertouzos, Michael, et al. *Made in America: Regaining the Productive Edge.* Cambridge, Mass.: The MIT Press, 1989.

Drucker, Peter. *Post-Capitalist Society.* New York: HarperCollins, 1993.

Edelman, Marian Wright. *The Measure of Our Success: A Letter to My Children and Yours.* Boston: Beacon Press, 1992.

Gardner, John W. *On Leadership.* New York: Free Press, 1990.

Hofstede, Geert. "Management Scientists Are Human." *Management Science,* January 1994, pp. 4–13.

Jacobs, Michael T. *Short-Term America: The Causes and Cures of Our Business Myopia.* Boston, Harvard Business School Press, 1991.

Naisbitt, John, and Pat Aburdene. *Megatrends 2000.* New York: William A. Morrow, 1990.

Oakley, Ed, and Doug Krug. *Enlightened Leadership: Getting to the Heart of Change.* New York: Simon & Schuster, 1993.

Peters, Tom. *Liberation Management: Necessary Disorganization for the Nanosecond Nineties.* New York: Alfred A. Knopf, 1992.

_____. *The Pursuit of Wow! Every Person's Guide to Topsy-Turvy Times.* New York: Vintage Books, 1994.

Pritchett, Price. *Service Excellence!* Dallas: Pritchett & Associates, 1994.

Rieger, Bradley J. "Lessons in Productivity and People." *Training and Development,* October 1995, pp. 56–58.

2

PERSONAL AND ORGANIZATIONAL VALUES

Before you read this or subsequent chapters in this book, take time to ask and begin to answer the following questions:

- What are values?
- Are there differences between organizational and personal values?
- Is there some overlap in organizational and personal values?
- What are your most important values in how you treat others? Where did they come from—parents, including grandparents? teachers? peers? others?
- Do more mature individuals have more mature values?
- Are our values as a society changing?
- What importance do we put on ethics, honesty, loyalty, trust, and commitment, among other values?
- What importance do we put on courtesy, compassion, dependability, and perseverance, among other personal values?
- What importance do we put on equity and fairness, entrepreneurship, teamwork, and leadership, among other organizational values?
- Which of these values are most important in how other people treat you?

After studying this chapter, you should be able to:

1. Define values generally and specifically for yourself.
2. Discuss organizational or corporate values that work in common with personal values.
3. Discuss unique personal values that hold the key to most people's success.
4. Discuss the organizational values that are common to most organizations' success.
5. Examine personal and corporate values and their impact on the organization of work.
6. Examine a successful businessperson and determine how values impact the conduct of business and employee relationships.
7. Define and apply the following terms and concepts (in order of first occurrence):

- **values**
- **personal values**
- **corporate/organizational values**
- **business ethics**
- **honesty/integrity**
- **loyalty**

- commitment
- stewardship
- attitudes
- courtesy
- compassion
- perseverance

- action orientation
- equity
- entrepreneurship
- teamwork
- visionary leadership

DEFINITIONS AND PURPOSES

Human relationships are based on our personal and organizational values.

In this chapter, we study the personal and organizational values that are the basis of all human relations. We are in a position to interact effectively with other human beings—human relations—only when we know what we stand for and what the underlying principles of behavior are. In short, we can experience meaningful human relations only when we know the underlying values.

Values are those customs or qualities within a society that are regarded in a particular way as guiding principles for behavior and action. **Personal values** are those values that individuals hold and allow to guide their activities including work. **Corporate values** are a composite of these personal values and more. There is a synergistic effect to corporate values; that is, the sum of all the parts is greater than the individual values. To turn around the long-term decline in America's productivity level requires implementation and adherence to a set of values, and the use of valid behavioral science principles in decision making and problem solving.

The values and principles to be considered include:

- Business ethics
- Commitment
- Honesty/integrity
- Loyalty
- Mutual trust/mutual respect

- Courtesy
- Work/leisure attitudes
- Visionary leadership
- Action orientation
- Quality products and services

We will start with some values that are both personal and corporate.

COMBINED PERSONAL AND ORGANIZATIONAL VALUES

Some values are critical to successful organization performance.

Some values are so critical to the successful performance of an organization that they pervade both personal and organizational life. Examples are mutual trust and respect, honesty/integrity, loyalty, and many others. The discussion of quality and service from Chapter 1 also fits into the categories of desirable common or universal values.

BUSINESS AND WORK ETHICS

The most basic values governing personal and corporate lives are ethics. **Business ethics** can be defined as taking into consideration the effects of one's decisions on many publics—employees, customers, even competitors. Failure to consider these diverse publics results in unnecessary firings, reorganizations, and personal frustrations that stifle an organization. These are painful human costs that can be avoided by considering the fundamental themes of human relations such as empathy, human dignity, and individual differences. The golden rule or an adaptation thereof makes decision making and action in the ethical areas much easier: "Do unto others as you would have them do unto you."

Organizational ethics emulate the boss's ethics.

Organizational ethics emulate the ethics of the boss. Some research has shown that just because an organization has a "code of ethics" does not make it more ethical. To the contrary, there is some evidence that having a code causes employees to rely more on it than their own innate senses of right and wrong.[1]

Professor Mark Pastin writes that "the ethics of a person or firm is simply *the most fundamental ground rules by which the person or firm acts*. Understanding these ground rules is the key to understanding how organizations function and to changing the way they function."[2]

A useful approach for making ethical decisions is to ask and answer 12 questions developed by Laura Nash:

1. Have you defined the problem accurately?
2. How would you define the problem if you stood on the other side of the fence?
3. How did this situation occur in the first place?
4. To whom and what do you give your loyalties as a person and as a member of the corporation?
5. What is your intention in making this decision?
6. How does this intention compare with the likely results?
7. Whom could your decision or action injure?
8. Can you engage the affected parties in a discussion of the problem before you make your decision?
9. Are you confident that your position will be as valid over a long period of time as it seems now?
10. Could you disclose without qualms your decision or action to your boss, your CEO, the board of directors, your family, or society as a whole?
11. What is the symbolic potential of your action if understood? if misunderstood?
12. Under what conditions would you allow exceptions to your stand?[3]

Some of the best business ethics advice available comes from Kenneth Blanchard and Norman Vincent Peale's *The Power of Ethical Management*. They suggest three "ethics check" questions:

1. *Is it legal?* Will I be violating either civil law or company policy?
2. *Is it balanced?* Is it fair to all concerned in the short term as well as the long term? Does it promote win–win relationships?

3. *How will it make me feel about myself?* Will it make me proud? Would I feel good if my decision was published in the newspaper? Would I feel good if my family knew about it?[4]

Blanchard and Peale also remind us that the most difficult part of being ethical is *doing* what is right, not *deciding* what is right. Of course, it is easy to say we would do one thing or decide to do something in an abstract situation but it is quite another to act in an ethical manner. Figure 2–1 reviews five principles of ethical power for individuals.[5]

All of the previous questions can be applied to individuals. We also need to ask the questions "Is the work ethic alive and well, or dying?" and "What can we do to improve the work ethic?" Art Carey says that a decline in our work ethic began after World War II when we began to enjoy material prosperity.[6]

HONESTY/INTEGRITY

Honesty is the value of refraining from lying, cheating, or stealing; it is being truthful, trustworthy, and sincere. Fundamental principles such as "honesty is the best policy" and "giving a fair day's work for a fair day's pay" and the preeminence of truth are still worthwhile values that can help to strengthen our organizations. Even when the truth hurts, it is best in the long run to be open and honest with others in our human relationships. Failure to do so simply allows us to dig ourselves deeper into a hole—whether on an employment or a personal level.

In his book, *Honesty in the Workplace,* Kevin Murphy explores an understanding of the psychology surrounding workplace honesty. He says:

> If you are concerned about ethics, dishonesty and crime in the workplace, the best thing you can do is promote programs, ideas and a workplace environment that encourage a healthy commitment to the organization. . . . People who identify with the organization are less likely to steal from it or to engage in behavior that harms it.[7]

FIGURE 2–1 Five Principles of Ethical Power for Individuals.

1. *Purpose.* I see myself as being an ethically sound person. I let my conscience be my guide. No matter what happens, I am always able to face the mirror, look myself straight in the eye, and feel good about myself.

2. *Pride.* I do feel good about myself. I don't need the acceptance of other people to feel important. A balanced self-esteem keeps my ego and my desire to be accepted from influencing my decisions.

3. *Patience.* I believe that things will eventually work out well. I don't need everything to happen right now.

4. *Persistence.* I stick to my purpose, especially when it seems inconvenient to do so! My behavior is consistent with my intentions. As Churchill said, "Never, never, never give up!"

5. *Perspective.* I take time to enter each day quietly in a mood of reflection. This helps me to get myself focused and allows me to listen to my inner self and to see things more clearly.

---

tính chân thật và ngay thẳng

A related view of honesty is integrity. Arthur C. Nielsen, Jr., CEO of the Nielsen marketing research and ratings company, relates that integrity is the willingness to take charge, be decisive, and suffer the consequences of defeat—that is, be able to accept the blame when things go wrong. He suggests that integrity is a sense of responsibility that extends not only to personal principles but to others—"to customers, to employers, to fellow workers. This kind of integrity means more than adherence to some vague code of business ethics. It means always doing what is right, as simple and as terribly difficult as that sometimes may be."[8]

> Integrity is not a conditional word. It doesn't blow in the wind or change with the weather. It is your inner image of yourself, and if you look in there and see a man who won't cheat, then you know he never will.
> —John D. MacDonald, *The Turquoise Lament*

Honesty, integrity, and ethics in making business decisions have significant long-term effects. Bad integrity, bad ethics, and bad decisions eventually drive away customers and suppliers and certainly demoralize employees.

PROFILE OF HUMAN BEHAVIOR

JAMES STOVALL

James Stovall purchased B&M Wood Products of Manor, Georgia, in 1974 at the age of 26 in a highly leveraged buyout. At the time, B&M had sales of $400,000 and employed 12 people; projected sales for 1997 are over $5,000,000, and 43 persons are employed. The primary products of the company are fence posts, poles, lumber, and metal farm gates. In 1991, Stovall incorporated B&M Consulting Company, an environmental consulting service and timber harvesting operation. Revenues for B&M Consulting in 1997 are projected to be almost $4,000,000. Sales for wood-related operations in other countries are over $2,000,000 and expanding.

When asked about the importance of personal and organizational values, Stovall said: "I believe that right usually prevails over wrong, although it may take time. Our company is managed for the long term; therefore, we do not compromise the integrity of the company or our employees to make a quick profit. I will not ask an employee to perform a task that I would not be willing to perform. In our organization, we value honesty, loyalty, integrity, commitment, and good work ethics.

"I value the label 'an honest man' and try to daily earn that reputation. The reputation of honesty within an organization and among its customers is a valuable commodity. I value honesty as the most important quality an employee can possess. . . . Second to honesty, loyalty is the next most important quality of an employee. All of us depend on the company for our livelihoods, and we need to work together as a team. Mistakes can be tolerated when a worker is loyal and willing to use the mistake as a learning experience."

Stovall has instituted a lottery system that rewards employees based on points accumulated during the month. Points are awarded for production, safety, attendance, punctuality, and good ideas. Employees are divided into groups with one winner per group. The employees are motivated by group pressure and monetary reward at a relatively small expense to the company.

James Stovall's B&M Wood Products is an integrated, value-added organization. They begin harvesting their product in the woods with a company harvesting crew and end the process by delivering the finished product on a company truck equipped with a loader to unload the product for their customer. They have control over the entire process and believe that this kind of value-added integration will enable their company to enjoy a long life span.

In the year 2000, Stovall predicts that an organization like his will be composed of "small groups" of contractors doing a lot of the employee-intensive work. Other work will be performed overseas wherever the political environment is conducive to business. Organizations will not have large numbers of employees working in one place, but operations will be scattered around the globe. Supervisory jobs that were once performed by workers with experience, but not much education, will be performed by college graduates familiar with work teams, statistical process control, just-in-time inventories, and quality control. "The work environment will provide little opportunity for the unskilled worker. Businesses will be searching for skilled, healthy, drug-free workers. Workers who fit this description will command high salaries, while the unskilled will find few jobs available, making the U.S. less competitive in the world market."

LOYALTY

Employee **loyalty** refers to being aware, having the foresight to appreciate and involve employees, and rewarding and being responsive to employee needs. Treating employees with respect creates loyalty and a healthy work environment. Like the other values and principles discussed here, loyalty is fundamental to long-term success in an employer–employee relationship.

William Werther writes that:

> Employee loyalty can do wonders for a company if it's channeled in the right direction. Yet, not only do executives perceive employee loyalty in their organizations as low, but they are not quite sure how to raise it. . . . For loyalty at work to flow freely, however, it must begin somewhere. That place is senior management, whose members realize that the loyalty they earn for the organization reflects the loyalty the organization gives to its member.[9]

Employee loyalty is a two-way street. Who is on the street is not as important as knowing that there is a reciprocal relationship. Management usually begins the relationship with an offer of employment but then may cease to honor its side of the contract, preferring instead to expect the employee to be eternally loyal. Many would argue that management loses considerable credibility and productivity with its employees because of this cavalier, take-the-employees-for-granted attitude.

MUTUAL TRUST AND RESPECT

Like honesty and loyalty, mutual trust and mutual respect are dominating factors in achieving the proper balance between employers and employees. But respect and trust go beyond honesty and loyalty, which are by definition related to customers. Respect and trust are the cornerstones of employees' relationships. Without them the relationships are destined to be short lived—in spirit if not in time.

Leaders must earn their trust. A leader without trust will have no followers. That does not mean that we must always agree with the leader; it means that we must always know where that leader stands. Trust is the conviction that leaders mean what they say—whether in national politics, business, or other types of organizations.

Trust and respect must be earned.

Trust and respect must be earned and developed over time. They cannot be mandated. Both personal and corporate trust are based on predictability, dependability, and faith as well as open communication. Open communications may create stresses in organizations, but, as we shall see, all stress is not bad.

No matter how much trust and respect are present, however, the success of the organization is dependent on the motivation to perform either as individuals or as part of a group. The key to effective teamwork is developing mutual respect and trust. Of course, like loyalty, both are appropriate in personal as well as organizational relationships. The primary focus in this book, however, is determining ways to be more productive in organizations.

THE KNOWING AND LEARNING ENTITY—INDIVIDUALS AND ORGANIZATIONS

How successful we and our organizations are depends in large part on our knowledge and willingness to learn. As individuals, we must be increasingly "quick studies," capable of rapidly grasping a concept essential for both our business and personal activities.

Can "anyone" learn or teach? Of course, the customer can always teach the businessperson a lot by walking out of the store or refusing to buy shoddy products. The lesson is not complete, however, unless there is a willingness to listen and observe, and an understanding that the person did not buy because the products or services were inferior. It is important to pay attention to details like customer service, courtesy, and some of the other values discussed in this section.

We must be perceptive and knowledgeable workers capable of getting "the big picture." Further, we must utilize general skills to comprehend, master, and apply knowledge to varying situations.

> For all employees, including managers, "learning is the new form of labor. [It's] no longer a separate activity that occurs either before one enters the workplace or in remote classroom settings. . . . Learning is the heart of productive activity."[10]

Leadership and management can be defined, analyzed, and learned, but it usually takes long hours of study, research, and constant learning. People do not become leaders or managers just because they have the words in their job titles. They have to learn and keep on learning if they are to be successful leaders and managers.

COMMITMENT AND RENEWAL

Commitment is an attachment to an organization that allows people to do things on their own willingly. Managers need to get others to make a commitment to people, goals, values, and systems. People need commitment for themselves and their organizations. A commitment to improved quality and doing things right the first time has become the keystone of renewed productivity and profitability in many organizations.

Commitment, like trust and loyalty, is a two-way street.

Honoring a commitment to one's job, word, and each other, including employees, employers, and customers, is a fundamental value to which we must return. Robert Waterman cites eight major attributes of corporate renewal, shown in Figure 2–2. His definition notes that commitment results from management's ability to turn grand causes into small actions so that everyone can contribute to the mission. The renewal factor is the opportunity that transforms threat into issue, issue into cause, cause into quest. Enthusiasm is generated. Everyone is pulling for the same purpose regardless of how small the task may be or seem.

The complacent manager merely presides. Instead, what is needed is renewal of commitment to the organization. Waterman's renewal factors apply to people as well as organizations. In summary, the attributes say that people should be prepared for diverse opportunities through (1) both internal and external information; (2) seeking stability in our relationships in the form of teamwork and trust, adaptability, and flexibility; and (3) decisive and visible commitment to achieve goals.

QUALITY, SERVICE, AND STEWARDSHIP

Hewlett-Packard is notable for its commitment to people and values such as quality. For retail and other types of business firms, honesty and high ethics mean good business. Customers demand quality and service in an increasingly competitive environment.

FIGURE 2–2 Waterman's Eight Attributes of Corporate Renewal.

Robert Waterman cites eight major attributes of corporate renewal. Those same eight factors may be applied to people in the renewing organizations:

1. Informed opportunism based on information and opportunity
2. Direction and empowerment within defined boundaries and delegated control
3. Familiar facts and congenial controls within existing contexts
4. External, different ideas from others (customers, competitors, etc.)
5. High value placed on teamwork and trust but inevitably politics and power are in the workplace
6. Stability, consistency, and norms within ever-changing conditions
7. Visible management backed by symbolic behavior and rules
8. Commitment to act toward a central purpose[11]

Clearly, providing quality products and services is not just a matter of "being nice" to customers and employees. In fact, it means showing and acting on real, substantial concern for employees and providing *real*, substantive service for customers. Peter Drucker notes that

> Everybody in retailing talks of "service" as the key to success, if not to survival. So do the new retailers. But they mean something different.
>
> For traditional merchants, service means salespeople who personally take care of an individual customer. But the new retailers employ very few salespeople. Service to them means that customers do not need a salesperson, do not have to spend time trying to find one, do not have to ask, do not have to wait. It means that the customers know where goods are the moment they enter the store, in what colors and sizes, and at what price. It means providing information.[12]

One pattern for conducting business in any organization is exemplified by the maxim, "Profit through service, survival through profit." Only when an organization gives value in the form of high-quality products and services can it expect to survive in the long run. Thus, the bottom line is to provide quality and service—that's the real reason to be in business or any other organization.

Service is the reason for any organization.

Professor Leonard Berry offers "Seven Rules of Service" regarding quality. He says "quality service" is:

1. Defined by the customer
2. A journey, a full-court press, all the time; continuously changing needs and expectations
3. Everyone's job
4. Inseparable from leadership and communication; leaders coach, praise, and model service; face-to-face communication; communicate to inspire, not to command; communicate by deeds, not words
5. Inseparable from integrity
6. A design issue
7. Keeping the service promise: "Not promising more than you can reliably deliver."[13]

Another positive view of service is offered by Peter Block, author of *The Empowered Manager,* and now *Stewardship.* Block says that organizations practicing stewardship offer equity, partnership, and choice at all levels for their employees. **Stewardship** is the willingness to be accountable for the well-being of the larger organization by operating in service, rather than in control, of those around us. Managers who act as stewards choose service over self-interest and hold themselves accountable to all over whom they exercise power.[14]

OTHER COMMON VALUES

COMPETITIVENESS. There is a competitive intensity in business. Foreign competition, new technology, deregulation, and other variables such as market maturity have caused firms to go out of business or lose ground because of their reliance on "doing things the way they have always been done." There is a need to identify a sustainable advantage and to determine how large that advantage is and how it can be achieved and sustained. It is important to ascertain sustainable advantage and value as well as earnings in establishing the success of an organization.

PATIENCE.   Patience is a unique value for both individuals and organizations. Not all or many entities possess this valuable attribute, but it can spell the difference between success and failure in business or personal relationships. Patience is the ability to accept delay graciously.

In a world filled with reasons to react, a quiet, understanding response may be the one example that brings peace and serenity to those around you—including employees and customers. Of course, there is a limit to what any organization can or should do to show its patience, but this quality may be the one that sets it apart from the competition.

CONFIDENCE.   Confidence is a two-pronged value—*self-confidence* and *confidence in others*—that needs cultivation from both an individual and corporate perspective. Individuals need self-confidence before they can build confidence in and with others; organizations, too, need the self-confidence that they can handle an appointed task.

Confidence is based on applying skills.

Good examples of confidence are students who are about to graduate and enter the world of work full time. They need self-confidence that they can do a job—not unrealistic expectations, but a spirit of "can do" based on the applications of their learned skills. To succeed at whatever people are doing, they need to develop skills and a strong belief in their capabilities. The key to achieving a goal is confidence in the ability to control one's life or perceived self-effectiveness.

A corporate example of confidence is seen in the members of a construction firm who know that they can handle a project even though they may not have done that particular type of job before. They can be self-confident that they will be successful if they have performed well and built their confidence on similar, smaller jobs.

The successful leader knows that his or her subordinates are going to make errors as part of a growing process. It is important that confidence in others be genuine, not phony. If the confidence turns out to be a facade and there is no genuine trust of subordinates, the negative effects may outweigh any short-term positive effects achieved by the initial phony trust.

DIVERSITY AND FUN.   Two last contemporary values are diversity and fun. Although seemingly unrelated, they have more in common than meets the eye initially. Our societies are too uptight. In deciding to act on certain matters like personnel staffing, we worry about minor things like "sameness," "personality," and a *personal* (although probably biased) assessment of "can he or she do the job?" The latter is, of course, very important, but there are better ways to assess it than by subjectively stating a feeling that a person can or cannot do the job. Let 'em try it!

The stereotyping of and outright discrimination against certain segments of our society cause us considerable loss of talent. Whether the stereotypes are based on gender, ethnic origin, religious preferences, or any number of other classifications, they have a negative effect not just on the talent pool but on the morale of the existing workforce.

Valuable advice is to loosen up and let the marketplace operate. When a woman does a construction job better than the men applying for the job, then let her do it—do it well—and have *fun* doing it. That's what is meant by loosening up: Don't get hung up on the stereotypes that suggest a group can or cannot do certain things. *Celebrate the diversity and enjoy the facts of individual differences that we are not all the same.* In fact, we complement one another rather well, and that makes for more effective teamwork and total organizational effectiveness.

PERSONAL VALUES

As noted earlier, organizational values are in large part a synergistic composite of individual, personal values. How we conduct our personal work activities and lives in general determines the total ethics of organizations.

An NBC–*Wall Street Journal* poll of Americans shows that the vast majority—75 percent—believe that traditional values have grown weaker. They define traditional values as "honesty, integrity, respect, trustworthiness, loyalty, commitment, self-discipline, caring," among other attributes. On discussing the poll, one writer concludes, "Everything in life that works really boils down to good people doing their best to do what's right. That was true yesterday. It's true today. And it'll be true tomorrow, when the debate about 'traditional values' will still be going on."[15]

ATTITUDE AND HUMOR

A fundamental concept and value of human relationships is attitude. By itself, it is not all that important; it is the *result* of attitudes that counts. We have learned that it is not desirable to measure people's performance based on attitude. On the other hand, a person's approach toward customers and other employees may be a critical portion of the job.

Attitudes are predispositions, mental states, emotions, or moods. Contrary to popular opinion, they are not easily measured nor is it appropriate to measure performance based solely on attitude. Above all, it is important to maintain positive attitudes about ourselves, our work associates, even our bosses. As inept or as horrible as we may think some of our work associates or bosses are, it is best to assume that they are doing the best they can at their jobs, and that we should do the same.

If there are great differences between managers' expectations and employee performance, then other arrangements—training, job changes, and so on—can be made. Initially, however, it makes sense to assume a positive attitude and trust one another.

Elwood Chapman notes that positive attitudes are appreciated and that the most popular and productive people in any work environment are usually those with the best attitudes. Their positive attitudes cause the following results:

- Inject humor into what otherwise would be just work. Everyone misses these individuals when they are on vacation.

- Add to the team spirit by "bonding" everyone together in a more positive and productive mood. Many are unofficial leaders greatly appreciated by supervisors.
- Make it easier for coworkers to maintain their upbeat attitudes. This, in turn, helps coworkers maintain productivity and enhance their own careers.[16]

Attitudes are important.

The wrong attitude may become a turnoff for others and spell defeat for ourselves if not held in check. If people spend most of their time griping about their jobs or whining about other organizational issues, opportunities for networking and possible change or advancement may be forgone. There is nothing wrong with the person who takes time off from work to enjoy family, hobbies, and leisurely relaxation activities. In fact, the converse is probably true—that there is something wrong with the workaholic who feels guilty about being away from work. We enjoy our leisure activities—and should—but we should also enjoy our work activities.

A positive mental outlook and action that puts emphasis on drive and determination to help see dreams come true are part of positive attitudes. On a macroscopic basis, they may be measured to determine the morale of an organization. But the attitudes of individuals toward their jobs and total organizations are what counts. Figure 2–3 shows the ABCs of a positive attitude.

Humor is related to attitude. In *Hope for the Troubled Heart,* Dr. Billy Graham observed that a keen sense of humor helps us to

- Overlook the unbecoming
- Understand the unconventional
- Tolerate the unpleasant
- Overcome the unexpected, and
- Outlast the unbearable

Another observer says that he noticed a grim attitude on the part of many executives who address workers on a new project. Of course, undertaking a new project is serious business but the writer says: "If a person lacks a sense of humor, I would never put him in charge of anything or anyone, because I see only a one-dimensional boob who is capable only of mediocrity."[17]

COURTESY/ENTHUSIASM

Closely related to attitudes and mutual respect is the handling of all publics—especially customers and coworkers—with courtesy. **Courtesy** goes beyond politeness or kindness. It means being civil to other people—customers, coworkers, subordinates, even the boss! Life is too short not to be courteous; you should always make time for courtesy.

Courtesy can spell the difference between profit and loss.

Courtesy is so important to the successful conduct of business that it can spell the difference between profit and loss, between survival and extinction of an organization. It is important in acquiring new customers and employees, as well as in keeping old customers and employees. Research indicates that almost 75 percent of banking customers cite teller courtesy as a prime consideration in choosing a financial institution.[18]

FIGURE 2–3 A Positive Attitude Is as Simple as ABC. Source: "A Positive Attitude Is as Simple as ABC," *The Coloradoan* (Ft. Collins), March 28, 1992, p. B5. Reprinted with permission.

Avoid negative sources—people, places, things, and habits.
Believe in yourself.
Consider things from every angle.
Don't give up, and don't give in.
Enjoy life today; yesterday is gone, and tomorrow may never come.
Family and friends are hidden treasures. Seek them and enjoy their riches.
Give more than you planned to give.
Hang on to your dreams.
Ignore those who try to discourage you.
Just do it!
Keep on trying. No matter how hard it seems, it will get easier.
Love yourself first and most.
Make it happen.
Never lie, cheat, or steal. Always strike a fair deal.
Open your eyes, and see things as they really are.
Practice makes perfect.
Quitters never win, and winners never quit.
Read, study, and learn about everything important in your life.
Stop procrastinating.
Take control of your own destiny.
Understand yourself in order to better understand others.
Visualize it.
Want it more than anything.
"Xccelerate" your efforts.
You are unique of all God's creations. Nothing can replace you.
Zero in on your target, and go for it!
—Wanda Carter
St. Augustine, Florida

Other research suggests that as the population increases, especially in some areas, we will become less courteous to each other.[19] The "in-your-face" rudeness brought on by some conditions in the 1980s and early 1990s may accelerate the seeming lack of courtesy. Overcrowding, changes in social status, and an ascendancy of special interest groups all contribute to an increasing concern for and, it is hoped, a return to courtesy.

How employees are treated by their bosses and other parts of management is also a fundamental value. Most people respond more positively to polite, considerate instructions than to orders. An ordinary conversation between boss and subordinate does not have to be rude or punctuated with "barbs" from the boss. Related to this type of interaction is the amount of enthusiasm that bosses exhibit and, in turn, can generate in others.

Be "fired up" with enthusiasm, or you may be fired with enthusiasm.

Finding ways to generate and maintain enthusiasm regarding people, product, and organizational mission is very important to successful leaders. Means of increasing enthusiasm include training and development, and

> ## SHORT COURSE IN HUMAN RELATIONS
> - Five most important words: YOU DID A GOOD JOB.
> - Four most important words: WHAT IS YOUR OPINION?
> - Three most important words: IF YOU PLEASE.
> - Two most important words: THANK YOU.
> - One most important word: WE.
> - Least important word: I.

healthy competition among internal groups—not a negative type of competition but an approach that says "We want to do better than we have done before." In essence, then, the competition is with self.

> Enthusiasm is one of the most powerful engines of success. When you do a thing, do it with your might. Put your whole soul into it. Stamp it with your own personality. Be active, be energetic, be enthusiastic and faithful, and you will accomplish your object. Nothing great was ever achieved without enthusiasm.
>
> —Ralph Waldo Emerson, *Circles*

COMPASSION/CARING

Compassion and a caring attitude are closely related to the theme of empathy introduced in Chapter 1. **Compassion** is a feeling for and understanding of another person's difficult situation. Tied to it is a desire to help alleviate or ease associated discomfort with either the physical or psychological situation. It is impossible for a person to always understand another's perspective. There may be similar circumstances, but because each individual is different, the feelings and resulting behaviors will also be different.

As managers, as family members, just as human beings, we should try to put ourselves in others' footsteps. How does this person feel? How would he or she react if experiencing something like a job dispute or layoff? Our organizations and the people in them will judge us by how we treat people. If we treat them without regard for their feelings or in other cavalier fashion, they will judge us harshly. Significant costs in morale and job performance are associated with a lack of caring.

DEPENDABILITY/RELIABILITY

Be dependable, reliable, and perseverant.

Dependability and reliability are very basic values. There is not a lot to say regarding them other than "be on time," "be predictable (it is hoped, in a positive sense!)" and, in a broad sense, "do a good job." These are truly fundamental values that provide the contrast between effective and productive organizations and those ineffective, less productive entities. Turned-on, positive people who can be depended on to turn out reliable products and services make the difference in those organizations.

Like so many other values discussed in this chapter, dependability and reliability are two-way streets in which both employees and employers expect their bosses and subordinates to be dependable and reliable—in short, "to be there."

PERSEVERANCE/DILIGENCE

Closely related to dependability and reliability are perseverance and diligence. Suzanne Chazin has called **perseverance** the ultimate key to success, noting that it can be more important than talent, brains, or luck. She says it is a simple trait that anyone can master and suggests that "successful people understand that no one makes it to the top in a single bound. What truly sets them apart is their willingness to keep putting one step in front of the other—no matter how rough the terrain."[20]

Tom Peters tells how to succeed in business by really trying harder than others and what separates winners from losers:

- *Attention to details:* superb execution will win the day.
- *Culture counts:* spirit, energy, and professionalism are important.
- *Keep meticulous books:* not necessarily complex but accurate and timely. Present a crystal clear picture of how your business is working.
- *Perseverance itself:* learn from early mistakes. Peters says that Sam Walton (Wal-Mart) and Anita Roddick (The Body Shop) "learned from their early pratfalls, made adjustment after adjustment, and eventually came up with a winning formula."[21]

Another frequently heard phrase for perseverance or diligence is "stick-to-it-ive-ness." Regardless of what we call them, these two values are fundamental distinctions that make a difference in successful individuals and organizations.

SELF-DISCIPLINE

Self-discipline is the only real discipline.

Unfortunately, *self-discipline* is a frequently used but redundant misnomer. There is only one type of discipline (not disciplinary action) and that is self-discipline. Surely, discipline—defined as a state of order and readiness in an organization—should be encouraged by management and others, but in the final analysis, discipline has to come from the individual.

Discipline is frequently confused with disciplinary action, which is externally imposed and may be viewed as punitive. Discipline—whether an externally "imposed" state of order or real self-discipline—is positive. Discipline is discussed further in Chapter 12, and disciplinary action in Chapter 13. These personal values are presented here as a beginning for further development of your values.

ACTION ORIENTATION

One could argue that inaction does less harm than some limited, albeit well-intentioned, action. But there are certainly cases where inaction has caused irreparable harm. The 1989 *Exxon Valdez* fiasco on the part of the company, or the state and federal governments' inaction or inability to act rapidly enough, is a classic example of an inaction orientation.

There are many excellent examples of what **action orientation** really means. They usually emphasize concepts such as "Try it, at least," "Ready! Fire! Aim!," "Do it now," and other quick-response mechanisms such as ad hoc teams.

Some of the preconditions for effective ad hoc teams are that they should be just that—ad hoc, of limited duration, impermanent committees that begin to consume lots of people's time. They should also have a minimum number of members on the team, report to a fairly high level of management, and follow the "KISS" formula—"Keep It Sweet and Simple"!

ACTION PROJECT 2–1 INDIVIDUAL GOALS AND VALUES (INDIVIDUAL EXERCISE)

The following survey is designed to start you thinking about certain goals and values—now and in the future. Like most of the exercises in this book, there are no right or wrong answers. The demographic information (age, gender, and major) is for classification and tabulation purposes only.

AGE: _____ MALE OR FEMALE: _____ MAJOR: _____

On Questions 1 through 6, you are asked to rank goals in order of preference (eca = extracurricular activities, 1 = most prefer, 6 = least prefer). On Questions 7 through 9, check the appropriate answer.

1. As a college student, rank your present "living" goals:

_____ money _____ where to live _____ career _____ family _____ friends _____ eca

2. In 5 years, how will your goal preferences rank?

_____ money _____ where to live _____ career _____ family _____ friends _____ eca

3. In 10 years, how will your goal preferences rank?

_____ money _____ where to live _____ career _____ family _____ friends _____ eca

4. In 20 years, how will your goal preferences rank?

_____ money _____ where to live _____ career _____ family _____ friends _____ eca

5. In 40 years, how will your goal preferences rank?

_____ money _____ where to live _____ career _____ family _____ friends _____ eca

6. Rank these compensation benefits in order of preference if all offered are of equal value:

    _____ cost-of-living increase

    _____ opportunity to buy stock at reduced rate every year

    _____ medical and life insurance

    _____ paid 15-week leave of absence every 5 years

DO NOT RANK THE FOLLOWING. Check the appropriate answer.

7. How often do you change career goals (if more than 5 years leave blank)?

    _____ every term _____ every year _____ every 2 years _____ every 5 years

8. For your career goals, do you feel

    _____ overeducated _____ educated enough _____ undereducated

9. Have your parents influenced your chosen career goals?

    _____ yes _____ no _____ partial input

There is no excuse for unplanned, organizational procrastination. When you make up your mind to do something—consensus—just do it! Of course, *planned* delays or personal emergencies can postpone action, but for the most part, once a decision is made, take action. Incidentally, Japanese managers are noted for taking more time to decide—to arrive at consensus—but once the decision is made, the action follows at a pace much quicker than most American implementations.

EQUITY/FAIRNESS

The author is fond of repeating the oft-quoted "three principles of real estate: location! location! and location!" (or, contemporarily, "financing! financing! and financing!"). There are similar, corollary principles in management and employee relations—specifically, "three principles of human resource management: equity! equity! and equity!" In short, **equity** means fairness, which may manifest itself in internal, external, or individual consistency within an organization.

Three types of equity: internal, external, and individual.

These equity principles are really quite true and fundamental to effective compensation and other human resource management. One type of equity is *internal equity*, how fairly each job is paid within an organization. A second type is *external equity*, how pay for a job compares to pay for jobs in other, perhaps competing, organizations. Finally, there is *individual equity* or performance pay, based on how well individuals perform in their jobs.

In fact, emphasis on short-term equity based on performance is increasing. Of course, long-term equity is important too so that job incumbents perceive fairness in pay and other employee treatment. But two researchers find that

> perceived fairness no longer means job security, steady cradle-to-grave growth, and ever-increasing benefits. Rather, employees should expect appropriate rewards based in large part on their performance during the past year, as well as the company's performance. . . . Flexibility is changing from a longer-term, financially-based curve to a shorter-term, performance-based series of sharp turns [adjustments].[22]

Regardless of whether it is long-term or short-term equity, the concepts of equity and fairness have always been important to American workers. Their importance appears to be increasing. Roberta Maynard found that fairness, openness, and honesty are consistently mentioned as qualities that employees most appreciate in a boss. Experts say that bosses can learn to be great by doing the following:

- Be a good and willing communicator.
- Specify job performance expectations.
- Make contact daily with as many team members as possible.
- Loosen the reins.
- Have a sense of humor and admit mistakes.
- Provide direction and strive to be consistent.
- Look for ways to improve and to learn from others.

Maynard concludes that in the future, bosses will succeed if they have the ability to promote teamwork and manage a diverse workplace.[23]

ENTREPRENEURSHIP/RISK TAKING

Entrepreneurship adds value.

Closely related to the action orientation is the risk taking of entrepreneurship. **Entrepreneurship** is the creation of wealth by adding value. Of course, there are risks in the action orientation—risks that we will be wrong, too soon with a decision, and so on. But there is a risk that we will lose market or a key person because of inaction, or because of drawn-out negotiations or unnecessary detail and "staffing" through an organization. By the time someone finds something acceptable after many revisions, the opportunity is lost.

The effective leader knows that there is risk inherent in leading and in making decisions. It is important to "risk" failure rather than to survive mediocrity. Vic Sussman writes that failure is not to be feared, but that it is a normal way to map the unknown and be a great tutor. He offers several specific suggestions:

1. Stop using the "F" [failure] word.
2. Don't take it [failure] personally.
3. Be prepared [insulate yourself by mapping a catastrophe plan].
4. Learn to fail intelligently.
5. Never say die.[24]

Women, in particular, are learning to take on the entrepreneurial role. Joline Godfrey, author of *Our Wildest Dreams: Women Entrepreneurs Making Money, Having Fun, Doing Good*, writes that young women have learned

> to cooperate, be responsive and communicate, bring practices once considered unbusinesslike to the business of business. In the days when partnerships and alliances were less important and "dog eat dog" was the prevailing sentiment, the qualities women exhibited were considered too soft for commercial enterprise. But it turns out that reciprocity and respect are key to effective partnership; that win–win has strategic benefits; and that in a world of diverse needs, points of view and stakeholder claims, sensitivity to others is a competitive advantage."[25]

Let the entrepreneurs work and grow in an organization by loosening the restrictions so common to bureaucratic organizations. Naturally, you don't want to free all employees to do anything that whim suggests to them, but allow them to make some mistakes within predefined constraints. In an organizational sense, that is *delegated authority,* a topic that will be discussed in later chapters.

TEAMWORK/COOPERATION/COLLEGIALITY

Teamwork is working together to identify and solve group-related work problems. Teamwork has become a fashionable buzzword in recent years and for good reason. Americans have always cherished their independence and individuality—sometimes at the expense of cooperation and teamwork. Discussions of Japanese management are peppered with references to their working together for consensus versus the individual decision making of Americans. It is becoming clear that if Americans and others are to be more successful managers of their organizations, they must become team members and leaders. Figure 2–4 shows a valuable team builder's checklist that emphasizes the roles of all members but especially the leader's roles.

FIGURE 2–4 Team Builder's Checklist

1. Does each team member, including myself, have a crystal clear understanding of the agreed goals of the team? _____

2. Is every team member, including myself, sufficiently committed to the team goals to devote the necessary effort to achieve them? _____

3. Does every team member, including myself, clearly understand his or her assigned role on the team and the importance of that role to team success? _____

4. Is every team member, including myself, committed to fulfilling his or her assigned role to the best of his or her ability? _____

5. Does every team member, including myself, clearly understand the plan for reaching team goals and, especially, does every team member understand precisely the part of the planned activity he or she is responsible for? _____

6. Does every team member, including myself, understand and accept the performance standards for individual activity and the total team activity necessary for the team to achieve its goals? _____

7. Am I providing frequent, timely, and useful feedback on each team member's performance, and to the team as a whole on team performances? _____

8. Am I providing the coaching and supervision necessary to help each team member and the group as a whole reach the required performance standards? _____

9. Am I providing the initiative, the enthusiasm, the sense of purpose, and an example of the appropriate behavior and attitudes that team members expect of their leader? _____

10. Am I creating and maintaining a supportive group climate, and am I constructively controlling the group process? _____

A spirit of cooperation and collegiality should pervade organizations. By definition, an organization means teamwork toward common goals and objectives. Teamwork is essential in athletic teams, businesses, and musical groups, and in civil, religious, and other kinds of organizations.

Teamwork can be carried too far, lessening the degree of individual motivation. There should always be opportunities for individual growth as well as team development. Not everything has to be or should be done as a team. There needs to be a balance between teamwork and individual effort.

A final lesson for universal teamwork is provided by Marian Edelman:

Remember and help America remember that the fellowship of human beings is more important than the fellowship of race and class and gender in a democratic society. Be decent and fair and insist that others be so in your presence. Don't tell, laugh at, or in any way acquiesce to racial, ethnic, religious, or gender jokes or to any practices intended to demean rather than enhance another human being. Walk away from them. Stare them down. Make them unacceptable in your homes, religious congregations, and clubs. Through daily moral consciousness counter the proliferating voices of racial and ethnic and religious division that are gaining respectability over the land, including on college campuses. Let's face up to rather than ignore our growing racial problems, which are America's historical and future Achilles' heel.[26]

ACTION PROJECT 2–2   GROUP VALUES (GROUP EXERCISE)

The object is to rank order five people based on how well you respect each one. First, arrive at your own individual answers (take 5 to 10 minutes). Then your instructor may ask you to meet with a group to compare and discuss your answers.

Scenario: Five people are stranded on two islands near each other, both surrounded by an ocean full of sharks. On one island there are two men, and on the other there are two women and one man. Melanie and her boyfriend, Brian, are on opposite islands and want to be together.

Melanie decides she needs help so she approaches Lynn and asks for help. Lynn's reply is that she's busy assembling a radio to signal for help and doesn't want to be bothered. Melanie then approaches Joe and again asks for help. Joe has been gathering wood to build a raft and will help only if she makes love with him. Melanie finally makes it to the other island and is happy to see Brian. Brian, however, saw what Melanie did to get across and no longer wants to have anything to do with her. Dave admits that he's always loved Melanie and the two get married.

Each person in the scenario has a reward:

1. Lynn represents intellect and with the radio signal all are found and rescued.
2. Dave finds happiness by receiving what he's always hoped for—Melanie's love.
3. Joe represents power and uses it to get people to do what he wants and control their actions.
4. Melanie gets true love from a man she didn't expect it from and the meaning of a good relationship.
5. Brian represents morality and doesn't lose his sense of morality by not letting Melanie get away with something and then ignoring it.

Rank the five individuals in order of your respect for them (1 = most prefer). Then, compare your rankings with others in your group.

YOUR INDIVIDUAL RANKING	GROUP RANKING		ANALYSIS/REASONS
_____	Brian	_____	_____
_____	Dave	_____	_____
_____	Joe	_____	_____
_____	Lynn	_____	_____
_____	Melanie	_____	_____

VISIONARY LEADERSHIP

An old adage says "Where there is no vision, the people perish." That's good and timely advice for nations, businesses, and other organizations. Where there is no **visionary leadership,** having the foresight to set a direction for a specific goal, organizations fail and people are hurt through poverty, unemployment, and misunderstandings.

John Gardner, former secretary of Health, Education, and Welfare, says that

> Leaders have a significant role in creating the state of mind that is the society. They can serve as symbols of the moral unity of the society. They can express the values that hold the society together. Most important, they can conceive and articulate goals that lift people out of their petty preoccupations, carry them above the conflicts that tear a society apart, and unite them in the pursuit of objectives worthy of their best efforts.[27]

We must continue to improve our visions for the future—and then act on them; that's what leadership is all about. Organizations that do business as usual suffer in the long term. Tom Peters, Nancy Austin, and many others point out the importance of having that vision and leadership if we are to succeed. Organizations and individuals both need to know what their objectives and goals are. People need time to reflect—and plan. Organizations like Disney, General Electric, McDonald's, and Wal-Mart are where they are today because their founders and successive leaders had entrepreneurial spirit and vision, and demonstrated the leadership necessary to be successful.

Human relations problems have many different causes. Five of the most common follow:

Your talents

1. Every person brings a unique set of talents, ambitions, and work experience to a job. These personal attitudes change over time, often as a result of the degree of success or failure the person experiences in the work world. Matching so many unique sets of personal qualities to a standardized technology can create problems.

Organization needs

2. The organizational aspects of a company, such as its size, geographic location, economic health, and degree of automation, define the scope of work and the activity in each work division. Frequent arbitrary structural definitions often cause difficulties in human relations.

Technological growth

3. Innovations in technology and production methods generally require the restructuring of job roles and responsibilities. Radical changes in basic organizational structure can cause severe strains between workers and management and thus create intense problems in human relations.

Need for responsibility

4. Promotions of individuals to positions of greater responsibility and authority generally create a need for changed behavior patterns between the new supervisors and their former peers, which, in turn, can create human relations problems.

Inexperienced workers

5. Inexperienced or young workers may not be able to perform their roles or tasks in work groups in a competent manner. The time they require to adjust can not only create problems with production schedules but can also lead to particular kinds of human relations problems between them and their coworkers and supervisors.

SELF-APPRAISAL

Since human relations problems have many different causes and perspectives, it might be interesting to identify your feelings about the five causes just listed. Then, it might be interesting to share them with members of your class. Listing your immediate feelings may help you to develop your own value clarifications as well as to determine your place in the working world.

1. Every person brings a unique set of talents, ambitions, and experience to a job. What three outstanding things do you feel that you can bring to a job?

   a. _____

   b. _____

   c. _____

2. With regard to the organizational aspects of a company,

   a. In what size company would you like to work?
      (1) 10–50 employees, (2) 50–150 employees, (3) over 150 employees

   b. Where would you like your company located?
      (1) locally, (2) within 100 miles of home, (3) anywhere in the United States, (4) outside the United States

3. Do you enjoy changes at work?
   a. Look forward to change.
   b. Occasionally enjoy changes.
   c. Seldom like to see change.
   d. Change makes it difficult to get the work done.
4. Promotions mean greater responsibility and authority. In my next job I would like to see a promotion
   a. In three months.
   b. In six months.
   c. In one year.
   d. When I deserve it.
5. One way to handle untrained and inexperienced workers is to
   a. Have training classes frequently for new employees.
   b. Hire only experienced employees.
   c. Have a trainee work with you to learn the trade.

Your ideas may change in a few months or remain the same. In any case, if you compare your answers with others and share your feelings about your answers, you may clarify some of your attitudes about work and discover some of your expectations of a career.

SUMMARY

All of the values and principles discussed in this chapter have the following as common elements: goal accomplishment, performed under highly competitive conditions, with genuine concern for employees and customers. There is evidence that better managed employees provide better service to the customers or constituents who are the ultimate reason for being in business, whether a profit or not-for-profit organization.

People are prepared for interactions with other human beings only when they know the underlying values or principles of human behavior. Values are those customs or qualities that are regarded as guiding principles for behavior and action. There are at least three sets of values: personal values, corporate or organizational values, and those that combine personal and corporate values.

Despite significant progress in managing our organizations better, widespread realizations of the internationally competitive business environment and business failures suggest that there is still room for improvement. The behavioral sciences have tremendous potential for improving total organizational effectiveness.

Specific combinations of personal and organizational values include business ethics, honesty, loyalty, mutual trust, commitment to organizational and personal quality, and service. Some of the values basic to the successful conduct of personal relationships are positive attitudes, courtesy, compassion, dependability, perseverance, and self-discipline.

Organizational values worthy of our attention include an action orientation, equity and fairness, entrepreneurship, teamwork, and visionary leadership. These values and their implementation are fundamental to our continued transformation out of a relative productivity decline.

Finally, we are challenged by human relations problems that have many different causes. Among the most common causes are individual talents, organizational needs, technological change, need to accept responsibility, and the need to train inexperienced workers in human as well as technological skills.

<table>
<tr><td>CASE STUDY
2–1</td><td></td></tr>
</table>

THE GOOD COPS

Pat Friel is a shift commander for the Fort Manitowac Police Department. He started as a rookie policeman 15 years ago and worked his way through the ranks to his present position. Pat is a perceptive and observant investigator of crimes—felonies, misdemeanors, and even traffic violations.

Manny Chavez, Judy Brent, and George Williams are younger patrol officers under Pat's command. They look up to and respect Pat as a role model. Police work requires teamwork and trust among officers and their supervisors if officers are to avoid being put in "harm's way." The relationships among this police group are very good in that there is an organizational climate of openness and social recognition of others' needs.

In fact, the climate of openness sometimes degenerates into pretty loose control of the group. Pat and the other officers spend a lot of time together—more than an hour per shift—in coffee shops and "bagel bars" around town. On the other hand, they spend considerable time in training and are in fact prepared to protect and serve the population in emergency situations. By definition, they experience some personal risk taking and organizational stress in their jobs.

The rates of serious crime and minor offenses are average but increasing throughout the Fort Manitowac community. Staffing levels within the department are also average in comparison to communities of similar population and other demographic characteristics. Competence and morale in the department are fairly high compared to previous police administrations where morale was very low and turnover of "good cops" was high.

1. Is there an attitude problem in terms of the work–leisure balance? Is there an honesty/integrity problem; that is, are the taxpayers getting their "money's worth"?

2. Should Pat and others spend as much time as they do in the coffee shops and bagel bars? (*Hint:* Weigh the pros and cons of police presence throughout the community with the appearance of "goofing off" on taxpayers' time.)

3. Are there other facts that you need to know before analyzing and recommending a solution to this case?

4. Are there any other ethical questions and/or value issues that you see in this case?

THE ETHICAL NURSE

Violet "Vi" Curtis is a registered nurse who graduated from Uptown University some years ago with a baccalaureate degree in nursing and completed a master's degree in clinical family nursing. Since receiving her master's degree, Vi has been employed as a nurse practitioner by the Metropolitan City Health Department, working with a number of individuals and families needing the services of a nurse practitioner.

Vi is a good, professional nurse. She helps her clients by providing them first-class nursing care and advice. The challenges of working within a big-city bureaucracy are becoming more strenuous for Vi. Limited municipal budgets are declining, and paperwork for each case is increasing. In fact, Vi has decided to leave the city health department and begin her own business as a nurse practitioner.

Starting one's own business involves many functions—financing, marketing, and accounting as well as producing the product or services. Vi is not concerned about her capabilities to provide quality care as a nurse practitioner. She also has other well-qualified individuals interested and willing to work for her if her business grows.

One of Vi's major concerns is that she does not have a marketing plan. She does not have a client base outside of the city health department. She knows that many of her current clients would become future, private clients but she is not sure how to go about attracting them. She has the mailing list for the city health department's clients available to her on computer and wonders if it would be ethical to mail announcements and other promotional literature to them.

1. Can you help Vi resolve her ethical dilemma?
2. Should she use the city health department's list?
3. Can you identify some factors that would start her toward developing a plan?
4. How can you reconcile Vi's entrepreneurial and ethical dilemma?

DISCUSSION AND STUDY QUESTIONS—TO KEEP YOU THINKING . . . _____

1. What are your most important guiding values?
2. What are the differences and similarities between personal and organizational values?
3. What are important "ethics check" questions? What are important principles of ethical power for individuals and organizations?
4. How do honesty, loyalty, and mutual trust impact business and employee relationships?
5. How do attitudes and other personal values impact business and employee relationships?
6. What are important organizational values?
7. What do action orientation, equity, entrepreneurship, teamwork, and visionary leadership have in common? (*Hint:* Supply a simple, one- or two-word answer.)
8. What are major human relations challenges or problems?

NOTES

1. Henry W. Tulloch and W. Scott Bauman, *The Management of Business Conduct* (Charlottesville, Va.: Center for Applied Ethics, University of Virginia, 1981), p. 9.

2. Mark Pastin, *The Hard Problems of Management: Gaining the Ethics Edge* (San Francisco: Jossey-Bass, 1986), p. xii (italics in original).

3. Laura L. Nash, "Ethics Without the Sermon," *Harvard Business Review*, November–December 1981, pp. 79–90.

4. Kenneth Blanchard and Norman Vincent Peale, *The Power of Ethical Management* (New York: Fawcett Crest, 1988), p. 20.

5. Ibid., p. 79.

6. Art Carey quoted in Patricia Romano, "Work Hard to Improve Work Ethic," *The Coloradoan* (Ft. Collins), May 13, 1996, p. D6.

7. Kevin Murphy, quoted in Carol Borchert, "Book Addresses Honesty in the Workplace," *Comment*, November 12, 1992, p. 4.

8. "Nielsen Shares Secrets of Success," *Beta Gamma Sigma* [professional business] *Newsletter*, Summer 1988, p. 2.

9. William B. Werther, Jr., "Loyalty at Work," *Harvard Business Review*, March–April 1988, pp. 28, 35.

10. Shoshana Zuboff, *In the Age of the Smart Machine: The Future of Work and Power* (New York: Basic Books, 1988), p. 395.

11. "How the Best Get Better," *Business Week*, September 14, 1987, p. 99.

12. Peter F. Drucker, "The Retail Revolution," *The Wall Street Journal*, July 15, 1993, p. A14.

13. Based on research and private communication from Dr. Leonard Berry, chair and professor of marketing, Texas A & M University.

14. Peter Block, *Stewardship: Choosing Service Over Self-Interest* (San Francisco: Berrett-Koehler Publishers, 1996).

15. Judith Clabes, "Be a Good Person, and Values Follow," *Rocky Mountain News*, June 25, 1993, p. 38C.

16. Elwood N. Chapman, *Your Attitude Is Showing*, 7th ed. (New York: Macmillan, 1993), p. 4.

17. Donald G. Smith, "Humorlessness Is No Joke," *The Wall Street Journal*, April 1, 1996, p. A14.

18. Barry Leeds, " 'Mystery Shopping' Offers Clues to Quality Service," *Bank Marketing*, November 1992, pp. 24–26.

19. John D. Long, "Common Courtesy: Less Common?" *Business Horizons*, January–February 1990, pp. 133–143.

20. Suzanne Chazin, "The Ultimate Key to Success," *Reader's Digest*, April 1992, pp. 21, 26.

21. Tom Peters, "How to Succeed in Small Business by Really Trying Harder than Others," *Rocky Mountain News*, November 17, 1992, p. 95.

22. Mircea Manicatide and Virginia Pennell, "Key Developments in Compensation Management," *HR Focus*, October 1992, pp. 3–4.

23. Roberta Maynard, "How to Be a Great Boss," *Nation's Business*, December 1991, pp. 44–45.

24. Vic Sussman, "Don't Fear Failure," *Reader's Digest*, June 1990, pp. 116–118.

25. Joline Godfrey, "Young Women Find a New Way to Succeed as Entrepreneurs," *Rocky Mountain News*, June 8, 1993, p. 43A.

26. Marian Wright Edelman, *The Measure of Our Success: A Letter to My Children and Yours* (Boston: Beacon Press, 1992), p. 54.

27. John W. Gardner, "The Antileadership Vaccine," Annual Report of the Carnegie Corporation (New York: Carnegie Corporation, 1965), p. 12.

RECOMMENDED READING

Aaron, Hugh. "Do the Right Thing in Business." *The Wall Street Journal*, June 21, 1993, p. A10.

Belasco, James A., and Ralph C. Stayer. *Flight of the Buffalo: Soaring to Excellence, Learning to Let Employees Lead.* New York: Warner Books, 1993.

Cheney, Lynne. "Hard Work: Once as American as Apple Pie." *The Wall Street Journal*, April 6, 1993, p. A14.

Collins, James C. *Beyond Entrepreneurship: Turning Your Business into an Enduring Great Company.* Englewood Cliffs, N.J.: Prentice Hall, 1992.

Covey, Stephen R. *The Seven Habits of Highly Effective People.* New York: Simon & Schuster, 1989.

Edelman, Marian Wright. *The Measure of Our Success: A Letter to My Children and Yours.* Boston: Beacon Press, 1992.

Egan, Gerard. *Adding Value: A Systematic Guide to Business-Driven Management and Leadership.* San Francisco: Jossey-Bass, 1993.

Galin, Michele. "Work and Family." *Business Week*, June 28, 1993, pp. 80–88.

Gray Matters: A Business Ethics Game. Baltimore, Md.: Martin Marietta, 1992.

Herman, Roger E. *Keeping Good People: Strategies for Solving the Dilemma of the Decade.* New York: McGraw-Hill, 1991.

Hoekstra, Pete. "Mandated Cooperation: A '90s Oxymoron." *The Wall Street Journal*, June 7, 1993, p. A14.

Jacobs, Michael T. *Short-Term America: The Causes and Cures of Our Business Myopia.* Boston: Harvard Business School Press, 1991.

Jellison, Jerald M. *Overcoming Resistance: A Practical Guide to Producing Change in the Workplace.* New York: Simon & Schuster, 1993.

Long, John D. "Common Courtesy: Less Common?" *Business Horizons,* January–February 1990, pp. 133–143.

Murphy, Kevin. *Honesty in the Workplace.* Pacific Grove, Calif.: Brooks-Cole, 1993.

Senge, Peter. "Building Learning Organizations." *Journal for Quality & Participation,* March 1992, pp. 59–72.

Thorbeck, John. "The Turnaround Value of Values." *Harvard Business Review,* January–February 1991, pp. 52–61.

PART 2
INDIVIDUAL CHALLENGES

GETTING TO KNOW OURSELVES AND OUR OPPORTUNITIES

3

PERSONAL DEVELOPMENT: STRESS, TIME, AND CAREER MANAGEMENT

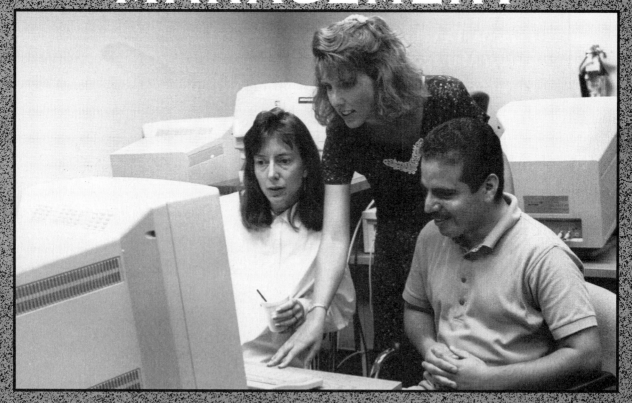

Here are a few questions to think about before starting to read this chapter. In fact, these questions need to be answered before you can begin a meaningful career. Talk with classmates and others about your answers.

- Is stress good or bad? What types of stress are good? What types are bad?
- What roles do stress and time play in my personal development?
- How can I better manage my time? Who manages my time—me or others?
- Whose responsibility is career development?
- When should I start thinking about my career development?
- What do I want to be doing five years from now? ten? twenty?
- How many times do I anticipate changing jobs before then?
- How do I measure success?

Learning Goals

After studying this chapter, you should be able to:

1. Distinguish between stress and tension, and between distress and eustress.
2. Describe the differences between Type A, H, and B behaviors.
3. List at least four ways to manage stress.
4. Set time priorities consistent with goals.
5. Use various tools and techniques of time control.
6. Improve work habits including reading, paperwork, telephone, and workplace habits.
7. Discuss the stages in career development and career advancement.
8. Develop your own personal action plans for career development.
9. Define and apply the following terms and concepts (in order of first occurrence):

- **work**
- **stress**
- **eustress**
- **distress**
- **Type A behavior**
- **Type H behavior**
- **Type B behavior**
- **workaholic**
- **anger**
- **career development**
- **career paths**
- **résumé**
- **flextime**
- **job sharing**
- **telecommuting**

PLANS FOR PERSONAL DEVELOPMENT

Introducing the concepts of career and other types of personal development early in this book helps to put the rest of the book in perspective. How we meet individual, group, and organizational challenges and adapt to change and different cultures can be personally rewarding.

Work—purposeful activity—is as natural as other life relationships. People thrive on things they do well, and work can be one of those things. To make work and life truly rewarding, it is necessary to have personal development and career plans. Having a goal and a flexible charted course of action enables planning for all the other human relations opportunities that arise in life.

STRESS

Among the factors impacting our personal development is stress. Not all stress is bad. Positive stress and tension, in large part, create and play major roles in personal development. Stress and tension also help us learn how to cope with multiple demands and develop our personal skills.

Stress refers to pressure, strain, or force on a system. Human stress includes physical and psychological stress. Too much of either can lead to fatigue or damage of the affected system.

According to Hans Selye, an expert on stress, there are two types of stress. **Eustress** is the positive type that has its foundations in meeting the challenges of a task or job. This type of stress manifests itself in achievement and accomplishment. The effects of eustress are beneficial in that they help us to overcome obstacles.

Distress is negative in that it allows us to be overpowered. Anger, loss of control, and feelings of inadequacy and insecurity are all manifestations of distress. We teeter on the edge of collapse because of these phenomena. If not restrained, serious physical and psychological health problems can result.

Stress and tension are natural. We need them to do our best work. We need them to get the adrenalin flowing. So we cannot hope to—nor would we want to—eliminate all excitement and accompanying stress from our jobs. Too much stress and tension on or off the job, however, can have a negative effect. In most cases the person, not the job, creates the tension. Many causes of stress originate off the job and serve to disrupt job performance.

Most stress is created by the person, not the job.

Negative stressors result in lower and poorer production, difficult relationships with other workers, inadequate attention and concentration, memory lapses, tardiness, and absenteeism. About 80 percent of the emotional problems of employees are caused by distress. The good supervisor must be prepared to help with these problems.

A promotion frequently creates added stress that can ruin a person's work and spill over into his or her home life. Some persons welcome and thrive on heavy stress and pressure at work. Some recognize when they have had enough and refuse an advancement—which often confounds people in management. Most people want the promotion, but don't want the added headaches, stresses, and responsibilities that accompany it.

**ACTION PROJECT
3-1**   STRESS-PRONE PERSONALITY QUIZ (INDIVIDUAL EXERCISE)

Rate yourself using the following scale on how you typically react in each of the situations given:

4 = very often   3 = frequently   2 = sometimes   1 = very seldom

1. I try to do as much as possible in the least amount of time. _____
2. I become impatient with delays or interruptions. _____
3. I have to win at games to enjoy myself. _____
4. I find myself speeding up the car to get through amber lights. _____
5. I hesitate to ask for or indicate I need help with a problem. _____
6. I seek the respect and admiration of others. _____
7. I am critical of the way others do their work. _____
8. I have the habit of looking at my watch or clock often. _____
9. I strive to better my position and achievements. _____
10. I spread myself "too thin" in terms of time. _____
11. I have the habit of doing more than one thing at a time. _____
12. I get angry or irritable. _____
13. I have little time for hobbies or time by myself. _____
14. I have a tendency to talk quickly or hasten conversations. _____
15. I consider myself hard-driving. _____
16. My friends and relatives consider me to be hard-driving. _____
17. I have a tendency to get involved in multiple projects. _____
18. I have a lot of deadlines in my work. _____
19. I feel guilty when I relax and do nothing during leisure time. _____
20. I take on too many responsibilities. _____

Now, add your ratings. Use the following guidelines to determine your susceptibility to stress:

20–30 Nonproductive

30–50 Good balance

50–60 Too tense

60+   Good candidate for heart disease, especially if hostile

TYPES A, H, AND B BEHAVIOR

Type A is impatient, goal oriented.

Type A persons are highly competitive, feel time pressures, and may have several projects going at the same time. The Type A person is likely to set personal deadlines or quotas for work and home at least once a week. The Type A person frequently brings work home. Such persons are highly achievement oriented and push themselves to near capacity. Hard-driving Type A students earn more academic honors than do their peers.

Some Type A persons are at more health risk than other Type A's. Research shows that it is not being a hard worker that puts a person at high risk of having a heart attack. It is being a hostile, hard worker. Redford Williams, M.D., director of the Behavioral Medicine Research Center at Duke University, observes that the most dangerous Type A characteristic is hostility. Anger, cynicism, and aggression are strong expressions of hostility. **Type H,** then, is a subset of Type A behavior. The "H" refers to hostility, and some Type A people show a lot of hostility. Recent studies show that hostility is the trait most closely associated with heart disease. Dr. Williams told an American Heart Association forum that, of all the aspects originally associated with the Type A personality, only those traits related to hostility contribute to coronary disease.[1]

Type H stands for hostility.

Type A workers may be called workaholics, fast paced, competitive, and impatient but these traits do not contribute to disease. However, Type H workers who are hostile and display anger, cynicism, and aggression are risking health problems.

Type B persons put their time in at work and seldom bring work home. They are more inclined to have interests in sports or leisure activities. Time is not a master, and proving their worth to themselves or to others is not a strong requirement of their personalities. They can be as intelligent as Type A's, but they do not work hard to prove it. Type B persons are less likely to demand strong control of their lives and environments. The heartbeat is much quicker to slow down after mental stress in the Type B person than in the hostile Type H.

SELF-APPRAISAL

Are You a Type H? Measure Your Hostility

1. Do you think you have to yell at subordinates so they don't mess up? _____
2. Do you assume cashiers will shortchange you if they can? _____
3. If your child spills milk, do you immediately yell? _____
4. After an irritating encounter, do you feel shaky or breathless? _____
5. Do you feel your anger is justified? Do you feel an urge to punish people? ___
6. Do you get angry every time you stand in line? get behind the wheel? _____

"Yes" answers show you are Type H, but check here to see how far it has progressed. (A "Yes" to Question 6 shows the highest level of hostility; to Question 1 the lowest.):

- A "Yes" to Questions 1 or 2 indicates cynical mistrust—that you expect the worst from people and take it personally.
- A "Yes" to Question 3 shows that you are expressing anger—whether your responses are automatic or slightly disguised.

- A "Yes" to Question 4 shows that your body is experiencing the effects of hostility.
- A "Yes" to Question 5 indicates reactions that are aggressively hostile.
- A "Yes" to Question 6 means that hostility has become a habit.[2]

WORKAHOLICS: FORTUNE'S FAVORITE CHILDREN

Workaholics exhibit many type A traits. A **workaholic** is a person who takes great satisfaction in work but may carry that commitment to an extreme preoccupation. They put in long hours, often neglecting their families. They cut subordinates loose and compete ferociously. Emphasis has moved away from trying to change basic personality traits to modifying behavior. Hans Selye, an expert in the field, has said that a race horse cannot become a snail; the best it can become is a slow trotter. It is usually part of the person's makeup and is difficult to change—the trait is even noticeable in childhood.

Workaholics enjoy their work; it is not a sacrifice or an imposition. What sets them apart is their attitude toward work, not the number of hours they work. Work is the dominant role in life, and the mate and family may seem to suffer; inactivity is intolerable and having free time means boredom. Even vacations are hard to take.

Workaholism in all probability is permanent and can only be modified. Yet as Winston Churchill stated, "Those whose work and pleasures are one are fortune's favorite children." At times, workaholism can become a problem for individuals and organizations. Figure 3–1 lists some of its symptoms and gives tips on coping with workaholism.

HOW TO SURVIVE STRESS

Stress is more than a matter of emotional problems and personality conflicts: It is a problem that affects the corporate balance sheet. Manifestations of stress such as ulcers, stroke, heart attack, alcoholism, drug dependency, and social breakdowns can also lead to low productivity, absenteeism, hospitalization, and premature death.

Several corporate programs are designed to take stress out of the job, or at least to minimize distress and reduce costs. Texas Instruments and John Hancock Mutual Life Insurance companies hold sessions that teach relaxation and coping skills. Several companies have built gyms and wellness centers. PepsiCo provides worker incentives that include rebates on fees for programs for losing weight and keeping it off. Adolph Coors Company holds stress classes, including one on the stress of child rearing.

A person undergoing stress feels "keyed up." Stress is usually accompanied by feelings of arousal or agitation. The problem is that when such arousal occurs, thoughts and actions become more primitive. As people become more and more agitated, their thoughts become more simplistic; they

FIGURE 3–1 How to Detect and Treat Workaholism.

Symptoms

- Rigid, inflexible, narrow, and overfocused in their thinking.
- Need to be in control and often engage in ritualistic behavior.
- Unable to delegate work; overly concerned about details.
- Can't say no; poor at setting priorities.
- Intolerant, impatient, and demanding of others, poor personal relationships.
- Not team players, uncooperative.
- Can't handle criticism; need constant approval of work.
- Can't rest or relax; constant feelings of inadequacy, guilt, and loneliness.

Tips

- Focus on results, not hours at the workplace; manage by objective.
- Restructure jobs that carry too much responsibility.
- Find a steady pace at work; create challenges that don't involve crises.
- Don't deliberate over minor decisions; use time wisely.
- Learn to delegate tasks and do so without interfering.
- Schedule time away from the office or workplace.
- Develop friends and relationships outside of work.
- Determine what you are avoiding by overworking.
- Do not take work home and avoid thinking about work at home.[3]

notice less in the environment, revert to older habits, and all complicated responses in their repertoire disappear.

When it is said that a piece of metal is "stressed," it means that the stationary metal is being acted on. Tension is the result of this stress. Notice that stress occurs when something external has been applied. The implication for us is that if an individual sees himself or herself as passive and his or her fate as being controlled by others, that person is more susceptible to stress in the form of unplanned external events. On the other hand, a person whose self-concept is more active is less susceptible to stress.

MAKE STRESS WORK FOR YOU

Don't fight tension.

Don't fight tension—use it. Built-up tensions can cause grave trouble, and telling ourselves not to be tense rarely works. We cannot always remove the source of our tensions. However, when you are tense, you are temporarily more energetic, alert, and aggressive. Start doing a job you have been putting off for a long time or one that seems to be a tremendous task. You will enjoy the feeling of accomplishment that such drive can give; your tension will ease and perhaps even disappear.

Tackle one thing at a time.

Tackle one thing at a time. Anxiety gives us a restless dissatisfaction with ourselves when we attempt to do too many things at once. For example, you find that you are not as successful at work as you would like so you decide to go to night school to work on your degree. You barely get started and you are asked to join a civic club that would provide some good contacts. You wish you had more money to buy better clothes, and you think of moonlighting to buy a new wardrobe. If you suffer persistent anxiety by starting things, dropping them, and becoming hopelessly distracted, then tackle one thing at a time. Stick with it until you have done all you can do about it.

Laugh at yourself.

Finally, laugh at yourself on occasion. The way to tell whether you are leaning too heavily toward role playing or pretense is to ask yourself, "When was the last time I had a good laugh at my own expense?" In fact, the following rules for stress management offer humorous but helpful, tongue-in-cheek advice.

THREE RULES FOR STRESS MANAGEMENT

1. If you can't flee, flow.
2. Don't sweat the small stuff.
3. It's all small stuff!

Situations are not inherently stressful.

We have to get away from the assumption that a situation is inherently stressful or nonstressful. We are the ones who put the labels there. We can also remove them. The feeling is often that stress will go on forever. It is not the stress itself that is painful and disabling but the impression that it will never end. It is this erroneous projection of a feeling, rather than the pain itself, that reduces people's ability to cope.

People like to control their own fate.

People like to see themselves as able to control their own fate. A primary contributor to stress is the feeling of "losing control." The painfulness of the subsequent stress may result not from the actual fact of losing control, but from the individual's unwillingness to admit that he or she is capable of losing control.

If people can accept both their strengths and their weaknesses, they can control stress. If they regard themselves as persons who are capable of controlling events, even while recognizing that there are occasions when they cannot, then they will be in a much better position to manage stress. If they are unable to adapt, a physical or mental breakdown may result.

CONTROLLING ANGER

Anger is an emotional feeling of distress as opposed to the physical manifestation of anger—hostility. Anger may be a manifestation of stress, but it is not a productive result. All jobs have or maybe should have an element of at least positive stress. Anger and loss of control because of the stress can have fatal consequences.

SURVIVING STRESS

Here is a seven-step survival plan. Remember to PLEASE yourself to a "T."

P **Plan.** Disorganization can breed stress. Having too many projects going on simultaneously often leads to confusion and forgetfulness when uncompleted projects are hanging over your head. When possible, take on projects one at a time and work on them until completed.

L **Learn to tolerate.** Many of us set unreasonable goals, and, since we can never be perfect, we often have a sense of failure no matter how well we perform. So set reasonable goals for yourself.

E **Enjoy life.** You need to escape occasionally from the pressures of life and have fun. Find activities that are absorbing and enjoyable no matter what your level of ability or skill at doing them.

A **Assert positive attitudes.** Learn to praise the things you like in others. Focus on the good qualities that those around you possess.

S **Set tolerance limits.** Intolerance of others leads to frustration and anger. An attempt to really understand the way other people feel can make you more accepting of them.

E **Exercise.** First, check with your doctor before beginning any exercise program. Then, select an exercise program you will enjoy. You will be more likely to stay with a program you yourself chose, especially if you pick one that you really enjoy rather than one that is drudgery.

T **Talk out tensions.** Find a friend, a member of the clergy, a counselor, or a psychologist with whom you can be open. Expressing your bottled-up tension to a sympathetic ear can be incredibly helpful in relieving that tension. Even if no solutions are reached, you may feel better about addressing your problems after releasing these tensions.

Various psychologists advise that controlling your emotions is an important skill. Anger signals that something is wrong. It is often a sign of faulty communications, and it has negative consequences. Psychologists Plas and Hoover-Dempsey advocate that everyone should plan in advance how to react to negative feedback.

> Learning to understand your emotions and coping with them when problems arise can make a tremendous difference in how you are perceived by others. Whenever anger flares at work, remember that good communication often makes hostility disappear. So even if a conversation is interrupted, make sure you get back to it. When you can effectively replace anger with good communication, you've learned one of the hardest but most important lessons of building effective interoffice relationships.[4]

Some companies, in an effort to manage anger, are implementing strict rules that prohibit angry behavior.[5] Similarly, psychologist Jerry Deffenbacher says that it is unrealistic to expect to eliminate anger:

The goal of intervention should be on *anger management*, not anger elimination. It is idealistic to believe that anger will or can ever be eliminated. Frustration, pain, injustice, and disagreement will continue. People become ill, jobs are lost, relationships end, others are inconsiderate and obnoxious. Even when anger regarding these events is well managed, a realist residue of mild anger (e.g., frustration, disappointment, annoyance, irritation) remains, and difficult choices remain to be made and implemented.[6]

AVOIDING BURNOUT

A recognized syndrome related to stress is job burnout, which follows a period of self-induced stress. Individuals in the counseling occupations such as lawyers, nurses, teachers, and mental health professionals are especially prone to burnout. As we increase the number of professional workers in counseling occupations, the opportunities for burnout will increase. Recognizing the symptoms, phases, and methods of overcoming burnout will help reduce its impact.

SYMPTOMS OF BURNOUT (BEYOND STRESS)

1. Chronic fatigue and low energy.
2. Irritability and negative attitude.
3. Idealistic, inflexible, and indecisive viewpoints.

FOUR PHASES OF BURNOUT

1. Emotional exhaustion.
2. Cynicism and defensiveness.
3. Isolation, tendency to eat alone and act antisocial.
4. Defeatism, feeling of having been unsuccessful with all job effort having been fruitless.

HOW TO OVERCOME BURNOUT

1. List priorities. Schedule yourself to do less.
2. Make goals that are achievable.
3. Compartmentalize by focusing on one job at a time.
4. Make changes in your job routine. Even schedule fun times.
5. Listen to your body. Your listless feeling may indicate you need more exercise, a better diet, or more sleep.
6. Develop a detached concern. Be concerned with your clients, but don't make them your problems. Build support groups by having contacts with people outside of work.

Another potentially positive and negative stressor is time. Time can be a positive stressor if we manage it, rather than letting it manage us. But if we become constantly rushed for time, always having to take our work home with us and working all of the time, then time becomes a negative stressor.

How we manage our time is also a major determinant of our personal development. All of us have the same amount of time in any given day. What we do with that time can determine our priorities, our future opportunities, our career options, and can help determine how successful we are.

WE ALL HAVE THE SAME AMOUNT OF TIME

Keep a "to do" list.

It makes good business sense to keep a calendar of appointments and a "to do" list. There will be a big payoff for a small amount of time spent each morning or evening in planning for the upcoming day. In addition to this planning time, we all need some "quiet" time during the day to get organized, to set priorities, and to think.

Some people's internal clocks and habits allow them to do their planning and organizing early in the morning; others prefer late evening. Regardless, we all have the same amount of time per day and planning it can help us maximize its use.

If you have difficulty losing or keeping track of time, it might be helpful to keep a detailed sample log of your time for a week or two. To see how you are doing, record your time in 10-, 15-, or 30-minute intervals and, then, at the end of the week categorize and tabulate how you spent your time (see Figure 3–2).

FIGURE 3–2 Log for Intermittent Time Analysis.

DAY OF THE WEEK_____	DATE_____	
Time:	Activity:	Interruptions:
pre-6 A.M.		
6:00 A.M.		
6:15		
6:30		
6:45		
7:00		
7:15		
7:30		
7:45		
8:00		
8:15		
8:30		
8:45		
9:00		
9:15		
9:30		
9:45		

Time	
10:00	
10:15	
10:30	
10:45	
11:00	
11:15	
11:30	
11:45	
noon	
12:15 P.M.	
12:30	
12:45	
1:00	
1:15	
1:30	
1:45	
2:00	
2:15	
2:30	
2:45	
3:00	
3:15	
3:30	
3:45	
4:00	
4:15	
4:30	
4:45	
5:00	
5:15	
5:30	
5:45	
6:00	
6:15	
6:30	
6:45	
7:00	
7:15	
7:30	
7:45	
8:00	
8:15	
8:30	
8:45	
9:00	
9:15	
9:30	
9:45	
10:00	
post-10 P.M.	

SET PRIORITIES ON YOUR TIME

The key to time management is setting priorities.[7] Most time management authorities recommend keeping a prioritized "to do" list. Tasks to be accomplished on a given day are listed with a space for assigning a priority code. One way to order daily tasks is by using the ABC priority system. The "A" is for activities with the highest priority, "B" for medium priority, and "C" for low priority. After this "first cut" at prioritizing the list, the A's can be prioritized as A_1, A_2, A_3, and so on. Likewise for the B's and C's. Work on the A's first or at least during your peak hours of performance. Alan Lakein explains:

> Some people do as many items as possible on their lists. They get a very high percentage of tasks done, but their effectiveness is low because the tasks they've done are mostly of C-priority. Others like to start at the top of the list and go right down it, again with little regard to what's important. The best way is to take your list and label each item according to ABC priority, delegate as much as you can, and then polish off the list accordingly.[8]

Figure 3–3 shows a prioritized daily "to do" list. Using a prioritized list allows us to spend 80 percent of our time on the most important items rather than the all-too-common practice of spending 80 percent of our time on routine activities.

THE TELEPHONE PARADOX

Being put on "hold" is not all bad.

The telephone can be a tremendous time saver. A quick call can answer questions that must be determined before you can proceed on an A-priority project. On the other hand, if you are put on hold, the telephone can be a time

---

FIGURE 3–3 Abbreviated Example of Daily "to Do" List.

C_2	_____	Call Morgan about Reardon project
B_1	_____	Complete paper on "Tech Transfer" for next month
A_1	_____	Finish report due next Friday
A_2	_____	Work on proposal for SBA
C_3	_____	Arrange itinerary for next month's trip—call travel agent
B_2	_____	Plan local travel and appointments for next week
A_4	_____	Letter to Bill Jones (fire problem)
A_3	_____	Refine goals with boss (make appointment)
B_4	_____	Call Johnsen about maintenance service
B_5	_____	Call City of Greeley engineer about new process they want
C_1	_____	Revise filing system
B_3	_____	Recreation time—call M.R.

waster. It need not be. Have work such as reading in front of you to do while on hold. Stay on hold, reading and working on papers, if you want to so that you and the person you are calling do not get into a game of "telephone tag," or calling each other back.

Avoid "telephone tag." If you are away from your workplace, try to group the return of telephone calls. Again, be in control of your own time where possible. And, as Robert Townsend recommended in *Up the Organization,* there is nothing wrong with answering your own telephone—when you want to do so.

MANAGE YOUR OWN TIME

Although it is not possible to make time for certain activities, it is essential to take time for yourself. Be in control of your own schedule so that you can work on A-priority projects. Organize your schedule and workplace to the point that they work for you. Table 3–1 presents ten summary tips for effective time management.

Iacocca's time planning. On a longer term scale, it is necessary to set priorities on an annual basis. Planning time for major projects and also for major relaxation are equally important. Lee Iacocca, in his autobiography, tells about the importance of planning and time.

> The ability to concentrate and to use your time well is everything if you want to succeed in business—or almost anywhere else, for that matter. Ever since college I've always worked hard during the week while trying to keep my weekends free for family and recreation. . . . Every Sunday night I get the adrenalin going again by making an outline of what I want to accomplish during the upcoming week. . . .
>
> I'm constantly amazed by the number of people who can't seem to control their own schedules. Over the years, I've had many executives come to me and say with pride: "Boy, last year I worked so hard that I didn't take any vacation." . . . I always feel like responding: "You dummy. You mean to tell me that you can take responsibility for an $80 million project and you can't plan two weeks out of the year to go off with your family and have some fun?"[9]

Increasingly, most managers want their subordinates to take vacations to avoid burnout. Of course, the vacation has to be planned so that it is not a bad time for the business.

TABLE 3–1 Ten Tips for Effective Time Management

1. Keep an intermittent time log for a week or two to see how you spend your time.
2. Plan daily, intermediate, and long-term goals.
3. Keep "to do" lists.
4. Prioritize activities.
5. Schedule your time realistically.
6. Improve your communication skills, including meeting management.
7. Make big projects manageable.
8. Balance your personal and professional life.
9. Organize your physical space.
10. Control interruptions and be willing to say "no."

YOUR DESK OR OTHER WORKPLACE

There has always been a running battle between the "clean desk" and the "cluttered desk" advocates. The former say that "a cluttered desk is a sign of a cluttered mind," while the latter argue that "a cluttered desk is a sign of genius." Regardless, the work area should be arranged comfortably for the principal workers. They should have close access to their tools and machines of production.

A survey of 100 executives by Accountemps, a temporary employment service, found that "people with neat desks stand a much better chance of promotion than coworkers with messy desks."[10] But there were perceived differences between top executives and middle managers. Desks used by middle managers were much more likely to be cluttered than those of the top executives, according to the survey.

A clean desk, however, doesn't guarantee job success—just as a messy desk would not be the only factor considered in a promotion or demotion. It is a point that many managers have a strong opinion about, and may consider with other factors in advancement or firings. What you want to achieve is a work space that is organized so that you have no more than ten items on your desk at a time and you are able to find what you need without lost time.[11]

ACTION PROJECT 3–2   TYPICAL TIME WASTERS (INDIVIDUAL EXERCISE)

This exercise is designed to give you some insight into some typical time wasters which may currently be part of your lifestyle. Please complete the form by rating yourself using the following scale:

4 = very often   3 = frequently   2 = sometimes   1 = very seldom

1. Indecision regarding what to do next _____
2. Daydreaming _____
3. Drawn-out conversations _____
4. Lack of concentration _____
5. Procrastination _____
6. Unclear priorities _____
7. Unnecessary socializing _____
8. Prolonged phone calls _____
9. Excessive TV watching _____
10. Little self-direction _____
11. Inability to say "no" _____
12. Too many commitments _____
13. Stressed out/too anxious _____
14. Partying _____
15. Inability to find anything _____

16. Not using time between classes (and all other short periods) _____
17. Shuffling papers _____
18. Staring at the books _____
19. Oversleeping _____
20. Trouble getting organized _____

Now, add your ratings. Use the following guidelines to determine your time efficiency:

20–30   Relatively time efficient

30–50   Good balance

50–60   You waste a lot of time

60+   Good candidate for time management course

MEETINGS—TIME WASTERS? OR COMMUNICATION TOOLS?

WHERE TO MEET?

Management by Walking Around (MBWA).

As with the telephone, meetings and where to have them are a dilemma. Tradition suggests that the subordinate goes to the boss's office—out of deference to status and to "save" the boss time in getting to the meeting. Techniques such as MBWA, "Management by Walking Around," practiced at Hewlett-Packard and other companies, have changed that.

There is some benefit to be gained by going to the other person's office. You usually remain in control of your time by being able to exit more freely than if someone is in your workplace. That doesn't always work, but it's worth a try. Even if someone is in your office or workplace, you can still control the meeting and her/his departure by your summary of the meeting and movement away from or out of your workplace.

FORMAL MEETINGS

Use an agenda.

Meetings are information dissemination and participation tools.

Meeting convenors should solicit agenda items from participants, distribute the agenda in advance, and begin and end the meeting at a prestated time. A further dilemma about meetings is how often to have them. Having meetings just because they are routinely scheduled at that time is a time waster if there are no agenda items to be discussed. The irony of not having regular meetings is that the people who complain the most about meetings are the same ones who, in the absence of meetings, complain that they don't know what is going on in their organization.

Meetings also provide an opportunity for significant participation, a topic to be discussed later in this book. Strive to obtain balanced participation; control the long-winded and draw out the silent.

SEVERAL RULES FOR EFFECTIVE MEETINGS AND THEIR LEADERSHIP

A. Preparation for meeting
- Limit the number of participants to those persons who are needed to reach a decision on the topic confronting the group.
- Schedule the meeting properly: (1) allocate time according to the relative importance of each topic, and (2) schedule meetings before natural quitting time, such as lunch.
- Determine the specific purpose of the meeting in your own mind.
- Develop and distribute the agenda in advance.

B. Leading the meeting
- Start the meeting on time. Do not wait for latecomers.
- Start with the most important item on the agenda. Then stick to the agenda; permit only emergency interruptions.
- Be sensitive to hidden agendas and the social–emotional needs of members.
- Summarize group progress and restate conclusions to ensure agreement.
- Make specific assignments for the next meeting.
- End the meeting on time to allow participants to plan their own time effectively.

C. Follow-up meeting
- Distribute the minutes or a summary of the proceedings. It is especially important to communicate group decisions to the group members.

Unless you know what your time is worth and how to evaluate the time cost of what you do, it is almost impossible to make a correct decision or to evaluate properly what action to take in a given situation. Too many people spend $50 worth of time on a $1 job. Table 3–2 illustrates what your time is worth by the hour, based on 244 eight-hour working days per year (a five-day week less vacation and holidays).

The chart shows the broad average of the entire day based on annual income. You should also decide what your priority of time is for each activity in which you are engaged. Some things you do are more important, and more profitable, than others.

CAREER DEVELOPMENT

INDIVIDUAL RESPONSIBILITY

The individual has the primary responsibility for his or her career development. **Career development** includes all of the activities necessary to help individuals

TABLE 3–2 What Is Your Time Worth?

IF YOUR ANNUAL EARNINGS ARE	EVERY HOUR IS WORTH
$10,000	$5.12
12,000	6.15
15,000	7.68
18,000	9.22
20,000	10.25
25,000	12.81
30,000	15.37
35,000	17.93
40,000	20.49
50,000	25.61
60,000	30.74
75,000	38.42
100,000	51.23

Career development starts with self-aware-ness.

become aware of and acquire the knowledge, skills, and competence to perform different jobs. Career development, like time management, is a personal, goal-oriented activity. No one can set your goals or plan your career for you.

No matter how sophisticated an organization's training program or job rotation system might be, you will usually have to take the initiative in planning your career. Career development starts with a self-awareness—knowing where you are and where you want to be in five, ten, or twenty years. Any gaps between your present situation and your future goals provide the basis for career planning.

PROFILE OF HUMAN BEHAVIOR

NORMAN O. VLASS

Norman Vlass has enjoyed a varied and productive career pattern over 35 years. Most of that time he worked for the Hewlett-Packard Company (H-P) as marketing and personnel managers. He has managerial-level business experience in marketing products and services to domestic and international locations, including Western Europe, Asia, and selected foreign countries. His areas of expertise include sales and distribution, contract negotiation, sales training, major product management, management recruiting, and leadership development.

As a senior human resource manager, Norman was responsible for training and employee development programs, compensation, counseling, and computer support. Norm retired from H-P in 1990 after 22 years and began work full time as an instructor in management and marketing for a major university. He was voted outstanding teacher by his college's students in 1993.

Unlike his distinguished and fruitful career at H-P, Norm's first job was as a chemical fertilizer salesman. He jokes that he started his career by selling fertilizer and continues to do so today—only in larger quantities!

Norm Vlass's career has been a stressful one in a positive sense—even as a fertilizer salesman he challenged himself to go beyond quotas and to develop new markets. He gives the example of driving into a small western U.S. town at midafternoon. Instead of checking into the motel and watching television before his next day's appointments, Norm scouted the town and started making calls that afternoon. That's a good example of positive or "happy" stress—eustress.

To this day, Norm enjoys positive health, balancing his life between family, community projects including membership on several boards of directors, and his teaching job. Of all the items discussed in this chapter, Norm says: "Time management is the most important; goal setting is the key to good time management." He does not view stress management as a major focus area, but as noted, he balances many potentially stressful activities. One time management tool Norm uses is managing meetings: "Have a set agenda and stick to it. Without an agenda, you don't have a meeting."

Career development is the responsibility of the individual, according to Norm. "Career management is a function of training and development. [The] company should provide some of the tools—not the motivation." Individuals have the responsibility for their careers, and they must develop new technological and interpersonal skills. He continues: "Leadership skills have the potential to either make or break the professional manager in the future as we reach into a global community with increased competition for markets and qualified management personnel. The words *courage, commitment, perseverance,* and *integrity* continue to fit the leader profile with a continued focus on values and ethics in business and personal relationships."

Vlass predicts that by the year 2000, "human resource managers will take on more of a leadership role in organizations," that "human resource managers will need to be the best equipped to understand and teach managers," that "higher levels of individual productivity will be *expected*," and that there will be "more focus on automation and internal skill development of the workforce." He explains that when the human resource manager (HRM) has "the ability to speak the language of management in a knowledgeable way that enhances communication, the position of HRM speaks with more credibility in relationships with other functional managers within an organization. Without this skill, the HRM limits his or her ability to speak with credibility and represent the authority of the HRM position."

Individuals must be willing to take short-term trade-offs for long-term gains. Some positions may be lateral transfers in today's increasingly flat organizations. An individual must also be prepared to leave an organization and perhaps a geographic region. The most important aspect of career development is to keep one's options open.

There are several stages in a person's career and life development. Become aware of career opportunities by talking with job counselors and researching literature such as the *Occupational Outlook Handbook* published by the U.S. Department of Labor. Current job opportunities as well as longer term forecasts of job demands are available in current periodicals, such as *The Wall Street Journal, USA Today,* and industry-specific journals.

One way of looking at a person's career and life development is through age, career phase, and manifestations of these.

AGES	CAREER PHASES	MANIFESTATIONS
Less than 25	Pulling up roots	Break with parents; establish own identity
25–31	Provisional adulthood	A period of trial and autonomy
32–40	Transitional period	Questioning of self, life, values
41–49	Settling down	Resolved to own/others' infallibility/mortality
50–60	Potential plateauing/midlife crisis	Career reassessment; "What will be, will be"
Over 60	Reestablishment	Maturity/late career changes; continued growth, retirement, or decline

ORGANIZATIONAL RESPONSIBILITY

Organizations can help you in various stages of your career development process. Many organizations are involved in some type of career development activity, ranging from one-on-one counseling to announcing available training and development seminars. To capitalize on an employer's help, you need to recognize the stages in career development.

STAGES IN CAREER DEVELOPMENT

1. Job search
2. Settling down and settling in
3. Changing with the organization
4. Midcareer changes and personal crises (burnout, lack of job challenge, plateauing, etc.)
5. Changing jobs within and outside of the organization
6. Preparing for retirement; identifying and grooming potential successors
7. Continuing to work, but at a reduced rate, in retirement

Career development is a part of an organization's human resources planning.

An organization's career development program will be more meaningful if it is a formalized process included in the organization's human resources planning. That means that your manager as well as a centralized database should have knowledge of your skills, training, and career aspirations and that these data are used in making personnel decisions. It pays to take the initiative in discussing these items with your manager and, if appropriate, personnel and career counselors in your organization.

Whether or not an organization incorporates career planning into its human resources development process may be a determinant in where you decide to work. Some organizations have taken on part of the responsibility for helping employees grow and prepare for lateral, upward, and sometimes retrenchment moves. Human resources planning and assessment of abilities and skills are part of career planning. Career planning programs also include demand analysis, career pathing, and career advancement.

DEMAND

Many careers are cyclical. Engineers, lawyers, and medical doctors are classic examples of fluctuating but fairly constant high-demand careers.

Demand for nurses and teachers has also fluctuated heavily in recent years, partly because of increased technology and population. As health care services rely on more sophisticated technology, there is less demand for nurses who do not have technical skills and more demand for clinical nursing specialists and other technologists.

The demand for secondary school teachers, once considered a glutted market, is variable. Some school districts now have to recruit teachers the way businesses recruit managers. Others may be cutting back or experiencing hiring freezes or even layoffs because of cost-cutting measures.

Businesses, too, have their opportunity areas. Demand for sales and marketing jobs and for computer specialists continues to grow. The outlook for first-level and middle managers may continue to be less than optimal because of the "lean-and-mean" downsizing or "rightsizing" approaches to management advocated in the 1990s. Still, there will always be a shortage of really good managers—in other words, there is always room for a truly outstanding leader/manager. The primary factor in individual career advancement is the quality of current job performance.

CAREER PATHING

Career planning involves making detailed plans relating to career goals. Included in these plans will be career options and potential career paths. **Career paths** are alternative progressions planned by both the individual and the organization through jobs in an organization. Figure 3–4 shows an example of possible career paths in a savings and loan or bank branch office. Titles may vary and there may be additional steps, such as assistant cashier or administrative assistant. The point is to indicate alternative paths to promotion within an organization.

Once the career paths are known, it is necessary to determine what skills, knowledge, and abilities a person needs to follow those paths. If analysis shows that a person does not have certain skills or training, then another career decision point and training needs analysis are immediately available. The individual and the organization are in a position to take action to move the person through the alternative career paths.

CAREER ADVANCEMENT

Certain steps should be followed to ensure success in pursuing a career. Learning how to learn, learning your current job well, and identifying and understanding potential "next jobs" are important first steps in the pursuit of a career.

FIGURE 3–4 Potential Career Paths in a Financial Institution Branch Office.

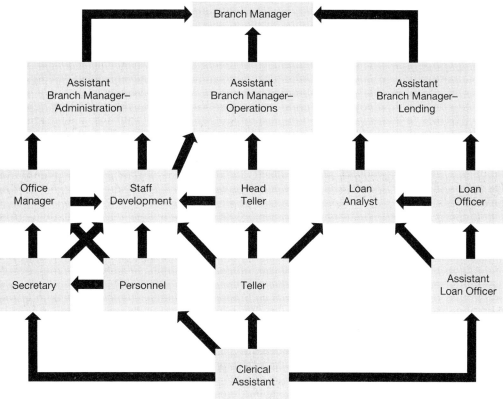

How well you do your current job—including being a student—is the best but not the only indicator of promotability and success in another job. Good performance in one job is not a perfect predictor of good performance in another, perhaps higher level, job. Additional assessment techniques are needed to predict success. But poor performance in the current job is a very good predictor of nonpromotability or failure in another job. One of the truest pieces of advice on career development is to produce in your current job in order to get ahead.

STEPS IN CAREER ADVANCEMENT

1. Learn how to learn.
2. Learn your job.
3. Perform your job well.
4. Know your potential "next jobs."
5. Try to understand your next jobs.
6. Find a mentor and network.
7. Build a performance database.
8. Make clear career choices.

Have a career plan. The plan may change, but if you don't have a goal or a career plan, then anything will do, won't it? Seek the help of mentors and networks. A mentor is an advocate of yours who takes you under his or her wing to advise, encourage, and facilitate contacts for you. Networking is the construction and nurturing of information networks for business and social use in and outside of an organization. Mentoring and networking are not gender based anymore. For years men have networked via the "good ol' boy" circuit. Team sports and other athletic activities have been one basis for these networks. Now women are also formalizing networks as well as capitalizing on informal activities such as aerobics classes and health clubs.

In addition to doing your current job well, it is necessary that it be well documented for performance appraisal and promotion purposes. Build your own database or record of your achievements even if management doesn't require it.

In a sense, you are being encouraged to keep a "brag sheet," but it is really a working document for a **résumé**—a summary of your accomplishments and goals. Keep your résumé up to date at all times, even if you think you don't have a lot of accomplishments. You can include part-time and summer jobs, extracurricular activities, and interests like specific sports. You never know when job or other social interest opportunities will present themselves to you, and you want to be prepared.

Finally, make clear career choices. Ask others in a job about the demands, expectations, and frustrations of the job before taking it. Jobs change but it is important for the job applicant to learn as much as possible before making a career commitment.

ALTERNATIVE SCHEDULE CHOICES

During the early 1990s *mommy track* became a familiar term for career women who also wanted to have more time for motherhood. The term itself is unfortunate because it could be deemed patronizing, but the concept can help men and women make a comfortable and productive reconciliation of roles if employers make effective use of talented employees' skills.

Several alternatives exist for accomplishing alternative schedule choices:

There are many alternatives other than 8-to-5 work.

1. *Alternative career paths.* Individuals work part time for a salary and may receive longevity credit for part-time work, but they lower their odds of becoming partners or other senior-level managers.
2. *Extended leave.* Employees can take up to three years off—with benefits and the guarantee of a comparable job on return.
3. *Flexible scheduling.* Employees create customized schedules and work at home, allowing a "phase-in" after leave.
4. *Flextime.* Any employee has the right to shift the standard workday forward or back as long as they work a "common core" of hours. **Flextime** allows employees to set their own work schedules within defined limits. Flexible time is most frequently used in service and retail industries to accommodate peak hours, but it can be adapted to manufacturing operations. Hewlett-Packard, Federal Express, and Merck are just a few of the types of manufacturing and service companies that have used flextime successfully.

5. *Job sharing.* **Job sharing** occurs when two or more employees share a title, workload, salary, benefits, and vacation. Job sharing allows individuals who might have time constraints because of other work, home, or school responsibilities, to be productive for their organizations by dividing a job usually held by one individual, into jobs held by two or more employees.

   There may be some additional requirements for coordinating and managing variable work schedules, but the benefits of acquiring the peak mental and physical skills of individuals outweigh the drawbacks. One of the major advantages is that it allows for cross-training of employees and sets the stage for skill-based pay systems. Although many managers remain highly resistant to job sharing, research of 131 companies shows that job sharing increases employee motivation, loyalty, and commitment.[12]

6. *Telecommuting.* Employees are allowed to limit the time they spend in the office by using personal computers, fax machines, and electronic mail at home. **Telecommuting** has already allowed organizations to improve their productivity by allowing employees to work when and where they are at their peak or prime times of performance. Telecommuting eliminates commuting time as well, leading to a more environmentally sound and safe existence.

   > Telecommuting is the springboard for a reengineering of how work is done. The more than 6 million employees who telecommute do so during work hours and are in fairly regular contact with the office. There are already signs that in the future the telecommuting concept will evolve into the idea that work can and will be done anytime and anyplace.[13]

Another consideration in career advancement is created by opportunities for dual-career couples and geographic transfer. Many career opportunities arise for one individual where it becomes problematic for the partner to secure meaningful employment or to leave an established, successful job. As a result, there is a rise in commuter marriages.

Franklin Becker at Cornell University says that the key to the office of the future is diversity. "Diversity is going to take on many different forms, including age, ethnicity, gender, and work style. The key shift will be to support the varied ways in which people actually work, emphasizing performance" instead of focusing on just being visibly present at the office all day.[14]

Flextime, job sharing, telecommuting, and other alternative choices continue to become increasingly popular. Because home computers can now be part of networks through modems and fax machines, it is much easier to modify schedules and, in fact, to be even more productive than at the office.

ACTION PROJECT 3–3 CAREER DEVELOPMENT (GROUP EXERCISE)

The following exercise requires that you choose/recommend your replacement.

> You are the manager of a men's wear department at a major department store. You have just been promoted and will be moving to another store. You have two full-time and three part-time employees from whom you

must choose a replacement to assume your position. The job requires 40 hours a week, and the starting pay is $22,000 yearly. You are looking for someone who is reliable and industrious.

These are the five candidates:

FRANK—Full-time employee, 32 years old, family man with two children; been with the store for two years; great public relations, no management skills, makes mistakes due to sloppiness.

CHARMAINE—Full-time employee, 17 years old, high school drop-out; been with store for six months; quick learner, makes few mistakes, does not plan on attending college.

GREG—Part-time employee, 21 years old; been with the store for three years; most knowledgeable in business aspects, excellent with customers, will be leaving in two years due to college graduation.

LISA—Part-time employee, 58 years old; been with the store 15 years, working twelve hours a week; most familiar with store routine, makes few mistakes, good public relations, health is failing—misses work about three days a month due to illness.

SUSAN—Part-time employee, 25 years old, pregnant; college graduate with degree in marketing; been with store for two years; best overall worker but prefers part-time hours.

First, rank order your preferences for the person to get the job (1 = first preference). Then, compare your rankings with others in your group.

YOUR INDIVIDUAL RANKING		GROUP RANKING	ANALYSIS/REASONS
_____	Charmaine	_____	_____
_____	Frank	_____	_____
_____	Greg	_____	_____
_____	Lisa	_____	_____
_____	Susan	_____	_____

SUCCESS

Being ready to act is the key to capitalizing on opportunities—and opportunities along with hard work are the keys to success. Success is not just a destination—it is a journey.

The concepts of "success" and "failure" as fundamental motivating forces are constantly being redefined. More and more, people are realizing that success can be measured by personal standards as well as by public ones. Some people listen to different drummers.

Success can be defined in terms of one's attitudes or material wealth. But is material wealth an adequate dimension by itself? Does it depend on how and why you acquire wealth?

Success is goal oriented. If you set demanding but attainable goals and achieve them, you are successful. If you perform well in your job, as well as in other relationships within your family and other social institutions, you are successful.

Success depends on your goals.

SUCCESS IS RESPECT

Success is attitudinal.

Success is not a popularity contest.

A more universal meaning of success relates to the attitudes of others. Respect from others is a more recognized dimension of success than any other. People need to be accepted by others. A person is successful who has gained the respect of intelligent men and women. Respect does not necessarily imply admiration nor popularity. Respect means that a person is recognized and given consideration. The person doesn't have to be loved, or even liked, to be successful. Individuals should have respect from some, preferably a majority, of their coworkers, customers, and others with whom they interact.

MATURITY

Success includes being magnanimous.

A mature attitude is another sign of success. Magnanimity, or the ability to rise above petty matters, is in itself a sign of maturity and success. The art of being successful includes being concerned with the important rather than the petty. Positive attitudes have a profound effect on success.

Negative attitudes and preoccupation with what is wrong with one's self, others, the organization, or society can drain energies away from the important matters and from ultimate success. We may spend our time tilting at windmills in a Don Quixotic manner while success is getting away—or we win the battle and lose the war.

Whether applied to international relations, national politics, or interoffice squabbles, magnanimity is a means of translating hostility into harmony and success. There are times when it is better to "turn the other cheek." Obviously there is also a limit beyond which we cannot go in both international and interpersonal relations.

No suggestion is made of not taking a firm stand on major issues. But, as in time management, it is important to make sure the issues are really important before we spend the majority of our time and emotional energies on them. From a likability viewpoint, magnanimity does much to facilitate human relationships.

YOU DON'T HAVE TO BE PERFECT TO BE SUCCESSFUL

Success does not necessarily imply perfection. Effective workers aim for success—not perfection—because the pressure and discouragement that perfectionists feel leads to decreases in productivity and creativity. Success, then, is a matter of feeling that we are doing our very best and having our boss, coworkers, customers, and others respect, acknowledge, and accept our efforts.

If you are a compulsive perfectionist, you may find it hard to believe that you can enjoy life to the maximum or find true happiness without aiming for perfection. You can put this notion to the test. On a piece of paper, list a wide range of activities such as mowing the lawn, preparing a meal, writing a report for work. Record the actual satisfaction you get from each activity by scoring it from 0 to 100 percent. Now estimate how perfectly you do each activity, again using a scale of 0 to 100. I call this an "Antiperfectionism Sheet." It will help you break the illusory connection between perfection and satisfaction.

Here's how it works: A physician I know was convinced he had to be perfect at all times. No matter how much he accomplished he would always raise his standards slightly higher and then he'd feel miserable. I persuaded him to do some research on his moods and accomplishments, using the Antiperfectionism Sheet. One weekend a pipe broke at his home and flooded the kitchen. It took a long time, but he did manage to stop the leak. Since he was such a novice at plumbing, had taken a long time, and required considerable guidance from a neighbor, he recorded his expertise as only 20 percent. On the other hand, he estimated his level of satisfaction with the job as 99 percent. By contrast, he received low degrees of satisfaction from some activities on which he did an outstanding job.

This experience with the Antiperfectionism Sheet persuaded him that he did not have to be perfect at something to enjoy it. Furthermore, striving for perfection and performing exceptionally did not guarantee happiness, but tended, rather, to be associated with less satisfaction. He concluded he could either give up his compulsive drive for perfection and settle for joyous living and high productivity, or cling to his compulsions and settle for emotional anguish and modest productivity. Which would you choose? Put yourself to the test.

President Theodore Roosevelt summarized the maturity, magnanimity, and orientation necessary to be successful in one's personal and career development:

> It is not the critic who counts, nor the man who points out how the strong man stumbles or where the doer of deeds could have done them better. The credit belongs to the man who is actually in the arena, whose face is marred by dust and sweat and blood. And who strives valiantly. Who errs and comes short again and again. Who knows the great enthusiasms, the great devotions and spends himself in a worthy cause. Who at the best knows in the end the triumph of high achievement and who at the worst, if he fails, at least fails while daring greatly. So that his place will never be with those cold and timid souls who knew neither victory nor defeat.

Finally, a quote from former secretary of Health, Education, and Welfare, John W. Gardner, is appropriate to close this chapter:

The things you learn in maturity aren't simple things such as acquiring information and skills. You learn not to engage in self-destructive behavior. You learn not to burn up energy in anxiety. You discover how to manage your tensions. You learn that self-pity and resentment are among the most toxic of drugs. You find that the world loves talent but pays off on character. You come to understand that most people are neither for you nor against you; they are thinking about themselves. You learn that no matter how hard you try to please, some people in this world are not going to love you—a lesson that is at first troubling and then really quite relaxing.[15]

SUMMARY

We need eustress—or positive stress—to help us to develop personally and professionally. However, distress, or negative stress, can be dysfunctional. Stress is natural but can be our worst enemy when it leads to emotional and physical ills. People with Type A behavior seem to be compulsive, hard-working achievers and are more likely to experience associated physical ailments, especially if their Type A behavior is associated with hostility, or Type H behavior.

Negative stress, or even too much positive stress, can lead to burnout. People who are fatigued and irritable express negative attitudes and make "missteaks." Feelings of burnout can be overcome in part by managing time.

Time management is largely a matter of scheduling activities and setting priorities. When we are in control of our own time, we manage our schedule and make time for ourselves. Telephones and meetings can be either time savers or time wasters depending on how we manage them and get them to work for us.

Both stress and time factors contribute to career development and success. Our jobs, environment, and lifestyle work together to create an ambiance that allows us to be successful. By not letting the petty things bother us, we give ourselves more time to concentrate on our important goals. Success should not be confused with perfection.

Focus on one job at a time and even schedule fun times; this helps to overcome the failure syndrome. Build support groups by having contacts with people outside of work. Finally, develop a somewhat detached concern for problems at work; this helps and can spell success in life as well as work. Recognize that personal and career development are primarily individual responsibilities. Organizations can help guide current and prospective employees through careers by providing realistic job previews and assessments of individuals' skills and abilities. There may even be times when it is advantageous for employees to "move on" to other opportunities.

Ultimately, success depends in large measure on how well we (1) cope with stress and tension; (2) manage our time, meetings, and other human interactions; and (3) plan and otherwise manage our personal careers.

IS THERE LIFE AFTER COLLEGE?

Bill Kuck graduated from the Business Division of Andaluska County Community College three years ago. He is a very personable individual and was well liked by fellow students, teachers, and coworkers—when he was working! But Bill has not worked more than a total of four months since he graduated, living on dwindling family income and inheritances.

His first position was salesperson in a shoe store near his college. He had worked there part time while in school, but his full-time job fell apart. The reasons are not entirely clear. The Andaluska economy was deteriorating, but others in the store had survived. Bill knew he would have to work harder under these economic circumstances, but did not; so he was laid off. He spent a lot of time talking with customers, but just wasn't able to make sales.

Bill thought about going to the state university for further education, but did not have the money to do it, so he took a temporary job as custodian at the college. He worked late at night and had a hard time getting to work on time. His supervisor was critical of his performance, and his job was not extended.

At this point Bill began to experience some health problems, including headaches, lethargy, and fatigue. He tried to get another job by talking with his buddies at the gym, but was not successful. He was getting very depressed.

1. What do you think Bill's problem is?
2. Is there a place for stress in this case? What kind of stress?
3. Has Bill planned out a career?
4. What other factors might influence Bill?

I DON'T HAVE ENOUGH TIME

Joan Flickinger is a branch manager for Home National Bank in the growing suburban community of Sylvan Dale. Ten years ago she had started at another suburban branch as teller, and was gradually promoted to assistant manager. When the Sylvan Dale office opened, she was promoted to branch manager.

Joan sat in her office at 6:15 P.M. wondering why she had not accomplished more that day. She had arrived just after 8 A.M. as usual. Her day had been filled by appointments with subordinates and customers, and was fairly typical, she thought, insofar as day-to-day operations were concerned.

She was frustrated because she had not spent any time on the report that the main office expected from her next week on expansion plans for her branch of Home National Bank. She knew that she would have to take that work home with her again tonight. It was difficult to work on it, in addition to spending time with her family—her husband and two teenage daughters. Joan had never really had any training in staff development positions and found it difficult to write such reports.

Joan's administrative assistant, Sue Tate, schedules appointments for her. The last meeting for the day was scheduled for 4:30, right after the office closed, with Sue. Sue wanted to talk about a raise because of her normal responsibilities in answering the phone, scheduling appointments, working for other branch officers, and typing correspondence and reports for the main office. The request for a raise had been unexpected by Joan, and the meeting was a little tense at times. It lasted over an hour and a half. No resolution was achieved.

1. What is Joan's problem?
2. Could career development and a career path help alleviate some of Joan's problem?
3. What should Joan do about her problem?

<table>
<tr><td>CASE STUDY
3-3</td></tr>
</table>

THERE'S NO PLACE TO GO

Joe Renfro graduated from Hilltop High School three years ago. He attended Empire Community College for almost a year but dropped out because "his studies just were not interesting."

After leaving Empire, Joe took a job as a shipping dock laborer at the semiconductor manufacturing facility of Addison-Bauer Company (ABC). ABC is a fairly large manufacturer, marketer, and supplier of semiconductors to various domestic and foreign companies. More and more of ABC's operations are being automated, but there are job opportunities for individuals with appropriate skills.

Joe has tested high for machine aptitudes and even some computer skills, but his instructors did not have the time or inclination to help him develop these skills. He has good interpersonal skills—as his friends and instructors say, "He's a good kid"—but he has not developed any technical much less conceptual skills.

1. Who has the primary responsibility for Joe's career development and progression?
2. Does ABC have some responsibility or even an obligation to themselves to help Joe acquire usable skills? Or to help him progress through their organization?
3. Discuss the pros and cons of who has responsibilities for Joe's career progression. Did Hilltop High School and Empire Community College have some responsibilities?
4. Do you perceive any organizational weakness in the ABC company? What information would you have to acquire before you could make an intelligent, rational decision?

DISCUSSION AND STUDY QUESTIONS—TO KEEP YOU THINKING. . . _____

1. Why did we introduce, study, and discuss personal development—coping with stress, time management, and career progression—now? Why not at the end of the book, or at the end of the academic term?
2. What are the differences between "eustress" and "distress"?
3. Why are workaholics "Fortune's favorite children"?
4. Can or should anger be eliminated?
5. What is meant by "the telephone paradox"?
6. Are meetings time wasters or communication tools?
7. Who has the responsibilities for career development?

8. What are career paths? How can they help you?

9. What are examples of alternative schedule choices?

10. What is success?

NOTES

1. David Levine, "The Secrets of People Who Never Get Sick," *Good Housekeeping,* December 1995, pp. 70–73.

2. "Are You a Type H?" *USA Weekend,* July 7–9, 1989, p. 8.

3. John Butterfield, "Unload Stress for '94," *USA Weekend,* December 31, 1993–January 2, 1994, p. 18.

4. Jeanne M. Plas and Kathleen V. Hoover-Dempsey, "Keeping Anger in Check," *National Business Employment Weekly,* Spring 1989, pp. 18, 20.

5. Mark P. Couch, "Fight Fire with Fire to Squelch Anger in Workplace," *Fort Collins Coloradoan,* October 9, 1995, p. C1.

6. Jerry L. Deffenbacher, "Anger Reduction," in A. Siegman and T. Smith, *Anger, Hostility and the Heart* (Hillsdale, N.J.: Lawrence Erlbaum, 1994), p. 267.

7. Lesley Alderman, "You Can Achieve More in a Lot Less Time by Following Five Key Steps," *Money,* October 1995, pp. 37–38.

8. Alan Lakein, *How to Get Control of Your Time and Your Life* (New York: Signet, 1973), p. 28.

9. Lee Iacocca with William Novak, *Iacocca: An Autobiography* (New York: Bantam, 1984), p. 20.

10. "Clean Desk for Success," *USA Today,* June 28, 1985, p. 1.

11. Hal Lancaster, "Managing Your Career: Is Your Messy Desk a Sign You're Busy or Just Disorganized?" *The Wall Street Journal,* January 30, 1996, p. B1.

12. Malia Boyd, "Job Sharers Are More Motivated," *Incentive,* February 1995, p. 13.

13. Julie Cohen Mason, "Workplace 2000: The Death of 9 to 5?" *Management Review,* January 1993, p. 15.

14. Ibid., p. 16.

15. John W. Gardner, Commencement Address at Stanford University, Palo Alto, California, June 16, 1991.

RECOMMENDED READING

Badger, James M. "14 Tips for Managing Stress on the Job." *American Journal of Nursing,* September 1995, pp. 1–33.

Barner, Robert. "The New Career Strategist." *Futurist,* September/October 1994, pp. 8–14.

Boyd, Malia. "Job Sharers Are More Motivated." *Incentive,* February 1995, p. 13.

Buhler, Patricia. "Managing in the 90s." *Supervision,* July 1995, pp. 24–26.

Ferner, Jack D. *Successful Time Management: A Self-Teaching Guide.* 2nd ed. New York: John Wiley & Sons, 1995.

Geber, Sara Zeff. *How to Manage Stress for Success.* New York: AMACOM, 1996.

Goleman, Daniel. *Emotional Intelligence.* New York: Bantam, 1995.

LeBoeuf, Michael. *Working Smart: How to Accomplish More in Half the Time.* New York: Warner Books, 1993.

Mayer, Jeffrey J. *Winning the Fight between You and Your Desk.* New York: HarperCollins Publishers, 1995.

Orpen, Christopher. "The Effects of Organizational and Individual Career Management on Career Success." *International Journal of Manpower,* 1994, pp. 27–37.

Schaubroeck, John; Ganster, Daniel C.; and Kemmerer, Barbara E. "Job Complexity, 'Type A' Behavior, and Cardiovascular Disorder: A Prospective Study." *Academy of Management Journal,* April 1994, pp. 426–439.

Siegman, Aron W. and T. Smith. *Anger, Hostility and the Heart.* Hillsdale, N.J.: Lawrence Erlbaum, 1994.

Silva, Karen E. *Meetings That Work.* Burr Ridge, Ill.: Richard D. Irwin, 1994.

Stewart, Thomas A. "Planning a Career in a World without Managers." *Fortune,* March 20, 1995, pp. 72–80.

Vaughn, Robert H. "Career Management Using Job Trees: Charting a Path through the Changing Organizations." *Human Resource Planning,* 1994, pp. 43–55.

4

PERSONAL PROBLEMS AND COUNSELING: ALCOHOL, DRUGS, AND SEX

Again here are some questions to start you thinking about topics in the chapter. You know the answers to some already and you will find answers to the others in the chapter.

- To whom would you go with a personal problem at work? to a friend, your supervisor, or a counselor?
- Do you think that people should vent their feelings or try to keep themselves under control?
- Which is better, to let problem employees go or try to rehabilitate them?
- What can you do for the employee who is an alcoholic or drug abuser?
- Is drug testing "fair" at the workplace?
- Do you think that you could recognize the point at which the alcoholic or drug abuser was performing his or her job ineffectively?
- Does sexual liaison on or off the job create problems in the workplace?
- What is sexual harassment?
- Who can help counsel with personal problems?

LEARNING GOALS

After studying this chapter, you should be able to:

1. Identify personal problems that affect employees at work.
2. Determine the extent of the problems.
3. Discuss the growing problems of alcoholism and drug addiction in business and be able to recognize some symptoms of alcoholics and drug abusers, recognize some "slang" terms used by drug abusers, and develop some background in how to deal with alcoholics and drug abusers in the workplace.
4. Recognize the legal and moral aspects of sexual harassment.
5. Discuss the pros and cons of supervisors being trained to act as counselors on the job.
6. Compare the differences between directive and nondirective counseling.
7. Identify what company and post-treatment programs can do to help affected employees.
8. Define and apply the following terms and concepts (in order of first occurrence):

- **alcoholic (industrial definition)**
- **prodromal phase of alcohol addiction**
- **drug abuse**
- **polydrug user**
- **depressants**
- **stimulants**

- hallucinogens
- designer drugs
- sexism
- sexual harassment

- homosexual
- nondirective counseling
- cooperative counseling
- employee assistance programs

TYPES OF PERSONAL PROBLEMS

This chapter addresses recognition of, counseling, and treatment for the problems of employees. Emphasis is given to problems of alcohol, other drugs, and sexism/sexual harassment in the workplace. More important, attention is given to counseling and the organization's response to employees who have these problems.

Everybody has problems! The magnitude of the problems and what, if anything, to do about them become challenges for management. How extensive are the problems and how do they manifest themselves? Only a recluse would not recognize the alcohol, drug, and sexism problems that exist in society and the workplace today. There are also more subtle problems that keep members of the workforce from being as productive as they could be.

Most dealings with people do not involve unpleasant experiences or misunderstandings, but things do happen that are disturbing enough to cause management to become interested in some of the basic concepts of counseling employees.

HOW TO IDENTIFY SOMEONE WITH A PROBLEM

Sudden behavior changes may signal distress.

People who are coping with personal problems at work frequently show signs of emotional distress. Management psychologist Harry Levinson, an author of books on executive leadership and publisher of the *Levinson Letter*, a twice-monthly newsletter on alcoholism and work group behavior,[1] identifies three behavioral changes that signal to coworkers and friends that emotional first aid is needed. These behaviors are discussed in the following paragraphs.

EXAGGERATED BEHAVIOR

An emotionally disturbed person's behavior patterns may become highly exaggerated. For example, an orderly person will become excessively meticulous. Or a quiet person will become extremely withdrawn. Or a friendly person will appear to be in a perpetual life-of-the-party mood. When ordinary behavior is exaggerated in this fashion, it is often a sign of stress. The troubled person tries to hide stress symptoms by acting as if everything were normal. In fact, everything is not normal, and because such behavior is an act, it will be discernible to those who are familiar with the person's normal behavior.

DISTRESS SYMPTOMS

A number of distress symptoms are apparent even to nonprofessional eyes. Disturbed persons are seldom able to concentrate and may be highly agitated. If they are worried and fearful, they may be jittery and perspire freely. They may be startled by loud noises or by the sudden appearance of the boss. If they are depressed or grieving, they may speak in dejected, exhausted tones. They may lose weight or seem to be suffering from lack of sleep. Some are likely to be constantly irritable; others will cry for the slightest reason.

RADICAL CHANGE SYMPTOMS

When someone's behavior at work changes radically, it may indicate severe stress. In such cases, irrational thoughts and actions will become apparent. For example, a quiet unassuming clerk with no official authority to do so might begin to issue orders to coworkers in an authoritarian manner. Or an ordinarily controlled and sober person might return from lunch under the influence of alcohol. Or an executive noted for forceful decision making might become incapable of making decisions about the most trivial matters.

ALCOHOLISM

It is almost a cliché that the increased complexities of modern life have added to nearly everyone's share of tensions, guilts, anxieties, and inhibitions. Alcohol consumption can increase tension as well as guilt and anxiety. Excessive alcohol consumption also reduces efficiency, sensitivity, and caution—three essential qualities for good job performance. The industrial definition of an **alcoholic** is any employee whose repeated overindulgence in alcohol sharply reduces job effectiveness and dependability.

HOW WIDESPREAD IS THE PROBLEM?

The problem of alcoholism for business is not just with chronic alcoholics, but with the social drinker as well. Nevertheless, some progress in reducing alcoholism is being made. Organizations like MADD (Mothers Against Drunk Driving) and SADD (Students Against Drunk Driving) have begun to have an impact nationally in reducing drunk driving and in reducing overall alcohol consumption. The introduction of wine coolers and low-alcohol and nonalcoholic beers are also examples of the reduction in alcohol consumption.

Ten percent of drinkers are alcoholics; few obtain help.

The National Council on Alcoholism estimates that 10 percent of the 110 million people who drink alcohol in the United States suffer from alcoholism. Of that 11 million, only about 700,000 to 1 million are undergoing treatment with Alcoholics Anonymous or similar organizations. Thus, there are about 10 million alcoholics who are not being treated.

PROBLEM DRINKERS AND INDUSTRY

Alcoholism is a personal problem of many employees that affects job performance. Many companies are getting tougher about drinking during the workday—at lunch, for example. In fact, drinking off the job and its influence on workers has become a matter of corporate policy. The National Council on Alcoholism lists some of the other costs:

1. The alcoholic employee is absent approximately three times as often as the nonalcoholic employee.
2. On-the-job accidents for alcoholic employees are two to four times more frequent than among nonalcoholic employees, and off-the-job accidents for alcoholics are four to six times as numerous.
3. Sickness and accident benefits paid out for alcoholic employees are three times greater than for nonalcoholic employees.
4. In one auto assembly plant, 363 out of 746 grievances filed during one year, or 48.6 percent, were alcohol related.

To these costs we must add intangibles such as loss of experienced employees, job friction, lower morale, waste of supervisory time, bad decisions, and damaged customer and public relations. Education may be a better answer to the problem than pre-employment alcohol testing. As popular as testing before hiring may seem, it is incredibly naive in that it merely screens out potential employees who exercise poor judgment by using alcohol within 10 to 15 hours before testing.[2]

SPOTTING AN ALCOHOLIC

Watch for decrease in quantity or quality of work.

Supervisors should keep records of absenteeism and investigate causes of on-the-job accidents. They should be suspicious if there is a decline in the quality or amount of work produced by a usually competent individual. Figure 4–1 outlines several signs that will indicate if the problem is due to excessive drinking. These are some of the more common signs of alcohol (and certain drug) intoxication:

1. **Physical signs.** Bloodshot or bleary eyes, trembling hands, flushed face, irritability, nervousness, alcohol smell on breath or as body odor, slurred or sloppy speech.
2. **Behavioral signs.** Impaired judgment, argumentative and insulting attitude, sudden changes of mood, fluctuating work output, avoidance of supervisor, use of breath purifiers, lowered work quality, increased absenteeism and lateness, longer lunch hours, early departures from work.

    The four phases of alcohol addiction according to studies conducted by E. M. Jellinek and replicated many times by others[3] are as follows:

1. **Prealcoholic phase.** The individual's use of alcohol is socially motivated.
2. **Prodromal phase** (*prodromal* means warning or signaling disease). The behavior that heralds the change to this phase is the occurrence of "blackouts" or amnesia-like periods during drinking.

FIGURE 4–1 Signs of Alcoholism and Stages that the Alcoholic Passes through from Inconsistent Performance to the Time of Termination.

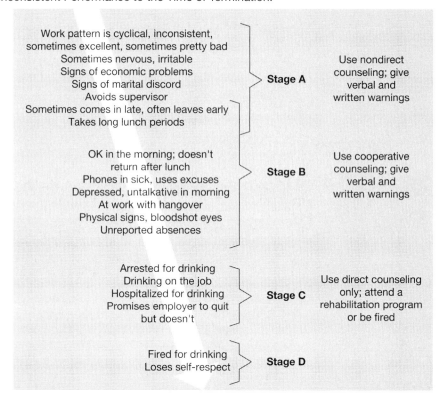

Work pattern is cyclical, inconsistent, sometimes excellent, sometimes pretty bad Sometimes nervous, irritable Signs of economic problems Signs of marital discord Avoids supervisor Sometimes comes in late, often leaves early Takes long lunch periods **Stage A**	Use nondirect counseling; give verbal and written warnings
OK in the morning; doesn't return after lunch Phones in sick, uses excuses Depressed, untalkative in morning At work with hangover Physical signs, bloodshot eyes Unreported absences **Stage B**	Use cooperative counseling; give verbal and written warnings
Arrested for drinking Drinking on the job Hospitalized for drinking Promises employer to quit but doesn't **Stage C**	Use direct counseling only; attend a rehabilitation program or be fired
Fired for drinking Loses self-respect **Stage D**	

3. **Crucial phase.** The key symptom is loss of control, setting up of a chain reaction; the drinker can no longer control the amount he or she will have once starting to drink. The drinker may be able to maintain a job and social footing but is close to the last and chronic stage.

4. **Chronic phase.** Characterized by beginning to drink early in the day, almost daily intoxication, and day-long drinking phenomena. Drinker may begin to experience vague fears, anxiety, tremors, or other mental and physical symptoms.

DEALING WITH ALCOHOLICS

The manager becomes concerned when employee drinking interferes with doing a good job.

It cannot be stated too strongly that it is only when the use of alcohol interferes with work that the supervisor is obligated to recognize the problem and come to grips with it. When employees' drinking habits create no problems at work, they are not of concern to the supervisor. The sensible managerial view is the one that says, "What my employees do during their leisure time is no business of mine. It becomes my business when drinking prevents them from doing their jobs properly."

Early identification of alcoholism is important, and the earliest cause for action is poor work performance. Supervisors who suspect that an employee's work difficulties may be due to problem drinking should discuss the poor performance and seek to determine the cause without making accusations.

The matter should be treated *confidentially* and discussed with no one else except counseling or medical personnel.

ACTION PROJECT 4–1   TWENTY ALCOHOL-RELATED QUESTIONS FOR YOUTH (INDIVIDUAL EXERCISE)

Instructions: Circle the appropriate answer:

YES   NO   1. Do you lose time from school due to drinking?
YES   NO   2. Do you drink because you are shy with other people?
YES   NO   3. Do you drink to build up your self-confidence?
YES   NO   4. Do you drink alone?
YES   NO   5. Is drinking affecting your reputation—or do you care?
YES   NO   6. Do you drink to escape from study or home worries?
YES   NO   7. Do you feel guilty or "bummed out" after drinking?
YES   NO   8. Does it bother you if someone says that maybe you drink too much?
YES   NO   9. Do you have to take a drink when you go out on a date?
YES   NO   10. Do you make out (in general) better when you drink?
YES   NO   11. Do you get into financial troubles over buying liquor?
YES   NO   12. Do you feel a sense of power when you drink?
YES   NO   13. Have you started hanging out with a crowd where "booze" is easy to get?
YES   NO   14. Have you lost friends since you've started drinking?
YES   NO   15. Do your friends drink *less* than you do?
YES   NO   16. Do you drink until the bottle is empty?
YES   NO   17. Have you ever had a complete loss of memory from drinking?
YES   NO   18. Have you ever been to a hospital or been busted due to drunk driving?
YES   NO   19. Do you "turn off" any studies or lectures about drinking?
YES   NO   20. Do you *think* you have a problem with alcohol?

One YES answer indicates danger, two a high probability, and three a clear problem.

Once the problem has been identified and admitted by the employee, neither the supervisor nor the employee should entertain any notions that the problem will cure itself. If there is no company program, it will be necessary to work out some kind of personal rehabilitation plan. Advice on how to do this can be obtained from doctors, counseling personnel, psychiatrists, governmental agencies, or Alcoholics Anonymous. There is no one "best" way in which to handle an employee with a drinking problem, but there are some general rules worth observing.

Exact no promises.

1. The supervisor should not exact or demand any promise the employee might make to stop drinking. Alcoholics are often incapable of keeping promises of that nature.

Don't moralize.

2. Supervisors should not moralize or lecture—it is a waste of time.

Shape up or ship out.

3. It is not a waste of time to threaten dismissal if the threat is sincere. "Shape up or ship out!" is the best threat. They must continue to work in order to survive.

Keep it confidential.

4. The problem should be kept confidential. There is nothing to gain and much to lose when someone's personal problems are broadcast to the world at large.

THE 12 STEPS OF ALCOHOLICS ANONYMOUS FACILITATION

1. We admitted we were powerless over alcohol—that our lives had become unmanageable.

2. Came to believe that a power greater than ourselves could restore us to sanity.

3. Made a decision to turn our will and our lives over to the care of God as we understood Him.

4. Made a searching and fearless moral inventory of ourselves.

5. Admitted to God, to ourselves, and to another human being the exact nature of our wrongs.

6. Were entirely ready to have God remove all these defects of character.

7. Humbly asked Him to remove our shortcomings.

8. Made a list of all persons we had harmed and became willing to make amends to them all.

9. Made direct amends to such people wherever possible, except when to do so would injure them or others.

10. Continued to take personal inventory and when we were wrong promptly admitted it.

11. Sought through prayer and meditation to improve our conscious contact with God as we understood Him, praying only for knowledge of His will for us and the power to carry that out.

12. Having had a spiritual awakening as a result of these steps, we tried to carry this message to alcoholics and to practice these principles in all our affairs.

Also, it makes good sense to try to assist someone in whom the company has made a substantial investment of time and money by training.

DRUG ABUSE

Drug abuse is the condition of individuals who are "hooked" on drugs of any type to the point that they cannot function without them. Unfortunately, substance abuse in the workplace cuts across all geographic boundaries and industries. Compared to companies who have screened out and cut drug usage, drug abusers cost their companies (1) three times more in medical claims, (2) five times more in workers' compensation claims, and (3) four times more in accidents on the job. The Research Triangle Institute has determined that the cost of drug abuse in the American workplace is more than $25.8 billion a year.[4]

Other, more recent estimates of drug abuse run even higher, but there is agreement that it is a major cost factor to American industry. A California study estimates that every dollar spent on treatment programs saves seven dollars in crime, health care, and welfare costs. According to the Office of National Drug Control Policy in Washington, the federal, state, and local governments spend roughly $25 billion on drug control efforts every year. Two other agencies put the price higher: A Brandeis University study estimates the yearly cost is $67 billion, with almost 70 percent attributable to drug-related crime, and a Columbia University study puts the cost of health care triggered by alcohol and drug abuse at $75 billion.[5]

Companies face reduced revenue and productivity, theft, increased insurance costs, and low morale as a result of drug abuse. Some recommendations to erase or at least reduce drug use in the workforce include firing employees for drug trafficking, developing drug training seminars for managers, and publicizing to potential applicants that drug testing will be done, sometimes unannounced. It is also important to explain addiction on and off the job.

A major problem of drug abuse is that only a few people are aware of the complexity of the issue. Medical reports, state laws, and psychological opinions differ widely from state to state. Despite the federal government's Comprehensive Drug Abuse and Prevention Control Act, the Controlled Substances Act, and legislation on "designer drugs," the increase in drug abuse is startling. One difficulty that companies face is that often supervisors and management do not understand the "lingo," what the drugs look like, or even the symptoms exhibited by the user.

Companies that are working with drug abusers under behavior medical treatment plans found that four out of five people recover. These data were released after surveying 2,400 companies. A motto used is "Try to get to people with problems before they become problem people."

Many people are polydrug users.

One West Coast representative for a rehabilitation program stated that half the people in the program between the ages of 20 and 35 are **polydrug users;** that is, the employee is taking more than one drug. Therefore it is not uncommon to have people in the program who are alcoholics and drug addicts. People responsible for rehabilitation programs often used the word "drug" to refer to both alcohol and drugs, because the treatment is often similar.

We must dissuade ourselves of the notion that the ordinary stresses of life constitute a disease that needs medication. We cannot expect stress-free, pain-free existence. Americans sometimes become conditioned from infancy to believe there is a pill for every ill. A contrasting view is credited to Winston Churchill: "Most of the world's work is done by people who do not feel very well all of the time."

MARIJUANA

Marijuana and other, much stronger, more dangerous drugs are hawked openly and competitively at rock concerts and at other gatherings of young people. But the ambiguities of the political and social situation do not make drugs any less dangerous, and not just in terms of getting arrested. And there are other costs associated with drug use: ". . . drug use, including marijuana use, causes considerable damage in our workplaces. Few Americans realize that three-fourths of regular drug users are employed. According to the U.S. Chamber of Commerce, employed drug users are 33% less productive than their nonabusing colleagues. They are likely to incur 300% higher medical costs and benefits."[6]

Most researchers agree that frequent use of marijuana, or its use in combination with other drugs or alcohol, is hazardous. In addition, researchers say that regular pot smoking during the day at school plays havoc with learning. Studies show that reasoning is impaired after a joint is smoked. Researchers know that not all the answers are in on marijuana. But they add that evidence is growing that it makes good sense to avoid heavy use of this controversial substance.

COCAINE

Cocaine (or "coke") is the alkaloid derived from the leaves of the coca plant. Its primary source is the eastern slopes of the Andes mountains, and it can be bought in the United States for about five times the price of gold per ounce.

Cocaine and some of its derivatives, including "crack" and "crank," have become even more addictive, universally used, and dangerous. Today it is the drug of choice for perhaps millions of upwardly mobile citizens.

The pattern of constant use can lead to a psychological dependence, the effects of which are not all that different from addiction. Moreover, there is growing clinical evidence that when coke is taken in its most potent and dangerous forms—injected in a solution or chemically converted and smoked in the process called *freebasing*—it may indeed become addictive. Cocaine can damage the liver, cause malnutrition, and, especially among those with cardiac problems, increase the risk of heart attack.

HARD DRUGS

Heroin and opium belong to that class of drugs known as narcotics, or "hard drugs." Hard drugs cause physical addiction in the user. Physical addiction means that the body develops a tolerance for the chemical and alters its activities to correspond to the amount of the drug used. As a result, the user has to use more and more of the drug to get any kicks or the pleasure of what addicts call "the rush."

The more of the drug that is consumed, the greater the physical dependency that develops. The greater the dependency, the harder it becomes to stop usage.

DEPRESSANTS

Other kinds of dangerous drugs are called "soft drugs," but not because they are any mellower than the hard ones. **Depressants** are designed to relax a person, but they can become addicting. Barbiturates (sleeping pills) are physically addicting, and the body develops a tolerance to barbiturates that is similar to narcotics tolerance. Some doctors believe that it is more difficult to cure a barbiturate addiction than it is to cure heroin addiction. The sudden cessation of barbiturates can cause convulsions and has been known to cause death, particularly when alcohol has been consumed. Large doses of barbiturates and alcohol, taken together, can kill.

Symptoms of use include confusion, difficulty in thinking, impairment of judgment, and marked swings in mood between elation and depression. There may be increased irritability and inability to control fighting or weeping.

STIMULANTS

Stimulants or "pep pills" act directly on the central nervous system, producing a feeling of excitation, energy, and the ability to go without sleep for prolonged periods. There is often a loss of appetite, and during such periods the user's body expends its reserve of energy, thus resulting in a "blackout." Amphetamines or methamphetamines are stimulants that are known as "speed," "dexies," "uppers," "bennies," or any of several other street names.

"Crashing down" can cause psychological depression.

Besides causing blackouts, amphetamines can also present withdrawal problems. When someone has become addicted to amphetamines and is suddenly cut off from them, withdrawal will result in severe psychological depression, laced with bouts of paranoia. "Crashing" or coming down from an amphetamine high may cause weeks of psychological distress. The abuser may exhibit nervousness, tremors of the hands, dilated pupils, dryness of the mouth, and heavy perspiration. In short, the person abusing stimulants may exhibit dangerous, aggressive behavior that resembles paranoid schizophrenia.

HALLUCINOGENS

Hallucinogens alter time and space perceptions. Mescaline, peyote, mushrooms, "angel dust" (PCP), and LSD cause hallucinations and alter time and space perceptions. Some people have reported very unpleasant hallucinations; others have described their "trips" as very pleasant. In the early days of LSD experimentation, great success was reported concerning its use with terminal cancer patients. However, its use in the United States is prohibited for many legal and medical reasons.

DESIGNER DRUGS

Synthetic drugs are dangerous, too.

Designer drugs are tailor-made, synthetic drugs. The degree of potency and duration of their effect can be laboratory controlled. Because one or two minor changes in the molecular structure of the chemical compounds can change the overall effect of the drugs, they are especially dangerous.

Gary L. Henderson, pharmacologist and toxicologist at the University of California at Davis (the individual who coined the term designer drugs), says that we face an enormous challenge because of the synthetics. "Designer drugs can be made cheaply and easily and sold for enormous profits. They are very difficult to detect and we know little about their biological and side effects. More important, they seem to be proliferating at an alarming rate. They are the drugs of abuse of the future."[7]

ADDICTS ON THE JOB

Symptoms and drug taking can be concealed.

It appears not only that drug addicts hold a wide variety of jobs but that their drug use goes undetected for long periods. According to the subjects interviewed in one study, heroin addiction on the job can be masked through careful manipulation of the "high" by shooting only enough heroin to prevent withdrawal symptoms. If the worker-addict begins to feel drowsy, he simply moves about a great deal to reduce this effect.

If any questions about unusual behavior are asked by supervisors or fellow workers, subjects give a wide variety of excuses, the major ones being fatigue caused by family problems, anxiety, night school, or noisy neighbors. Another excuse, usually offered by older addicts, is that their unusual behavior results from either a hangover or a drink on the job. Drug abuse is usually not the stated reason for dismissal. Instead, poor job performance, lateness, and absenteeism, among other reasons, are cited.

Figure 4–2 shows commonly detected drugs from workplace testing. Although the number has been declining from the late 1980s to the early 1990s, the number of drug-positive workers is still significant.

CONFRONTING DRUG ABUSE

Listed here are specific recommendations for supervisors to consider in handling the drug problem:

1. The first step is education. Consider establishing programs for managers and employees to arm them with the facts and heighten their consciousness of alcohol- and drug-related behavior.

2. Establish a program and develop a company policy. Include members of security, the legal department, personnel, the union, supervisory

FIGURE 4–2 Commonly Detected Drugs in General Workplace Testing. Source: Based on more than 9 million tests conducted by SmithKline Beecham Clinical Laboratories, "News Release," October 12, 1993, pp. 1, 3.

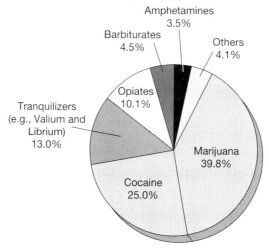

personnel, the workforce, medical specialists, and top management. If the problem is perceived as the sole responsibility of a single group, policy and program will inevitably be slanted and biased.

3. Consider employing recovered (or "recovering") former addicts from certified treatment programs. In addition to the fulfillment of their regular duties, they can lend a personal expertise to your company program.

Drug abuse and alcoholism in the workplace can be counteracted. Job applications and drug testing can help screen job applicants. Workers who abuse drugs or alcohol may be detected through searches, but all these activities must be handled carefully to avoid legal action. Drug testing by private employers has received a chilly reception in some courts, although the U.S. Supreme Court has ruled that the federal government may test workers in sensitive or safety-related jobs.

EXPRESS YOUR OPINION

Many companies are now using urinalysis to detect for traces of drugs including alcohol. Abstinence for a period of time before the test will throw off the results of the test. But some companies use spot-checks or unannounced tests. What do you think? Are these tests an invasion of privacy? What are the arguments for and against corporate prohibition of drug usage even off the job? Does it make a difference if the job is in a "sensitive" industry such as nuclear power generation, air traffic control, or law enforcement?

SEX AND THE WORKPLACE

Human sexuality probably doesn't need a lot of definition for most readers of this book. The author is reminded of the young daughter who was a good student but was very satisfied with a C in her sex education class. She was afraid if she got a better grade, her dad would worry! And, if she got a poorer grade, she would worry!

Sexual liaisons in the workplace may cause organizational grief.

Sexism, job discrimination based on gender, is illegal and is discussed later in the chapter on job discrimination (Chapter 16). Sexual liaisons in the workplace are another concern because of the impact they may have on other employees. This is especially true if there is a boss–subordinate relationship involved. The parties concerned are probably setting themselves up for embarrassment and grief, if not worse. Regardless of the emotions and feelings—or whether everything is highly moral—there may be organizational repercussions.

Mary Cunningham was a staff assistant–strategic planner at Bendix, a conglomerate aerospace engineering and equipment company, where Bill Agee was a senior executive. Agee sought the professional advice of Cunningham and because of that came to be viewed by others in management as weak and subject to easy influence. After they left the company, they were married, but considerable personal damage had been inflicted on both.

The fact of two people falling in love does not mean they lose their business judgment. But when the relationship is between boss and subordinate, coworkers may feel uncomfortable, suspicious, or threatened. One example of potential problems is where two employees become involved romantically while working on a project; when the project is finished, one of the employees gets a promotion but the other one quits to join a major competitor.[8] Either of the employees may be put in a compromising position.

Violence in the workplace is more common than we like to admit. As more couples enter the workplace, the battered mate is seen more often with bruises and with feelings of guilt and shame. Such an employee can be your coworker or an employee under your supervision. It is impossible for us all to be in optimal emotional balance all the time. We all occasionally "blow up," and we depend on others to help us overcome our moments of stress; management depends on supervisors to see that it is done.

SEXUAL HARASSMENT

Sexual harassment is offensive to at least one party.

Sexual harassment is any unwanted attention of a sexual nature that occurs in the process of working or seeking work that interferes with a person's work ability. Unlike sexual liaisons, which are a function of mutual consent, sexual harassment is offensive to at least one of the parties. It may be blatant, involving physical touch, but is often verbally or visually offensive because of innuendo, jokes, or stares.

Section 703 of Title VII of the Civil Rights Act of 1964 makes sexual harassment illegal. The final amendment to the Equal Employment Opportunity Commission (EEOC) guidelines states that sexual harassment includes unwelcome sexual advances, requests for sexual favors, and other verbal or physical conduct of a sexual nature made as a condition of employment or advancement.

Case law holds that "sexist remarks" and "insistent and vicious looks" are sexual harassment. Specifically, the following situations have been found to be sexual harassment:

- A boss says to his secretary, "You deserve a pat on the fanny for a good job."
- Joking about sex in regard to women's bodies. The women employees get very uncomfortable, and the men enjoy every minute of it.
- Requiring a female lobby attendant to wear a skimpy uniform that the company claimed was part of its dress code.
- A female employee has been having an affair with the head of her division. She tells him she wants to break it off. He replies that she will lose out on the promotion she has been expecting.
- The company has a number of vending machines which require service twice a week. An outside male services these machines. Every time he comes to the company he remarks to the female receptionist that she looks sexy and asks her to go on dates with him. The receptionist is fed up with his behavior and tells her boss how she feels.[9]

As you can see from the examples, sexual harassment includes acts of outside vendors as well as employees. Companies such as Hewlett-Packard have posted notices in their lobbies asking that the company be made aware of improper advances or remarks between vendors and employees.

The supervisor *is* the company.

The courts and the EEOC hold the employer responsible for acts of sexual harassment in the workplace regardless of whether or not the employer knew of the conduct. Unless the company can show that it took immediate and appropriate corrective action, it is liable for its employees' actions—even if it had a policy against harassment. In *Meritor Savings Bank vs. Vinson,* the court upheld the EEOC's expanded interpretation of sex discrimination under Title VII of the Civil Rights law of 1964. It made it clear that employers have a duty to provide a workplace free from a sexually hostile, abusive, or offensive atmosphere.

Sexual harassment victims are not always women. Young men are sometimes sexually harassed in industries such as hotel/hospitality and food service. Physical, visual, and verbal acts may be just as offensive and unwelcome to men as they are to women. Would it make any difference if the roles were reversed in the foregoing incidents (that is, if the "harasser" were a woman, and the "harassee" were a man)?

What causes sexual harassment? Without getting deeply into the psychology of abnormal behavior, some of the organizational causes of sexual harassment may be (1) more competition for coveted upper-management slots, (2) more empowerment for both men and women, and (3) homefront stereotypes carrying over into the workplace. Regardless of the reasons, no company should have room for any types of stereotypes or harassment.

PREVENTING SEXUAL HARASSMENT

According to a survey conducted by *Personnel* magazine, the majority of medium and large companies have a formal policy on sexual harassment. The survey found that confidentiality is a major concern of employees who are hesitant to report an incident of sexual harassment. Companies use dress codes to prevent incidents, and surveys, hot lines, and complaint boxes to encourage employees to report harassment.[10]

The key to eliminating or at least reducing sexual harassment is prevention. The EEOC guidelines make a strong claim that prevention is the best tool for controlling sexual harassment. Guidelines suggest that the employer should:

1. Be familiar with the varying forms of sexual harassment that can take place (particularly quid pro quo and hostile environment).
2. Use EEOC guidelines and case law to clearly define sexual harassment and explain the various types to employees.
3. Establish a written sexual harassment policy.
4. Communicate this policy to all employees on a regular basis.
5. Strongly denounce sexual harassment and confirm that it will not be tolerated and connect sexual harassment violations to disciplinary remedies.
6. Inform all employees of their legal rights to complain about sexual harassment under Title VII of the Civil Rights Act of 1964.[11]

To avoid aggravating sexual harassment, it is important that employers:

- Do **not** ignore complaints just because they are not formally filed.
- Do **not** ignore complaints because they allegedly happened several years ago.
- Do **not** try to convince an employee not to complain and do **not** defend the offensive behavior as "only joking."

- Do **not** dismiss an employee who complains as a way to remove potential problems for the agency.
- Do **not** put off taking action simply because an allegedly harassed employee asks that no action be taken.[12]

Prevention requires active management support.

For a sexual harassment prevention program to be effective, it must have the full understanding and support of management. Written policies that are distributed throughout the organization are also important preventive measures. Sanctions and mechanisms for complaint procedures should be a part of those policies. Finally, counseling should be available to individuals who have been victims of harassment.

HOMOSEXUALITY

Homosexual is "the most generally accepted designation for same-sex orientation."[13] The word derives from a combination of *homo-*, the Greek form of "same" and "sexual," late Latin. As used here, the term *homosexual* means the entire range of same-sex affections and relations, male to male and female to female. Some might prefer different terms like *gay* or *lesbian*, but those terms have different meanings: "The mistaken belief that the homo- component represents the Latin word for 'man' has probably contributed to resistance to the expression among lesbians."[14]

Lesbianism can mean many things: a self-experienced state of awareness for the same sex; a preference, affectional and/or sexual in nature; or a political choice—a conscious rejection of patriarchy, of traditional roles of women, of limitations placed on women's control of their own lives. It can mean any or all of these things, but homosexuality is still the more all-encompassing, easily definable term.

Is homosexuality predetermined or acquired (environmentally determined)? Considerable research remains to be done on homosexuality and its effects at work. In the summer of 1993, Dean Hamer, a genetics researcher with the National Institutes of Health, released a study that said:

> There is at least a 99.5% chance we have identified the genetic marker for sexual orientation. . . . Since people don't choose their genes, they can't possibly choose their sexual orientation.
> But, Hamer continues, "homosexuality is not completely genetic and not necessarily determined by genes in every individual."[15]

It is unconscionable to discriminate against or harass people based on any false criteria such as ethnic origin, gender, sexual preference, etc. Additional information on discrimination appears in Chapter 16, on job and pay discrimination.

WHO CAN HELP WITH PROBLEMS?

The main purpose of counseling is to discover an employee's principal problem and to find a way of handling it. First, one must find a way to understand the employee, to help him or her recognize that area of concern and deal with it objectively. An empathetic supervisor may condemn the problem but not the employee. Perhaps the hardest part of counseling is for the employee to accept help and the counselor to give it.

Remember the advice from Chapter 3 to make tension work for you—do not fight it, but use it in a positive sense. Suggestions there included a type of self-counseling to prioritize our activities to tackle one thing at a time and to enjoy an occasional laugh at our own expense. But there are also other sources of help: friends, supervisors, and professional counselors.

Sometimes we can be the source of help to solve our own problems, but frequently we need outside help. Who can we turn to? Regardless of our answer, we need someone who will listen to and help us act on our problems.

FRIENDS

Friends, supervisors, or specialists can help those under stress.

Perhaps the closest confidant an employee can find to discuss a situation with is a friend at the plant or office. A friend will tend to be receptive, open, and willing to listen without passing judgment. These qualities can be found in some, but not all, superiors. In the informal setting the "counselor-friend" can give empathy and friendly advice. Usually there is little pressure for the employee to follow the friend's advice, and the problem does not become public knowledge.

When some people recognize that a coworker is upset, they may be reluctant to talk about their perceptions. They may feel that it is a private affair and that discussing it will only add to the distress. But there are circumstances in which it is permissible to intrude on another person's privacy at work. The first is when help is requested, which is certainly not an intrusion. The second is when two people have worked well together and one has strong evidence that the other's job performance is falling down. Calling attention to work-related problems often enables people to open up and talk about their personal problems. What is needed is a "listening" friend who can keep a confidence.

SUPERVISORS

An employee's most logical step is to go to a listening supervisor with his or her minor problems. Good supervisors will soon discover whether they are capable of handling particular situations. If the supervisors are inexperienced, they should consult with their superiors or an expert in the field before having an interview with the employee. It is wise to call in an expert's opinion early in a case involving drugs, alcohol, or legal entanglements.

Beginning supervisors are often reluctant to discuss subordinates' personal problems because they feel poorly equipped to deal with such matters. Nevertheless, the longer they work in supervisory positions, the more practice they will get in dealing with personal problems because, inevitably, some employees will need to talk about disturbing aspects of their lives and jobs.

Counseling takes time but so does finding and training replacements.

Experienced supervisors know that well-conducted counseling is hard and tiring work, especially when they have to deal with hostile and critical subordinates. They learn how to avoid being pushed into defensive postures and how to remain calm. But no matter how good they get, such encounters always use up a lot of energy.

The major limitation that most supervisors experience in counseling is time. Follow-up is often essential for effective counseling, and that can consume a great deal of time. In the long run, if insufficient time is set aside for counseling, more problems may result with an even greater loss of time.

Suppose that a supervisor never took the time to counsel an employee with problems but that employee's inefficiencies resulted in the loss of an hour's worth of work every day for three weeks. Wouldn't three or four hours of counseling be a better investment of time?

SPECIALISTS OR COUNSELORS

Calling in specialists is advisable in cases of abortion, adoption, and marital strife.

The personnel director, the attorney, and the physician all become counselors in one circumstance or another. Personnel directors by their very role can act as uninvolved third parties in labor disputes, salary placements, and job transfers. Company physicians or attorneys can perform the role of a counselor very effectively. Some company psychologists give yearly emotional checkups. An emotional checkup might discover undue tension and nervousness that need attention in the same way that a physical examination would detect the danger of high blood pressure.

Some companies have instituted various kinds of counseling programs to deal with specific personal needs. Companies hire specialists mostly in hopes that they will improve employee performance and free managers from trying to deal with problems beyond their expertise. Employees with serious problems don't leave them at home, which can render a worker practically useless.

Company counselors should either help solve the problems themselves or refer the employees to local resources. People should learn what services are available in their own communities.

COMPARISONS OF SUPERVISORS AND TRAINED COUNSELORS

Specialists help to free managers.

The relative advantages of training supervisory staff as counselors or hiring expert personnel to handle the task are compared in Table 4–1. It is clear from the table that both approaches have distinct advantages. One disadvantage of hiring experts is that programs using experts have had great difficulties winning the acceptance of supervisory personnel. Apparently, many supervisors feel threatened by such programs because they fear that employees will criticize them unjustly. Advice in how to counsel will help the supervisors to overcome their criticisms.

TABLE 4–1 Comparisons of Trained Supervisors and Specialists as Counselors

ADVANTAGES OF TRAINED SUPERVISORS	ADVANTAGES OF EXPERTS[1]
1. More available to employees	1. Usually more skillful
2. More natural relationships	2. Less bias and more confidential
3. More aware of the employee's job performance	3. Less conflict with other employee roles
4. No need to introduce the outside person to conflict	4. Less emotional involvement

[1]Personnel directors, psychologists, medical specialists.

DIRECTIVE METHOD

The traditional method of counseling is called *directive* because the counselor directs and controls the form, flow, and content of the exchange between counselor and counselee. Even though it may be impossible for one person to understand exactly the attitudes of another, there are times when a person in a confused state wants concrete advice that can be given by such guidance. Asking questions, making a diagnosis, and giving advice are characteristic of the direct counseling approach. Counseling is often expected in an organization with a strong formal chain of command.

Directive method gives advice and reassurance.

Directive methods usually appeal to novice supervisors, because they often seem to be the easiest paths to follow in troubled situations. These methods are fast and seem to require little skill, but are relied on much too heavily.

ADVICE.   This is the most common type of counseling available. It is easy to give good advice—if you know what is suitable.

This doesn't mean the counselor should not answer direct questions requiring factual answers. Factual answers and opinions clearly labeled as opinions are often necessary and helpful. But when emotional problems are under consideration, direct advice seldom is helpful unless solicited.

REASSURANCE.   There is nothing wrong with reassurance—in the right place and at the right time. It especially encourages new and timid workers.

NONDIRECTIVE METHOD

Nondirective method requires active listening.

Nondirective counseling, also known as "client-centered therapy," is the method that often lends itself to current human relations practices in industry. In large measure, it is the way in which professionally trained people practice active listening as a counseling technique. Nondirective counseling is so named because, up to a point, the counselor lets the client determine the direction of the discussion. The counselor listens without making judgments and helps the client to clarify alternatives.

Catharsis is talking out one's feelings.

The basic concept of nondirective counseling holds that by skillful, active listening a counselor can help a client to release pent-up emotions. The process of obtaining relief from psychic and emotional tensions by talking about deeply felt emotions is called *catharsis.* Only after the client experiences catharsis and feels free of the weight of locked-in emotions can he or she then identify and solve personal problems in a rational frame of mind, and with minimum direction or advice from the counselor.

The ultimate goal of nondirective counseling is to stimulate the growth of self-recognition and self-knowledge. The theory and the goal are based on the belief that clients are responsible for their own behaviors and that they will solve their own problems once these problems are recognized fully. It holds further that self-recognition can develop only when the counselor establishes what professionals call a "permissive atmosphere," one in which the counselor remains neutral and accepts all statements and actions without passing judgment. In this method there is a belief that the client can solve personal problems if given the opportunity to do so and that every person basically is interested in doing the right thing.

Nondirective counselors follow four basic practices when conducting counseling interviews. Each is discussed in the following paragraphs.

READINESS.   Nondirective counselors know that it pays to learn as much as possible about the client before the initial appointment. In most companies, personnel files will be open for counselors' inspection.

ACTIVE LISTENING.   Nondirective counselors listen for all positive and negative feelings. They don't interrupt. Often they repeat statements they don't understand to the client until both understand the intended meaning.

A nondirective counselor does not give advice.

NO ADVICE.   Nondirective counselors can answer questions about company policies and procedures, but if the client asks, "What should I do?" about a personal problem, they will not answer it. They believe that if the client expresses everything he or she thinks and feels about the problem, sooner or later the client will come up with self-generated advice. Further, they believe that the best advice is always self-generated.

One inquiry that works well is "Would you like to tell me about it?" Do not pursue lines of inquiry that can be answered with "yes" or "no." An occasional contradiction by the employee himself or herself usually indicates confusion, which is often a preliminary step in the clarification process.

CLARIFICATION.   When the client does begin to arrive at solutions, the nondirective counselor encourages the exploration of the ideas through to their logical consequences. Counselors may offer occasional questions and suggestions at this stage. They help to clarify alternative courses of action as clearly as possible, but they require the client to make the decisions.

What a troubled employee needs to do is let it all out and stimulate self-help. What a counselor needs to do is try to empathize—and, in some cases, sympathize. Finally, at the risk of being redundant, the counselor needs to listen.

COOPERATIVE COUNSELING

Cooperative counseling blends direct and nondirect counseling.

Somewhere between directive and nondirective counseling lies the style called **cooperative counseling.** It is a blend of the direct guidance and authority typical of directive counseling and the nonjudgmental, active listening behavior typical of nondirective techniques. This form of counseling is especially effective during appraisal and evaluation interviews, but it also has been useful in counseling employees with personal problems. When using this method, the counselor's role is neither that of a judge nor of a sympathetic listener, but a complex mixture of the two.

In cooperative counseling, the counselor tries to stimulate the client's thinking by asking specific, nonthreatening questions at the beginning of the interview (see Figure 4–3.) These questions are directive in that they determine the subject of the interview, but they are also nondirective in that the client is encouraged to express emotions as well as thoughts and attitudes. If the expression of these emotions brings tears or anger, the counselor should remain sympathetic and patient until the outburst is over. When nonthreatening questioning works, it stimulates honest, deeply felt communication very quickly.

FIGURE 4–3 In Cooperative Counseling the Counselor Stimulates the Client's Thinking by Asking Nonthreatening Questions at the Beginning of the Interview.

"Mirroring".   This style also uses the nondirective device called *mirroring,* that is, restating a client's own words not only to reflect and clarify the client's feelings but as material from which to form nonthreatening questions. Silences and pauses for thought are also customary in cooperative counseling, but they are not as long lasting or as frequent as in nondirective practice.

Because of its combination of directive and nondirective features, cooperative counseling is particularly effective in dealing with some alcoholics and drug addicts. Its nondirective aspects encourage and stimulate honest communication quickly; its directive features allow the counselor to set realistic behavior limits for troublesome employees.

COMPARISONS OF COUNSELING METHODS

Table 4–2 summarizes the different features of directive, nondirective, and cooperative counseling.

COMPANY PROGRAMS

Companies can institute programs to help deal with problems of alcohol and drug abuse and sexual harassment. Programs are best developed quietly without fanfare. Since alcoholism and drug abuse are medical–personnel matters, all the safeguards of confidentiality should be observed.

When employees are referred by their supervisors, or when they come on their own, they are given a series of physical and psychological tests and then referred to various agencies, such as Alcoholics Anonymous, the Employee Assistance Program (discussed later), or the local chapter of the National Council

TABLE 4–2 Comparisons of Various Counseling Techniques

METHOD	DIRECTIVE COUNSELING:	COOPERATIVE COUNSELING:	NONDIRECTIVE COUNSELING:
	JUDGE	JUDGE-HELPER	HELPER
Objective	To communicate, to evaluate, to persuade the employee	To communicate, to evaluate, to stimulate self-help	To stimulate growth and self-help
Assumptions	Employee desires to correct known weaknesses	People will change if defensive feelings are removed	Growth can occur without correcting faults
Attitude	People profit from criticism, appreciate help	One can respect the feelings of others if one understands them	Discussion develops new and mutual trust
Motivation	Use positive or negative incentives	Help overcome resistance to change; use positive incentives	Increase freedom; increase responsibility
Risk	Loss of loyalty; inhibition of independence; face-saving problems created	Need for change may not develop	Employee may lack ideas; change may be other than what the superior had in mind
Gains	Success is most probable when employee respects interviewer	Develops favorable attitude toward superior that increases probability of success	Almost assured of improvement in some respects

on Alcohol. Employees select a rehabilitation agency of their own choice, and weekly consultations with the company's medical staff are held thereafter.

Company programs can also provide psychological assistance and "money management" education during a layoff. Emotional distress is one by-product of excessive debt.[16] Some suggestions for organizations considering downsizing include the following:

- Provide warnings of layoffs.
- Make terminations crisp and professional.
- Be aware that employees will probably carry some hostility and anger into the session.
- Take threats seriously.
- Concentrate on teaching financial concepts rather than developing individual plans.
- Help employees assess their current situation and develop an appropriate financial strategy.
- Remember the remaining employees and consider their feelings.[17]

A GUIDE FOR MANAGERS AND SUPERVISORS

Don't let laypeople diagnose medical problems.

Be alert to changes in the work and behavioral patterns of all personnel under your supervision. Document particular instances in which an employee's job performance fails to meet minimum established standards. Do not attempt to diagnose medical or behavioral causes for work deterioration.

PROFILE OF HUMAN BEHAVIOR

MARTA BROSZ

Two Sioux Falls chemical dependency programs, one decades old and one brand new, have been cited as the best at turning children and adults away from drugs and alcohol.

Project Awareness, a 22-year-old program designed to teach children to abstain from drugs and alcohol, has been named South Dakota's top drug prevention program. The newly created Minnehaha County Jail Treatment Program, which weans inmates away from drugs, is the outstanding treatment program.

Overseeing both is Marta Brosz, executive director of Carroll Institute, and herself the state's outstanding treatment professional. "Project Awareness has been around for twenty-two years and developed innovative programs in schools, including its student assistance program. They've been working in ongoing school programs," said Gilbert Sudbeck, director of the alcohol and drug abuse division of the state Health Department.

"The in-jail program is fairly new and was simply given an award for doing comprehensive alcohol and drug treatment within the jail system. That's something that's fairly unique. It's very cost effective and efficient."

One of the state's pioneer drug programs, Project Awareness, teaches children of all ages in schools around the region about drugs and chemical addiction. Project counselors working out of Sioux Falls' schools conducted 1,233 programs that educated 16,088 people last year.

"They're in our building," said Jan Nicolay, Washington High School principal. "When young people want to talk to somebody, they don't want to have to wait for somebody."

With children learning at an ever-younger age about drugs from peers and media, early prevention is key, Brosz said. "Elementary kids are so sophisticated," she said. "You give them a pretest in drug awareness and they get 100 percent."

Brosz has been with Carroll Institute since 1983, working her way from counselor to director in May 1986. She has developed standardized testing procedures for prospective counselors as part of an international consortium that includes forty states and several countries. "Marta's been very active on a national level in relation to South Dakota participation in an international consortium of drug and alcohol counselors," Sudbeck said.

Since the Minnehaha County jail started its treatment program about two years ago, roughly 500 inmates have participated. Of 229 inmates who completed the program, 62 percent had abstained from alcohol and drugs one year later, a survey indicated. Eight out of ten were working at least part time.

Minnehaha County's program isn't unique. Rapid City also offers such a program, but the jail program in Sioux Falls is more comprehensive, efficient, and effective, advocates said, "Other counties can follow suit if they get the funding," Brosz said.

SOURCE: Mike Trautmann, *Argus Leader* (Sioux Falls, South Dakota), August 23, 1993, p. B2. Reprinted by permission.

Conduct a corrective interview with the employee when the documented record of his or her unsatisfactory performance warrants. At the end of the interview, inform the employee that the services of the Employee Assistance Program (EAP), discussed in a following section, are available if a personal problem is causing the poor performance. Such programs are frequently available in areas served by the National Council on Alcoholism.

If the employee's performance continues to deteriorate, conduct a second interview and take whatever first-step disciplinary action is warranted. Inform the employee that failure to improve job performance will result in further disciplinary action up to and including termination. Conclude with a strong recommendation that the individual use the services of the EAP on a confidential basis. If deterioration of performance continues, conduct a third interview.

Conclude by offering the employee the choice between accepting the services of the EAP or being terminated because of unsatisfactory job performance. Avoid diagnosing a problem or confronting the employee with what you suspect might be the problem. Termination is always for a cause related to job performance standards.

Give complete documentation of the employee's job performance problems and arrange for referral to the counselor as soon as possible if the employee chooses that alternative. If the employee refuses help or if his or her performance remains unsatisfactory, the manager will take the appropriate disciplinary action or dismiss the individual from employment.

Use firm, consistent procedures. Any deviation from firm and consistent administration of these procedures because of misguided feelings of sympathy or other reasons will delay needed treatment and create an extreme risk to the employee's health and ultimate recovery. It is important that the supervisor not focus his or her attention on a "witch hunt" for alcoholism or other problems. The only criterion used for referral to the EAP is deteriorating job performance. The program places the responsibility for needed diagnosis, counseling, and treatment in the hands of qualified professionals.

Management can minimize the impact of sex in the workplace by maintaining an open environment where affected parties may talk about the situation. The same type of counseling that is available for extensive alcohol and drug users should be available for the individual caught up in a potential sex involvement. And, remember, in the workplace, a couple falling in love and getting married poses less of a problem than a couple getting "unmarried" or divorced and still trying to work together.

ACTION PROJECT 4–2   WHAT KIND OF COUNSELOR ARE YOU? (INDIVIDUAL EXERCISE)

Instructions: This project presents five situations. You are to select one of the four responses that most nearly fits the typical answer you might give in such a situation. When you are finished, you will relate your answers to the counseling style you may be displaying at work.

1. You are a supervisor interviewing a young job applicant who says: "I am determined to be successful, and to me that means 'being in charge.' That's

more important to me than anything else, and if I have to climb over others on the way up—well, that's the way things are in business."

_____a. You see yourself as a deeply ambitious person. Is that it?

_____b. What do you suppose is behind this strong determination of yours to get ahead?

_____c. Would you be interested in taking some tests to determine in what area you might expect to be most successful? It might be of real help to you, although it is possible with your drive that you could be successful in a number of fields.

_____d. Strong ambition can be a real asset to any person. Are you really sure, though, that you mean it when you say you're not adverse to climbing over those who get in your way? Couldn't that turn out to do you more harm than good?

2. You are a supervisor, and the occasion is the first annual formal performance review with a female employee. Her work was excellent the first few months, but has gradually deteriorated until now it is barely satisfactory. You discuss her poor performance, and she blurts out to you: "I think my problem with my work is that I'm so lonely! I don't have any friends, and I can't seem to make any no matter how hard I try. For some reason I feel like I'll never have anyone I can really call a friend."

_____a. Well, I'll tell you what I can do. I can arrange for you to join a small social group at the "Y." I send quite a few people there who have difficulty in making friends. This gives them something to do and permits them to make friends slowly and at their own pace. How does that sound to you?

_____b. Possibly if you could tell me a little more about how you are trying to make friends, we could get a clearer idea of what is involved.

_____c. It's gone on so long it almost has you convinced. Is that what you mean?

_____d. That's a pretty unhappy situation, to be without friends, and one that I would really work on. There are a number of things that you might do to learn how to make friends, and the sooner you start, the better.

3. You are the parent of a second-year university student who suddenly brings up the subject of switching majors, and says: "This other field seems to offer a greater chance for personal success. I won't be so dependent on others in trying to reach my goals. It will mean switching majors completely, and an extra year or so of college, but I am still young and I want to get started in the right field as soon as I graduate."

_____a. Whether this is the field in which you'll stay, no one can say but it seems to me that you are thinking more for yourself.

_____b. Have you thought of the possibility of working out a combination major? It seems a shame to just toss out all you've learned so far.

_____c. I take it that you've decided that you'd do better to change.

_____d. How much study have you given this new field?

4. A close friend calls at your office to tell you of a business venture he is enthusiastic about. He says: "All I need is enough money to get this thing started.

It can't miss! Whoever provides the finances to get this off the ground will be in on a sure winner. I'm ready to go as soon as I locate the working capital!"

_____ a. If you think it wise, I could give you the name of an investment counselor who'd be glad to go over the proposition with you and possibly give you some good leads on how to seek financial support.

_____ b. That's fine! One must feel sure of himself if he expects to make a go of something. To go into something hesitantly can really make it get all mixed up. You're on the right track and I wish you success.

_____ c. If you could get the cash to start, do you feel sure you could make a go of it?

_____ d. Have you figured out what the risks are yet?

5. You enter the company cafeteria just in time for a late lunch and notice a fellow supervisor whom you see only occasionally. She hasn't finished eating and is sitting at a table alone in the almost empty cafeteria, so you join her. After a minute or two of discussing current company goings-on, she suddenly says very seriously: "I came to work here the same time Joe did. I know he's after Walt's job when Walt retires, but I'm sure going to try to get it even though Joe has more experience. I am just as ambitious, and I have just as much on the ball. I am not going to let that stuffed-shirt get that promotion if I can help it!"

_____ a. It's a fine thing to try to get ahead, but do you think that by starting out with such an attitude toward him that you are going about it correctly?

_____ b. And that will probably take a lot of careful planning and thinking. You'll want to go carefully.

_____ c. He really makes you want to beat him out, does he?

_____ d. Let's wait a minute here. Why is it so important for you to get ahead of this man?

ANALYSIS

Each of the answers to the five previous situations is related to one of the four types of supervisors—ranging from the "blunt accusatory supervisor" who discourages discussions to the overprotective "mother hen." Somewhere in between is the type that encourages a two-way communication between the employee and the supervisor.

Read the description of the four types; then see the answers that give you the type of supervisor that is related to each response.

Judge—You assume the validity of the person's statement and give it added value by indicating your personal judgment.

If you agree with this statement, you give it added support; if you disagree or question it, you encourage the person to defend it. Neither approach sets up a proper perspective for clear analytical discussion.

DA (*District Attorney*)—You assume the validity of the person's statement and probe to get more information or find a hidden motive.

This often comes across as being blunt or accusatory and discourages communication. The other party very likely will become uncomfortable and on the defensive and is apt to close the subject as quickly as possible. The other person wants discussion, not a cross questioning!

MLH (*Mother's Little Helper*)—You assume the validity of the statement, and you not only agree but also have supportive suggestions and advice to offer, possibly even personal help.

This attitude eliminates any discussion of the statement; the results can be extremely varied—from encouragement on one hand to unwanted meddling on the other.

CRM (*Check for the Real Meaning*)—Without accepting the statement as being valid, but by repeating it, rephrasing it, or summarizing it, you invite further discussion by indicating your neutrality and your willingness to be a good listener.

In this further discussion, you check for the real meaning because you cannot know how serious a person is prior to in-depth discussion. In spite of what people say, they may be

- Inviting serious discussion
- Thinking out loud
- Trying to impress you
- Deeply troubled and seeking comfort through discussion or other circumstances

Only if you check for the real meaning, in a neutral manner, do you encourage meaningful two-way communication that may reveal the other person's true thoughts.

SCORE YOUR TEST

SITUATION 1	SITUATION 2	SITUATION 3	SITUATION 4	SITUATION 5
a. CRM	a. MLH	a. J	a. MLH	a. J
b. DA	b. DA	b. MLH	b. J	b. MLH
c. MLH	c. CRM	c. CRM	c. CRM	c. CRM
d. J	d. J	d. DA	d. DA	d. DA

Do you like what you found out? If you answered three or more situations with a district attorney response, there is some tendency to act the same way in a real-life situation. Or did you tend to be "mother's little helper," the meddling overprotective supervisor? It is true that some situations require a judge or a mother's little helper, but some employees resent an MLH as much as a DA and fail to open up when they have problems. If you received five CRMs, your peers might question your scoring, or they might be eager to have you as a supervisor!

FOLLOW-UP DISCUSSION QUESTIONS

What relationship do you find between these character types and directive counseling, nondirective counseling, and cooperative counseling? Is Mother's Little Helper more likely to give directive or nondirective counseling? _____

_____

Which style is likely to give the most direct counseling? _____
Which is the best style for these situations? _____

_____

_____

Why? _____

_____

EMPLOYEE ASSISTANCE PROGRAMS

Employee assistance programs (EAPs) provide counseling and other remedies to employees having substance abuse, emotional, or other personal problems as well as some work-related problems such as downsizing. "Although EAPs used to focus mainly on alcohol and drug abuse, today they address stress management, family and marital problems, workplace violence and the emotional disruption that can accompany downsizing."[18] According to one survey, utilization of EAPs has increased 10 percent to 15 percent over the past few years. And they are frequently called on to help with corporate downsizing and reorganization. Of 198 companies surveyed, 73 percent said their EAPs cover these workplace concerns.[19]

The first step in an EAP involves the maintenance of performance records and the application of corrective measures when performance falls below standard. The second phase constitutes the link between the work context and community treatment resources. Two experts recommend that management should address (1) the effect of program participation on disciplinary procedures, (2) the disposition of information about employees' participation in the program, and (3) the evaluation of results over time.[20]

Employee assistance programs can help employers cope with the effects that personal employee problems such as drug abuse and alcoholism have on job performance. Because poor employee performance can mean substantial economic losses, companies have turned increasingly to various forms of EAPs in an effort to step up production and reduce costs.

POST-TREATMENT PROCEDURES

FOLLOW-UP IF THE EMPLOYEE IMPROVES

The employee must be assured that job security will not be jeopardized if he or she obtains the recommended treatment, progresses toward control of the illness, and job performance improves.

The employee should also be advised not to expect any special privileges or exemptions from standard personnel administration practices.

If a relapse occurs, close follow-up and coordination between the supervisor and the company medical director is of utmost importance. In spite of relapses, many persons ultimately control their disease.

FOLLOW-UP IF THE EMPLOYEE DOES NOT IMPROVE

If the employee refuses help or accepts treatment but makes no progress toward rehabilitation, and job performance remains poor or deteriorates further, supervisors must take the action they would normally take in cases of unsatisfactory job performance.

Of course, many approaches to rehabilitation are possible. It is important to remember that alcoholism, drug abuse, or sexual misconduct are usually symptoms of other deeper social and psychological problems and that, for rehabilitation to actually work, these problems must be taken into account.

SUMMARY

Personal problems cannot always be left at home. Sometimes they travel to work. At work personal problems are reflected in (1) exaggerated behavior, (2) specific distress, and (3) radical changes. Once distress is recognized, friends and coworkers can often help each other through the rough times. Their main counseling tool is the practice of active listening. Effective self-counseling is also a technique that can be learned to good advantage.

Both professionally trained counselors and supervisory staff perform counseling functions. These functions are very tiring and time consuming but necessary, and sometimes rewarding. The three major counseling styles are (1) the traditional directive, (2) the newer nondirective, and (3) the cooperative, a combination of the first two. In directive counseling, the counselor directs the subject matter; in nondirective counseling, the subject is allowed to develop spontaneously. Cooperative counseling combines features of the first two types and is particularly useful when dealing with alcoholics and drug addicts.

Alcoholism is a major disease that does great damage to our national productivity and results in great waste of human resources. Drug addiction, although perhaps not as prevalent, is increasing throughout the entire population, and some companies have instituted counseling programs to help their afflicted employees lick these disabling problems.

Sexual liaisons and sexual harassment are also becoming more significant problems in the workplace. Research on homosexuality and its effects on the workplace continues.

When a case of alcoholism, drug abuse, or sexual harassment is encountered, company policy often recognizes the problem as an illness that can be cured and offers the employee help through an employee assistance program. Such a program is based on counseling. If, after many trials, the employee refuses help and his or her job performance does not improve, two choices are left—leave the company or undertake self-cure, which is very difficult.

**CASE STUDY
4–1**

THE SWEET SMELL OF GRASS

Tom Nowak walked to his office on Monday morning to find Dan Porter waiting for him at his door. "Tom, I would like to see you right away in my office." Tom was surprised at the sudden approach that his boss had used the first thing on a Monday morning. It must be serious, he thought, as they walked down the hall together. He thought that they had always had a stable, amicable relationship.

"What's up?" asked Tom, trying to keep from sounding too apprehensive as they arrived at Dan's office.

"Sit down, Tom, it's important. It involves some of the men in your department." Dan was obviously disturbed. "You have been responsible for the shipping room for several years, and I haven't had any serious reason to doubt how you handle your men or the decisions you make in that department. But this new development upsets me."

Dan continued, "I've heard, and occasionally seen, a group of your boys, a clique, seem to take their breaks surreptitiously in out-of-the-way places, the rest room, and behind the loading dock. I've heard the reason is because they're smoking marijuana. Is that true, Tom?"

"You might be right, Dan. I really don't know, but I suspect it."

"Have you ever confronted them with the idea? Have you asked them outright?"

"No," said Tom quietly, "and I am not sure it's a good idea."

"Why not," replied Dan quickly and rather irately, "do you have a better idea?"

"The first reason is that they would probably lie if I asked them outright if they were smoking pot. They would lie for fear of losing their jobs. Another is I am not their mother or guardian of their morals. Their break time is strictly their own. Oh, I know it's illegal, and the company could get into trouble even though we don't control their breaks. However, we might be opening 'Pandora's box' if we approach it head on."

"What do you mean by a crack like that, Tom?" inquired Dan.

"You know as well as I do," said Tom, "that there are some guys under you that have openly discussed the effects of pot and who have admitted trying it. I don't have to name them, you know them."

Dan looked perplexed. "You're right, but they haven't stepped out of line at work to my knowledge. If we condone its use at work we have a problem. It is illegal, you know. We just can't take the risk that it is being done on company time."

1. What would be your approach to solve the immediate problem?

2. If you were to counsel any of the employees, which counseling approach would you use?

3. Should Tom and Dan try to solve the problem between themselves or should they confer with others?

4. There is no company policy on the matter; should they develop one?

CASE STUDY 4–2 — JUST A LITTLE LARCENY—I'LL DRINK TO THAT

In the opinion of Bob Ruppert, hospital administrator, the theft of various items ranging in value from $1 to $100 has become a major problem at the Bisbee Memorial Hospital. And it is increasing. At the recent monthly supervisors' meeting, Ruppert stated, "All the evidence we have been able to gather seems to indicate that the problem is serious and the loss is quite large. We must take steps to stop our loss. Hopefully, we can take care of it on an individual basis. I hope so. I have no idea whether it is the problem of a few or many."

A few days later you are in the home of a long-time friend who works at the hospital with you, but not under your supervision. Darryl Gossage has been with the company as a maintenance man for more than fifteen years and has been considered one of the company's most competent men in his field. You also knew his drinking habits were getting worse, and some of your friends say that he has become an alcoholic.

This particular Saturday Darryl has imbibed rather heavily and as you chat with him in the garage you notice a microscope with the initials BMH marked on the side. You mention to him, "Isn't that one of our microscopes, Darryl?"

"Yah," Darryl replies hesitantly, "it needs fixing." Casually, you go over to the microscope and check it out. It appears to be in good order.

1. What would you say? Do you make an accusation or let it pass?
2. Do you ignore it and ask Darryl for suggestions on what can be done about theft of hospital property?
3. What is the best way to handle Darryl's possible "light finger" problem?
4. If you think Darryl's drinking is now a serious problem, how would you handle it?

CASE STUDY 4–3

LOVE IN BLOOM OR...?

Fran is a good-looking, 19-year-old student who works full time at a small fast-food restaurant. Fran is working to accumulate enough money for college and a new car. The manager of the restaurant, Pat, is also a college student and about four years older than Fran. There is an assistant manager for each of the work shifts, and Fran would like to be promoted to that position for the extra pay and status. Pat likes Fran and has made no secret about it. In fact, several times Pat has asked Fran out to movies after work and suggested that they take their breaks in Pat's car. Pat has openly commented on Fran's attractive qualities. Fran has rejected Pat's advances. Pat appears to be "hurt" and has told Fran that unless they can take breaks together and date, Fran doesn't stand a chance of becoming an assistant manager.

1. What do you think—is this sexual harassment or just "love in bloom"?
2. What can Fran do?
3. Would it make a difference to know that Fran is a young man and Pat a young woman? Go back through the case and see if there are any differences.

DISCUSSION AND STUDY QUESTIONS—TO KEEP YOU THINKING . . . ───

1. Compare the advantages of having trained supervisors doing counseling versus the advantages of a trained expert doing the counseling of employees.
2. Describe the four basic practices nondirective counselors follow when they are counseling.
3. Describe the four stages of alcoholism and the types of counseling that might be given for the first three stages.
4. Depressants and stimulants are both legal drugs but can be abused. For what reasons are each of them prescribed?
5. Comment in your own words on Winston Churchill's statement: "Most of the world's work is done by people who do not feel very well all of the time."
6. How can you recognize alcoholism and other drug dependency?
7. What are appropriate steps for preventing sexual harassment?
8. Is homosexuality predetermined, acquired, or a combination?

NOTES

1. Catherine M. Petrini, "Work Groups on the Wagon," *Training and Development,* April 1995, p. 11.
2. Kevin Murphy, "Why Pre-Employment Alcohol Testing Is Such a Bad Idea," *Business Horizons,* September–October 1995, pp. 69–74.
3. Jean Kinney and Gwen Leaton, *Loosening tghe Grip: A Handbook of Alcohol Information* (St. Louis, Mo.: C.V. Mosby, 1983), pp. 55–56.
4. Victor Schacter and Thomas E. Geidt, "Cracking Down on Drugs,"*Across the Board,* November 1985, p. 28.
5. "Drug Abuse Costing America Billions," (Columbus, Georgia) *Ledger-Enquirer,* February 4, 1996, pp. A7–A8.
6. Donna E. Shalala, "Say 'No' to Legalization of Marijuana," *The Wall Street Journal,* August 18, 1995, p. A8.
7. Gary L. Henderson, "They're Cheap and Easy to Make," *USA Today,* July 29, 1985, p. 8A.
8. "Ticklish Questions," *Across the Board,* April 1996, pp. 46–52.
9. "Dealing with Harassment," *Colorado Business,* July 1983, p. 11.
10. Diane Feldman, "Sexual Harassment: Policies and Prevention," *Personnel,* September 1987, pp. 12–17.
11. Ruth Ann Strickland, "Sexual Harassment: A Legal Perspective for Public Administrators," *Public Personnel Management,* Winter 1995, p. 504.
12. Ibid.
13. Wayne R. Dynes, ed., *Encyclopedia of Homosexuality* (New York: Garland, 1990), p. 555.
14. Ibid.
15. Sue Lindsay, "Homosexuality Inherited, Scientist Says," *Rocky Mountain News,* October 15, 1993, p. 6A.
16. Barbara O'Neill, "Americans and Their Debt: Right-Sizing for the '90s," *Journal of Financial Planning,* January 1995, pp. 20–28.
17. Carla Joinson, "Easing the Pain of Layoffs," *HR Magazine,* February 1995, pp. 68–74.
18. Christina Many, "Beyond Drug and Alcohol Abuse," *Business Insurance,* June 26, 1995, p. 3.
19. Ibid., pp. 3–4.
20. Steven H. Appelbaum and Barbara T. Shapiro, "The ABCs of EAPs," *Personnel,* July 1989, pp. 39–46.

RECOMMENDED READING

Appelbaum, Steven H., and Barbara T. Shapiro. "The ABCs of EAPs." *Personnel,* July 1989, pp. 39–46.

Bacon, Donald C. "See You in Court." *Nation's Business,* July 1989, pp. 16–26.

Broad, Mary L. "HRD Innovation for Substance Abuse Prevention." *Training and Development,* February 1996, pp. 58–66.

Champagne, Paul J., and R. Bruce McAfee. "Auditing Sexual Harassment." *Personnel Journal,* June 1989, pp. 124–138.

Dynes, Wayne R., ed. *Encyclopedia of Homosexuality.* New York: Garland, 1990.

Frank, Richard G., and Thomas G. McGuire. "Estimating Costs of Mental Health and Substance Abuse Coverage." *Health Affairs,* Fall 1995, pp. 102–115.

Greiff, James. "When an Employee's Performance Slumps." *Nation's Business,* January 1989, pp. 44–45.

Kupfer, Andrew. "Is Drug Testing Good or Bad?" *Fortune,* December 19, 1988, pp. 133–135.

Leonard, Bill. "Performance Testing Can Add an Extra Margin of Safety." *HR Magazine,* February 1996, pp. 61–64.

Mangan, Doreen. "An Rx for Drug Abuse." *Small Business Reports,* May 1992, pp. 28–38.

Masi, Dale A., and Seymour J. Friedland. "EAP Action and Options." *Personnel Journal,* June 1988, pp. 61–67.

Masterson, James F., M.D. *The Search for the Real Self: Unmasking the Personality Disorders of Our Age.* New York: The Free Press, 1988.

Scanlon, Walter F. *Alcoholism and Drug Abuse in the Workplace: Managing Care and Costs through Employee Assistance Programs.* 2nd ed. New York: Praeger Publishers, 1991.

Sharp, Tom S. "Workplace Policies Fight Substance Abuse." *Personnel Journal,* June 1993, p. 33.

U.S. Department of Justice. Drug Enforcement Administration, Fact Sheets. Washington, D.C.: GPO, 1987. Later editions available.

Woititz, Janet G. *Struggle for Intimacy: Dedicated to Adult Children of Alcoholics.* Pompano Beach, Fla.: Health Communications, 1985.

Wrich, James T. "Beyond Testing: Coping with Drugs at Work." *Harvard Business Review,* January–February 1988, pp. 120–127, 130.

5

HUMAN MOTIVATION

Here are some questions that may stimulate your thinking. The answers to some will be found in the readings; other answers will come from your experiences and personal opinions.

- How are you motivated? What "turns you on"?
- Why do people work when they don't need the money? Is money the most important incentive, or are other reasons equally important?
- What makes some people work harder than others?
- Does everyone have the same needs? Are needs hierarchical?
- Are people motivated internally or externally?
- How can routine jobs be redesigned to be more productive and satisfying?
- Do managers motivate subordinates by listening to them?

LEARNING GOALS

After studying this chapter, you should be able to:

1. Describe what motivation means to you.
2. Explain how the individual's need to be motivated may differ from the company's and supervisor's need to motivate.
3. Describe the schools of psychology and how they relate to motivation.
4. Discuss the various behavior defense mechanisms we exhibit when we cannot achieve our goals easily.
5. Describe the five elements of Maslow's hierarchy of needs. Contrast them with Herzberg's hygiene or maintenance approach and motivators.
6. Contrast intrinsic motivators from extrinsic motivators and list several of each type.
7. Compare the expectancy, equity, and needs approaches to motivation.
8. Describe the nature of incentives and their relationship to motivation.
9. Summarize some of the important methods of job enrichment.
10. Describe barriers to achievement and how to overcome them.
11. Define and apply the following terms and concepts (in order of first occurrence):

- **motivation**
- **goal congruency**
- **behavior modification**

- **reinforcement**
- **belonging needs**
- **self-actualization**

- hygiene/motivation approach
- expectancy approach to motivation
- equity approach to motivation
- ERG approach to motivation
- incentive
- intrinsic motivators
- defense mechanisms

- job design
- job enrichment
- job enlargement
- job rotation
- job sharing
- core job dimensions

This chapter is devoted solely to human motivation processes and accompanying strategies for improving them. Chapter 6, Job Performance and Morale, includes discussions of individual job satisfaction, group morale, and the desired result of motivation—enhanced job performance and productivity.

WHAT IS MOTIVATION ALL ABOUT?

Motivation is an internal concept based on a person's needs and the fulfillment of those needs. Too often, we think of motivating another person. But, as we shall see, it is not something that we do to or for another person, nor is it externally imposing a set of needs on that other person. In its simplest sense, motivation is need fulfillment.

Motivation is what inspires people to act. It instills a belief that what people are doing on the job is important. At work, motivation is achieved naturally because work is defined as any activity or effort undertaken to accomplish a goal. All workers are motivated to some degree. Some are more motivated than others.

In the business world, motivation is used to describe the drive that impels an individual to work. A truly motivated person is one who wants to work. Both employees and employers are interested in understanding motivation. If workers know what strengthens and what weakens their motivation, they can often perform more effectively to find more satisfaction in their jobs. Employers want to know what motivates the employees so that they can get them to work harder. The motivation to work is integral both to successful organizations and to employee job satisfaction. Thus both employees and employers must understand it better.

MOTIVATION AND BEHAVIOR

Motivation is an internal need satisfied by external expression.

A common understanding of the word *motivation* is that it is something stemming from within a person. Motivation is an internal need that is satisfied through an external expression. The achievement of the goal or the obtaining of the incentive is the external factor that the public sees, but the reason why people are moved or motivated to achieve it may not always be obvious.

Concept of individual differences revisited.

People are motivated to perform similar actions by very different internal drives. Recall that individual differences are those unique emotional, physical, and social qualities about each individual human being. The concept of individual differences is illustrated by the fact that two employees work hard to get raises but for different reasons. To one, the raise is important because it will provide more money; to the other, the higher status that the raise signifies is a stronger motivation than the money. Capitalizing on fulfilling these different needs is a job of the leader/manager. It could be argued that this is manipulative, but it is really a good job of matching needs and abilities. The resulting positive behavior is the expected outcome.

Also, similar internal motivations can have different results. Two employees who feel a strong need for job security may handle their needs in very different ways. One might decide to work hard but never to "rock the boat" for fear of being fired. The other might choose to be innovative, even at the risk of being controversial, as a way of becoming indispensable.

MOTIVATION AND ORGANIZATIONS

Management often refers to employees as "resources" or "assets," which means that employees are valuable, profit-making parts of a business organization. Studies of motivation try to discover what incentives will cause workers to work and increase their value as assets. Managers care about their workers' personal motivations because those motivations affect production rates. Therefore, they try to structure, by incentive systems, the motivations of workers. They cannot motivate the workers—only the workers themselves can do that.

Management can facilitate achievement of workers' goals, such as personal salary maximization, autonomy, and empowerment, while at the same time accomplishing organizational objectives (see Figure 5–1). The objective of **goal congruency** is to maximize the overlap between organizational objectives and individuals' goals.

Ivy League professor and management theorist Chris Argyris examined the proposition that individual growth needs and organizational objectives are often in conflict. He found that as people mature, they grow more independent and want to make more decisions for themselves. They want to take on more responsibility, to become more competent. He also found that some organizations exert pressures that directly oppose these patterns of self-actualization. In the interest

FIGURE 5–1 Goal Congruency. The Objective Is to Make the Shaded Area as Congruent as Possible.

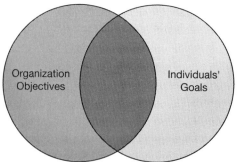

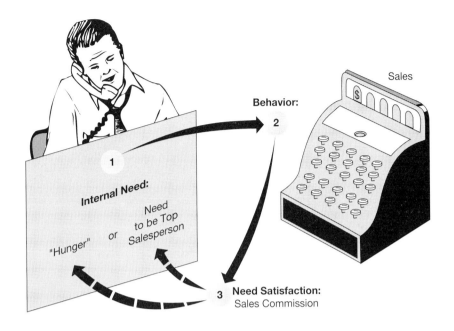

Behavior:
2

Sales

1
Internal Need:
"Hunger" or Need to be Top Salesperson

3 Need Satisfaction:
Sales Commission

of efficiency, organizations require employees to submit to rigid forms of authority, demand few skills of them, and make as many decisions as possible for them.

Argyris believes that the "incongruence between the individual and the organization can provide the basis for a continued challenge that, as it is fulfilled, will tend to help people to enhance their own growth and to develop organizations that will tend to be viable and effective."[1]

Motivation can be understood in its simplest form as a three-step process: (1) an internal need exists, (2) a behavioral action or direction is taken to satisfy that need, and (3) the satisfaction of that need is accomplished. Note that the need is internally, not externally, imposed. The need may be economic, social, or psychological. For example, you may have a desire for food that can be satisfied by various actions: grabbing a snack or waiting several hours for a more substantial meal. Another example would be a social or psychological need to be the top salesperson in a division.

The achievement of a goal is satisfying, and the tension release is gratifying, but the feeling of satisfaction is usually short-lived. The "glow" of achieving a goal lasts but a few minutes to an hour, and seldom more than a day. Thus, how can the individual's motivation become more long lasting? The answer in part is in different schools of psychology and concepts of motivation.

PSYCHOLOGY AND ITS IMPACT ON MOTIVATION

Three schools of psychology have had a great impact on people's beliefs about motivation. None of the ideas is more right than others; they only represent

FIGURE 5–2 Iceberg Theory: A Large Portion of Our Personality Is Hidden from Our Conscious Perception.

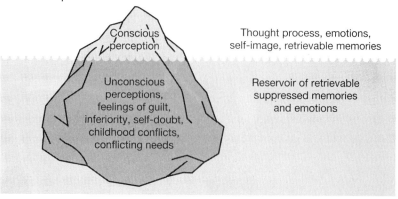

different ways of perceiving motivation and how to motivate. They are the psychoanalytic, the behaviorist, and the humanistic schools of behavior.

PSYCHOANALYTIC SCHOOL

"Iceberg" theory.

Sigmund Freud, the founder of the psychoanalytic process, stressed the complexity of human motivation and pointed out that the outward manifestation of an individual's psyche is like the tip of a submerged iceberg (Figure 5–2). Freud believed that the interpersonal and social environments determined the outcome of the individual's life and death efforts. To Freud, the physical environment is experienced rather than observed; that is, we may hit the submerged iceberg without knowing it. On the other hand, it may be necessary for us to hit or feel the iceberg if we are to know what our true motivations are.

BEHAVIORIST SCHOOL

Behavior modification.

More than thirty years ago, psychologist B. F. Skinner developed a behavior modification theory that is relatively easy to understand but is sometimes difficult to implement. **Behavior modification** is the process of influencing behavior by rewarding the individual for proper responses and failing to reward for improper responses. It involves the principle of conditioning and the principle of reinforcement. Conditioning involves rewarding desired behavior and not rewarding undesirable behavior.

Principle of reinforcement.

Repeated rewards are called **reinforcement.** Skinner found that, for effective reinforcement, a carefully planned schedule must be followed. Rewards must be timed properly to be effective. The most effective rewards are those that immediately follow the desired behavior.

Positive rewards, such as praise or food, are generally more effective than negative reinforcement, such as punishment. The basic approach is to reinforce desired behavior and ignore undesirable actions. Over a period of time, the reinforced behavior will tend to be repeated, and the unrewarded will tend to disappear. Punishment of undesired behavior is to be avoided as contributing to feelings of restraint and actions of rebellion.

Behavior modification has some intriguing possibilities for motivation. One of the best documented examples of the potential of behavior modification in industry is at the Emery Air Freight Company. The supervisors at the company were trained to praise work done correctly by the employees, such as keeping records of all their activities, improving delivery times, or responding quickly to telephone requests. The program saved over $2 million in four years.

HUMAN RELATIONS SCHOOL

Many people search for universal guidelines and principles that are applicable to all organizations. They seem to believe in the *classical organizational theory.* This theory says that employees are lazy, work only for money, and need to be supervised closely if they are to produce up to standard.

The human relations school, on the other hand, was developed by a contrasting or opposite viewpoint. Its supporters believe in looking to people rather than to the organization for resolving interpersonal problems or opportunities. There is a heavy emphasis on the study of informal groups, group decision making, employee satisfaction, and leadership styles. People have many different feelings and collectively develop a group personality that should be managed differently from that of other groups. From an academic point of view, the human relations approach is now being classified as neoclassical when compared with the classical (rigid) organizational theory. Primary examples of the human relations needs approach are Maslow's hierarchy of needs and Herzberg's hygiene/motivation concept.

MASLOW'S BASIC NEEDS

Internal need fulfillment is the basis for motivation. Whether those motives arise out of fear, determination, goal setting, or whatever source, the identification and fulfillment of individuals' needs congruent with organizational objectives become an important management task.

Abraham Maslow conjectured that basic needs are the same for all human beings.[2] He found that, although different cultures satisfy these needs in different ways, the needs themselves remain the same. What are these basic needs or instincts that motivate people to act in the ways that they do?

Identifying needs in one's self and in others can be difficult for a variety of reasons. First, while five basic needs have been defined, they result in endlessly varying activities. The expression of these needs is influenced by both a person's present surroundings and by past experiences and is different in different individuals. To complicate matters further, basic needs are often more unconscious than conscious. For example, someone who feels hungry and eats to satisfy that "felt" hunger may actually be needing love or security (see Figure 5–3).

FIGURE 5–3 Maslow's Hierarchy of Needs.

PHYSIOLOGICAL NEEDS

Not much can motivate a person who has not reasonably satisfied his or her basic physiological needs. Maslow suggested that when a person is starving, the only need that is important is food. Gandhi put it another way: "Even God cannot talk to a hungry man except in terms of bread."

Maslow's five basic needs start with the physiological needs.

The physiological needs include such basics as food and drink, sleep, clean air, satisfactory temperature, and protection from the elements by clothing and shelter. When the primary physical needs are satisfied, other physical instincts may take their place, such as sexual desires and the sensual desires of taste, smell, and touch. For most people, the physical needs are indirectly satisfied with the money earned from the work they do.

SAFETY OR SECURITY NEEDS

People also want to feel safe from harm. In most adults, the safety needs are expressed by the desire to be stable and secure. To prefer the familiar and the known to the unfamiliar and the unknown reflects the basic need for safety.

Your chosen career may reflect your need for security.

The type of career we choose may reflect our need for security. Such careers might be teaching, accounting, or civil service. Are you thinking of working for a large, stable company whose growth and future is predictable? Is your choice in the changing fields of aerospace or electronics, or is it in a more stable area, such as food processing or the fire department? If you find that these stabilizing factors fit your outlook on a career, then your need for security is very strong.

SOCIAL OR BELONGING NEEDS

People need a sense of belonging.

Once people have basically satisfied their physiological and safety needs, they feel an urge for acceptance, affection, and the feeling of belonging. This need expresses itself in a desire to be loved by someone and to have someone to love. It is important to remember that a person needs to give as well as receive affection. Supervisors can see the strength of the social need by observing cliques during coffee breaks or groups leaving work together. What management needs to do is capitalize on this need during work hours.

The social needs may more aptly be called the **belonging needs** or team spirit needs. Teamwork and team spirit are often more important than individual achievement, but many leaders and administrators underestimate their importance. We want to be successful as a group or team as well as individually.

ESTEEM NEEDS

Maslow classifies the needs for esteem into two categories: (1) the desire for a sense of internal worth and (2) the desire for prestige or reputation that can only be conferred by other people. People who value themselves have highly developed feelings of confidence, worth, strength, capability, and adequacy. Lack of self-esteem produces feelings of inferiority, inadequacy, weakness, and helplessness. These feelings of self-dislike lead to discouragement and a sense of failure.

Management often recognizes that individual needs can be satisfied better with "status" symbols than with money. The executives have their status symbols in forms of private dining rooms, carpeted offices, and keys to the executive washroom.

Status symbols satisfy the self-esteem need.

Supervisors also recognize that individual needs often can be satisfied better with status symbols than with money. Blue-collar workers, although they may sneer at executive symbols, have many status symbols of their own. The shop foreman or union boss may rate the end locker or wear some distinctive symbol, such as a jacket or badge, to denote his or her position. A word processor may gain self-esteem by serving as a private secretary rather than as a member of the word processing section. A salesperson gains status by driving a company car or by receiving a new car from the company every three years.

Belonging need can be in conflict with the esteem need.

Sometimes our needs are in conflict. The need to be an integrated, accepted member of a group may conflict with the need to be a leader. A good worker who is selected as a supervisor may become an ambivalent leader because the need to be an accepted member of the group proves stronger than the ego drive to be a supervisor.

SELF-ACTUALIZATION NEEDS

The need for self-fulfillment, the realization of one's fullest potential, is called **self-actualization.** Needs for self-fulfillment are demonstrated by doing a job well merely for the sake of doing it well and by striving toward more creative endeavors of all kinds. Maslow distinguishes the needs concerned with physiology, safety, belonging, and esteem as "deficiency" needs—without their satisfaction, people lack the necessary components for developing healthy personalities. Self-actualization is a "growth" need. Healthy people are those who are free to concern themselves mainly with satisfying their needs for continual growth and fulfillment both on and off the job.

THE HIERARCHY OF NEEDS

Maslow explains the five categories of needs in terms of a hierarchy and says that one need must be relatively well satisfied before the next in line can become a driving force. Although this description of a hierarchy of needs is convenient, it is slightly misleading. One need does not require full satisfaction before the next need on the hierarchical ladder makes itself felt.

People are constantly driven by internal forces—they are increasingly motivated toward new goals. One of the chief reasons for the pleasurable feelings accompanying the achievement of a goal being short-lived is that another goal, based on the same or a different need, soon takes its place. When a need is satisfied, it no longer motivates. The ever-changing nature of needs plays an important role in the theory and practice of incentive systems and job development programs. The truly motivated person will look for opportunities to satisfy his or her desires, as demonstrated in "To the Kid on the End of the Bench" (Figure 5–4).

FIGURE 5–4 To Be Motivated to Long-Term Goals Means Determination, Sacrifice, and Strong Desire. Compliments of United Technologies, Box 360, Hartford, Connecticut 06141.

TO THE KID ON THE END OF THE BENCH

Champions once sat where you're sitting, kid.

The Football Hall of Fame (and every other Hall of Fame) is filled with names of people who sat, week after week, without getting a spot of mud on their well-laundered uniforms.

Generals, senators, surgeons, prize-winning novelists, professors, business executives started on the end of a bench, too.

Don't sit and study your shoe tops. Keep your eye on the game. Watch for defensive lapses.

Look for offensive opportunities.

If you don't think you're in a great spot, wait until you see how many would like to take it away from you at next spring practice.

What you do from the bench this season could put you on the field next season, as a player, or back in the grandstand as a spectator.

SELF-APPRAISAL

Can You Recognize the Need?

Each of the following work situations stresses the denial of one of four basic needs: (1) security, (2) social, (3) self-esteem, and (4) self-actualization. After each situation write the number of the need being denied. Refer to the text if necessary. (Answers are given at the end of the chapter.)

1. A rumor of imminent layoffs is being circulated in the company, and the employees are upset. _____

2. A new employee felt "left out" when she was not asked to join her fellow workers for coffee. _____

3. A machine operator developed a way to cut production time. His supervisor adopted the plan for operators on similar machines without giving him credit. The man was resentful. _____

4. A man who had worked hard on behalf of the union wished to be elected shop steward. At the last election, he was not nominated, and he felt let down by his friends. _____

5. A worker received $15 extra in his weekly paycheck. He felt ashamed that he did not report the mistake. _____

6. A group of employees liked to go for coffee together. The boss divided them into two groups and made them go at different times. The employees were unhappy about the ruling. _____

7. An employee who felt he could not work smoothly with others wanted to take a human relations course. The course required him to leave work fifteen minutes early once a week, and he offered to make up the loss by coming in fifteen minutes early on those days. The supervisor denied his request, thereby causing the employee a setback in his planning. _____

8. A store manager set a goal of a 15 percent sales increase in the next six months. She failed to attain her goal, but she did increase sales by 5 percent. She was keenly disappointed. _____

9. A salesman is worried because he has experienced a substantial drop in sales for no apparent reason. _____

10. A manager resented having to cancel, at the last minute, elaborate plans for a camping trip with his family. _____

| EXPRESS YOUR OPINION | You have now read Maslow's hierarchy of needs. Let us assume that most of your physiological needs are satisfied and concentrate on your psychological needs. Sometimes, the self-esteem need seems to prevail, for instance, when you need considerable recognition as an individual. At other times, there may be a strong need for social acceptance to overcome a loneliness in your daily life. Which need seems to be the strongest and most desirable need to satisfy in the next few months? Can you say why? What one accomplishment could satisfy it most?

What do you think is the strongest need of your closest friend? Is it the same as yours? What is the strongest need of your parents? Do you think that people may go through life cycles that at different stages reflect the importance of different needs? |
|---|---|

HERZBERG'S HYGIENE/MOTIVATION APPROACH

Another, but complementary, approach to motivation by need fulfillment is provided by Frederick Herzberg. In an attempt to provide global satisfaction for an organization's workforce, Herzberg classified needs into two categories.

SATISFIERS AND DISSATISFIERS

Herzberg found that the factors that make a job satisfying are separate from the factors that make it dissatisfying. For example, offering workers more money can lead to less dissatisfaction, but not to true job satisfaction. Employees who hold jobs that they consider intrinsically rewarding are satisfied with their jobs; with less rewarding work, they become less satisfied. Offering them more money does not replace the opportunity of doing fulfilling work.

Workers are often in a neutral position—neither happy nor unhappy, but simply doing their jobs. Certain negative job factors decrease job satisfaction, and alleviating them brings employees back to a neutral position. Other positive factors can create employee satisfaction on the job. Without them, the employees again drop back to neutral, without turning into dissatisfied employees.

MOTIVATION-MAINTENANCE APPROACH

Satisfying a hygiene factor keeps us from being unhappy.

Herzberg believes certain factors are used to keep a person from being unhappy (Table 5–1), much in the same way that food keeps us from being hungry. Having a fine breakfast in the morning does not keep us from being hungry in the afternoon. Such is the case of motivation in industry. For example, a salary raise makes us happy, but not forever. Six months or a year later, we feel that we are deserving of a raise again, for one of many reasons. In Herzberg's terminology, money and fringe benefits are known as "negative motivators." Their absence from a job unquestionably will make people unhappy, but their presence doesn't necessarily make them happier or more productive.

TABLE 5–1 Hygiene Factors and Growth Needs

HYGIENE MAINTENANCE FACTORS	MOTIVATORS AND GROWTH NEEDS
Salary, status, and security	Growth and advancement to higher level tasks
Company policies and administration	Achievement
Supervision	Recognition for achievement
Work environment and interpersonal relations	Interest in the task
	Responsibility for enlarged task

SOURCE: Frederick Herzberg et al., *The Motivation to Work* (New York: John Wiley, 1959), p. 81.

But . . . satisfying a hygiene factor does not make us happy or productive.

Hygiene factors are conditions conducive to maintaining mental and physical health. Satisfying the hygiene maintenance factors only keeps us from being unhappy. Whether people's behavior is motivated by physical needs, security needs, or social needs, once these "appetites" are satisfied, they cease to be motivated, and will become "hungry" again. We find that more money in routine amounts, such as the annual raise, is largely taken for granted, anticipated before it arrives, and viewed as a justly deserved reward for past services, not as a stimulus to a new effort.

Another way of viewing Herzberg's approach is that, once certain maintenance factors are present, they are adequate and keep a person from being unhappy. Such factors are company policies, supervision, interpersonal relationships, status, money, and security. However, the strong factors that motivate persons to do more on the job are really the opportunities for professional growth, responsibility, work itself, recognition, and achievement.

Dissatisfiers relate more to hygiene factors.

When employees are asked what is dissatisfying in their jobs, they usually complain about things that are not associated with the actual work itself but rather with the work environment. These complaints include such matters as supervision, relations with others, physical conditions, organizational policies, administrative practices, pay, fringe benefits, status, and job security. Such complaints suggest that the context within which the work is done "is unfair or disorganized and as such represents . . . an unhealthy psychological work environment."[3]

Satisfiers relate more to the job itself.

When employees are asked what satisfies them about their work, they will describe aspects of the job itself. Employees are satisfied when the work they do interests them, when they achieve job goals and receive recognition for their achievements, and when they grow in responsibility. Factors that lead to job satisfaction are directly related to the need for self-actualization.

In summary, Herzberg believes that both **hygiene** and **motivation** needs must be satisfied. Employees with exciting jobs will usually be willing to tolerate unpleasant circumstances, such as low pay or an unfriendly supervisor. However, the fewer the possibilities for growth and personal fulfillment on a job, the greater the number of hygiene factors that must be offered in compensation. Workers want something back for what they give. If they can't get personal satisfaction, then they will seek satisfaction in other ways.

**ACTION PROJECT
5–1**

SELF-MOTIVATION COMES WHEN YOU HAVE GOALS
(INDIVIDUAL EXERCISE)

Answer the following questions as they pertain to you. You should not be asked to turn your answers in or to react to these questions in class, unless you wish to verbalize your feelings. The idea for this exercise is to see if you can focus on your needs and goals at this point in your life.

1. What is your number one, most important, physiological need at this time?

   _____

2. What is your number one security need at this time? Is it being basically satisfied? _____

3. What is your number one social need at this time? Is it being basically satisfied?

_____

4. What is your number one self-esteem need at this time? Is it being basically satisfied? _____

5. What one goal would you like to accomplish in three months? _____

_____

6. What one goal would you like to accomplish in three years? _____

_____

7. What would you like to accomplish for yourself personally in the next three years? _____

8. What would you like to accomplish for your family in the next three years?

_____

9. What would you like to accomplish in business in the next five years? _____

_____

Every month for the next six months review your list and see how you are doing. Are your goals realistic? Are you really working to make your dreams come true, or are you keeping them as fantasies? You are free to change your goals, but if you change them all, you may be running away from the challenges of life.

OTHER APPROACHES TO MOTIVATION

Considerable research has been done on motivation, leading to additional theories, such as the expectancy approach, equity approach, ERG approach, and others.

EXPECTANCY APPROACH

How we expect to do influences how we do.

The **expectancy approach** relates to the strength of an individual's belief that a particular course of action will result in a given outcome (reward). That belief is a function of expectation itself (expectancy), the method for making it happen (instrumentality), and the degree of attractiveness of a behavioral goal (valence) that the individual places on the outcome (reward). The formula for the relationship is shown in Figure 5–5.

FIGURE 5–5 Formula for Expectancy Approach.

Motivation	=	(or is a function of) Expectancy × Instrumentality × Valence
where		
Expectancy	=	the person's belief that effort will result in performance
Instrumentality	=	the person's belief that performance will be rewarded
Valence	=	the perceived strength or value of receiving the rewards

A good example of the expectancy approach is the grade that you expect to earn in a class. That grade influences how hard you work and the value you place on the outcome. In the example just given, the grade is the expectancy. The instrumentality is how hard you work to achieve that grade, and the valence is how much you want a particular grade. The reward is the grade itself.

EQUITY APPROACH

The **equity approach** places emphasis for motivation on perceived fairness. Its basis is that workers strive to maintain balance between their own inputs and their rewards in comparison to other workers with whom they compare themselves.

Equity is in the eye of the beholder.

The concept is comparative in that our perception of fairness is based on how we see others rewarded for more or less effort. If individuals perceive inequity, they can reduce that inequity by working harder, by seeking other rewards, or by a variety of other actions. Can you think of other ways to reduce inequity?

Workers compare their input/output ratio with others' input/output ratios. Figure 5–6 shows the relationship and consequences of imbalances in the input/output ratios. Rewards can take the form of monetary or nonmonetary rewards such as recognition, praise, advancement opportunities, or special privileges. If the perceived inequity is because the individuals are being overrewarded,

FIGURE 5–6 Equity Approach Ratios and Consequences.

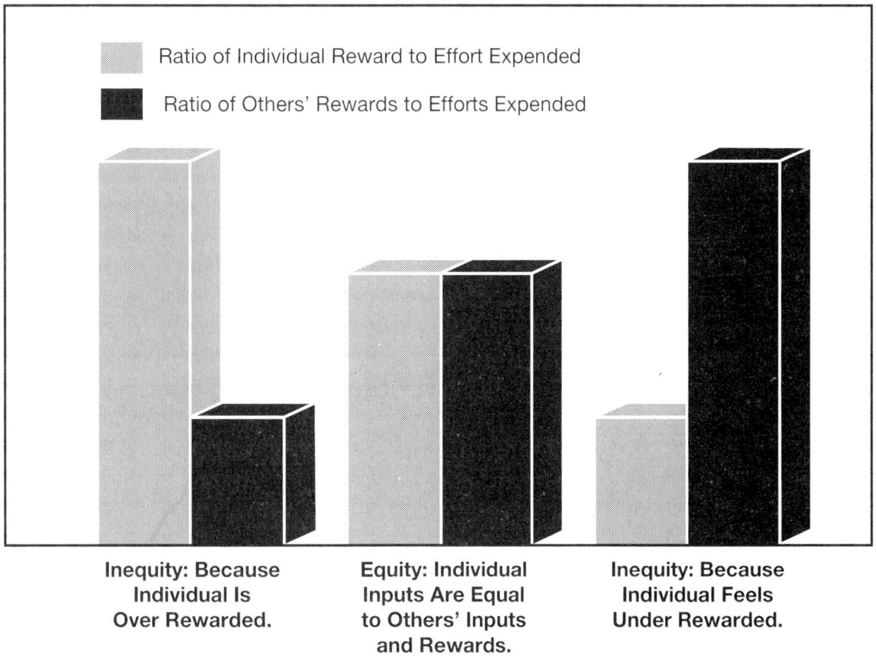

Ratio of Individual Reward to Effort Expended

Ratio of Others' Rewards to Efforts Expended

Inequity: Because Individual Is Over Rewarded.

Equity: Individual Inputs Are Equal to Others' Inputs and Rewards.

Inequity: Because Individual Feels Under Rewarded.

they may be resented or feel guilty because they are receiving more than deserved. If the inequity is because the individuals are being underrewarded, they may "slack off." Equity results in feelings of fairness.

ERG APPROACH

Another modern model is the **ERG approach,** based on the work of Clayton Alderfer.[4] Like other needs-based models, Alderfer's model looks at three sets of needs: (1) existence (subsistence) needs, (2) relatedness (social) needs, and (3) growth needs. This approach recognizes that although there is no one best way to motivate all employees, there are some broad guidelines or models to follow and a recognizable hierarchy that makes motivation problems easier to resolve. Effective managers learn to know employees and tailor motivation techniques to meet their needs.[5]

The ERG approach follows a hierarchical, stair-step structure similar to Maslow's hierarchy of needs. The existence (E) needs include all forms of material and physical needs, and must be relatively satisfied; if frustrated, the E needs will be more important. The relatedness (R) needs are the next step up in the hierarchy and involve relationships with other people; if they are not relatively satisfied, both the R and E needs are important. Growth (G) needs include creative efforts and are the pinnacle or top order of needs; if they are not relatively satisfied, they will be greatly desired. Thus, real motivation is based on growth, not existence or even relatedness.

OTHER MOTIVATIONAL PROCESSES

Considerable research has been done on other specific needs that affect motivation, including achievement, affiliation, and power. The achievement approach holds that a person's performance is a function of the strength of that individual's need for achievement. The affiliation approach measures the need to be with other people in meaningful relationships including business. The power approach measures the need for control and influence over others.

Another type of motivation is *tensional* or *deficiency motivation.* In essence, Freud's approach is the tensional or "a-deficiency-must-exist-before-you-can-have-a-motivating-situation" approach. *Hedonistic motivation* is another type. The hedonists believe that an individual will try to attain or maintain a pleasant state, and strive to change or leave an unpleasant state: "If it feels good, do it; if it hurts, don't do it." Yet other types of motivation are the *"pull"* or *positive stick-and-carrot approach,* the *"push"* or *negative K.I.T.A. (kick in the "pants")* approach, or the *growth, self-actualization ("be everything you can be")* approach. Growth motivation is a more positive type that puts emphasis on the individual and psychological growth of the human being.

The *management-by-objectives/results* method is an example of motivation that is practiced in industry. The supervisor and the employee together develop realistic goals for the employee to accomplish by some future date, usually six months to a year. Emphasis is then placed on results. The employee's next appraisal or review is based on how well he or she has met the established goals. In some firms, it becomes a method by which employees can set their own goals and recognize how they will be evaluated later.

There is a time and place for all approaches. Try the following self-appraisal exercise. It will probably lead you toward establishing internal motivation. Develop a determination to accomplish your goals and focus on your strengths, not on your weaknesses.

SELF-APPRAISAL
Goal-Setting Exercise

Here is an exercise that will help you zero in on goal setting. Write down something you personally would like to accomplish in three months.

MY GOAL FOR THREE MONTHS: _____

By writing something down, you have committed yourself and established a deadline. Don't procrastinate—work for it. Now list something you would like to accomplish in three years.

MY GOAL FOR THREE YEARS: _____

Neither goal should be so easy that you will naturally reach it through the course of events. Be willing to make a few sacrifices to achieve them. If you have enough stamina, you will write your goals on the cover of your notebook as a constant reminder of what you are striving for. If you have enough self-confidence, you will share your goals, not dreams, with others in your class.

INCENTIVES

THE NATURE OF INCENTIVES

What is the incentive to be motivated? An **incentive** is anything other than the job itself that motivates employees to produce. Incentive systems, which are based on external manipulation, are products of an external control management philosophy. According to this approach, people are viewed as passive and must be persuaded, rewarded, pushed, punished, or otherwise externally controlled into action.

WHEN DOES AN INCENTIVE BECOME A RIGHT?

Today, about the only plan left that can be called a true incentive plan is the monetary reward offered to workers if they increase their standard output. Most other rewards offered as incentives are today considered workers' rights. Rights do not have incentive value; they are taken for granted. Employees who feel underpaid do not work any harder when their wages are raised—their responses are to feel less dissatisfied and to feel that deficiencies have been remedied.

Most managers also want to see rewards as incentives. However, many of these incentive schemes have been a source of frustration, because they have not increased output consistently. One reason for this disappointing state of affairs can be explained by Maslow's principle: A need that is satisfied ceases to motivate. Employees adjust rapidly to changing conditions, particularly when they are for the better.

Management is thus in the awkward position of offering incentives that are basically irrelevant. As Douglas McGregor, a college president and management theorist who was introduced in Chapter 1, said:

> . . . the carrot and stick theory does not work at all once man has reached an adequate subsistence level and is motivated primarily by higher needs. Management cannot provide a man with self-respect, or with the respect of his fellows, or with the satisfaction of needs for self-fulfillment. It can create conditions such that he is encouraged and enabled to seek such satisfaction for himself, or it can thwart him by failing to create those conditions.[6]

But to create these conditions the manager must know a great deal about human nature.

INTRINSIC AND EXTRINSIC MOTIVATORS

Intrinsic motivators take place on the job and help us to enjoy working, in contrast to extrinsic motivators, which can only be enjoyed off the job. During the past forty years, the growth of employee benefits has become an important aspect of the payroll. They are no longer "fringes." In some organizations, they amount to 50 percent of payroll. Companies provide sick leave, paid vacations, medical and dental plans, and free legal aid. All these plans were established in hopes that employees would show more loyalty and more motivation. Ironically, in most cases an employee can enjoy the fringe benefits only when off the job.

Often extrinsic motivators are needed to prod people into doing new or more difficult jobs or into acquiring rudimentary skills. In fact, there is a danger that extrinsic rewards may undermine intrinsic motivation—that we may undermine a person's intrinsic interest in an activity by inducing him or her to engage in it only as a means to some extrinsic goal. The joy of performing a task for itself may disappear when it is done simply for the reward offered by the supervisor.

Intrinsic motivators benefit employees on the job. Logically, people work harder when they are provided with comforts and when work is enjoyable. In one University of Michigan survey, 1,533 workers were asked to rate the importance of various aspects of work, and intrinsic motivators led the list. Of the five top-ranked features, only the fifth had to do with tangible economic benefits:

1. Interesting work
2. Enough help and equipment to get the job done
3. Sufficient information to get the job done
4. Enough authority to do the job
5. Good pay

YOUR EPITAPH (INDIVIDUAL EXERCISE)

Suppose you were to die tomorrow! How would you like people to remember you? What words would you like to be said about your personality during your eulogy? What kind of accomplishments would you like listed?

Now make out your own epitaph. List your name, date of birth, and date of death—tomorrow. Then list your accomplishments.

Finally, below the epitaph, list the accomplishments you wished you had done. Perhaps these are the goals and tasks you would like to accomplish in the future!

During your working career you may have held many or only a few jobs, but within a short time you were able to state that you enjoyed the job or were looking eagerly for another. Concentrate on one company and list the major extrinsic motivators. Now list the company's intrinsic motivators.

Now ask yourself, if you enjoyed the job, was it because of the extrinsic or the intrinsic motivators? If you disliked the job, was it because of the extrinsic or the intrinsic motivators?

By your own experience and the experiences that might be shared by others in the class, which seems to be the most important? Which motivators do companies tend to advertise and spend most of their time developing? Why?

BARRIERS TO ACHIEVEMENT

Regardless of the type of motivation, the end result of motivation should be performance. A formula for performance is

$$Performance = Function (Ability \times Motivation)$$

It is necessary to have both the ability and motivation to perform. If either ability or motivation is low, the performance will be low.

Reactions to frustrations can be conscious or unconscious.

Even if motivation and ability are high, some personal goals and needs may not be met. Certainly when we have an internal need and decide consciously or unconsciously to satisfy that need, we may exhibit certain behavior to reduce tension. Notice in Figure 5–7 that barriers can deter us from reaching our goals.

Barriers cause frustrations that persist and become stronger. Some external barriers encountered by employees are discriminatory practices, hostile supervisors, monotonous jobs, and economic insecurity. Some internal barriers that frustrate employees are poor work habits, a dysfunctional personality, or a poor aptitude to do a particular job.

In some cases, by strengthening motivation (e.g., internal drive or external reward systems), it is possible to overcome the barrier. In other cases, it is not possible to overcome the barriers, and behavior defense mechanisms are the result. **Defense mechanisms** are ways in which an individual may try to reduce the tensions caused by frustrations.

COMMON DEFENSE MECHANISMS

Aggression.

Aggression or hostility may be of a direct verbal or a physical type that is expressed in the form of attacks against persons perceived to be the cause of frustration. *Displaced aggression* can be observed in a supervisor who feels that he or she is not able to communicate with a superior and in turn will verbally abuse his or her subordinates.

FIGURE 5–7 Barriers to the Motivation Process.

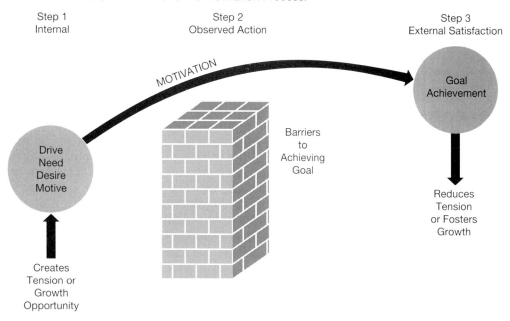

Step 1
Internal

Step 2
Observed Action

Step 3
External Satisfaction

MOTIVATION

Goal
Achievement

Drive
Need
Desire
Motive

Barriers
to
Achieving
Goal

Reduces
Tension
or Fosters
Growth

Creates
Tension or
Growth
Opportunity

Individuals who can tolerate a high degree of abuse or aggression by others are said to have a high degree of tolerance to frustration. People with an "inner calm" are able to handle their own frustrations as well as those of others more easily.

Regression. *Regression* is defined as reverting to an earlier form of behavior to find satisfaction. It can be seen best through "childish actions," such as temper tantrums or pouting. We can even see this in the case of a newly appointed supervisor who starts doing segments of the old job he or she enjoyed because he or she cannot master the duties of the new position.

Fixation. *Fixation* behavior is the persistence of doing the same thing over and over again in the same way. Have you known a mechanic who is determined to put a bolt in a particular hole? He continues to force it until he strips the threads. Such behavior can continue even when several demonstrations show that it won't work. This type of stubbornness can also be seen when a salesperson has been taught to use several sales techniques but slips back into an old worn-out technique that has become ineffective.

Resignation. *Resignation* is displayed when someone gives up all sense of emotional or personal involvement. By failing to achieve some goal, a person may lose any positive concern about his or her job and adopt an apathetic attitude toward the situation.

Withdrawal. Such behavior can lead to *withdrawal,* in which the frustrated individual simply removes himself or herself from the situation in question—either physically or psychologically. A person who is not able to cope with a business adversary may avoid situations that would put him in contact with that individual. A person who becomes the butt of jibes and jokes may become a loner by adopting withdrawal behavior.

Repression.

Repressive behavior is exhibited by the person who blocks out from the conscious mind those cognitive associations that are disturbing. It is an unrealistic form of behavior, since it implies that the problem will simply go away if one doesn't think about it.

Compensation, rationalization, projection.

Other common reactions are *compensation, rationalization,* and *projection.* The office clerk who is frustrated with his limited education may try to compensate by using multisyllable words and complicated language to impress others. Or the manager who is frustrated with having little or no authority may attempt to impress others by her "bossiness," which is really a form of rationalization. Or an employee may compensate when he has been passed over several times for a promotion by saying, "It would hardly have been worth the small difference in pay; I can find other good ways to spend my time." Projection is the act of subscribing to someone else's attitudes or thoughts. It can take the form of blaming others for your own thoughts, feelings, and behaviors. Some employees continually blame others because they sincerely believe that they themselves are not at fault for their own actions.

Defense mechanisms are common in all of us and very often unconscious. Unless used to an extreme degree, defensive behavior is considered quite normal; perhaps not acceptable at all times, but certainly normal.

JOB DESIGN

The world is filled with boring jobs. Managers must rely on incentives to encourage workers to perform their jobs well because many jobs cannot be made satisfying to all people. But managers can have a great influence on the design of even the dullest jobs. Ideally, jobs should be structured to expand workers' capabilities. Workers can be motivated most effectively when managers allow employees to assume responsibility and participate in a productive way in making decisions (see Figure 5–8).

Job design includes all the variables that will increase the quality and quantity of worker performance. It is a conscious effort to organize tasks, duties, and responsibilities into a work unit.

Try to create a job where the person is self-motivated.

Jim Tunney, motivational speaker and NFL referee, says: "Most of the time people go through life doing the things they do because they're supposed to do them. They've been conditioned."[7] The management challenge is to get people to motivate themselves by helping them realize their own strengths and weaknesses, by helping them achieve self-confidence and belief in themselves and their capabilities. Although the following approaches are not equally effective, they give a solid foundation for understanding how jobs can be designed to be challenging.

HORIZONTAL JOB LOADING

Horizontal job loading assumes that, if employees are given more work to do at the same level at which they are currently performing, they will be motivated to work harder and also be more satisfied with their work. For example,

FIGURE 5–8 Workers Can Be Motivated Most Effectively When Managers Allow Employees to Assume Responsibility and to Participate in a Productive Way in Making Decisions. Michael Mayman/Photo Researchers.

an assembler is told to put together 1,000 parts instead of the 500 previously required. Horizontal job loading does not motivate.

VERTICAL JOB LOADING

Greater challenge or re-sponsibility motivates.

Vertical job loading changes jobs to include larger areas of responsibility. Jobs are restructured so that they will become *intrinsically* more interesting. The worker is motivated because the job is more challenging and more meaningful. For instance, a dishwasher's job would be changed vertically if he or she were also made responsible for keeping track of worn and broken dishes and for reporting defects to a supervisor.

Vertical loading implies that employees should be given as much responsibility as possible. Employees should be encouraged to be accountable for their work, with little supervision. Vertical job loading includes the idea of "closure": Employees have an understanding of the organization of which they are a part. They are no longer just cogs in a wheel but instead can participate in and contribute to the entire work process. To provide for closure, tasks that belong together logically are grouped into one job—steps that one employee can carry through from beginning to end.

Thus vertical job loading means:

1. Less direct control of the employee
2. Increased personal accountability
3. Assignment of complete tasks
4. Greater freedom on the job
5. Better skill utilization

A clerk at a bank remembers her job well. Even a machine would have grown bored with it. "My job was to pull invoices and checks out of envelopes and stack them into three piles: one under $10, another between $10 and $25, and a third over $25. Then I passed the piles on to the next person. After two months of this I was so bored I would have quit within another month." After two more years she was still at the bank, but instead of performing a tiny task in the paper mill, she handled all the processing for twenty-two corporate accounts. "Handling your own accounts is a lot more interesting, and you feel like you have accomplished something."

JOB ENRICHMENT

The term **job enrichment** gained popularity when **job enlargement** began to be mistaken for horizontal job loading. *Job development* is another term in current use. Job enrichment and development indicate the fundamental principles of vertical job loading.

Overspecializing leads to boredom.

For at least 50 years, industry has been committed to breaking down jobs into their smallest possible components and stringing them out along assembly lines. Managers, assuming that work was inevitably boring, tried to boost morale and productivity by improving benefits and working conditions. We are now finding that the impact of boredom on productivity outweighs the benefits of extreme specialization.

Change of tasks relieves the monotony.

JOB ROTATION AND JOB SHARING.   In **job rotation,** workers learn to do all the different activities necessary in one operation or unit of work. Teams that are used to working together adapt well to the rotation method. Job rotation can be subjected easily to horizontal loading. The monotony may be relieved by rotating similarly meaningless tasks, but this does not help to make the job more significant. However, it is quite possible to arrange for vertical job rotation, where both routine and complex tasks are passed around and new skills have to be applied to each job in the operation.

As noted in Chapter 3, **job sharing** allows individuals who might have time constraints because of other work, home, or school responsibilities to be productive for their organizations by dividing a job usually held by one individual into jobs held by two or more employees. The ultimate purpose of job design efforts is to improve performance and quality of work life, concepts we will examine in the next chapter.

DELEGATION

Delegation of authority is a motivator.

Another way to satisfy the needs for achievement, recognition, and responsibility is to give employees a task and the authority to carry it out. Authority is one of the most important positive motivators delegated to employees by supervisors. If workers are allowed to have it, they may be willing to take on new challenges. Some leaders, however, are afraid to grant such authority, because an employee may make a poor decision that would embarrass the supervisor. Or worse, they are afraid that delegation will lessen their own authority.

Delegation of authority—including some "do's and don'ts"—is examined along with leadership in Chapter 11. In the meantime, look for new ways in which to expand, rather than to limit, your subordinates' scope of activities. Many supervisors do not use their time wisely because they are not delegating enough duties to their employees.

One company that does try new methods is Polaroid. It allows its scientists to pursue their own projects and order their own materials without checking with a supervisor. Film-assembly workers are allowed to run their machines at their own pace. At another company, marketing correspondents are allowed to send letters affixed with their signatures rather than with those of their executives.

FLEXIBILITY GIVES SELF-DIRECTION

"Sliding time" or "flex-time" helps employees decide for themselves.

Such giants as General Foods and Motorola banished time clocks years ago. Other companies have staggered the working hours to best fit the parking lot traffic flow. One company has five shifts starting every fifteen minutes. The morning shifts start at 8:00, 8:15, 8:30, 8:45, and 9:00 A.M. The evening shifts end at 4:00, 4:15, 4:30, 4:45, and 5:00 P.M. Each group puts in an eight-hour shift. But the employee can pick his or her time schedule. The factory or office workers can come in any time they like, provided that they are around for "core time," from 10:00 A.M. to 3:00 P.M., and that they put in a forty-hour week. Supervisors must trust their workers to maintain or increase productivity under decreased supervision, and supervisors must be prepared to deal with those few who abuse the system.[8]

LET WORKERS SEE THE END PRODUCT OF THEIR EFFORTS

In today's automated society, too often employees work on parts for pieces of equipment that they never see. It is common for employees to have no idea of the type of equipment that will hold their handiwork. Such a limiting view of the product can lead to a more complacent, bored attitude on the job. Some manufacturing firms have sent employees from their supply plants to assembly plants to see where their parts fit into the finished product. Other firms put the assembly-line workers on inspection jobs for one-week stints. Said one welder, "I now see metal damage, missing welds, and framing fits that I never would have noticed before." The employee who sees more of the company as a whole can identify with it in more positive terms. There is a greater chance of loyalty and motivation under these conditions.

LISTENING SUPERVISORS

Listening to employees motivates more than talking to them.

Studies seem to indicate that employees who have listening supervisors have higher morale than those who do not. To be an effective communicator, it is necessary to know far more than the rules for writing memos or making effective speeches. It is important to develop an insight into human motives and aspirations of employees to interact effectively. Realizing the importance of effective listening to an organization's effectiveness, Xerox and the American Management Society have developed and conducted listening clinics.

As one manager said, "I don't understand why the employees don't perform better." In reply another manager commented: "Perhaps they don't want to be treated better, but want to be better utilized, and the only way we can find out how to make things better is to listen to them."

JOB CHARACTERISTICS MODEL

Job characteristics model.

By analyzing jobs and providing five **core job dimensions,** managers can increase high internal work motivation and quality work performance of employees. Also, as illustrated in Figure 5–9, workers are more satisfied with their jobs, rarely absent from work, and more loyal to their company when five core job characteristics are implemented. Hackman and Oldham[9] define five core tasks and two interpersonal dimensions.

CORE TASK DIMENSIONS. The following are key influences on employee motivation:

- **Skill variety.** The degree to which the job requires performing a variety of operations, and the degree to which employees must use a variety of procedures in their work.
- **Task identity.** The extent to which employees can identify and complete an entire piece of work.
- **Task significance.** The extent to which the job has a strong impact on others and their work.

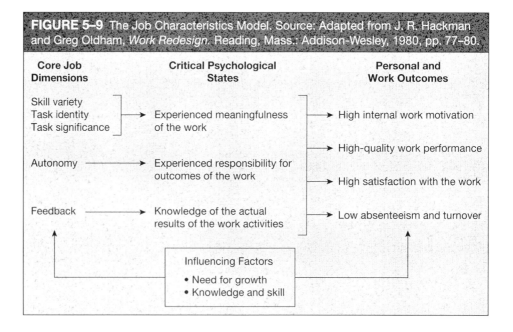

FIGURE 5–9 The Job Characteristics Model. Source: Adapted from J. R. Hackman and Greg Oldham, *Work Redesign.* Reading, Mass.: Addison-Wesley, 1980, pp. 77–80.

- **Autonomy.** The extent to which employees have a say in scheduling and controlling decisions affecting their work.
- **Feedback.** The degree to which employees receive information regarding level and quality of performance.

INTERPERSONAL DIMENSIONS. The following are job characteristics that influence the degree to which employees relate well with others on the job:

- **Dealing with others.** The degree to which a job requires employees to deal with others (customers, other organizations' employees) to complete their work.
- **Friendship opportunities.** The degree to which a job allows employees to talk with and establish informal relationships with others at work.

PROFILE OF HUMAN BEHAVIOR

E. RACHEL HUBKA

"Motivating Part-Timers to be Entrepreneurs"
Motivating part-time workers has become something of an art at Rachel's Bus Company in Chicago. From the time E. Rachel Hubka, the company's president, started the business in 1989, she has looked for ways to hire good workers and help them develop.

Now, the company's 120 mostly part-time drivers enjoy a benefits package that includes holiday and vacation pay and bonuses for perfect attendance. In addition, they get a chance to develop their own entrepreneurial skills in a way that not only enriches them but also helps the company.

The firm contracts with the Chicago Board of Education to transport children to and from school. Hubka is also building revenue by offering trips for private groups.

She recognized a few years ago that helping her drivers become more professional would enhance the company's image. (Lack of respect from children and their parents was a regular source of employee complaints and morale problems.) Hubka also believed that increasing drivers' professionalism would help Rachel's stand out among its thirty-five area competitors and would improve the firm's chances of cultivating repeat private-trip business.

To foster a professional attitude, Hubka provides all drivers with business cards. She helps them with their personal appearance and manner, and she teaches them how to talk effectively with customers and ask for their business. She also throws in a powerful incentive for the drivers: a chance to earn more.

Private jobs are rotated among drivers, who get one-third of the revenue from their trips. Drivers who bring in business or are requested by name get an additional 10 percent of the job's invoice.

For her most aggressive driver-entrepreneurs, the revenue from those jobs represents as much as two-thirds of their paychecks. For some, it has turned a $7,500-a-year job into one that generates more than $20,000 in income. The company's revenues from private jobs have risen to about 15 percent of total revenues. Hubka wants it to be 25 percent in a few years and 40 percent eventually.

"If I can teach drivers to become more professional in their dealings with the public, that makes their job easier," Hubka says. "And if they have any interest in becoming entrepreneurs—as I did—this shows them how to do it."

SOURCE: Roberta Maynard, "Motivation: Nurturing Part-Timers to be Entrepreneurs," *Nation's Business*, March 1996, p. 10. Reprinted by permission, Copyright 1996, U.S. Chamber of Commerce.

SUMMARY

Motivation refers to any activity with a goal toward which the action is oriented. In business, that motivational action is called work. To want to act is true motivation.

Motivation is an internal state, which may be triggered by incentives. We all have highly individualized reasons for acting in the ways that we do. Therefore, while some generalizations can safely be made about the nature of motivation, it is inadvisable to judge the reasons for motivation on behavior alone.

Because organizations are responsible for job structure and content, they are largely responsible for workers' responsibilities to satisfy their personal needs—needs that provide the motivating force for their work. Organizations and individuals must constantly reevaluate their mutual satisfactions and dissatisfactions in an attempt to balance each other's needs.

At least three schools of psychology can be studied as they relate to motivation. Sigmund Freud founded the psychoanalytic school of thought, which states that much of a person's motivational thrust is hidden in the unconscious realm of the brain. Therefore the reason for a person's motivation is hard to discover. B. F. Skinner believes that people can be motivated to act through behavior modification, which involves the rewarding of desired behavior and the ignoring of undesirable behavior. Any attention to a behavior, either positive or negative, will enforce such a behavior. The third school of thought was developed by Abraham Maslow and Frederick Herzberg, who widened the scope of motivational theory with their observations on the hierarchy of needs and hygiene/motivation factors, respectively. Several contemporary motivation concepts include the expectancy, equity, and ERG approaches.

Incentives are punishments and rewards that are extrinsic to the job itself. They are used to try to motivate people to work better or harder. The carrot-and-stick management philosophy is a way of describing incentives. Basically, incentives are designed to push or pull employees to perform their jobs even better.

Motivating factors are intrinsic to the job. True motivation must come from the job itself—only the job can be satisfying. Part of feeling self-fulfilled is having the sense of utilizing one's energy in a fruitful way. Only when workers feel that they are achieving something in spite of the routine nature of the work are their jobs satisfying. However, managers cannot always change the structures of jobs so that they give more responsibility and decision-making power to employees.

Horizontal job loading only increases workers' duties at the same level, without giving workers higher levels of responsibility. Vertical job loading, on the other hand, adds dimension to jobs. Employees are made responsible for entire operations, including many levels of tasks and skills. Job rotation is the concept of trading jobs, which often relieves monotony and can increase responsibility. Through job enlargement programs, assembly lines have been disbanded and teams formed that build entire assemblies together. *Job enrichment* or *job development* is the term now used to indicate vertical job loading methods.

The job characteristics model outlines five core job dimensions—skill variety, task identity, task significance, autonomy, and feedback—that provide high external motivation, high-quality work performance, high satisfaction with work, and low absenteeism and turnover.

CASE STUDY 5-1

HOW DO YOU MOTIVATE MOTEL MAIDS?

All Western Motels are part of a franchise operation with six interests in the San Diego area. For the last several years, employee turnover, especially among the lower salaried workers, has been a major problem. The turnover rate for maids alone reached the level of three employees per month per motel. This computes to the staggering figure of 45 percent on an annual basis.

The maid is probably the most potent representative of a motel, even though she is seldom, if ever, seen by the guests. It is the way in which she performs her work that will determine, to a large extent, whether a guest will return to the motel for a second stay—and motels survive on repeat business. "Repeaters" make a house's reputation—especially through word-of-mouth advertising, which is the best and the cheapest kind!

Not only were the motels faced with the expense of hiring, processing, and bonding employees, but low morale was producing a low-grade, careless approach to the job. In several instances, a complete refund of rent monies had to be made. In addition, maids quit without notice, and the cost to train a new applicant was becoming intolerable.

The maids for the Western concerns were being paid the top wages in the area for related employment. These wages were not at all high, however, because no motel can afford to increase its overhead appreciably. The working conditions seemed good. The women were allowed one gratis meal per shift at the motel's coffee shops, and they were allowed to use the pool facilities during their off-hours at four of the locations.

The managers tried to interview the workers who had left their employ, but they could get no useful information from them. They spoke in generalities, such as "I'm just tired of working here." Finally, the operators approached the franchise's main office in Phoenix, and a general meeting of the concerned managers was called. You were chosen as the franchise representative to the conference.

The meeting was held on September 19 and 20 at one of the San Diego locations. Five of the motels sent representatives. One manager claimed that the whole thing was "just a waste of time and money." After lunch, on the first day, your group sat down to discuss the situation.

It was the general consensus of the group that the fidelity of the employees toward the company should be increased. Personal identity and pride in their jobs seemed to be the ingredients most lacking. But how could these feelings be induced into a role such as that of a maid?

1. Put yourself in the role of the motel maid. What physical changes could be made to enhance the job?
2. Personal identity and pride in the job should be given top priority in redesigning the position. Can changes be made in uniform, job functions, reporting times, personal recognition, or off-duty privileges to enhance the employees' personal identity?
3. What psychological factors can be developed to help the maids' personal images?
4. What intrinsic motivators can help the situation?

CASE STUDY 5–2

THE "HOOKY" CASE

The XYZ Corporation of Midland, Nebraska, manufactures and distributes water pumps for irrigation systems. Its products are outstanding and are much sought after by individual farmers and agricultural corporations. The company is well financed and its products are marketed through the company's own marketing and sales organizations rather than manufacturers' representatives. Because its pumps are so well accepted, the marketing function is less demanding than that in similar companies.

Nevertheless, XYZ has an extensive geographical marketing organization throughout the United States as well as international operations. Similar to other organizations, they have a fairly extensive hierarchy in production, marketing, finance, personnel, and other staff departments. Their marketing function is organized with geographical regions, divisions, and departments.

Frank Taylor, Midwest division manager for XYZ, has been selected to attend an all-expense-paid two-week course on management development at a state university. Frank is 49 years old and has been with the company for twenty years. He has held several sales and marketing positions with XYZ and other employers before XYZ.

While in these jobs, Frank attended many technical, marketing, and management development courses and seminars. Consequently, he is not sure whether he needs to attend the present course, but he did want to visit the city and other organizations in the area where the course is being held. In fact, Frank takes his family with him to the city where the course is held but does not actually attend the class meetings.

1. What is the problem here?
2. What do you need to know that you don't know before you can recommend a solution?
3. What are several alternatives that you see?
4. What, if anything, should be done about Frank?

DISCUSSION AND STUDY QUESTIONS—TO KEEP YOU THINKING . . .

1. What are various schools of psychology and how do they relate to motivation?

2. Is all motivation based on "internal" motivation?

3. Describe barriers to achievement and how to overcome them.

4. Compare Maslow's need classification with Herzberg's hygiene/motivation approach; compare with Alderfer's ERG approach.

5. Compare the expectancy and equity approaches to motivation.

6. Explain the differences between intrinsic and extrinsic motivators.

7. What are the differences between horizontal and vertical job loading?

8. What are important job task and interpersonal dimensions that contribute to the quality of work life?

NOTES

1. Chris Argyris, *Integrating the Individual and the Organization* (New York: John Wiley, 1964), p. 7.

2. A. H. Maslow, *Motivation and Personality* (New York: Harper & Row, 1954).

3. Frederick Herzberg, Bernard Mausner, and Barbara Bloch Snyderman, *The Motivation to Work* (New York: John Wiley, 1959), p. 113.

4. Clayton Alderfer, *Existence, Relatedness, and Growth* (New York: The Free Press, 1972).

5. Pat Buhler, "Motivation: What Is Behind the Motivation of Employees?" *Supervision,* June 1988, pp. 18–20.

6. Douglas McGregor, *The Human Side of Enterprise* (New York: McGraw-Hill, 1960), pp. 121–122.

7. Jim Tunney, "Motivating People," *USA Today,* June 7, 1985, p. 13A.

8. David Hull, "No More 9 to 5?" *Computer Decisions,* June 1982, pp. 160–178.

9. Richard Hackman and Greg R. Oldham, *Work Redesign* (Reading, Mass.: Addison-Wesley, 1980), pp. 77–80.

RECOMMENDED READING

Barling, Julian. "Work and Family: In Search of More Effective Workplace Interventions." *Journal of Organizational Behavior,* 1994, pp. 63–73.

Baytos, Kimberly, and Brian H. Kleiner. "New Developments in Job Design." *Business Credit,* February 1995, pp. 22–25.

Brooks, Donald V. "Today's Compensation Systems: Rewarding the Wrong Things." *Canadian Manager,* December 1994, pp. 10–11.

Covey, Steven. *The 7 Habits of Highly Effective People.* New York: Simon & Schuster, 1989.

Creech, Regina. "Employee Motivation." *Management Quarterly,* Summer 1995, pp. 33–39.

Ford, Martin E. *Motivating Humans: Goals, Emotions, and Personal Agency Beliefs.* Newbury Park, Calif.: SAGE Publications, 1992.

Hines, Andy. "Jobs and Infotech: Work in the Information Society." *Futurist,* January/February 1994, pp. 9–13.

Lawler, Edward E., III. "From Job-based to Competency-based Organizations." *Journal of Organizational Behavior,* January 1994, pp. 3–15.

McClelland, David C., and David H. Burnham. "Power is the Great Motivator." January–February 1995, pp. 123–139.

Milas, Gene H. "How to Develop a Meaningful Employee Recognition Program." *Quality Progress,* May 1995, pp. 139–142.

Mitra, Atul, Nina Gupta, and G. Douglas Jenkins, Jr. "The Case of the Invisible Merit Raise: How People See Their Pay Raises." *Compensation and Benefits Review,* May/June 1995, pp. 71–76.

Mohrman, Susan A., Edward E. Lawler III, and Gerald E. Ledford, Jr. "Do Employees Involvement and TQM Programs Work?" *Journal for Quality and Participation,* January/February 1996, pp. 6–10.

Olgilvie, Heather. "Towards a Creative Environment." *Journal of Business Strategy,* September/October 1994, pp. 30–31.

Penzer, Erika. "Motivating Low-Wage Workers." *Incentive,* February 1990, pp. 47–51.

Pollock, Ted. "Six Keys to Improved Employee Motivation." *Production,* September 1995, pp. 12–13.

Robbins, Anthony. *Awaken the Giant Within.* New York: Summit Books, 1991.

Spitzer, Dean R. "The Seven Deadly Demotivators." *American Management Association,* November 1995, pp. 56–60.

Turner, Dan. "Redesigning the Service Organization." *Journal for Quality and Participation,* July/August 1994, pp. 28–33.

Uzzi, John A. "Work Effectiveness." *Managers Magazine,* October 1995, pp. 23–24.

Watson, Tom. "Linking Employee Motivation and Satisfaction to the Bottom Line." *CMA Magazine,* April 1994, p. 4.

Wilsey, Michael D. "Leadership and Human Motivation in the Workplace." *Quality Progress,* November 1995, pp. 85–88.

6

JOB PERFORMANCE AND MORALE

This chapter will help you discover certain feelings about your work. Begin by considering the following questions:

- How do human needs affect work performance?
- What is the ultimate goal of work activity? job satisfaction? high morale? job performance? improved quality of work life?
- What makes a job satisfying or dissatisfying? Do you like the people you work with? Do you socialize with them on and off the job?
- Are you treated as part of a team or as an employee with only specific duties to perform? Is your job boring or challenging? If you had your way, how would you change your job to make it more meaningful?
- Do we reward for knowledge, mastery of skills, results, or a combination of these?
- How do you feel about your organization's objectives? Do you think that the organization is interested in profits or cost savings only, or does it have the interests of its employees and society in mind?

LEARNING GOALS

After studying this chapter, you should be able to:

1. Define job performance, performance standards, and performance measurement.
2. Argue the merits and disadvantages of job descriptions.
3. Define the terms *morale* and *job satisfaction.* Understand the relationships among job performance, morale, and job satisfaction.
4. Define quality of work life and its relationship to total quality management.
5. Discuss the general attitudes of blue-collar workers and of white-collar workers toward their jobs in today's society.
6. Explain how and why employee surveys can be useful in studying morale. Explain how reviewing the company's records can tell us something about the employees' morale.
7. Describe how the physical environment can affect employees' morale.
8. Define and apply the following terms and concepts (in order of first occurrence):

- **job performance**
- **job description**
- **performance standards**
- **performance measurement**
- **pay-for-knowledge**
- **pay-for-mastery**

- job satisfaction
- referent others concept
- morale
- blue-collar jobs
- job cycle
- white-collar jobs
- wellness programs
- quality of work life
- total quality management
- whole job concept
- ergonomics
- decibel
- footcandle

JOB PERFORMANCE: THE KEY TO MORALE AND PRODUCTIVITY

The study of human relations involves the practical attempt to achieve the two separate goals of greater productivity at work and greater human satisfaction within the organization. Job performance provides the key to these two goals and the key to organizational effectiveness.

A beginning in determining the relationship between productivity and satisfaction is the source of both concepts—job performance. Effective **job performance** is best defined by (1) determining the job to be done, (2) determining the standards by which job completion is to be measured, and (3) tying the results to a reward system. What employees and management do in setting and meeting standards of performance determines organizational effectiveness.

Human satisfaction within the organization can be broken down into two aspects: *Job satisfaction* relates to the individual, whereas *morale* reflects the feelings of the group. After years of research on motivation, job satisfaction, and productivity, we still do not have agreement regarding a cause-and-effect relationship between any of these variables. Herzberg and many others have studied and written extensively on job satisfaction and related subjects for decades. The results regarding the relationship of job satisfaction and productivity are not always clear or well established.

Job satisfaction is a function of job performance.

What does seem clear is that there is a greater probability of job satisfaction resulting from effective job performance than the opposite. This finding is contrary to the thrust of the research in the 1960s and 1970s, which tried to establish job satisfaction as a cause of good performance.

THE JOB DESCRIPTION

Job descriptions are fundamental.

Job descriptions are changing with computer applications.

The **job description** is the beginning point in defining what is to be done on a job. The manner of preparing and updating job descriptions is changing with computer applications of human resource information systems (HRISs). They are much easier to keep up to date and therefore more useful to both employees and managers. The use of job descriptions as orientation devices and as the first step in job analysis remains important for all human resources managers. More important, they are a means of defining the expectations of job incumbents.

Some of the factors included in the job description are responsibilities, relationships, duties (tasks), and performance elements. The last two, tasks and performance elements, are relatively new additions. They add meaning to the description by allowing the incumbent to know what is expected, what is to be done, and how the performance standards will be applied—that is, how the performance will be evaluated.

Federal government's use of performance standards.

The Office of Personnel Management and other federal government agencies have made significant progress in recognizing the importance of setting performance standards for performance appraisals. The performance elements, tasks, and performance standards are utilized actively in goal setting, counseling, and evaluation. Figure 6–1 shows how tasks, performance elements, and standards can be built into the job description.

PERFORMANCE STANDARDS

In addition to the use of job descriptions to define job performance expectations, specific **performance standards** must be used as criteria for measuring performance. The standards can be arrived at through the management by objectives/results (MBO/R) process, or any other behaviorally-based, results-oriented system. Participation by the employee in setting the standards is a key aspect of this process.

FIGURE 6–1 Performance Elements, Tasks, and Standards for Research Administrator (RA), GS-13, 14.

PERFORMANCE ELEMENT	TASK	PERFORMANCE STANDARD[*] FULLY SATISFACTORY
I. Program Planning	1. Consult and interact with higher management research leader, scientists, cooperators, industry groups, and so on, in order to identify research gaps, needs, and priorities.	1. a. Essential internal and external groups are consulted prior to submission of program planning information to RA. b. Any sensitive program issues are communicated and/or documented in submission to RA.
	2. Develop implementation plan/proposal including justification statement and financial plans.	2. a. Research program and project priorities are communicated to RA on a timely basis. b. Annual Position Resource Management Plans sent to RA no later than (date). c. New or revised research proposals, including budget increase requests, sent to RA consistent with the budgetary cycle. d. Research proposals, documentation, and so on, responding to emergencies submitted on a timely basis.
II. Program Management	1. Provide program leadership.	1. a. Assures that new ideas, stimuli, and so on, are provided to research units/programs. b. Resources have been shifted, where appropriate, to support new or redirected research efforts. c. Multidisciplinary research efforts have been increased. d. Internal and external interest in the new or redirected research effort have been increased.
	2. Promote research productivity.	2. a. Publications (1) Referred journals _____ (2) Department series _____ (3) Trade publications _____ (4) Proceedings _____ (5) Book chapters _____ (6) Citation index _____ (7) Reviews _____ (8) Abstracts _____ (9) Mimeographed releases _____ (10) Popular publications _____

[*]This agency has three performance rating levels: meets standard, exceeds standard, does not meet standard; therefore, one performance standard is sufficient.

SOURCE: U.S. Office of Personnel Management, *Performance Standards Handbook,* April 1981, pp. 11–23.

People should be able to set their own targets of performance within organizational constraints. That does not mean "do your own thing"! It means setting your own standards of performance within the organizational constraints and mission. The manager determines what must be done, when, and by whom. Other requirements in setting performance standards include determining quantity and quality of work to be done, setting time schedules, and establishing cost and other budgetary constraints.

At a fully acceptable level of performance, a performance standard should have the following characteristics:

1. Enable the user to differentiate between acceptable and unacceptable results.

2. Present some challenge to the employee.

3. Be realistic—that is, be attainable by any qualified, proficient, and fully trained employee who has the necessary authority and resources.

4. Be a statement of the conditions that will exist and will measure a job activity when it is performed acceptably, expressed in terms of quantity, quality, time cost, effect obtained, manner of performance, or method of doing.

5. Relate to or express a time frame for accomplishment.

6. Be observable.[3]

People-oriented standards.

If the criteria are behaviorally oriented, as in behaviorally anchored rating scales (BARS), they provide standards that are people oriented. The scales (expected behavioral outcomes) are worded in terms of actual behavioral expectations and become part of a graphic scale. Multiple levels (usually seven or nine) on the scales correspond to expected behaviors at various levels of performance. The subordinates play a key role in establishing the BARS. Chapter 13 provides further discussion and examples of both MBO/R and BARS.

The secret to MBO/R is setting and maintaining high standards of performance. Setting standards too low yields low, or at best, mediocre performance. Top performers appreciate knowing that they have high standards to meet. They would be demoralized by low standards where mediocre performance is rewarded equally with excellent performance.

PERFORMANCE MEASUREMENT

Please note that the discussion of performance measurement in this section is different from and does not include performance appraisal, a topic to be discussed later, in Chapter 13.

Set standards in advance of performance.

Performance measurement determines how specific behaviors match predetermined performance standards. If desired performance has not been defined in advance of performance measurement—that is, if objective standards are lacking—how can the employee and the manager know when performance has been achieved? How can the subordinate know if he or she has performed well and thereby be satisfied with the job? Effort alone may influence one's job performance but is less important than measuring results. Both quality and quantity dimensions must be used in measuring results. The active participation of employees in setting their performance standards contributes to better job performance.

Feedback should be immediate, precise, and specific.

We all like to know how we are doing. To know that, we must have feedback. Performance measurement systems are based on feedback, which should be available *immediately, precisely,* and *specifically.* Most performance appraisal techniques currently in practice disregard the immediacy. Many performance evaluations are still performed only annually, if then. Monthly, weekly, or even daily feedback is preferred to provide employees with the necessary information to perform their jobs better. Likewise, the feedback should relate to precise behavior, specific performance, and desired behavioral outcomes.

Most job performance is difficult to measure objectively. External variables such as economic conditions might influence job performance and cannot usually be controlled by the individual. The measurement of performance is easier and more precise given predetermined criteria and standards.

A study by Graham Kenny and Alan Dunk[4] shows several performance measures that are useful to production managers:

PERFORMANCE MEASURE	RELATED ELEMENT
Variance between planned output and actual output	Product
Machine output rates	Machines
Variance between standard amounts of materials required for jobs and actual amounts used	Machines
Incidence of quality control problems	Product
Rate at which delivery schedules are met	Customers
Variance between standard times allowed for jobs and actual times taken	Employees
Scrap or waste levels	Material
Absenteeism levels of employees in department	Employees
Incidence of customer complaints	Customers
General output per employee	Employees
Accident levels of employees in department	Employees

REWARDING RESULTS

Employers have experienced difficulties in making the connection between performance and rewards. Jan Muczyk and Robert Hastings write:

> The sad truth of the matter is that in many organizations with productivity problems, the below-average, average, and above-average employees at all levels of the organization receive roughly identical rewards—and this applies to nonunionized organizations as well. Therefore, the extrinsic incentives for performing at high levels are absent from the workplace.[5]

Increasingly, organizations are moving toward skill-based pay, pay-for-knowledge, and pay-for-mastery systems. Skill-based pay and **pay-for-knowledge** plans put emphasis on abilities to complete certifiable skills rather than points for subjective job evaluations. Employees are paid for the number of different jobs that they can adequately perform or the amount of knowledge they possess.

The **pay-for-mastery** plan takes the concept one step further in requiring not just the knowledge and skills, but mastery of the work that employees perform. By acquiring job mastery, employees are able to identify and perform work assignments *better, easier, simpler,* and *timelier—BEST*:

> . . . the employer provides its clients with a product that is on time and is of the highest possible quality. In addition, the organization achieves profitable levels of output. By having teams of master employees, everyone wins. The employees receive higher levels of pay while performing jobs that are more interesting and in which they have greater levels of authority. The users of the provided goods and services receive a quality product on time and at a competitive price. The employers are able to enjoy a profit while having minimum labor and client problems. This is a goal of most organizations in a capitalistic-democratic society.[6]

Tying both monetary and nonmonetary rewards to performance is important. The ties should be both causative and timely; that is, a cause-and-effect relationship should be present as well as a timely reward. If the reward only comes once a year, it is too late to be considered a reward for performance. It is possible to give monetary reward increments more frequently if they are based on a computerized HRIS.

Of course, the monetary reward cannot always be tied immediately to performance, but nonmonetary praise and recognition can. Nonmonetary rewards can occur as often as necessary to reinforce feedback on job performance. *One of the most overlooked factors in rewarding performance is communicating recognition and praise for a job well done.* Praise and recognition can be frequently communicated orally and sometimes in writing for both public media and individual personnel files.

DETERMINANTS OF JOB PERFORMANCE

Job performance is multidimensional.

Job performance is more complicated than a unidimensional variable such as job satisfaction would suggest. The ability to perform on the job is based on such variables as rewards, coworkers, management competence, the intrinsic quality of the work itself, promotion opportunities, and other social and external conditions.

REWARDS. Monetary and nonmonetary rewards, such as recognition and job security, are usually at the top of the lists of variables affecting job performance. The overall tie between pay and performance has always been present but the relationship between an employee's behavioral performance and pay has too frequently been ignored.

Pay-for-performance.

Pay-for-performance plans provide a more direct link between good performance and its reward than do salary and wage levels. Regardless of whether the pay plan is for blue-collar piecework or rate of return on the balance sheet for executives, there is more of a cause-and-effect relationship between pay and performance than if a straight salary or wage is paid. The relationship of pay to job performance is often complicated by age, education, and occupational level, variables examined in the next section.

COWORKERS. The place of the work group in contributing to effective job performance has been well established by the Hawthorne and other studies. The importance of being continuously associated with fellow workers is stronger for some employees than the more direct monetary rewards.

From day one, new employees form impressions about coworkers that affect their job performance for the duration of their careers with that organization. Managers and supervisors, inasmuch as they are also coworkers, contribute to the social environment affecting job performance.

MANAGEMENT AND SUPERVISORY COMPETENCE. The expectations of employees about the competence of their supervisors and managers have increased with higher levels of education and with each generation. If managers do not have the technical and interpersonal competence expected by the employees, then the employees will not be as diligent in performing their jobs.

There is no substitute for interpersonal job contact and relationships by managers to ensure the commitment necessary for effective job performance.

At least one company, Hewlett-Packard, achieves this by following a philosophy of "management by walking (or wandering) around."

INTRINSIC QUALITY OF THE WORK ITSELF. Regardless of the extrinsic factors such as quality of management, coworkers, and pay, the internal aspects of how the job is designed are important determinants in how effectively the job is performed (see Figure 6–2). Job design and the autonomy and responsibility of employees are critical areas for most individuals. When jobs are too structured, employees lose interest in performing to maximum levels.

Recognition is another factor contributing to how "good" the job is and consequently how well the employee performs the job. The amount of recognition provided for individuals is a significant force having a direct bearing on how intensely they work.

PROMOTION OPPORTUNITIES. Not all employees want promotions, but the opportunities for promotion must be present. Unlike most of the foregoing factors where there is general commonality among most individuals, considerable individual differences are seen with regard to promotion opportunities.

Promotion opportunities must be present whether used or not.

Whether or not the promotion actually takes place is not as important for some employees as the opportunity. There is an analogy to Herzberg's dual-factor approach to motivation: The opportunity for promotion must be present to avoid dissatisfaction, but satisfaction is still not guaranteed. The "neutral" point of at least having the opportunities available is preferable to dissatisfaction and negative job attitudes and performance.

FIGURE 6–2 How Well the Job Is Designed Determines How Effectively the Job Is Performed.

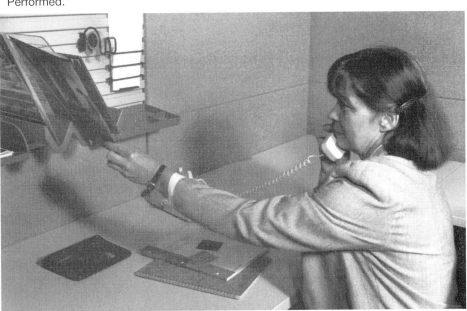

SIMILARITIES OF JOB PERFORMANCE TO JOB SATISFACTION. Not too surprisingly, these factors of pay, working conditions, promotion opportunities, and others are the same items that have been considered to be the determinants of job satisfaction by Herzberg and others. The variables are not means to an end of job satisfaction, but are effects of the end itself—effective job performance. Job satisfaction, on the other hand, is influenced by job performance itself, along with other variables.

JOB SATISFACTION AND MORALE

Job satisfaction is an individual perception.

Most career choices involve consideration or reconsideration of what one expects to get out of a job, that is, job satisfaction. **Job satisfaction** is a personal matter based on each individual's value system and attitudes about the job. Morale, on the other hand, is a group concept—a composite of all individuals' job satisfactions. Both job satisfaction and morale are based on attitude. Both are subjective, but it is essential that both be measured and heeded if the organization is to be highly productive.

Job satisfaction is in relationship to "referent others."

Job satisfaction is relative. Only when an individual considers his or her situation in relationship to others can job satisfaction be determined. This is the important referent others concept. The **referent others concept** is that individuals compare their rewards with others who have similar backgrounds, abilities, and responsibilities.

Morale is a composite of all individuals' job satisfactions.

Morale, that composite state of mind and emotions, affects our attitudes and willingness to work, which, in turn, affect those of others. People with high morale have confidence in themselves, in the future, and in others. High morale permits employees to take minor irritations in stride and work under pressure without blowing up.

Maintaining high morale is a continuous task.

Raising morale to a high level and maintaining it there is a continuous process that cannot be achieved simply through short-run devices such as pep talks or contests. High morale is usually slow to develop and difficult to maintain. Low morale develops more rapidly and is even more difficult to overcome. A positive—or negative—outlook on life and work is contagious in the workplace.

Whereas satisfaction is a person's attitude toward job or life, morale reflects the general tone or esprit de corps of a collective group of personalities. Each person either heightens the prospect for esprit de corps or lowers the outlook for cooperative effort.

THE VARIABLES OF JOB SATISFACTION

Knowing what to expect regarding the variables of job satisfaction will help managers predict and be prepared for changes in both individual job satisfaction and the morale of the entire organization. These variables are helpful in explaining job performance variances among different groups. Primary variables include age, years on the job, occupational field, organizational level, education, and gender.

Aggregate relationships.

All the variable relationships discussed are aggregates. There are many individual exceptions, but on balance the relationships represent the workforce population. Many researchers including Herzberg and the author have observed and studied the relationships in various organizational settings (see Figure 6–3).

Generally a positive but U-shaped relationship.

AGE. Generally, there is a positive correlation between age and job performance/satisfaction, but the specific effects remain uncertain. Unique relationships exist for certain age groups such as the very young (19 or younger) who are relatively high performers and well satisfied, and for individuals nearing retirement who experience some downturn in performance and satisfaction.

Fluctuations in attitudes of younger workers occur because of a new interest in work and a change in the workplace. Young people will perform well and experience high job satisfaction on initial employment. However, both performance and satisfaction can fall off rapidly and dramatically for several years until they reach their late twenties. Then, performance and satisfaction increase gradually with age—eventually surpassing the levels of initial employment.

Another positive but U-shaped curve.

YEARS ON THE JOB. Tenure on a particular job follows a very similar pattern. That is, the initial high performance and satisfaction are followed by a steep falling off or falling out during the first year of employment on any job. Both remain low for several years before turning upward.

FIGURE 6–3 Variables of Job Satisfaction. All the Relationships Shown Are Aggregated. Individual Differences Exist.

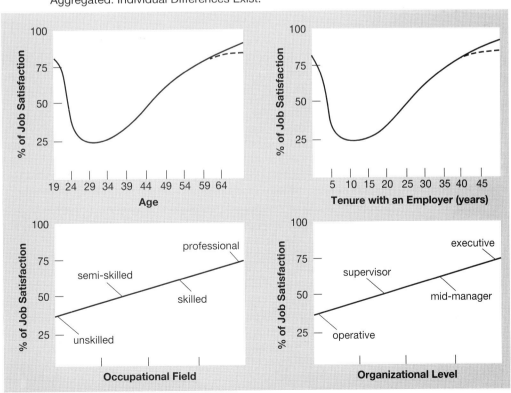

If individuals repeatedly leave organizations during this falling-off period and take different jobs, they are perpetually in flux: initially feeling almost euphoric about their new jobs, and a short time later feeling dissatisfied and unproductive. Absenteeism and turnover are manifested in this situation. If employees keep moving through this cycle from job to job, they become "job-hoppers" and experience personal costs as well as the costs of turnover to their organizations.

Satisfaction increases with complexity and status of job.

OCCUPATIONAL FIELD.   Differences exist in job performance and satisfaction among various occupational groups, but there is generally a positive relationship between complexity of the job and performance/satisfaction. Historically, less skilled workers need more job security than the cosmopolitan or professional workers. Unskilled workers are less mobile and more dependent on local organizations including, in some cases, their unions.

One encouraging fact emerges from studies of job satisfaction: The higher the level of occupation, the higher the morale. Laborers and other nontechnical employees are generally lower performers and are less satisfied than technical, skilled, and professional workers.

ORGANIZATIONAL LEVEL.   There is a similar positive relationship between job performance and satisfaction and organizational level. The performance and satisfaction levels of individuals are probably as much a function of level as they are a function of occupational field. As an individual ascends a hierarchical organization, he or she experiences opportunities for higher job performance and consequently opportunities for higher job satisfaction.

Negative relationship of education to satisfaction.

EDUCATION.   Higher educational level does not necessarily mean greater job satisfaction. This may be due in part to increased expectations prompted by higher levels of education. Exceptions to this trend may be found at the level of graduate education, especially at the doctoral and postdoctoral levels in medicine and other disciplines.

The increased expectations brought about by higher education may be offset somewhat by the increase in promotions based on occupational and organizational levels. Similarly, the rising educational level of the general population may account for the relative dissatisfaction of younger, but more educated, workers.

The gap between job satisfaction for men and women narrows.

GENDER.   In the past, men have reported a higher degree of job satisfaction than women. More recently, differences have diminished due in part to more equal opportunities for employment and advancement. Women have placed higher priorities on coworkers and working conditions than men.

BLUE-COLLAR CHALLENGE

Today's jobs are not as likely to bring the same satisfaction earned by such craftsmen as the cabinetmaker or blacksmith of the last century. **Blue-collar jobs** are principally physical jobs, including construction, manufacturing, and some service industries. Work skills are now linked to machine operations, and what we make is mostly the product of other machines and other workers. The mechanized worker stands at a psychological distance from his or her work and is not identified with the end product. This type of employee is often confined to a fixed workstation and is expected to leave it only with permission. Such restrictions can affect one's attitude toward work.

An important determinant of job satisfaction is the length of the **job cycle**—how long it takes to perform an operation before starting over. For a college professor, the work cycle is often a semester. For a skilled craftsman, it may be weeks. For the worker on the assembly line, it may last only a minute: "The job can get sickening, if it is only plugging in ignition wires. You get through with one motor, turn around, and there's another motor staring you in the face."

Most people like variety in their work rhythm; they may work fast for a while and then slow down gradually as the day wears on. Such change of pace helps to reduce both fatigue and job boredom. The assembly line offers few provisions for worker preference. The pace is set and the worker usually cannot change it. Therefore, the machine may be a worse autocrat than any supervisor.

To make work more enjoyable, many employees invent games that supply new goals. When job pressure is not tightly paced, the worker may experiment with various speeds and set various output goals. Social games frequently provide another form of diversion.

JOB SATISFACTION IN THE WHITE-COLLAR WORLD

White-collar jobs are principally office work, corporate management, and some professionals. Banks, retail stores, hospitals, and service industries are providing more white-collar jobs than ever before. White-collar jobs are usually more flexible than blue-collar jobs because they are not as strictly tied to production quotas. Working hours are often more flexible, and the procedures for doing a job are usually not as rigid. Even so, white-collar workers also often feel dead-ended in their work.

Industrial psychology has found that a job title such as "staff assistant" may provide a sense of advancement to an employee who was doing almost the same job when it was called "chief clerk." Copywriters, programmers, and laboratory technicians all must exhibit initiative and creativity. Such positions require a deep concentration and present a varied work pace, both of which tend to raise employee morale.

The big problem for collar color seems to occur in the "middle years." At this stage of their lives, nearly twice as many blue-collar as white-collar workers were dissatisfied with their jobs. One reason for this overall dissatisfaction with work may be that blue-collar workers can experience an "economic squeeze" during their middle years. Blue-collar workers usually achieve their top earnings earlier in life, whereas white-collar workers do not plateau early, but begin to reap the rewards of their greater education in their thirties.

An increasing number of pink-collar workers, including paraprofessionals in health care and other fields, are experiencing both pay and status dissatisfactions. Pink-collar workers also include waitresses, nurses' aides, and many office workers. Any of these jobs may be considered "dirty collars" at times, depending on their job content and surrounding management practices.

A short job cycle can cause boredom.

The machine can be more of a taskmaster than the supervisor.

White-collar jobs are more flexible.

A change in title can mean higher job satisfaction.

Blue-collar workers achieve earning plateau before white-collar workers.

Pink-collar workers are dissatisfied.

MORALE AND THE CHANGING WORKFORCE

The more successful the company, the more likely the employee is to show loyalty. If a company is experiencing a good production record, it is wise to share such information with employees. Employees of today demonstrate a higher morale in small companies than in large ones. An employee from a multinational company commented, "Oh, I am only one of a thousand employees; they don't care what my name is as long as I turn out so many parts an hour." Consider the statement, "I am lost in this joint; the management only knows me as employee number 456."

Every day from 3 to 7 percent of the workforce is missing, representing a loss of well over $100 million a year in absentee wages. Absenteeism also incurs the significant expenses of training workers to fill in for absentees, disruption of production, and overstaffing to minimize the impact of absenteeism. Companies most apt to have no-shows are those that offer sick leave pay and those that keep scant records and are lax about employee absences.

Autonomy and creative opportunities are important variables for younger, better educated workers. Younger workers expect and are required to have greater creativity and decision-making abilities in high-tech and other contemporary organizations. Research in hospitals and other health care organizations confirms the expectations and demands of a younger, changing workforce. Younger, better educated doctors and nurses as well as paraprofessionals expect autonomy and independent decision-making ability along with a cooperative team effort.

Problems arise when the employee's salary comes close to the supervisor's.

It may seem to employees that the longer they work, the higher their salaries become, but the closer their salaries come to their supervisors' salaries, the more likely their morale will drop. The thinking behind this is "Why should I work to become a supervisor when I will only receive a few cents more an hour for that much more responsibility? It isn't worth it." Likewise, the supervisor may feel that he or she is underpaid, because there is no wage premium attached to responsibility. As an employer, be sure to make that span of earnings between the employee and the supervisor enough, roughly 30 percent, to make it seem worthwhile to both of them. An employee should see a substantial monetary increase in accepting a supervisory role, and the supervisor should feel compensated for the task.

Wellness programs.

A large number of companies are changing their attitudes toward employee health. Organizations are taking a stance of "wellness" and illness prevention rather than health insurance and rehabilitation. Many companies are actively helping employees to maintain and improve their health through wellness programs. **Wellness programs** are company-sponsored programs whose purpose is to improve and maintain employees' physical and mental health and productivity.

Such firms are building swimming pools, gymnasiums, jogging tracks, squash and tennis courts, locker rooms, and saunas to keep employees healthy. Low-calorie menus in company cafeterias promote workers' health as well. Some companies give bonuses to employees who do not take any sick days. A status-free environment is now available at many gyms, sports, and health programs offered by some companies, and in health clubs and fitness centers across the nation (see Figure 6–4).

FIGURE 6–4 A Status-Free Environment Is Offered in Fitness Centers.

**ACTION PROJECT
6–1**

DECIDE HOW SATISFIED YOU ARE WITH YOUR JOB
(INDIVIDUAL EXERCISE)

No job is perfect. But when do you know it's time to bail out? Take this quiz. Answer each item true or false.

1. My job fits my personality.
2. I like my coworkers.
3. I'm seen as a valuable member of the organization.
4. My work is challenging.
5. Time goes quickly at work.
6. At the end of the day, I feel "tired" but a healthy type of tired.
7. I'm comfortable with the idea of staying in my current position for a while longer.
8. Generally, I feel happy about my work situation.
9. The three things I value most in a job (e.g., prestige, independence, salary, responsibilities, good coworkers) are present.
10. My boss and I have a good relationship.

11. In the past few months, I've been free from minor illnesses and other stress reactions (e.g., poor sleeping, poor eating habits, forgetfulness) due to my job.

12. I feel enthusiastic about coming to work.

13. I don't worry about being laid off.

14. My friends and family comment that I seem satisfied with my job.

15. If I asked to work on a new project, I'd probably be allowed to.

16. I can fill in my job description with my own style.

17. I seldom miss work or feel a need to leave my work area.

18. It's easy to concentrate on my duties.

19. There is little I would improve in my job.

20. The problems I encounter on my job are temporary.

Other job satisfaction quizzes often give a rating scale to determine whether a job is right for you. Only you can judge. How do your true answers stack up against the false ones? Are the items most meaningful to you present in your job? Overall, are you happy?

If so, continue to enjoy your work. If not, don't stay because it's the easier thing to do. Feeling stressed because you have a job you don't like will take more of a toll than looking for another position.

SOURCE: Patricia Romano, "Decide How Satisfied You Are with Your Job," *The Coloradoan* (Ft. Collins), October 4, 1993, p. D7. Reprinted with permission.

QUALITY OF WORK LIFE AND RELATED CONCEPTS

The concept of quality of work life (QWL) has been around for some time, but it remains an elusive term. To some, it means "humane" work; to others, it means an environmentally healthy and equitable organization. For our purposes, let us define **quality of work life** as the concept of making work meaningful for employees in an organizational environment where they are motivated to perform well and are satisfied with their work.

Several characteristics or criteria are used when assessing QWL programs:[7]

- Adequate and fair compensation
- Safe and healthy environment
- Immediate opportunity for development and use of human capacities
- Future opportunity for continued growth and security
- Social integration in the workforce—the opportunity to achieve personal identity and self-esteem
- Employee rights to privacy, speech, equity, and due process
- Balance between work and total life space—the extent to which a

person's work has a balanced role, not demanding so much time, effort, or other inputs so as to severely disrupt leisure and family time

- Social relevance—the degree to which the worker views what the organization does as socially responsible and therefore of social value

The purposes of these QWL features are to make the organization a more comfortable and otherwise satisfying as well as more productive place to work. In Chapter 5, we discussed Hackman and Oldham's job characteristics model (see Figure 5–9). Knowing those skills, task identities, and their significance makes it possible for the individual to perform better and experience higher job satisfaction.

TOTAL QUALITY MANAGEMENT REVISITED

Recall that in Chapter 1 we defined **total quality management** (TQM) as a comprehensive approach to quality that encourages everyone in the organization to provide customers with reliable products and services. To carry that definition further, TQM also refers to the following:

1. Complete commitment to quality products and services to customers
2. Organizational support to accomplish goals
3. Analyses of customers' needs so as to satisfy or exceed them

This type of commitment is healthy and positive for employees as well as customers. It is important for the employees' organization to support them in their efforts to serve customers and not be a hindrance. A major research interest is how well employees do in satisfying customers' needs—customer satisfaction—if the employees themselves are dissatisfied—job dissatisfaction. *Prima facie* evidence suggests a direct correlation between the two types of satisfaction.

JOB PERFORMANCE, MORALE, AND PRODUCTIVITY

EFFECTIVE JOB PERFORMANCE RESULTS IN JOB SATISFACTION

No direct link between job satisfaction and production.

If employees don't have the tools and managerial latitude to perform, they can be neither satisfied nor productive. Efforts have been made for years to establish a link between job satisfaction, morale, and productivity—largely to no avail. There is no direct link because the relationship between job satisfaction and productivity is more a matter of perception than a direct link.

Again, there is an analogy to Herzberg's dual-factor theory: If relative job satisfaction is present, higher productivity is still not guaranteed because of other variables such as job design, organizational hierarchy, and age of the organization. But if relative job satisfaction is not present, long-term productivity gains are very difficult to achieve.

Performance and productivity relationship.

The relationship between high-quality job performance and productivity is more direct. The whole point of job performance is to accomplish useful, productive jobs. Total organizational effectiveness is based on how productive and efficient each individual is in the organization. Enabling individuals to perform well and to be satisfied in their jobs contributes to accomplishment of organizational objectives.

There is a delicate balance between too much pressure for productivity and high morale. Too little pressure results in a goof-off organization. Too much pressure results in a damn-the-organization, I'll-only-do-what's-necessary attitude. When management shows consideration and concern for the individual differences of workers, increased job performance and consequently increased job satisfaction are the results (see Figure 6–5).

Turnarounds at American companies.

American car manufacturers continue to struggle with the ragged reputation that they turn out cars inferior to those made by Asian or European manufacturers, and that American workers are not sufficiently productive. Nevertheless, there have been stunning turnarounds at American manufacturers. By increasing participation of the blue-collar employees through informal discussions, GM reversed declines in production and morale at its Tarrytown plant. Within a few months, the percentage of bad welds, for example, dropped from 35 percent to 1.5 percent. And when the small voluntary program of worker participation was expanded to the plant's 3,800 employees, 95 percent of them took part.

Giving workers a greater voice in their jobs can improve productivity by bringing about declines in grievances, absenteeism, and waste. Similar advances are being experienced at GM's Saturn plant in Tennessee.

FIGURE 6–5 The Delicate Balance for Productivity Pressure.

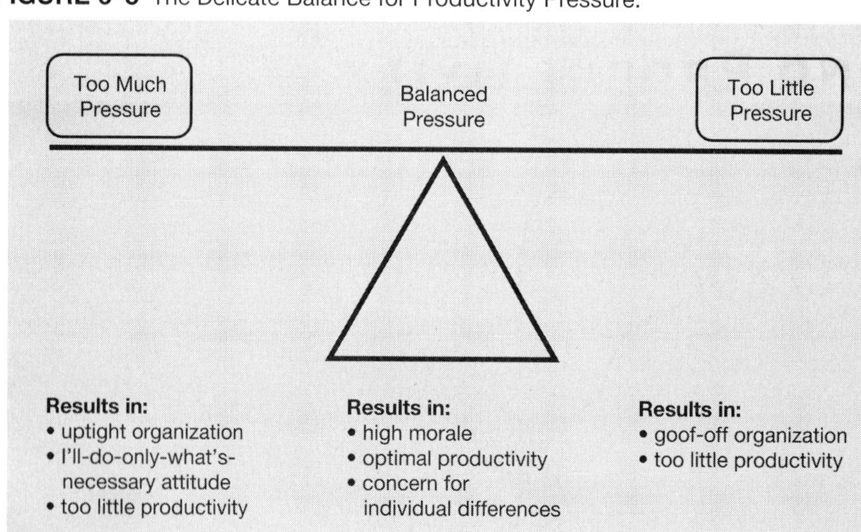

Too Much Pressure

Balanced Pressure

Too Little Pressure

Results in:
• uptight organization
• I'll-do-only-what's-necessary attitude
• too little productivity

Results in:
• high morale
• optimal productivity
• concern for individual differences

Results in:
• goof-off organization
• too little productivity

MAKING DULL JOBS MORE INTERESTING

Industry is trying to inject interest and incentive into jobs that have historically been monotonous. The trend toward job enrichment is constantly evolving because of innovations in many areas, but consider the following ways to combat monotony:

1. Allow workers to form natural work units. Work is distributed so that each person performing a task is identified with the job.
2. Combine tasks both horizontally and vertically where appropriate to allow workers to perform an entire job.
3. Where possible allow workers to establish direct relationships with their clients or ultimate users of their products or services.
4. Communicate end product or service feedback to workers so that workers know how they are performing.

The whole job concept.

The **whole job concept** holds the worker responsible for the assembling, finishing, and testing of a complete unit instead of for one small, repetitive task. In one plant, rejects dropped from 23 percent to 1 percent in the six months following the change from the assembly-line concept to the whole job concept. The company also found that absenteeism dropped from 8 percent to 1 percent and that productivity increased.

Quality circles.

Encouraging job participation is another method of job enrichment—helping hourly employees to realize that they are not part of a machine and challenging employees to use their thinking abilities. The worker is involved in problem solving and planning instead of routinely performing duties. Decision making leads to expansion of responsibilities, and work teams hold regular "rap" sessions to express complaints. Likewise, voluntary quality circles meet regularly to solve problems. Most employees opt for and participate actively in quality circles.

EXPRESS YOUR OPINION   Does everyone want to have challenging, enriched jobs?

DIAGNOSING AND MAINTAINING MORALE

Organizations, like any organisms, are subject to inertia and static; that is, they can become resistant to any kind of change or innovation. They easily accumulate practices and policies that can overload their systems. Checking up on morale can be preventive medicine as well as a way to begin a cure for a diseased corporate body. And when treatment is given, further checkups are often useful to reveal whether it has been successful or not.

PROFILE OF HUMAN BEHAVIOR

LIZ ROEDIGER

Liz Roediger is a person who likes—even "loves"—her job as receptionist/secretary, and it shows. All you have to do is call her place of business, a subsidiary of a *Fortune 500* company, and you are welcomed by Liz's very pleasant and professional greeting, and a concern that you are served as a customer.

As a receptionist/secretary at her current and similar past jobs, including a year-long stint with a federal government agency, her employers, supervisors, and coworkers all benefit from her enthusiasm and dedication to serving the customer. She works closely with top management, new product development, sales, and other marketing personnel. Former and current employers are generous in their praise of Liz's skills and job performance. Her job requires her to have knowledge of computers and communication devices and to learn new skills as technology expands.

Regarding performance and morale, Liz says: "Job performance has always been and will continue to be most important to me. Being the best that I can be affects everyone around me. I have the ability to make the best or the worst of a good or bad situation. Morale includes being a professional and creating the mood around me. Being around a low-morale workplace and people who can sometimes be negative is difficult for me as I believe it is for most of us. My belief is that we all have the ability to make our surroundings exactly what we want them to be."

Liz acknowledges that there are some jobs that may be more dull than others, but she tries to make those jobs more interesting: "I, like others, have likes and dislikes; if I accept the things that I find dull and boring, I can assure myself that it is okay to feel this way and go on from there. Turning dull jobs from a negative into a positive works for me."

Liz feels that diagnosing and maintaining morale is a form of communication: "I find that listening, instead of being heard, is best in most cases. Taking time to listen to others' needs and responding in a positive form of verbal or physical expression can change a room full of what I believe to be negatives into positives. . . .

"Motivating others by creating the proper physical, cultural, and managerial environment needs to come from the top. Everyone should be treated, first and foremost, as people. All of us could be motivated with a few well-chosen words such as 'would you, please,' and 'thank you.'"

Concerning quality of work life and quality of management, Liz notes that: "Quality of work life makes the difference between unhappiness and professionalism in my job. Doing what I enjoy and doing it in the best way I can makes for quality work. . . . Quality of management/quality work is important to me in creating an office that works together as a team. I look up to good management, and it is always easier to work with personnel who treat employees with appreciation."

Liz Roediger concludes: "Job performance and morale in the workplace need to start with people doing what they want to do and not settle for anything else. If we are doing what we enjoy, instead of what we don't enjoy, we will be able to do a great job, and the joy we have in our jobs will be a plus and very significant in our morale and performance."

Morale is not static, and because it is constantly changing, it must be continuously assessed. Several methods are available for diagnosing and maintaining morale, including records analysis, informal and formal surveys, and above all listening. Bruce Pfau, managing director of quality consulting for the Hay Group of management consultants, sees a trend toward increased employee surveys, citing a 300 percent increase between 1989 and 1992. The reasons include the following:

- Downsizing is over for many companies that are now realizing their new "lean and mean" workforces need attention.
- Employees are viewed as good conduits to and from customers about the quality of company goods and services.
- Companies view surveys as a means of determining obstacles to quality.
- A survey gives the company candid insights and suggestions to enhance performance that would be hard to come by on a nonconfidential basis.

Pfau concludes, " . . . employee surveys allow companies to reliably and objectively determine what employees have to say, avoiding anecdotal data which may slant the facts. . . ."[8]

ANALYSIS OF RECORDS

Check company records first.

The first method of analysis to ascertain employee morale is examination of company records. Heavy absenteeism, excessive tardiness, long lunch hours, quitting early, and poor safety records could indicate low morale. Low production and a high rate of spoilage may be another indication. Finally, personnel records show the percentage of employee turnover, which in some industries can be expected to be 10 to 20 percent, or even higher.

Turnover can indicate morale problems.

The following records should be maintained and give some indication of employee morale. These should be reviewed before a company survey is attempted:

1. Labor turnover
2. Production records
3. Waste and spoilage
4. Absenteeism
5. Tardiness
6. Grievance reports
7. Exit interviews
8. Safety records
9. Medical reports
10. Suggestion boxes

INFORMAL QUESTIONS AND ANSWERS

The personnel department and supervisors can learn much from employees and one another about morale. They can ask questions and listen to employees and other managers. One pitfall is for supervisors and management to assume that morale is high or low. They can easily be mistaken in their understanding of what employees are really thinking and feeling.

One method of finding out what employees think is for human resources specialists to hold confidential, informal interviews with employees. The success of this method depends on the impartiality of the interviewer and the degree of trust that the employee feels. Employees with complaints often prefer to remain anonymous for fear of reprisals.

Exit interviews.
Employees who are leaving the company are often more than willing to talk about the negative aspects of their jobs. Some companies conduct exit interviews or send letters to elicit such information. Opinions from former employees can be helpful, but companies that wait to ask questions until employees leave may already have serious trouble with morale.

FORMAL SURVEYS

Employee surveys are the most comprehensive way in which to study morale. In a survey, everyone is asked to respond to the same questions so that management can get an accurate view of the general level of morale. Surveys can be conducted by impartial interviewers or by questionnaires. One common way of combining survey approaches is to distribute a questionnaire to pinpoint problem areas and then use the interview technique to get more details.

The basic approach has a great deal to do with how valid a survey is. Indifference, resistance, or fear on the part of management is easily sensed by employees. The approach should always be, "What can be learned from the study?" rather than "Who can we blame?" If management wants to know whether employees are content with their working hours, it should ask, "Do you like your working hours? What hours would you prefer?" An example of a poor question is "How do you like your pay and benefits?" It asks for too much information at once, and the answers cannot be interpreted precisely.

Objective surveys ask multiple-choice questions.
Multiple-choice questions are popular on questionnaires because, with standardized responses, objective and longitudinal trends can be measured. Objective surveys generally use a direct approach, asking specific questions and categorizing the answers. The chief advantages to these types of surveys are that they can be administered and analyzed very easily and they can be scored by a computer, if desired. The results can give statistical data that is easily measured.

Descriptive surveys ask you to write out how you feel.
Descriptive surveys encourage employees to express their feelings on a topic in their own words. Questions such as "How fairly do you feel the company treats you?" and "In what positive ways could the company improve its employee–employer relationships?" require the employee to express his or her feelings. Usually, the first questions of a descriptive survey are an attempt to get employees to express their own attitudes about the company and their workstations. The last part of the survey usually attempts to ask in a participative way how employees would improve the employee–employer relationship if they had an opportunity to do so. Such surveys can be conducted by interview or individual questionnaire. The important considerations are that employees are assured that what they think is important and that their responses will not be identified by management except in a positive way, perhaps as a part of a suggestion system.

EMPLOYEE RESPONSES AND FOLLOW-THROUGH

Just conducting a morale survey tends to boost morale because it indicates to employees that the company is interested in what they think. Questionnaires that don't require employees to identify themselves add to the validity of the answers. Surveys conducted by mail do not generate as much response as do surveys conducted personally on the job.

Morale surveys have a tendency to raise morale temporarily.

Morale surveys may raise morale, but only for as long as employees believe their opinions are contributing to change. Surveys irritate employees when they feel that their answers are not given true consideration. Employers who are afraid to publish findings because they do not want to attract attention to problem areas take the chance of actually causing problems by encouraging only negative rumors. Management should be prepared to follow through with remedies for the problem areas indicated by the survey. If management cannot effect change, it must be prepared to explain to employees why change is not possible at that time.

ACTION PROJECT 6–2   MORALE AND PRODUCTIVITY (INDIVIDUAL EXERCISE)

A. DEFINITIONS

1. **Morale**—A group of emotions and attitudes (state of mind) that determines our desire to work. High morale means satisfied and motivated employees, but it does not necessarily mean high production.

2. **Job satisfaction**—Individual perceptions on how well certain job-related factors are being fulfilled.

3. **Productivity**—All of the steps, functions, and processes required to produce a product or service. The level of production is determined by physical resources, worker skills, individual worker satisfaction, and all workers' morale.

   Two examples of how job satisfaction is affected by production:

   a. Employees may have high morale but lack the required new machinery to improve production. Consequent job satisfaction will be low.

   b. Employees in a company with high productivity and profit will tend to have high morale. Individual employees will tend to have high job satisfaction despite individual differences.

B. SELF-TEST

Please answer the following questions about your organization using the following scale. Use your current or last job (even if it was part time or within your family) as a reference point:

5–very much or like   3–neutral   1–very little or dislike

GROUP 1

5	4	3	2	1	1.	What is your personal job satisfaction level?
5	4	3	2	1	2.	What is the organizational morale level?
5	4	3	2	1	3.	Do you like your job?
5	4	3	2	1	4.	Do you like the people you work with?
5	4	3	2	1	5.	Do you feel the organization is successful?
5	4	3	2	1	6.	Do you trust your coworkers?
5	4	3	2	1	7.	Are your coworkers happy with their jobs?
5	4	3	2	1	8.	Are you willing to put in overtime when required?
5	4	3	2	1	9.	What do you feel your job performance is?
5	4	3	2	1	10.	Are you optimistic about the future of the organization?
___	___	___	___	___		Total Group 1 Score

GROUP 2

5	4	3	2	1	1.	If your coworkers are motivated, does this motivate you?
5	4	3	2	1	2.	Does the organization require a certain performance level?
5	4	3	2	1	3.	Are you rewarded for high performance?
5	4	3	2	1	4.	How important is quick task completion?
5	4	3	2	1	5.	Could performance be improved?
5	4	3	2	1	6.	Is your job flexible?
5	4	3	2	1	7.	Are communication channels good in your organization?
5	4	3	2	1	8.	Does your company have adequate physical resources for high production?
5	4	3	2	1	9.	Are you and your coworkers skilled and trained well?
5	4	3	2	1	10.	Do you feel that the quality of goods or services your organization produces is high?
___	___	___	___	___		Total Group 2 Score

C. SCORING

Group 1 total score equals the vertical coordinate on the following graph. Group 2 total score equals the horizontal coordinate on the graph. Plot the points:

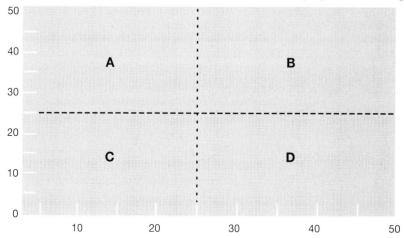

Ratings:
A = high morale with low productivity
B = high morale with high productivity
C = low morale with low productivity
D = low morale with high productivity

An organization's objective should be to reach section B. Sections A, C, and D indicate that changes may be needed.

PHYSICAL ENVIRONMENT AND MORALE

It is worthwhile to study the effects of the environment on individuals. The explosion tragedies and mass fatalities in Mexico City and in Bhopal, India, and the potential for reoccurrence are matters for concern. Hazardous conditions can obviously have a negative effect on workers.

ERGONOMICS

Ergonomics is the study of work, focusing on the dynamics of man/machine interfaces and the best design to accommodate humans. Ergonomic specialists focus on the relationship of people to uses of work space. In addition, emphasis is placed on intrinsic motivators in industrial circles. Much is said these days about noise, visual and toxic pollution, and the emotional fatigue that results from a poor working environment.

Once called *human engineering,* ergonomics involves designing workstations for maximum performance and in a way that makes the job more suitable to the employee. This requires studying not only size and shape of chairs and workbenches, but also areas of lighting, music, sound, color, and temperature.

Many people spend major portions of their workdays seated. Men's bodies require a different kind of chair than do most women's postures, but little attention is usually given to this kind of detail.[9]

NOISE POLLUTION AFFECTS MORALE

There are two effects of noise: biological and psychosociological. Both can adversely affect morale. It has been suspected for some time that as many as 10 million workers may have suffered hearing loss due to excessive noise. A number of physicians are certain that job noises are a factor in some neurotic and psychotic illnesses.

Noise can be a source of psychological and physical stress.

In a study entitled "Affectiveness of Noise on People," prepared for the Environmental Protection Agency, Dr. James D. Miller of the Center Institute for the Deaf in Saint Louis wrote, "There is no definite evidence that noise can induce either neurotic or psychotic illness." However, his report added, "But all the facts show speech interference, hearing loss, annoyance, and the arousal and distraction clearly support the contention that noises can act as sources of psychological distress."[10] Distress can, in turn, contribute to "such unpleasant symptoms as nausea, headaches, instability, argumentativeness, sexual impotence, change in general mood and general anxiety." Other studies show that noise contributes to a breakdown in communications and can produce irritable and depressed feelings, as well as a short attention span and hyperactivity.

Decibels measure noise.

The difficulties in controlling sound are to find acceptable standards and feasible ways of controlling it. The limits are measured in **decibels** on a logarithmic scale that runs from the threshold of hearing 1 dB(A) (one decibel on the A audiometric scale) through normal conversation (about 50 decibels), to

FIGURE 6–6 Average Hourly Noise Level Scale. Source: Daniel A. Girando and George S. Everly, *Controlling Stress and Tension: A Holistic Approach* (Englewood Cliffs, N.J.: Prentice Hall, 1979), p. 99.

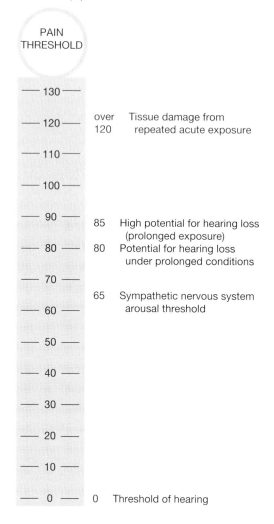

PAIN THRESHOLD

— 130 —

— 120 —   over 120   Tissue damage from repeated acute exposure

— 110 —

— 100 —

— 90 —   85   High potential for hearing loss (prolonged exposure)

— 80 —   80   Potential for hearing loss under prolonged conditions

— 70 —

65   Sympathetic nervous system arousal threshold

— 60 —

— 50 —

— 40 —

— 30 —

— 20 —

— 10 —

— 0 —   0   Threshold of hearing

the level of hearing impairment (85 decibels, if continuous), to that of acute pain (135 decibels) (see Figure 6–6).

VISUAL POLLUTION

Eye strain from CRTs and VDTs.

Eye strain from cathode-ray tubes (CRTs), video display terminals (VDTs), and other close work is of increasing concern to employees, unions, and managers. Office workers in particular are bombarded by "visual shock" and monotony from viewing VDTs. In some cases, the bombardment is literally from hazardous radiation of unshielded CRTs. Pregnant women may be especially at risk in using VDTs. Miscarriage rates are higher than normal among women who work with VDTs.[11]

ASSESS YOUR NOISE LEVEL

The following list shows the noise levels for common activities we are exposed to daily. They are measured in decibels. Calculate your average hourly level of noise exposure for a typical eight-hour day.

ACTIVITY	DB(A) × HRS/DAY		
Rocket engine	180 ×	=	
Jet plane takeoff	150 ×	=	
Police/fire sirens at 100 feet	138 ×	=	
Pneumatic (air) drill at 5 feet	125 ×	=	
Live rock concert	125 ×	=	
Loud rock music (recorded)	115 ×	=	
Train passing at 10 feet	108 ×	=	
Heavy manufacturing plant	100 ×	=	
Large truck at 90 feet	98 ×	=	
10-hp outboard motor at 50 feet	88 ×	=	
Heavy freeway or city traffic at 5 feet	85 ×	=	
Bus ride	85 ×	=	
Average assembly line	75 ×	=	
Department store	65 ×	=	
Average office	65 ×	=	
Classroom	64 ×	=	
Conversation at 3 feet	63 ×	=	
Average residential street	55 ×	=	
Air conditioner	55 ×	=	
Average domestic noises	48 ×	=	
Quiet radio at home	42 ×	=	
Library	38 ×	=	
Quiet auditorium	30 ×	=	
Whisper at 5 feet	20 ×	=	
	Total noise level	=	_____

Add 10 minutes for each time a noise or sound annoys you or disrupts your concentration on a task.

_____

Total noise level ÷ 8   =   _____.
This is your average
hourly noise level.

SOURCE: Daniel A. Girdano and George S. Everly, *Controlling Stress and Tension: A Holistic Approach* (Englewood Cliffs, N.J.: Prentice Hall, 1979), p. 99.

LIGHTING

Lighting is expressed in footcandles.

Lighting levels are generally expressed in footcandles. One **footcandle** is equal to the light of one candle at a distance of one foot, as established by the Illuminating Engineering Society (an industry group that publishes lighting standards that are widely followed by electrical contractors when lighting is installed). The average level of light nationally in commercial buildings is 125 footcandles. It is estimated that candle power runs from 10 for a hotel lobby to 150 for a proofreading activity.

Supervisors should be aware that incandescent lighting is more economical to install, but more expensive to maintain than is fluorescent lighting. Perhaps the greatest problem is not the lack of candle power or the illumination of direct glare from lighting fixtures or windows; rather, it is the reflected glare from furniture and contrasting dark shadows that usually cause more eye fatigue and low production than lack of lighting.

In considering the adequacy of illumination, it is necessary to take into account the lighting of the total "visual field" rather than the light of the "field of observation." For instance, the light from the outside may be brighter than that at the desk; thus, if a person is facing a window, he or she must adjust visually to the combined value of the light rather than to that of the work space alone. If one eye receives more light than the other, the adjustment is similarly disturbing. The implication is that the whole area should be illuminated uniformly. Fatigue and low morale also are experienced when the illumination changes too rapidly for the pupil to contract and relax comfortably.

Increasing use of computers is a matter of concern because some arrangements and lighting thwart employee productivity. Adjustable task lighting should be combined with indirect, ceiling-mounted or ambient light. Workers at computer terminals should also have a visual path enabling them to focus on objects at least ten feet away while taking breaks.[12]

COLORS AND SPACE

Color exerts a definite psychological effect and also has a reflective quality. Light green and sky blue, for example, reflect approximately 40 percent of the light they receive, but dark red reflects only about 16 percent. The lighting of a factory can be improved by the use of pastel-colored paint.

In analyzing the color spectrum, we find that red increases restlessness, attracts attention, and speeds decisions. As a result, bright red is a poor choice for large office areas in which people will be working continuously, but it is a good choice for areas in which people meet to enter and exit and where fast movement is encouraged. Pale blue is the most restful of the colors, whereas green slows muscular responses, steadies the nerves, and encourages reflective thinking.

Exit doors can be hard to find in large factories, but the exit door in one factory is plainly marked by bright colors high above the door and, as a guide to finding the door, a thirty-foot-tall arrow reinforces the identification (see Figure 6–7). Research indicates that proper use of color tones and combinations reduces fatigue, increases efficiency, decreases accidents, and improves housekeeping.

Like Garfield the cat, employees "need their space"—whether in the office or factory. Attention needs to be given to designing flexibility into work space to accommodate changes in technology and company growth. Long-term planning can minimize the costs of growth and change.

FIGURE 6–7 Supergraphics Add Color, Show the Way, and Help Morale.

SUMMARY

How individuals perform is a function of how well their jobs are defined, how they fit in with their work groups, and how adaptive the organization can be in accommodating their abilities and skills. High-tech and white-collar workers especially need considerable latitude in adapting to their organizations.

Effective job performance is a key to job satisfaction and morale. Life satisfaction is also influenced by job satisfaction. Employees experience relative job satisfaction not as an end in itself but as a means to job performance. We need to identify and facilitate job performance as both the means and the end of organizational effectiveness.

Quality of work life includes all the variables that make work meaningful for employees in an organizational environment where they are motivated to perform well and are satisfied with their work. QWL factors include adequate and fair compensation, a safe and healthy environment, social integration in the workforce, and certain employee rights. Total quality management is a comprehensive approach to quality that encourages everyone in the organization to provide customers with reliable products and services.

Morale, like health, requires attention. It is a composite of feelings, and maintaining high morale is a continuous task for management. It appears that younger workers are more dissatisfied with work because they have higher expectations.

Conducting surveys and exit interviews are two ways in which employee morale can be determined. Descriptive surveys ask respondents to write down how they feel. Noise pollution, lighting, and colors all affect the attitudes of employees. Color has become more important than before in personalizing one's work space.

If employees are to perform at optimal levels, they need autonomy and other intrinsic job qualities in order to contribute to overall organizational effectiveness. Well-managed companies build in creative opportunities for their employees. They allow them to perform dynamic jobs and grow in a safe environment.

CASE STUDY
6–1

THEFT IN THE SERVICE STATION

Scott Hays is owner and manager of a service station in the downtown area of a large city. He employs twelve men, four of whom he hired just a month ago when he decided to extend the business hours.

When Scott conducted an inventory this morning of the tires that the station had in stock, he discovered that four tires were missing. His first thought was that someone had broken in when the station was closed, but he could find no evidence of this. Scott also discounted the idea that someone had managed to sneak into the garage and steal the tires while the station was open. Surely someone would have seen that happen. The only possibility left was employee theft.

Scott had conducted his last inventory just a few days before he had hired the new men. Since that time he had a sales slip for every tire sold, except for the four missing tires. Scott began considering his men. Could one of them have stolen the tires? This had never happened before!

Scott began to suspect two of his men in earnest. Pete, who is the station mechanic, has worked for Scott for a number of years. Until recently Pete's performance has been good. But a few weeks ago, Scott caught Pete in the process of overbilling a customer for work done on his car. Scott corrected Pete's error without much thought until later, when he found that Pete had written two bills. There was a higher amount listed for the customer and the lower one for the station, thus enabling him to pocket the difference. When Scott confronted Pete, he apologized. Pete said he had never done it before and would never do it again. His reason was that temptation was too strong.

The other man Scott suspected was Dave. Dave had to be corrected on more than one occasion for not giving the proper change back to customers. Were these shortchanges honest mistakes? They only seemed to happen when Scott was away from the station. Dave is apparently in financial trouble, because last week he requested an advance on his next paycheck. Yesterday Scott found out that Dave had been asking some of the men if he could borrow money. Scott wonders if Dave stole the tires for the money he would get for them. If you were Scott, what steps would you now take?

1. Would you fire Dave and Pete? Would you release all four new men?
2. Would you call a meeting of all the employees and discuss the matter? Would you tell them that you felt one of them was a thief?
3. Would you demand that they all take a polygraph test?
4. Would you tell them that if it didn't happen again you would forget it?

MORALE POLLUTION

Have you ever experienced an increasing foul odor from your refrigerator and on inspection been unable to locate the source? In such cases it becomes necessary to investigate, to find the curdled milk or spoiled fruit. There is sometimes a parallel in organizations—in a person who over the years has soured in attitude to the point where the radiation from him pollutes the system's morale.

In one such case, the member was an original employee in a large and successful organization. He had been a central figure in the top management groups and had the perquisites that go with the status. But he had not, in his own eyes, kept pace with the upward mobility of his peers. So far as position was concerned, James Whitmore, 55, had been put in charge of an essential, but to him peripheral, component of the business. He sulks unhappily. His subordinates know that they have a discontented, demoralized boss, and they do not feel represented properly to the rest of the company.

1. What options are available to solve this morale problem that has affected Whitmore's division?
2. What do you believe is the best option, considering the company? considering the employee?

DISCUSSION AND STUDY QUESTIONS—TO KEEP YOU THINKING...

1. What is the relationship between job performance and job satisfaction? between job performance and job standards?
2. What is the relationship between quality of work life and total quality management?
3. What are the determinants of effective job performance?
4. What are the pros and cons of having job descriptions for all employees?
5. What are some methods that an organization can use to determine morale?
6. Generally, what are the relationships of the following to job satisfaction:
   a. age
   b. occupational field
   c. organizational level
   d. job experience with an employer
7. Explain some of the psychological and physical effects that can result from noise and visual pollution.

NOTES

1. Tom Peters, *Thriving on Chaos: Handbook for a Management Revolution* (New York: Alfred A. Knopf, 1988), p. 501.
2. Philip C. Grant, "What Use Is a Job Description?" *Personnel Journal,* February 1988, pp. 45–53.
3. Richard Henderson, *Compensation Management: Rewarding Performance,* 6th ed. (Englewood Cliffs, N.J.: Prentice Hall, 1994), pp. 424–425.
4. Graham Kenny and Alan Dunk, "The Utility of Performance Measures: Production Managers' Perceptions," *IEEE Transactions on Engineering Management,* February 1989, pp. 47–48.
5. Jan Muczyk and Robert Hastings, "In Defense of Enlightened Hardball Management," *Business Horizons,* July–August 1985, p. 24.

6. Henderson, *Compensation Management,* p. 409.
7. Richard E. Walton, "Quality of Work Life: What Is It?" *Sloan Management Review,* Fall 1973, pp. 11–21.
8. Bruce Pfau, quoted in Christine B. Needham, "Firms Look Inside for Help," *Rocky Mountain News,* January 7, 1993, p. 10L.
9. "The Chair Ain't Broke, But They Fixed It," *The Wall Street Journal,* May 2, 1988, p. 25.
10. Sheldon Cohen, "Sound Effects on Behavior," *Psychology Today,* October 1981, pp. 38–49.
11. "Latest Study on VDTs Adds to Safety Fears," *The Wall Street Journal,* October 20, 1988, p. B1.
12. Jeffrey L. Skeggs, "Effective Lighting Needed Now for Computers to Come," *The Office,* October 1988, pp. 74–75.

RECOMMENDED READING

Alexander, John O. "Toward Real Performance: The Circuit-Breaker Technique." *Supervisory Management,* April 1989, pp. 5–13.

Allerton, Haidee. "The Elements of Performance Management." *Training & Development,* December 1995, pp. 9–10.

Ariss, Sonny S., and Sherman A. Timmins. "Employee Education and Job Performance: Does Education Matter?" *Public Personnel Management,* Spring 1989, pp. 1–9.

Covey, Steven. *The 7 Habits of Highly Effective People.* New York: Simon & Schuster, 1989.

Herzberg, Frederick. *Work and the Nature of Man.* Cleveland, Ohio: World Publishing, 1966.

Jaffe, Dennis T., and Cynthia D. Scott. *Take This Job and Love It: How to Change Your Work without Changing Your Job.* New York: Simon & Schuster, 1988.

Magee, Richard H., Mary Finn Magee, and Melinda Magee Davies. "A Performance Planning Primer." *Training,* May 1985, pp. 99–101, 129–131.

Novak, Alys. "A Vision for the Future: Ergonomics." *Colorado Business Magazine,* March 1988, pp. 56–61.

Prichard, Robert D. *Measuring and Improving Organizational Productivity: A Practical Guide.* New York: Praeger Publishers, 1990.

Reichheld, Frederick F. "Solving the Productivity Puzzle." *The Wall Street Journal,* March 4, 1996, p. A4.

Robbins, Anthony. *Awaken the Giant Within.* New York: Summit Books, 1991.

Trunzo, James. "Office Computers Create Glaring Problems." *The Wall Street Journal,* October 5, 1987, p. 24.

Walton, Richard E. "From Control to Commitment in the Workplace." *Harvard Business Review,* March–April 1985, pp. 76–84.

Weiner, Edith, and Arnold Brown. *Office Biology: Or Why Tuesday Is Your Most Productive Day and Other Relevant Facts for Survival in the Workplace.* New York: MasterMedia, 1993.

Weiss, Alan. *Managing for Peak Performance: A Guide to the Power (and Pitfalls) of Personal Style.* New York: Harper & Row, 1989.

PART 3

GROUP CHALLENGES

GETTING TO KNOW AND INTERACTING WITH OTHERS

7

INTERPERSONAL AND INFORMAL COMMUNICATION

Here are a few questions to think about as you read this chapter. The answers to some of these questions can be found in your reading; others can only be answered based on your own experiences. Your feelings and ideas about these questions might well be shared with others.

- Is it easier for you to speak or to listen?
- Do you have to work just as hard listening to a speech as you do when preparing a speech?
- Does body language contradict your verbal messages? Which is more honest? Why?
- What are various types of communication networks?
- What are barriers to effective communication?
- What are some examples of ways in which we communicate our feelings visually?
- Should organizations try to "stamp out" the grapevine? Can the grapevine have any useful purpose?

LEARNING GOALS

After studying this chapter, you should be able to:

1. Restate in your own words the idea that "meanings are in the person, not in the message."
2. Describe the communication process and discuss barriers to effective communication.
3. Describe the importance of the following elements in communication:
   a. Attitudes
   b. Emotions
   c. Roles
   d. Nonverbal behavior
   e. Feedback
   f. Perception
4. Describe why listening is an active, not a passive, activity. List six general guidelines for more effective listening.
5. Define and give examples of the four basic levels of communication:
   a. Conventional
   b. Exploratory
   c. Participative
   d. Intimate

6. Describe how proxemics affects our actions.

7. Describe at least five ways by which we can interpret people's feelings through body language.

8. Argue for the importance of the "grapevine" in business organizations and describe:

   a. The people who use it

   b. Its accuracy

   c. Its uses

9. Define and apply the following terms and concepts (in order of first occurrence):

   - communication
   - perception
   - feedback
   - self-disclosure
   - listening
   - distortion
   - filtering
   - semantics
   - body language
   - kinesics
   - proxemics
   - neurolinguistic programming (NLP)
   - whole brain theories
   - informal communication
   - grapevine
   - rumor

THE MEANING OF COMMUNICATION

Communication is simple, isn't it? It's just a matter of A saying to B, "Do this or that activity," and B hearing what A said. Rarely is it that simple—and even then note that B only *hears* A; nothing was said about understanding or acting on what A said. More than 70 to 80 percent of our work lives are spent receiving messages, but we are usually not trained to be listeners. We receive education and training in sending verbal messages—speech—but very little in receiving them.

This chapter is about the not-so-simple interpersonal communication processes, including sending and receiving—listening and understanding—as well as nonverbal communication. We will explore several fundamental principles for helping us to be better communicators, especially better listeners. The next chapter addresses the more formal types of communications in organizations.

Communication is the process of transferring information and understanding *from* one or more persons *to* one or more persons. In the simplest form of communication, one person transfers information to another. In more complex kinds of communication, members of a group transfer information to other members of a group. Comprehension is the only test of a message's success as communication. If the message is *understood*, communication has succeeded. If it is not, communication has failed.

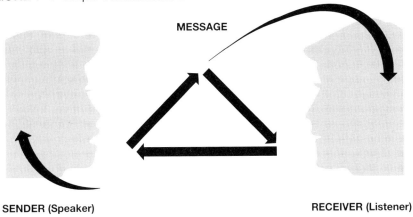

FIGURE 7–1 Simple Communication.

MESSAGE

SENDER (Speaker)

RECEIVER (Listener)

Figure 7–1 shows a simple model of the communication process. In it a speaker (sender) transmits a message to a listener (receiver), who sends back another message.

Communication of all types is so common but so complex that it continues to justify study. We think because we all communicate so frequently in one way or another that we have expertise in communication processes. It is surprising that we don't do a better job, given our experience. But we have a tendency to concentrate on the transmittal process (speaking and writing) rather than the receiving process (listening, reading, and understanding). We think we know more than we do about communication.

There is an old story about three Englishmen riding on a bus. The bus stops. The first man says, "I say there, is this Wembley?" "No," says the second man, "this is Thursday." "So am I," says the third, "let's have a drink." Moral: All too often we hear only what we want to hear!

MEANINGS ARE WITHIN US

The meaning of words exists within ourselves.

How many times have you asked someone, "What do you mean by that?" How many times have you had to answer that question yourself? How do you answer it? Consult a dictionary? Probably not. Most people confronted with that question assemble their thoughts into new combinations of words and phrases and try to get the meaning across in different words. The meaning doesn't change, but the words do. *Meaning* exists *within ourselves,* not in the words we use to express that meaning. The meaning of a message is also called its *semantic* content.

Meaning is that which is intended to be understood. Except in the case of mathematical and some scientific communications, meaning is always *subjective.* Objective meaning in mathematics and science can be communicated because, in those "language systems," one term is never allowed to have more than one meaning. Nor can a term have an ambiguous meaning. "Plus" can never mean "minus," nor can it ever imply "equal to." The rules of mathematical language leave absolutely no room for disagreement, but the word "happy" can mean

100 different things to 100 different people. It can also mean ten different things to the same person in ten different sets of circumstances.

Subjective meaning has multiple meanings.

A word's *subjective* meaning is the *personal significance* of that word to an individual. For some people, "rock music" means stimulating, exciting rhythms, singable melodies, and amusing or provocative lyrics. To others, it means a noisy assault on human ears, with no discernible melodies and inaudible or asinine lyrics. Almost every word we use has different emotional and intellectual meanings for each of us. Even the most ordinary, everyday term will have an astonishing variety of meanings attached to it because the *meaning attached to any object or experience is always experienced personally.*

Semantic meaning cannot be fixed.

The more our messages relate to and overlap the other person's mental and emotional experiences, the more effectively we communicate with each other. And, just as experiences are constantly changing, so are meanings. Thus, meaning can never be fixed permanently. Because no two people can ever give *exactly* the same meaning to anything, good communication demands a high tolerance for ambiguity, especially because the more abstract the term, the more meanings it can have. Consider some of the different meanings that words such as "justice," "freedom," and "faith" have for different people.

Because so many words have ambiguous meanings, to understand fully someone's meaning, we must pay as much attention to the person speaking as to the words being spoken. Voice tones, facial gestures, and body language communicate more meaning than words convey. Effective communicators are person oriented, not word oriented. They know that, although one word may have many meanings, people always give their own meanings to all words.

PERCEPTION

Perception is an individual view of facts and emotions, but our organizational and total worlds are more complex than one person's view. Perceptions are the way in which we interpret circumstances to be—either accurately or in a distorted manner.

Our value systems have a profound effect on what we see or hear happening. We are also influenced by our needs for economic, social, and psychological fulfillment: recognition, love, and self-worth, among others. In other words, we frequently see and hear what our backgrounds would have us perceive.

THE COMMUNICATION PROCESS

Communication is largely a matter of style. Psychologist Robert Hecht says that

> Paying attention to communication styles when you do business can help you avoid people problems. As the old song title explains, "It Ain't What You Do, It's the Way That You Do It." Becoming a student of communication styles can help you be more persuasive, working with other people's natures rather than against them. . . .

Each of us, it seems, has a preferred way of approaching people, tasks, and time. Adapting occasionally to another's communication style can yield impressive results.[1]

Hecht recognizes four basic styles of communicators and advocates using different styles to meet the needs of the intended receiver:

- A **forecaster** is interested in ideas; is imaginative, visionary, innovative.
- An **associator** is interested in personal relationships; is agreeable, adaptable, perceptive.
- A **systematizer** is impressed by details, plans, order; seems rational, steady, methodical.
- An **energizer** is results-now oriented; is spirited, dynamic, decisive, impatient.[2]

To speak coherently, we must select 10 percent of the words and thoughts in our minds and discard or "put on hold" the remaining 90 percent at the same time that we are speaking. It is an amazingly complex process. When we listen, we can hear and comprehend at least double the number of words that we can speak. Therefore, it would seem that listening to and understanding a message would be easier than speaking it, because listening requires less mental activity than does speaking. In our culture, however, verbal messages are frequently received inaccurately, understood poorly, and garbled in retelling. If you have played the "Pass It Along" whisper game, you know how garbled the message may become.

The keys to effective verbal communication are speaking clearly, listening actively, and providing ample feedback—supplemented, when necessary, by "getting it in writing." Having ideas and not knowing how to express them is the same as not having them at all.

MODELS

One way to find out what takes place during any changing process is to construct a model of the process. A model is a visual representation that names, describes, and classifies the separate parts of the process. It also shows how the separate parts connect, interact, and influence one another.

The simple model shown in Figure 7–1 omits so many parts of the communication process that it could be applied just as logically to a temperature control system. Figure 7–2, although still quite simple, shows a more sophisticated model of human communication. In Figure 7–2 the clarity of the transmission is shown as a function of the speaker's attitudes, emotions, role relationships with the listener, and nonverbal behavior. Similarly, the clarity or the reception is shown as a function of the listener's attitudes, emotions, role relationships with the speaker, and nonverbal behavior. **Feedback** is the process of reacting to a person's message, either verbally or nonverbally. The listener is shown as responding to the message by either positive or negative feedback or by a combination of both. Barriers that cause a decrease in communication effectiveness are discussed later in this chapter.

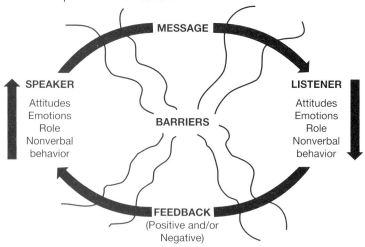

FIGURE 7–2 Complex Communication.

TYPES OF COMMUNICATION NETWORKS

Figure 7–3 shows various types of communication networks. In the chain network, members communicate sequentially. In the wheel network, all communications flow through a central figure. The Y network allows one individual to be the central focal point for three individuals. The circle network allows each person to communicate directly with only two others. In the all-channel network, any member can communicate with any other member but there is one who is considered to be the leader. Finally, in the star network, any member can communicate directly with any other individual.

The relevancy of the different types of networks is very important. Some individuals, leaders, or other persons who play a central role in communication, may become overloaded with communications. They may receive and send too much information to function effectively. Notice that in the centralized networks like the wheel or Y, the central figure has more communications than any other individual. Other members may feel isolated, and satisfaction with the group decreases. Conversely, the circle or star networks do not have a central position. All members have equal opportunities for communication interactions.

ACTION PROJECT 7–1   A PERCEPTION PROJECT (GROUP EXERCISE)

This exercise can be used in a group training session in the following manner: Everyone in the group is given a copy of the following paragraph. One person is asked to read it out loud, and the rest of the group follows along.

> The boys' arrows were nearly gone so they sat down on the grass and stopped hunting. Over at the edge of the woods they saw Henry making a

FIGURE 7–3 Types of Communication Networks.

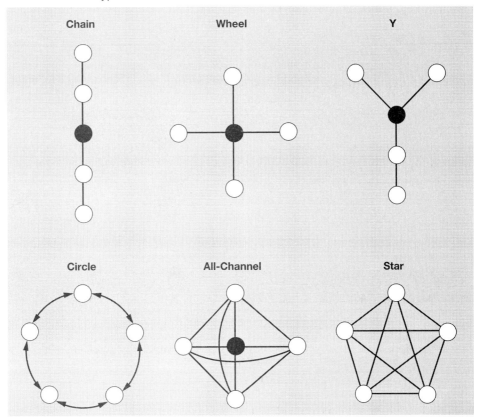

Chain · Wheel · Y · Circle · All-Channel · Star

bow to a little girl who was coming down the road. She had tears in her dress and tears in her eyes. She gave Henry a note which he brought over to the group of young hunters. Read to the boys, it caused great excitement. After a minute but rapid examination of their weapons they ran down the valley. Does were standing at the edge of the woods making an excellent target.

A discussion of what happens to the person who reads the paragraph aloud should follow the reading. You will be surprised how deceiving words can be!

A classic example of this phenomenon is the famous drawing of the woman shown in Figure 7–4. Look carefully. What do you see first—a fashionably dressed young woman or a much older woman with a scarf over her head? Actually, both figures are present. The younger woman is looking away from you, to your left at an angle. The older woman is also looking to your left but toward you at an angle. Do you see them both? Which one you see first and whether or not you can see them both is a matter of perception—your view of facts, age, and physical characteristics.

FIGURE 7–4 What Do You See—a Young Woman, an Old Woman, or Both?

SPEAKING

Speaking is a form of communication that should be confirmed in writing if it is lengthy, complex, or technical. Studies have shown that college freshmen, immediately following a ten-minute lecture, retain only 50 percent of it and forget half of that material within forty-eight hours.

Matters important to a subordinate are particularly susceptible to misinterpretation and should be confirmed in writing. The most common example is the spoken promise of a raise or promotion, which is often misinterpreted after a lapse of time. About 30 percent of a message is lost or distorted after having passed through the first two recipients. When communication is urgent, intermediate layers of communication should be skipped and the message given directly to the person affected.

VOICE TONE

"There are no dull subjects . . . only dull ways of talking."[3] The basic point and purpose of our communication must be clear. But our intent and enthusiasm for the subject matter must also be clear.

Often the tone of our voice will indicate our emotional state to others even if we are not aware of it. To those who know how to interpret them, voice tones can transmit as much or more emotional information as words. Loudly pitched voices can communicate anger no matter how emotionally neutral the dictionary meanings of the words being shouted. Anger can also be conveyed by very intense whispering. The same emotion can be expressed by different tones of voice, and people differ in their reactions to these tones.

EMOTIONS

Emotions can make it hard to listen accurately.

Perhaps the most important emotional factor in good communication is desire. If the desire to understand one's self and others is strong, then understanding usually results. However, one of the largest drawbacks to effective communication is that, as humans, we do not separate ourselves from our emotions. In fact we identify with them. *We become our emotions.* We say, "I am angry" or "I am sad." The intensities of our feelings color everything we think and talk about. When we talk about a problem, we cannot help seeing it in terms of our own past experience and in terms of how we feel at that very moment. Naturally, this can make it more difficult to see the other person's point of view—especially if he or she is also in the throes of some strong emotion.

SENSITIVITY TO OTHERS

Sensitivity to others begins with the *desire* to communicate, which involves the desire to perceive other people's meanings as well as the desire to express one's own. Sensitive people are willing to make the necessary effort to try to understand other frames of reference and other sets of values. Sensitivity to others also requires the ability to recognize and identify one's own responses and perceptions as well as those of others. It is impossible to be sensitive to other people if you are not sensitive to yourself.

SELF-DISCLOSURE

When people communicate with each other, especially face to face, their physical and emotional states of being are to some degree exposed. **Self-disclosure** is the act of opening up your personality—your weaknesses as well as your strengths—to others. This exposure is sometimes disturbing, because our culture places a high value on self-concealment. In a competitive society, concealment is frequently more useful than is self-exposure or self-revelation. If we were to reveal more of ourselves to each other, we would understand each other better.

When people wish to reveal themselves to each other, they talk about *personal* matters such as loves and hates, beliefs and fears, worries and anxieties, and perceptions about work, about themselves, and about each other. Of course, the atmosphere for self-disclosure must be one of mutual acceptance and goodwill, or mutual self-defense systems will automatically switch our psychic "early-warning systems" on to "red alert," thereby raising defensive barriers and short-circuiting communication.

LISTENING

Listening is an active, not passive, activity.[4] Listening can be described as a combination of (1) *hearing*—the physical reception of sound; (2) *understanding*—the interpretation and comprehension of the message; (3) *remembering*—the ability to retain what has been heard; and (4) *acting*—responding by either action or inaction. It is not enough to hear. It is necessary to understand, remember, and act.

The "echo chamber" is not worthwhile feedback.

Henry Thoreau once wrote, "It takes two to speak the truth—one to speak and another to hear." Sometimes people think that they are communicating when all they are really doing is talking a lot and taking some time to get the feedback on what they have said. This has been called the echo-chamber approach to communication. Feedback is important, but there is much more to listening than just feedback.

Bad listening can result in people being injured or killed. The sinking of the *Titanic,* the attack on Pearl Harbor, the Waco, Texas, incident, and some disasters such as the one in Bhopal, India, are classic examples of breakdowns in communication and judgment. Messages were sent; however the listening process broke down.

We are a wasteful society compared to other cultures; we waste our natural resources and energy. And we waste our communication abilities compared to other cultures: We waste our words both in sending and receiving.

In primitive societies, where writing is unknown and *all* messages are transmitted by speech, the accuracy of the transmission is much higher than in countries with high literacy rates. This indicates that illiterate people know how to listen and remember messages better than do literate people.

We just don't listen carefully. Two researchers have suggested that one of the reasons that we are not more careful is because we don't view communication from different listening perspectives. Bennett and Wood say that there are three perspectives or listening styles called results, process, and reasons. Results-style listeners want to hear the bottom line only. Process-style listeners want to be led into a subject with some background on how it all came about, before getting to the bottom line. Reasons-style listeners must be convinced that whatever is being proposed is reasonable, logical, and correct for the situation.[5]

Good listening is paying attention to what is said.

How many times have you had a conversation with someone and not heard a word that was said? Have you ever wanted to shake someone and force him or her into "paying attention" to you while you were speaking? Most people have these experiences from time to time. Listening is a form of *paying attention,* which is an active process involving much more than hearing and seeing. When we pay attention to each other, we are *focusing* our awareness on what is being said and are excluding other external and internal stimuli. This is not always easy, because our senses are constantly scanning the environment for incoming stimuli, much like switched-on radar screens, and our minds are often preoccupied with our own thoughts.

Under normal circumstances, people listen with only about 25 percent efficiency.[6] Good management requires listening more. People who force themselves to talk less begin to lose the desire to talk too much and, in turn, begin to enjoy listening instead. The ability to listen well is not an inherent trait. It is a learned behavior. When we come into this world, we don't have a built-in knowledge of how to listen. That skill must be developed.[7] Unfortunately, it is not developed systematically in our school systems. We teach reading, writing, speaking, and numerous other abilities, but not listening. In the business world Steil has found that, as one advances in management, listening ability becomes increasingly critical.

Problem of preoccupation.

Most of us can speak at about 140 words per minute, but we can comprehend at a much faster rate. This permits us to take mental excursions into other areas as we listen. If we are preoccupied, we can slip away from the conversation quickly to think of another topic. Later we return, hoping not to have missed anything important.

Problem of prejudgment.

Opinions and prejudices can also cause poor listening. The style of the speaker's clothes, facial expression, posture, accent, color of skin, mannerisms, or age can cause a listener to react emotionally and tune out. Trying to put aside preconceived ideas or prejudgments when a person is speaking allows us to open our minds to worthwhile listening.

One sales manager tried to judge the percentage of the sales presentation dialog that was carried out by his own salesperson and the percentage done by prospects—generally hospital purchasing agents, heads of housekeeping, and hospital department heads. He found that there was usually an inverse correlation between the amount of talking by his salesperson and the amount of the resulting order. The "high-percentage talkers" tended to be the newer people in the field, whereas the "low-percentage talkers" were the more experienced and successful ones.

There are no specific rules to follow for effective listening, because what might work well for one person might not work for another. There are, however, some general guidelines that will help you to construct your own rules for more successful listening.

GOOD LISTENING HABITS

1. **Listen without evaluating.** Listen as well as you can without passing judgment. A good listener is not judgmental and doesn't preguess what the speaker is saying.

2. **Don't anticipate.** Sometimes we think we know what people are going to say before they say it—and we say it for them (especially type A personalities)! Often we are wrong. Don't jump the gun by anticipating the next statement; stay in the present and listen.

3. **Avoid excessive note taking.** Note taking is important when we realize that we forget one-third to one-half of what we hear within eight hours. If we prepare a brief, meaningful record, we greatly improve the probability of remembering what was said. If too much time is spent on note taking, real listening suffers.

4. **Don't try to "get" everything.** Listen for the major themes being made rather than for isolated facts.

5. **Don't fake attention.** The same time and energy that are used to fake attention can be put to good use by really paying attention. Actually, it takes less energy than faking does. Acting is hard work.

6. **Review.** Periodically review the portion of the talk given so far. Plan to tell the contents to someone within eight hours.

BARRIERS TO COMMUNICATION

The communication process is complex enough by itself, but there are many barriers that block communication. These include distortion, language/ semantics, defensiveness, noise, and mistrust, among other emotional responses. Let us now examine each of these barriers.

DISTORTION

There are so many distractions to the communication process. Environmental considerations, other demands on our time, and thought processes are just a few of the things that can distract and consequently distort the communication process. **Distortion** includes any distractions like stereotyping. For example, one experiment shows that at any given time in a college classroom, 60 percent are off on a mental trip of their own, 20 percent of both men and women are thinking about sex, and the remaining 20 percent are paying attention to the lecture! No wonder there is distortion and we fail to hear, let alone understand, what is being said.

Figure 7–5 shows an area of distortion common in most communication. The area or arc of distortion is a function of what the sender intends to communicate, and what both the sender and receiver actually do communicate. There may always be some distortion, but effort should be made to minimize the area and to avoid deceitful practices that increase misunderstandings.

Stereotyping is an unfortunate type of distortion. Our preconceived notions or ideas about people, situations, or cultures get in the way of the truth. Remember the wag who said: "Don't confuse me with the facts, my mind is made up!" As noted, we hear and perceive what we want to hear.

Filtering is another example of distortion where the receiver hears only what she or he wants to hear. The receiver only acknowledges certain information and may use that information to make the message more clear.

FIGURE 7–5 Area of Communication Distortion.

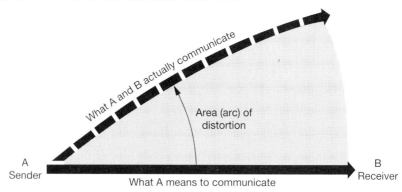

Here is a topic that might develop some strong contrasting feelings between people. Pair off with another student and take opposite views on the topic. Argue for five minutes for your special viewpoint; then engage in Carl Rogers's *Repeat My View* game, where the receiver has to repeat the view of the sender. See if you don't develop a new appreciation or understanding for the other person's point of view.

Thousands, perhaps even millions, of illegal aliens are in the United States, and many are working in our industries. They are depriving our citizens of potential employment; they are not paying taxes, yet they are receiving welfare.

Many businesses feel that they must compete in the open marketplace. If they can pay illegal aliens less than the prevailing wage rate, they can in turn sell a product cheaper to the public. By such a method, the public benefits. It is certainly cheaper than sending our raw goods or parts to a foreign country to be processed or assembled and then bringing them back to the United States to sell.

Are you for or against aliens remaining in the United States?

LANGUAGE/SEMANTICS

There are honest differences in language, among cultures, and even within families. **Semantics** refers to the meanings given to individual words. Each of us may give different meanings to the same word. We may even give different meanings to the same word under different circumstances. The word "love" has many different meanings. Another example is that a parent may ask teenagers what they are going to do with their lives—meaning, what occupations, what job expectations, and so on are contemplated. The teenagers, on the other hand, may perceive the question to mean life-style expectations—and there will probably be a different time perspective as well. That is, the parent probably means for a career or lifetime; the teenager may mean the next five years at the most.

DEFENSIVENESS

Good communication depends on the organizational and communication climate or culture. If there are not too many taboo subjects in the organization or between boss and subordinate, we can expect an entirely different climate than if all transactions are conducted at arm's length, that is, with suspicion or wariness on the part of both sender and receiver. Supportive and defensive characteristics are contrasted in Figure 7–6.

The defensive climate can be distinguished from a supportive climate where there is more mutuality of objectives, openness, and understanding. The supportive climate is recognized as follows:

1. People seem interested; they listen.
2. People don't seem hurried; they imply by body movements that they are not bored/not busy, and that they want to hear what an individual has to say.

FIGURE 7-6 A Contrast of Communication Climates. Source: Adapted from Jack R. Gibb, "Defensive Communication," *Journal of Communication,* September 1961, pp. 141–148.

DEFENSIVE CLIMATE		SUPPORTIVE CLIMATE
Evaluation	Communication that appears to "judge" the other person increases defensiveness.	Description
Control	Communication that is used to control the receiver evokes resistance.	Problem orientation
Strategy	Perception of the sender engaging in a strategy involving ambiguous motivations causes receivers to become defensive.	Spontaneity
Neutrality	Perception that neutrality in communication indicates a lack of concern for the receivers' welfare causes receivers to become defensive.	Empathy
Superiority	Communication that indicates superiority in power, wealth, or in other ways arouses defensiveness.	Equality (as human beings)
Certainty	Dogmatic speakers who seem to know the answers, to require no data, tend to put others on guard.	Provisionalism (willing to listen)

3. People who are receivers invite the sender to proceed by asking questions that are directly tied to the sender's preceding statements.

4. People who are receivers don't judge or criticize what is being said for the sake of criticism but request clarification and allow time to correct misunderstandings.

NOISE

The sender must often compete with a number of other stimuli in getting the message through to the receiver; that is, there is physical noise or other externally generated sensations in the system or process. "Noise is . . . an irritant that can prevent employees from working efficiently, and which can prevent managers from being able to collect their thoughts."[8] Physical noise is but one of the many sources of confusion and therefore a barrier to effective communication. So-called background noise may include loud or even soft music or noise in an office, and, depending on the ears of the listener, either hard-rock or elevator music may be distracting to people trying to work in nearby environments.

Machinery or some other physical noise is a bad enough distractor, but when human-generated noise like loud conversation takes place nearby, it can be equally or even more distracting because of the irregular peaks and valleys of decibels. Some organizations have attempted to cope with the problem by restricting phone calls during certain hours of the day or by providing "think tanks" where employees can go to work in a stress-free environment. Employees who work in offices where noise control is not institutionalized can reduce noise by not using the telephone at certain hours, coming early to the office or staying late, or even by using earplugs or earphones that mask sporadic noise.

MISTRUST

There may be a distinct mistrust between the sender and receiver of a message. That mistrust can be a barrier to effective communication. In the workplace, such a condition can be very negative and telling in explaining poor performance and productivity. According to a survey by pollster Louis Harris, an organizational climate with restructuring, mergers, and acquisitions may be contributing to the workers' mistrust of management. The survey revealed that top executives, when questioned about worker feelings, do not always show a thorough understanding of their employees.[9]

There is a direct link between employee communication and the trust relationship between management and employees. Understanding the goals of the organization and the results of their work give meaning to employee efforts. Valorie McClelland finds that five factors are essential in building communication trust: openness, feedback, congruity, autonomy, and shared values. Mistrust can arise from mixed signals sent by management. Managers need to consider the consistency of their communication to their audiences. Finally, to achieve better communication and less mistrust, managers must consider emerging issues and plan together to make decisions consistent with long-term goals.[10]

FEEDBACK

Have you ever heard the three principles of real estate marketing/selling? Location, location, location! Or financing, financing, financing! Likewise, there are three similar principles of communication: feedback, feedback, feedback! Our communications are only as good as the message that gets through—and the sender needs to know that; that is, the sender needs feedback.

Feedback connects, influences, and interacts with all the other parts of the communication process. Originally, the term *feedback* was used by engineers to refer to the transfer of electrical energy from the output to the input of the same electrical circuit. In computer technology, feedback is used to describe a computer's coded responses or answers to messages. These responses are usually very simple. "Correct," "incorrect," and "not enough data" are the most common. In this manner, the computer "tells" the source of the message whether the message has been received accurately or not. In similar fashion, people tell one another whether their messages are being received correctly or not.

Feedback is verbal and visual.

In face-to-face communication, both the listener and the speaker continuously give feedback to each other (1) nonverbally, by nodding agreement or disagreement, frowning or smiling, yawning or engaging in or avoiding eye contact, and (2) verbally, by the relevance of their questions and responses in relation to what is being discussed.

Those responses likely to be perceived as rewarding (smiles or nods of agreement) are called *positive feedback.* Those perceived as punishing (yawns, signs of inattention) are called *negative feedback.* Feedback enables us to recognize misunderstandings while they are happening so that the messages can be modified and redefined until the confusion is cleared away.

Feedback in its broadest usage includes *all* the verbal and nonverbal responses to a message that are perceived by the sender of that message. Constructive and responsible feedback is:

1. Specific, *not* general
2. Focused on behavior, not the person
3. Considerate of the needs of the receiver
4. Focused on something the receiver can act on
5. Solicited, not imposed
6. Shared information, not advice
7. Well-timed and not overloading
8. Concerned with "what" and "how," not "why"
9. Checked for accuracy

SILENCE

Have you ever decided to let silence speak for you? Silence is a type of feedback. Some experts feel that it is never good to rush in and break the silence in a small conversation. Remember, the more secure the person, the less fearful he or she is of silence. This technique appears to be contrary to what you have learned in speech classes. However, here are some reasons for believing that "silence is golden."

Silent power is used frequently by interviewers and others to force a person to speak. Another example of silence is the *silence of uncertainty*; if a person has a thoughtful look of concentration, it may be risky to break the concentration if you are trying to convince someone or to communicate a specific message. The more important the subject, the greater the patience required: *Silent accord* accompanied by a smile or a nod is a good way in which to respect their choice of communication. *Silent disapproval* may be accompanied by a studied frown, pursed lips, or a shake of the head. Don't rush to speak—wait for the person to verbalize his or her feelings. If you wait for the person to verbalize those feelings, then you can direct your comments to the misgivings rather than to a mere guess.

ACTION PROJECT 7–2 ONE-WAY AND TWO-WAY COMMUNICATION (GROUP EXERCISE)

Have you ever wondered how well you are understood? Can you really tell others exactly what you are thinking? Here is your opportunity to prove to yourself how well you can tell others what is on your mind. To set the stage for the exercise, remember this story:

> This is the case of the night supervisor in a machine shop who didn't know how to do a job on a lathe because there was no blueprint available. The day supervisor was angry, being telephoned at home, but described the

blueprint over the phone. Since the supervisor was angry, the night foreman hesitated to ask any questions. The result of the telephone conversation was seen the next day in $1,000 worth of ruined parts.

Suggestions for the blueprint/drawings are provided in the Instructor's Manual, but you can use any moderately complex drawings such as combinations of circles, rectangles, triangles, or other geometric forms.

PART 1: NO FEEDBACK

Your instructor will ask the class to pair off and move your chairs so that you are sitting back to back. One partner will be able to see the chalkboard and the other will not. The partner who can see the chalkboard will then describe the configuration that is drawn there. The other partner will draw what he hears described on a piece of paper. It is important that the student who is drawing asks no questions and gives no verbal feedback to the other.

The person giving the instructions will be the day supervisor. The other individual will be the night supervisor and will have to have a full blank sheet of paper ready to draw the sketch.

PART 2: CHECK RESULTS

After everyone has finished the drawing, all the night supervisors may turn around and compare their sketches with the configuration drawn on the chalkboard.

PART 3: FEEDBACK

This time the students will reverse roles. The person who first drew the sketch now describes the second configuration to the other partner. This time questions may be asked by both individuals. Repeating questions and repeating answers sometimes helps both to understand just what is meant.

PART 4: CHECK RESULTS

Again after everyone has finished the drawing, all of the night supervisors can check their work. There should be real improvement.

LEVELS OF VERBAL COMMUNICATION

There are four levels of verbal communication (see Figure 7–7). We communicate with strangers and casual acquaintances on the *conventional* level. Conversation on this level is fairly impersonal. It consists of conventional attempts to be polite, to get acquainted, to fill silences, or to seek or convey incidental information or relieve tensions. Remarks such as "Hi, there!," "Do you have the time?," and "Good morning, Homer" show only that we acknowledge the presence of the other person. These comments may open the door to further communication, but are minimal attempts at communicating.

On the second, *exploratory*, level, communication is fact and problem oriented. Here, too, conversation is usually impersonal. Many times our relationships with our coworkers, neighbors, and business contacts are developed on

FIGURE 7–7 Levels of Communication in Building a Relationship.

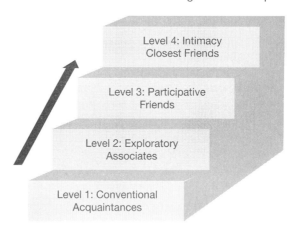

Level 4: Intimacy
Closest Friends

Level 3: Participative
Friends

Level 2: Exploratory
Associates

Level 1: Conventional
Acquaintances

this level and remain on this level for many years. Your relationship is friendly, but not open to very much self-disclosure. The topics of conversation are almost always related to business, not to personal matters. Classroom lectures are usually conducted on the exploratory level. Often in personal transactions a relationship must be established on this level before the participants can move on to the third level.

The third level is *participative*. Here people talk about themselves and engage in self-disclosure. They express their own feelings, describe their own experiences, and discuss their own ideas. While these are *personal subjects*, they are expressed in *fairly safe* ways: "I feel happiest with people my own age" or "I would say that I am more conservative now than I was five years ago." The fourth level, *intimacy*, we reserve for only a select few. Here again people reveal themselves, but now they expose themselves intimately to one another in ways that involve risk: "I get the feeling that you don't really care about me" or "I want you to know I've been on drugs." Intimate relationships are characterized by communication of this kind, which evolves from deeply felt mutual understanding.

NONVERBAL COMMUNICATIONS

BODY LANGUAGE

Body language can convey the opposite of our words.

Body language, or in more scientific terms, **kinesics,** is using your eyes to understand how a person feels without depending on verbal communication. Any nonflexive or reflexive movement of the body can communicate something to the outside world and it often does so more honestly than can verbal communication.

Studies show that at least 70 percent of what is really being communicated between individuals is done nonverbally.[11] This type of communication involves various dimensions: body posture, eye contact, gestures, distance, and proximity, among others.

Our eyes, hands, and bodies send and receive communication signals constantly. Some thirty-three separate major head and facial movements that communicate specific messages have been isolated. When engaged in nonflirtatious conversation, nearly all men and women and boys and girls tend to imitate the sitting and standing postures of someone they admire. People may cross their arms and legs and orient their bodies in specific "withdrawal" postures to shut out people who are perceived as threatening. And most people, regardless of sex or age, will touch each other when they are deeply moved by strong emotions.

But avoid rigid interpretations of body language.

Here is a tip: You might consider deliberately mirroring movements to enhance rapport when you feel that would be useful. And remember to avoid rigid interpretations of nonverbal clues. Never make an interpretation based on a single clue or read too much into the body language. Maybe some people just fold their arms a lot!

POSTURE

Studying a person's posture is a good clue as to how an individual feels about himself or herself. Stooping indicates that the person has the burden of the world on his shoulders, whereas a rigid walk or stance may indicate emotional stress.

Body language even speaks to muggers. Two researchers secretly videotaped people walking in Manhattan's garment district on three working days between 10 A.M. and 12 noon.[12] Each pedestrian was taped for six to eight seconds. The researchers assembled sixty taped segments of an equal number of men and women of varying ages. Then twelve prisoners who had been convicted of assaults on persons were asked how "muggable" the people videotaped were. More than half the convicts rated the same twenty people as either easy or very easy victims. Movements that characterized easy victims included their strides, which were either very long or very short, and their postures, which were awkward. Overall, the people rated most muggable walked as if they were in conflict with themselves.

EYE CONTACT

Everyone knows that a few seconds of eye contact can transmit meanings that might require hundreds of words if spoken. Such idioms as "to make eyes at," "to keep an eye on," or "if looks could kill" reflect the importance of eye contact in many kinds of communication. Someone who sits at a crowded lunch counter looking straight ahead and an airplane passenger who sits with tightly closed eyes are both communicating that they do not wish to speak or be spoken to. And their message is usually interpreted correctly without any need for words.

SPACE OR PROXEMICS

Proxemics is the physical distance that people put between themselves. There are two types of space as a form of communication: social and public. In the social type, for example, the distance in a normal business transaction would be four to seven feet. This distance is used for casual social gatherings, but it can be used as a manipulative tool by a salesperson as well. As the salesperson steps closer to the client, he or she invades the client's inner circle, making the customer feel uncomfortable. The salesperson pressures the client psychologically into a sale. The social space of seven to twelve feet is used for more formal business relations. It is the distance between the "big boss" and you—a way of showing the boss's authority. This distance also allows other activity with another person around without being rude. Public space of twelve to twenty-five feet, as in a teaching situation, allows many to focus their attention on one or more persons.

You will discover that, the closer an individual chooses to sit to another, the more comfortable that person feels about the relationship. In business, the more confident a person is, the closer he or she will decide, even subconsciously, to sit to a partner or associate. Notice that two coworkers sit closer to each other than do the employee and the "boss."

TOUCHING

When we allow ourselves to touch and be touched, we become more open and vulnerable to one another. This openness, in turn, creates a greater sense of receptivity and, consequently, a greater willingness to listen attentively and try to understand the other person's point of view.

We trust those more whom we allow to touch us.

There is an interesting relation between the words "touch" and "tact." The word *tact* derives from the Latin word for "touch." The psychological relationship between the two terms has not been lost altogether, for every day we say of a tactless person that he or she has a "heavy touch." We do *not* trust tactless people because they are likely to wound or betray us. We do trust those we allow to touch us and those we feel it is safe to touch. Trust, or the lack of it, often determines the kind of feedback that is generated during a conversation.

NEUROLINGUISTIC PROGRAMMING AND WHOLE BRAIN THEORIES

Observation and intuition are part of NLP.

Body language has now become part of the study of communications. People have distinctive ways of expressing themselves. Observation and intuition along with verbal and nonverbal language have become the means of neurolinguistic programming. **Neurolinguistic programming (NLP)** is a model for understanding human behavior and a set of communication and learning techniques, based on the belief that people have preferred modes of acquiring and processing information.[13]

NLP indicates that people have a preferred way of learning and communicating. It is a communication technique that is easily learned. *Neuro* refers to the human nervous system and the way it receives and uses communication. *Linguistic* refers to the manner of communication including the words, tone, inflection, and timing. The *programming* aspect refers to the mechanisms for achieving consistency of responses, given the message and manner of communication. It is becoming increasingly important in obtaining the total message of communications.

NLP is not unlike whole brain theories of learning. **Whole brain theories** are based on a presumed preference for one of the two hemispheres of the brain. The right brain is believed to be the seat of creativity and emotion while the left brain is the seat of logic and reason.

PROFILE OF HUMAN BEHAVIOR

VICTORIA "VICKI" LYONS

Victoria Lyons is a professional communicator who "practices what she preaches." Vicki is the technology coordinator serving fifty school districts with short- and long-term technology consultation to incorporate technology as a tool in K–12 curricular areas. She also now teaches or has taught business communications, executive profile development, and other business courses at the secondary, community college, and university levels. Vicki is the author of *Business Writing: Strategies for Word Processing* published by Prentice Hall.

Vicki says that she enjoys "being in informal communication situations. I can see people as individuals and understand their personal motivation. I find informal settings to be more conducive to people feeling more free to communicate and find it is easier to build trust and camaraderie. . . . Every individual brings to any communication process a wealth of knowledge and ability to comprehend and internalize the needs/wants of the people involved. Individuals must use their listening abilities and be able to use their body language and words to convey a sincere message of interest and appreciation for what others are communicating. I find myself treating all people—peers, superiors, students, adults, and children—in a manner that I would like to be treated. This may sound like a cliché, but I find in relating to people as people that I am better able to interact with them on common ground and with common respect."

With regard to perception and voice tone in speaking, Vicki says that "Awareness of one's own communication style helps tremendously with perceiving another's communication style. How I am perceived by others has a direct impact on how my ability to communicate takes place—either positively or negatively. Therefore, I am immensely tuned to others to gauge their reactions to my words and how I say them. This constant awareness helps me change my tone or my message, depending on how I think they are perceiving my message. Although perception is important in formal communications, it is of utmost importance in interpersonal and informal communications because the direct action or reaction of individuals in this context can resolve or enhance conflict, help to reach consensus or put up barriers, and close the line of communication or keep it open in the future. . . . Many times, how something is said is more important in interpersonal communications, than what words are actually spoken. In working with adult learners, they bring to the teacher–student relationship many years of learning in settings where they are the recipients of information and have not had the opportunity to express their knowledge and understanding of many things."

Regarding listening habits and barriers to communication, Vicki comments that "Fully listening to all words and being in tune to the needs of the speaker are absolutely necessary in informal and interpersonal communications. It is not enough to just nod your head while thinking of other things or making a judgment. This activity leads to a complete breakdown in the communication process. All people, from babies to the elderly, want to be listened to and want someone to take interest in their ideas. For example, when I am working with teams of teachers in school districts as they are planning a long-range technology plan, we work very closely in small teams and in one-on-one situations. I must actively listen to each of them, which gives me the opportunity to learn what each one brings to the table and what each person's hidden agenda may be."

Victoria Lyons finds the largest barrier in interpersonal communication is the prejudice that each of us brings to any communication—that is, the knowledge we think we have about another person based on our experience or based on misinformation. She concludes: "Effective communicators must be able to identify when judgments are being made on sound factual information and when they are being made on anecdotal information, media portrayal of individuals, or lack of experience. Working in the educational arena for my professional life, I have worked with vice chancellors of universities, directors of programs of university systems, leaders in state education departments, nontraditional students who have returned to school after fifteen years because their factory jobs no longer exist, students who are first-generation college students from rural or inner-city communities, people whose self-image has deteriorated over many years because our 'society' has a media image of what a successful person is, and many in between. In each case, when I am able to continue to see the individual as a person and not as a 'position' in career or in life, our ability to communicate is strengthened."

INFORMAL CHANNELS

Although informal organizations are bound by no chart on the wall, they are bound by convention, custom, and culture. **Informal communications** grow out of the *social* interactions among people who work together. These communications do not appear as formal patterns of relationships on organization charts. Most theorists believe that informal relationships cannot be charted because they change so rapidly and are so complex. One of the major functions that informal channels serve is that of providing communication routes for members of small groups. Every successful business has at least one healthy, if invisible, communication channel through which to conduct the messages of the informal organization. One major source of employees' information about their companies is the grapevine.

THE GRAPEVINE

The grapevine is the unofficial news carrier.

The **grapevine** is the informal channel of communications between people. It is fast and selective in disseminating limited information. The term is believed to have come into use during the Civil War when the first telegraph lines, used to carry military intelligence, were strung from tree to tree in the pattern of a grapevine. Often messages were garbled or interfered with, and so all rumors, or unofficial messages, came to be known as carried "by the grapevine."

In a complex organization, depending on its size, there can be dozens or hundreds of grapevines. They carry information that is not, or cannot be, transmitted by formal means. Information of this sort includes "I wouldn't ask for that raise today, if I were you. The boss is in a foul mood, and you'd better wait until her mood changes."

You can't eliminate the grapevine.

However, it is impossible to predict the direction, speed, accuracy, or final content of a message carried by the grapevine. Messages may be abbreviated, magnified, restructured, elaborated, or generally twisted out of shape. Sometimes official messages must be issued to counteract the inaccuracies of the grapevine. At other times, the grapevine can spread information very quickly and accurately.

Even though the grapevine's reliability can never be determined with complete certainty, it does serve some useful functions.

The grapevine develops relationships.

1. It satisfies a need that employees have to enjoy friendly relations with their fellow employees.

2. It helps workers make sense out of their work environment, especially in interpreting unclear orders from supervisors.

It also releases anxieties.

3. It acts as a safety valve. When people are confused and unclear about what is going to happen to them, they use the grapevine to release their anxieties. When they feel powerless to direct their destinies, passing a rumor along the grapevine is a way of expressing and releasing negative energy.

4. When people gossip about someone who is not present, they often pass judgment. Some people pass judgment on others to find out where they stand. It is a way of dealing with self-doubt and insecurity.

Research indicates that the grapevine has a role to play in socializing employees to a company, initiating behavioral change, disciplining employees, and providing information. To increase the accuracy of grapevine messages, regular management contact should provide honest, reliable information.[14]

RUMOR

Rumor has no standard of evidence, no basis but feelings.

The grapevine is the channel through which information is disseminated and is based on limited information. A **rumor,** by contrast, is information based on speculation, wishes, or imagination. Rumor is sometimes used as a synonym for the grapevine, but a rumor is not a grapevine message. A rumor has no secure evidence or reliable person's word behind it. Rumors can be correct, but more often they are not. Generally, rumors are spread by people who are very interested in the subject. In the course of a day, the details of a rumor may change, but the theme will remain the same. Sometimes rumors are agents for

Rumor is more often untrue.

wish fulfillments. Why would Mary and Herman start a rumor that everyone in the office is going to get a $25 monthly raise?

Probably just saying it out loud makes them feel good, and they may think that, if the words are said long enough and loud enough to enough people it just might come true. The problem with rumors is that they are especially subject to distortion because people *are* interested in the subject matter and distort those details that don't interest them. They enlarge and elaborate the ones that do.

Stop rumors quickly.

Managers who wish to stop rumor mongering should try to stop only those that are important—rumors that affect morale and productivity. Those should be nipped in the bud as quickly as possible. Face-to-face conversations or group meetings are the best methods for stopping dangerous rumors from spreading. But the person denying the rumor must be known for honesty and be willing to answer questions on the subject.

Rumors express a feeling, may indicate insecurity.

Upwardly moving rumors can provide managers with an understanding of feelings among the workforce. Managers who learn to ask questions such as "What does that rumor mean—is someone insecure and afraid of being fired?" or "Is someone really quitting?" are often provided with truthful answers via the grapevine. Labor relations mediators always make it their business to listen to the rumors that union and company officials spread about each other. They believe that such rumors are projections of fears and that, if they can learn what each side is afraid of, they can achieve a better understanding of complex issues.

ACTION PROJECT 7–3   HOW DO I COMMUNICATE? (INDIVIDUAL-DYAD EXERCISE)

Complete the following exercise on a separate sheet of paper by rating each question on a scale of 1 to 5 (where 5 = strongly agree/very high). When you are through, ask a friend, classmate, or other associate to rate you using the same scale. Then, compare your responses. Too much disparity suggests room for concern and improvement.

	STRONGLY DISAGREE	DISAGREE	NEUTRAL	AGREE	STRONGLY AGREE
1. I think before talking.	1	2	3	4	5
2. I think before writing.	1	2	3	4	5
3. I listen to others without distraction.	1	2	3	4	5
4. I listen to others without interrupting.	1	2	3	4	5
5. I encourage feedback from others by soliciting questions and by other verbal means.	1	2	3	4	5
6. I encourage feedback from others by my body language.	1	2	3	4	5
7. I am careful in selecting understandable words and phrases.	1	2	3	4	5
8. I am brief and to the point in communications.	1	2	3	4	5
9. I encourage free exchange of ideas by withholding judgment about others' ideas.	1	2	3	4	5
10. I listen even if I don't like the person who is talking or otherwise communicating.	1	2	3	4	5
11. I encourage others to communicate by my facial expressions and body language.	1	2	3	4	5
12. I restate what I understand others to have said and/or ask questions to clarify positions.	1	2	3	4	5

Communication is the process by which information and understanding are transferred from one person to another. Effective communication enables people to exercise control over their environment. It is an essential tool for the establishment and maintenance of good social and working relationships. If the messages being communicated are not understood, then communication is poor or nonexistent. Effective communication is a dynamic process that involves constant change and interaction among all the elements that comprise it.

The meaning of a message is always subjective, because meanings reside in people, not in words. A word's meaning is the significance that word has for both speaker and listener, and that significance is likely to vary greatly from person to person. Good communication requires paying as much attention to the person speaking as to the verbal message itself, because so many words have such ambiguous meanings. Barriers to effective communications include distortion, language/semantics, defensiveness, noise, mistrust, and other emotional responses. Failure to listen is another major barrier.

Effective listening depends on paying attention and focusing. It requires understanding, remembering, and acting, as well as hearing. Although there are no specific rules that everyone must follow to become a good listener, there are some general guidelines for acquiring good listening habits.

The communication process can be described in terms of a model in which attitudes, emotions, roles, nonverbal behaviors, perceptions, and feedback are interacting constantly. There are four levels of communication that depend on the degree of intimacy existing between speaker and listener: conventional, exploratory, participative, and intimate.

Body language, or kinesics, is interpreting a person's attitudes by observing his or her body movement. Nonverbal cues are usually more honest than are verbal cues. But remember to avoid rigid interpretations of nonverbal clues, particularly those based on a single clue. Proxemics is the distance people put between themselves. The closer they are to each other, the more comfortable they are in their relationship.

The grapevine is used by nearly everyone in an organization at one time or another. It can carry accurate messages with amazing speed. It can also distort and filter messages beyond recognition. Rumors and facts are carried by the grapevine. Good managers pay attention to grapevine communications as a way of staying in touch with workers' thoughts and feelings.

CASE STUDY 7–1	BODY LANGUAGE SPEAKS LOUDLY IN THE ESCROW OFFICE

An escrow department of a large national bank recently hired a new employee. Monica Chatman is twenty-five years old and single. Prior to being hired as an escrow officer, she worked as a teller and later as a secretary of an escrow office in another firm. Before leaving her former location, Monica was given some training in escrow procedures. Monica is an attractive woman, and this is highlighted by her stylish, yet conservative, method of dress, as seen in her preference for coordinated pantsuits and dress suits.

Although Monica has had previous on-the-job training in escrow, she has not yet reached complete proficiency. In some areas she is still in need of further training and advice. The person closest to Monica, both in physical distance and job responsibilities, is John Baxter—the only other escrow officer. When Monica was hired, she was informed by the department supervisor that John would be the person to go to for help and advice, primarily because both she and John would be working on the same tract of homes for some time.

Being a rather shy person Monica has not made a habit of asking John for his help. She has tended to keep to herself for the most part, and John has not gone out of his way to help break the ice between them. At any rate, Monica doesn't really know if John is capable of giving her any worthy advice, let alone taking the time to help her. Judging from appearances, she feels that John is a pretty sloppy individual both in appearance and in his work. He seems to have trouble handling his own duties. It looks as if he is always a week behind in his work. His desk is constantly a mess. Besides, John's clothes look almost as if he has slept in them.

In spite of his overly casual appearance and method of handling his work, John is competent and qualified in the escrow business. When Monica began working in the department a few weeks back, John had planned on giving her any assistance she would need in handling her new position. However, John soon began to feel that Monica really didn't want his help. Even though Monica seems shy, John believes that she is more stuck up and cold than anything else. To friends, John will readily admit that he is a little chauvinistic when it comes to women, and he has admitted to a close friend in the bank that he is somewhat jealous of Monica's promotions all the way from teller to escrow officer by the age of twenty-five. He also finds it irritating that Monica manages to type so quickly and has her desk clean at the end of each day. It is also John's opinion that Monica looks down on his appearance. As a family man he cannot afford the quality of clothes that Monica, as a single woman, wears each day. As far as John is concerned at the present time, if Monica wishes any help from him, she will have to come and ask for it.

As the supervisor of the escrow department, you have become aware of the problem existing between Monica and John. They should be working together and yet they are not.

1. Given the information supplied, what would you identify as the main problem?

2. What steps would you take to improve the situation?

3. From the description of Monica, what other assumptions might you make about her personality? Could these assumptions lead to faulty generalizations?

4. From the description of John, what other assumptions might you make about his personality? Could these assumptions lead to faulty generalizations?

5. How can you, as supervisor, help both Monica and John overcome their misconceptions of each other?

CASE STUDY 7–2

THERE'S A RUMOR ABOUT MY PROMOTION

Bill Hackaday has worked for the Denver branch of the Tamlon Corporation for three years and is now a junior executive in the Engineering Department. Bill has just returned from a two-week vacation.

This morning Randy Meyers, a coworker and good friend, stops Bill on his way into the building. "Congratulations, Bill. From what I hear, you will apparently be in your own office soon."

"What are you talking about, Randy? I'm not due for a promotion yet."

"I didn't think you were, but the rumor is that Mr. Lundquist is going to promote you."

This information has Bill puzzled. He knows that there are others in line for promotion before him. But then again, he knows that his work is good and that a promotion at this time would be ideal because he is about to be married. With the promotion he could consider purchasing a new home.

When Bill entered the plant, he was not approached by anyone else about the promotion. When he passed Mr. Lundquist in the hallway he mentioned nothing about a promotion. That evening, as Bill prepared to leave work, Mary Stewart, a coworker in the department, asked, "Is it true that you'll be leaving us soon, Bill? I heard that you were being transferred to the Atlanta branch this summer."

"I haven't been told anything about it. Where did you hear about it?"

"Oh, I don't know, someone mentioned it last week and said to keep it quiet until you got back. The word is that either you'll be promoted or transferred to the Atlanta branch."

"But don't you think someone would have said something to me by now?" inquired Bill.

"It sure seems so. I suppose it could be another false rumor. Do you remember the one that was going around last month?"

This information has Bill concerned. He'd like a promotion, but the last thing he wants right now is a transfer.

1. What would you do if you were Bill?
2. What kinds of signs is Bill getting? Are there hidden agendas here?
3. Should you try to track down the source of the rumor, or ignore it and go ahead with your future plans?
4. Should you discuss the rumor or your personal plans with Mr. Lundquist?
5. Are there other ways of checking the validity of the rumor?

DISCUSSION AND STUDY QUESTIONS—TO KEEP YOU THINKING...

1. What are major barriers to effective communication?
2. Describe what is meant by the echo-chamber effect in listening.
3. How does perception affect communication?
4. Explain what is meant by the phrase "meanings are within us."
5. Explain how to combat a rumor.

NOTES

1. Robert M. Hecht, "Key Words: Use the Right 'Communication Style,'" *Success*, December 1989, p. 14.

2. Ibid.

3. Ralph Proodian, "There Are No Dull Subjects," *The Wall Street Journal*, January 4, 1985, p. 18.

4. Margaret Brody, "Listen Up! Do You Really Hear What People Are Saying?" *The American Salesman*, June 1994, pp. 14–15.

5. Ruth T. Bennett and Rosemary V. Wood, "Effective Communication via Listening Styles," *Business*, April–June 1989, pp. 45–48.

6. Glenn Pearce, "Doing Something about Your Listening Skills," *Supervisory Management*, March 1989, pp. 29–34.

7. Jo Procter, "You Haven't Heard a Word I Said: Getting Managers to Listen," *IEEE Transactions on Professional Communication*, March 1994, pp. 18–20.

8. J. H. Foegen, "Quiet, Please!" *SAM Advanced Management Journal*, Winter 1987, p. 17.

9. Louis Harris cited in Stanley J. Modic, "Whatever It Is, It's Not Working," *Industry Week*, July 17, 1989, p. 27.

10. Valorie McClelland, "Employees We Trust," *Personnel Administrator*, September 1988, pp. 137–139.

11. C. Barnum and N. Wolniansky, "Taking Cues from Body Language," *Management Review*, June 1989, pp. 59–60.

12. Betty Grayson and Morris Stein, "Body Language That Speaks to Muggers," *Psychology Today*, August 1980, p. 20.

13. Barbara Dastoor, "Speaking Their Language," *Training and Development*, June 1993, pp. 17–20.

14. David Cathmoir Nicoll, "Acknowledge and Use Your Grapevine," *Management Decision*, 1994, pp. 25–30.

RECOMMENDED READING

Dastoor, Barbara. "Speaking Their Language." *Training and Development*, June 1993, pp. 17–20.

Doyle, Michael, and David Straus. *How to Make Meetings Work.* New York: Berkley Publishing Company, 1993.

Flesch, Rudolf. *The Art of Plain Talk.* New York: Harper & Row, 1946. Also *The Art of Readable Writing.* New York: Harper & Row, 1949.

Galpin, Timothy. "Pruning the Grapevine." *Training & Development*, April 1995, pp. 28–33.

Gunning, Robert. *The Techniques of Clear Writing.* New York: McGraw-Hill, 1952. Gunning also developed the fog index.

Harris, Carol. "NLP: A Pathway to Personal Effectiveness." *Personnel Management*, July 1992, pp. 44–47.

Heyman, Richard. *Why Didn't You Say That in the First Place? How to Be Understood at Work.* San Francisco: Josey-Bass Publishers, 1994.

Knippen, Jay T., and Thad B. Green. "How the Manager Can Use Active Listening." *Public Personnel Management*, Summer 1994, pp. 357–59.

McNerney, Donald J. "Improve Your Communication Skills." *HR Focus*, October 1994, p. 22.

Scully, John P. "People: The Imperfect Communicators." *Quality Progress*, April 1995, pp. 37–39.

Silva, Karen E. *Meetings That Work.* Burr Ridge, Ill.: Richard D. Irwin, 1994.

Slizewski, Patricia. "Tips for Active Listening." *HR Focus*, May 1995, p. 7.

Smith, Bob. "Care and Feeding of the Office Grapevine." *American Management Association*, February 1996, p. 6.

Stuart, Peggy. "Learning-Style Theories." *Personnel Journal*, September 1992, p. 91. Includes a discussion of NLP and whole brain theories.

8

ORGANIZATIONAL DESIGN AND FORMAL COMMUNICATION

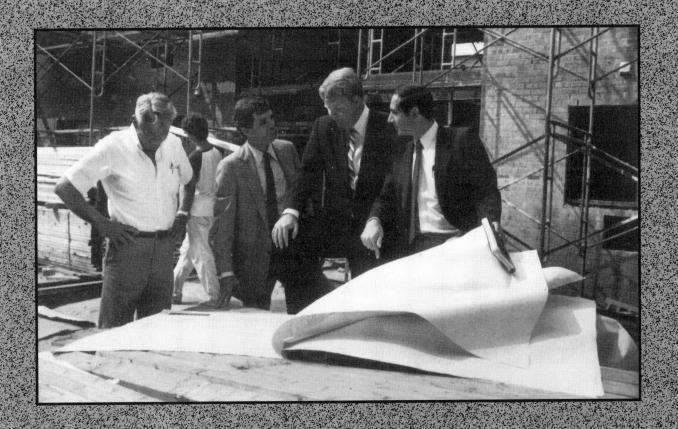

Here are some more questions to challenge your reading and to stimulate your thinking. Not all the answers to these questions will be found in the chapter. Some can only be answered from your own perspective.

- Why is organizational design important to communication?
- What are staff and line functions, and why are they sometimes confused with each other?
- Would you rather work for a tall or a flat organizational-type firm?
- How do formal communications differ from informal ones?
- Why do some supervisors distort messages?
- How can you use the "positive sandwich" technique? Is the positive sandwich technique phony?
- How is cyberspace changing the way we conduct business?
- How are virtual organizations changing the way we conduct business?
- Does the employer have the right to monitor employees' electronic mail (e-mail) and voice mail?
- What are some ways to make the written word easier to read?
- What are some of the international symbols that all people seem to understand?

LEARNING GOALS

After studying this chapter, you should be able to:

1. Compare and contrast organizational design and organizational structure.
2. List the advantages and disadvantages for each of the three types of organizations: line, line–staff, and matrix.
3. Describe the kind of information that vertical communication usually conveys, both upward and downward. Describe the basic elements involved in improving upward and downward communication.
4. Understand the Pygmalion (self-fulfilling prophecy) effect.
5. Explain the importance of good horizontal communication in coordinated group effort and how it can be improved.
6. Identify and discuss examples of virtual organizations, including telecommuting, hotelling, and virtual companies.
7. Identify guideposts for more effective writing and easier reading levels.
8. Know how electronic communications changed organizational communication.

9. Define and apply the following terms and concepts (in order of first occurrence):

- organizational communication
- organizational structure
- organizational design
- flat organizational structure
- span of management
- compulsory advisory service
- completed development work
- project management
- matrix organization

- formal communications
- organization chart
- horizontal communications
- vertical communications
- self-fulfilling prophecy
- positive sandwich technique
- cyberspace
- telecommuting
- hotelling
- virtual company

COMMUNICATING IN ORGANIZATIONS

So many of the human relations problems that we encounter today have their origin in organizational communication or miscommunication. **Organizational communication** is any communication that takes place within a total organization—usually formal and written messages, as opposed to informal, interpersonal communication. This chapter explores the differences in communication among various types of organizations, including more formal types of communications—channels, charts, and groups—within the organizational structure. **Organizational structure** is characterized by mechanisms including communications that are used to coordinate and control the activities of organizational members.

If a group is to cooperate in accomplishing a common purpose, that purpose must be known to all group members, and to be known to all, it must in some way be communicated. All cooperative activities take place within a framework of communication. Without effective communication, there is no cooperation.

An organization comes into being when (1) there are individuals able to communicate with one another (2) who are willing to act (3) to accomplish a common purpose. These are the three basic elements necessary for any organization, and all are equally important for the effective functioning of the organization.

Good communications unify group behavior.

In today's work organizations, communication is the foundation on which all other functions rest. Communication serves not only to transfer information and to help understanding among individuals and groups, but it also unifies group behavior. Unified behavior provides the basis for continuous group cooperation. The simplicity of the organizational structure itself can facilitate good communication.

The organization's structure must be built around the firm's long-range objectives.

Organizational design is the macroscopic term that includes an organization's structure and its processes for decision making, communication and performance management. An organization's structure limits the freedom of individuals to achieve a larger goal. That goal may be questionable or it may conflict with other larger goals. Workers who object to the organization's purposes will not accept the structure of the organization because they do not accept the objectives.

TALL AND FLAT ORGANIZATIONAL STRUCTURES

In complex organizations, there are usually several levels of management, but only one or two levels of workers. Supervisors interact with the employees daily and manage their work closely. Tall and flat organizational structures affect the managerial span of control and, ultimately, communication effectiveness.

Fewer controls are found in flat structures.

A **flat organizational structure,** with widely distributed authority and fewer strict controls, is a good environment for people who like to work independently. A successful flat organization depends primarily on alert supervisors who make good decisions and take responsibility. Poor supervision in a flat organization can lead quickly to management problems because of fewer divisions of labor.

Flat structure allows for a wider span of management.

Entrusting each supervisor with a greater number of subordinates reduces the number of supervisors needed and thus reduces supervisory salaries, which may constitute a large part of the firm's operating costs. If efficiency can be maintained, then the organization will benefit financially through the use of this broader span of control or span of management.

The greater the number of management levels, or the taller the structure, the longer it takes for a message to reach the proper level for action and the more numerous the possibilities for communication breakdown. Some companies, as a result, have been trying to reduce the number of their intermediate management levels without overloading the managers.

The taller the structure, the poorer the communications.

Given an equal number of persons in each organization, an axiom concerning the tall and flat organizational structures is evident: the taller the structure, or the more numerous the levels of management, the poorer the communication; the flatter the structure or the fewer the levels of management, the better the chances that accurate information is being transmitted (see Figure 8–1).

SPAN OF MANAGEMENT

The number supervised is the span of management.

Studies on organizational structure suggest that one person can effectively and directly supervise from twelve to as many as forty people. This number is called the *span of control* or **span of management.** If most workers are doing the same tasks, and the variety of demands is not too great, a manager can supervise many people. Other determining factors for span of management are the geographical

FIGURE 8–1 Organizational Differences Caused by Different Spans of Management for the Same Number of Operative Employees (48).

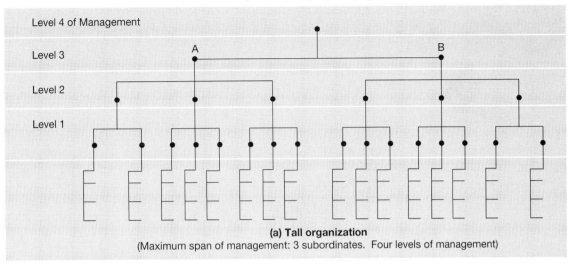

(a) Tall organization
(Maximum span of management: 3 subordinates. Four levels of management)

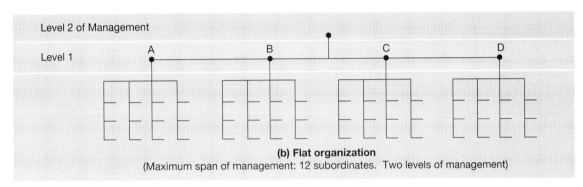

(b) Flat organization
(Maximum span of management: 12 subordinates. Two levels of management)

separation, the experience, and the training of employees and supervisors/managers. As managers ascend the company hierarchy, the number of persons they can supervise effectively diminishes because of the complexity and diversity of the jobs supervised. The span of management is also defined as the number of people with whom one can have meaningful daily face-to-face contact.

LIMITING THE SPAN OF MANAGEMENT. When a supervisor has extensive responsibilities, the workers may feel that no personal attention is being given to their work and their problems. The supervisor may also have difficulty training, communicating with, and controlling the workers if the span is too wide. To remedy the situation, a supervisor can break up the span, either by delegating some authority to informal team leaders or by asking experienced people to serve as trainers. It is important to organize the work so that there is more time for the human relations aspect so vital to any company.

STRETCHING THE SPAN OF MANAGEMENT. Enlarging the span and producing a flatter organization facilitates communications. Bottlenecks caused by too many levels can then be eliminated.

Broadening the span of management lessens the red tape.

The advantage of broadening the supervisory span is less red tape. The structure is compacted, so that operations require a shorter chain of command. A broader span also encourages more extensive delegation and more general, rather than close, supervision. All these factors can raise employee morale.

EXPRESS YOUR OPINION

Consider how many persons each supervisor must manage in your company and whether you consider the span of control is more typical of a tall or a flat organization. Would you consider your company as having a tall or a flat organizational structure? Now that you have made such a determination, do you feel that it is the best type of structure for your company?

Do you feel that the number of people in the company is likely to determine the type of organizational structure? Is the nature of the business or the leadership more important as to the type of organizational structure that will be developed within the company? Rank the following three factors in terms of importance in developing an organizational structure: the size of the company, the nature of the business, and the leadership style used.

ACTION PROJECT 8–1   DRAW YOUR ORGANIZATION CHART (INDIVIDUAL EXERCISE)

Draw the organization chart (hierarchy) for your organization (it may be a student organization, your temporary job, or some social organization).

1.   Show job titles of two or three organizational levels above you.

2.   Show your job title and others on your organizational level (circle your job title).

3.   Show job titles of two or three organizational levels below you.

Suggestion: This exercise is a great "ice-breaker" and may be useful in "putting yourself in perspective" and in discussing your role and status in the organization. You can also add the span of management for each level—that is, the number of individuals reporting directly to each manager.

STAFF AND LINE ORGANIZATIONS

The words *staff* and *line* are the classical terms used to define the traditional divisions of labor in complex organizations. They stem from nineteenth-century military usage and are still employed by the military. In business and industry, generally speaking, a line function is one that contributes directly to the main activity of the business; a staff function is one that assists the line function in an advisory or administrative capacity. Much of the heavy distinction between line and staff is disappearing with downsized organizations.

SEEKING AND GIVING ADVICE

The concept of **compulsory advisory service** states that the advice and counsel of others must at least be heard by decision makers. The advice may not be heeded, but the decision maker must take others' counsel and listen to it. Listening with an open mind to what other people have to say can greatly enlarge the potential of making a good decision. Other people can also act as sounding boards—providing a chance to hear how ideas sound.

Completed development work is a corollary to compulsory advisory service. It means doing a thorough job of problem definition, analysis, weighing of alternatives, and solution recommendations. People who complete their work do not give half-baked advice.

People who make a practice of not consulting others take greater risks in making decisions because they isolate themselves from feedback. On the other hand, by seeking too much advice too much of the time, a person can not only appear to be incapable of making a decision independently but can also undermine his or her own confidence.

LINE STRUCTURE

The supervisor usually functions according to a line structure of authority. In other words, authority is delegated downward in a clearly defined line, from the individual who is the supreme authority, to a subordinate, to a lower subordinate, and so on. The military is a prime example of a tightly structured line organization.

In this type of organizational structure, authority is delegated from the top management to the middle managers, who delegate it to the supervisors, who exercise it over their workers. Many more levels may be included, but the basic chain of command remains the same.

GENERAL STAFF AND SPECIALIZED STAFF

There are two separate types of staff: general and specialized. General staff personnel usually assist division managers in a variety of ways. Specialized staff usually contribute specific skills in very narrow areas of expertise. Examples of general staff include accounting and human resource management. Market research and production planning are examples of positions that require specialized staff.

Staff persons are usually better informed of company activities.

General staff are much more mobile than are line personnel because of the nature of their jobs, especially in factories. Their jobs tend to cut across horizontal divisions and consequently they are much better informed about company affairs than line managers. In recent years, there has been a reduction in general staff. Many companies are downsizing and attempting to save money and increase efficiency by clearing out staff members at headquarters.

Staff persons have a greater motivation to communicate.

Specialized staff personnel often find themselves in conflict with line managers because the line managers fear that new production methods will

FIGURE 8–2 Types of Staff Positions.

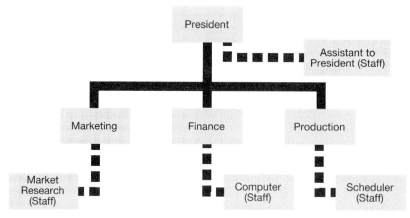

Staff must sell ideas, not give commands.

render their jobs obsolete. Poor communications, hostility, and even sabotage are not uncommon between line and staff personnel. While many specialists lack command or line authority, they have greater motivation to communicate because they realize that their success depends on selling their ideas to others. A specialist has a shorter communication chain to higher management, which, as a result, usually gives him or her more mobility than operating workers (see Figure 8–2).

The concept of group work teams has become an important aspect of modern organizational theory. Traditional organizations utilized a pattern of one-to-one relationships between organization members in which supervisors dealt with subordinates individually. Modern concepts emphasize group relationships and task force teams in accord with the new emphasis on better human relations and fuller participation among and by all employees. The manager must have a good grasp not only of group dynamics but of each person involved.

Group participation is, in fact, sometimes referred to as human relations because its primary function is to give employees a voice in what they do and how they do it. Available evidence indicates that, when a solution to a problem is worked out by the group to be affected by the change, it is accepted much more readily than when it is superimposed from above.

PROJECT MANAGEMENT

Some unique communication problems arise in project management. **Project management** is a method for managing short-term, specific tasks. Most projects are completed by use of project teams or a special type of matrix organization. The **matrix organization** is a team of people brought together from different departments to work on a product or project. Temporarily, a person may have people report to him or her who are normally above or below in rank.

FIGURE 8–3 Matrix Organization Structure.

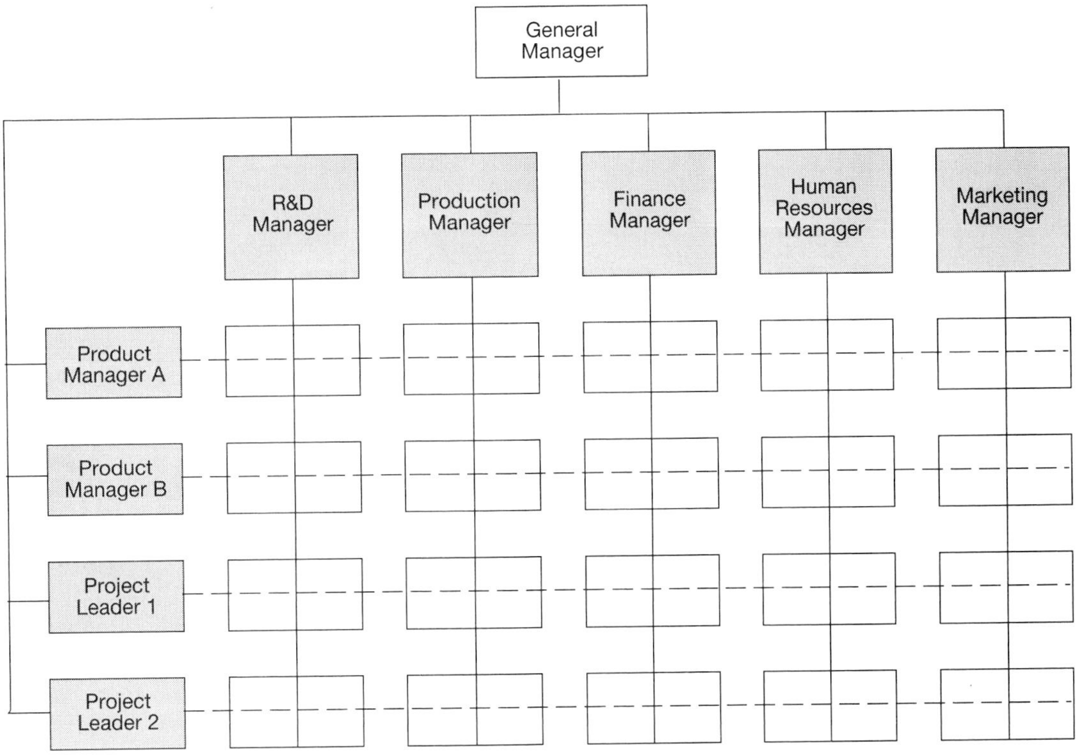

PROJECT TEAMS AND MATRIX ORGANIZATIONS

Under a team project, a boss may report to an employee.

A matrix is often a temporary structure.

The project manager may have no permanent authority in the organizational structure, but be an expert in the specific project and as such coordinate, direct, and control the various members of the project team. In effect, a matrix organization is a second form of organization overlaid on the line chain of command (Figure 8–3).

Computer engineers, those who install electronic data processing equipment or automated machinery, often function in this capacity. As short-term programs are established, special groups are created to handle them. This arrangement results in temporary structures and can put a strain on relationships, or it can help break down the rigid barriers of formal communications (see Figure 8–4). Product managers or project leaders have temporary authority over their projects because they report to a general manager the same as the functional managers.

Integrated machine production and data processing can be developed into what might be called a "horizontal plane." Such a combination of two different units into a workable team cuts across superior–subordinate relationships that may be affecting the jobs of employees in different areas. This new matrix plan superimposes a new vertical structure whose chain of command can help to solve or cause obvious difficulties.

Project managers who have to solve new problems must learn to deal horizontally with their peers and diagonally with workers at different levels. Following established, formal, vertical routes is costlier, takes more time, and is too disruptive.

FIGURE 8–4 A Matrix Organization or Project Team as Related to the Regular Chain of Command.

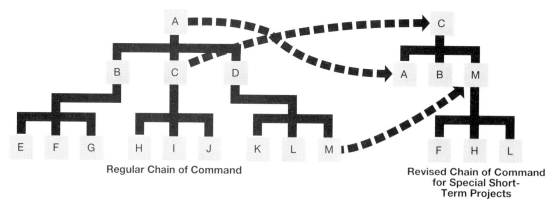

Regular Chain of Command

Revised Chain of Command for Special Short-Term Projects

PROBLEMS AND THEIR PREVENTION IN MATRIX ORGANIZATIONS

The matrix design has many benefits, but to reap them managers need to know how to prevent and treat its problems.[1]

1. **Problem.** There is a tendency toward anarchy or no recognizable boss. This can happen quickly if the project is about to confront a crisis. The solution is to establish more structure and to have one person oversee the project until the situation can be resolved.

2. **Problem.** A power struggle can take place early in a matrix organization. One answer is to develop a balance of power or dual command. Strong statements of equal strength and friendly competition must be stressed. If this method does not work, then an overseer must be appointed.

3. **Problem.** Severe groupthink can emerge. That may lead to many meetings at which only group decisions are made. Such an attitude could be fatal to a project. Responsibilities must be established as to workloads and decisions that can be made by individuals as well as to duties that can be decided only by the group.

Keeping the channels of communication open and clear, especially in a matrix organization, can make the difference between an effective and ineffective organization.

COMMUNICATION CHANNELS

Formal communication is a part of all organizations.

Communication channels are the paths along which messages travel from one person to another, or from one group to another, or both. All organizations use both formal and informal channels of communication. Formal channels are the communication chains and networks that determine the direction and flow of official messages to all the different members and divisions of an organization.

Formal communication channels are an integral part of any organizational structure. They stem from the rules and customs that govern the distribution of authority, rank, and type of work within the organization.

FORMAL COMMUNICATIONS

Formal communications are structured, stable methods of communicating between people and their superiors, subordinates, or peers. Customs are followed with regard to authority, rank, and type of work. Official communications usually must travel between and within separate divisions, along structural paths.

In complex organizations, there are usually several levels of management, but only one or two levels of workers. Management levels tend to increase in number and complexity, but worker levels tend to remain stationary. The greater the number of levels of managers, the longer the communication chain and the greater the possibilities for communication breakdowns. The move toward flatter organizations has the positive benefits of reducing levels of communication. There is less room for autonomy and self-expression in tall organizations with many levels of management hierarchy. Consequently, the types of people working in those organizations usually receive more direction and control. Conversely, flat organizations with fewer levels of management require flexibility and versatility on the parts of both supervisors and their employees.

ORGANIZATION CHARTS

Organization charts show the formal channel of communication.

An **organization chart** showing an organization's structure is a kind of anatomical drawing indicating the formal, *official* channels through which messages must travel. Flowing around the formal structure are complicated, ever-changing networks of informal, *unofficial* channels.

An organization chart cannot indicate *all* the formal channels, only the major ones. A chart that showed all the formal paths that messages must travel would look more like a maze or a Chinese puzzle than a chart. For example, administrative assistants are seldom shown on charts, but in large organizations most messages are routed through these individuals. The efficiency of a communication system often depends on how well the administrative assistants of vice presidents are relating to one another.

The organization chart is not sacred. Charting the organization makes sense to give some continuity for management and other employees. But new organization theory suggests that "we are not hapless beings caught in the grip of forces we can do little about. . . . Organization has been made by man; it can be changed by man. . . . The fault is not in organization, in short; it is in our worship of it."[2]

CHAIN OF COMMAND

An organization chart shows the chain of command but, again, those formal channels should not be set in stone. Experience has suggested that, by following the principle of the chain of command, with accountability following one level at a time from the top of the company to the bottom, an organization can have a more efficient, productive operation and a more cohesive workforce. The main purpose of the organizational chain of command is to establish responsibility and effective communication at every level. This approach offers several advantages, including having decisions made on the spot.[3]

HORIZONTAL COMMUNICATIONS

Horizontal communications are used when members at the same level in the hierarchy of authority communicate with one another; that is, one worker to another or one manager to another. Horizontal channels operate both formally and informally, and officially and unofficially. A sales manager who tells a plant manager to increase production next month because a clever advertising campaign has paid off and sales are pouring in would use formal channels for the message. But the plant manager might have given the sales manager a great idea for the advertising campaign over a drink a few months previously—surely an informal situation. Many workers and managers use informal horizontal channels often and with great success. They rely on friendships and favors given and owed as a way to ignore or expedite requests, to evade rules, or to change the work flow.

The problems associated with horizontal communications seldom stem from a lack of messages among individuals or groups but, rather, from the large numbers and various types of messages that are sent and received. Work is often duplicated unnecessarily or is delayed inordinately because information needed in one department is available only in another, and sometimes no one in the department needing the information knows that it exists.

VERTICAL COMMUNICATIONS

Vertical communications flow in two directions, up and down. However, although downward and upward communications travel along the same paths, the content, nature, and problems of the two vary considerably. The differences between them can be compared to the force of water when it flows up or down. Downward communication is like water streaming down from a waterfall. It pours down easily with great force and wets a large area; upward communication is like a small spurt of water shooting up from a fountain against the pull of gravity. The higher it travels, the more it loses its force. Official top-to-bottom communication channels flow down with great force and reach a great many people, but official bottom-to-top channels flow up with difficulty and reach relatively few people, as shown in Figure 8–5.

It is easier to communicate downward than upward.

FIGURE 8–5 Differences between Downward and Upward Communications.

MANAGER

MANAGER

DOWNWARD
COMMUNICATIONS
HIT WITH
IMPACT

UPWARD
COMMUNICATIONS
MAY DRIFT UP OR
MAY NOT EVEN
REACH THE
INTENDED
PERSON

EMPLOYEE

EMPLOYEE

DOWNWARD COMMUNICATIONS

To increase the effectiveness of their firms, many executives have decided to shift decision making related to everyday operations downward to middle-level employees, who are closer to operations and to the customer.

Downward communication is the fastest form of communication.

Downward communication is the fastest form in the vertical chain of communication, is accepted more at face value, and is reacted to more vigorously. Matters that affect employees directly, such as salaries, job security, and fringe benefits, are of real interest to them. Studies show that this type of information ranks highest with employees, whether they are managers, supervisors, or shop workers.

Managers only *think*
they know the problems
of their employees!

One problem of downward communiqués is that many managers think they understand the problems of their employees; however, their employees are not likely to agree. This fundamental difference in perception tends to exist at each level in an organization, thereby making communication more difficult.

Often managers become overconfident and take less care with their downward communications. Other, more successful companies hold regularly scheduled meetings of their management personnel each Monday morning where everyone is required to stand up. Things tend to get accomplished in a hurry. Many banks, savings and loan associations, and retail stores do this during the fifteen-minute period just prior to the morning opening. There is an increasing use of short meetings that include warm-up exercises and singing of company songs—spinoffs of Japanese management ideas.

WRITTEN VERSUS ORAL DOWNWARD COMMUNICATIONS

Written communications traveling along downward channels range from handwritten messages pinned to bulletin boards to typed interoffice memos, printed job descriptions, circulars, handbooks, job manuals, and electronic mail. The number of internal publications and memoranda as well as external publications continues to increase.

Research suggests that those who rely principally on memos, letters, and manuals for communicating messages downward not only fall short of achieving understanding, credibility, and acceptance, but they actually contribute to new problems of misunderstandings, disbelief, and rejection. Incredible amounts of time, money, and materials are wasted on written communications that serve little purpose.

Sharing information in a brief verbal meeting can serve at least two purposes: (1) less paperwork and (2) better interpersonal communication, relationships, and overall understanding.

When emotions are
"high," communicate
with them in person.

Some employees are informed best in writing, some orally, and some both ways. And there are those who must be told repeatedly for the message to have any substantial impact. Any tender topics are best handled orally rather than in writing. Firing an employee or arbitrating conflicts among workers is best handled in person. When emotions are high or financial stakes are great, face-to-face communications are a must.

Many companies have begun to change their basic views about internal communication systems. One corporation banished its "Never say it—write it!" slogan and replaced it with "Talk it over—jot it down." No one denies that written, downward communication serves an extremely important function when complex, hard-to-remember facts and details must be transmitted precisely and preserved with care. But paper is often the wrong medium for the "getting-things-done" kind of message that demands quick decisions in response.

SELF-FULFILLING PROPHECY

Do you believe in self-fulfilling prophecy? The **self-fulfilling prophecy** means that what you expect of others determines the reactions of others. If you expect low achievement, people will produce little. If treated as inferior, lazy, materialistic, or irresponsible, people become so. People in different organizational settings, if treated as responsible, independent, understanding, goal achieving, and creative, tend to become so. The term *Pygmalion management* is derived from this concept. Management can expect elegant performance from an employee if the training is good and, most important, if the expectations and responsibilities are high enough. Is there some truth in this theory that is expressed by leaders through their actions and attitudes?

EXPRESS YOUR OPINION	Do you believe that there is some truth to the self-fulfilling prophecy or the Pygmalion theory? Do you believe that your parents or teachers may have influenced you either in a positive or negative way? Can you name people who have influenced you in your accomplishments or career direction? It is usually easier to see how others have influenced us, but harder to see how we have influenced others. Whom do you feel you have influenced through the self-fulfilling prophecy? Have you expressed such feelings subtly to a coworker or to those at home?
	Do you suppose that such an attitude or belief in the Pygmalion theory might be an excuse for not being successful? "I am not successful, because my father didn't expect much out of me!" Can we overcome such a negative influence?

HOW TO HANDLE BAD NEWS

Managers frequently must transmit negative messages, such as denying salary raises, job promotions, or transfers. The positive sandwich may work most effectively in these situations.

Use the "positive sandwich" to handle negative news.

Basically, the **positive sandwich technique** provides bad news between slices of good feelings and can be used in handling negative news. Start with a good slice of bread spread generously with good news and information that is true and supportive. Then express the bad news quickly and simply as a slice of thin ham, followed up with another piece of bread bearing supportive reasons and assurances.

Whether the message is written or oral, you have to prevent the disappointing news from turning your subordinate against you. The opening remarks or sentences should strengthen whatever good feeling exists. Certainly, by asserting the bad news right at the beginning, you would be giving too much emphasis to it and jeopardizing existing goodwill. Equally vital to bad news situations is the last third of the positive sandwich, a positive ending. A positive closing can tip the scales toward the retention of the employee's goodwill.

There is another viewpoint on delivering bad news. Get it out of the way first and then positively reinforce the recipient of the bad news. Advocates of this approach say the positive sandwich technique is phony and only prolongs the inevitable. What do you think?

Upward communication occurs when someone in a lower position in the company communicates information, ideas, suggestions, opinions, or grievances to someone higher. When a typist drops a suggestion in the company suggestion box, or a supervisor reports a breakdown in the machinery to the plant manager, or a copyeditor suggests a sales campaign to the advertising manager, or the results of a survey about workers' attitudes are distributed to the vice president—all of these communications travel by upward routes.

The first step toward building a successful upward communication program is to gain the endorsement of top management. Next, an anonymous communication audit of all employees will provide insight into how employees understand the goals of the business and how employees feel about their jobs and the communication climate. Including open-ended questions in the survey will provide better opportunity for employees to express their true concerns.

The best "open door" is when the supervisor walks out to the workers.

Other mechanisms that are available for encouraging upward communications include (1) employee–management meetings, (2) speak-out sessions, (3) quality circles, (4) employee ombudsmen positions, (5) newsletters, and (6) the open-door policy. Employees consider access to upper management, involvement in decision making, information about the business, feedback to suggestions, and a climate of trust to be the most effective methods of communication.[4]

For upward communications to be effective, managerial staffs and their subordinate employees must work together in a spirit of trust and goodwill. Suppose that a company maintains a conspicuously placed suggestion box that gets a great deal of use but that the employees never receive managerial feedback on any of their suggestions; they will probably take a cynical view of management's sincerity. On the other hand, when workers know that their messages are treated with respect and attention, the company benefits in at least four important ways. The acronym OPEN gives good reason why upward communications are of value.

BEING OPEN PROVIDES GOOD REASONS FOR GOOD UPWARD COMMUNICATIONS

O **Offers ideas.** Employees often have valuable ideas and suggestions about increasing product quality and production rates. The research and design department does not have a monopoly on all good ideas.

P **Prevents problems.** When messages travel upward easily, managers can stay informed about potentially troublesome situations and prevent union problems.

E **Encourages acceptance.** Effective upward communication reveals to management the degree of acceptance and credibility that company policies have among employees.

N **Notable participation.** Free, open upward communication stimulates employees to work more willingly when they have some say in planning or evaluating those policies.

Another factor in upward communication is the increasing emphasis on quality management (TQM and other ideas) discussed earlier. If employees are free to emphasize quality and even shut down operations when quality is substandard, then communication must be open in all directions—especially upward.

In the following *Profile of Human Behavior,* Larry Denny explains that formal documentation, "constant communication among the people," and other concepts are vital to the success and survival of businesses. He continues by noting that "internal communication can break down as the number of employees grows" so it is important to facilitate communication by keeping all channels open.

PROFILE OF HUMAN BEHAVIOR

LARRY DENNY

"Doing Well What Comes Naturally"
When Larry Denny decided to draw up a quality management program for Den-Con, his Oklahoma City firm, he wasn't taking on a terrific burden.

What his program really amounted to, Denny says, was "the documentation of what we already had under way; we described in detail the very precise flow of everything we were doing, and why we were doing it."

That document of perhaps thirty pages has grown about ten times as thick since 1983, "but we don't do things a lot differently," Denny says. Instead, his small company, which manufactures oil-drilling equipment, has defined ever more precisely how it does well what it does. Denny's systematic attention to quality permitted his small firm to survive—and then to thrive—despite the drop in world oil prices in the 1980s and the resulting drop in drilling.

Denny had only three or four employees when he drew up his first quality program (he now has thirteen). Such tiny firms must practice what amounts to total quality management, even if they do not give it that label. The essentials of TQM—among them, an intense focus on the customer, constant communication among the people in the business, and an unflagging awareness of anything that might signal a problem—are vital not just to the success but to the very survival of the smallest businesses.

When success comes and survival is no longer the immediate issue, a company's growth can weaken its commitment to quality management. What is most convenient or efficient internally can start to seem more important than what's best for the customer. Internal communication can break down as the number of employees grows.

Thanks to the momentum built up when it was small, the business may grow and prosper for years, but eventually sales lag or customer complaints rise. It's at this stage that many large and medium size companies turn to formal total quality management programs, in a frequently successful—but often painful— effort to recapture the spark that helped make them big in the first place.

As Patrick L. Townsend, a quality consultant and coauthor with Joan E. Gebhardt of *Quality in Action* (John Wiley & Sons), puts it: "The principles are the same," whether the company is large or small; "the trick is to apply them consciously."

Larry Denny's Den-Con is a case in point. So successful has he been at using his quality program to withstand the energy industry's economic reverses that Den-Con was designated a 1992 Blue Chip Enterprise for Oklahoma in the national competition sponsored by Connecticut Mutual Life Insurance Co., the U.S. Chamber of Commerce, and *Nation's Business.*

Denny started his business in California in 1975 and moved it to Oklahoma City in 1981. After many years of working for larger companies, he says, "there were a lot of things I wanted to do with my own company."

He started with a strong bias in favor of prevention—a central tenet of the quality movement. For example, he knew that he didn't want to heat-treat the castings for his products himself; he wanted to buy castings that were heat-treated and ready to use, even though they would be more expensive. That way, there wouldn't be any question, if cracks or other defects showed up in the castings, that they were the foundry's responsibility. By establishing such ground rules at the start, Denny didn't eliminate all problems—but he did prevent many *chronic* problems that would have been inevitable otherwise.

Den-Con makes pipe-handling tools—in particular, devices that grip pipe as it is being put down into a hole—of a kind that are common throughout the industry. A reputation for high quality can be tremendously important to a company that makes such products, especially if it is a small firm like Den-Con. "Small companies in our industry are given no tolerance for error," Denny says.

When he entered the international marketplace, he recalls, he was trying to sell to multinational drilling contractors, in competition with a much larger company. Better delivery and lower prices alone wouldn't be enough; he had to find some way to make Den-Con credible despite its size. Den-Con's quality program "allowed us to go out to the industry and show people, when they questioned our credibility, that we knew what we were doing," he says.

Although most of Denny's customers are much larger companies, most of his suppliers are small enough that he's an important customer to them. He has cultivated relationships with them of the kind that are typical of TQM companies. "We've made no secret of the fact that everybody is constantly being evaluated," he says. "There are a lot of shops out there that want the work. On the other hand, we're loyal." Den-Con has been working with its principal foundry, for example, since 1981.

For all of its TQM characteristics, Den-Con may not count as a TQM company in the strictest sense, because Denny hasn't methodically embraced all the elements that most experts believe should be part of a complete quality plan. He places no special emphasis on employee empowerment, for example, or on building teams.

And that's just the point: In a very small company, where so much of TQM comes naturally, the idea should be to move into conscious, formal TQM as it is needed, and where it will do the most good.

SOURCE: Michael Barrier, "Doing Well What Comes Naturally," *Nation's Business*, September 1992, pp. 25–26. Reprinted by permission. Copyright © 1992, U.S. Chamber of Commerce.

SMALL GROUP COMMUNICATIONS

Groups satisfy needs.

Most people spend a great deal of time communicating in small groups. Our lives revolve around our families, classes, work teams, quality circles, athletic teams, and committees—and this list could be extended much further. The groups that most influence people's behavior become their reference groups: the groups with whom values, attitudes, and beliefs are shared. Groups also provide people with opportunities to satisfy their needs for recognition and achievement. They satisfy other wishes too, such as those for dominance and autonomy.

A person with high credibility has great influence.

Small-group interaction is dynamic and involves a lot of feedback. The social relations within a small group influence the kind of communication that takes place, and, in turn, the nature of the communication will influence social relations. For example, a person who has high credibility will have much more influence than will someone of high status but low credibility. High credibility confers a kind of power on the person who has it.

In business organizations especially, the power relations within a group determine to a large extent the kind of communication that exists. When power is concentrated in too few high-status people, lower status group members will feel that their needs are not being met, and communication will be less than effective. Communication is also affected within a group by the degree of cooperation and competition among the group members. Additional information on group behavior and dynamics is presented in Chapter 9.

ACTION PROJECT 8–2   HIDDEN AGENDAS IN GROUP DISCUSSIONS (GROUP EXERCISE)

Working with a group and achieving a common goal can be very satisfying. However, we all have different backgrounds and different motives for our actions. In groups you will be asked to arrive at a group consensus, and individual contributions will not be considered in the final evaluation.

However, each member of the group will have a hidden agenda to try to achieve. Thus two things will be taking place at once. The group will try to arrive at a group decision, and each person will try to accomplish his or her personal goal.

INSTRUCTIONS

Part 1: Formation of Groups
Form groups of five persons. After the members of the group become acquainted, read the following problem.

Part 2: The Problem
An employee in your manufacturing company was caught selling marijuana. During the review of his records it was discovered that he had been warned about smoking marijuana on the job. It was noted in his records that he was arrested for selling drugs off the company grounds. The records also revealed that the nineteen-year-old employee comes from a very poor background with divorced parents and an alcoholic father. He is currently living with his mother who had a nervous breakdown after the divorce.

Which one of the following possible solutions would you recommend?

1. Fire the employee.
2. Send him to the police and let them handle the problem.
3. Give him one more warning with the understanding that the next infraction means losing his job.
4. Release the young employee with a verbal warning.
5. Work with the local authorities and recommend a one-year probation. Keep him in your employ as long as he obeys the probation rules.
6. Recommend he attend a rehabilitation clinic.

DISCUSSION

Part 1: Hidden Agenda

On some occasions people will have hidden agendas, some of which may be subconscious. Such agenda items may be to impress one's boss, or to influence the group by dominating the discussion, or to try to influence the group to make a decision that will be in some way beneficial to the person in question. Now each of you will be given a hidden agenda item by the instructor to try to accomplish. Be sure not to reveal your hidden agenda to the group.

Part 2: Arrive at an Answer

The instructor will give you ten to fifteen minutes to arrive at a group answer.

SHARING YOUR GROUP'S ANSWER

One person from each group will announce to the rest of the class the group decision and explain why it was felt to be the best answer.

REGROUPING

Part 1: Sharing Your Hidden Agenda

Now share your hidden agenda with the group. Did you achieve your objective? Did others in the group discover your hidden motive? They shouldn't have!

Part 2: Changing Your Mind

Now that you have heard the feelings of other groups, would your group change its opinion? Is it sometimes best to wait to make decisions on some matters until more opinions have been collected?

CYBERSPACE: ELECTRONIC COMMUNICATION AND VIRTUAL ORGANIZATIONS

As we move into the twenty-first century, computers and electronic media are transforming organizational communication. Mainframe computers and technologically sophisticated electronic switching systems first made transfer of information easier. Then, minicomputers and personal computers, and now cyberspace, make this information transfer an everyday occurrence.

Cyberspace is a term used to describe "the *medium* in which electronic communications flow and computer software operates . . . in general, the term is now used to refer to the concept of global systems interconnection whereby every computer and telecommunications network will come to have access to the same information space."[5] By 2000 this mass interconnection will provide a single source of electronic data and communications that will be crucial to the operations of all businesses.

The electronic revolution promises fast communications.

The electronic revolution is promising that business at the turn of the century will be fast, more efficient, and challenging. Now is the time to prepare to adjust to that environment. Easy access to cyberspace is rapidly changing the way we conduct business via electronic communication and virtual organizations.

ELECTRONIC COMMUNICATION

Everyday, more than one billion e-mail messages travel over the Internet. In 1996, more than 30 million users accessed Internet with a projected 200 million users by 2000. There are more than 159 nations connected, more than 60,000 organizations worldwide, and more than one million business computers online. This confirms the importance of e-mail as a business communication tool and further opens the global marketplace because communication is now with coworkers and with clients around the globe.[6]

Businesses now utilize the Internet and the World Wide Web for these tasks:

- Provide technical support of products.
- Post business news.
- Introduce new products.
- List product lines with links for downloading detailed product information.[7]

E-mail and voice mail privacy issues are a concern of businesses and employees today. Linda Bluso, an attorney in a Cleveland-based law firm, states that employees' claims and grievances often stem from employers' monitoring of employees' messages. "The difficulty is that employees tend to believe that information on e-mail systems at work [is] private and confidential and not for the eyes of employers," says Bluso. However, the computer system is owned and operated by the employer.[8]

Because this technology has advanced so quickly, legal guidelines have not kept pace. In 1986, the Electronic Communications Privacy Act (ECPA) was passed by Congress to provide "protection against unauthorized interception of electronic communications. . . . Section 405 of Senate Bill 652 (The Telecommunications Competition and Deregulation Act of 1995) introduced in March 1995, . . . would broaden ECPA. . . ."[9]

Companies can help avoid these legal problems by following these guidelines:

- Eliminate references to "personal," "private," or "confidential" when referring to e-mail, voice mail, or access passwords.
- Remind employees periodically that electronic communication

equipment is the property of the company for conducting company business and that monitoring of transmissions may occur.

- Review state and federal laws as well as any case law that has or might develop in this area.[10]

VIRTUAL ORGANIZATIONS

Some organization functions may exist solely in computer systems.

These new technologies relax "the need to locate employees close to each other. In the future, some organizational functions may exist solely in computer systems."[11] Currently there are five examples of virtual organizational forms:

1. **Telecommuting,** or working from home by computer has been steadily growing in favor since the 1980s. More than six million Americans are now telecommuters. Workers sometimes complain of social isolation when working from home on computers the entire workweek.

2. **Hot-desk** arrangements exist in reengineered office environments where individual desks have been abandoned and employees are allocated a desk each day. All that is common each day is their telephone number and computer network access. Companies utilizing this concept have reported social hostility toward this system. Digital Equipment Corporation and IBM have implemented variations of this concept in Europe.

3. **Hotelling** refers to workers who spend most of their working hours with clients and, therefore, need no desk in their company. Such employees stay in contact with colleagues by computer and voice mail. The consultant firm of Ernst & Young uses hotelling and provides cubicle space when workers "visit" their home base.

4. **Virtual teams** exist when people collaborate closely but in a variety of locations. Mercury Telecommunications, because of massive expansion, uses virtual teamworking. Employees are unified through information technologies and by skilled team coordinators who provide the needed sense of common identity and mission. Employees are provided office space when they need to be at the company base.[12]

5. **Virtual company** refers to organizations that start a business with no physical office space and run the company relying mostly on cyberspace for connectivity between both customers and coworkers. Stefanie Syman, who started a virtual business that later acquired physical space, offers these suggestions to other virtual novices: "I recommend nearly paranoid attention to detail, compulsive use of lists, and a level of communication with other staff that might at first seem excessive. Aim for a near Packwoodian thoroughness when recording events of the day, and then make sure to share this information with the right staff members. That way you'll be sure that more than one fallible individual holds the keys to your business."[13]

As Christopher Barnatt, University of Nottingham, reminds us:

> The more we can interact with each other through technology, the more transparent computers and communications systems will appear, the more we will forget we are working through them, and the greater will be the quality of the business relationships we may foster across new

"virtual" organizational working patterns. After all, although the tools of cyberspace may be cold, logical and horrendously complex, their application will continue to allow the culture and camaraderie—the battle, the losing and the winning—of business life to be conducted not just more efficiently, but also more effectively.[14]

FACSIMILE AND OTHER TELECOMMUNICATIONS TECHNOLOGIES

Facsimile, one of the oldest electronic communications media, allows clerical staffs to transmit entire documents over telephone lines in as little as fifteen seconds. Improvements in fax technology, and reduced costs of equipment and long-distance charges, are expected to contribute to its increased use.

New scanning and printing technologies and maturing international standards have advanced facsimile (fax) machines to the point that worldwide communication is possible. The personal computer-fax machine is another variation on electronic communication. The chief advantages of a personal computer (PC) fax are cost, convenience, control, clarity, and consolidation. In many cases, the disadvantage of a PC fax is that it is designed to serve individuals, not groups. A stand-alone fax machine, on the other hand, can be shared by several people. Handwritten symbol recognition, which allows a person to write directly onto a flat display screen and then convert the handwriting into text, and voice input may change the way data are input into computers.

Many companies use audiotapes and videotapes as well as teleconferencing instead of formal minutes and reports for their meetings. The application of telecommunications equipment (the combination of telephone and computer technologies) can improve the ease and efficiency of conducting business.

Seven advantages of telecommunications technology to enhance pure organizational communication are (1) avoiding intraoffice and intercompany communication delays by using voice messaging systems, (2) broadening market reach with portable computers and electronic mail, (3) accessing up-to-date information via online databases, (4) keeping geographically dispersed units in touch with each other using facsimile transmissions and electronic mail, (5) simplifying scheduling and facilitating ongoing business relationships, (6) making equipment more productive by linking more than one computer to a printer or workstation, and (7) increasing the quality of decision making by having complete and current information available when needed.[15]

WRITTEN WORD

The most durable of all means of communication is the written word. Perhaps when facts need to be presented, nothing surpasses the written word, for it provides a historical document for future reference. A few of the factors used to determine the readability of material are the number of syllables and words in a sentence, the number of sentences in a paragraph, and the number of personal references.

TABLE 8–1 Guidepost for Effective Writing

READING LEVEL	FAIRLY EASY	STANDARD	FAIRLY DIFFICULT	DIFFICULT
Average sentence length in words	14	17	21	25
Syllables per 100 words	142	150	158	166
Personal references per 100 words (I, you, us)	10	6	4	3
Typical publications	Newspaper	Magazine	Literary	Scholarly

SOURCE: Rudolph Flesch, *The Art of Plain Talk* (New York: Harper & Row, 1949). See also Robert Gunning, *The Technique of Clear Writing* (New York: McGraw-Hill, 1952).

The three averages (sentence length, syllables, and personal references) are applied to a scale that gives the reading-ease score (see Table 8–1.) For example, an average sentence length of 17 words, with about 150 syllables for each 100 words and 6 personal references per 100 words, would be considered average. The greater the number of syllables and words in a sentence, the more difficult the sentence is to read and understand. The greater the number of personal references in a passage, the easier the passage is to read. From these studies the Prudential Insurance Company developed guideposts for more effective writing. Shorter sentences do not mean duller or degrading sentences but, rather, sentences that are more easily understood by more people.

VISUAL SYMBOLS

Besides the written word, we communicate in other graphic ways—and more universally. The world speaks a babel of a thousand tongues, but wouldn't it be nice to travel anywhere in the world and be able to find the restroom or the ticket agent in any airport? Or wouldn't it be nice for a three-year-old in Gambia and a three-year-old in Indiana to recognize "Danger—Don't Touch!" instantly? This is not easily accomplished; for example, how would a pictograph of a man in trousers and a woman in a skirt go over in India, where Hindu men sometimes wear a *dhoti* that may resemble a skirt, and women sometimes wear trousers?

Traffic symbols are more or less standard in Europe, thanks to an inter-country agreement that makes it possible to drive from Italy to Denmark with nothing more than a smile and a map (Figure 8–6). But there are still some problems worldwide. A triangle, which means "caution" in France, means "stop" in England, "yield" and "helicopter landing" in the United States, and "birth control" in India.

We find that we react to symbols or pictures and draw certain inferences from them. The color red or black may derive positive or negative responses. The use of these colors in a sign may invoke actions that were not intended by the signmaker.

FIGURE 8–6 International or Universal Symbols Help People Communicate. The United States Is Now Using Symbols the Rest of the World Has Been Using for Decades.

INFORMATION   HOTEL INFORMATION   NO SMOKING

RAIL TRANSPORTATION   COFFEE SHOP   TOILETS

SUMMARY

Traditional concepts of staff and line have changed in recent years. With those changes have come innovations in communication techniques between the divisions. Integrated work teams composed of both line and staff personnel create much better human relations among employees and contribute greatly to better small-group communications.

Two kinds of communication channels serve to accomplish effective communication: formal and informal. Formal channels are the official paths by which official messages travel. They are called the vertical and horizontal channels because they relate to and grow out of the vertical and horizontal relationships pictured on an organization's structural chart. Informal channels stem from the unofficial, social relationships existing between individuals who work together, and they serve to transmit unofficial messages.

Although the downward and upward channels both move vertically, the nature, content, and volume of messages going up or down are completely different. The downward channel is dominated by orders from above dealing with policies and procedures. Vast amounts of printed matter are generated in the top-down channel in the form of memos and reports.

Horizontal channels exist for members of the same organizational rank to communicate with one another. Horizontal communications can be observed on a formal organization chart, but they also exhibit a number of characteristics associated with the informal modes of communication. It has been demonstrated that open horizontal communication is essential for the success of any complex organization, from the managerial level to the assembly line.

The information technologies continue to develop rapidly and improve communication and the quality of our decisions. In addition, advanced technologies are changing forever how business is conducted. Easy access to cyberspace is rapidly changing the way we conduct business via electronic communication and virtual organizations.

We are more informative in written language if we keep our average sentences between fifteen and eighteen words. There is a need for constant, open communications among and within small groups and more formal organizations, and between organizations.

CASE STUDY 8–1

HOW CAN THE STAFF COMMUNICATE MORE EFFECTIVELY WITH LINE PERSONNEL?

Good communication between staff and line personnel is important in all organizations, and it can be said that effective communication plays a significant role in determining the overall success of any organization. However, when the communication process between staff and line personnel is less than effective, problems can develop, as seen in the following illustration.

Jay Galler, who manages the personnel department of a large industrial plant of about 200 employees, recently distributed to all employees a detailed questionnaire that required the employees to fill in information about their job title, number of years with the company, salary rate, and a description of their job responsibilities. The form stated that the purpose of the questionnaire would be to provide management with updated material concerning personnel classifications. The form stated that all employees should return the form on or before the coming Friday, which gave the workers five days in which to fill out all the information needed. Jay announced to each department that he would tour the plant on Friday morning and pick up all the forms that had not yet been turned in to the personnel department.

The updating of the personnel classifications was requested by the plant manager. The reason was to review all the job duties with the possibility of reclassifying some of the positions, in some cases to provide a more equitable pay rate, which would mean a pay raise for some.

At the end of the week, before Jay's tour of the plant, fewer than 20 percent of the questionnaires had been returned to the personnel office. After touring the plant, Jay had collected only an additional dozen forms.

Obviously, an accurate study of the wages and salary schedules could not be done because of the lack of necessary data. There appears to be a problem between line and staff, more specifically the passing of information from the line personnel to the staff, a common problem.

1. How will the line personnel suffer as a result of not filling out the questionnaire?
2. How could Jay have made his communication more effective?
3. Was Jay's method the best way of distributing the forms? Is there a better way? Should Jay have departmental meetings to discuss the form?
4. What information should be included on the memo regarding the questionnaire?

WORK DELEGATION AND DUAL COMMAND

Frank Colella works in an aircraft plant as a dispatcher in production control. According to his immediate supervisor, Frank's duty is to determine the priority of shop orders for completion in each department. On this particular Saturday, Frank was assigned to the turret lathe department and only a few people were working. Frank was working this day under a lower level supervisor by the name of Mike. Since Mike's department was behind in production, he told Frank to make an inventory of all the orders in his department, not just those that could be completed quickly to reduce the backlog. Frank told Mike he could not follow the order, since his immediate supervisor had given him specific instructions. Mike replied, "This is my department, I should know what is best; I am the supervisor, and I run the department." Frank again refused and Mike called his general supervisor, who told Frank that the matter would be referred to the superintendent on Monday and that Frank would be fired.

1. Who is right in this situation, Mike or Frank?
2. How would you resolve the problem of dual authority?
3. What action would you take if you were the superintendent, and why?
   a. Fire Frank.
   b. Reprimand him.
   c. Do nothing.
   d. Commend him for following the orders of his immediate supervisor.

DISCUSSION AND STUDY QUESTIONS—TO KEEP YOU THINKING . . . _____

1. How do formal communications differ from informal ones?
2. Why is organizational structure important in communications?
3. How do the processes and effects of downward communications differ from upward communications?
4. How are vertical messages likely to be different depending on whether they move up or down?
5. What is the Pygmalion (self-fulfilling prophecy) effect and how does it impact management?
6. What purpose(s) do small-group communications accomplish besides the obvious transmittal and receiving of information?
7. What are current examples of electronic communications that facilitate better organizational communication?

NOTES _____

1. Stanley M. Davis and Paul R. Lawrence, "Problems of Matrix Organizations," *Harvard Business Review*, May–June 1978, pp. 34–37.

2. Jerry Buckley, "The New Organization Man," *U.S. News and World Report*, January 16, 1989, p. 50.

3. Andre Nelson, "A Supervisory Principle—Chain of Command," *Supervision*, May 1988, pp. 14–17.

4. Valorie A. McClelland, "Upward Communication: Is Anyone Listening?" *Personnel Journal*, June 1988, pp. 124–131.

5. Christopher Barnatt, "Office Space, Cyberspace, and Virtual Organization," *Journal of General Management,* Summer 1995, pp. 78–91.

6. Rick Mendosa, "The E-Mail Race," *Hispanic Business,* April 1996, p. 52.

7. Robert Tuten and Charles Olentine, "Internet: The AirWave of the Future," *Poultry Digest,* March 1966, p. 30.

8. "Employee E-Mail: Is It Really Private?" *Nation's Business,* March 1966, p. 10.

9. William N. Bockanic and Marc P. Lynn, "Electronic Communications: They May Not Be as Private as You Think," *Journal of Systems Management,* November/December 1995, pp. 64–65.

10. "Employee E-Mail: Is It Really Private?" *Nation's Business,* March 1966, p.10.

11. Christopher Barnatt, "Office Space, Cyberspace, and Virtual Organization," *Journal of General Management,* Summer 1995, pp. 78–91.

12. Ibid.

13. Stefanie Syman, "There Are No Water Coolers in Cyberspace," *The Wall Street Journal,* May 6, 1996, p. A12.

14. Barnatt, "Office Space, Cyberspace, and Virtual Organization."

15. Theresa Engstrom, "Seven Business Reasons to Turn to Telecommunications," *Working Woman,* August 1987, pp. 44–47, 84.

RECOMMENDED READING

Davidson, Duncan, Duane Dickson, and James Trice. "Rightsizing for Success." *Business Forum,* Winter/Spring 1993, pp. 10–12.

Jacob, Rahul. "The Struggle to Create an Organization for the 21st Century." *Fortune,* April 3, 1995, pp. 90–99.

Hoffman, Richard C. "The Effect of Hierarchical Level and Receiver Status on Managerial Communications." *Journal of Managerial Issues,* Summer 1995, pp. 222–240.

Hunsaker, Phil. *Communicating at Work.* New York: Simon & Schuster, 1993.

Keidel, Robert W. "Rethinking Organizational Design." *Academy of Management Executive,* November 1994, pp. 12–30.

McCollum, James K., and J. Daniel Sherman. "The Matrix Structure: Bane or Benefit to High Tech Organizations?" *Project Management Journal,* June 1993, pp. 23–26.

Mercer, Michael W. *How Winners Do It: High Impact Skills For Your Career Success.* Englewood Cliffs, N.J.: Prentice Hall, 1994.

Munter, Mary. *Guide to Managerial Communication.* Englewood Cliffs, N.J.: Prentice Hall, 1982.

Naisbitt, John, and Patricia Aburdene. *Re-Inventing the Corporation: Transforming Your Job and Your Company for the New Information Society.* New York: Warner Books, 1985.

Odiorne, George S. "Ethics for the Nineties." *Manage,* April 1988, pp. 8–14, 33.

Peters, Tom. *Liberation Management: Necessary Disorganization for the Nanosecond Nineties.* New York: Alfred A. Knopf, 1992.

Shannon, John H., and David A. Rosenthal. "Electronic Mail and Privacy: Can the Conflicts Be Resolved?" *Business Forum,* Winter/Spring 1993, pp. 31–34.

9

GROUP BEHAVIOR AND CONFLICT MANAGEMENT

TO START YOU THINKING

Here are some questions to stimulate your thinking and open avenues of discussion before you read the chapter.

- What is a group? What determines if it is effective?
- What attracts you to another person or group of people?
- How do you obtain consensus in group behavior and decision making?
- Are there major differences in behavior, power, and control between formal and informal groups?
- Why should groupthink be avoided?
- What is the difference between task leaders and social leaders?
- When is conflict good for an organization? When is it bad?

LEARNING GOALS

After studying this chapter, you should be able to:

1. Understand groups and their characteristics.
2. Appreciate propositions about group dynamics.
3. Understand consensus building and its advantages and disadvantages.
4. Understand and differentiate task-related and maintenance-related roles.
5. Cope with inconsistencies and ambiguities of group and role behavior.
6. Understand role prescriptions and role behaviors.
7. Explain the role of groupthink in decision making.
8. Develop a plan for effective conflict management.
9. Define and apply the following terms and concepts (in order of first occurrence):

- group dynamics
- group
- norms
- group cohesiveness
- consensus
- task-related roles
- maintenance-related roles
- role prescriptions

- role behaviors
- role conflict
- role ambiguity
- informal groups
- groupthink
- cooperative conflict theory
- C-type conflict
- A-type conflict

GROUP DYNAMICS

The demands of meeting individual challenges are minuscule compared to being effective in groups. Sheer numbers and the accompanying arithmetic or geometric interactions possible among groups make the task of managing groups challenging. Groups, like individuals, have and develop their own personalities.

Group dynamics are the social processes by which small groups interact. The term also refers to the collective effect that individuals have on each other. The sense of belonging, prestige, and shared perceptions can dramatically affect one's individual behavior.

Interaction, interdependence, and communication are the keys to group activity. There must be some commonality of objectives and interdependency of individuals to accomplish those objectives. Thus communication among those individuals is imperative to successful fulfillment of group goals.

WHAT IS A GROUP?

A **group** is a collection of people who either meet personally or in absentia for the purpose of accomplishing a social or work objective. This definition is more contemporary than those traditionally used but with modern communications techniques, it is quite possible to have a meeting or other interactions with individuals separated by thousands of miles.

Groups are usually involved in meetings, task forces, or teams. All these activities are affected by many variables, including the size of the group and the predisposition to work together to accomplish an objective. Figure 9-1 shows the various factors that influence group task accomplishment. Groups evolve into teams. It is incorrect to assume or think that just because you have a collection of people that you have an effective team.

Major determinants of group effectiveness are norms of the individuals, size of the group, and degree of cohesiveness in the group. Status of group members also affects effectiveness and success of the group and will be discussed in the chapter on power and status.

FIGURE 9–1 Factors Influencing Group Task Accomplishment.

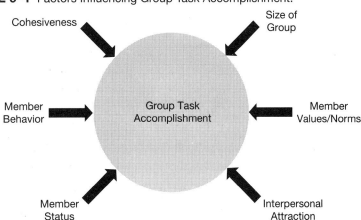

Norms

Norms are ideas or values that a group has regarding expected behaviors of individuals and group members. Both individuals and groups have values. Individuals bring their values to the group, which in turn, develops group norms.

Norms are usually unwritten but are powerful devices for assuring group conformity. Feelings run strong about right and wrong conduct of group members. In one sense, the group norms are summations of the individual members' values, but they are larger than the sum. They are, in effect, synergistic or larger than the sum of the parts. They can be very strong or less effective depending on the character, morals, and integrity of the individuals comprising the group.

Consider the example of a team who assembles aircraft or automotive products. The values that individuals attach to money, human life, and congeniality of a group all affect the speed and quality of production output. If the members are on a pay-for-piecework basis, their output may be guided by numbers of products they can produce and other variables. If the product is safety related and might endanger its end user if not properly produced, their output may be more balanced with concern for quality and safety. Similarly, and perhaps most important, if an individual wants to be a part of the group, he or she must cooperate with the group members. These individual values all contribute to the formation of a group norm and standards of behavior.

Group Composition

Why are we attracted to some individuals? Certainly the task goals of the workplace may almost force attachment if not attraction. More likely, and in voluntary associations, we are attracted to work with others because of similar attitudes, opinions, behavior, goals, age, education, and personality. Continued exposure and frequent interaction are also reasons for interpersonal attraction.

Another reason groups are composed the way they are is perceived attractiveness or desirability of association. As we discussed "perception" in the communication chapters, it follows that if we perceive an association with a person as having desirable consequences, then we can anticipate that relationship will be rewarding. If we grow to like an individual through association and interaction, the relationship becomes mutually rewarding.

Size of Group

The overall effectiveness of a group is influenced significantly by its size. Two-person groups can be very effective depending on interpersonal attraction and task goals. But groups are more commonly thought of as having more than two people. Group size minimums are not as important as maximums. Two to seven individuals may function very effectively as a group.

The desirable number for an effective group seems to be five, although some experts would say it is seven members. Below five, for the most part, each person in the group says something to each other person. In groups over seven, the low participators tend to stop talking to each other and speak more to the leader. Subconsciously this situation becomes more formal, and real interaction generally declines. The tendency for stronger directive leaders to emerge generally increases visibly as size increases.

There also must be recognition by each group member that each way of thought has its own validity. The failure of group members to grant these recognitions to each other inevitably results in the failure to communicate. Successful communication among the different members of a group depends on something more than a common language. Experts trained in using precise technical vocabularies have difficulty communicating with laypersons. Even in ordinary everyday language, different words have different meanings for different people, as discussed in Chapter 7.

Figure 9-2 compares communication and complexity of interaction in small groups (six members) and large groups (sixteen members). As group size increases, consensus becomes increasingly difficult to achieve. Thus, consensus will be facilitated by limiting the size of the group working on any particular project and maximizing each person's opportunity to participate and contribute. Otherwise, if the group is too large, a "false consensus" (nominal agreement only) is obtained.

There is an inverse relationship between group size and the ability of the group to function efficiently and effectively. Factors influencing the optimal size of a group include the group's purpose and individuals' needs for influence, interaction, and interdependency. As group size increases, up to a point, the skills and resources of the total group increases. Unique skills and status may be added if a person with perceived high prestige is added to the group. If prestige or status differences are too great among group members, a negative effect on cohesiveness may result.

FIGURE 9–2 Complexity of Interaction in Small and Large Groups.

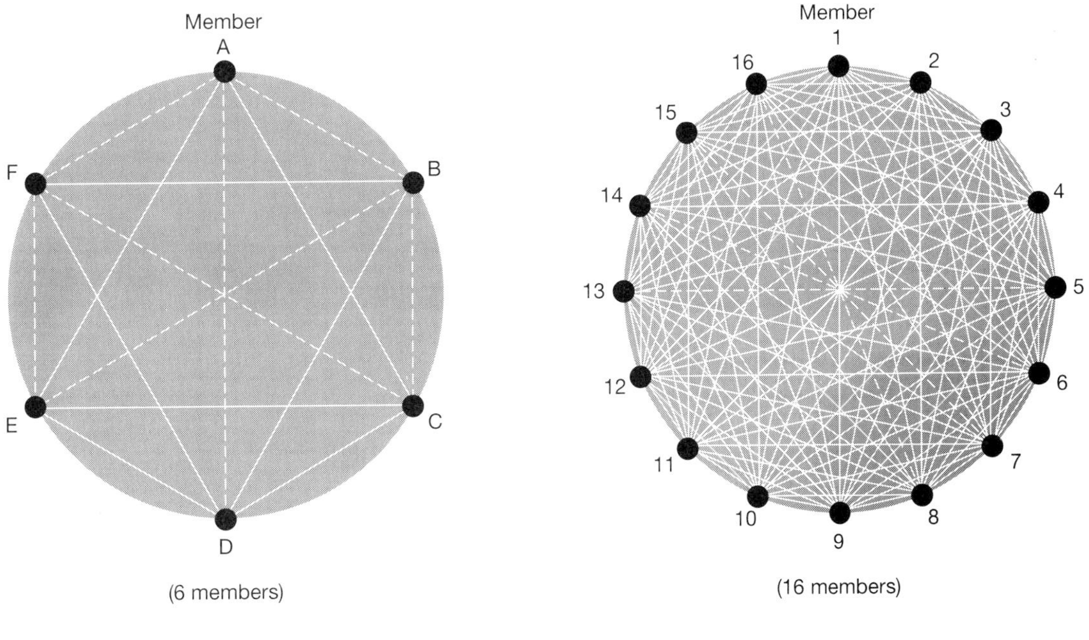

(6 members)

(16 members)

GROUP COHESIVENESS

Group cohesiveness is both a cause and effect of group size and ability to reach consensus. A highly consensual group exhibits high group cohesiveness; similarly, a highly cohesive group (where group members' desires to remain a part of the group are high) can reach consensus more readily because of their mutuality.

Related to the group's cohesiveness are the types of decisions and emotions affecting the group. Emotional or affective conflict results in consensus being reached largely due to avoidance or withdrawal from group processes—the "I don't care" and "Anything, just to get this over with" syndromes—even in important decisions affecting group members. Difficult decisions or particularly troublesome decisions are handled on an ad hoc basis rather than as part of a cohesive, well-functioning group. Figure 9-3 lists several characteristics of group dynamics and consensus building.

FIGURE 9–3 How Do You Obtain Consensus?

Building a group into a cohesive, consensual team requires the following:

1. Recognition that groups are everywhere—in all kinds of settings.
2. Recognition that groups have power—in numbers.
3. Recognition that groups have positive and negative outcomes:
   a. Positive outcomes may include better (more thought-through) decisions, acceptance, and actions.
   b. Negative outcomes may include unnecessary group conformity and "groupthink," a term to be discussed later.
4. Hard work—especially among professionals.
5. Leadership guidance and facilitation.
6. Extensive communication, including interpersonal dialogue.
7. Give and take—giving and taking of advice, and giving and taking of constructive criticism.
8. Group-oriented communications—not highly opinionated or "me" statements.
9. Restatement of decision-making processes—not final solutions, in which individuals become locked onto a position and therefore put into a defensive posture.
10. Limiting group size to a workable number (maybe five to seven) of affected individuals in order to avoid a "false consensus" (nominal agreement only to get the group process completed).

GROUP CONSENSUS

Consensus is an attempt to arrive at a solution acceptable to most group members. How do you obtain consensus among members? You communicate and work at it—and it is hard work. It requires management guidance and some processing; that is, working with and through the group on decision making, communication, or the process as well as the end product.

Obtaining consensus is hard work.

Obtaining consensus requires extensive communication, especially, but not limited to, interpersonal dialogue either between two or a small number of individuals, or within a group. The process requires a lot of give and take: the giving and taking of advice and the giving and taking of constructive criticism.

The communicative behaviors of group members can either facilitate or hinder group consensus. If the communications are group oriented, they will have a positive effect on group consensus. Highly opinionated or "me" statements—"I'm an expert, and if you don't agree with me, you're wrong!"—have a negative effect on the group.

Even the terminology employed can affect the group's behavior. Efforts need to be made to secure agreement, adaptation, and compromise instead of getting "locked in" or becoming defensive about one's position. A very practical approach to this is to ask group members to describe their process, not "What do you think should be done?" The latter locks them onto a position or solution, and they become defensive of their decisions.

As noted in the previous section on cohesiveness, decisions can become emotional, ad hoc, and hurried. In contrast, when the discussions, decisions, and even differences of opinion take place on a higher and rational plane, it is much more possible to achieve true consensus for a decision.

Group rapport and trust develop high morale.

If a group is composed of five persons, each contributing his or her own personality, soon a new personality develops—that of the group. Group rapport and trust in each other develops. The growth encouraged by all relates to the height of the morale that can be achieved by the group. However, the larger the group, the more elusive the feeling of group morale and the harder it is to determine.

ACTION PROJECT 9–1 CAN YOU COME TO A CONSENSUS? (GROUP EXERCISE)

Wayout University, like other institutions of higher learning, is experiencing grade inflation: steadily increasing grade levels in its seven colleges. Students and faculty alike are perpetually concerned with the grading systems employed. The topic of grades is frequently broached in both formal and informal settings. Today, a problem-solving conference on grades has been convened by Harry Benedict, a student government representative. *Note:* Harry doesn't show up for the meeting but all the other invitees do. Can you reach some consensus regarding what, if anything, to do about grade inflation?

ROLE FOR BILLY STILLMAN

You have been associate dean of students at Wayout for the past five years. You are becoming increasingly alarmed at the number of student problems and drop-outs. You feel strongly that the grading system has something to do with these rates.

ROLE FOR PAT FOSTER

You are the assistant dean in the College of Physical Sciences. Your responsibilities include ensuring that undergraduate instruction in your college meets the standards of accrediting associations of various disciplines and screening applicants for graduate study in your college. You are concerned about the grading systems but need some measure of student performance in order to carry out your responsibilities.

ROLE FOR LYNN SAMSON

You are a professor of mathematics. You are dissatisfied with the grading system because you believe it imposes artificial barriers among students. You do realize that all students are not born with bachelor's degrees stamped on their birth certificates and that some students do unsatisfactory work for various reasons. You are also particularly concerned with the importance of rewarding the exceptional student and want a system that does so.

ROLE FOR MARION JOHNSON

As an average student, you get easily discouraged when your grades are not as high as your expectations. Consequently, you are suffering some physiological and psychological health problems.

ROLE FOR FRANCIS ALBRIGHT

You are an exceptionally good student in that you study hard, get excellent grades, and get involved in class and out-of-class discussions. You are well respected by your peers and professors. You expect to be rewarded for your efforts and achievements.

CHANGING SOCIAL VALUES

Individuals and groups are influenced by changing social values. The up-heaval of the 1960s and the evolution of the 1970s—the civil rights movement, the women's liberation movement—had a tremendous effect on our society. The individualism of the 1980s and 1990s also changed the character and destiny of American organizations. People continue to question the routine paths that their careers are expected to take. Women realize that they have new options and men can also grow and develop in new ways in their work lives.

The individual looking for personal growth and development these days is no longer satisfied to stay in one job for years on end, no matter how large the paycheck or secure the situation. We hear of many instances of people who are driven by sheer boredom to try something different.

Two-career couples are common.

The two-career couple is now a norm. Husbands and wives may alternate in job changing. The author knows a young, former bank president who is now

"Mr. Mom" at home with his preschool children while his wife works outside the home. Both are enjoying the relationship.

EARLY CAREER CHANGES

The "trying twenties."

There are life decisions to be made in the "trying twenties." People in this age group may be preparing for a career, marriage, and a family. There seems to be the idea that during this age people can overcome all if they apply their minds and wills to life—that destiny is within their control. Perhaps this is a necessary self-deception that can help them to achieve their goals and to succeed.

The great majority of young people in America still believe in the work ethic, the idea that hard work and getting ahead are essential for a full and satisfying life. It is with this spirit of enthusiasm that many young people begin working at their first "real" jobs.

MIDCAREER ADJUSTMENTS

Higher up the ladder competition becomes greater.

Career consultants often help clients by encouraging them to review their backgrounds in terms of what they have to offer prospective employers. Three important aspects are experience, education, and breadth of background. A person midway in his or her career can usually offer experience, but may find education lacking. Formal education may be a determining factor in the choice between two experienced persons for a position or a promotion.

As an employee moves up the ladder of success, the competition becomes stiffer, and reeducation is one answer. Returning to the classroom may scare the middle-aged person, but more persons of all ages are returning to further their education. The evening college classroom or industrial programs have two features: (1) providing the means by which to learn up-to-date methods of handling work problems and (2) offering new vantage points through which the individual can perceive himself or herself in relationship to the world.

Breadth of background helps acceptance of responsibility.

The breadth of one's background can show that a person is willing to accept greater responsibility. Such experience can prove at a later time to a potential employer that this applicant has accepted responsibility, either in a company or in the community. The employer who hires workers older than forty years of age usually perceives these qualities:

1. Stability that comes with maturity
2. A serious attitude toward the job
3. More reliability, less absenteeism, and proven steady work habits
4. A sense of responsibility and loyalty
5. A tendency not to be distracted by outside interests or influences

Noting these advantages, many employers now make it a practice to include older workers in every working unit. They find that mature employees have a stabilizing influence on the group as a whole. McDonald's restaurants provide classic examples of this change in social values and work groups.

ACTION PROJECT 9–2   HOW DO YOU RESPOND? (INDIVIDUAL EXERCISE)

The following exercise measures how you and others respond to certain role behaviors in group situations. In each case, circle your response to the question:

"HOW DO YOU RESPOND WHEN . . . ?"	REALLY TURNED OFF	TURNED OFF	TURNED ON	REALLY TURNED ON	
	1	2	3	4	5
1. Another group member says that he or she knows how to solve a problem, but you don't think the individual really does know how.	1	2	3	4	5
2. A coworker will not take a stand when pressed for an opinion or a decision.	1	2	3	4	5
3. Another coworker has confronted you and expressed desire to help alleviate a workload problem you have.	1	2	3	4	5
4. Your boss is bugging you about the pet project assigned to you last week for presentation to the board (you are on schedule).	1	2	3	4	5
5. The president and the board of directors have different views on the company's long-range objectives and direction.	1	2	3	4	5
6. Coworkers use different approaches to achieve similar results; some take more time but allow more job freedom.	1	2	3	4	5
7. Two subordinates of yours, doing the same task-oriented job, have different styles of working. The first worker is always three to five minutes late to work, takes more than an hour for lunch, and sometimes leaves work early. The second worker is consistently punctual, quite often stays late, and will work on the weekends if need be. Both produce at about the same level.	1	2	3	4	5
8. After five years at your 40–45 hour/week job, your old boss quits. His replacement now assigns you work that takes at least 55–60 hours/week to complete.	1	2	3	4	5
9. Department A at Company X uses flextime and Department B uses straight time (8 to 5, Mon.–Fri.) to schedule their workers.	1	2	3	4	5
10. Company P has a very conservative upper-management strategy team. Just one month ago, Company P was taken over in a hostile merger by Company Q. Company Q's upper-management strategy team has a very aggressive reputation.	1	2	3	4	5

Your instructor may ask you to share your responses with others in the class for discussion purposes. The real value of this exercise is to compare and discuss responses on individual items. If you want to add your scores, the total will give you a very rough indicator of your overall reaction to work situations. If the total score is below 20 or above 40, or if you are "really turned off" too often, you may want to check your responses.

GROUP ROLES

Group roles are shared expectations of how group members are to perform in their positions. Group roles are developed because of activities, interactions, and sentiments of others in a group as well as self-expectations. There is an informal

FIGURE 9–4 Task and Maintenance Roles of Group Members.

EXAMPLES OF TASK-RELATED ROLES	EXAMPLES OF MAINTENANCE-RELATED ROLES
Objective(s) clarifier	Consensus seeker; mutual support
Planner	Encourager; facilitator
Organizer	Mediator
Seeker of information (acquire and provide facts)	Gatekeeper, relevant to group norms
Leader	Compromiser
Coordinator	Communicator
Energizer	Standard setter
Evaluator	Observer
Summarizer	Evaluator
	Reconciliator; tension reducer

testing of each group member to see if there is a good fit. How well an individual fits into a group depends on the factors discussed earlier: norms, social class, interpersonal attraction, group cohesiveness, and size.

Roles of group members may be divided into task-related and maintenance-related roles. **Task-related roles** are those behavioral expectations that directly aid in the accomplishment of group objectives. Task roles include helping define problems, acquiring and providing facts, and summarizing group deliberations. **Maintenance-related roles** are those behavioral expectations directly related to the well-being and development of the group. Examples of these roles are consensus-seeker, facilitator, and reconciliator. These and other roles are shown in Figure 9-4. Group roles are also a function of role prescriptions and roles behaviors, as shown in the following discussion.

ROLE PRESCRIPTIONS AND ROLE BEHAVIORS

Doing as others expect you to do is playing the role.

What we say and do are largely matters of expectations, role prescriptions, and role behaviors. The things that people are expected to do are known as **role prescriptions;** the things that they actually do are known as **role behaviors.** To the extent that role behaviors match the appropriate role prescriptions, within a company, for example, an individual is said to be effective or successful. It is assumed that the individual is in fact contributing to company goal achievement.

Roles are the sum of expectations.

The role prescription is the set of expectations that affects a particular role, such as a manager's position. All the different people with whom one comes into contact collectively form one's multiple role.

Performance evaluation is essentially a matter of determining the degree to which the role prescription and role behavior match. It is an attempt to equate organizational goal attainment with the individual contribution. What is really important insofar as an organization is concerned is not how much an individual does but how much of what he or she does is organizationally relevant as determined by his or her role.

The role is thus the sum total of expectations placed on the person by the supervisors, subordinates, peers, customers, vendors, and others, depending on the person's particular job.

Role Conflict and Ambiguity

One must be able to integrate these expectations, as well as one's own, into a coherent psychological pattern if one expects to perform successfully. If, however, the individual lacks a clear understanding of these expectations and if they conflict with one another or his or her own expectations, the individual experiences **role conflict** and will be unable to satisfy some of these expectations. **Role ambiguity** exists when a person is not too sure about how to act or perform in a given situation.

Research suggests that, when there is a sizable discrepancy between a manager's concept of his or her role and the employees' role expectations of that job, motivation and efficiency tend to be poor. For example, if managers see themselves as mediators and developers of compromises between management and labor, but both management and the union expect them to be hard-nosed negotiators, role conflict develops.

Even when top management has learned to live with varying role expectations, many employees find their function in a company much easier when their role prescription is defined clearly. The lack of a job description or role definition sometimes accounts for employees saying, "Oh, I don't know, I just feel uncomfortable on the job. I guess I really don't know what the boss expects of me."

GROUP BEHAVIOR

The behavior that goes on in a committee or other small group can be viewed as positive and negative reactions to questions and answers. Negative reactions include showing disagreement, tension, or antagonism. Positive reactions include showing agreement, tension release, and friendly solidarity.

There are about twice as many positive reactions in most meetings as there are negative reactions. One might suppose that the more successful the meeting, the more positive the reactions. But evidence does not support this view. Rather, there appears to be a kind of optimum balance between disagreements and agreements. Too few disagreements may be an indication of the lack of involvement and interest in the task, or that the atmosphere is so inhibited and constrained that nobody dares to disagree. When ill feelings arise about some critical point, a chain reaction tends to set in, and logical or practical demands of the task may cease to be governing factors.

DIFFERENCES BETWEEN FORMAL AND INFORMAL GROUPS

Formal groups are function, task, or job oriented at work. These groups are usually comprised of supervisors, managers or leaders, and other employees. **Informal groups,** on the other hand, are much more people oriented. They concentrate on sentiments derived from activities and interaction of the group members. The informal organization is more directed by group norms and privileges than the formal rules and regulations with the formal group. Figure 9-5 compares characteristics of formal and informal groups.

FIGURE 9–5 Comparisons of Formal and Informal Groups.

CONCEPT	FORMAL GROUP	INFORMAL GROUP
GENERAL ORIENTATION:	Official, formal	Unofficial, informal
PRIMARY COMPARISON:	Formal, delegated authority	Political prowess
BEHAVIOR GUIDELINES:	Rules and regulations	Norms and privileges
POWER SOURCE:	From management	From group members
CONTROL SOURCE:	Rewards and punishment	Group entitlements

GROUPTHINK

There is a downside to group cohesiveness, the harmony and consensus approach: the risk that everyone in the group will start to think alike. "Groupthink" sets in. **Groupthink** is a deterioration of the decision-making processes because of in-group pressures to think alike.

Groupthink may inhibit thinking.

A strong sense of group unity and a feeling that "we" are on the right track can lead to finding the quickest, but not the best, answer. Closely knit groups sometimes suffer from the illusion of unanimity—that is, no one wants to break up the cohesiveness of the group. Group leaders may also assume, wrongly, that silence on the part of a member means consent or agreement.

Illusion of unanimity.

Members of a group may indulge in self-censorship, failing to mention a legitimate idea contrary to the group's direction. They feel that the idea is not really what the group wants to hear. Many of us want so much to be a member of the team that we will not oppose the general trend.

Self-censorship.

Shared stereotypes of the opposition are another aspect of groupthink: "Well, all those people feel the same way, but what do they know?" "They really aren't that important. Actually, we have to discount the cranks." Such group behavior can even lead people to feel that, if you think differently from the group, you are of the opposition or you don't want to be part of the team. So many of us want to be members of the team that we will not oppose the general trend.

Shared stereotypes.

Groupthink can also generate the illusion of invulnerability. "After all, we have been a leader in the field for many years; why shouldn't people accept our results?" The idea that our group cannot be wrong because we think alike leads to feelings of grandeur and infallibility. Very successful companies are likely to find that their committees fall into the groupthink syndrome. Do you have a strong leader of your committees who states an opinion before others, setting the stage for groupthink? Such group leaders expect the committee to rubber stamp predetermined decisions.

Groupthink creates a sense of infallibility.

TASK LEADERS OR SOCIAL LEADERS

When people are active in a group meeting, they may be characterized by actions of two types: the task leader and the social leader. The *task leader* feels that the accomplishment of the task is important. The ability to define the problem, the best way to handle it, and the time restriction become of paramount importance. The

A task leader wants to get the job done.

Think of a national issue, a company decision, or a well-known local situation in which a group or committee has fallen into the trap of "groupthink." Consider an international situation (e.g., the selling of new cars) or competition between companies. Review the four aspects of groupthink.

1. Illusion of unanimity
2. Self-censorship
3. Shared stereotypes of the opposition
4. Illusion of invulnerability

Give reasons to each point listed for why the group, committee, or company has succumbed to groupthink.

feelings of the individual members are of lesser concern. Task leaders are willing to "forgive and forget" if someone's feelings are hurt or if someone tramples on their emotions. The accomplishment of the goal, success, and self-ego are their trademarks.

The *social leader* is concerned with the feelings of each member and that each has an opportunity to participate. An agreement on a solution to a problem is only possible if there is compatibility among the members. The social leader will resent the "takeover" tactics of the task leader and will move in for a reassessment, compromise, or evaluation.

CONFLICT MANAGEMENT: COOPERATION AND/OR COMPETITION

Goals are important in conflict management.

Morton Deutsch, a noted social psychologist, determined that how people in a team, group, or organization believe their goals are related is important in understanding how effectively they work together.[1] This **cooperative conflict theory** is a powerful way to understand conflict. Research confirms that when people believe their goals are compatible, they know that as one succeeds, others succeed. There is increased cooperation because when one person is successful, others are helped in reaching their goals. This fosters a win–win climate with team collaboration.

On the other hand, people may believe their goals are competitive—if one wins, others lose. A competitive employee needs to prove that he or she is the most capable and that his or her ideas are superior; other people's successes are frustrating. Competitive goal strategy fosters competition in a win–lose climate.[2]

FIGURE 9–6 Cooperative Conflict Theory. Reprinted with Permission from Dean Tjosvold. *Learning to Manage Conflict: Getting People to Work Together Productively*, p.45. Copyright ©1993 Dean Tjosvold. First published by Lexington Books [now Jossey-Bass Inc., San Francisco]. All rights reserved.

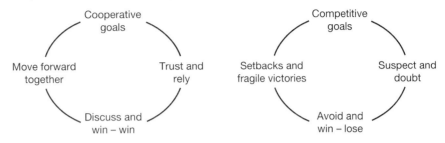

Employees' views of professional and organizational goals as cooperative or competitive affect employees' orientation and intentions toward one another, as illustrated in Figure 9-6. Those viewing goals in a cooperative climate want others to be effective and view others as wanting them to be effective because it is in everyone's best interest. They believe that their risks and efforts will be supported and reciprocated and trust they can rely on coworkers.

Cooperative employees know others' views.

Research confirms that employees in cooperation share information, know each other's points of view, exchange resources, assist and support each other, and use higher quality reasoning. This helps cooperators complete tasks quicker, reach high-quality solutions together, reduce stress, strengthen work relationships, and foster future collaboration.

In this climate of trust, cooperatives can manage their conflicts productively—freely speaking their minds, revealing their frustrations, and talking out their anger. In working for win–win solutions that strengthen the cooperative relationship, they explore alternative perspectives, creatively integrate differing views, and feel confident that they will continue to work together cooperatively.

Competitive employees foster suspicion.

Those who view goals as competitive, on the other hand, foster the suspicion that people only want to look out for their own interests, even at the expense of others. This mistrust halts the flow of information and resources and creates unproductive conflict that deters productivity, increases stress, and decreases morale. Confrontations are often harsh because of a win–lose attitude.

Studying and discussing competitive and cooperative conflict as a team, group, and organization is a way for people to change from ineffective conflicts to productive conflict management.[3]

DISCUSS HOW TO HANDLE CONFLICT WITH YOUR ANTAGONIST

When—not "if"—conflicts arise, it is important to work through them to mutual understanding. The conflicts may not always be resolved but they ought to be communicated to one another, and managed. Conflicts do not just go away; and the result of conflict may be to disagree, but the parties at least ought to know the areas of disagreement.

TEAMS AND CONFLICT MANAGEMENT

Organizations are depending on teams, from top-management teams to self-directed work teams. The underlying assumption in the movement to team-based management is that teams will increase organizational productivity because teams foster higher creativity, energy, and performance.[5]

Likewise, cross-functional teams have been hailed by academics, practitioners, and the business press alike as the miracle cure for companies in the 1990s. Indeed, the increased autonomy and open communication fostered by teams create an atmosphere in which innovative ideas can be developed into products and services that are more responsive to customers' needs than ever before.[6]

Conflict *can* improve team effectiveness.

Being a team member provides the employee with the opportunity to reach beyond the job being performed and become involved with achieving organizational goals. In addition, team involvement enhances decision making, builds consensus, increases support for action, and provides a cooperative, goal-oriented culture—critical factors when the coordinated efforts of employees are essential to reaching organizational goals. "Conflict *can* improve team effectiveness. The problem is that, once aroused, conflict is difficult to control. Sometimes it remains task focused, facilitating creativity, open communication, and team integration. In other instances, it loses its focus and undermines creativity, open communication, and integrated effort."[7]

All teams are not effective: The reality of teams and their effectiveness is often different from the promise. As a result, while offering the potential of major breakthroughs, ineffective teams increase the amount of time needed to make a decision. This is largely due to the ineffective use of conflict management in teamwork.

CONFLICT IN THE ORGANIZATION

Conflict is a natural, healthy part of any organization. It can, however, be painful when not managed productively. Carrying a grudge has no positive benefits and can have negative consequences.

INDIVIDUAL CONFLICTS. Jimmy Calano and Jeff Salzman of CareerTrack offer strategies for managing conflict successfully by harnessing the

Dean Tjosvold provides several guides for action and pitfalls to avoid in conflict management:

ACTION GUIDES FOR CONFLICT MANAGEMENT

- Distinguish between the conflict over the issue and the one over how conflicts are being managed.
- Recognize that characterizing the other as arrogant and closed-minded grows out of competitive conflict.
- Take the first steps toward discussing openly how conflicts are being managed.
- Check assumptions that the other is unwilling to improve conflict management.
- Deal with competitive, negative attitudes.
- Try to remain open-minded and fair.
- Focus on working together to improve conflict management.
- Discuss the costs of the destructive conflict and the mutual benefits of productive conflict.
- Signal that the conflict can be constructively resolved.
- Avoid blaming and affronting social face.
- Demonstrate that you are trying to understand the other's perspective.
- Counter the negative perceptions your antagonist has of you by changing behaviors.
- Empower your antagonist by offering options to choose.
- Know and be prepared to use alternatives to a negotiated agreement.

PITFALLS TO AVOID IN CONFLICT MANAGEMENT

- Keep arguments rational and task oriented, even when competitive and negative attitudes are getting in the way.
- Assume that discussing how the conflict is being managed is too personal and will escalate the conflict.
- Assume you alone must manage conflict.
- Assume your opponent alone must change.
- Believe that the conflict means that the other wants to be frustrating and mean.
- Convince yourself that your antagonist does not want to manage conflict based on indirect evidence.
- Wait for the other to make the first move to prove good intentions.[9]

---

power in conflict and transforming it to achieve personal success. Some points they recommend follow:

1. Choose the time and place carefully when addressing conflict. Avoid initiating conflict in public or in front of uninvolved people. Remember to "praise in public and criticize in private."
2. Change behaviors not people. Fix the problem instead of fixing the blame on another. Instead of wasting energy trying to convince a coworker that he or she is to blame, concentrate on a win–win solution.
3. Agree on something. Establish basic goals that are common to all involved. This creates a positive foundation, minimizing defensiveness and fostering cooperation and problem solving, by looking at different ways common goals can be achieved.
4. Use "I" language. State your case in relation to how you feel instead of attacking another person. For example, "I'm not happy with the progress of our project" is more effective in approaching problem solving than "You don't have the report done on time!"
5. Figure out where you went wrong or how you may have contributed to the conflict and admit it. Perhaps you were late in providing information. If so, start the confrontation with, "I know that I was late getting the data to you initially."
6. Criticize concretely. Don't be vague by saying, "You are unprofessional." Be concrete by stating, "The report is three days late and in the wrong format." Being concrete provides guidelines for improvement.
7. Bow out for awhile. When emotions are high, take some time—a few hours or a day—to allow both parties to move from the blame stage to the solution stage.
8. Embrace conflicts. Bring up problems and annoyances as they happen to build honest relationships.
9. Find the win–win solution. When emotions are high, it is human nature to lock into your position. Break out of your resolve to win and defeat your coworker and consider new possibilities that provide a win–win solution.[10]

> Thomas Capozzoli describes the nature of conflict as neither good nor bad:
>
> > Conflict is not something that is a tangible product but it lies in the minds of the people who are parties to it. However, it does become tangible when it manifests itself in arguing, brooding, or fighting. The problem lies with the inability for people to manage and resolve it effectively. If managed effectively, conflict can be constructive. If not, conflict can be a destructive force in people and organizations.[11]

Conflict is constructive when:

- People grow and change positively from the conflict.
- The conflict provides a win–win solution.
- Involvement is increased for everyone affected by the conflict.
- Team cohesiveness is increased.

Conflict is destructive when:

- The problem is not resolved.
- It drains energy from more important issues.
- It destroys the team spirit.
- The team or individuals become divided.

TEAM CONFLICTS.   Conflict in teams serves a productive purpose when it is focused on the differing perspectives and judgments of how to reach an organizational goal. Conflict becomes unproductive and harmful to team effectiveness when it focuses on another team member rather than an issue. Personal attacks often diminish team cohesion.[12] On the other hand, conflict is a natural, healthy occurrence when people work together and prevents complacency in teams, which deters growth.

MAKING CONFLICT A SUCCESSFUL COMPONENT OF TEAM INTERACTIONS

Effective team members view conflict positively.

Teams that are seen as effective use conflict as an advantage to build discussion and foster creative thinking. Effective teams improve decision making and acceptance of those decisions by team members. Ineffective teams do a less successful job of managing and resolving their differences. Ineffective team members view conflict as a burden—something to avoid. Avoiding conflict leads to weak decisions and underutilized teams.

Ineffective team members view conflict as a burden.

Research confirms that there are two types of conflicts that all teams experience: C-type conflict and A-type conflict. Whether the outcomes of team conflict are positive or negative is generally dependent on whether the conflict was C-type or A-type.

C-TYPE CONFLICT.   Differences of opinion will always happen among team members—when they deal with topics essential to completion of organizational goals, team effectiveness generally improves. This is termed *cognitive conflict* by some researchers; this text refers to this positive conflict interaction as C-type conflict. In an extensive team conflict study, Allen C. Amason and other researchers found that:

> This type of disagreement is a natural part of a properly functioning team. Natural, because as team members gather to make important decisions, they bring different ideas, opinions, and perspectives to the table. C-type conflict occurs as team members examine, compare, and reconcile these differences. This process is key to the team's ability to reach high-quality solutions that are understood and accepted by all team members.[13]

Managers generally agree that C-type conflict improves overall team effectiveness.

C-type conflict improves team effectiveness because team members participate in frank communication and broad consideration of different alternatives, facilitating creative problem solving with innovative thinking and improving the quality of decision making. Furthermore, team members are more committed to the decisions made through C-type conflict.

A-TYPE CONFLICT.   The downside of conflict is that, when used ineffectively, it can harm the team and create hostility among a team's members. As a result, the quality of decision making actually declines along with the commitment and understanding necessary to get the decision successfully implemented.

Unlike disagreements over substantive issue-oriented matters, which seem to be largely beneficial, disagreements over personalized, individually oriented matters are largely detrimental to team performance. Conflict theorists collectively call these types of disagreements *affective conflict*—this text will refer to this destructive conflict as A-type conflict. **A-type conflict** lowers team effectiveness by provoking hostility, distrust, cynicism, and apathy among team members.

The descriptions given to A-type conflict in organizational teams focus on personalized anger or resentment and hostility, usually pinpointing certain individuals instead of organizational goals. A-type conflict emerges when C-type conflict becomes "contaminated." This anger, when directed at individuals, may span team boundaries and spread to other areas of the organization. Amason et al. remind us that:

> Unlike C-type conflict, A-type conflict undermines team effectiveness by preventing teams from engaging in the kinds of activities that are critical to team effectiveness. A-type conflict fosters cynicism, distrust, and avoidance, thereby obstructing open communication and integration. When that happens, not only does the quality of solutions decline, but commitment to the team itself erodes because team members no longer associate themselves with the team's actions.
>
> Effective teams learn to combine the diverse capabilities of their members. In contrast, team members who are distrustful of or apathetic toward one another are not willing to engage in the types of discussions necessary to synthesize their different perspectives. As a consequence, the creativity and quality of the team's decisions suffer.
>
> Likewise, team members who are hostile or cynical are not likely to understand, much less commit to, decisions that were made largely without their participation. Thus, in the best case, these members are unable to carry out the decision because they do not understand it. In the worst case, these disgruntled team members are unwilling to work to implement the decision as intended. A-type conflict also undermines a team's ability to function effectively in the future. Team members who have been burned by A-type conflicts are less likely to participate fully in future meetings.[14]

Since research suggests that conflict can be both beneficial and detrimental to team effectiveness, it is important to implement C-type conflict and discourage A-type conflict in groups, as illustrated in Figure 9-7.

C-type conflict enhances team effectiveness by improving both the quality of decisions and the chances that decisions will be successfully implemented. At the same time, A-type conflict reduces team effectiveness by decreasing quality and undermining the understanding and commitment necessary for successful implementation of a decision.

FIGURE 9–7 Outcomes of C-type and A-type Conflict. Source: Adapted from Allen C. Amason, Kenneth R. Thompson, Wayne A. Hockwarter, and Allison W. Harrison, "Conflict: An Important Dimension in Successful Management Teams," *Organizational Dynamics*, Autumn 1995, p. 27.

DECISION-MAKING INTERACTION FLOW	
A-TYPE CONFLICT	**C-TYPE CONFLICT**
Destructive conflict	Better decisions
Reduced progress	Increased commitment
Poorer decisions	Increased cohesiveness
Decreased commitment	Increased empathy
Decreased cohesiveness	Increased understanding
Decreased empathy	

MANAGING C-TYPE CONFLICT WHILE AVOIDING A-TYPE CONFLICT

Because experience tells us that teams with successful outcomes are those that utilize C-type conflict while avoiding A-type conflict, it is important to note the key characteristics that exist in C-type conflict. According to the research, these characteristics are focused on activity, creativity, open communication, and integration.

FOCUSED ACTIVITY. Effective teams focus on the problem and stay close to the task, reaching decisions quickly and efficiently. Less effective teams stray from the central task, dwelling over insignificant points, replacing task goals with social facilitation. Because of this, less focused groups take longer to define problems and develop solutions more quickly than groups that are more focused.

CREATIVITY. Effective teams develop a climate that fosters creativity by encouraging members to consider problems from different angles and discover new and diverse solutions to the problems. C-type conflict is a central force for team creativity. By fostering open communication that encourages differing opinions and creative suggestions, a team is cultivating C-type conflict.

OPEN COMMUNICATION. Teams are more effective when they have more open communication and a culture that promotes free speech and open disagreement with others' viewpoints, free from the threat of hostility, animosity, or retribution. Open communications are the key to achieving genuine team member participation, thereby increasing quality of decision making and strengthening team agreement and acceptance. Less effective teams seem to have less open communications in which team members offer only guarded responses and are fearful of expressing their true opinions.

Outspoken, honest, and sincere communication may produce some disagreement and conflict. However, when team members view the conflict as task oriented, or C-type conflict that is meant to enrich the team's overall effectiveness, they tend to react positively. Only when the conflict seems to be A-type does communication start to undermine team effectiveness by starting self-serving disagreements, by promoting the interests of one team member at the expense of another, and by adopting a defensive stance.

INTEGRATION. All team members are utilized in effective teams. Effective teams using C-type conflict are aware of how crucial it is to include and get the best from all team members. When teams fail to make the fullest possible use of all team members, there is often a disproportionate contribution between members. Why go to the trouble to form a team when the benefit is lost because only a few team members participate in the decision-making process?

Leaders can make their teams more effective by including all team members—asking for opinions of less active team members and moderating the input from members who overpower the discussion. Integration and participation are crucial for obtaining a commitment to the decisions that are made:

> Teams that encourage discussion, debate, and integration can gain higher levels of satisfaction from their members than teams that ignore their differences. The ability to manage conflict so that team members feel free to state their concerns or opinions, even when those concerns or opinions counter the majority, is key to achieving integration of the team members. Obviously, the role of the team leader is central in getting each member of the team involved, as well as building the sort of culture that will improve the team's effectiveness.[15]

TEAM LEADERS AND CONFLICT MANAGEMENT

Team leaders are responsible for managing conflict.

The team leader has the responsibility for managing conflict within the team. Because effective teams are increasingly valuable to organizations, people who are successful at leading or facilitating team interactions play an ever increasingly important role in organizations around the world. Effective team leaders and coaches perfect their conflict management skills including diagnosis by these means:

- Determine when members are suppressing their ideas to avoid conflict.
- Determine if divergent or unpopular ideas are being rejected or ignored.
- Keep tabs on whether conflict is constructive and task related.
- Recognize when members try to smooth over conflict rather than confront it.

Likewise, leaders and coaches intervene by these means:

- Draw out and summarize opposing positions.
- Steer conflict away from personalities and toward task-related issues.
- Tolerate and sustain task-related conflict even when it makes some members (including the leader) uncomfortable.
- Help the team recognize that task-related conflict encourages innovation and creativity.[16]

PROFILE OF HUMAN BEHAVIOR

BRIAN WILSON

Meet one manager who went from "supervisor" to "team developer." Brian Wilson knows what it's like working for a company where management calls the shots, giving orders in one-way communiqués. That's the way it was when he began working at GE, in the early 1980s.

"Back then, it was 'Do as I say,' " says Wilson, who started as an hourly employee, producing numerical control products on the third shift. "Management gave directives and associates performed them, right or wrong, no questions asked."

But those days at the Charlottesville, Virginia, plant are long gone. General Electric Co. has since merged with Japan's Fanuc Ltd. to form GE Fanuc Automation North America, Inc. The U.S. Department of Labor has listed the company as a clearinghouse workplace for its outstanding team leadership. And Wilson is a part of management—sort of.

BECOMING A "TEAM DEVELOPER"

Over the past five years, traditional roles at GE have changed dramatically. Wilson, once a supervisor, is now "team developer" of production operations. He heads up three teams with a total of forty-three associates; there are approximately forty-two teams at the plant.

"Today, management works to support the associates," he says. "We go directly to the people on the front lines—those responsible for implementing the ideas. That's been good for the teams and for the business." So good, in fact, that last year was the best in the company's history. But the gains haven't come without some challenges. When the program first began, consultants and supervisors recruited representatives from manufacturing, marketing, engineering, human resources, and the hourly employees. For more than six months the group, led by Robert Collins—a CEO with a vision—met and discussed how to develop GE Fanuc into a team-based workforce.

"In the beginning, we had a number of people who wanted to opt out. But we wouldn't let them." Wilson explains how the company dealt with the resistance. "You hate to say something is mandatory, but it was. But we knew there couldn't be gains without some pain. So we stuck with it.

"We had a situation where some people had been working together side by side for ten or fifteen years, and hadn't had to speak to each other. Suddenly, they had to.

"Many people were used to taking orders," he continues in a powerful voice that sounds as if it used to give them. . . "We had to learn that when we made decisions as a team, we had to stick with them. And when things didn't happen the way we had planned, we had to bring it back to the meetings and discuss it."

As he speaks, it becomes increasingly apparent why Wilson was selected to help initiate the company into a new era. He is a man who leads by example, and unabashedly admits, "I'm still learning to let go of the reins."

TEAM MEETINGS

Progress is charted through weekly team meetings, where associates set the agenda. In the beginning, associates and team developers were given hours of training in problem solving, conflict management, and goal setting—all of which occurred on site during regular working hours. Continuing education is still available, and once a month, the entire workforce gathers for an operations review, led by Collins. There, monthly business results are reviewed with associates, who are also given an opportunity to participate in a Q&A session with senior management.

Wilson says the key to success has been management's commitment to change and open communication. And the results have gone way beyond profit margins. "It's helped me deal with people in and out of this environment," he says. "It's been a complement to my own life."

"In January, one of my work teams presented at the operations review," he says, returning to the discussion about the plant. "They were asked to share some of their best practices." The team was commended for a newly created cross-training program, in which the associates rotate jobs every three weeks.

"I'm really proud of them," Wilson says. "And this is just the beginning. The sky's the limit."

SOURCE: "Winning Team Plays: The Dream Team," *Supervisory Management*, May 1995, p. 10. Reprinted from May 1995 issue of Supervisory Management by special permission, copyright © 1995 by American Management Association. All rights reserved.

**ACTION PROJECT
9–3**   FORCED-LADDER CHOICES
(INDIVIDUAL AND GROUP EXERCISE)

For this exercise your instructor will ask you to rank the following statements in order of personal feelings, putting the most distasteful one at the top of the ladder. *Note:* Use the parentheticals to write on the numbered rungs of the ladder. It is important that you distribute your choices among all the lines. What matters most is how strong your feelings are. When you are finished, your instructor will break the class into groups of five to discuss your decisions. The groups will then be asked to arrive at a group conclusion. You may cross out, draw arrows, or make changes, but arrive at a final group decision.

1. A man reports his neighbor to the IRS because he heard him mention how he falsified his deductions on his income tax forms. (income tax)

2. A family man with two children and a concern for the population explosion has a vasectomy without consulting his wife. She wants more children and he doesn't. (father)

3. A man believes one should have complete freedom of personal choice. He feels that he should be able to play golf where he pleases and with whom he pleases. So he builds a golf course and operates a segregated club to keep out blacks. (golf club)

4. Two men get their kicks at night by going to Greenwich Village and harassing homosexuals. (two men)

5. A son criticizes his dad for working in a plant that makes munitions to sell to foreign governments. His father tells him to shut up because the money he makes helps send the boy to college. (blue-collar worker)

6. A cop turns his son in for smoking pot. (cop)

Complete your individual feelings rankings first; then wait for your group to work out its rankings.

INDIVIDUAL FEELINGS	GROUP FEELINGS
1. _____	1. _____
2. _____	2. _____
3. _____	3. _____
4. _____	4. _____
5. _____	5. _____
6. _____	6. _____

1. Does personal ego interfere with making logical deductions? Please explain.
   _____

2. When someone in the group challenged you on your opinion, did you lash back, withdraw, or simply refuse to listen to them? Please explain. _____
   _____

3. Did the most aggressive and talkative person win over most of the group? How about the most reserved member; was he or she in control? Please explain. _____
   _____

SUMMARY

Groups have a powerful influence on the success or failure of our organizations. If the group perceives itself as being cohesive, it will be much more likely to succeed. On the other hand, the perception of the group as a habitual failure naturally affects the outcome of further efforts and a vicious cycle of cause-and-effect failure is created. Athletic teams are classic examples of this phenomenon.

The success of groups is influenced by group size and cohesiveness, interpersonal attraction, as well as individual behavior, status, values, or norms of members. Changing social values contribute to the makeup of work groups; increasingly, there are many midcareer changes and a mix of age, gender, and other demographic groups in the workplace.

A key to effective group behavior is the ability of the group to reach consensus. And the key and the challenge to obtaining consensus is keeping discussions on a high, rational plane. Concerted effort by the group leader and group members (limited to a small, cohesive group) to be fair, open, and trusting will help achieve consensus. Above all, universal participation and contribution by all group members will enhance the quality of the process and the decisions.

How people in a group, team, or organization believe their goals are related is important in understanding how effectively they work together. When people believe their goals are compatible, cooperation increases because they know that as one succeeds, others succeed. Conversely, when people believe their goals are competitive, the competition fosters a win–lose climate.

Teams that encourage C-type conflict are productive and effective. Teams utilizing A-type conflict, which is directed toward individuals instead of goals and problems, are unproductive and ineffective. It is important, then, for team leaders to implement C-type conflict and discourage A-type conflict in groups.

CASE STUDY 9–1

WHO'S THE BOSS?

Sam and Sarah Cerenti are a husband-and-wife team operating a small manufacturing facility in Riverside, California. Sam is in charge of design and production of their printed T-shirts, sweatshirts, and other novelty items—many of which are related to ski and other sports industries. Sam's background includes working as a mechanical engineer for a major manufacturing company.

Sarah is responsible for marketing and public relations for the small firm. Unlike Sam, Sarah does not have a formal education in business or engineering but is "picking up the business as she goes along." When a major contract customer presents an idea for a unique, marketable T-shirt and sweatshirt to Sarah, she replies that "We just don't have time in the schedule to produce it." The customer knows that the product will sell because he has done the market research at a chain of health clubs and has orders in hand for several hundred shirts. The customer is put off by Sarah and is ready to take his business elsewhere.

1. What is the problem here? Are there role conflicts?
2. Has Sarah overstepped her authority? Are any of the following factors contributing problems?
   a. Authority definition
   b. Group or role behavior
   c. Management style
   d. Consensus decision making
3. What would you suggest that Sarah, Sam, and the customer do?

CASE STUDY 9–2

CHARLIE HAS A CHANCE TO GET AHEAD

Charlie is employed as an accountant in a small assembly plant in the Midwest. In his seven years at Astro-Technology, he has become acquainted with most of the 200 employees and enjoys the atmosphere of his office and the company attitude toward him. However, in the past three years, he has not received a promotion, and there is little chance for one in the near future. The raises he has received have not kept up with inflation. He has discussed the situation frequently with his wife, Rita, who is working as a personnel officer at a research firm in town. Although Rita has never told Charlie, she feels that her job has more status than his. Even though Charlie earns slightly more income, she has more flexible hours, more holidays with pay, better company fringe benefits, and apparently more status when the two companies' organizational charts are compared. Rita enjoys her present position and the salary she receives. Their two daughters are doing well in grammar school and are active in the Girl Scouts and their local swim team.

A month ago Charlie heard of a new position for an accountant in his company's home office in Dallas. He knows that his company has a practice of promoting from within, and his supervisor feels that he would have a good chance of getting the position. It would mean an immediate 15 percent raise in pay; more prestige, because he would have a private office; and more opportunities for promotions. He applied for the position, but was afraid to tell his wife. When the interview was scheduled, he informed Rita that he had to go to Dallas for a seminar.

Charlie was impressed with Dallas and the possible neighborhoods from which his family could select to make their home. The home office was impressive! Dark walnut and chrome were everywhere, and the personnel in the office were very friendly. After a tour of the facility he had an interview with five managers. A week later he was informed that he was one of the three finalists. He was excited and eager to accept the position if it was offered to him. That night, when he told Rita, she was upset. The move would mean they would have to leave their lovely home that they had been remodeling during the last seven years. The girls would have to find new friends.

Finally, and most important, could Rita find a job as good as the one she has? It seemed unfair to force her to move and give up a good job, just so Charlie could satisfy his own ego. It turned into a real argument. Charlie wants to move and Rita does not. Charlie wants to achieve more in his career and Rita is happy with her current job and their present lifestyle.

1. What points can Charlie use to justify the move and his attitudes about advancing in his career?

2. What points can Rita use to justify staying where they are? What points can she make to say that the status quo is satisfactory for them?

DISCUSSION AND STUDY QUESTIONS—TO KEEP YOU THINKING . . ._____

1. What determines group effectiveness?

2. What are the major differences in behavior, power, and control between formal and informal groups?

3. What are examples of task-related and maintenance-related roles?

4. What can be done to minimize the effects of groupthink?

5. What is the difference in cooperative and competitive goal conflicts?

6. Discuss some points for dealing effectively with individual conflict.

7. Compare and contrast C-type and A-type conflict.

8. List the key characteristics of C-type conflict. How are these characteristics dealt with in A-type conflict?

NOTES

1. M. Deutsch, "Sixty Years of Conflict," *The International Journal of Conflict Management,* January 1990, pp. 237–263.

2. Dean Tjosvold, *Learning to Manage Conflict: Getting People to Work Together Productively* (New York: MacMillan, 1993), pp. 44–46.

3. Ibid.

4. Dave Mason, in James A. Wall, Jr. and Ronda Roberts Callister, "Conflict and Its Management," *Journal of Management,* May–June 1995, pp. 515–558.

5. Valerie I. Sessa, "Using Perspective Taking to Manage Conflict and Affect in Teams," *Journal of Applied Behavioral Science,* March 1996, pp. 101–115.

6. Katherine Zoe Andrews, "Cross-Functional Teams: Are They Always the Right Move?" *Harvard Business Review,* November/December 1995, pp. 12–13.

7. Allen C. Amason, Kenneth R. Thompson, Wayne A. Hochwarter, and Allison W. Harrison, "Conflict: An Important Dimension in Successful Management Teams," *Organizational Dynamics,* Autumn 1995, p. 29.

8. In Richard J. Mayer, *Conflict Management: The Courage to Confront* (Columbus, Ohio: Battelle Press, 1995), p. 3.

9. Tjosvold, *Learning to Manage Conflict,* pp. 48–49.

10. Jimmy Calano and Jeff Salzman, "How to Turn HEAT Into Light," *Working Woman,* March 1988, pp. 122–123.

11. Thomas K. Capozzoli, "Conflict Resolution—A Key Ingredient in Successful Teams," *Supervision,* December 1995, pp. 3–5.

12. Erich Brockmann, "Removing the Paradox of Conflict from Group Decisions," *Academy of Management Executive,* May 1996, pp. 51–62.

13. Amason et al., "Conflict: An Important Dimension," p. 22.

14. Ibid., p. 25.

15. Ibid., p. 29.

16. Greg Burns, "The Secrets of Team Facilitation," *Training & Development,* June 1995, p. 49.

RECOMMENDED READING

Bazerman, M. H., and M. A. Neale. *Negotiating Rationally.* New York: Free Press, 1992.

Bolman, L. G., and T. E. Deal. "What Makes a Team Work?" *Organizational Dynamics,* 1992, pp. 34–44.

Combs, Gail B. "Take Steps to Solve Dilemma of Team Misfits." *HRMagazine,* May 1994, pp. 127–128.

Hackman, J. Richard, ed. *Groups That Work (and Those That Don't).* San Francisco: Jossey-Bass, 1990.

Jehn, K. A. "Enhancing Effectiveness: An Investigation of Advantages and Disadvantages of Value-based Intragroup Conflict." *International Journal of Conflict Management,* Vol. 5, 1994, pp. 223–238.

Katzenbach, J. R., and D. K. Smith. *The Wisdom of Teams.* Boston: Harvard Business School Press, 1993.

Mayer, Richard J. *Conflict Management: The Courage to Confront.* Columbus, Ohio: Battelle Press, 1995.

Rahim, M. A. *Managing Conflict in Organizations.* 2nd ed. Westport, Conn.: Praeger, 1993.

Sherer, Jill. "Resolving Conflict." *Hospital & Health Networks,* April 20, 1994, pp. 52–55.

Tjosvold, Dean. *Learning to Manage Conflict: Getting People to Work Together Productively.* New York: Macmillan Publishing Company, 1993.

_____. *Managing Conflict: The Key to Making Your Organization Work.* Minneapolis: Team Media, 1989.

Yarborough, Mary Helen. "Use Peer Review for Conflict Resolution." *HR Focus,* October 1994, p. 21.

10

POWER AND STATUS

Here are some questions to start you thinking about power and status in organizations.

- How do you define power?
- Is it important for individuals to perceive themselves as powerful if they want to exercise power?
- Is "playing politics" necessarily bad?
- Where does power come from? Is power a function of perception?
- How and why do you measure power in organizations?
- What determines your status?
- Do you agree with the following statement: "If people think they have status, they have status"?
- How would you rate different occupations in terms of status? Do some jobs have more prestige, even though they produce less income than other positions in the marketplace?

LEARNING GOALS

After studying this chapter, you should be able to:

1. Differentiate between personal and organizational or position power.
2. Understand the norm of reciprocity as it pertains to power relationships.
3. Know what types of people are powerful and what makes them powerful.
4. Understand the relationships between power, perception, and organizational politics.
5. Distinguish between "playing politics" and "power plays."
6. Distinguish between various sources and types of power, including
   a. Referent power
   b. Connection power
   c. Reward power
   d. Expert power
   e. Information power
7. Explain how differences in job status are expressed by
   a. Task differentiation
   b. Professionalism
   c. Hours and pay
   d. Work environment
   e. Clothing and other belongings
   f. Communications

8. Explain the major determinants of status.
9. Define and apply the following terms and concepts (in order of first occurrence)

- power
- organizational power
- personal power
- norm of reciprocity
- perception
- expert power
- referent power
- legitimate power
- connection power

- playing politics
- power plays
- status
- social stratification
- status symbols
- professional
- status inconsistency
- status anxiety

DEFINITION OF POWER

Power is a person's ability to influence others, not just their behavior. The amount of power that an individual possesses is determined by his or her organizational and personal power.

Organizational power is derived from higher authority.

Organizational power refers to the capacity of managers to exert influence over others. It is derived from higher level authority and is delegated downward in an organization. The greatest organizational power is the power of doing a good job—the power of and authority of being right, having the knowledge, and being a proficient expert in one's discipline. **Personal power,** on the other hand, is obtained from the acceptance of followers, not from higher level management.

Personal power is obtained from acceptance of followers.

There is certainly an instinct for power in many of us. Most people do not like to admit that they want power, which is why they never get it. Those who do have power may go to endless lengths to mask that fact. The contemporary American style of power is to pretend that one has none, because to confess that one has power is to make oneself responsible for using it. The masters of power instinctively try to control every situation in which they find themselves and try to place as much of an obligation as possible on another person.

We have various reasons for working: (1) money (need), (2) pleasure, (3) identification in society, (4) escape, and (5) power. Companies consciously or unconsciously have noticed that the opportunity to acquire and wield power motivates people. Therefore there tends to be a built-in or "house" power game that is established by the management. Most corporations find it in their interest to encourage power games, because providing an opportunity to obtain power is cheaper than giving raises.

Hedrick Smith, PBS correspondent, writes in *The Power Game* that "Power is the ability to make something happen or to keep it from happening." He continues:

In short, the most vital ingredients of power are often the intangibles. Information and knowledge are power. Visibility is power. A sense of timing is power. Trust and integrity are power. Personal energy is power; so is self-confidence. Showmanship is power. Likability is power. . . . Winning is power. Sometimes, the illusion of power is power.[1]

Power is only as useful as it is recognized by those over whom it is exercised. There is a quid pro quo for power; that is, individuals over whom it is exercised accept it. This is known as the acceptance of authority or power. Coercion or force may have been used to effect the acceptance, but it is nevertheless not really effective until it is accepted.

Norm of reciprocity creates an obligation.

Related to the acceptance of power is another concept known as the norm of reciprocity. The **norm of reciprocity** states that people feel an obligation to return pay or other consideration to another for continuance of a mutually beneficial relationship.

WHO ARE THE POWERFUL?

Heads of private and public organizations including government wield a great amount of power. The stereotype of the powerful individual is the tycoon billionaire who can buy and sell properties at will, including the services of individuals. To be sure, many of the very powerful have amassed large private fortunes; even more are the heads of publicly held corporations. Figure 10–1 shows some of the most powerful people in corporate America according to one annual survey. Note that more than half of those listed in 1987 are now out of their powerful offices. In addition to IBM, Sears, Apple, and others cited, major changes were forced in top leadership at General Motors, Westinghouse, Eastman Kodak, and many others.

The individuals shown in Figure 10–1 and others like them are extremely powerful, but there are many others beneath the surface of these and similar private and public organizations who wield considerable power. What makes one person powerful and another not, even though they have both formal organizational and personal power? Before individuals can be considered powerful, they must possess the confidence and trust of those over whom they would exercise power. They must also have the self-confidence that they can use power to the satisfaction of subordinates, bosses, and other coworkers.

Chief of staff position has power.

Behind-the-scenes power brokers are common. The chief of staff position in many organizations possesses considerable power but does not always share the glory (or disdain!) from others. Consider the chiefs of staff for all the presidents of the United States that you can remember—do they not wield considerable power in who gets the ear of or who gets to see the president? Just the recent presidents—Ford, Carter, Reagan, Bush, and Clinton—have had powerful individuals in Dick Cheney (later secretary of defense), Jodi Powell, Don Regan, James Baker (later secretary of state), John Sununu, and Leon Panetta, to name a few.

1987	CORPORATE ORGANIZATION	1996
John Akers	IBM	Out
Edward Brennen	Sears, Roebuck	Out
Warren Buffett (diversified investor; temporary CEO of Salomon, Inc.)	Berkshire Hathaway	Warren Buffett
Robert Crandall	AMR (American Airlines)	Robert Crandall
Michael Eisner	Disney	Michael Eisner
Robert Goizueta	Coca-Cola	Robert Goizueta
Katherine Graham	Washington-Post	Out
John Gutfreund	Salomon, Inc.	Out
Lee Iacocca	Chrysler	Out
Rupert Murdoch	New Corporation, Ltd. (Fox media et al.)	Rupert Murdoch
John F. "Jack" Welch	General Electric	Jack Welch
John Young	Hewlett-Packard	Out
John Sculley	Apple	Out

MORE POWER TO YA!

Power can exist in different forms that vary in their degree of forcefulness. The manager can use a number of means for building a power base:

1. Proficiency—knowing the job better than anyone else
2. Position—one's place in the hierarchy
3. Praise—the perceived ability to reward
4. Punishment—the perceived ability to damage
5. Politics—access to stakeholders in the organization
6. Personality—one's personal characteristics
7. Persuasion—the cultivated skill of changing beliefs
8. Performance—doing the job better through greater expenditures of time and effort
9. Potential—convincing others of what one might be able to do someday
10. Protégé—involving others in one's connections to an influential person

The more power managers can accrue, the more resources they can command. With more resources, the managers' subordinates can do their jobs better.[2]

Sometimes the power is hidden even further from view. James Baker and Don Regan were both active chiefs of staff, but the real power broker behind President Reagan was his wife, Nancy—who ultimately arranged the removal of Regan. Parallel situations exist in other organizations, including city governments, educational institutions, and the military where the chief of staff role has achieved formal status.

PROFILE OF HUMAN BEHAVIOR

G. DALE MEYER

Dr. G. Dale Meyer is both a professor and a businessperson (an entrepreneur and consultant). During his academic career he has risen to distinguished professor status at the University of Colorado–Boulder, having received an endowed chair and the university's lifetime teaching award, the President's Teaching Scholar. Professor Meyer left university life for several years to found and serve as CEO of the Western Management Corporation, a strategic assessment, broker, and equity ownership firm in more than 300 entrepreneurial companies.

He is presently the Anderson Professor of Entrepreneurial Development and President of the United States Association of Small Business and Entrepreneurship (USASBE), an affiliate of the International Council of Small Business (ICSB) where he serves on the board of directors. Dr. Meyer also serves on the boards of five other companies.

"Power is a form of influence," says Meyer. "There are many power bases including holding a position of authority, being an expert in something other people need in order to succeed or reach goals, and coercion or autocratic, top-down power. In today's culture in the United States, coercive power is an alien concept. Over the long run, people will not, and in fact should not, tolerate coercive, dogmatic techniques of leadership or management style."

"In fact, dispersing the power throughout an organization actually creates *more* influence. I like to call it 'leading from behind.' In other words, by delegating and inspiring all people to be responsible for the whole, visions and missions are accomplished much more effectively and efficiently than when an individual or small coterie of people attempt to control everything. The leader becomes a reference person whose strategies are internalized by those who are responsible for implementation (although strategy making should also be participative)."

". . . it takes a very secure person to distribute her/his power in a process which might look to an outsider like giving up control. But yielding authority (a form of power) to a wider group of people means that the responsibility for performance is more generally shared by others. Things get done. The right things get done. Yet, the ultimate responsibility still rests with the leader and it becomes much more possible to accomplish the widely internalized goals. Also, an effective leader is a visionary *and* a moderate risk taker."

"In addition to the increased performance that wide empowerment brings to an organization, there is an ethical issue as well. All individuals have something to contribute to the whole. The leader can find the theretofore hidden capabilities of another individual and support the utilization and growth of those capabilities. This renewal allows the empowered person to feel his/her dignity as a human being. Small successes build other larger successes. Self-worth is enhanced. The leader believes in his/her ability to bring out the best in others. Such empowerment creates a win–win outcome. And, it's simply the right thing to do."

POWER AND PERCEPTION

Power is a function of perception.

Are perception and power strange bedfellows? Not really, for power is more a function of perception than anything else. The strengths of both personal and organizational power are a matter of perception. Important perceived questions are "Can the boss or any other powerful individual reward or punish me?" "Is the boss competent?" and "Does he or she have the formal position or earned respect from me to exercise power?"

Perception is a matter of individuals' beholding what others believe, think, or see to be truly representative of a situation. If an individual is perceived as having power, he or she has power—at least in the eye of the beholder. If they are not perceived as having power, they have a serious flaw in conducting business effectively for their organizations. Self-confidence and self-perception are part of this process as well.

LEADERSHIP POWER IS DERIVED

Leaders are given power by group consensus.

It is common practice to grant leadership power to people who already have some authority. But leaders are given their power only by group consensus, without necessarily having any special status, such as position, skill, or education, to recommend them. Leaders gain power within a group gradually, by establishing trust and recognition.

Power is largely a matter of perception. If the leader is perceived to have power, then that leader's ability to lead and otherwise exercise influence over a group is enhanced. The distinguishing difference between a leader and an authority figure is that the group chooses the leaders (see Figure 10–2). We will examine those leadership processes in greater detail in Chapter 11.

EXPRESS YOUR OPINION

What are the attributes of leaders/managers that make them powerful? Are they considered to have the following attributes? envisioner? empowerer? champion? encourager? listener? person with knowledge? others?

SOURCES AND TYPES OF POWER

What are the real sources of power? Power is derived from various sources, including personal expertise and from informal leadership skills that enable managers to obtain the loyalty and support of others.[3] You do not have to take power away from others to increase your power base.

You do not have to be the highest ranking individual to be the most powerful. The power of the informal group is strong—and just because a person has formal organizational power does not make him or her more powerful than someone else who has strong personal power.

Let's examine the sources. Figure 10–3 shows a continuum of the sources and types of power.

EXPERT POWER

Expert power is personal power based on skill and knowledge. The power of expertise is a most important source. Does the person who exercises the power know what he or she is talking about? If the answer is "yes," he or she has the authority or power because of that knowledge and competence. Such power is important in organizations where there may not be a direct boss–subordinate

FIGURE 10-3 A Continuum of Power Types.

relationship between individuals but cooperation is essential if objectives are to be achieved.

INFORMATION POWER

He or she who holds the information has the power—at least the power of information. If someone else—a boss, subordinate, or other decision maker—needs certain information and you have that information, you also have power.

Expert and information power are based on knowledge.

Information power is similar to but different from expert power in that they are both sharing knowledge or information, but the power of expertise is based more on education and knowledge held than is the latter, which is based on information held. For example, a person may be very smart and know a subject backward and forward, but he or she may lack essential skills and information in passing that knowledge along.

REFERENT POWER

Influence based on **referent power** reflects faith in and following of the leader. A person has referent power if others identify with him or her. This type of power comes as close as any to the charismatic approach or following that is so often talked about. People like to be with or follow this type of powerful person.

People follow individuals they admire.

People like and follow individuals in whom they see characteristics they admire. They are emotionally attached—perhaps even mesmerized—by this kind of power. They are probably liked personally and may be perceived as a role model or mentor. Individuals with referent power are just plain liked better than others.

LEGITIMATE POWER

Legitimate power is based on position and exists because people believe a person has a legitimate right to influence them. It is power delegated from within an organization. Employees feel obligated to follow the power because of the formal position.

Response to legitimate power is routine.

Response to legitimate power is almost automatic. The power is so entrenched that a response is routine. If power is exercised over something that is standard operating procedure, a routine response can be expected. There are cultural and social expectations by peers that legitimate power will be followed. A spin-off of legitimate power is representative power—like that of a union steward or public relations officer who is an important liaison with management.

REWARD POWER

Reward power is just what it sounds like—the holder has the power to reward. A person is influenced by the powerholder who can offer a reward and whether that reward satisfies a fundamental need. If people think that their efforts will meet the powerholder's objectives and if they think their efforts will be rewarded, they will follow.

Not all rewards are tangible; a leader can exercise reward power by complimenting another. Reward power is positive reinforcement using various types of incentives such as pay raises, promotions, praise, and recognition. Reward power is most closely related to motivation: It is a matter of finding out what motivates others and attempting to reward them accordingly.

CONNECTION POWER

Closely related to rewards, **connection power** allows the holder to reward others through a network of connections with influential people. As noted before, power is largely a matter of perception, and if the holder is viewed as having powerful connections, the holder has power. An individual may not have strong personal or organizational power, but if he or she has connections with people who do, that individual can exercise that connection power.

A person with connections has power.

COERCIVE POWER

Figure 10–4 offers several summary suggestions for eliminating negative reactions to the exercise of power.

FIGURE 10–4 Steps for Minimizing Negative Reactions to Power. Adapted from Robert Baron, "Power in Organizations: Using It Wisely," *Behavior in Organizations*, 2nd ed. (Boston: Allyn & Bacon, 1986) p. 353.

1. "It is better to be liked than feared." The general rule is, in most situations, referent power is preferable to coercive power.
2. Always know what you're doing. It is crucial for persons wishing to exercise power over others to establish a high level of expertise. To the extent that they do, this may enhance their performance.
3. Be legitimate; don't overstep the bounds. Managers have legitimate power over their subordinates to change subordinates' behavior in some ways but not others. It is very important that these boundaries not be overstepped.
4. Style counts—always use the velvet glove. Many managers are unsure about how to give directions to their subordinates; most people strongly dislike being told what to do; it makes them angry. Instructions that are phrased as requests rather than commands can prevent employees from feeling that their egos have been squashed.

On the continuum of personal to organizational power, coercive power is most typical of organizational power. Here the powerholder has the power to punish. Like reward power, it is largely a matter of perception but also fact if it is the boss who holds the power. The threat of punishment is as strong as the actual act of punishment as we know from the study of discipline and disciplinary action. Punishment or the threat of it works better in law than in management; it is advisable to minimize the use of coercive power because it hurts human relations and productivity.

ACTION PROJECT
10–1

WHO HAS THE POWER? AND WHAT KIND OF POWER IS IT?
(INDIVIDUAL AND/OR GROUP EXERCISE)

George Schwartz is CEO of Schwartz Enterprises, Inc. (SEI). SEI is a conglomerate food processor and supplier. They have been very active in acquiring subsidiary companies who now compete with one another as profit centers.

George is concerned that various executives within the company use quite different styles of management. By itself, this does not present a problem and is to be expected because of the vigorous acquisition strategies followed by SEI. On the other hand, George wants to learn more about the decisions that are being made by key executives at SEI. Some are causing discontent and morale problems, and George thinks some decisions are a misuse or abuse of power.

Below are several scenarios of actions being taken by key Schwartz executives. See if you can identify the power styles or types being used by those individuals. Write the type of power in the appropriate blank. Your instructor will probably then ask you to discuss your choices either individually or in groups. Be prepared to defend your choices.

POWER TYPE (WRITE IN BLANK): EXECUTIVE ACTION

_____ Frank Lefler is VP of purchasing for SEI. Frank recently bought several motors and other products at a considerable discount before prices went up based on useful data that he acquired from data banks, suppliers' price sheets, and telephone conversations with suppliers.

_____ Marjorie Cummins is VP of marketing. She has authority over salespeople and other marketing personnel. In addition, she knows where the potential large customers are and can refer these personnel to them for large orders—she knows her global territories very well.

_____ Sally Brown is an office manager for one of the larger subsidiaries. She has many personnel reporting to her and can schedule overtime and days off, and also has the potential for terminating unsatisfactory performers, since many of these people report directly to her but work in other corporate and subsidiary offices.

_____ Jose Rodriquez is a plant manager for another one of the subsidiaries. Jose has been with the company for more than twenty years and worked his way up the chain of command. He is very well liked by his subordinates who "would go to hell and back for him" in the words of one of his subordinates.

_____ John Bolger is VP of R&D for one of the major subsidiaries as well as the corporate offices. John is extremely well qualified through education and experience in his fields. Whenever there is doubt about the viability of a process or even the potential for a new market, John's opinion is sought.

_____ Jodie Foster is executive VP of SEI. She earned her position because of her formal education and work background, which includes being president of one of the largest subsidiaries. She reports directly to Mr. Schwartz and has most of the presidents of the subsidiaries reporting directly to her.

_____ Benny Mandang is a superintendent over several foremen and all of the workers at one of the subsidiary companies. Benny "runs" the plant and determines who will be hired and promoted and who gets raises.

POLITICS

The manifestation of power is a series of political trade-offs. Always present is the idea of "you scratch my back, and I'll scratch yours," or a reciprocal agreement to help one another.

Some groups and individuals have formal power to control others directly. Other groups have power to impact others by slowing performance and productivity. Any group can impact others by advancing or withholding power in the form of services rendered or economic sanctions. This is known as "playing politics." The term generally has a negative connotation, but fortunately it is not all bad. **Playing politics** is a positive way of distributing power in offices and organizations. Using politics at work is an artform.[4] Much of that power distribution and its impact come with experience, but it may serve you well to study the following.

Politics is a way of distributing power.

OFFICE POLITICS

Business, or the conduct of any transaction, is by definition a process of give-and-take. If we are to be successful in our transactions, we have to be sensitive to others, their needs and aspirations. Office politics means tuning into others and their reactions. Specific examples of office politics activities include these:

- Congeniality toward coworkers, including bosses and subordinates
- Unusual praise for bosses' or subordinates' work
- Helping a coworker who is struggling with a work-related problem
- Taking action solely to satisfy the boss
- Sharing information in articles or reports
- Communicating positively and selectively; that is, knowing when to say nothing

Do you see any compromises in your values if you engage in these activities?

ORGANIZATIONAL POLITICS

Positive strategies for becoming more powerful.

Various pragmatic strategies have been developed for becoming more politically powerful and effective. When all else fails, do what is right—in your own mind, or seek the advice of a trusted counselor. Help others to achieve their objectives and thereby build your own power. Find a mentor who has connection power. Make alliances and work from a position of strength in numbers. Finally, practice power by example—the action of work well done will speak more loudly than all the status symbols in the world.

There are also illegitimate strategies that include blackmail, character assassination, and physical force. These unscrupulous methods are self-serving, and no matter how nasty you may be or think you are, there is always someone who can make you look like an amateur! There are many professional "politicians" who know how to play the game—and those politicians are not all in government!

POWER PLAYS

Read the signs of power plays.

Power plays refer to actions taken behind the scenes to get what you want. Power players don't want publicity. It is better to set things up quietly and patiently, so that what they want is offered to them. Confrontation produces friction and friction slows progress.

How can you recognize the power plays at work? A person shows outward signs of power. There is a solid presence suggesting that the person belongs where he or she is, with a certain immobility, steady eyes, and quiet hands. Nothing can substitute for the combination of self-control and personal magnetism.

Rocklike immobility in times of crisis gives an impression that a person is in control. People who sit still acquire a reputation for common sense and reliability. If you wish to develop such a posture, try not to shift your eyes or blink a lot. Look straight at the person with whom you are conversing and keep your gaze on the person longer than he or she does on you. A relaxed mouth is very helpful, because pursed lips, lip biting, or twitching the corners of the mouth can show frustration or nervousness.[5]

High-stakes players never ask for favors, but grant them willingly and make sure that there is no way of returning them. They take advantage of these situations in their favor. Such persons establish territorial imperatives by pushing their things gradually toward you or leaving their possessions around.

POWER RELATIONSHIPS

Good leaders obtain authority from groups.

People who have authority are not necessarily leaders. All leaders have authority, but all authoritarians are not leaders. Good leaders derive their authority from the group.

EXTERNAL POWER IS DERIVED

External power stems from multiple sources.

Authority, or externally derived power, usually stems from position or rank. Heads of small firms and managers of departments have authority because of their job positions. The director of a corporation will influence numbers of people because of the considerable authority he or she has in the organization. Because of the power vested in the position of the presidency of the United States, a president's policies influence the destinies of the nation and all its people.

External power may also come from knowledge or expertise. For example, a group applying for a grant may turn for leadership to someone who has applied for grants successfully in the past. A company interested in building a nuclear power plant will look to the most educated and experienced experts in the field of nuclear physics for leadership. Our leaders need—must have—the autonomy and power to lead if they are to be effective.

Michael Korda, author of *Power: How to Get It and How to Use It,* has said we no longer have power brokers. He cites Ronald Reagan as a charismatic, powerful individual but states:

> Those who are not willing to delegate at least some power will eventually lose their own (power)—and their freedom. People who cannot take orders are in no position to give orders when they themselves are placed in positions of authority. We have gradually transformed our system of government into a town meeting of over 250 million people in which everyone has an equal right to prevent things from being done, but in which no one person can effectively control or begin anything.[6]

A frequent criticism heard of organizations today is that it takes too long to get some things done. Korda tells us why, in part, and leads to the suggestions that we need to capitalize on our power sources and exercise power to produce effective goods and services in a timely fashion.

POWER MEASUREMENTS

How do we know if we are doing a good job? How do we know if we are getting things done effectively? We measure it. Measurements of power include the following:

- Estimating potential influence by examining the outcomes of contested decisions in an organization
- Assessing power by examining each party's available sources of power and the constraints on its use
- Examining reputational indicators of power, an approach that assumes a relatively stable power distribution exists at a given point of time, that organization members know who has how much power, and that they are willing to talk candidly about the power distribution[7]

Other, more objective indicators of power include status symbols such as a person's position title, office location and furnishings, and salary. Special privileges provide an indication of the person's power in the organization. A weakness in this kind of measure is the possibility that status symbols may lag shifts in power or that some powerful persons may prefer to avoid obvious status symbols.[8]

THE SOCIAL BASIS OF STATUS

DEFINITION

Status is ranking by prestige as seen by others.

Status is the term applied to the *ranking or ordering of people into relative positions of prestige and the social rewards offered with such positions.* Status involves a two-way transaction that must include at least two people. One person may claim status, but status is not achieved unless the other person confers it. In other words, status is earned. People of similar social status recognize one another by their social similarities, such as speech, mannerisms, and ways of dressing.

People of the same rank consider one another equals. The various status levels are acknowledged and maintained on the basis of social differences that separate people from one another. In the assignment of status roles, certain differences are emphasized, whereas other differences—as well as similarities—are ignored. Which characteristics become the bases for social position depends on what is considered important to a particular society.

Some of the most common characteristics used to classify people are (1) wealth and possessions; (2) education; (3) appointed authority; (4) ethnic background, religion, or race; (5) ancestry; (6) income; (7) occupation; and (8) political and economic power. The significance of ancestry, ethnic origin, or kinship is more important in some countries than others. In China, Great Britain, Kenya, and other African countries, these factors are more important than in the United States. Similarly, level of education has more significance in European countries than it does in the United States.

EXPRESS YOUR OPINION	Does it make sense to classify or stereotype people by any means? Do you have ethical or moral reservations about such classifications?

SOCIAL STRATIFICATION

Social stratification is the ranking of people within society, by others, into higher and lower social positions to produce a hierarchy of respect or prestige. The things that people want, such as money, position, or security, are all in short supply and are distributed unevenly. The status system is a way of recognizing this uneven distribution of social values; that is, it is a way of according the people at or near the top the respect due them for having the most of what society wants.

Status recognizes uneven social values.

We can do little to change our heredity, race, or ethnic background, but if we desire, we can change our education, income, occupation, or power. Some may be able to upgrade themselves through a form of status over which they have some control; for example, those who try to enhance their prestige or status by using power.

STATUS SYMBOLS

There are all kinds of **status symbols,** external evidence of value that individuals attach to behaviors, people, and "things." The attainment of power and rank are considered normal work goals, and this process plays an important role in organizational incentive systems. In fact, the privileges attached to high-status positions are sometimes even more important to workers than is the money they earn.

Importance of jobs is often determined by the symbols.

The more observable the tasks, the easier it is to discern status. In physical or manual work, the levels of skill and responsibility a job requires are readily apparent. In offices, however, everyone shuffles papers and, because jobs tend to look similar, more obvious external signs of status are needed. The importance of jobs, then, remains to be judged by the symbols attached to them.

Generally, the larger the organization, the more preoccupied are its workers with status symbols. Large organizations operate much like the military, with highly visible status symbols serving as a way of communicating authority. Because of the close personal contacts usually present in small companies, where everybody knows who has the power, symbols of authority are not as necessary.

HOURS AND PAY

Salary has more status than wages. Why?

Hourly workers who are required to punch time clocks do not have the same amount of status as those who receive fixed salaries—even though the hourly employees may earn more money. Working during fixed daily hours usually carries less prestige than being paid to complete specific projects. Only "important" employees are given the freedom to work around the clock or to not show up at all.

Fixed working hours have less prestige.

Employees often indicate their high status by being casual about the hours they work: arriving late, leaving early, taking long lunch hours and breaks, and randomly leaving workstations to chat with other workers. Lower status employees must observe rigid work schedules and strict eating and resting periods. So-called "hourly" employees can actually be paid for minutes worked and may even have to request permission to go to the bathroom.

Relative pay standards within organizations do not apply consistently within the larger society. A relatively high wage may indicate monetary *compensation* to make up for low status. For example, a construction worker doing manual labor usually has less social prestige than does an office clerk. Yet construction workers make two to three times more money than do office clerks.

Despite the difference in pay, certain people wish to change from being a blue-collar worker to a white-collar worker. Why? (1) Supervision is more relaxed. (2) If the white-collar job is nonunion, there is less likelihood of being harassed and having to follow the many rules of unions. (3) Informal dialogue replaces the formal interview in the hiring process. (4) Grievances are likely to be handled through counseling by the supervisor rather than through a rigid grievance system.

WORK ENVIRONMENT

Status can be conferred by any agreed-on formula. The placement of a machinist's machine, the location of a parking spot, the location of a personal locker—all can carry status significance. Working near the end of the production line

TABLE 10–1 Office Furniture Allotment

1. Department head or equivalent	Desk, table, credenza, swivel chair, four to six arm chairs, 12' chalkboard, files as required
2. Section head	Desk, table, swivel chair, four to six side chairs, 8' chalkboard, two bookcases, files as required
3. Supervisor	Desk, table, swivel chair, two side chairs, bookcase, chalkboard space, four-drawer file
4. Scientist or engineer	Desk, swivel chair, side chair, chalkboard space, bookcase, four-drawer file cabinet
5. Secretary, clerical, etc.	Desk, swivel chair, file, furniture as authorized by department head
6. Draft, tech, hourly, etc.	No furniture

usually carries more status than working near the beginning because the finished product is more valuable. Working on the eighth floor with the salespeople can imply less status than working on the tenth floor near the manager's office. Do you agree with these implications?

The aspects of the work environment that go beyond meeting utilitarian needs are usually placed there for the sake of status. Just about any environmental factor can be incorporated into creating a desired image: size of facility, layout and size of work areas, furniture, colors, decorations, temperature, humidity, ventilation, noise, and lighting are all status indicators.

Table 10–1 lists the furnishings allowed the various occupations in a small research firm in California. In this company the furnishings obviously indicate precise levels of status.

Within organizations, the value of certain status symbols depends on high demand and limited supply. If all the offices are already plush, then the size and location of work areas will indicate the status. For example, in most companies the few corner offices have premium status, followed by the rarely available offices with windows. Windowless offices are more numerous and, hence, lower in status. In offices with no windows, lighting is often used as a status criterion.

Corner offices have higher status.

Normally, higher status is attached to the people having better working conditions. The better the working conditions, the higher the status. That is why white-collar jobs usually carry more status than blue-collar jobs of equal skill and pay. The status value given to different conditions has a supply-and-demand effect similar to that in economics. When supply is adequate relative to demand, the status value will be less than when demand exceeds supply. For example, if there were a great demand for plumbers and carpenters and few trained, their status would go up; likewise, if the demand for nurses and druggists were low, the status of these professions would drop.

Better working conditions mean higher status.

CLOTHING AND CARS

Throughout history, dress has been an important way in which to determine people's status. The mass production of clothing in the twentieth century has

FIGURE 10–5 Many People Expect Some Government Employees and Others to Wear Readily Identifiable Clothing on the Job. Spectra.

eliminated many traditional status distinctions based on dress. Today, "dirt" rather than fashion is the determining factor in the different attitudes that white- and blue-collar workers have about their work clothing. The basic dress distinction between the two groups is that white-collar workers can wear fashionable street clothes to work and blue-collar workers must wear clothes to protect them from dirt.

Career apparel can affect morale.

Lab technicians, nurses, waiters and waitresses, police personnel, and many other people employed in service industries wear uniforms to work every day. People expect the police, flight attendants, and nurses to wear readily identifiable clothing on the job (see Figure 10–5). Some banks, public utilities, and insurance companies also provide "work clothes" for employees. The advantage of career apparel is that it tends to boost employee morale, at least temporarily; it improves the public image, it is tax deductible for the employer or the employee, and the relative cost is small when compared with what a person would normally pay for a work wardrobe . The disadvantage is the absolute cost. There is also a loss of individuality, and the apparel program may become old and dull after a few years.

Some American workers seem to like the convenience of uniforms. Honda provides each worker with eight and launders and mends them. "It saves deciding what to wear to work," said one worker. Company uniforms are a cultural value in Japan. "In Japan, what counts most is the group relationship and one's ability to conform to it." Individualism is frowned on. An old Japanese aphorism holds that "the nail that sticks out usually gets hammered down." Janet Guthrie, the first woman to compete in the Indianapolis 500, writes that "In an age of individual affluence and mobility formerly unknown, the automobile rivals clothing as a statement of social, professional and political position, philosophical affiliation and wealth."[9]

FIGURE 10–6 Those Who Want Promotions Have Different Speech Patterns

THOSE DESIRING PROMOTION MOST

1. Are more guarded with their communications.
2. Minimize disagreements with supervisors.
3. Filter out or minimize their problems.
4. Stick more to "Business" talk.
5. Communicate more with superiors.

HOW STATUS AFFECTS COMMUNICATION

Status affects the manner in which people communicate with one another. The ability to move upward in the organizational hierarchy greatly affects the nature of communication (see Figure 10–6). Talking with a supervisor, even about the job, is a form of socialization often used to gain favor with supervisors. Employees may minimize actual disagreements with their supervisors to put themselves in favorable light.

A study done in three large industrial organizations found that information communicated to supervisors is heavily filtered when it reflects incompetence and thus threatens the security or progress of subordinates. The study discovered that the more people aspire to move upward, the less accurate is their communication upward.[10] Another study concluded that, when low-ranking members of an organization are in a position to move upward, they are exceedingly guarded in their relations with those of higher rank who can interfere with their progress.[11]

The more one wants to move up, the less accurate the communication.

Good communicators have a better chance of having their ideas accepted by the boss than noncommunicative individuals. The ability to communicate well can itself be status producing.

JOB STATUS

What makes one job "better" than another? high pay? prestige? good working conditions? job security?

The answer is that there is no single deciding factor. Truly great jobs offer all of the above and more. Yet some careers that seem most enviable to outsiders often have hidden drawbacks. Airline pilots, for example, are well paid but must work grueling hours. Jobs, after all, are a complicated mix of pluses and minuses, and most people know the ins and outs of only their own personal work.[12]

The 1992 study by Branch and Luciano ranks 100 jobs based on qualities including pay, security, prestige, and overall satisfaction. Action Project 10–2 extracts 27 of those 100 jobs and compares them to a 1981 Gallup poll that found that relative rankings of certain professions had not changed appreciably in thirty years.[13] Try your hand at ranking the overall attractiveness, pay, respectability, prestige, and status of jobs. How do they compare with the 1992 and 1981 results? Can you explain the differences or trends?

ACTION PROJECT 10–2 TRY YOUR HAND AT JOB STATUS RANKING

RANK	1981	1992	YOUR RANKING
1.	MD	Biologist	
2.	Judge	Geologist	
3.	Clergy	Physician	
4.	Banker	College math professor	
5.	Lawyer	High school principal	
6.	Public school principal	Sociologist	
7.	Business executive	Pharmacist	
8.	Public school teacher	Urban planner	
9.	Funeral director	Civil engineer	
10.	Local political office holder	Veterinarian	
11.	Advertising practitioner	Aeronautical engineer	
12.	Realtor	Chemist	
13.		Electrical engineer	
14.		Bank officer	
15.		High school teacher	
16.		Lawyer	
17.		Army officer	
18.		Dentist	
19.		Grade school teacher	
20.		Architect	
21.		Sculptor	
22.		Airline pilot	
23.		Orchestral musician	
24.		Librarian	
25.		Purchasing manager	
26.		Film director	
27.		Funeral director	

Note: These are only the top 27 jobs; there are 73 other jobs ranked in the 1992 study.

SOURCES: "Professions: Contributions to Society, Stress, Prestige," Gallup Report No. 193, October 1981, p. 17; and Shelly Branch and Lani Luciano, "Money's Best Jobs in America," *Money,* February 1992, p. 68.

TITLES AND POSITIONS

Job titles promote status distinctions. An executive has more job status than a shipping clerk, a secretary more status than a typist, a journeyman more status than an apprentice.

Status distinctions sometimes make us forget that many different kinds of work are necessary for the smooth functioning of our total society. They tend to separate us and to add to existing social and political tensions, particularly in large cities.

The secretary's status is determined in part by boss's status.

The same job title can carry differences in status caused by the status of the organization or the supervisor. The salesperson for an international company has a "better" job than does the salesperson working for a local manufacturer. The secretary to the senior vice president has more status than does the secretary to the sales division manager. The architect who designs huge office buildings can be more influential with colleagues than can the architect who designs only small dwellings.

PROFESSIONALISM

Professionals are experts.

Sometimes the only difference between an "occupation" and a "profession" is the social status accorded to various jobs. A **professional** is a career type that is recognized by others as a profession. It is determined primarily by a college degree and/or special licensing. Attempts to "upgrade" or "professionalize" occupations are attempts to gain greater social recognition for certain kinds of work. Sometimes the nature of the work warrants such desires to raise status, sometimes it does not.

ASPECTS OF A PROFESSION

1. Career is restricted to credentials and professional training. More requirements limit the number who will enter the field; examples: law school and medical school.
2. Activities that do not enhance one's prestige are dropped.
3. Tasks that already have status are claimed as part of the profession.
4. The profession is consulted early in the decision making.
5. The words of the more professional "experts" are challenged less.
6. More "life and death" decisions are left to professionals.
7. Peer review is common.
8. Licenses are applied for and renewed because of continuing education.

STATUS INCONSISTENCY AND AMBIGUITIES

Status inconsistency is any discrepancy due to different status assignments awarded by society. The indicators of status include title, pay position, and symbols. Each of these is a barometer that measures a different aspect of status. As

Today as more and more people attend college in hopes of upgrading their status and more career fields are requiring more professional training, some interesting things are developing. In many areas of the United States, more than 50 percent of the high school graduates will continue their education by going to college.

Many fields state that they are professionals or experts. Such career areas are requiring that people pass more tests or take more college courses to be accepted into the realm of the professionals. For example, in the past twenty years the real estate field in California has gradually required more and more professional or college coursework to receive the designation of "realtor."

With more people attempting to become "professional," will the term have less meaning in the next century? Further, as more people are becoming more educated, are they challenging the words of the "experts" or professionals now more than they did five or ten years ago? Should the public question professionals, such as lawyers, doctors, dentists, engineers, and educators more or less than they do now? Why? Is this questioning authority? What is your opinion?

If all roles have the same status, life is consistent.

long as all these status indicators give approximately the same readings, status is not likely to cause trouble to the individual or the organization. But when such indicators of status give inconsistent measures, personnel unrest and dissatisfaction will ensue.

Ambiguous situations in which the status position of an individual or group has not been established clearly can be troublesome. In a sense, status symbols are characterized by a "culture lag," because they do not keep up with technological and organizational changes. Newly created groups obviously suffer status identification, because there is no easy placement using the present status indicator.

At work, people with seniority do *not* always have the highest status jobs or earn the most money. Office jobs may pay less than factory jobs, even though it is generally agreed that office workers enjoy higher occupational status. Sometimes supervisors earn less than the employees under them.

Inconsistent measures may result in personnel unrest and dissatisfaction. The more prestigious group members expect to occupy the more prestigious jobs. The longer service, better educated employee expects extra respect, but may not receive it. The employee with a prestigious family background and education who works in a low-status job may feel uncomfortable and may demonstrate aggression. Employees who enjoy status consistency are less likely to feel the stress and difficulties than are those who do not.

Different status rankings for roles lead to inconsistencies.

One can anticipate that "status anxiety" would show itself when an employee is unable to cope with his or her expected status. **Status anxiety** is difficulty in changing role behavior to each of the status roles. Certainly status anxieties are not helped by the fact that the indicators of status are often complex and not easily discerned. When there is status inconsistency in the various roles that a person is asked to perform, one can see how status anxiety is likely to be higher.

ACTION PROJECT 10–3   AFTER THE BOMB (GROUP EXERCISE)

This exercise bases status on necessity. Six people are sealed in a bomb shelter for several weeks. It is believed that an atomic bomb has been dropped somewhere in the vicinity. There is an oxygen leak, so two of the six persons will have to sacrifice themselves so that there will be enough oxygen left for the remaining four persons to survive until the "safety light" goes on. Who should be asked to volunteer? Each person in a group will be asked to play a part and justify why he/she should not volunteer. The group has 20 minutes to decide what to do.

ROLE 1.   A medical doctor—a general practitioner, 40 years of age, in good health, and has done extensive traveling.

ROLE 2.   A pregnant mother of two children—25 years of age, enjoys cooking, gardening, and knows many of the "pioneering ways of living," such as canning, candle making, etc.

ROLE 3.   A teacher (this role can be played by a man or a woman)—32 years of age, a high-school teacher with experience teaching math, English, and history.

ROLE 4.   A teenage athlete—a boy age 17, excellent student in school, and has taken many survival trips into the desert and mountains.

ROLE 5.   A carpenter—28 years of age, with experience in plumbing, cement work, and some knowledge of electricity.

ROLE 6.   A politician—a senator from one of the major states in the union, 45 years of age, and very knowledgeable in government organization and mass transportation. (This role can be played by a man or woman.)

(EXTRA ROLE IF NECESSARY)

ROLE 7.   A civil engineer—age 55, married twice, has had high positions with several companies building bridges, highways, and government buildings.

Each group must discuss which two persons should go within the next 20 minutes. In fact, each group must establish a rank order as to who is the most important (most important = 1).

MOST IMPORTANT

1. _____

2. _____

3. _____

4. _____

5. _____

6. _____

7. _____

DISCUSSION QUESTIONS

1. Did the real world of status influence your decisions within your artificial world, or was a new status hierarchy developed? Why? _____

   _____

2. Was your group influenced by the "talkers" within the group? Did the "talkers" influence the final decisions? _____

   _____

3. Does a "fight for life" change our perspective? _____

   _____

4. Did the number of people of each sex influence the final decision? _____

   _____

5. How did the results of your group compare with the results of other groups within your class? How do you account for the differences among groups?

   _____

SUCCESS AND FAILURE

Success breeds success—confidence is gained when enterprises meet with favorable responses and feelings of accomplishment. Similarly, failure breeds failure—unless realistic goals are set and adequately met, individuals can come to believe that they do everything wrong—all the time. The perception of the self as a habitual failure affects the outcome of further efforts and a vicious cycle of cause and effect is created.

In most cases, high status is a symbol of success, and many people assume that they will feel successful when they attain a higher status. In fact, however, achieving higher status brings feelings of true success only when feelings of genuine achievement are experienced. Genuine achievements require constant challenge. Success is based on a continuum of changing goals that can be envisioned and then met. When successive challenges are not offered, only stagnation and frustration result.

Genuine achievement requires constant challenge.

The levels of job status influence the ability to achieve feelings of success. Usually, the lower the job status, the greater the specification of the work routine. This means that there is relatively little opportunity for creativity, judgment, and initiative to come into play. Usually, the higher the job level, the greater the opportunity to tackle new problems. The motivation to experience increased self-esteem through dealing successfully with new problems should not be underestimated. And it is probably best to remember that success is never final and that failure is seldom fatal.

Failure is seldom fatal.

The two basic sources of power are personal and organizational. Organizational power refers to the capacity of managers to exert influence over others. It is derived from higher level authority and is delegated downward in an organization. Personal power, on the other hand, is obtained from the acceptance of followers, not from higher level management.

Power is only as useful as it is accepted and recognized by those over whom it is exercised. Increasingly, in today's organizations, the people who have the knowledge and information, have the power.

Other types of power include legitimate power, which is based on organizational position; referent power, which is based on personal power; expert power based on skill and knowledge; and reward and coercive power based on the ability of the powerholder to reward or punish others. Connection power is based on the powerholder's ability to relate to influential people.

Politics is one means of gaining and using power. "Playing politics" is the process of advancing or withholding power in the form of services rendered or economic sanctions. It is a way of distributing power in offices and other organizations.

Status is rated according to relative rank. Status positions are rewarded in different ways according to rank. While higher status can be claimed by someone, it does not actually exist unless it is acknowledged by others. Society establishes specific behaviors and symbols by which status is acknowledged.

A salary has more status—and usually more benefits—than wages, and fixed working hours have less prestige than flexible hours. Likewise, office workers have more status than laborers, because office work is "clean," even though the pay may well be less than that of the blue-collar worker. The location of offices, the clothes that people wear, and people's perceived physical height seem to affect the status people are given.

The ability to succeed affects self-esteem. Achieving higher status is perceived as a sign of success only when the individual has set a goal and met it, gaining status in the process. Self-worth is so important that workers in the most mundane jobs find ways in which to achieve a sense of success.

CASE STUDY 10–1

THE POWERFUL PROFESSOR

Max Stillwell is a senior professor in the College of Applied Sciences at the State University of New Hampton. He has been on the faculty for more than twenty years and served as dean of the college for ten of those years. After his "retirement" from the dean's job five years ago, he went back to full-time teaching.

As a dean, Max exercised considerable monetary control over his own and other college budgets. Nevertheless, he never thought of himself as particularly powerful. He continues to serve on a number of university-wide committees and is frequently called on for advice in his area of expertise—training and development. In fact, colleagues in the College of Extended Learning (CEL) frequently ask him to serve as a committee member on graduate students' committees.

One of Max's friends who is a CEL faculty member, John Dickinson, asked Max to serve as a speaker at a summer conference sponsored by CEL. John made it clear initially that there would be no honorarium or other remuneration, but Max still agreed to give the talk. One of the reasons Max accepted was that he wanted to learn more about the particular subject that he was asked to talk about. He rationalized that this experience would give him the opportunity to learn. In fact, he did conduct research and learn quite a bit about the subject before giving the talk, which was acclaimed successful by both John and the participants at the conference.

Another reason that Max accepted was that he and John, among others in CEL, were friends. He wanted to maintain that friendship. He told John he was accepting for the friendship reason, but he also knew that John might be able to repay the favor at another time.

1. What kinds of power has Max had in the past?
2. What kinds of power did Max exercise in giving the talk?
3. What kinds of power did John exercise in asking Max to give the talk?
4. Do you see the different sources and types of power at work?
5. Do you see an example of the norm of reciprocity at work?
6. Do you think most of Max's power is from personal or organizational sources? informal or formal sources?

CASE STUDY 10–2

STATUS REVERSAL

How would you feel if a person who had worked under you for a long time suddenly became your boss, taking a job you had wanted and for which you felt qualified? Doubtless you would have feelings of disappointment, competitiveness, anger, and insecurity.

Status reversal is a frequent problem at all levels in organizations. But when it occurs at the pinnacle of a complex organization, which badly needs the optimum talent and experience of both people involved, it represents a problem of considerable consequence. A difficult relationship problem between two key officers need not be felt with the same intensity by both parties for it to cause damage.

In this case, each executive was highly ambivalent about the other prior to the reversal of their status. When the status reversal was announced, Alan McLean, the man who had been senior, generated negative attitudes. By contrast, the new superior, Norman Menninger, became more positive, tolerant, understanding, and caring toward his former boss. In this instance, both parties concerned recognized that they had to do something. Their experience and norms of their organization were such that they felt that in the best interests of human relations and the company something should be done. So they came to you, a coworker.

1. Is this a short-term or a long-term problem?
2. Is it best to bring in an outside consultant on the problem?
3. Should counseling take place and, if so, what kind of counseling?
4. What specific steps can be taken to solve this problem?

DISCUSSION AND STUDY QUESTIONS—TO KEEP YOU THINKING . . . _____

1. What is the role of "perception" in power? Especially, reward power and coercive power?
2. What are the differences between "connection power" and "referent power"?
3. Is "social stratification" an example of stereotyping?
4. What are the major determinants of status?
5. How does status affect communication?
6. What are distinguishing aspects of a profession?
7. What is the relationship between power and politics?

NOTES _____

1. Hedrick Smith, *The Power Game: How Washington Works* (New York: Random House, 1988), pp. xxii, 42.
2. Adapted from J. Kenneth Matejka, D. Ashworth, and Diane Dodd-McCue, "More Power to Ya!" *Management Quarterly,* Winter 1985–1986, pp. 33–36.
3. Gary Bielous, "Seven Power Bases and How to Effectively Use Them," *Supervision,* October 1995, pp. 14–16.
4. Peter Jaques, "A User's Guide to Office Politics—Some Guidelines," *Management Services,* April 1994, pp. 16–17.
5. Julias Fast, *Body Language in the Workplace* (New York: Penguin), 1994.
6. Michael Korda, "The Gradual Decline and Total Collapse of Nearly Everyone," *Family Weekly,* August 29, 1982, p. 5.
7. Gary A. Yukl, *Organizational Behavior and Personnel Psychology,* rev. ed. (Homewood, Ill.: Richard D. Irwin, 1984), p. 221.
8. Ibid.
9. Janet Guthrie, "Scaling Down Status," *Working Woman,* December 1983, p. 74.
10. Phillip B. Applewhite, *Organizational Behavior* (Englewood Cliffs, N.J.: Prentice Hall, 1965), p. 60.
11. Ibid., pp. 95–96.
12. Shelly Branch and Lani Luciano, "Money's Best Jobs in America," *Money,* February 1992, p. 66.
13. "Professions: Contributions to Society, Stress, Prestige," *Gallup Report* No. 193, October 1981, p. 17.

RECOMMENDED READING _____

Benton, Debra A. *Lions Don't Need to Roar: Using the Power of Professional Presence to Stand Out, Fit in and Move Ahead.* New York: Warner Books, 1992.

Buhler, Patricia. "Navigating the Waters of Organizational Politics." *Supervision,* September 1994, pp. 24–26.

Clement, Ronald. W. "Culture, Leadership, and Power: The Keys to Organizational Change." *Business Horizons,* January–February 1994, pp. 33–39.

Cohen, Allan R., and David L. Bradford. *Influence Without Authority.* New York: John Wiley, 1990.

Davids, Meryl. "Where *Style* Meets Substance." *Journal of Business Strategy,* 1995, pp. 49–60.

Edwards, Owen. *Upward Nobility: How to Succeed in Business Without Losing Your Soul.* New York: Crown, 1991.

Eisenstodt, Gale. "Information Power." *Forbes,* June 21, 1993, pp. 44–45.

Ferris, Gerald R., Dwight D. Frink, Maria Carmen Galang, and Jing Zhou. "Perceptions of Organizational Politics: Prediction, Stress-Related Implications, and Outcomes." *Human Relations,* February 1996, pp. 233–266.

Fimbel, Nancie. "Communicating Realistically: Taking Account of Politics In Internal Business Communications." *Journal of Business Communication,* January 1994, pp. 7–26.

Fuchsberg, Gilbert. "Chief Executives See Their Power Shrink." *The Wall Street Journal,* March 15, 1993, p. B1.

Haddock, Patricia. "Communicating Personal Power." *Supervision,* July 1995, p. 20.

Kalbfleisch, Pamela J., and Michael J. Cody, Eds. *Gender, Power, and Communication in Human Relationships.* Hillsdale, N.J.: L. Erlbaum Associates, 1995.

Osborn, Michelle. "The 'New Power Look': At Ease." *USA Weekend*, February 5–7, 1993, p. 22.

Pfeffer, Jeffrey. *Managing with Power.* Marshfield, Mass.: Pitman, 1992.

Richardson, Bill, and John Thompson. "Strategy Evaluation in Powerful Environments: A Multi-Competence Approach." *Leadership & Organization Development Journal*, 1995, pp. 17–25.

Toffler, Alvin. *Powershift: Knowledge, Wealth and Violence at the Edge of the 21st Century.* New York: Bantam Books, 1990.

PART 4

ORGANIZATIONAL CHALLENGES

WE LEAD, DEVELOP, AND DECIDE

11
LEADERSHIP

Look at these questions before reading the chapter. Some answers may be found in the chapter; others can only be answered by personal opinion.

- Is there an ideal leader for all situations?
- What are the personality traits of leaders?
- What kind of leader is needed for a crisis?
- Do leaders have more intelligence than their followers?
- What is the function of a leader in a group?
- When is close supervision or general supervision best for most Americans?
- What traits of Theory Z could Americans adopt in their culture?
- What is the best type of leader in classroom or group discussion?
- How can we measure leader behavior?
- What type of leader are you? Why?
- Free-rein leadership means almost no control by the leader; therefore it should not be used by supervisors. Do you agree?

Learning Goals

After studying this chapter, you should be able to:

1. Distinguish between leadership and management.
2. Discuss the roles that a task leader and a social leader play in groups. Determine if there are any common traits for leaders.
3. Explain various continua and models of leadership.
4. Explain the advantages and disadvantages of the following styles of leadership behavior and how they relate to McGregor's theories of leadership:
   a. Autocratic
   b. Participative
   c. Free rein
5. What are the features of Theory Z?
6. Discuss the "contingency model" and give examples of the model in practice.
7. Explain the path–goal process of leadership and subordinate effectiveness.
8. Name the characteristics of transformational leadership.
9. Define and apply the following terms and concepts (in order of first occurrence)

- **leadership**
- **task leader**
- **social leader**
- **autocratic leader (X-type leader)**

- participative leader (Y-type leader)
- benevolent autocrat
- leadership continuum
- free-rein leaders
- Theory Z
- Managerial Grid
- contingency model
- organizational engineering
- path–goal approach
- situational leadership
- transformational leaders
- catalytic leadership
- delegation
- substitutes for leadership

WHAT IS LEADERSHIP?

BREAKING THROUGH THE MYTHS

Leadership, like common sense, is somewhat elusive and not so common. Leadership is such an elusive concept partly because people do not define themselves in leadership terms. Someone coming home from a community meeting might say, "I sure got them to come around to my point of view" or "I was surprised at how carefully they listened to what I had to say." But if asked, "Did you lead the group?" that person would be apt to answer, "Well, not really." Furthermore, followers are unclear about their reasons for choosing leaders.

Boards of directors of business organizations complain, "What we need are more leaders, not managers!" Whole nations cry, "We need vision. Don't read the polls and then act. Get out front!" Isn't that leadership?

DEFINING LEADERSHIP

Inspiration, sales ability, and persuasion cannot have any impact unless there is some measure of *influence* over the audience or group. A person may be good at making dramatic speeches but not inspire anyone to become a follower. The best propaganda in the world may not convince anybody. The most persuasive arguments may fall on deaf ears. Only if a group wishes to be influenced can a leader function.

Leadership is goal directed.

Leadership can be defined as the ability to influence the goal-directed actions and behaviors of others. Leaders are going places and have the ability to inspire others to go along. The ability to cause others to follow a common goal is one sure way of recognizing leadership. Aristotle said the leader must have *ethos*—the moral character to persuade; *pathos*—the ability to move people emotionally; and *logos*—the intellect to give people solid, logical reasons for action. We need leaders in our governments and organizations who exhibit all three of these qualities.

Leaders initiate change.

Leaders initiate change, either by making decisions or by encouraging others to make them. A group's trust in its leader is affected by the quality of his or her decisions. Whether or not the decisions are good, people who follow leaders must accept the decisions made and the process used in making them.

The CEOs of several large organizations state that "dynamic and effective leadership includes creating and articulating a vision and plan; being customer driven; and creating the necessary environment."[1]

One executive, Kevin J. Jenkins, president and CEO of Canadian Airlines, said:

> Taking time to paint a picture of the future is important. . . . Without a clear sense of direction, even the best of efforts will dissolve into a series of projects and plans that ultimately go nowhere. When your efforts are aligned and integrated, you can achieve amazing results. . . .
>
> To create a foundation for success, the leader's job is to demonstrate commitment to change by removing roadblocks; providing the necessary resources, such as education, training, and work structures; and inviting contributions from all involved, including employee and labor groups.
>
> Successful leadership enables more than just those at the top of the organization to take the helm. Yet leaders must resist the temptation to take back the controls when the going gets tough. The effective use of power is knowing when to stand back and when to step in.[2]

FOLLOWING LEADERS

There is nearly always an element of uncertainty or confusion that prompts people to choose and follow a leader. Sometimes followers are attracted to a leader who represents their values. They are willing to place themselves under the leadership of someone who can help them to refine and act on values. Those values must be made attractive and acceptable to the followers. A good leader must be able to develop and work with subordinates.

Groups need leaders to reduce uncertainty and confusion. If a group is functioning smoothly, very little leadership may be required. Leadership can have an important effect on a group's morale, especially since one of its chief functions is to keep the group focused on its goals. When it becomes necessary to stabilize unstable situations, aggressive leadership is required.

BEING A LEADER

The leader must also be a follower. A good leader must give and take depending on the situation. As group goals and tasks change, new leaders and shifts in power result. As work is delegated, authority roles change. Leadership in a group depends on the group standards and the leadership rules that are acceptable.

A classic example of the type of leader who also follows is Peter Ueberroth. Ueberroth organized the 1984 Olympics in Los Angeles and then became major league baseball commissioner. During the one-and-a-half-day baseball strike in 1985, Ueberroth was credited by club owners and players with keeping the talks going even after the strike began. Keeping the talks going prevented gridlock and an impasse. Ueberroth himself, however, denied any role in solving the strike.

More recently, Ueberroth led an effort to Rebuild Los Angeles (RLA). He was a high-profile leader and drew criticism resulting in his resignation. But his underlying leadership style was effective in getting others mobilized. Upon his resignation, he said: "I'll still be at RLA meetings. I'll just be at the back of the room instead of the front." Although he was officially a cochair of the group, he was recognized as a "first among equals" and much of the structure and tone of RLA was set by him.[3]

WHEN IS A LEADER BEST?

A leader is best
When people barely know he exists,
Not so good when people obey and acclaim him,
Worst when they despise him.
Fail to honor people
They fail to honor you;
But of a good leader, who talks little,
When his work is done, his aim fulfilled,
They will all say, "We did this ourselves."

Lao-tzu, 6th century B.C. Chinese philosopher

Well-functioning groups never remain leaderless, but a group doesn't necessarily have only one leader. A group *can* have one leader, but every member of a group can also be a leader. Some leaders prefer to monopolize power; other leaders rely on all or several members of the group to display leadership individually.

Group members who trust one another can mutually influence group decision making. People may hold back their abilities to lead for many reasons—perhaps because they lack confidence in themselves, perhaps because the situation does not allow leadership. However, *all people are potential leaders.* And, given the desire and the opportunity, people can develop into effective leaders.

All people are potential leaders.

PROFILE OF HUMAN BEHAVIOR

ALBERT C. (AL) YATES

Dr. Albert C. Yates is president of Colorado State University (CSU) and chancellor of the Colorado State University System. In addition to his presidency of CSU, as chancellor of the system, he oversees the operations of the University of Southern Colorado and Fort Lewis College.

Dr. Yates began his college studies at Memphis State University, where he graduated magna cum laude with degrees in chemistry and mathematics in 1965. He went on to earn his doctorate in theoretical chemical physics from Indiana University at Bloomington in 1968. He has served as associate university dean for graduate education and research at the University of Cincinnati, and executive vice president and provost at Washington State University. In several of these associations, he was deeply influenced by the leadership research and practice of a former president of the University of Cincinnati and professor of management at the University of Southern California, Dr. Warren Bennis.

Another of his favorite writers and political theorists—Niccolo Machiavelli—said: "There is nothing more difficult to take in hand, more perilous to conduct, or more uncertain in its success, than to take the lead in the introduction of a new order of things." These words helped him develop a vision and understand how people work. The president of the university's governing board said: "He has created relationships. . . . He has served as a coalition builder, as a spokesperson, as a person who leads the charge on issues affecting higher education."[4]

Al Yates views his presidency as that of a coach to a team: "We are a team—a team of people with individual strengths and insights and ambitions." He does not believe that leadership is just about him but that it involves all faculty, staff and students: " . . . please know that the success of our time here does not depend upon me (alone)." Success depends on all of us—collectively and individually. It depends on the extent to which we commit ourselves and earnestly try to make a difference.

"To assume a position of leadership requires that one accepts certain special obligations, and chief among these is the obligation to lead with optimism and hope. In accepting such positions of responsibility, each of us must be willing to forgo the luxury of being negative, or depressed, or cynical.

"We should observe, too, that the weight of our opinions is often more than is deserved; and that means we must measure our comments with care and dare not abuse the privilege of leadership. Let us remember, always, to accept responsibility for our words, as well as our actions. One of the keys to becoming an effective leader is to develop the ability to subjugate one's own feelings and ego on behalf of the people and the institution one is attempting to nurture and support. If you are not able to do at least these things, then the impact of your leadership will be minimal; you may even be revealed—to yourself and others—as an impostor."

Al says that "Over time I have learned that one of the true tests of able leadership is the achievement of an appropriate balance between attention given to day-to-day operational needs and that given to the requirements of a broader perspective and long-term directions . . . the 'vision' has to come first; allow the long-term perspective to prescribe our daily choices and priorities."

Yates quotes Warren Bennis as saying that many organizations are unsuccessful in their attempts to strike this necessary balance: "Most organizations are overmanaged and underled." He chooses the following words of Bennis to define the difference between leaders and managers:

> Managing is about efficiency. Leading is about effectiveness. . . . Management is about systems, controls, procedures, policies, structure. Leadership is about trust—about people.
>
> Leadership is about innovating and initiating. Management is about copying, about managing the status quo. Leadership is creative, adaptive and agile. Leadership looks at the horizon, not just at the bottom line. . . . What leaders do is inspire people, empower them. They pull rather than push.

SOURCES: "Introductory Speech to Fall Leadership Conference," Colorado State University, Estes Park, Colorado, September 23, 1991; Julie Poppen, "(Yate's) Term in Office Is Transforming CSU," *Fort Collins Coloradoan*, June 2, 1996, pp. A1, A8.

For many years, social scientists tried to isolate and analyze the personal characteristics necessary for effective leadership. Most of these attempts were found to be unsound because the research conclusions were based on predetermined models of leadership. Many of the lists of traits were anecdotal—that is, based on one "great man" or another who exhibited certain traits. Then respondents would draw up a list of what they thought leaders should be.

Today, researchers have examined more aspects of the human personality than were even conceived of twenty-five years ago—and remarkably few consistent leadership traits have been isolated.

Honesty, perseverance, good judgment, self-confidence, creativity, and enthusiasm are just a few of the traits important for leadership that are frequently identified by successful CEOs and other leaders of organizations.

Such traits as height, weight, appearance, self-control, dominance, alertness, cheerfulness, and geniality usually have little relation to leadership. Nevertheless, some of the reasons for selecting leaders and spokesmen for the 1985 airline hostage situation in Beirut were their height, physical appearance, and dominance. See Figure 11–1 for a checklist that addresses more substantive measures of leadership.

Korzes and Posner studied thousands of managers and found that the traits most admired in leaders were honesty, competency, forward-looking ability, inspiration, and intelligence. They concluded that to be effective, five principles must guide leaders:

1. **Challenge the process.** They are pioneers and innovators—people who are willing to step into the unknown. They encourage those with ideas.
2. **Inspire a shared vision.** They are incredibly enthusiastic and spend time gazing across the horizon.
3. **Enable others to act.** They do not act by themselves but are team players from top to bottom of their organizations.
4. **Model the way.** They serve as role models.
5. **Encourage the heart.** They encourage fun and simple celebrations of accomplishments.[5]

Leader's IQ is usually higher than the average of the group.

Intelligence has only a relative relationship. Leaders usually have a higher intelligence than the average of those they lead, whether it is a group of manual laborers or a group of professional technicians. The intelligence of a leader may not be much greater than that of his or her peers, but the leader is able to see the relationship between the task at hand and the personalities of those who must perform it.

A leader's perception of the followers enables him or her to motivate group members into action. Other traits or leadership behavior dimensions include emphasis on performance, giving of praise/recognition, training/coaching, conflict management and critical analysis and inspiration.

	SATISFACTORY	NEEDS IMPROVEMENT
1. Have you assessed the degree to which others perceive your status as leader, the extent of formal authority granted your position, and the informal authority others grant to you in recognition of your knowledge, experience, and demonstrated effectiveness?		
2. Are you aware of the various norms that your work group has developed? Do you know the workers' standards of behavior, especially those affecting the quality and quantity of work?		
3. Have you decided how much freedom you will extend to employees in establishing work standards and how far they can go collectively without interfering with the attainment of the organization's goals?		
4. Can you tolerate the dual loyalty of others—to their friends or work group as well as to you?		
5. Have you identified the informal leaders in your organization, those individuals to whom others look for guidance or approval, even though they have no formal authority?		
6. Have you established a communications network that serves the leadership needs in the most effective fashion?		
7. Do you prepare your subordinates for organizational changes that will affect their status, security, or job responsibilities?		
8. Have you taken appropriate steps to win the confidence of others in your ability to handle change by demonstrating the reliability of your previous decisions?		
9. Do you provide sufficient opportunity for others to participate in plans for implementing change so that they will accept the rationale of new standards of performance?		
10. Do you maintain a watch over new standards during the settling-in period that follows change, regularly reinforcing or adjusting the standards to accommodate nanticipated circumstances?		

SOCIAL POPULARITY

Being popular implies a desire for friendly personal interaction. A leader can be very decisive and even unpleasant during a group discussion and very amiable among friends in a social setting.

The potential leader does not always have to be the most articulate or outspoken member of the group. Frequently, the leader holds back and does not tell or even suggest what a group should do. Potential leaders must be good listeners. Accordingly, they are well liked but they don't set out to be well liked by being "pushy."

Leaders can help achieve consensus.

Well-liked people do have an advantage in that they can bring group members "around" and help achieve consensus. Group members concerned with social relations often act as leaders in attempts to keep the group unified. We will examine informal group leadership further at the end of this chapter.

GROUP RELATIONSHIPS

The "social leader" and the "task leader."

A group might develop two types of leaders, the "social leader" and the "task leader, " each one having his or her own function and each complementing the other in achieving the goal with a minimum of conflict. The **task leader** contributes most to the achievement of the task, but difficulty may arise because, in playing this role, the task leader may irritate people and injure the unity of the group. **Social leaders** are concerned with the group working together and everyone understanding the others' points of view. Seldom can one person fill both roles, so it is important that leaders form a coalition.

Leaders must create a win–win environment. A win–win environment is one in which all parties—the organization, the leader, and the followers—win.

FUNCTIONAL ROLES

There are times when leaders must make decisions. The leader's wishes certainly have weight in making choices—the extent of that weight depends on the distribution of power within the group. Leaders can help to clarify possible alternatives and prevent groups from stalemating or turning into debating societies.

Leaders can help clarify alternatives.

In some cases, the leader may make the decision by default. The chance of the decision being acceptable to the group is enhanced if the group participates in the decision. The leader also has training and people development responsibility (see Figure 11–2). A wise person said that "leadership is providing a greenhouse environment for the seeding, growth and development of its major asset: people."

A leader can act as an arbitrator for the group. In this function, the leader does not usually participate directly in the group process, for instance, when group decisions are being made. Instead, the leader tries to stay uninvolved and neutral. In this arbitration role, the leader listens to all sides of the argument and helps group members to arrive at a solution or, ultimately, takes action to decide the issue alone. A leader is often put in the position of arbitrator to prevent serious group splintering.

LEADERSHIP STYLES

Along with different leadership traits and functions, the *styles* in which leaders perform can also be identified. Theorists of leadership behavior styles do not dismiss the force of leaders' personalities, but they find that

FIGURE 11–2 Leadership Includes Training.

Leadership styles depend in part on personalities.

leaders use leadership styles consistent with their personalities. For example, someone who has trouble trusting other people's judgment will tend toward an authoritarian leadership style. Someone else will choose to be authoritarian simply as a way of saving time. One person's lack of trust and the other's desire for efficiency are both consistent with the authoritarian leadership style.

The various styles or approaches to leadership are based on types of control that leaders exercise in a group and their behavior toward group members, and are discussed in the following sections.

ACTION PROJECT 11–1 WHAT MAKES A SUCCESSFUL LEADER?

Name two or three people you consider to be successful leaders in several categories: business, education, government, religion, or other groupings. They do not have to be nationally known, but they should be important to you. Identify important traits and actions they have taken that you identify with them.

After you have completed your list and accompanying characteristics, compare them with class members. Are some leaders frequently mentioned?

BUSINESS LEADER	TRAITS	ACTIONS
EDUCATION LEADER		
GOVERNMENT LEADER		
RELIGIOUS LEADER		

THEORY X AND THEORY Y LEADERS

McGregor's X and Y theories.

One scale of leadership qualities is based on (1) the forces at work within a leader, (2) the forces at work within followers, and (3) the arena in which the leader and followers interact. This framework, developed by Douglas McGregor, is known popularly as the X and Y theories of leadership. During the period of "sweatshop" labor in the early twentieth century, the leadership style demonstrated by supervisors was primarily that of an **autocratic** or **X-type leader.** And some still hold this view—that people work mostly for money and status rewards.

However, McGregor believed that leaders can have a feeling for the employee as well as for the accomplishment of the company goal. The **participative,** or **Y leader,** believes that many people naturally aspire to independent responsibility and self-fulfillment and, further, that people need to feel respected as being capable of assuming responsibility and correcting mistakes on their own. In brief, the X leader is interested in production; the Y leader is interested in employees. It remains a challenge to combine the two extremes.

AUTOCRATIC LEADERS

Autocratic, or X, leaders leave no doubt about who is in charge. They use the power they have acquired by their rank, knowledge, or skills to reward and punish as they see fit. Their ability to command is the major or sole method by which things get done. This posture does not imply hostility or negativity but, rather, sureness of will. Authoritarian leaders give orders and assume that people will respond obediently. This style is usually perceived as "hard sell," and subordinates are permitted little freedom.

A spin-off of the autocratic leader is the **benevolent autocrat.** This person is still an autocrat but uses his or her reward power to manipulate or sell the subordinates on the goals of the autocratic leader. Do you see a degree of phoniness in the benevolent autocrat? Who would you rather work for—an autocrat or a benevolent autocrat?

PARTICIPATIVE AND DEMOCRATIC LEADERS

Participative leaders decide after group input.

Participative, or Y, leaders invite decision sharing. Their style calls for subordinates to exercise high degrees of responsibility and freedom. They use as little authoritarian control as possible and are concerned with group interrelationships as well as with getting the job done.

True democratic leaders confer final authority to the group.

The two types of participative leaders are *consultive leaders,* who require a high degree of involvement from employees but make it clear that they alone have the authority to make final decisions, and *democratic leaders,* who confer final authority to the group and abide by whatever the group decides, with no exceptions.

Participative leaders do not try to disguise their power to make the final decision, particularly when faced with crises. But they also encourage employees to contribute opinions and information and to participate in the decision-making process as much as possible.

Participative leaders request and expect constant feedback, a practice that provides them with the best available information, ideas, suggestions, talent, and experience. When people participate in making the decisions that affect their lives, they support those decisions more enthusiastically and try hard to make them work.

Ambiguities of the Y theory.

There are ambiguities attached to participative leadership, for it certainly does not mean that one considers the employee first and the company second. The employee-centered supervisor who gets the best results tends to recognize that high production is also among his or her responsibilities. The major difference between participative leadership and autocratic "leadership" is that participative leaders give their subordinates a share in decision making and communicate more openly with employees than the autocrat.

Table 11–1 compares the two leadership styles. Which one is more comfortable for you?

TABLE 11–1 Traits of Autocratic and Participative Leaders

AUTOCRATIC STYLE: X THEORY TRAITS	PARTICIPATIVE STYLE: Y THEORY TRAITS
Task oriented	Employee oriented
Interested in details	Interested in generalizing
Efficiency minded	Democratic to very permissive
Time and motion studies	Sensitive to individual's needs
Product oriented	People oriented
Interested in promoting oneself	Aware of morale
Fast decision maker	Slow decision maker
Somewhat extroverted	Somewhat introverted
Self-appointed or company appointed	Group appointed
Close supervision	General supervision
Task specialist	Maintenance specialist
Paternalistic	Democratic

FIGURE 11–3 Relationship of Leader's Authority to Followers' Freedom.

FIGURE 11–3 Relationship of Leader's Authority to Followers' Freedom.

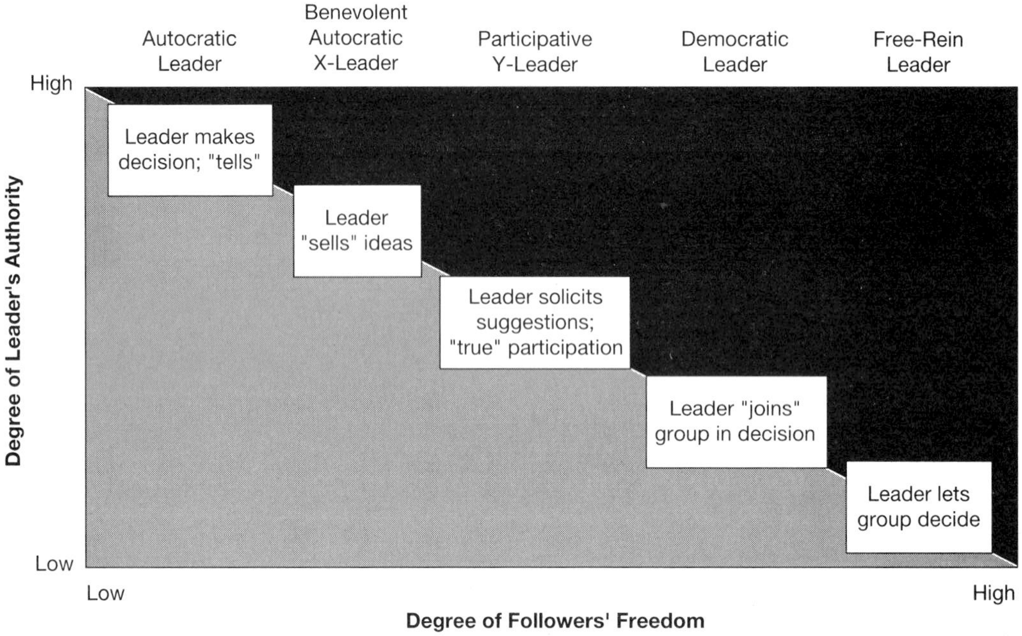

CONTINUUM OF LEADERSHIP BEHAVIOR

The **leadership continuum** plots alternative ways for leaders to approach decision making, depending on how much participation they want their subordinates to have. Figure 11–3 shows the relationship of the leader's authority to followers' freedom. At the left, the autocratic leader makes and announces the decision. The benevolent autocratic or X leader presents ideas and sells the decision. The participative, or Y leader seeks suggestions before making a decision—"true participation," not phony selling or abdication. The democratic leader decides with the group, on a "one-person, one-vote" basis. The free-rein leader asks the group to decide on its own.

FREE-REIN LEADERS

Free-rein leaders are nondirective.

Free-rein leaders are also referred to as *laissez-faire leaders* or *group-centered leaders.* Free-rein leaders are almost completely nondirective. They communicate goals and guidelines and then allow employees to meet them without issuing further directions, unless specifically requested. One goal is to involve all non-leaders in participating as equally as possible in a project.

This leadership system offers the most effective use of time and resources. The highest possible degree of authority is vested in the group—it is almost as if the group were leaderless. This laissez-faire atmosphere can motivate people to initiate and carry out complex work plans efficiently and responsibly. Guidelines are established by a good free-rein leader, but day-to-day direction is seldom used.

Examples of the free-rein leadership system are route sales representatives; certain professional workers, such as engineers, scientists, and teachers; and research and development personnel.

SYSTEMS LEADERSHIP AND SUPPORTIVE RELATIONSHIPS

An integrated model of leadership behaviors was proposed by Rensis Likert and associates at the University of Michigan, Institute for Social Research. They categorized four systems of management leadership, which they called System 4, based on these principles:

- Supportive relationships—leaders show confidence and trust in subordinates
- Wide participation in group decision making, goal setting, and control
- Motivation based on trust and involvement
- Substantial communication and cooperative teamwork

Each member experiences support.

The *principle of supportive relationships* means that the leadership of the organization is such that it ensures maximum probability that in all interactions with the organization, each member will view the experience as supportive and one that builds and maintains a sense of personal worth.

THEORY Z

Taking the leadership alphabet one more step, William Ouchi of the University of California at Los Angeles wrote *Theory Z*. As American firms struggle with high employee turnover and some worker alienation, Ouchi pointed to a management style used in Japan. **Theory Z,** founded in strong Japanese cultural tradition, uses ideas like consensus building, mutual loyalty, and cooperation from both American and Japanese management.

Table 11–2 shows a combined organizational type, Z, based on American, or type A, organizations and Japanese, or type J, organizations. Note that there is a major difference in treatment of employment and career paths in the organizations.

TABLE 11–2 Characteristics of Type A, Type J, and Type Z Organizations

TYPE A (AMERICAN)	TYPE J (JAPANESE)	TYPE Z (MODIFIED AMERICAN)
Short-term employment	Lifetime employment	Long-term employment
Individual decision making	Consensual decision making	Consensual decision making
Individual responsibility	Collective responsibility	Individual responsibility
Rapid evaluation and promotion	Slow evaluation and promotion	Slow evaluation and promotion
Explicit, formalized control	Implicit, informal control	Implicit, informal control with explicit, formalized measures
Specialized career path	Nonspecialized career path	Moderately specialized career path
Segmented concern	Holistic concern	Holistic concern, including family

SOURCE: Adapted from William G. Ouchi and Alfred M. Jaeger, "Type Z Organization: Stability in the Midst of Mobility," *Academy of Management Review,* April 1978, pp. 308, 311.

LONG-RANGE PLANNING

The basis of Theory Z is futurism. Businesses and governments look five, ten, even twenty years ahead to try to build lasting prosperity. One reason that some companies are not under constant pressure for fast profits is that much of Japanese industry is owned by banks and not by individual shareholders.

CONSENSUS DECISION MAKING

Corporate decisions are reached by a tedious process of collective compromise that can sometimes involve as many as sixty to eighty individuals, each of whom holds a potential veto. The process of consensus building is slow, but once an agreement is reached, no one attempts to sabotage or slow down the project.

MUTUAL TRUST AND LOYALTY

Companies are developed to create a powerful bond between the workers and their firms. Managers are famous for inspiring loyalty, long hours, and high-quality production in their workers. A top executive briefs the employees once a month on sales and production goals, and employees are encouraged to air their complaints. Four times a year the workers attend company-paid parties. These are features of Sony, not in Japan, but in the plant in San Diego, California.

NONSPECIALIZED CAREERS

Personnel are moved regularly from one department to the next. In the process, they become experts in the structure and the internal workings of the company, not specialists in marketing, finance, or production. It sounds like a way to develop conceptual skills.

STRONG COMPANY IMAGE AND DIRECTION

A strong company image and a strong sense of direction often mean a weak union organization. Japan has fewer strikes and less labor unrest than any other major industrial power.

Many Japanese employees wear the company "costume." Even employees of Japanese companies within the United States wear the company uniforms. At Sony the universal blue-gray jacket is the firm's way of saying that Sony is a working company, a blue-collar company all the way from top to bottom.

QUALITY OVER QUANTITY

Japanese workers are not only encouraged but are actually expected to make quality control their top priority. At Matsushita Electric, workers are instilled with the notion that each one of them is a quality control inspector. If they spot a faulty item in the production process, they are encouraged to shut down the whole assembly line to fix it. There is even furious competition between Hitachi and Sony in statistical battles to achieve the lowest defect rate for products.

SUBSISTENCE-LEVEL WAGES, BUT REAL BONUSES

Adequate wages are paid, but real bonuses are given to all workers if the company is successful each year. When a recession or other problem affects a firm, the company does not threaten the employees with layoffs, but will pare down paychecks for everyone, including top executives.

FEW PROMOTIONS AND LIFETIME EMPLOYMENT

In Japan, a large portion—approaching 35 percent—of the workforce is covered by a paternalistic employment practice. Since few people job-hop, there are fewer promotions. Yet since no one else is promoted, no one feels that he or she is falling behind.

Promotions may come as infrequently as once every ten years in Japan; such a glacial pace would drive any fast-moving U.S. manager crazy. Employees in Japan view their company as an extension of their family lives. Indeed many of them equate the importance of their company with that of their own life.

EXPRESS YOUR OPINION

Many people say "Let's get on the bandwagon and use Theory Z in our company. If Japan can use it successfully, why can't we?"

Do you think that we can adopt Theory Z within our culture? Looking at the theory, analyze where you think we as a nation, or your company, can adapt most easily to each major idea. Where are we as a culture least likely to accept such ideas?

1. Long-range planning
2. Consensus decision making
3. Mutual trust and loyalty between management and worker
4. Nonspecialized careers
5. Strong company image and direction
6. Quality over quantity
7. Subsistence-level wages, but real bonuses
8. Few promotions and lifetime employment

MANAGERIAL (LEADERSHIP) GRID

Another approach to measuring and depicting leader behavior was developed by Robert Blake and Jane Mouton.[6] The **Managerial Grid**® is a model based on a matrix of values 1 through 9 for two primary variables: a manager's concern for people and management's concern for production. A 9 by 9 matrix yields 81 possible combinations, but the most important styles fall into five categories:

- 1,1 ("What's the Use?") Management—low concern for both people and production
- 9,1 ("Get-the-Job-Done"—at people cost) Management—high concern for production, low concern for people
- 5,5 ("Status Quo"—organization) Management—balanced concern for both people and production
- 1,9 ("Keep Everybody Happy"—at cost of production) Management—low concern for production, high concern for people
- 9,9 ("Pinnacle"—team) Management—high concern for both people and production

It may seem desirable to pursue the 9,9 management style as the "best" style for all occasions, but there is another school of thought that suggests the appropriate style is contingent on the situation. We examine the contingency model in the next section and situational leadership in a later section.

CONTINGENCY MODEL

The **contingency model** was developed by business and management psychologist Fred E. Fiedler at the University of Washington. According to Fiedler, anyone can become a good leader, given the right circumstances. Effective leadership is not the function of any one particular management style but, rather, of matching the right style to the right job at the right time. By making an organizational change, it is possible to create a circumstance that will stimulate a person's positive leadership potential. Fiedler writes:

> The evidence suggests that neither the directive nor nondirective approach is consistently more effective. Each approach works better under certain conditions. You cannot run a committee in a completely directive and autocratic manner unless it consists of "yes" men and women. Nor would it make much sense to be very participative in working on an assembly line.[7]

To use the contingency model, we must first identify a manager's leadership style. We must then analyze the job situation and determine the best possible combination of leader and job for that particular moment in time.

IDENTIFYING THE STYLE

Least-preferred coworker test identifies style.

Identifying a leader's style can often be difficult. To make the task easier, Fiedler devised a *least preferred coworker test,* in which people are asked to characterize their least preferred coworker, past or present. From more than fifteen years of test data, Fiedler found that relationship-motivated leaders usually describe their least preferred coworker as "untrustworthy" or "unreliable personally," whereas task-motivated leaders describe their least preferred coworker as "lazy," "unintelligent," or one who inhibits the completion of difficult jobs. In this test, leaders usually fall somewhere between the two extremes, but in a manner that still allows us to identify their styles.

In the contingency model, there are two basic leadership styles: the relationship-motivated style and the task-motivated style. The relationship leader is motivated primarily by relating to people. These leaders are stimulated by forming and maintaining good work relationships with their subordinates and in doing this can get jobs done very well—in certain situations.

At the other end of the scale are the task leaders, who "could never just baby-sit a company." These leaders need many task challenges to be stimulated. The companies and situations that need task-style leaders involve risk taking and crises.

DETERMINING THE SITUATION—MATCHING THE STYLE

The situation is determined by three principal factors:

1. **Leader–member relations:** the nature of the interpersonal relationship between the leader and follower, expressed in terms of good through poor
2. **Task structure:** the nature of the subordinate's task, described as "structured" or "unstructured," associated with the amount of creative freedom allowed the subordinate to accomplish the task
3. **Position power:** the degree to which the position itself enables the leader to get group members to comply with and accept his or her direction

Fiedler analyzes job situations to discover (1) to what extent the job situation will call for a strong work relationship and (2) to what extent it will call for the completion of difficult jobs. His conclusion is that relationship-motivated leaders do best in situations that are relatively difficult to lead, whereas task-motivated leaders do best in situations that are either very difficult or very easy to lead (see Table 11–3).

Frequent evaluations of jobs should be encouraged. And leaders should not be afraid to change leadership positions. Such changes occur during the process of **organizational engineering,** which is a method of creating and

TABLE 11–3 Matching the Leader to the Situation, According to Fiedler's Contingency Model

SITUATION			LEADER STYLE NEEDED
Leader–Member Relations	Task Structure	Leader Position Power	
Good	Structured	Strong	Task
Good	Structured	Weak	Task
Good	Unstructured	Strong	Task
Good	Unstructured	Weak	Relationship
Poor	Structured	Strong	Relationship
Poor	Structured	Weak	Relationship
Poor	Unstructured	Strong	Can be either
Poor	Unstructured	Weak	Task

maintaining effective leadership. The approach is a lot easier than firing or trying to change supervisors who lose their effectiveness because the leadership needs of their job situation have changed.

THE PATH–GOAL APPROACH

According to the **path–goal approach** to leadership, the leader's behavior is based on two classes of factors: subordinate characteristics and environmental factors. The subordinate characteristics include ability, locus of control, authoritarianism, needs, and motives. Characteristics of the work environment include subordinates' tasks, the primary work group, and the formal authority systems.

Figure 11–4 illustrates the path–goal process. Note that each of the three behaviors or environmental factors interacts with the others to reach, eventually, the target goals: motivated behavior, satisfied employees, leader acceptance, and effective performance. Like any other leadership approach, the purpose of studying the path–goal process is not to build a monument to the

FIGURE 11–4 A Path–Goal Spiral with Emphasis on Both Leader and Employee Effectiveness.

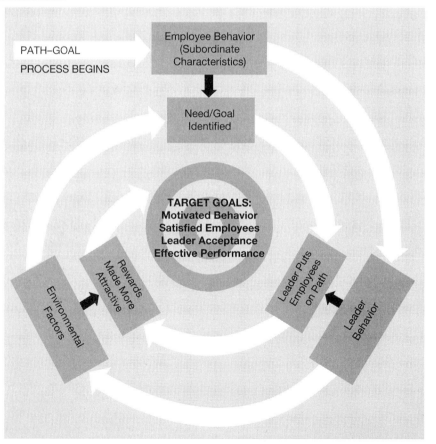

leader but to put the emphasis on total organizational effectiveness—by both leaders and subordinates.

Here are some of the findings of path–goal studies:

1. When the task or work situation is ambiguous, a directive style of leadership is desirable. When task demands are clear, directiveness is a hindrance.
2. Supportive leadership has its most positive effect on satisfaction for subordinates who work on stressful, frustrating, or dissatisfying tasks.
3. In nonrepetitive ego-involving tasks, employees are more satisfied under a participative style of leadership than a nonparticipative style.[8]

Path–goal lays out a path to achieve goals.

As the label implies, the path–goal approach lays out a path by which to achieve goals. If the goals, and the tasks necessary to accomplish them, are well defined, then a motivating and rewarding situation exists. The leader's behavior is effective because of its impact on a subordinate's perception of the goals and the paths to those goals.

MANAGEMENT BY OBJECTIVES/RESULTS

MBO/R has success if properly implemented.

Management by objectives/results (MBO/R), formerly called management by objectives, is a goal-setting and performance-appraisal process in which boss and subordinate mutually determine specific goals for the employee to meet within a given time frame. MBO/R is discussed in Chapter 12 as an appraisal method, but it has also had success in its goal-setting applications. If an autocratic leader tries to impose his or her objectives or goals on the organization, and calls that MBO, no wonder it doesn't work.

The failure of MBO/R may be a result of a poor fit between the process itself and the organizational environment in which it is implemented. The traditional, highly participative, and permissive MBO process will fail if it is introduced in organizations whose leaders are not inclined to be participative or permissive.[9]

SITUATIONAL APPROACH

The **situational leadership** approach, developed by Hersey and Blanchard, suggests the leader match styles to followers' readiness levels.[10] Basically, the approach is a spin-off of the contingency model and states that there are two dimensions to leadership: task behavior and relationship behavior. These two dimensions form a four-quadrant matrix such as that shown in Figure 11–5. The bell-shaped curve becomes a "development cycle" indicating growth in follower readiness. Note that the readiness curve is read from *right to left*. As a follower's readiness level increases, *and* as the relationship and task levels change, the style of the leader changes. For example, if the follower is new, the task behavior of the leader is high and relationship low, the leader would be in a "tell" mode. As the individual progresses and the relationship behavior

FIGURE 11–5 Situational Leadership Behavior Model. Source: Paul Hersey and Kenneth H. Blanchard, *Management of Organizational Behavior,* 5th ed. (Englewood Cliffs, N.J.: Prentice Hall, 1988), p. 182.

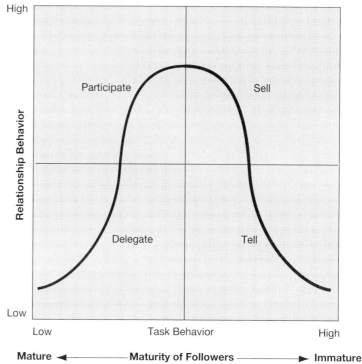

increases, the leader would be in the "sell" mode on through the "participate" stage, where the task is low but relationship is high. Finally, with a fully developed follower, the leadership style can shift to one of "delegate," low relationship and low task behavior.

TRANSFORMATIONAL APPROACH

One last approach to the measurement of leader behavior is transformational leadership. Just as the name implies, **transformational leaders** are capable of effecting major changes in their organizations because of their vision and willingness to give individual consideration to and empower employees through intellectual stimulation. Leader charisma may be part of the process as well, but the major characteristic is employee empowerment.

There are all kinds of good examples of transformational leaders: Lee Iacocca transformed the Chrysler Corporation. Jack Welch at General Electric, the late Sam Walton at Wal-Mart, Dr. Albert Yates cited earlier in the *Profile of Human Behavior,* General Colin Powell, and a multitude of other leaders at departmental and local government levels all provide examples.

An interesting observation about the concept and the examples given is that transformational leaders inspire others to empower their immediate and other subordinates to be transformational as well. One of the main benefits of the approach is that it is quickly demonstrated that leadership is not a one-person show. Again, in the preceding examples, Iacocca, Welch, Walton, and others provided or are providing for strong successors.

Transformational leaders are long-term and development oriented.

Transformational leaders are concerned about both the long-term goals of the organization and the developmental needs of individuals in those organizations. They change individuals' awareness of issues by helping them look at old issues in new ways and by rising to the challenges of new problems. Walter Ulmer, president and CEO of the Center for Creative Leadership, says

> I think we have a significant flaw in much of the recent literature and training on leadership. That flaw is the failure to distinguish between two fundamental dimensions of organizational leadership: "operating" and "building." In the former, the leader is concerned with making the organization as efficient and immediately productive as it can be; in the latter, the leader is concerned with the continuing capacity of the organization to be efficient and productive.[11]

CATALYTIC LEADERSHIP

Catalytic leaders stimulate involvement and thinking by subordinates.

Leaders have been commanders, coaches, and facilitators. Now, there is a need for leaders to be catalysts. **Catalytic leadership** stimulates involvement and thinking by subordinates, allowing them to push the boundaries of their jobs, and helping them to venture into uncharted territories. Catalytic leadership is called for when there is high concern for diversity, a high degree of bottom-up rather than top-down control, and when employees desire opportunities for growth and creativity.

What qualities do leaders need in order to deal effectively with a wide variety of employees and to give subordinates the autonomy to take on responsibility and control? Seven qualities are at the core of catalytic leadership:[12]

1. Tolerance for ambiguity
2. Valuing difference
3. Capitalizing on change
4. Belief in the wisdom of the team
5. Maintaining a balance between product and process
6. Building responsibility and accountability
7. Inviting, using, and giving feedback effectively

Another aspect of catalytic leadership is for the CEO or other leader "to know that they do not have the objectivity, skills and experience to enact radical change. External, objective, apolitical and experienced catalysts and consultants are used to help navigate, find direction, and implement plans."[13]

Figure 11–6 shows the growth of leadership knowledge and provides a summary of the evolving approaches to leadership.

FIGURE 11–6 Evolving Approaches to Leadership.

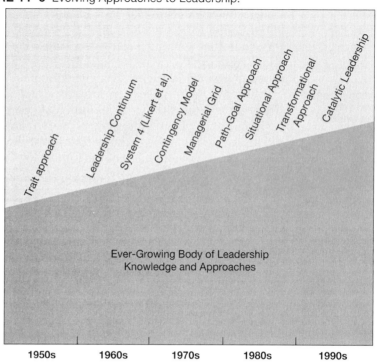

DELEGATION

Delegation requires assignment and implies acceptance as a contract.

Delegation is the assignment of authority to carry out a task to another person and that person's acceptance of the task. As with a contract, there must be an offer and an acceptance according to the terms of an agreement. The employee who accepts a job also accepts the responsibility for completing it. The acceptance of an assignment is thus two sided, carrying both the responsibility and the authority to do the job, although the two sides are not always equal in weight. For example, a subordinate may not have the authority to order the parts or employ the number of people necessary to complete a job that he or she has agreed to do.

To have the responsibility but not the authority to complete a task is an aggravating and depressing experience. Employees will eventually resent and resist supervisors who withhold authority when they try to delegate responsibility. Several important do's and don'ts of delegation are summarized in a study shown in Figure 11–7.

DELEGATION OF AUTHORITY

The delegation of authority means the granting of enough power to subordinates to enable them to accomplish a defined task. In the delegation process, the manager still retains overall authority and can, if need be, revoke all or part of the authority that he or she has granted to a subordinate.

FIGURE 11-7 Do's and Don'ts of Delegation.[14]	
DO	**DON'T**
Encourage the free flow of information.	Hoard information.
Focus on results.	Emphasize methods.
Delegate through dialogue.	Do all the talking yourself.
Fix firm deadlines.	Leave time uncertain.
Make sure the person has all necessary resources.	Give assignments without needed tools.
Delegate the entire task to one person.	Delegate half a task.
Give advice without interfering.	Fail to point out pitfalls.
Build control into the delegation process.	Impose controls as an afterthought.
Back up delegatees in legitimate disputes.	Leave persons to fight their own battles.
Give the delegatee full credit for his or her accomplishments.	Hog the glory or look for scapegoats.

Authority gives rise to an equal amount of responsibility. Responsibility arises with the acceptance of delegated authority, but the responsibility itself cannot be delegated, neither with nor separate from authority. The CEO of an organization has the ultimate responsibility for everything that happens in the organization. As that CEO or other leader delegates authority and it is accepted, then responsibility arises.

ACTION PROJECT 11-2 WHAT KIND OF BOSS WOULD YOU BE? (INDIVIDUAL EXERCISE)

INSTRUCTIONS

On the following pages, questions having a number of possible answers are given. Read the questions and then circle the letter for the answer that best describes your response. Please restrict yourself to the given choices. Do not write in the blanks now—they are for numerical scoring by yourself later.

1. What would your attitude be toward employees' working hours?
    a. Be a "stickler" for hours. _____
    b. Ignore latecomers and employees who leave early, providing you know they are putting the hours in. _____
    c. Ignore time altogether as long as they did their work. _____

2. If one of your employees lost his or her temper with you, would you
    a. fire the employee? _____
    b. try to placate the employee and suggest you discuss it at a more convenient time? _____
    c. insult the employee? _____
    d. treat the incident as if it had never happened, but watch the employee closely after that? _____
    e. treat the employee more casually? _____

3. How would you treat internal stealing of company and personal property?
   a. Put up notices to tell people it was happening. _____
   b. Call in a security firm. _____
   c. Ask your managers to keep watch. _____
   d. Ignore it and accept it as human nature. _____
   e. The first three. _____
4. If one of your junior members asked to see you about an alleged victimization by his or her department head, would you
   a. ignore it on the grounds that the person didn't know what he or she was doing? _____
   b. go to the department head in question and have a quiet word with him or her? _____
   c. have them both in the office to talk about it? _____
5. Do you think it is better to lead
   a. by example? _____
   b. by the rules? _____
   c. by common agreement? _____
   d. depending on the situation? _____
6. What do you think the primary purpose of the company should be?
   a. to make a profit _____
   b. to provide employment _____
7. Given two identical candidates of the same age, experience, and ability, which would you take?
   a. the one who had the most knowledge of your company _____
   b. the one who seemed to have the closest business philosophy to your own

   _____
   c. the more agreeable _____
   d. the one who seemed to need the job _____
8. You are faced with falling sales figures. How would you react?
   a. Change your entire sales staff. _____
   b. Offer incentives to the existing staff. _____
   c. Alter the product. _____
   d. Both a and c. _____
   e. Both b and c. _____
9. What do you think is the single most important fact in an employee's life?
   a. his or her success in the company _____
   b. his or her personal life _____
   c. money _____
10. As a new president of a firm, you found that it is failing. What action would you take?
   a. Cut back on the staff. _____

b. Expand staff because the more personnel there are, the more work they will perform. _____

c. Liquidate the company immediately, selling off the assets at a good profit, and then start again. _____

11. You are confronted with the need to terminate a senior person in the company. Would you

    a. do it yourself? _____

    b. expect the personnel officer to do it? _____

    c. make life so unpleasant for the person that he or she would have no alternative but to leave? _____

12. Do you think wages should be paid

    a. on merit or how well you perform? _____

    b. on years of service? _____

    c. equally—as everyone contributes something? _____

13. On the whole, do you think paperwork is

    a. necessary? _____

    b. wasteful? _____

    c. gets overcomplicated? _____

14. To which of the following philosophies would you subscribe?

    a. The early bird gets the worm. _____

    b. Slow and steady wins the race. _____

    c. Haste makes waste. _____

15. One of your department heads lies continuously. Would you

    a. demote him or her? _____

    b. fire him or her? _____

    c. make allowances and check everything he or she does? _____

    d. ask him or her to leave? _____

16. If your secretary complained of feeling ill and had not quite finished typing an urgent piece of work, would you

    a. ask him or her just to finish it and then go home? _____

    b. suggest that he or she stay on as long as possible? _____

    c. tell him or her to go home right away and make other arrangements, knowing that the work probably would not be finished in time? _____

17. If one of your staff members continually disagrees with you, would you

    a. begin to worry about your judgment? _____

    b. get rid of him or her? _____

    c. regard his or her attitude as the sign of a healthy, constructive mind? _____

18. Would you give your employees

    a. orders? _____

    b. instructions? _____

    c. suggestions? _____

19. Which of the following do you think is the main function of an employer?
    a. decision making _____
    b. personnel _____
    c. financial _____
    d. all three _____
20. If your company is running profitably and well, would you
    a. be content to let it continue that way? _____
    b. take on more work and, if necessary, buy more equipment? _____
    c. invest the profits outside the company? _____

SCORING YOUR TEST

Answers are listed below. Give yourself the number of points that correspond to the answer you gave to each question. Then total your score. Read the conclusions that follow.

1. a. 5	2. a. 5	3. a. 3	4. a. 5	5. a. 3
b. 3	b. 2	b. 3	b. 3	b. 5
c. 0	c. 0	c. 0	c. 0	c. 0
	d. 3	d. 0		d. 0
	e. 3	e. 5		

6. a. 5	7. a. 5	8. a. 5	9. a. 5	10. a. 3
b. 0	b. 3	b. 2	b. 0	b. 0
	c. 2	c. 3	c. 3	c. 5
	d. 0	d. 5		
		e. 4		

11. a. 5	12. a. 5	13. a. 0	14. a. 5	15. a. 3
b. 3	b. 0	b. 5	b. 0	b. 5
c. 0	c. 2	c. 3	c. 3	c. 0
				d. 3

16. a. 3	17. a. 0	18. a. 5	19. a. 4	20. a. 0
b. 5	b. 5	b. 3	b. 2	b. 5
c. 0	c. 2	c. 0	c. 3	c. 4
			d. 5	

CONCLUSIONS

11–27 points. You're pretty sociable. You might enjoy making money, but your firm would never actually make it if you were in charge. However, if the company failed, you would still have plenty of friends.

28–50 points. Your idea of a boss is someone friendly rather than astute, slow rather than fast, one who would do no more harm than good, but would hardly set the commercial world on fire.

51–72 points. You would be aware of the job at hand, but would probably make mistakes through lack of thorough convictions or any business philosophy. You would be adaptable, probably conscientious with good judgment, and well liked by your colleagues.

73–84 points. You would not take much interference from those weaker than yourself; you would be inclined to be ruthless, telling yourself that everyone finds their own level. Not always popular perhaps, but thought of as efficient.

85–100 points. You are either a master of industry or power mad. You prefer "yes" people. For you, what counts are figures and performance. On occasion, you might stay after everyone has left to check up on who was working; when, why, and how.

INFORMAL GROUP LEADERSHIP

The informal group leader is usually chosen by default; that is, there is not a formal election, but, by mutual assent and the process of elimination, the individual with the greatest status is chosen as informal leader. That person serves as an example and role model for others in the group.

The qualifications for informal leader includes primarily status, which is a function of age, knowledge, social skills, and other strengths. The group leader is not always the most popular group member but is viewed as the individual who can satisfy subordinates' leadership needs. Assuming leadership by presenting new ideas and helping to make decisions may make a person admired but not always liked. Part of "taking the risk" of leadership is that "taking a stand" does not always make a person popular with all group members.

"LEADERLESS" GROUPS

Finally, there is growing evidence that *some* groups may not need leaders, or more properly, that there are substitutes for leadership. **Substitutes for leadership** are a series of attributes that permit less direct leadership: subordinate ability, responsibility, routine tasks, and specific organizational plans. It is still too early to know how many groups fit into this category. The emphasis in the 1980s on "lean and mean" organizations and quality circles stimulated interest in reducing the number of formal leaders.

A number of factors can serve as substitutes for certain aspects of leadership. Examples of these factors are tasks with direct feedback, cohesive work groups, able and experienced subordinates, and unambiguous, routine jobs. Another substitute is self-leadership and self-control, requiring less direct intervention on the part of a formal leader.

Finally, more often than in the private sector, public sector managers tend to be leaderless and receive little policy guidance. This is true for both brief appointees and career officers serving long periods. Some rules for maintaining effective operation of an agency in the absence of leadership include:

1. Make normal decisions normally.
2. During leaderless periods, strive for greater cooperative bureaucratic efforts than would be normal during easier times.
3. Promote open information exchanges.
4. Do not permit process mechanics and red tape to take over the agency and its functions.
5. Do not permit petty turf and authority issues to assume undue importance.
6. Remember that a leader will eventually arrive to return things to normal.[15]

SUMMARY

Leaders initiate and facilitate change by interacting with members of groups to make decisions about matters having a high-risk or uncertainty factor. Followers follow because they already agree with the changes that the leader is initiating or because they want to be changed. Often, the best leadership is low-key. Listening and supporting others in an ethical manner spurs individual and organizational development.

Leadership is not always aggressive or autocratic; often the best test of effective leadership is how smoothly a group functions. Every situation calls for different leadership responses. Because of the many functional variables inherent in each situation, there are plenty of opportunities to demonstrate different leadership traits and styles.

Many people do not recognize the leadership potential in themselves. Considerable research into the personality traits of leaders has led to the conclusion that leadership is directly attributable to relatively few traits, such as self-confidence, energy, relative intelligence, perseverance, and enthusiasm. A leader's traits are not out of the ordinary, although they are highly developed. Being well liked socially and being well respected as a leader are two different things; they sometimes go together and sometimes not. Often, social leaders and idea leaders are mutually supportive.

The effectiveness of a leader is not always determined by the person's personality traits; effectiveness can also be measured in terms of the composite relationship of the group to the problem, the environment, the feasibility of the solution, and the leader. All situations do not require the same type of leader; some groups may not require a formal leader at all.

Two major leadership styles according to Douglas McGregor are the benevolent autocrat, or X leader, and the participative leader, or Y leader. There are many situations where one style works more effectively than the other. Theory Z, developed in Japan, is based on long-range planning, consensus decision making, company image, quality over quantity, and lifetime employment.

The contingency model identifies a manager's leadership style and then analyzes the job situation and matches the best leader for the job at that particular moment in time. Many other approaches are available for selecting the appropriate leadership style: a systems approach, the Managerial Grid, and the path–goal, situational, and transformational approaches. All of them boil down to fitting the leadership style to the situation where the leader is either an active or passive catalyst.

CASE STUDY 11–1

CONFLICT BETWEEN TWO STYLES OF SUPERVISION

Fire Station 13 is commanded by Captain Eric Collings. He has been in charge of the station for a period of six months, following his promotion and transfer from another fire station.

Station 13 is located in foothills outside a large community. The station's location, along with some additional factors, has led to a confrontation between Collings and the battalion chief, David Marx.

Chief Marx: "I don't care, Captain Collings, what the reasons are. There are rules and regulations that must be followed. As long as I am the battalion chief, it is my duty to see that the fire stations under my supervision perform properly, and that means these rules and regulations will be followed."

Captain Collings: "It is my opinion, with all due respect, Mr. Marx, that your insistence upon following fire department regulations to the letter is hindering my men in their job performance and hurting their morale. I can't help but feel that in this case the regulations should be eased or modified for the benefit of this station and its men."

Chief Marx: "We have a good public image as a result of our uniform rules. The public sees us as a neat, clean, efficient fire-fighting unit. You're asking me to bend the rules to make it easier for your own men. If I were to bend the rules for you, I'd be obligated to bend the rules for everyone, and that I won't do."

Captain Collings: "But sir, ours is the only station that is removed from the community. We fight brush fires, not structural fires. We seldom come into contact with the public and we are constantly in the dust. I can't help but feel that you're being too strict with the men about appearances. I agree that appearance is important, but keeping uniforms spotless and shoes highly shined is next to impossible here. And I don't think your reprimanding Johnson this afternoon was fair. We don't even have a cement floor beneath our trucks here. How can you expect him to remain clean when he has to lie in the dirt to make his safety checks of the truck?

"While I'm at it, sir, I would also like to say that I think your haircut and television policies are too strict. Ours is the only department that is forced to wear our hair this short. In comparison to many other fire departments, we look bald. I feel this, and the fact that you won't allow the men to watch television while relaxing on duty, is unfair to the men. These men are professionals, and they should be treated as such. They have asked me to speak to you about this, and I myself am in total agreement with them. As their captain, I am asking that you relax the regulations that are clearly too severe."

Chief Marx: "Captain, we have a good public image. We shall continue to have a good public image in spite of your protests. If you and your men find the situation unbearable, transfers can be made available."

1. If you were Captain Collings, would you accept things as they are or would you continue to protest the rules and regulations imposed on your station?

2. If you accepted the battalion chief's wishes for a strict code, how would you handle the supervision of the firemen? Would you inform your men of how you feel and how David Marx feels?

3. If your men then encouraged you to ignore the rules established by the chief, what would you do?

4. If you disobey the chief's orders, are you showing the firemen that it's all right for you to disobey, even though you expect them to obey you? Is this a situation of cognitive dissonance for the firemen—that is, are they being asked to hold two mutually contradictory viewpoints at the same time?

CASE STUDY
11–2

WHO LEADS: THE CHOSEN LEADER OR THE INFORMAL LEADER?

The Landau Construction Company recently contracted to erect the frames of houses as part of a federal housing project. Loren Franks is the supervisor for the company on this project, and the twelve people working for him were hired from the local union hall. Loren receives bonuses that are based on how rapidly projects are completed. The faster the project is completed, the more money he will get. Because of rain he is falling a little behind his schedule.

Loren has supervised most of the workers in the past and, on the whole, he considers them good, skilled carpenters. One of the men, a young and relatively new carpenter named Brian Baxter, has not worked for Loren before. Soon after work began on the project, Loren became aware of Brian and his popularity with the other workers. In the beginning, during coffee and lunch breaks, Brian was constantly asking the more experienced workers questions about the carpentry field. Because of his easygoing manner and his desire to learn, Brian soon became popular with all the workers.

After a few weeks, Loren noticed that Brian began to ask fewer questions about carpentry, and instead began to tell many humorous stories and jokes for the workers' entertainment, which presented no problem in itself. Loren became increasingly aware, however, that the workers were taking longer lunch hours and coffee breaks to listen to Brian. It seemed that Brian always had a story to finish or one last joke to tell before going back to work.

Loren counseled Brian twice about the problem, but this failed to produce results. During the two counseling conversations Loren got the impression that Brian was enjoying both his popularity and the situation, which worsened. Usually after an extended break, Loren would find many workers grouped around a single operation for which only one worker was needed, such as sweeping shavings. Loren found that the center of the group cluster would invariably be Brian. On these occasions, when Loren was forced to remind the carpenters that their work was not getting done, Brian would always laugh it off and have one last comment to make, which the men would wait to hear.

From all appearances, Brian has assumed informal control of the group. If you were Loren, how would you go about correcting the situation that exists?

1. Do you continue to counsel Brian or do you now go to the workers?

2. If you talk with the other carpenters, what do you say to them?

3. Are there other alternatives?

4. Would you "blacklist" Brian—that is, tell other supervisors not to hire him because he doesn't work hard enough?

DISCUSSION AND STUDY QUESTIONS—TO KEEP YOU THINKING . . .

1. Distinguish between leadership and management.

2. Describe the differences between task leaders and social leaders.

3. Discuss at least half of the many Theory X traits. Also, discuss at least half of the Theory Y traits.

4. Which features of Theory Z match the X or Y concepts? Is Theory Z more like X or more like Y?

5. Does participative management mean abdication of leadership? How is it different from free-rein leadership?

6. What are the bases for the path–goal process of leadership?

7. What are the bases for situational leadership?

8. What are the bases for transformational leadership?

NOTES

1. Karen Bemowski, "Leaders on Leadership," *Quality Progress,* January 1996, p. 43.

2. Ibid., pp. 43–44.

3. John R. Emshwiller, "Ueberroth Leaves Rebuild L.A. Effort Without Leader or Target of Criticism," *The Wall Street Journal,* May 24, 1993, p. A3.

4. Julie Poppen, "(Yate's) Term in Office Is Transforming CSU," *Fort Collins Coloradoan,* June 2, 1996, pp. A1, A8.

5. James M. Korzes and Barry Z. Posner, *The Leadership Challenge: How to Get Extraordinary Things Done in Organizations* (San Francisco: Jossey-Bass, 1987), pp. 8–13.

6. Robert Blake and Jane Mouton, *The Managerial Grid III* (Houston, Tex.: Gulf, 1985).

7. Fred E. Fiedler, "When to Lead, When to Stand Back: If You Want to Be a Directive Leader You'd Better Be Smart. Otherwise, Get Your Employees Involved," *Psychology Today,* September 1987, p. 26.

8. Robert J. House and Terence C. Mitchell, "Path–Goal Theory of Leadership," *Journal of Contemporary Business,* Autumn 1974, pp. 81–99; see also R. J. House, "Retrospective Comment," in L.E. Boone and D.D. Bowen, eds., *The Great Writing in Management and Organizational Behavior,* 2nd ed. (New York: Random House, 1987), pp. 354–364.

9. Jan P. Muczyk and Bernard C. Reimann, "MBO as a Complement to Effective Leadership," *Academy of Management Executive,* May 1989, pp. 131–138.

10. Paul Hersey and Kenneth H. Blanchard, *Management of Organizational Behavior* (Englewood Cliffs, N.J.: Prentice Hall, 1988) and personal communication with Ken Blanchard, August 1994.

11. Walter F. Ulmer, Jr., "Inside View," *Issues and Observations,* published by the Center for Creative Leadership, Greensboro, N.C., Third Quarter 1993, p. 6.

12. Lee Gardenswartz and Anita Roe, *Diverse Teams at Work: Capitalizing on the Power of Diversity* (Chicago: Irwin, 1994), p. 230.

13. Richard G. Ligus, "Implementing Radical Change: The Right Stuff," *Industrial Engineering,* May 1994, p. 29.

14. James M. Jenks and John M. Kelly, "Delegation: Key to Management Success," *Manage,* Second Quarter 1986, pp. 29, 31.

15. Richard E. Schmidt, "Management in a Leaderless Environment," *Bureaucrat,* Fall 1985, pp. 30–32.

RECOMMENDED READING

Bennis, Warren G. *An Invented Life: Reflections on Leadership and Change.* Reading, Mass.: Addison-Wesley, 1993.

_____ **and Robert Townsend.** *Reinventing Leadership: Strategies to Empower the Organization.* New York: William Morrow, 1995.

Blake, Robert R., and Anne Adams McCanse. *Leadership Dilemmas—Grid Solutions.* Houston, Tex.: Gulf, 1991.

Conger, Jay A. "Leadership: The Art of Empowering Others." *Academy of Management Executive,* February 1989, pp. 17–24.

De Pree, Max. *Leadership Is an Art.* New York: Doubleday, 1989.

_____. *Leadership Jazz.* New York: Doubleday, 1993.

Dinkmeyer, Don, and Daniel Eckstein. *Leadership by Encouragement.* Delray Beach, Fla.: St. Lucie Press, 1996.

Fiedler, Fred E. "When to Lead, When to Stand Back: If You Want to Be a Directive Leader You'd Better Be Smart. Otherwise, Get Your Employees Involved." *Psychology Today,* September 1987, pp. 26–27.

Jawaorski, Joseph. *Synchronicity: The Inner Path of Leadership.* San Francisco: Berrett-Koehler Publishers, 1996.

Kiechel, Walter, III. "The Case against Leaders." *Fortune,* November 23, 1988, pp. 217–218, 220.

Lawler, Edward E. *The Ultimate Advantage: Creating the High-Involvement Organization.* San Francisco: Jossey-Bass, 1992.

_____ **and Barry Markovsky, eds.** *Social Psychology of Groups.* Greenwich, Conn.: JAI Press, 1993.

Locke, Edwin A., and Gary P. Latham. *Goal Setting: A Motivational Technique That Works!* Englewood Cliffs, N.J.: Prentice Hall, 1984.

McGregor, Douglas. *The Human Side of Enterprise.* New York: McGraw-Hill, 1960.

Nahavandi, Afsaneh. *The Art and Science of Leadership.* Upper Saddle River, N.J.: Prentice Hall Business Publishing, 1997.

Ouchi, William. *Theory Z: How American Businesses Can Meet /the Japanese Challenge.* Reading, Mass.: Addison-Wesley, 1981.

Peters, Thomas J., and Nancy Austin. *A Passion for Excellence.* New York: Random House, 1985.

Sayles, Leonard R. *The Working Leader: The Triumph of High Performance over Conventional Management Principles.* New York: The Free Press, 1993.

Yukl, Gary A. *Leadership in Organizations.* 2nd ed. Englewood Cliffs, N.J.: Prentice Hall, 1989.

12

Orientation, Training, and Discipline

Take a look at these questions and check your reactions to them.

- How important is orientation to you in your job(s)? other organizations?
- What specific factors would you want covered in an orientation?
- Are you aware of how much a company's orientation can affect job attitudes?
- What is the difference between job training and general education?
- What are the differences between training and development?
- Do you know what *transactional analysis* means? Or such terms as *meditation, assertiveness training,* or *sensitivity training?*
- What are the differences among simulation, experiential training, and organizational training methods?
- What is the difference between discipline and disciplinary action?
- What is the relationship between discipline and training?

LEARNING GOALS

After studying this chapter, you should be able to:

1. Relate the need for employee orientation on a new job.
2. Distinguish between training and development.
3. Discuss training from the point of view of needs assessment, goals, methods, and follow-up.
4. Describe the "simulation techniques" used in training. Discuss how they simulate business situations.
   a. In-basket method
   b. Case method
   c. Management games
   d. Role playing
5. Discuss the following "experiential" methods of training. Develop ideas that are for and against each experiential method.
   a. Sensitivity training
   b. Transactional analysis
   c. Assertiveness training
   d. Meditation
6. Distinguish between aggressiveness and assertiveness.
7. Distinguish between meditation and biofeedback as fads and also as physiologically useful techniques.

8. Distinguish between discipline and disciplinary action. Discuss the relationship between discipline and training.

9. Define and apply the following terms and concepts (in order of first occurrence):

- orientation
- policy orientation (induction)
- procedural orientation (process orientation)
- inductive method (of orientation/learning/training)
- deductive method (of orientation/learning/training)
- training
- development
- learning
- on-the-job training (OJT)
- programmed instruction
- simulation
- in-basket training
- management games
- experiential methods
- role playing
- sensitivity training
- transactional analysis
- assertiveness training
- meditation
- biofeedback
- discipline
- disciplinary action

INTRODUCTION

This chapter complements the discussion of leadership roles from Chapter 11 in that it deals with functions that can make the leader's job easier and more effective: orientation, training, and discipline. Ultimately, the leader has responsibility for all these functions, but leaders can enhance their effectiveness by empowering others through employee orientation, preparedness (training), and a positive state of readiness for contingencies (which is how "discipline" is used here).

The topics of recruitment and hiring are outside the scope of this book. These topics are usually covered in human resource management (personnel) texts and courses. All managers play an important role in recruitment and hiring, but their role in developing employees once they are hired is frequently understated. So, let us view these development functions in chronological order: orientation first; then, training and development; and finally, discipline—again in the positive sense of readiness and willingness to do a job.

ORIENTATION

When new employees decide to take a job, they already have some impressions about the company for which they plan to work. The job interview will have given them a sense of the company's environment. However, the on-the-job impressions of the first few days greatly influence and solidify attitudes toward their jobs and the companies for which they work. **Orientation** is the formal means by which employees learn about their new employer, their jobs, and coworkers.

Orientation versus induction.

Orientation is concerned with accomplishing two major tasks: (1) informing employees of company policies and benefits and (2) making employees aware of locations and procedures that affect their abilities to do their jobs. Formally, the first point is called **policy orientation (induction),** and the second, **procedural orientation (process orientation).** Loosely, both tasks fall under the general concept of orientation—acquainting new employees with their job environment and coworkers and with company policies and procedures.

POLICY ORIENTATION

A general area with which new employees must become acquainted is department and company policies and practices. These orientation subjects usually include absentee policies, vacation times and amounts, holidays, disciplinary procedures, and how to fill out certain company forms. Employees will need to study the options for medical and other fringe benefits, use of the credit union, stock purchase plans, employee purchases and discounts, and retirement and insurance plans. Some companies find that detailed information should not be presented for about a week, or until after new employees have time to feel comfortable with more immediate concerns, such as the job, the coworkers, and the work environment.

PROCEDURAL ORIENTATION

New employees must learn the locations of things that are pertinent to their working lives: parking spaces, employee entrances and exits, time clocks, lockers, restrooms, bulletin boards, cafeteria, coffee and smoking areas, and work-related departments. It is a sad comment on a company's orientation program when a new employee is encountered wandering the halls in search of the restroom or the cafeteria. Further induction should include company procedures, uniforms, safety equipment, rest breaks, and details of pay.

Sponsors for new employees.

Some managers consider it good management practice for an established coworker to sponsor a new employee, at least during the first few days. In this way, a new employee can establish immediate rapport with a person in the same department, which helps the newcomer to overcome feelings of shyness and strangeness. The coworker is available to answer questions and to introduce the new employee to others. In general, coworker orientation is a good method for easing the new employee into the company environment. But the manager must be careful when choosing an individual for this responsibility.

TWO APPROACHES TO ORIENTATION

The inductive method: from part to whole.

Orientation is approached in two ways: moving from part to whole (inductive) or moving from whole to part (deductive) (Figure 12–1). The **inductive method**

FIGURE 12–1 Illustration of the Inductive and Deductive Methods of Orienting New Employees.

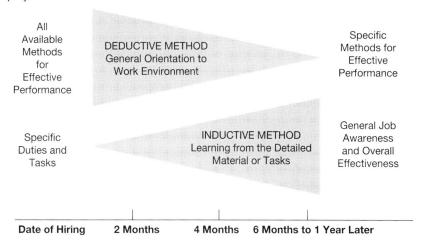

favors expansion of orientation. Employees are first instructed in the details of their jobs and necessary locations and procedures. Gradually, employees are exposed to more information. They learn the details of company benefits, the overall company objectives, how people and departments interrelate, and how the company relates to the community. Many new employees like to begin by learning their jobs and making themselves useful, and then gradually widen their scope. One disadvantage is that employees may form incorrect opinions about the company, opinions that are difficult to alter later on in orientation.

The deductive method: from whole to part.

In the **deductive method,** employees are first introduced to the company as a whole. The company is treated as a family that employees must get to know before beginning their job duties. The deductive method is learning from the whole to the part. During the first week, a film on the company is often shown, which focuses on the firm's products but also emphasizes employee security and company success. Early in the employee orientation a new recruit is aware of the steps in production and what part he or she will play in the process.

A disadvantage is that the newcomer may become anxious to get to work and learn his or her duties during this indoctrination period. However, the newcomer is learning to identify, associate, and feel comfortable with the firm. According to this view, it is better to train a good, productive, loyal employee first to become a statistician, a computer operator, or a labor relations specialist than to hire a highly trained outsider.

EXPRESS YOUR OPINION

Consider the company at which you work now or select a company you can relate to comfortably and determine whether you would use the deductive method or the inductive method of orientation. Consider not only the method that seems best for you but also the size of the company, the type of industry, and the turnover and longevity of the employees.

ORIENTATION IS KEY TO LONG-TERM PERFORMANCE AND MORALE

Orientation is a key to retention, morale, and performance. If employees are not properly oriented to their organization during the first few working days, both employees and organization suffer negative consequences for years to come. First impressions *are* lasting!

Turnover can be reduced by good orientation.

Studies have shown that turnover is relatively high in many organizations but can be substantially reduced by effective orientation. Corning, Inc., found that individuals who had been through several orientation sessions had a lower turnover rate than did those who had minimal orientation. Other benefits of effective employee orientation include stronger loyalty, lower absenteeism, and higher job satisfaction.[1]

One partner in a management consulting firm says of employee orientation:

> Of course, poor selection procedures can be at the root of the problem. But, more often than not, we fail to make new employees comfortable in a new and stressful environment. . . .
>
> Sometimes a new employee "falls between the cracks." The departmental supervisor thinks that "orientation" is a personnel department function; the personnel department thinks it is a departmental responsibility. And, in fact, nobody has developed a plan that recognizes short-, medium-, and long-term requirements.[2]

Orientation is a dual responsibility.

Orientation is the responsibility of both the employee's department and the human resource office. The orientation in the department is as important or more so than the personnel, paperwork orientation. The department should value (and celebrate!) employees from day one.

Joseph P. McCarthy, a human resources planner at Metropolitan Property and Casualty Insurance Company, says these are key elements of a program:

- **Supervisor's role.** The supervisor is the key contact for the new employee. The supervisor's role is supplemented by a four-page (easily readable) *Guide for Supervisors* that may be individualized for each employee.
- **Mentor's role.** The mentor is a coworker somewhere between a traditional high-level sponsor and a totally informal buddy.
- **Partnership with peers.** Promotes teamwork.
- **Self-development.** Each employee is accountable for her or his self-development.
- **Feedback.** Both informal and formal feedback is provided, including a specific third-month form citing the employees' own perception of their most satisfying accomplishment to date.
- **Orientation videos.** One video is a brief history of the organization; another features highlights on teamwork and creativity.[3]

Figure 12–2 shows an original orientation checklist to be used by a new employee's manager/leader. The human resource/personnel department would have a different list covering employee classification and records, safety, work rules, benefits, and other personnel-related activities. There may be some redundancy (duplication) between the manager/leader's

FIGURE 12–2 Manager/Leader's Orientation Checklist for New Employees.*

_____ A genuine, warm welcome from supervisors and coworkers (there should be room for fun and celebration)

_____ Preparation of coworkers (at least a telephone call in advance of introduction)

_____ Actual introduction to coworkers

_____ Introduction of employee to selected employees outside of the department

_____ Overview of job setting including tour of facility

_____ Assigning a volunteer mentor

_____ Providing an employee manual/handbook—enough information without overload:

      _____ Brief history of organization

      _____ Organizational overview

      _____ Other items included by personnel department

_____ List of specific job requirements:

      _____ Job responsibilities

      _____ New employee's position in organization

      _____ Work values

      _____ Work expectations of the employee

      _____ Emphasis on quantity and quality of work

_____ Critical facilities:

      _____ Copy machine

      _____ Restroom

      _____ Telephone and norms for use

      _____ Eating arrangements

      _____ Parking

      _____ Day care center

      _____ Credit union

      _____ Working hours

      _____ Breaks

      _____ Pay policies

      _____ Performance appraisal policies

*This checklist is not intended to include personnel department items such as benefits. The personnel department should have its own checklist for orientation.

checklist and the human resource department's checklist, but that is good— if they are coordinated.

Finally, new employees want answers to these questions:

- What's your definition of a top producer?
- How will you let them know when their performance is unsatisfactory?
- How can they register complaints effectively?
- How formal should their communication be within the organization— rough notes or typed memos?
- What is the best time to talk with you?
- When, if ever, should they call you at home?
- How much social interaction is expected or appreciated in the organization?[4]

TRAINING AND DEVELOPMENT RELATIONSHIPS

Learning and development are fundamental to all behavior modification. A person's success in an organization is determined in large part by education, including orientation, training, and development on and off the job.

Misunderstandings are costly; they waste time and often material. These are times when supervisors must train and direct employees in areas in which they have no experience on materials that are expensive and on procedures that are complex. Therefore, the likelihood of errors because of communication problems becomes more common in our technical world. It is wise then to consider training programs.

Training is hard to measure.

The effectiveness of training programs is difficult to measure, and there is no guarantee that a training program will enable an employee to perform a job successfully. However, the risk is even greater in the other direction: Without training, mistakes in skill and judgment are more possible. Often, training is a small risk when compared with the potential errors that result from no training. Regardless, training should be viewed as an entire process—not just the delivery of training.

WHAT IS TRAINING?

Training can change behavior.

Training is the process of transmitting and receiving information related to problem solving. It can be used in changing behavior as well as in learning skills and concepts. Training is specific in improving the trainee's abilities to perform in particular jobs. Educational programs transmit information for its own sake, with no expectation of how and when the information will be used—if ever. The specific purpose of training is to communicate information that is applicable to practical situations. After training, trainees should be able to demonstrate changes in behavior or performance that contribute to their abilities to deal skillfully with specific problems. Training, however, implies a

Training implies formal commitment of time.

formal commitment of time—be it ten minutes or six months—set aside to learn specific, directly applicable information.

Training takes two forms: traditional and human relations. *Traditional training* is concerned with learning skills and theoretical concepts that can be applied to performing the mechanics of a job. Traditional skills are oriented to the "how to" aspects of work. Human relations training passes on skills dealing with the ability to interact with others: coworkers with coworkers and supervisors with subordinates. *Human relations training* is concerned with the attitudes and assumptions that people have about their jobs, about themselves, and about other people.

Many kinds of training are vital to today's working world. Without it, misunderstandings are likely to occur, which often result in wasted time, money, and human energy and emotion. Nowadays, employees are rarely expected to work at tasks for which they receive no training. A manager who does not know how to work with people is at as severe a disadvantage as is a drill press operator who does not know how to run a drill press. Without job training, employees are put in the position of having to "muddle through" as best they can.

FIGURE 12–3 The Training and Development Process Cycle.

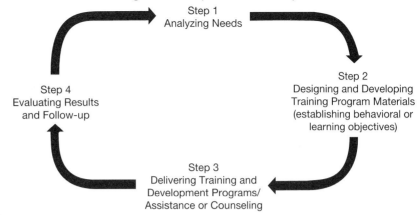

Training is a cyclical process involving at least four steps: (1) analyzing needs, (2) designing and developing training materials, (3) delivering training and development programs/assistance or counseling, and (4) evaluating results and follow-up (see Figure 12–3). All four steps are important, but too often only step 3 is considered training. One of the reasons that so much training is ineffective is because it addresses only one point in the cycle. If the delivery system does not meet a need, is improperly designed, or is not evaluated or followed up, it is little wonder that we do not know our jobs or whether training is effective.

WHAT IS DEVELOPMENT?

Development emphasizes increasing participants' abilities.

Development falls between specific training and general education. There is an expected payoff to the sponsoring organization but it is not always concerned with the participant's current job. **Development** activity puts emphasis on increasing the participant's abilities to perform effectively in other jobs as well as the current job.

The focus of development is on the general needs of the organization. The focus of training is on the present job and the almost immediate application of knowledge and skills to that job. Training is generally considered job specific and seeks to improve an individual's ability to perform a job or organizational role. Development is more oriented to the future and is broader in scope than training.[5]

Who has the responsibility for development? Just as managers and trainers have the responsibility for seeing that employees are trained, they both share the responsibility for development. Effort must be made to develop the discipline noted earlier, and to develop subordinates' capacities for and commitment to sharing responsibility for an organization's success. To be effective, the manager-as-developer must accomplish the following three major tasks:

1. Work with direct subordinates as a team to share responsibility collectively for managing the unit.

2. Determine and gain commitment to a common vision of the department's goals and purpose.

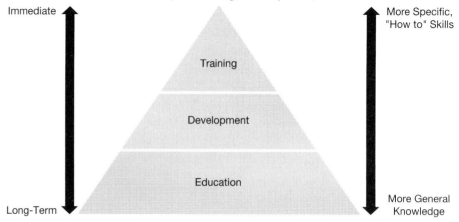

FIGURE 12–4 The Relationship of Training, Development, and Education.

Immediate

Long-Term

Training

Development

Education

More Specific,
"How to" Skills

More General
Knowledge

3. Work on the continuous development of individual subordinates' skills, especially in the managerial/interpersonal areas needed to be an effective member of the shared responsibility team.

The manager-as-developer then seeks to develop in subordinates the willingness and ability to share the responsibility for departmental success. The manager must shape subordinates into a powerful, cooperative, hardworking, dedicated, and responsible team.

Figure 12–4 shows a relationship between training, development, and education. One reason why the term *development* has come into more common usage in recent years is to cover the middle ground between training and education. Some, however, would argue that to define training as the imparting of more specific "how to" skills is too narrow a definition. What do you think?

WHAT IS LEARNING?

Learning means change. To learn is to change. **Learning** is a relatively permanent change in knowledge or skill produced by experience. Good learning outcomes depend on the following:

- Training design
- Trainee characteristics
- Work environment
- Opportunity to perform
- Transfer of learning onto the job
- Ability to perform, if motivated
- Occurrence and maintenance of knowledge transfer, if positive work climate[6]

Positive attitudes from everyone concerned with training and its spheres of potential influence help to make the learning process a worthwhile experience.

TABLE 12–1 Matching Areas of Training with Methods

AREAS OF TRAINING	METHOD OF TRAINING
1. New employee orientation	1. Classroom technique daily from 8 to 10 A.M. or 1 to 2 P.M.
2. Stockroom training	2. Videotape
3. Reservation desk training	3. Programmed manuals
4. Evaluation of program	4. Survey of participants and management

GOALS AND METHODS

Whether an employee comes to a job with previous experience or is trained by the company after being hired, job training of some kind, formal or informal, must occur. Often the most difficult problem in job training is recognizing the need for it. Managers must be convinced to allow time and money for training endeavors.

The training director or a committee on training may select areas that need training programs and prepare a priority list of those areas selected. Such a list might look like this:

1. New employee orientation
2. Stockroom
3. Reservation desk
4. Evaluation of programs

THE TRAINING MUST FIT THE NEED

First select the goals— then the methods.

A distinction must be made between training goals and the methods by which the goals are undertaken. Training methods are appropriate only according to the training goals. Methods can be compared only in terms of objectives. For instance, role playing does not help employees to learn more about running a drill, although it may help people learn how to become better managers. Therefore, training goals must be defined clearly before a specific program is undertaken (see Table 12–1). Once the goals are well formed, the methods fall into place. The content of a training program might not be learned adequately if the appropriate methods are not used.

It is, for instance, not enough to teach human relations without actually "doing" it. Instead of a lecture, some method involving interaction with other people must be employed. Case study and role playing are just two examples that we will examine under methods.

DEVELOPING MANAGERS

Managers can do much to develop their subordinates by delegating small and large tasks. Of course, it is difficult to delegate but one of the main purposes for doing so is employee development. Perhaps Theory Y leaders more often encourage the development of people. If the department operates effectively while the supervisor is on vacation, people are being developed.

There are several reasons why managers fail to develop good subordinates:

1. Managers are chosen for their technical excellence, but they have little or no training in human relations.
2. Managers would rather avoid training and prefer to hire proven managers from other companies.
3. Managers are interested in enhancing their own status rather than in helping their subordinates.
4. Managers know very little about their subordinates' potential, preferring to select a carbon copy of themselves when a promotional opportunity arises.

These factors contribute to the reasons for accelerating management development efforts. Whether management development is done inside or outside of the organization, there are real benefits to be acquired from formalized programs. Primary among the benefits is increased performance and productivity. But the training and development efforts must be germane to both the human relations and technical aspects of jobs.

PROFILE OF HUMAN BEHAVIOR

PAULA M. ANCONA

Paula Ancona has been writing the "Working Smarter" column for Scripps-Howard News Service since November 1988. The column is distributed to about 380 newspapers every week. "Working Smarter" gives readers in all professions and at all levels practical suggestions for improving their work lives. Paula writes about diverse topics such as job searches, sexual harassment, training, humor on the job, and dealing with a difficult boss. A collection of her columns is being published by Chamisa Press, Minneapolis, Minnesota. She has a bachelor of science in journalism from Bowling Green State University, is married, and has three children.

From 1988 through May 1992, Paula also was staff development director at *The Albuquerque Tribune.* She designed and supervised the *Tribune's* employee performance review system, planned and conducted in-house workshops, helped staff members meet individual skills goals, and wrote professional development articles for the in-house newsletter. She maintained a part-time schedule to accommodate the demands of her young family, sometimes telecommuting from home. Paula also conducted a series of reader focus groups that gathered information to help *Tribune* editors and staff members understand readers' needs.

On orientation, training, and discipline, Paula says "Orientation sets the tone for a new employee's work experience. The more an employer makes a new employee feel welcome and gives the basic information needed to jump right into the job, the better. Training is key to developing a strong work force and to bringing America up to speed in the global marketplace. Positive discipline, or guidance, should teach employees how to be more effective."

Paula continues: "There are many simple ways that employers can keep employee morale healthy. It is less a matter of money and perks than it is one of atmosphere, attitude of supervisors toward subordinates, and sincerely valuing employees. Example: Ways we tried to keep morale high at *The Albuquerque Tribune* included giving employees some flexibility with their work hours, celebrating awards with the entire staff, recognizing the unsung heroes of the office, and routinely welcoming employee input in newsroom decisions.

"Informal orientation sounds appealing because it seems simple and relaxed and inexpensive in terms of time and dollars. However, my experience is that if orientation is too informal it never gets done. Managers are just too busy cranking out work in their departments. If the organization doesn't mandate that new employees devote a day or two or more to learning about the organization and their jobs, and doesn't make it someone's specific responsibility, it doesn't happen. The employee is forced to learn it the hard way, as he or she works through the first few months. Oh, she (or he) might spend a few hours on the first day learning basics, such as how to use the phone or complete a certain task, but won't get a tour of the entire operation or learn about the company's customers or see how the job fits in with the bigger picture."

Paula believes that quality of work life is "very, very important. I know of a young executive who left his job because the atmosphere in his division was so negative, tense, and unfriendly that he dreaded going to work each morning. . . . He and many of his equally stressed-out colleagues found that they no longer were doing their best work because their manager had such a negative, hard-driving style. When the young executive moved to a new position in a different division, he felt his work improved in part because his new boss was more flexible, caring, and willing to let him run his own department."

In the future, Paula Ancona perceives that in organizations like hers, "training will become even more important because the news industry is changing very quickly to keep up with changing reader tastes, reader time constraints, and new technologies."

She anticipates that workplaces will "be more humane places to work, where diversity is encouraged, flexibility is seen as a positive solution to problems, and employees are valued as people not just producers of work. . . . Working people need to practice savvy self-management to make sure they get what they want out of their jobs and careers."

INSTRUCTIONAL METHODS

To instruct means to impart information, ideas, or skills so that they may be learned by others. Instruction can be made available not only through human teachers but also through literature, films, and computers—in fact, with any aid that provides students with materials from which to learn. The students' participation in this process is to learn what is presented to them.

On-the-Job Training

Good OJT requires a good trainer.

On-the-job training (OJT) is an example of applied instruction. In OJT, the burden is on the trainer—whether human or machine: it is generally assumed that, when a worker does not learn the job thoroughly, the teacher has not taught the job correctly. For an instructor to present material consistently, OJT should be preplanned. Information should be presented in manageable sections and in a logical sequence. To facilitate this process, the trainer should break down the job to be learned—either in writing or some other permanent record.

Regardless of what skill training is necessary to acquire a job, some on-the-job training is helpful. Without it, new employees learn only through trial and error. On-the-job training can include informal comments and suggestions from others, but supervised OJT is more effective.

A person new to a job is nervous, which makes it difficult to concentrate. The trainee must be put at ease and not feel rushed. Impatience, irritation, or criticism almost always terminate learning. The learner's accomplishments and efforts must be praised, helping to build self-confidence. A trainer should not interrupt when a trainee is performing correctly, because it will break the concentration. However, when a trainer sees that an error is going to be made, the trainer should interrupt, thereby preventing the error from occurring. A bad habit can be formed by doing something incorrectly just once. To correct an error, the trainer should return to the step immediately preceding the error.

Written Material

Probably the most popular way to disseminate general information is through the written word. Businesses like to keep employees informed of fundamental company background and policy. Well-designed pamphlets about company activities and job manuals containing specific job data often help employees to do their jobs more effectively.

Written material is good for details and easy access.

One advantage of manuals is the ease with which they can be used over and over again. Also, job-relevant information can be accumulated so that maximum accessibility is ensured. The mind is freed of learning many details when sources of information are available.

Written material, however, is often not read or is read superficially and soon forgotten. Writing is suitable for transmitting technical data, but it is not always useful for training that deals with emotions or attitudes.

Lectures

Lectures can present a considerable amount of material to a considerable number of people. As with written material, the lecture method is employed best to convey ideas. It is used in company training programs as the most reliable way in which to pass on information. Lectures do not cater to individual needs and they provide little opportunity for feedback. Question and answer periods, interspersed throughout or following a lecture, allow for some individual participation and should be used whenever possible.

Whether or not lectures are interesting depends on the material presented and the presentation. Lectures can be presented by anyone familiar with the information, but the listening rate often depends on the lecturer's speaking style. The most accomplished lecturers are able to sense the overall mood of the crowd, to which they respond spontaneously and appropriately.

PROGRAMMED AND COMPUTER-ASSISTED INSTRUCTION

Programmed instruction (PI), also called programmed learning, is a self-teaching method that is particularly useful for transmitting information or skills that need to be learned and placed in logical order. The "instructor" is replaced by an instruction booklet or a computer or both. It is possible to present programmed instruction entirely in written or computer form. PI presents what is to be learned in a brief, logical sequence, one step at a time.

Programmed learning can be carried out by the use of computers or booklets, depending on the need. The method is to present a small amount of information, followed by a simple question that requires an answer on the part of the learner. There is immediate feedback for each response as the learner finds the answer on the next page or elsewhere. The learner knows whether he or she is right or wrong immediately. Since the program is designed to have a low error rate, the learner is motivated further. The main advantage to such an individualized problem is that it is self-pacing. For remedial instruction, enrichment material, or short segments, this method works well.

Immediate feedback.

Self-pacing.

With traditional training methods unable to keep pace with demand, computers have been used to fill the gap. Computer-assisted instruction (CAI) has become the fastest-growing segment of the over $10 billion training industry. Although the costs of CAI are high, compared to costs for formulating and delivering teacher-led courses over a period of several years, the results favor CAI.

Knowledge-based or expert computer systems, based on artificial intelligence, contain information on particular subjects and can give user-specific advice. Combined with interactive video, expert systems can be used as "intelligent" tutors to teach tasks and skills. The systems can also be used in the work environment as an aid to on-the-job decision making. Expert systems move training away from the transfer of knowledge to the application of the system to goal-oriented tasks in the actual work environment.[7]

Advantages of PI and CAI include consistency, paced learning, and measurable objectives among others. But as appropriate as PI and CAI may be for tutoring or technical skills building, they are not as applicable for human relations training. Human relations information is best disseminated, even by videotape, and experienced through simulation and other experiential methods.

Both PI and CAI can reduce total training time appreciably and have the major advantage of immediate feedback. The major drawback is the cost of developing materials.

VIDEOTAPE

Videotape is used to instruct new employees on how to perform their jobs. An assembly line can be filmed from several positions by a video camera, and the finished videocassette can be installed in a monitor or screen above the workstation. A well-timed tape recording describing a multistepped job can supply more job understanding than can supervised on-the-job training.

The new employee can watch the process on the screen several times before trying the project. The employee can start or stop the videotape at any point desired, allowing the employee to learn at his or her own rate. Nervousness is minimized because the employee is not under the watchful eyes of a supervisor. Likewise, supervisors can use their valuable time to attend to other duties, with only spot-checks on the recruit for reassurance. Videotape can be used immediately after "shooting" the training sequence. Finally, it can be made in house with a limited staff.

SIMULATION METHODS

The **simulation** method is used to develop, in a controlled environment, a situation that is as near to real life as possible so that people can learn from their mistakes without affecting the real world. Car and aircraft simulators recreate real-life situations (see Figure 12–5). Astronauts work thousands of hours in a simulator of the space shuttle before taking their first flights.

IN-BASKET TECHNIQUE

Problem solving under a time limit.

In-basket training is structured around the familiar receptacle used for collecting incoming mail, memos, telephone messages, and reports. Materials that require problem solving are put into an in-basket, and the student plays the role of a manager responsible for solving the problems found in the basket. The students are given background information on the personalities and situations involved. Then, using their experience as a guide, students are asked to take the appropriate action within a short time period.

The in-basket method teaches planning and delegating.

The in-basket method has been used primarily to learn about effective management and supervision. The technique attempts to simulate real-life situations. Using a time limit helps to create the tension inherent in workday problem solving. The problems are organized to approximate work experience as closely as possible.

One typical in-basket approach is to ask students to assume the role of a manager who has just returned from a business trip and must leave again shortly on another trip. The student managers have twenty minutes in which to make decisions on materials that have accumulated in the in-basket. How well can the manager list priorities? What assumptions are made, and are they warranted? Is the work distribution planned adequately? Is the work delegated appropriately? Action Project 12–1 gives several examples of in-basket exercises. Notice that there may be some "reverse delegation" (trying to get the boss to solve the subordinate's problem).

FIGURE 12–5 Car Safety Simulation. Courtesy of General Motors.

ACTION PROJECT 12–1   ABBREVIATED IN-BASKET EXERCISE (INDIVIDUAL EXERCISE)

Assume that you are Pedro Ramirez, manager of the Lakeview irrigation project. It is 2:30 P.M. on Tuesday, October 18. You have been in an executive committee meeting most of the morning making final arrangements for the annual project inspection that is to be conducted by a visiting group of government officials. Conferences with members of this team will occupy virtually all your time for the next two days. The team will be arriving at 5:00 P.M., and you must leave the office by 4:00 P.M. to meet them at the airport.

While you were in conference, the morning mail was placed on your desk along with the interoffice memos and notices of phone calls shown. Your secretary has placed them at the top of the file of communications because they appear to be the most urgent ones. Read them carefully and then answer the question at the bottom. How would you dispose of each of the following communications? Remember that you must leave for the airport by 4:00 P.M. and that you will be with the visiting team and away from your desk during the next two days.

INTERPLANT MEMO (1)

Monday, Oct. 17, 4 P.M.

TO: Pedro Ramirez

FROM: Gonzalez, Maintenance Supt.

We have just received a call from the Lakeview Power Company telling us that all power to the project will be off from 7:00 A.M. until 9:00 A.M. on Wednesday morning in order to make emergency repairs on the high-voltage transformer serving the project. I urged them to change the time, but they said this was the only time they could do it without causing an even longer shutdown. I tried to reach you by phone, but you were in a meeting. We need to get together as soon as possible to figure out how we are going to handle the power outage.

PHONE CALL

The Offset Printing Company called while you were out. They want you to call them back. MESSAGE: The page proofs for the Lakeview Irrigation Management Conference a week from Saturday are ready for checking. Since you are the conference chairperson, they would like you to take a look at the page proofs as soon as possible. They wanted me to be sure to remind you that if the programs are to be printed in time for mailing, the printing of them must start no later than tomorrow morning.

INTERPLANT MEMO (2)

(no date)

TO: Pedro Ramirez, Manager

FROM: Joan Rider, Personnel Director

Pedro, the approval came through for a facilities supervisor. Do you want to write up a formal job description for me? Do you want to have a panel interview candidates for the job or do you want to handle the interviews yourself?

TELEGRAM

Oct. 18, 10:45 A.M.

Mr. Pedro Ramirez

Project Manager

Lakeview Irrigation Project

Too much water was sent down the Oasis lateral yesterday and all of our crops were flooded. We demand immediate reparations (monetary damages) for our farmers.

(Signed)

Y. Aguilar, President

Oasis Ditch Company

CASE STUDY METHOD

In the case method, a problem, or case, is presented in writing to an individual student or group. Cases are intended to simulate real-work situations and therefore include descriptions of the organizational structure and personalities involved. Group members study the problem and then offer their solutions. Because of group participation, group members are able to get immediate reactions to their ideas, as well as react to the ideas of others. Although groups are often led by a teacher or trainer, the group sessions can be so informal that they get off the track. However, this experimental approach makes traditional management principles more meaningful to group participants.

Case study assumes that in business practice there is no one "right" way in which to accomplish an objective. It involves the ability to justify management decisions, to give priorities to problems that are important to the company and its employees. For instance, a case study could involve an employee who was fired by a supervisor for using a company car for personal reasons. The employee has appealed to the grievance committee. As a member of the committee, each student would receive pertinent information to decide whether to (1) sustain the firing, (2) suspend the employee for a period of time without pay, or (3) reinstate the employee with full rights.

MANAGEMENT GAMES

Management games are games played by teams of employees that simulate competition engaged in by departments or other organizations. A management game is a form of problem solving. At least two teams, each of which represents an organization, make decisions concerning their company's operation. Decisions can be made about production, marketing, finance, human resource utilization, and other management challenges. Decisions are based on a set of specified economic theories, presented as a model of the economy.

Good judgment is the key.

Simple management games are not based on analyzing complex problems. Instead, emphasis is placed on making good judgments in a minimum amount of time, based on specific problems and limited rules. In simple games, effective strategies can be reached without making too many decisions and without having to use large amounts of managerial know-how. These management games may oversimplify business relationships and give the impression that running a company can be easy—when, in fact, even the simplest management decisions require the consideration of many factors. When the model is fairly simple, a referee can be responsible for calculating outcomes.

When the model is complex, a computer must be used. The game can be continuous: Teams receive all or part of the results of their decisions on which they make new decisions, thus continuing the game. Figure 12–6 is a diagram of the steps in a management game.

EXPERIENTIAL METHODS

There is an old saying, "Experience is the best teacher," but experience can also be very expensive if it is not conducted in a training environment. **Experiential methods** are any kind of training techniques in which the participants interact and express their feelings, experience the emotion, and examine the rationale and consequences of their decisions. Assertiveness training, transactional

FIGURE 12–6 Steps in a Management Game—an Important Aid in Teaching Production, Marketing, and Financial Concepts. Teamwork is the Key in Arriving at Decisions.

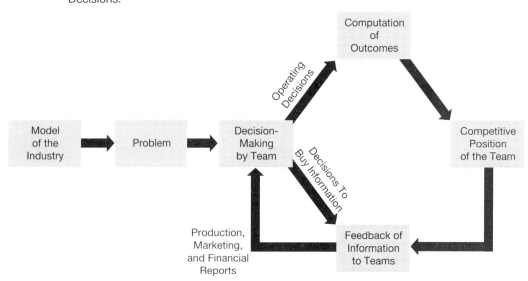

analysis, and meditation are all experiential and are often called human relations training programs. Another and clever way of thinking about experiential training is that it means to learn from the mistakes of others—you can never live long enough to make them all yourself!

Psychology is one of the most popular "games" or activities around. Each new activity leaves a new imprint on our thoughts and language. Each wave etches in its own peculiar vocabulary. The oldest game is role playing, followed by the sensitivity training and encounter groups of the 1950s and 1960s; during the 1970s and 1980s we were presented with transactional analysis (TA), meditation, and assertiveness training. Experiential cases and computer-assisted training became increasingly popular in the 1980s and 1990s. Whether the participant will be caught up in the wave of TA, meditation, or other experiential training is hard to say, but all these methods are based on experiences that each individual will *feel*.

ROLE PLAYING

Role playing, or preferably "role assumption," is both a simulation and experiential exercise in problem solving, designed primarily to aid in understanding human relations. Role playing works in small groups of two to eight people.

A group is given a situation that requires a decision. Participants are then given descriptions of the attitudes of the people they are to represent, which they develop and dramatize as best they can, using their own personalities. It is *not* acting, contrary to the sound of role playing. It is putting one's self and emotions into a situation; in fact, being one's self, not acting. There are no lines to memorize—all the characterizations are improvised.

Role playing is putting one's self into a situation.

The group works on the problems until they arrive at a solution that satisfies most of the participants. Some members of the group may act as observers. After each role-playing session, the observers comment on the process, giving feedback on communication skills, supervisory techniques, and attitudes expressed between supervisors and subordinates.

Videotape role playing.

Another variation is for one role to be played consistently by one person while another role is played successively by each group member. For example, a trainee plays a personnel director who interviews a particularly talkative job candidate. Application forms are provided and the talkative applicant is well versed in his or her role. A video- or audiotape may be used during the role-playing session. Afterward, the trainer and group members discuss the process, thus beginning to change each trainee's attitudes and behaviors. Listening to or watching the tapes can help the trainees become more aware of their actions. The authors have found the videotape method to be the most successful way to provide students with helpful insights into interviewing techniques through role playing in job interviews.

Executives also watch themselves in action. To their distress, they see themselves mocking their teammates, issuing authoritarian orders, and exhibiting impatience. Although their goal is to beat other teams, they discover that most of the conflicts are with persons on their side.

Sensitivity Training/Confidence and Team Building

How we function in teams.

The goals of confidence and team building, formerly and still called "sensitivity training," are for individuals to understand (1) how they function in a group setting, (2) how a group functions, and (3) how to develop team skills. **Sensitivity training** is concerned with "sensitivity" to one's feelings and the feelings of others. It differs from psychotherapy, whose purpose it is to delve deeply into inner motivations. The focus of sensitivity training is on observable "here and now" behavior rather than on assumptions about motives.

The T-group, or training group, differs radically from more traditional forms of training because it lacks the demonstrable goal that exists in role playing. In this situation you play "yourself." People who have been successful at "getting things done" find this experience frustrating and at first idiotic. With no problems to solve, participants are divested of their worldly status and authority. They are left to deal with other people without their formal relationships to back them up. Gradually group members learn to be more honest in their communication. As they become more open with one another, they trust one another more and accept other points of view. They learn to give and take leadership and make group decisions without using formal authority as a crutch.

Trainers can be important models with whom T-group members can identify. Ideally, a trainer should express feelings openly and honestly, should not become defensive and withdrawn under criticism, and should exhibit acceptance and trust of others. Trainers display different leadership patterns, from very directive to virtually nondirective and from a high expectancy of participants to accept emotional risk to a low expectancy. These variables should depend not only on the trainer's own preferences, but also on the constitution of the group itself. As a result, the styles and results of sensitivity groups vary greatly.

Transactional Analysis

Transactional analysis, or TA, is a method of studying communication by learning of the three ego states of child, adult, and parent. It was developed by the late Eric Berne, a psychiatrist who is best known for his book, *Games People Play,* and was popularized by Thomas Harris in *I'm OK—You're OK.* The leaders of TA believe that everyone's personality is made up of three parts, called *ego states.* An ego state is a pattern of behavior that a person develops as he or she grows up, which is based on a network of feelings and experiences he or she has.

The three ego states: child, adult, parent.

The *child ego state* exists when people feel and act as they did in childhood. The spontaneous expression of internal feelings of joy, frustration, or creative ideas, as well as wishes and fantasies, are all examples of the child ego state. The *adult ego state* can be expressed when people are thinking and acting rationally, gathering facts, estimating outcomes, and evaluating results. The *parent ego state* is best likened to how a parent would handle young children. Rules and laws, tradition, demonstrations of the correct way to do things, and protection can be seen as examples of the parent ego state.

In any of the three states, one can adopt very different attitudes toward oneself and those with whom one works. In the parent state, a person can be an "OK" supervisor by giving critiques rather than criticism and knowing how to be supportive. Or one can be an "OK" supervisor in the adult state by being

TABLE 12–2 Transactional Analysis of Parent, Adult, and Child

PARENT	ADULT	CHILD
Abides by rules and laws, do's and don'ts, truths, tradition	Is rational	Sees, hears, feels joy, frustration
Avoids inconsistency	Estimates	Is creative
Uses how-to's	Evaluates	Has wishes, fantasies, internal feelings
Teaches	Stores data	
Demonstrates	Figures out	
	Explores	
	Tests	

responsive and analytical. The child state can be seen as being a cooperative supervisor willing to help come up with creative ideas. Table 12–2 shows the TA of an adult, a parent, and a child.

I'm OK—you're OK.

People express how they feel about themselves and others as being OK or not OK, whether they are dealing with subordinates or superiors. They also reflect how they feel about others as being OK or not OK. Further, transactional analysis constructs the following classifications of the four possible life positions held with respect to oneself and to others:

1. I'm OK—you're OK.
2. I'm OK—you're not OK.
3. I'm not OK—you're OK.
4. I'm not OK—you're not OK.

By understanding ego states, as well as OK and not OK attitudes, we can make sense out of the different styles that people use. Some are so common that they are stereotypes. We may not like to use stereotypes, but like a mirror that distorts an image, it can still reflect some truth. The OK or not OK attitudes can be seen in the three ego states in Table 12–3.

TABLE 12–3 Transactional Analysis of the Not OK and OK Attitudes

PARENT		ADULT		CHILD	
NOT OK	OK	NOT OK	OK	NOT OK	OK
Dictator	Supportive	Compute	Communicator	Milquetoast	Negotiator
Do it my way	Informal critic	Always testing	Offering alternatives	Scatterbrain	Innovator

One study reports a resurgence of interest in TA as a strategy for organization change. The goals of organizational TA are still enhanced personal autonomy consisting of awareness, spontaneity, and intimacy. The overall goals are improved supervisory and other employee behavior, and improved organizational climate.[8]

ASSERTIVENESS TRAINING

Assertiveness training emphasizes the approach.

Assertiveness training teaches people to stand up for their feelings without resorting to one-upmanship. It encourages development of a straightforward, deliberate way of handling emotions and developing a personal authenticity.

The ultimate goal is to keep communications flowing back and forth between people—even in the face of strong feelings.

Assertiveness should not be confused with aggressiveness. Assertiveness allows you to express feelings constructively in a friendly manner. If both men and women would be warmer and more open, it would eliminate their anxieties about assertion. Straightforward, deliberate, and systematic rethinking is the first step toward a constructive change in our feelings and emotions.

HOW TO BE ASSERTIVE

Overcoming the anxiety that prevents us from behaving assertively is the first step. It all comes down to your ability to size up a situation and tackle it without letting the other person's negative reactions sidetrack you. Here are a few rules.

SAY IT DIRECTLY. It is natural to beat around the bush if you don't know how people will react. Recognize the other person's point of view, but be sure to get your own point across.

EXPRESS HOW YOU FEEL. If you have been asked to work overtime for at least three days a week for the last couple of months, express your feeling that you are tired of it. "I think I have done my part; perhaps it is time for others to put in their time."

BE SPECIFIC WITH A SOLUTION. "I don't mind working one night a week, but three is just too much. Besides, I feel that if I work overtime just one night a week I can do a better job all around." Ending with a strong positive note makes that request more reasonable and understandable to the listener.

ACTION PROJECT 12–2   ASSERTIVENESS TRAINING (GROUP EXERCISE)

This experiential exercise is designed to better develop assertiveness. Perhaps there are many times we have thought "I wish I had said. . . ." We are too shy, feel intimidated, or are not even conscious that we have not reacted more strongly and positively in a given situation. By actually taking an active role in a situation, we can become more confident and act more spontaneously.

Assertiveness training is very direct. By using group exercises, videotapes, and mirrors, one learns how to handle confrontations. Now you can learn how to better handle honesty, disagreements, and questions of authority and develop a more assertive behavior in posture and gestures.

TERMS

Aggressive behavior—Such behavior does not take into account feelings or rights of others. Aggression is an attempt to get one's own way regardless of others. Assertion is firmness, not an attack.

Overlearning—When you rehearse or role play assertive behavior, it is essential to continue practice until responses become almost automatic. This helps prevent becoming flustered in an actual situation.

GUIDELINES

Keep in mind the following points about assertiveness training:

1. Be direct in your feelings. State specifically how you feel, but not in anger.
2. A good way to prevent assertion from becoming aggression is to simply re-state your request as many times and as many ways as possible.
3. Express a possible solution to your situation. It should be a reasonable request.

Don't do the following:

1. Don't start an argument. If there is a settlement in an argument, it more often appears as a win–lose situation. A calm discussion is more likely to end in a win–win situation where both parties feel like they have arrived at a justifiable conclusion.
2. Don't try to belittle the other party by calling him or her stupid or not using common sense.
3. Don't use one-upmanship, by showing how much better you are in terms of words or actions. Don't demand certain action.

INSTRUCTIONS

Everyone in the class will be paired to practice this exercise. Find a partner within the classroom and together select one of the situations below. Then decide who will play each part. Role play the situation several times. After each attempt you and your partner should decide how it can be done better.

SITUATIONS

A. You were treated unfairly when the vacation schedule was made. The persons with the greatest seniority have first selection on which week or weeks to take their vacations. You have seniority over four other people but you were sick the one day the vacation schedule was made. Your attendance has been excellent by company standards, and you wish to move two people who selected the vacation time you wish. *Roles:* Manager and employee

B. You are returning a blouse or shirt with a seam that is coming loose for a cash refund. You do not have the sales slip, but the price and the name of the firm are listed on the sales tag attached to the item. The salesclerk states he cannot give a cash refund without a sales slip. *Roles:* Salesclerk and customer

C. You question the restaurant bill of $28.43. You cannot read the individual charges, but you feel you were overcharged by about $3.00. It is an expensive place and the restaurant is very busy. *Roles:* Cashier and customer

D. You question your professor about a test grade. You feel you have not been given enough points on an essay question and the total points for both the essay question and the objective questions were incorrectly added. The total points would affect your final exam grade. *Roles:* Professor and student

PROCEDURES

After putting yourself into a situation several times, answer the following questions.

1. What problem did you select? _____

_____

2. What was your most difficult action to overcome? Was it shyness, aggressiveness, or lack of confident voice tone and gestures? _____

_____

3. What more positive actions did you demonstrate by the time you did the last role-playing session? Was it a more calm attitude, a more confident, winning attitude, or stating a solution in a clearer way?_____

_____

_____

MEDITATION AND BIOFEEDBACK

In Western society, there has been experimentation with the Eastern esoteric psychologies of Zen, yoga, and meditation. In short, **meditation** is a method of silent thinking used to learn how to be calm and alert through relaxing and concentrating on a single thought. It is a process that neutralizes anxiety and allows the body and the mind to feel alert after meditation.

Certainly we can make better decisions if we are alert and calm. Other benefits of meditation are increased consciousness, cognition, and reasoning as they pertain to leadership and decision making.[9]

Biofeedback is a system of electronic recording and feeding back of information about physiological responses. These systems record tensions and allow people to monitor and modify their responses. These techniques can be very helpful in managing stress.

Physical benefits of meditation and biofeedback.

The reactions that occur when a person is practicing meditation or biofeedback are controlled mostly by the autonomic or involuntary nervous system, which produces movement in the cardiac and smooth muscle tissue and also controls the activation of the endocrine system. Some research shows that the major physiological change associated with these techniques is a decreased metabolic rate. This research was taken further to illustrate that autonomic responses can be controlled.

Many behaviorists believe that the potentials of biofeedback and meditation without drugs are great. We now need more research to prove these beliefs valid. A complement to physiological and psychological feedback is self-discipline, our next topic.

EXPRESS YOUR OPINION

Now that you have studied the simulation methods (in-basket, case study, and management games) and the experiential methods (role playing, sensitivity training, transactional analysis, assertiveness training, and meditation), would you consider the simulation method or the experiential method the most important for your company? Why?

Which technique (e.g., management games, TA, or assertiveness training) do you think would be the most beneficial for most of the employees in your organization? Why?

Would you hire an outsider to conduct such training programs or would you have them conducted in house by your own personnel? Why?

DISCIPLINE DEFINED

Discipline is positive.   One of the most common mistakes made in both management literature and practice is to refer to discipline as disciplinary action. **Discipline** is a noun that refers to a state of order, positive morale, and readiness to achieve organizational objectives effectively. It is brought about by learning and training. The result of this state is self-control, orderliness, efficiency, and effectiveness of a group or individual. **Disciplinary action,** on the other hand, is only one method of achieving discipline and usually more punitive. We will examine disciplinary procedures in the next chapter, but here we need to emphasize the positive state of discipline.

Order, readiness, and consistency are so important to an organization that is trying to be productive that we must do everything possible to bring about that order. Another way of viewing discipline is to think of it as subordinates who have commitment to organizational objectives. Members of an organization are made ready through learning and training to accomplish their tasks.

Military and athletic organizations recognize the importance of discipline and commitment to fulfilling their missions. Only if they are well prepared and committed to those missions will they be successful. And the responsibility for discipline lies with the leaders, as well as the self-discipline of individuals.

To ignore the positive aspects of discipline and training would be a serious shortcoming in any discussion of human behavior. They are at the very heart of what enhanced human relationships are about. How well a person is prepared for working within a group or organization is a function of discipline and training.

EMPHASIZE POSITIVE DISCIPLINE AND PERFORMANCE

The objective of positive discipline is to obtain top performance of organization members. Too much emphasis has been placed on negative disciplinary action that creates poor morale and low performance and productivity.

For supervisors to get top performance from their employees, the employees must be convinced that performance does make a difference. There are a number of ways to achieve this, including (1) reward performance, (2) "talk up" performance, (3) coach and counsel on performance, (4) measure performance and results, (5) delegate clearly and follow up, (6) give rewards for suggestions that lead to improved performance, (7) hold meetings that focus on performance, and (8) make performance satisfying.[10]

Personal discipline to do what has to be done, when it has to be done, is often cited as a quality necessary to be successful. If you create a positive rather than a negative environment, discipline—the state of order and commitment to get tasks done—will be high.

COMMITMENT

Traditional approaches to discipline, based on punishment, promote adversarial relationships between leaders and followers. A more effective approach now being used by many companies recognizes good performance and encourages employee commitment to the organization and its goals. Once employees see the discrepancy between actual and expected performance, the burden is on them to change.

Commitment is an attachment to an organization.

Recall that in Chapter 2, we defined commitment as "attachment to an organization that allows people to do things on their own willingly." A three-component model of organization commitment was used to study job withdrawal intentions, turnover, and absenteeism. *Affective, normative,* and *continuance* commitment were all studied. Affective commitment—emotional attachment to an organization characterized by acceptance of organizational values and willingness to stay with the organization—was the most predictive of turnover and absenteeism.[11]

A study of Washington State University graduates found that commitment to the supervisor was positively related to performance. Commitment was based on how well the employees internalized work; one way to do this is for employees to focus their efforts on supervisors rather than the organization.[12]

General Electric uses a commitment-oriented performance approach where employees are treated as responsible adults who are specifically accountable for acceptable performance. Contributions and commitment are recognized, as are inappropriate actions or inactions. There is still disciplinary action, but the emphasis is on the positive state of discipline. The system allows employees to be recognized positively for good performance.

Commitment is based on expectations.

Before individuals can feel a commitment, they must know the desired expectations. The level of commitment and expected performance is based on their job knowledge, abilities, and training to do their jobs. Only with improved performance brought about through education, training, and development can our workforces and other group members be more committed and disciplined, or ready to do their jobs.

SUMMARY

Orientation to the job is a form of training that can greatly affect a new employee's attitudes. Orientation familiarizes new employees with all the matters that don't pertain to performing the job itself but are vital to successful accomplishment of the job. New employees must also receive some on-the-job training. Even when they have previous job experience, no two jobs are the same. The success of OJT is up to the trainers, who should have a clear idea of training procedures.

Training is the practical side of education because it has to do with transmitting information to improve problem-solving abilities. Traditional training is concerned with mechanical and intellectual knowledge; human relations training is concerned with emotions and attitudes. The main purpose of any kind of training is for learning to take place. Learning occurs when students change. Differences are demonstrated by changes in behavior.

Development, including management education, takes place when the learning activity puts emphasis on increasing the participant's abilities to learn other aspects of jobs. Both employees and management have responsibility for development.

The effectiveness of training and development is determined in part by the attitudes of the participants: attitudes of students, teachers, and sponsoring companies. For training to be successful, companies must be clear about their training goals and then pick the training methods most applicable to these goals. The success of training programs is usually measured from the sponsoring company's viewpoint. Trainees may gain a lot personally, but if company goals are not met, the training has not "paid off."

Instructional training methods include written material, correspondence courses, lectures, conferences, programmed instruction, and the many kinds of audio and visual aids. Well-known simulation techniques include the in-basket method, the case method, management games, and role playing. They share the goal of solving problems that are as close to real-life problems as possible. Simulation methods employ many different styles, but they are always at least one step removed from reality.

Experiential methods advocate learning about self to be more effective in solving problems in human relations. Members of confidence building or sensitivity training groups learn to experience themselves and each other in an unstructured group context. Transactional analysis, assertiveness training, and meditation all relate to self-awareness and behavior change as people see themselves in a new perspective.

Positive discipline is really what human behavior is all about. Discipline is the state of being orderly and ready to carry out a commitment. The result of this state is self-control, orderliness, efficiency, and effectiveness of an individual or group. Commitment is the degree of attachment to an entity—individual or organization—and willingness to honor and stay with that entity.

CASE STUDY 12–1   TRAINING GARY FOR PROMOTION

Recently Don Taber, who is the supervisor of the Auto Repair Department of a large domestic and imported car dealership, was informed that he would be promoted to a position of higher management, that of the vice presidency of the dealership. He was also given instructions to select the most capable man in his department and to prepare him for taking over his current supervisory position.

There is one man in particular whom Don would like to promote, Gary Kurtz. He has been the lead mechanic for the company for a number of years. Gary is a reliable employee and has always performed his work with the utmost competence. Don feels that Gary possesses the ability to become a good leader. Along with Gary's knowledge of auto mechanics and his friendly attitude toward helping and training the other mechanics, he is always anxious to accept new responsibilities, and he is a man who enjoys working hard for the satisfaction of accomplishing goals that either he or others have set.

But it will be necessary to work with Gary first before placing him in charge of the department. Although Gary has many good leadership qualities, he does have certain weaknesses that need to be strengthened. In the past, when Don has been on vacation or away on company business, Gary has been placed in charge. On these occasions, when he was actually put in a position of authority, he was nervous and high-strung. When deadlines on repairs were required, he had a hard time scheduling his employees to finish the task. Under stress Gary has handled such situations poorly and has vented his unreasonable frustration on employees and even customers. During these times he also tends not to listen to the ideas of the other employees and instead considers his own opinion as final and binding.

It is Don's opinion that these weaknesses can be overcome with proper training and that he will be able to develop Gary's good qualities to an extent that he will be considered an effective leader by both the company and the employees who will be working for him.

1. How should Don go about developing Gary's good qualities and aiding Gary in correcting his poor ones?
2. What training aids or techniques might Don use in developing Gary's leadership ability?
3. Give reasons why certain techniques might develop certain leadership qualities.

CASE STUDY 12–2

SHOULD TRAINING BE REQUIRED?

Jim Barnes had just finished going over the production reports and was getting ready to go home when Larry Williams, the assembly superintendent and Jim's immediate boss, walked into the office. He immediately came to the point of his visit. The company training director was starting a series of training sessions on improving communication skills, to be held late in the day on Thursdays. Larry wanted Jim to take the course. The remark hurt Jim!

Jim replied that he thought his communications had been all right. Larry explained that his suggestion had not been a criticism. He tried to present the idea of Jim's attending as an opportunity for Jim to develop himself and to broaden his understanding of communications. But there was still no change in Jim's expression.

"Jim, just the fact that I am having trouble making you see that I have your interest at heart illustrates the kinds of problems we have in communicating. I know what I want to say, but you are getting a different picture. We discussed things like that when I took the course. If you take the course, you might use this conversation for a case problem."

Jim said he was sorry he misunderstood and promised he would let Larry know in a day or two. On the way home, Jim reasoned that he should be grateful that the boss wanted him to take some further job training. But he was already having trouble keeping his work current, without leaving early on Thursday afternoons. He had always been careful to keep his boss fully informed. Where had he failed? Besides, this class would also interfere with his Little League games.

"Damn, a suggestion from the boss is almost the same as an order," thought Jim. The next day Jim met with Mark Watkins, a coworker, to discuss his concern.

Mark said, "Relax, Larry probably made the same suggestion to other supervisors who report to him. Just forget the whole idea. Larry is from the new school, you know, forcing people to take management training programs, but they can't force you to take the class as long as you are producing. All they are interested in is profit."

Jim thought about this advice from a respected employee but decided he should take the course. However, some questions remained unanswered.

1. Should management expect a person to put in his or her own personal time on self-development?

2. If they want him or her to study, shouldn't they set it up on company time?

3. At what point are the demands on the supervisor's personal time for training programs excessive?

DISCUSSION AND STUDY QUESTIONS—TO KEEP YOU THINKING . . .

1. What items should be included in a new employee orientation?

2. Who has the responsibility for conducting the orientation?

3. What are the differences between training and development? between training and education?

4. Describe the training and development process cycle.

5. Describe the differences between simulation techniques and experiential methods?

6. What are the differences between assertiveness and aggressiveness?

7. What are the differences between discipline and disciplinary action?

8. What are the components of discipline?

NOTES

1. Robert L. Mathis and John H. Jackson, *Human Resource Management,* 7th ed. (Minneapolis: West Publishing Co., 1994), p. 268.

2. Kenneth G. Koehler, "Orientation: Key to Employee Performance and Morale," *CMA Magazine,* July–August 1992, p. 6.

3. Joseph P. McCarthy, "Focus from the Start," *HR Magazine,* September 1992, pp. 81, 83.

4. "New People Need a Good Orientation," *Managers Magazine,* August 1991, p. 25.

5. David E. Bartz, David Schwandt, and Larry Hillman, "Differences Between 'T' and 'D'," *Personnel Administrator,* June 1989, pp. 164–170.

6. Irwin L. Goldstein, *Training in Organizations: Needs Assessment, Development and Evaluation,* 3rd ed. (Pacific Grove, Calif.: Brooks/Cole, 1993), pp. 142–43.

7. Peter R. Kirrane and Diane E. Kirrane, "What Artificial Intelligence is Doing for Training," *Training: The Magazine of Human Resources Development,* July 1989, pp. 37–43.

8. Mark Neath, "Evaluating Transactional Analysis as a Change Strategy for Organizations," *Leadership & Organization Development Journal,* January 1995, pp. 13–16.

9. Harold S. Harung, Dennis P. Heaton, and Charles N. Alexander, "A Unified Theory of Leadership: Experience of Higher States of Consciousness in World-Class Leaders," *Leadership & Organization Development Journal,* July 1995, pp. 44–59.

10. Phillip C. Grant, "The Do's and Don'ts for Getting Top Performance," *Management Solutions,* May 1988, pp. 22–26.

11. Mark John Somers, "Organizational Commitment, Turnover and Absenteeism: An Examination of Direct and Interaction Effects," *Journal of Organization Behavior,* January 1995, pp. 49–58.

12. Thomas E. Becker and Daniel M. Eveleth, "Foci and Bases of Employee Commitment: Implications for Job Performance," *Academy of Management Journal,* Best Paper Proceedings 1995, pp. 307–312.

RECOMMENDED READING

Avishai, Bernard. "Companies Can't Make Up for Failing Schools." *The Wall Street Journal,* July 29, 1996, p. A10.

Craig, Robert L., ed. *Training and Development Handbook: A Guide to Human Resource Development.* 3rd ed. American Society for Training and Development. New York: McGraw-Hill, 1987.

Goldstein, Irwin L. *Training in Organizations: Needs Assessment, Development, and Evaluation.* 3rd. ed. Pacific Grove, Calif.: Brooks/Cole, 1993.

Jerris, Linda A. *Effective Employee Orientation.* New York: American Management Association, 1993.

Kanter, Rosabeth Moss. "Discipline!" *Harvard Business Review.* January–February 1992, p. 7.

Kiechel, Walter, III. "Getting Aggressiveness Right." *Fortune,* May 27, 1985, p. 180.

Kirkpatrick, Donald L. "Effective Supervisory Training and Development," Part 2. *Personnel,* January 1985, pp. 52–56.

————."Effective Supervisory Training and Development," Part 3. *Personnel,* February 1985, pp. 39–42.

Kolb, David A., Joyce S. Osland, and Irwin M. Rubin. *Organizational Behavior: An Experiential Approach.* 6th ed. Englewood Cliffs, N.J.: Prentice Hall, 1995.

Moyers, Bill D. *Healing and the Mind.* New York: Doubleday, 1993.

"Office Manual for Greenhorns. 12 Guidelines to Help New Employees Get Up to Speed." *Executive Female,* July–August 1993, p. 14.

Porter, Lyman and Lawrence E. McKibbin. *Management Education and Development: Drift or Thrust into the 21st Century.* New York: McGraw-Hill, 1988.

Robinson, Dana Gaines, and Jim Robinson. *Training for Impact.* San Francisco: Jossey-Bass, 1989.

Shandler, Donald. *Reengineering the Training Function: How to Align Training with the New Corporate Agenda.* Delray Beach, Fla.: St. Lucie Press, 1996.

Vaught, Bobby C., Frank Hay, and W. Wray Buchanan. *Employee Development Programs: An Organizational Approach.* New York: Greenwood, 1985.

13

APPRAISALS, PROMOTIONS, AND DISMISSALS

Here are some more questions to think about while reading the chapter.

- What, if anything, are the differences between performance appraisal and performance evaluation?
- Why is a job description important?
- What type of appraisal is the most difficult to conduct?
- What is meant by management by objectives? BARS?
- What are some of the "human errors" in rating employees?
- What are the various forms of employee benefits?
- What benefits are the most important to you? Why?
- How do you avoid or at least minimize layoffs?
- How do you handle disciplinary action, demotions, and dismissals?
- What three employee benefits are most important to you and your classmates? Why?

LEARNING GOALS

After studying this chapter, you should be able to:

1. Discuss the importance of the three basic purposes of performance appraisals.
2. Describe how, ideally, an interviewer should prepare for and conduct an appraisal interview.
3. Define and give the advantages and disadvantages of the following types of appraisal methods:
   a. Graphic rating scale
   b. Critical incident behavior
   c. Essay
   d. Field review
   e. Ranking
   f. Management by objectives (MBO)
   g. Self-evaluation
   h. Behaviorally anchored rating scales (BARS)
4. Discuss the following errors that supervisors make when appraising employees:
   a. Halo effect
   b. Personal bias
   c. Central tendency
   d. Recency bias

5. Discuss the difference between merit and ability promotions.
6. Describe how to handle demotions and firings.
7. Describe the various incentive plans.
8. Discuss the increasing importance of benefits in establishing better employee–employer relationships.
9. Define and apply the following terms and concepts (in order of first occurrence):

- **performance evaluation**
- **performance appraisal**
- **developmental purpose (of performance appraisals)**
- **graphic rating scale**
- **critical incident technique**
- **360-degree feedback**
- **field review**
- **peer appraisal**
- **upward appraisal**
- **management by objectives/results**
- **behaviorally anchored rating scales**
- **halo effect**
- **central tendency bias**
- **recency bias**
- **merit promotion**
- **ability promotion**
- **disciplinary action**
- **incentive**
- **benefits**

APPRAISAL/EVALUATION OF PERFORMANCE

All workers need to know whether they are doing a good job or not. **Performance evaluation** is a method by which to measure worker performance and let them know how they are doing. However, it is much more than a report card. There should be a distinction between backward-looking performance evaluations (history) and forward-looking performance appraisals (future as well as past and present). The **performance appraisal** looks at potential and promise for future development as well as past performance. Tom Peters, management consultant, makes a plea to measure constantly the things that are important:

> Performance appraisals should be ongoing, based upon a simple, written "contract" between the person being appraised and his/her boss. . . . The following attributes can turn performance appraisal from a minus to a plus:
>
> 1. "Appraisal" must be constant, not focused principally on the big annual (or semiannual) appraisal "event."
> 2. Appraisal is—and should be—very time-consuming.
> 3. There should be a small number of performance categories, and no forced ranking.
> 4. Minimize the complexity of formal evaluation procedures and forms.

5. Performance appraisal goals ought to be straightforward, emphasizing what you want to happen.

6. Make the pay decisions public.

7. Make formal appraisal a small part of overall recognition.[1]

Employees need to know if they are doing a good job.

All workers must sometimes wonder whether their supervisors think they are doing a good job or not. They may feel that management is either comparing them with other employees or judging their performance against a standard, and the employees are unable to decide which of these methods of appraisal is more fair.

Throughout history, people have evaluated one another's performances, measuring them against the codes of behavior, morals, and values that form the very fabric of society. A process of evaluation is necessary for any sort of understanding and communication. In the job situation, the performance appraisal and interview are equally important to both the employer and the employee.

Perhaps the most famous and effective performance appraisal of all time was addressed by God to the corrupt, idolatrous King Belshazzar, written on the wall of Belshazzar's palace by a disembodied hand: "You have been weighed in the balance and found wanting" (Daniel 5:27). The poor rating so upset Belshazzar that "he turned pale, he became limp in every limb, and his knees knocked together." He was slain shortly thereafter.

The consequences of poor performance appraisals are not, it is hoped, so harsh today. In fact, the opposite is true because of positive biases that enter into performance appraisal decisions. We will examine those biases later. First, let us look at the purposes of an appraisal.

PURPOSES OF AN APPRAISAL

Performance appraisals serve many purposes, but they can be sorted roughly into three categories: the administrative purpose, the informative purpose, and the developmental purpose. There is some well-founded criticism that (1) all performance appraisals contain a subjective element and (2) one performance appraisal technique cannot meet all these purposes. One public administration expert notes:

> I believe that these two purposes [developmental and judgmental] cannot easily be achieved simultaneously by the same instrument or even with different instruments in the same organization. Given the nature of things, judgmental uses quickly dominate in any system attempting or claiming to incorporate both purposes. Developmental systems require employees to be open about their doubts and weaknesses. If they have any fear that these "confessions" might be used against them in any way, the developmental process collapses.[2]

It helps to categorize the purposes and then examine the techniques and pitfalls of errors made in rating employees.

The Administrative/Operational Purpose

To see if the employee should be transferred, promoted, or terminated.

Performance appraisals are useful for management because they provide a method of allocating the resources of the organization. Specifically, they are or should be the means of deciding who is to be promoted, who is to be transferred, and who is to be terminated. In some companies, salaries are also determined by performance appraisals, but many companies use a seniority system, not because it is any more fair but because it is easier to operate, usually more objective, and creates less resentment among the employees. Performance appraisals compel supervisors to do some constructive thinking about both their subordinates and themselves.

The Informative Purpose

To inform employees how they are doing.

The informative purpose of a performance appraisal, which is more obvious than the administrative purpose, albeit not more important, is to let the employee know whether management thinks that the employee is doing a good job or not. Management can let the employee know what the company expects, what the employee can expect from the company, and what aspects of the work his or her supervisor feels need improvement. It can also show recognition for those aspects of the work that are outstanding. Finally, it is a way of helping each employee to perform his or her present job more efficiently and satisfyingly and also a way of helping each employee to prepare for possible advancement and promotion.

A Developmental Purpose

Developmental purpose is most important from employee viewpoint.

Notice the emphasis on the use of performance appraisal rather than performance evaluation. Evaluation has a connotation of looking back, as noted earlier; appraisal suggests forward-looking, future development. The **developmental purpose** of performance appraisal is the most important from the employee's viewpoint. Individuals need—and want—to know how they are doing so they can continue to develop their strengths and work on their weaknesses.

A developmental plan should be an integral part of any performance appraisal. How strengths and weaknesses are discovered is the subject of the methods section, which follows later in this chapter. First, it is important to seek some assurance that people know on what bases their performance is being appraised. Performance appraisal is just that—appraisal of job performance, and, if it is to be successful for any of the purposes discussed here, the job must be defined.

Job Description

The number of people who do not know what their job responsibilities are is amazing. If an employee does not know what is supposed to be done, the job cannot be performed successfully, and if a supervisor does not know what an employee is supposed to be doing, any appraisal will be meaningless.

Appraisals should be based on job descriptions.

The best way—and the legal way—in which to evaluate an employee is to decide how well the employee's assigned duties are being carried out. Before an appraisal can be made, a job description must exist. Job descriptions are often written, spelling out in a general way the responsibilities and tasks of a position. The job description of a mail clerk might read: "Receives and opens the mail; stamps the date received on each item; distributes the mail to the proper department or individual; picks up the mail from each department; prepares and stamps the necessary envelopes; wraps, addresses, and stamps packages; delivers the mail to the post office." The job description must be understood by both the employee and the supervisor before any meaningful performance appraisal can be made.

Behavioral dimensions—individual objectives and performance factors—are the basis for appraisal. To make the appraisal effective requires interaction between supervisor, others, and the employee—frequently in the form of an appraisal interview.

ADVANTAGES AND DISADVANTAGES OF APPRAISALS

ADVANTAGES OF APPRAISALS

1. Performance appraisal programs provide a basis on which the employee knows that he or she will be evaluated.
2. They motivate the employee by providing feedback on how he or she is doing.
3. They provide backup data for management decisions concerning merit increases, promotions, transfers, and dismissals.
4. They can be constructive rather than critical.
5. They allow for quicker discovery of good and bad performance.
6. Required periodic appraisal will force the supervisor to face up to and deal with the problems of poor performance.
7. Performance appraisal programs force superiors to communicate to subordinates their judgments of employee performance.

DISADVANTAGES OF APPRAISALS

1. Performance appraisal programs may demand too much from supervisors, but then that's their job.
2. Standards and ratings tend to vary widely and often unfairly.
3. Personal values and biases can replace organizational standards.
4. Because of poor communications, employees may not know how they are rated.
5. Managers tend to resist and avoid the task of making formal appraisals, particularly when critical judgments are involved.

THE APPRAISAL INTERVIEW

Performance appraisals cannot simply be handed to employees or put in their boxes or mailed to their homes because they serve as the formal basis for a discussion of the employee's performance between the employee and the supervisor. This discussion is known as the *appraisal interview.* It can be one of the most unpleasant tasks of a supervisor or one of the most satisfying. Which it is depends to a great degree on how good the employee's performance has been. But it also depends on how well the supervisor is prepared and conducts the interview.

PREPARING FOR THE INTERVIEW

Plan for a half-hour interview.

The employee should be given advance notice and opportunity to be involved in setting the time, place, and reasonable length of the interview. They should allow at least half an hour. The supervisor should put down in writing as much as possible pertaining to the employee's performance. The appraisal forms should be filled out and the supervisor should be prepared to justify each item. Time should be spent in reviewing the past reports of performance and in recalling what was covered in previous interviews. The supervisor should also remind the employee to prepare for the interview, to think about it ahead of time, and to jot down thoughts. A supervisor should consider what questions might be asked if he or she were in the employee's place and be prepared to answer those questions. The interview, however, should not be planned too rigidly. It should be flexible, for it is actually as much a discussion as it is an interview.

It is usually best *not* to have the interview immediately after a disciplinary action or a reprimand. The supervisor and employee should select a time when neither is likely to be under stress or tired; mornings are usually best (see Figure 13–1). The supervisor should arrange not to be interrupted and should provide a private and comfortable place in which to meet. Comfort for both supervisor and employee probably means no barriers such as desks.

HOW TO OPEN THE INTERVIEW

If an employee has been doing well, let it be known immediately.

If it is the employee's first appraisal interview, he or she should be told about the general purpose of the appraisal and the interview. If the performance of an employee has been outstanding, it is often a good practice to make this known at once, because the employee will accept more readily any suggestion or minor criticisms that the supervisor may want to make. If, however, the performance is something less than outstanding, it may be best to avoid a discussion of the employee's overall rating at the beginning. Indeed, it is often best to avoid starting with the past at all.

Let the interview be future oriented.

It is *very* important to emphasize the future development needs of the employee. If the supervisor opens with a discussion of the employee's future goals and plans, the interview will naturally go on to areas of improvement in the worker's present performance, and from there it will return to and cover

FIGURE 13–1 The Supervisor and Employee Should Select a Time for the Appraisal When Neither Is Likely to Be under Stress or Tired.

the past. If, however, the supervisor opens the appraisal interview with a discussion of the employee's past performance, the interview may bog down in a detailed discussion of a particular item and never get beyond the past.

DISCUSSION METHODS

An appraisal interview can be directive or permissive; that is, either the supervisor or the employee will direct its course. The ideal interview, however, will be neither, for both the supervisor and the employee have something to contribute; the whole discussion is about how the supervisor and the employee judge the performance of the employee, and therefore the participation of both is vital to a successful interview. The supervisor should encourage the employee to talk about himself or herself and the job. If possible, the employee should self-analyze the performance; people tend to believe what they have determined for themselves more readily than what they are told. If necessary, the supervisor can check his or her understanding of what the employee is saying by summarizing and clarifying the points in question.

The interview is partly a self-evaluation.

At times, however, the supervisor does enter into the discussion in a more assertive way, letting the employee know how the performance is being viewed and whether it meets these standards. The supervisor must let the employee know in what ways performance falls short and how it can be improved. In the

The interview is a joint effort.

final analysis, the appraisal interview is a joint problem-solving effort to which the supervisor and the employee both have something to contribute.

ENDING THE INTERVIEW

The interview should close when the supervisor has clarified what he or she intended to cover and the employee has likewise had a chance to review the issues that concern him or her. Organization practices vary, but most supervisors give a copy of the performance appraisal to the employee immediately after the interview. If, however, the appraisal and the interview have dealt with the employee's objectives and plans for achieving specific goals, that information is put into the report when the employee is given his or her copy. The employee should also be reassured as to the supervisor's interest and willingness to take up the discussion at another time.

TECHNIQUES AND CRITICISMS OF APPRAISALS

A number of appraisal methods are available, each with its own particular advantages and drawbacks. Many are beginning to question the overall effectiveness of performance appraisal systems—especially the forms themselves. One expert writes that it is time to emphasize performance *planning* by encouraging employees to go beyond what they believe is achievable. Emphasis is on goal setting and is forward focused rather than backward oriented.[3]

GRAPHIC RATING SCALE

The **graphic rating scale** or profile rating sheet usually lists the factors to be considered and the terms to be used. Figures 13–2 and 13–3 are abbreviated examples of such forms.

FIGURE 13–2 Graphic Rating Scale (or Profile Rating Sheet) Showing Visually How Well an Employee Is Performing on the Job (Partial Rating Sheet).

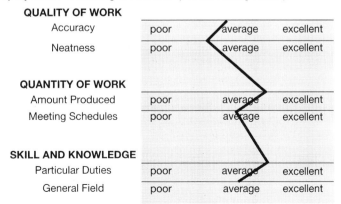

FIGURE 13-3 Example Performance Appraisal and Development Form (Abbreviated).

Part I Identifying Variables (names, department, SSN, dates, etc.)   *(left blank in example)*
Part II Review Progress in Meeting Objectives/Standards of Performance Set Last Period

Objectives:	Performance Factors:	Weighting	Rating:	Score:
	(as agreed to and/or modified during the period)	*(total 100%):*		

				5 = far exceeds standard		
				4 = exceeds standard		
				3 = meets standard		
(Each of the following is an example of items				2 = does not meet standard		
that would be tailored for each specific job):				1 = way below standard		
A. Improve customer service	1. Answers complaints promptly	24%	×	4	=	.96
	2. Calls back within 30 minutes					
	3. Reduces callbacks					
B. Take independent action	1. Shows initiative in work improvements	16%	×	3	=	.48
	2. Identifies/corrects errors					
	3. Develops new work tasks					
	4. Solves problems					
C. Improve people relations	1. Works cooperatively with others	24%	×	3.5	=	.84
	2. Recognizes needs/desires of others					
	3. Treats others with courtesy and respect					
	4. Inspires respect and confidence					
D. Improve effectiveness of supervision (over others, if applicable)	1. Leads/directs/utilizes subordinates	24%	×	4.5	=	1.08
	2. Conducts performance/development reviews on schedule					
	3. Administers personnel policies effectively/fairly among subordinates					
E. Scheduling reports for management and customers		12%	×	3.8	=	.46
F. Any other specific objectives and performance factors	(weight and rate, if needed)	___	×	___	=	___

X. Quality of work (see note at right)*   1. Completed work is accurate, neat, well organized, thorough and applicable

Y. Quantity of work (see note at right)*   1. Completed work compares to (a) standards for job, and (b) quantity produced by coworkers.

*All jobs have a quality and quantity of work dimension so unless one is more important than the other, the remaining objectives should automatically take them into consideration. This example does not include quality and quantity dimensions.

TOTALS   100%   3.82

Part III Summary of Overall Performance (left blank but same scale as in Part II)
Part IV Development Plan

A. For areas of improvement in current job and/or if employee did not meet standard, the following actions/objectives have been agreed to:
   1. _____
   2. _____
   3. _____

B. In preparation for possible advancement or career growth if employee is interested, the following actions/objectives are agreed to:
   1. _____
   2. _____
   3. _____

C. For job enrichment, if advancement or career growth is *not* an option, or if employee is not interested, the following have been agreed to:
   1. _____
   2. _____

Part V Signatures   *(left blank in example)*

The supervisor simply fills out the form, and when all supervisors are using the same form and all employees are being judged in the same terms, comparisons can be made more easily and will probably be fairer. Although the opinions and prejudices of the appraiser will still influence the rating, this is not necessarily a drawback, because the only way in which the element of subjectivity can be removed from an appraisal method is to eliminate the appraiser.

There are some important disadvantages, however. The categories and factors listed often tend to overlap, which makes it difficult for the conscientious supervisor to use the form (e.g., if the quantity and quality of an employee's work are excellent, how can the appraiser say that the employee's skill and knowledge are anything but excellent?). The method is also rather rigid and does not give a complete picture of the individual's past performance and future development potential. For these reasons, the method is often employed in conjunction with the essay appraisal, which is discussed later.

CRITICAL INCIDENT TECHNIQUE

Record good and bad incidents that have happened.

When the **critical incident technique** (CIT) method is used, the supervisor records the actual behavior observed, noting examples of insubordination or tardiness and instances of the employee using good or bad judgment. Keeping such records of all employees, however, demands much of the supervisor's time.

Dennis, a new deep-sea diver, was talking to a hard-hat worker on the oil platforms in the North Sea. "You know, Joe, I don't understand how little notes about my actions have popped up in my personnel folder back in Aberdeen, Scotland. Why, that's more than 500 miles away!" Phone calls can put the CIT to work in the appraisal of employees—at a distance of 500 miles away and out at sea. The behavioral accounts are recorded as anecdotes and put in the employee's personnel file. There is the negative connotation of "keeping a little black book" on the employees, but when done well, it can be the basis for essay appraisals.

A good discussion of the critical incident technique is provided in the following example:

> . . . a study of critical incidents in the life of a bank teller might focus on how that person would handle a situation where a customer is trying to cash a third-party check drawn on an account that has insufficient funds to cover it. The teller would be faced with the challenge of explaining to the customer that the bank could not honor the check, obviously a frustrating experience for the customer. Presumably, some tellers could handle the situation smoothly in a way that would not alienate the customer; others might be blunter and leave the customer angry with the bank in a situation in which it was merely an innocent bystander. A study of the ways in which "successful" versus "unsuccessful" tellers handle a specific bad-check incident might help in training future tellers. Thus, we see the value of studying critical incidents.[4]

ESSAY APPRAISAL

The essay appraisal requires the supervisor to write a paragraph or more about the employee's strengths and weaknesses, the quality and quantity of work, present skill and knowledge, and potential value to the company. Although this method probably gives a better and more fully rounded picture of the employee, it is likely to be more subjective than a simple graph or form. For this reason, an essay is not of much value for the purposes of comparison. In addition, essay writing is difficult and time consuming for the average supervisor, and more emphasis may be put on writing ability than other performance characteristics.

The following examples are actual sentences from military officer efficiency reports:

- This officer has talents but has kept them well hidden.
- Does not drink but is a good mixer.
- Can express a sentence in two paragraphs any time.
- A quiet, reticent, neat-appearing officer. Industrious, tenacious, diffident, careful, and neat. I do not wish to have this officer as a member of my command at any time.
- He has failed despite the opportunity to do so.
- His leadership is outstanding except for his lack of ability to get along with his subordinates.
- He hasn't any mental traits.
- Needs careful watching since he borders on the brilliant.
- Never makes the same mistake twice, but it seems he has made them all once.[5]

RANKING

Ranking compares the employee with other employees. This method is useful and justifiable in cases when several employees are being considered for promotion to a single position. It may also be used when it is necessary to lay off a part of the workforce. For any purposes other than these, however, a method of appraisal should be used that compares an employee with a job standard and not with fellow employees. Comparing a person with his or her peers will almost invariably create jealousy and bad feelings in a company's workforce.

360-DEGREE FEEDBACK

360-degree system solicits feedback from all stakeholders.

A recent technique of performance appraisal methods is a composite method called 360-degree feedback. The **360-degree feedback** system is a performance appraisal system that solicits feedback comments from all stakeholders in an employee's performance—not just the boss and the employee—but the boss's boss, peers, customers, even suppliers and others. Subsets of the 360-degree system are field review, peer appraisals, upward appraisals, and self-appraisals.

FIELD REVIEW.   **Field review** involves appraisal by a group rather than by an individual. The group can consist of fellow employees or several supervisors or a combination of these. It is sometimes used when there is reason to suspect prejudice or bias on the part of the employee's supervisor or when an employee wishes to appeal an appraisal.

The judgment of the group will usually be more fair and valid than will that of an individual, but field review is excessively time consuming, and it is not always easy to find a second supervisor who has any real firsthand knowledge of the employee. Some companies use the field method for all middle-management personnel on the grounds that they will arrive at a fairer evaluation and will overcome the personal biases of supervisors. Peer evaluations are a type of group review and also contribute to the fairness and validity of the appraisals.

PEER AND UPWARD APPRAISALS. There is strength in numbers. What this means regarding performance appraisal is that it makes sense to diversify the raters. It would probably be a mistake for an organization to adopt exclusively any method of appraisal. Putting all the appraisal responsibility with peers or subordinates would be as narrow and potentially biased as the typical system of having the boss exclusively appraise the subordinates.

Peer appraisal involves soliciting opinions and factual information from peers regarding an individual's performance. Peer systems are effective and gaining acceptance. One organization, Honeywell's commercial aviation division, puts technicians, factory workers, and support staff through performance review by groups of their peers—eventually all employees. Each person is rated on fourteen measures such as "how well the worker recognizes and solves problems" and "acts as a resource to others." One employee learned that he was pretty average—his colleagues suggested that "he keep them better informed about his whereabouts and his progress on projects." The advice struck a nerve: "If your supervisor says it, you might just say it's a personality conflict, . . . but when it comes from your peers, it's not real refutable."[6]

Upward appraisal includes obtaining feedback from subordinates on the supervisor's performance. Upward appraisals have the advantages of empowering employees and making appraisal decisions defensible against legal challenge because they are based on wider assessment data. But there are drawbacks: Managers may feel their position is being undermined or that subordinates will not be honest enough to make meaningful comments. If upward appraisal is to be effective, it should include the following:

- Anonymity for the subordinate respondents
- A manager having enough subordinates to facilitate that anonymity and also to ensure a reasonable sample on which to base feedback
- The focus of upward appraisal being on those aspects of managerial performance that subordinates are most able to comment on
- A sufficient degree of trust being built up to gain the managers' support for the exercise[7]

Once the appraisals are conducted, "don't sit on them." Expectations have been raised, and it is important to act on and follow through on findings.

SELF-APPRAISAL. Self-appraisal of job performance is also being adopted by more employers. The idea is to get employees to participate in their job reviews and create a dialog with the boss on performance evaluation. Self-appraisal provides timely, focused feedback, eliminating the anxiety of performance ambiguity and motivating the individual to take more responsibility for performance and growth.[8] More frequent evaluations are possible; in fact, the individual is in a position to appraise his or her performance monthly or even more often if he or she is working on a special project.

One system recommended is to have at least two separate appraisal meetings—one to find ways for the employee to do the job better and the other to determine if any improvement has actually occurred since the developmental meeting. The experience gained from discussing job performance with a supervisor during a performance feedback discussion helps employees learn to accept constructive criticism as the basis for personal and professional growth. The experience in the developmental appraisal process will help employees overcome the apprehension associated with the formal evaluation process.[9]

MANAGEMENT BY OBJECTIVES

MBO has goals set by both supervisor and employee.

Management by objectives/results (MBO/R) is a widely used appraisal system. Under this method the employee and the supervisor set common goals, discuss what the employee can accomplish during the next evaluation period, and agree on what is expected of the employee. This method follows four rules:

1. The superior and the subordinate together set specific objectives to be accomplished for which the subordinate is held directly responsible.
2. Both decide how the performance will be measured.
3. Both develop short-term targets to be accomplished within a given time frame.
4. The appraisal focuses on the results that have been achieved in accomplishing these goals (see Figure 13–4).

FIGURE 13–4 The Path Taken to Establish and Follow a Management by Objectives Program.

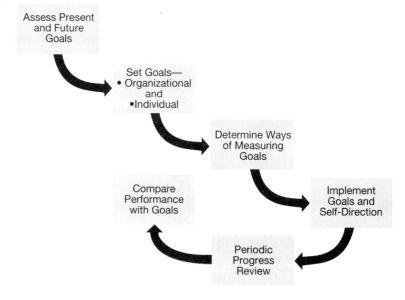

Difficulties with this method often arise when implementing the second rule, which is, of course, the basic problem of all the appraisal methods. How does one measure performance? Most goals are not easily measurable. Because it is an achievement-oriented method, management by objectives would seem to be a better instrument for measuring top- and middle-management performance than for measuring the performance of, say, a clerk-typist.

The supervisor and the subordinate may have occasional progress reviews and reevaluation meetings, but at the end of the set period of time, the subordinate is evaluated on the accomplishment of the agreed-on goals. Employees may be rewarded for their success by promotion or salary increase. If they have failed, they may be fired or transferred to a job that will give them needed training or supervision. Whatever the outcome, it will be based on the employees' accomplishment of the goals *they* had some part in setting and to which they had committed themselves.

BEHAVIORALLY ANCHORED RATING SCALES

Behaviorally anchored rating scales (BARS) identify expectations of performance in specific behavioral terms. The absence or presence of behaviors rather than subjective ratings or rankings become the basis for the appraisal. Figure 13–5 is an example of BARS for an office support clerk. The possible outcomes of specific behaviors become part of a linear graphic scale where dimensions of job performance are the anchor points.

FIGURE 13–5 Behaviorally Anchored Rating Scale.

JOB: OFFICE SUPPORT CLERK
DIMENSION: INTERPERSONAL RELATIONS

PERFORMANCE	BEHAVIORAL ANCHOR
1. Unacceptable	Clerk is rude, sharp, and intolerant of others, their opinions, and questions.
2. Very poor	Talks aimlessly with clients; may argue with rude customer.
3. Poor	Exhibits poor follow-through when answering requests for information.
4. Average	Maintains communication with coworkers in a timely manner.
5. Good	Facilitates communications through effective questioning and listening.
6. Very good	Consistently provides high-quality treatment and acceptance of unusual clients and/or situations.
7. Outstanding	Always polite and courteous with others regardless of what difficulties arise.

The BARS system is designed using a combination of the graphic rating scale and critical incident technique. To develop BARS scales, records are kept of critical incidents, and performance dimensions are developed and scaled to the incidents producing the final instrument.

PROFILE OF HUMAN BEHAVIOR

LINDA EGELAND

"Rustic and Wonderful"

She can't cook, she says, but Linda Egeland knows a thing or two about running a restaurant. She is a cofounder and the president of two successful restaurants in the Detroit area: the Moose Preserve Bar & Grill in Bloomfield Hills, an affluent northern suburb, and the Beaver Creek Tackle and Beer in Westland, a blue-collar community west of the city.

How about a bowl of venison chili, garnished with sour cream? Or hot pasties, the savory meat pies that are a staple of Michigan's Upper Peninsula? Or some Paul B onion rings?

These are just a few of the dishes that grace the menus at the two establishments, which have a hunting-and-fishing-lodge theme and an atmosphere as homey as the bar on television's "Cheers." "I hear again and again from our customers how good our staff is and how friendly they are," Egeland says. Furniture and accessories run from hickory tables and snowshoes to pine cones and deer-crossing signs. A mounted moose head, dubbed Jackson, greets visitors in the Moose Preserve's foyer.

Egeland, a former environmental chemist, and her husband, Victor Dzenowagis, an executive at Stroh Brewery Co., had dreamed of having a bar and restaurant of their own since their Michigan State University days, when they waited tables and tended bar at Dooley's in East Lansing.

For six years, says Egeland, who is 35, "we saved and saved and looked and looked," but they still didn't have the money to buy what they wanted. They asked three friends, including two who had also worked at Dooley's, to go in with them.

The five came up with $60,000 from savings and bought the Westland location, then known as Paddy's Pub, in 1986.

The pub was losing money, says Egeland, "but it was a pretty decent facility, and we got it for the money that we had."

In 1990, after they had turned Paddy's Pub into a success, they opened the Moose Preserve. But not without a fight. Restaurants in the area tended to be owned by chains or geared to expensive dining, and two well-regarded restaurateurs had failed at the site Egeland and her partners sought. Township officials, Egeland says, were "leery about some new young kids that have some bar in Westland coming to build a bar in their city."

The banks weren't eager, either, until the partners were able to sell a young loan officer on the concept: a place that serves casual but good food at a busy intersection within five miles of two major sports arenas. One is the Palace of Auburn Hills, where the Detroit Pistons play; the other is the Pontiac Silver

Dome, home of the Detroit Lions. The partners got $150,000 from the bank and, after promising to put $30,000 into landscaping the boarded-up property, they got the go-ahead from the township.

The partners' persistence helped their business become recognized as a state Blue Chip Enterprise in a program sponsored by the Connecticut Mutual Life Insurance Co., the U.S. Chamber of Commerce, and *Nation's Business* honoring small companies that have overcome challenges and emerged stronger. Combined revenue at the two restaurants exceeds $4 million annually, and employees number more than 100.

But it's not just the good food or the comfy surroundings that bring customers back. Or the big-screen TVs, the dart boards, or pool tables. It's not even the Mutt Wall of Fame, a wall with hundreds of pictures of customers' dogs that have been entered in the Moose Preserve's Mutt-of-the-Month contests. The secret, says Egeland, is that owners and staff members alike work at "making the customers believe that we really do care about them and we really appreciate their business and want them to come back."

When hiring, Egeland and her partners look for people who are outgoing, energetic, and quick to smile, and who have an attitude that says they want to work for the company and will do anything they have to do. "We'll take that over experience any day," says Egeland.

SOURCE: Sharon Nelton, "Rustic and Wonderful," *Nation's Business*, December 1993, p. 18. Reprinted by permission. Copyright © 1993, U.S. Chamber of Commerce.

EXPRESS YOUR OPINION	What kinds of performance appraisal techniques does your employer or other organization use? How effective are they? Your teacher uses performance appraisal techniques; analyze their effectiveness and fairness— that is, are graphic types of appraisals more objective? Do essay appraisals leave too much room for subjectivity?

FREQUENT ERRORS MADE IN RATING EMPLOYEES

Supervisors make a number of mistakes when they fill out performance appraisals. Most of them are the sorts of mistakes we all make when we misjudge friends and acquaintances. Most errors are due to the way that raters process information. Too frequently, supervisors try to recall appraisal situations using "memory-based" processing instead of "on-line" processing, which produces more accurate results.[10]

HALO EFFECT

One area of performance influences other areas.

The **halo effect** exists when a supervisor or other rater assumes that if an employee is above average in one area, the employee is above average in all areas. Many people attribute nonexistent virtues or accomplishments to those to whom they are attracted. Another term for this assumption is constant error: Considering the employee to be excellent in one particular area, the supervisor goes on to say that he or she is excellent in all areas. It is similar to another natural tendency, that of rating a person as "excellent" rather than "above average" or flattering a worker rather than leaving room for improvement. The halo effect can also work in reverse. If a person strikes us as unpleasant, we may assume that he or she is an inefficient worker.

PERSONAL BIAS

Favoritism to certain groups, races, or gender.

Personal bias is difficult to avoid. Every human being has prejudices of one sort or another. Preference may be given to employees of the same race or the opposite sex or to workers who belong to the same club as the supervisor. Intelligent or good-looking persons may receive better ratings than their actual job performances deserve. On the other hand, supervisors are often aware of their prejudices and may attempt to compensate for them, actually giving individuals against whom they are biased better performance appraisals than they really merit.

CENTRAL TENDENCY

Central tendency bias assumes all people are average.

When **central tendency bias** prevails, the supervisor completes all the forms in about the same way for all the employees so that they all come out about average. In an attempt to be fair, the supervisor does not discriminate among different workers or among the different areas of performance of an individual. In fact, treating everyone as average is unfair to the outstanding performers especially. It is also unfair in the long run to the substandard performer who needs constructive criticism and needs to change performance behavior.

RECENCY BIAS

Recency bias occurs when an employee may receive a higher or lower appraisal depending on his or her most recent performance. Supervisors have a tendency to judge an employee's performance for the whole rating period based on the employee's actions within the week just before the appraisal. The good or bad incidents of the last week are fresh in the mind; the achievements or failures of a year ago are forgotten. There is also a natural and quite proper hesitation to rehash a recent incident, particularly when it is one in which the employee looked bad. Nevertheless, the performance appraisal is a rating for an entire period.

Mr. Smith is a supervisor for the Crummy Concrete Company. The team he supervises consists of Nick, Pedro, and Donald. Nick is the outstanding employee on the team, but last week he and Mr. Smith had a bitter argument. Donald, on the other hand, is only an average worker, but during the past week he has volunteered several times to stay a little late and help clean the machinery. Smith is about to submit his semiannual performance appraisal of his work team to top management. He wants to be a fair supervisor, but he will have a natural tendency to rate Donald higher than his overall performance during the past six months deserves and to rate Nick lower. If he had kept records of the actual performance of the men on the job through a critical incident or other technique and reviewed them prior to filling in the appraisals, his ratings might have been more accurate.

ACTION PROJECT 13–1   RATING EMPLOYEES (GROUP EXERCISE)

INSTRUCTIONS

The supervisor completed the semiannual appraisal form of an employee yesterday and has scheduled a thirty-minute interview period with the employee today to discuss the following ratings:

Quality of work	Dependability and initiative
Quantity of work	Ethics and standards of behavior
Work habits	Personal qualities
Work attitudes	Overall work performance
Relationships with others	

The supervisor tried to be honest in the appraisal, but is fearful that the employee will feel it to be unfair. Thus, the supervisor is not looking forward to the interview. The employee feels that the rating is unfair in three areas (work attitudes, relationships with others, and overall work performance).

PROCEDURE

The class will be divided into two groups. Everyone in group 1 will play the role of the supervisor. Everyone in group 2 will play the role of the employee. When the groups are segregated, each of the employees should choose the occupation they want to role-play. Some possibilities: assembly person for computer plant, clerk, or salesperson.

Next, break into pairs (one supervisor and one employee) and take a few minutes to get used to your role (the supervisor should review the important points of a good interview).

Now role-play the interview for fifteen minutes. The supervisor should do his or her best to defend the appraisal and at the same time build up the employee so that the employee's next rating will be better.

After the role-playing sequence the supervisor is to do a self-rating by completing Form A, and the employee is to rate the supervisor by completing Form B. When completed, get together and compare forms.

Form A
Supervisor's Appraisal of Own Interview Technique

	YES	MORE OR LESS	NO
1. Did I put the employee at ease?	_____	_____	_____
2. Did I ask the employee's opinion about how he or she was doing on the job?	_____	_____	_____
3. Did I make good points clear?	_____	_____	_____
4. Did we clarify any disagreements over job performance?	_____	_____	_____
5. Did I give the employee a chance to ask me any questions about job performance?	_____	_____	_____
6. Did I listen to any of the suggestions the employee brought up and indicate I cared about them?	_____	_____	_____
7. Did I establish job performance objectives for the future with the employee?	_____	_____	_____
8. Do I know more about the employee's personal ambition as a result of this interview?	_____	_____	_____
9. Did I leave the door open for any future discussions on subjects of mutual interest?	_____	_____	_____
10. Did I make the employee feel he or she is important to self and to our company?	_____	_____	_____

After you have finished, your instructor may open a class discussion regarding the appraisal interview.

Form B
Employee's Appraisal of the Supervisor's Interview Technique

	YES	MORE OR LESS	NO
1. Did the supervisor make me feel comfortable?	_____	_____	_____
2. Did he or she ask my opinion about my job performance?	_____	_____	_____
3. Did he or she make my good points clear?	_____	_____	_____
4. Did we clarify any disagreements over my job performance?	_____	_____	_____
5. Was I given a chance to ask questions about my job performance?	_____	_____	_____
6. Did the supervisor listen to any of the suggestions I brought up and give me the feeling that he or she cared about them?	_____	_____	_____
7. Did the supervisor establish my job performance for the future?	_____	_____	_____
8. Does the supervisor know more about my own personal ambition as a result of this interview?	_____	_____	_____
9. Did the supervisor leave the door open for any future discussions on subjects of mutual interest?	_____	_____	_____
10. Did the supervisor make me feel important to myself and the company?	_____	_____	_____

After you have finished, your instructor may again open a class discussion regarding the appraisal interview.

Tradition, laws, and the availability of qualified candidates within a company influence whether a position becomes "open" to the general public or is filled by an in-house promotion. First-level management positions are usually filled by in-house promotions, which are often determined by the immediate supervisor. For middle-management positions, competition is also opened to people outside the organization.

It is common practice for companies to check for internal talent first before searching elsewhere. You should remember this when you are given expanded duties. It may be a method of testing you for a promotion.

Managers often need a way to determine who should be promoted and who should be terminated. A simple tool, known as a promotable people or replacement chart, can make it easier to identify and analyze employee potential. The first step is to sketch a chain of command with each job title in a separate box. Then color boxes blue for employees with excellent growth potential and use green for those with moderate growth potential. Questionable employees, or those too new to evaluate, or marginal performers can be colored yellow. Poor producers, those due or overdue for termination, would be colored red. At a glance, the completed chart will point out critical employee opportunities or problems.[11]

WHAT PROMOTION MEANS

To many people, job improvement or promotion means regular wage increases, more security, and perhaps an easier job. However, this is not always true. An easier job is not possible in some industries because of the fast-paced demand for new technology, and increased security is never guaranteed. As for wage increases, some people turn down promotions because the increase in pay does not seem to equal the increase in responsibilities. Promotion usually results in the following:

- More responsibility
- More authority
- More hours
- More communication
- More meetings
- More learning
- More development
- More management skills necessary
- More of a large number of similar factors

Promotion does not always mean more money. Some individuals can outearn the boss and still keep their jobs by working on commissions and other means. Most NFL quarterbacks and many other sport superstars outearn their coaches. Outstanding achievers in many industries may outearn their bosses without serious consequences.

PROMOTION BASED ON MERIT OR ABILITY

Merit is based on performance.

Merit promotion is based on past performance rather than on the ability to perform the duties of the advanced position. If promotion is to be an incentive for an employee, the best performing employee should be advanced if that person wants to be promoted. However, differences in employee merit may not be readily measurable, so that, when you make a promotion based on merit, the person who was not promoted may feel that favoritism was involved. Another difficulty with merit promotions is that it is hard to evaluate many on-the-job performances, such as that of the salesperson trying to sell a product that is in short supply.

Ability is based on potential.

Ability promotion is based on the potential that an employee has to hold an advanced position. In awarding promotions, there is also the question of ability—the potential to perform well in advanced jobs. Larry is doing a good, even a great, job in his present position, but on the surface he does not show the potential for additional responsibility. Charlie, however, is doing only adequate work, but he has poor supervision and the job is not challenging. A promotion to a more difficult assignment may cause him to blossom.

Walter Ulmer asks a penetrating question:

> Does your system of selecting the right people for promotion—as good as it is—do everything it should for your organization? (The high percentage of managers who are promoted and then are seen to fail should be viewed as a national disgrace. Something is missing, including reliable definitions of "success" and "failure." Evaluation of candidates from multiple perspectives—not just from the perspective of the boss—might be a powerful part of the solution. Opportunities for monitored development on the job after structured feedback should help. But the true criteria for promotion remain unclear in almost all organizations.)[12]

THE EMPLOYEE WHO DOES NOT WANT TO BE PROMOTED

In our culture a person who doesn't want a promotion used to be considered either weird or lazy. Now, that person may want to concentrate on quality of current lifestyle, feel accomplishment in the current job, or prefer a lateral transfer to a different job, not a promotion. People who really do not want to be promoted may come to feel that failure to show interest in advancement is a black mark against their records. Thus, some individuals accept a promotion when they are not suited for it, thereby putting the "Peter principle" into practice. Unfortunately, it is at a high cost to themselves and to the organization.

Promotion doesn't satisfy everyone.

For these reasons, a clear recognition of each employee's psychological needs is valuable both to the person and to the company.

DISCIPLINARY ACTION

In the last chapter, we defined **disciplinary action** as one method of achieving discipline, the desired state of order and readiness in an organization. Disciplinary action has traditionally been punishment for an infraction of rules or violation of an accepted group norm.

Disciplinary action may be punitive.

Disciplinary action usually involves several steps: an oral reprimand, written warnings, suspension, and eventually termination, if necessary. Resorting to disciplinary action may be lessened by (1) *smart hiring* using background checks and extensive interviews, (2) *performance appraisals* with clear goals and objectives, (3) *training and development* to improve skills and increase performance, and (4) *rewarding* performance and goal achievement. In short, accentuate the positive in discipline and dealing with employees, and avoid the negative consequences of disciplinary action.

Knowing when and how to use disciplinary action is frequently a tough call. One supervision expert lists the following five worst disciplinary mistakes of a supervisor:

- Being inconsistent
- Losing your temper
- Praising too much—allowing staff to become "praise junkies" who pursue objectives not for performance but for praise
- Avoiding any disciplinary action entirely
- Playing Mr./Mrs. Nice Guy[13]

Procedurally correct performance appraisals are important in court rulings.

The importance of having a procedurally correct performance appraisal system is strengthened by recent court and administrative rulings. There is a need to adopt procedural due process for performance appraisal systems to rate employee job performance accurately because those ratings may be challenged. Legal problems regarding employee disciplinary measures can be prevented by making sure that employee disciplinary actions follow prescribed guidelines. Before imposing disciplinary actions, employers should ensure the following:

- Employees have been given advance notice of disciplinary action.
- Disciplinary rules are reasonable.
- Offenses have been properly investigated.
- Investigations are conducted objectively.
- Rules are enforced equally.
- Penalties are related to the severity of offenses.[14]

DEMOTIONS AND DISMISSALS

We have examined the positive aspects of appraisals, performance, and promotions. There is also a negative side when it is necessary to demote or dismiss an employee. Fortunately, there are actions that managers and others can take to make demotions and dismissals more humane and less vulnerable to litigation.

WARNINGS

Employees should be given written warnings of demotion or dismissal. In cases involving unsatisfactory performance, particularly for permanent employees, warnings in *addition* to the scheduled evaluation reports should be given before action is taken.

In most cases, permanent employees may not be dismissed for reasons of unsatisfactory performance unless documented evidence is available. Performance evaluation reports—scheduled and unscheduled—provide a written record of specific deficiencies. *Employees' deficiencies affecting job performance that are not recorded on performance evaluation reports cannot be used properly as a basis for dismissal.*

HOW TO HANDLE A DEMOTION

A demotion is required when an employee does not have the ability to perform specific tasks or when economic conditions within the company dictate staff changes. In the former case, an employee is usually aware that he or she is not performing to expectations. There is no need to be abusive about the poor performance, especially if you have given encouragement and alternatives such as retraining to perform better and have issued written warnings of the impending demotion. Your best approach is to be *firm.*

Make clear statements about the poor performance, using actual incidents. If you are not clear, the employee may feel that the demotion is your fault, not his or hers, and attribute the demotion to personality problems between the two of you. Remember, it is the performance that is unacceptable, not the employee. An assignment that is less taxing physically or emotionally or one that requires less current technology may be the answer. Remember, a demotion is not a dismissal.

The *positive sandwich technique* is ideal in a demotion situation, as demonstrated by the following example:

The positive sandwich technique is bad news between slices of good feelings.

> Charlie, you have been with us about six months now. You have been able to adapt to the company and the employees seem to like you. You have a sincere desire to put out an honest day's work. That I like, Charlie!
>
> However, I wouldn't be fair if I told you that your performance has been up to par. We can't have so many mathematical errors in your docking and loading reports. As you have discovered, it has a domino effect all the way up to the accounting department.
>
> Now, we don't want to let you go because we feel you have potential, but not in your present position. I was thinking, Charlie, perhaps things would work out better for both you and the firm if we moved you to another position. Here is a description of the job I had in mind. I feel it is the type of job that is more suited to your nature and ability.
>
> Unfortunately, the pay is a little less, but if you can do the job well you can be making as much in three months as you are now. They have a good crew over there and you would still be reporting to me. I want you to know I have confidence in you, Charlie.

This approach leaves Charlie with some self-respect and also gives him the alternative of either accepting the demotion or leaving the firm. Using this technique, you seem to put Charlie in charge of his destiny, although you as the supervisor have decided that Charlie is no longer going to continue in the present position.

HOW DO YOU FIRE AN EMPLOYEE?

Place yourself in a typical supervisory situation. When you analyze your department realistically and plan for its future goals, you come to the conclusion that loyal people in your department are shouldering the responsibility for one person who is not producing. You can see that it is unfair over a period of time for others continually to support the burden of the freeloader. In time, both morale and production will be lower if the problem continues. The solution to your problem is to "unhire" an employee.

Before you reach the decision to terminate a person's employment, ask yourself some questions:

1. Did I give ample warning? You are not being fair with the individual unless in performance reviews you have given constructive suggestions on how to improve his or her work or mend his or her ways.

2. Do I have a qualified replacement ready to step into the vacancy? You must be certain that the change will bring about a significant improvement. At least the *potential* for improvement must exist.

3. Is the *primary* responsibility for failure the employee's—or mine? Did you pick the right person for the job? Did the person receive the necessary training and supervision? Perhaps all the person needs is a new manager, not a new employer.

The release of an employee should be handled delicately for the good of the employee, the company's image, and the morale of other employees. Recall the characteristics of positive, constructive feedback discussed in the communications chapters. Constructive feedback should have these characteristics, among others:

- Specific, not general
- Focused on behavior, not the person
- Considerate of the needs of the receiver
- Checked for accuracy

Care in firing can also head off a lawsuit that may charge discrimination because of age, sex, or race.[15] But don't sugar-coat the problem, because the fired employee may be unaware that he or she has been fired.

Timing of the firing is very important, and it should never be done near the employee's birthday or anniversary. Some experts suggest that such an interview should be done at the beginning of the week. Ironically, some advisors recommend that several weeks before Christmas is a better time for dismissals than waiting until after the first of the year. According to this theory, the holidays are a good time to give notice because people are naturally networking at that time of year during parties and other festivities. It's much better than in January when they are left out in the cold, both literally and figuratively.

EXPRESS YOUR OPINION	What do you think—if the decision has been made, is it more humane to give notice of dismissal several weeks before Christmas, or should you wait until after the first of the year?

Certainly the supervisor should do the firing personally and not rely on a stranger from personnel, and the bad news should be communicated in a conference room or the employee's office, so that the boss can exit easily once the message is delivered. The location of the meeting room should also be off the beaten path, in case the employee erupts when told that he or she is being let go.

Being fired can even be a positive experience for an employee, despite its initial pain. Let an employee go in a way that lets him or her maintain self-esteem. There may be other areas in which the individual can perform more effectively and be happier. Thus, on the positive side, you may help an employee to recognize the opportunities involved in being fired and open new avenues to be explored.

Do recognize the importance of terminating an employee once other alternatives have been exhausted. Don't avoid the unpleasant because a bad situation will not get better by itself. A bad employee—especially a manager—can have very negative effects on the rest of the organization.

Harvey Gittler tells the story of an abusive manager (Jack) who was allowed to stay in the position of plant manager for seven years because the "bottom line looked good." Gittler concludes:

> Never mind the human carnage [other employees who quit or were crucified]; the bottom line looked good. . . . It is not the Jacks of the world who should be indicted; they are sick, pathetic men. It is their bosses who should be indicted for allowing abusive management to continue even for a day.[16]

LAYOFFS

With increasing economic uncertainties and technological advances, the number of layoffs is increasing. There is an uncertainty inherent in human resources forecasting that makes careful workforce reduction planning a necessity. The workforce can be reduced in several ways:

1. Attrition
2. Induced retirements
3. Selective dismissals
4. Layoffs

Attrition, the loss of employees in the normal course of events, may not reduce the workforce rapidly enough. Induced retirements such as (1) "the golden handshake," where an employee under 70 is given a financial inducement to retire, and (2) "window plans," where employees have a fixed period of time to resign, are costly. Layoffs, too, may be costly but their negative impact can be reduced by contingency and outplacement planning. Layoffs assume the possibility of recall.

The organization should make plans for reductions and communicate the existence of those plans to their employees, no matter how good business and economic times may seem. Sound human resources planning suggests that personnel administrators should always know not only what the job needs are, but also where the personnel surpluses are located. These should be available at any given time in the form of some type of personnel database.

Whether reductions are determined by seniority, performance, potential appraisal records, or some other means, a reduction plan should be communicated to employees before the plan needs to be implemented. Finally, outplacement services provided by the company as an employee benefit can help soften the blow for the individual and the company. The "survivors" of a layoff will judge the company harshly and experience very low morale if the cuts are made without an understandable plan.

ACTION PROJECT 13–2   PROMOTIONS AND DISMISSALS (INDIVIDUAL OR GROUP EXERCISE)

The organization you work for has decided to reduce the size of the department that you manage. The decision has been made to promote one person to a supervisory position and to dismiss one employee. The decision as to who will be promoted and dismissed has been left up to you. The employees in your department are listed below.

Rank each employee for promotion or dismissal. A "1" in the promotion column would be your preference for promotion. A "1" in the dismissal column would signify the employee you consider most eligible for dismissal.

PROMOTE	DISMISS	
_____	_____	BRIAN: Eighteen years on the job, seven years to retirement. Solid employee but little potential for growth.
_____	_____	LAURIE: Seven years of experience. Informal employee spokesperson and leader. Tends to create unrest and conflict among employees toward management.
_____	_____	GREG: Ten years on the job. Produces passable work. Popular around office and close personal friend from your college days. You hired him personally, shortly after gaining your current position.
_____	_____	DALE: Four years of experience. Most prolific producer. Quiet, prefers to work alone and never mixes socially with coworkers. Looked on suspiciously by coworkers.
_____	_____	NORM: Twenty-three years on the job, two years to retirement. Former productivity leader for most of his career but has lost enthusiasm lately and currently his productivity is poor.
_____	_____	SALLY: Recently hired. Sally was highly recruited and was considered an excellent prospect. Her productivity has been way below standards and expectations. Has had problems adjusting to coworkers.

On what basis did you make your rankings? Now, compare your individual rankings with others in your group.

Your Individual Ranking for			Group Ranking for	
PROMOTION	DISMISSAL		PROMOTION	DISMISSAL
_____	_____	Brian	_____	_____
_____	_____	Laurie	_____	_____
_____	_____	Greg	_____	_____
_____	_____	Dale	_____	_____
_____	_____	Norm	_____	_____
_____	_____	Sally	_____	_____

SALARIES AND WAGES AS REWARDS

Just as we have seen that a good performance appraisal is a way of telling the employee that the employer appreciates his or her work, a reward is another way of communicating the same information. That reward is usually monetary but can also be in the form of important nonmonetary recognition.

On most levels of an organization, the usual procedure followed when a supervisor recognizes superior performance is to develop a good performance appraisal followed by a promotion, bonus, raise, or a combination of these. The supervisor rewards a high level of achievement over a short period of time with a substantial pay raise that the employee will likely receive for the rest of his or her working life. The supervisor does this in the hope that the high level of achievement will continue.

Salaries consist of base pay and benefits. The base pay is more important than benefits, in both practical and psychological terms. An employee must feel that his or her base pay is fair and adequate: An employer cannot make up in benefits for what is lacking in the basic wages, because a below-average wage plan with good benefits provides security but little substance for immediate necessities.

Salary can mean purchasing power, status, respect, and appreciation.

Workers need the reassurance that wages can give them; although the company may have been good to them in the past, they need to have their feelings of worth updated periodically. Thus most companies give yearly raises. Indeed, in a great many organizations, except for general pay raises, these are usually the only raises that an employee receives. The employee may be practically guaranteed a raise, but status, appreciation, respect—all the intangible benefits that are bestowed with a merit raise—are not always realized; the raise simply means that the employee has been there for another year. Other means of recognizing employee performance such as commissions and profit sharing help motivate employees.

INCENTIVE PLANS

An **incentive** is an inducement offered to influence future performance of an individual, a team, or a total organizational unit. Pay-for-knowledge and pay-for-performance systems are increasing in usage, at least as supplements to salaries and wages.

Each of the four wage incentive plans outlined in this section has certain advantages and disadvantages. Many such plans have been devised only to be abandoned and replaced by others. Regardless of which wage incentive plan is adopted, all must take several factors into consideration:

1. The wage paid must be related to the individual's output.
2. The wage plan must make adequate provision for learners and new employees.

3. The plan must be easy to administer, easy to understand by the employees, and easy to relate to costs.

Andrall E. Pearson, former president of PepsiCo, advocates paying for the best:

> Make sure every unit rewards its best achievers appropriately. Sometimes, better performers get bigger raises than less-accomplished people, but the differences are so slight as to be demotivating. . . . Top performers relish the challenge of ever-higher goals. What demoralizes them is a climate that rewards mediocrity and excellence equally.[17]

COMMISSIONS

In this system, which is generally used for salespeople, income received is based on a percentage of sales. Many salespeople receive a base salary in addition; others have a guaranteed minimum wage.

A commission pay structure is a classic example of an incentive pay system: The more you produce, sell, or otherwise work, the more you get paid. The downside to a pure commission structure is that external variables may be affecting production or sales. Perhaps the salesperson is working very hard in the short term, tending to business, and taking care of customers, but the sales just aren't coming. Compared to someone who is not working hard but enjoys the benefits of a healthy salary, salespeople may perceive an inequity. Equity is what compensation and rewards are all about. It behooves management to find a balance between commission pay and retaining good employees.

PROFIT-SHARING PLANS

These plans are simply a method of distributing a portion of a company's profits among its employees. Such plans provide an incentive for efficiency, innovation, and cooperation among an organization's workforce. Usually the profits are distributed annually, sometimes in the form of a Christmas bonus. Profit sharing is a way of enabling a company to give a pay increase to all its employees without being saddled with such an increase indefinitely.

It has the disadvantage, however, of rewarding all workers indiscriminately, just as the group incentive raises reward all employees in a particular group without attempting to differentiate between the efficient and the inefficient.

MERIT INCREASES

Merit increases are wage increases awarded for excellent performance.

These are increases in pay given to employees who have received excellent performance appraisals. The system has the advantage of being uncomplicated, and the raises received under such a method probably communicate more of the intangibles (status, appreciation, respect) than do raises received under any other system. Unfortunately, the method also can produce considerable ill will and jealousy, and, because the employee receives raises almost entirely at the discretion of a supervisor, the system is only as fair or unfair as the supervisor is.

CASH BONUSES

A bonus is a reward for outstanding performance over a short period.

Cash bonuses are money given to employees for outstanding performance, as a sort of one-time merit increase. As a practical matter, raises, once granted, are difficult to rescind. Bonuses, on the other hand, can vary from year to year with an employee's performance. It is far better to give bonuses for good performances over a short period. Theory Z companies rely heavily on the cash bonus system.

EMPLOYEE BENEFITS

Employee **benefits** are forms of tangible compensation given to employees other than direct pay. Employees will make sacrifices for and be loyal to a company when they feel that the company, in turn, will make sacrifices for and be loyal to them. Thus a utility crew may take great personal risks to keep telephone service open during a flood, or the employees of a store might accept a pay cut when the store is faced with a financial crisis. Less dramatic, but no less important, is the worker who will stay on the job for an extra ten to fifteen minutes to explain something to a supervisor. On the other hand, when employees are in trouble, they rightly expect the company to make sacrifices also. It is here that benefits come in, for the greater part of such benefits is in the form of insurance: medical plans, sick pay, group life insurance, pensions, and credit unions.

Common benefits are vacations, group life insurance, and medical plans, but they range all the way from organ transplants to group auto insurance to company-paid legal fees. The list in Table 13–1 is only a partial listing.

"Cafeteria-style" compensation.

Because of the many benefits available, organizations have been able to offer "cafeteria-style" packages from which employees can select the benefits they want. Such packages are tailored to the needs of the individual employee. Different people have different needs and desires. For example, younger employees prefer

TABLE 13–1 Types of Benefits Provided by Companies

Social security	Workers' compensation
Group life insurance	Supplemental unemployment benefits
Medical plans	Credit unions
Pension plans	Annuity programs
Stock purchase plans	Education aid
Recreational aid	Vacation with pay
Paid holidays	Paid birthday off
Company discount stores	Profit sharing
Loans	Group dental plans
Flexible time schedules	Child care centers

higher salaries to extensive retirement plans. Female employees, married employees, and employees with children usually consider a medical plan to be the most desirable benefit, especially if it includes maternity benefits.

Stock options appeal primarily to single employees and professional employees. A psychological advantage to these benefit packages is that, by participating in the formulation of their own packages, the employees are more satisfied with their own roles in the programs, and thus the benefits they receive are more "visible" and tangible.

If employees do not know what they are being paid, they cannot appreciate it. Benefits can often amount to more than 35 percent of a worker's base salary. These benefits ought to be communicated to them. One means of communicating this information is shown in Figure 13–6.

FIGURE 13–6 A Letter Showing Employees What They Earn in Salary and Benefits.

Dear _____

After preparing your W-2 this year, we thought you might be interested in knowing the total amount paid to you by the firm for salary, incentive compensation, and benefit programs during the year.

Your annual salary amounted to $_____ plus incentive compensation of $_____ for a total of $_____

The firm also paid the following amount for a comprehensive program of benefits:

1.	Medical/dental insurance	_____
2.	Life insurance	_____
3.	Accidental death and dismemberment	_____
4.	Disability	_____
5.	FICA (social security) employer's share	_____
6.	Workers' compensation	_____
7.	Unemployment insurance	_____
	Total benefits paid	$_____

Also last year the following amount was contributed to your pension plan by the company:

$_____

The total annual compensation paid to you during the year amounts to:

Salary	_____
Incentive	_____
Benefits	_____
Pensions	_____
Total	$_____

On behalf of all of us, thank you for your fine contributions. We look forward to working with you during the coming year.

Sincerely,

Performance is what's important in performance appraisal—personality idiosyncrasies are not. Performance appraisals serve many purposes. They let management know the quality of the company's personnel, they compel the supervisor to think constructively about subordinates and about himself or herself, and they inform the employee of what management thinks about the job that he or she is doing.

There are several types of appraisal methods. The 360-degree feedback system solicits appraisals of an employee's performance from all stakeholders including bosses, peers, customers, and suppliers. The essay appraisal requires the supervisor to write a paragraph about the employee's performance. The graphic rating scale is a form listing a number of performance factors; the supervisor states on the form whether the employee is poor, average, or excellent in a number of performance areas. In the critical incident technique, the supervisor keeps track of incidents and examples as they occur. The field review is the appraisal of an employee by a group of persons. Ranking is a method whereby the employee is compared with fellow employees. Management by objectives places emphasis on the employee's goals and the methods whereby those goals can be achieved. A system using behaviorally anchored rating scales permits performance to be measured against predetermined standards that have been set mutually by boss and subordinate. The use of peer, subordinate, and self-appraisal is increasing rapidly.

There are also a number of errors that supervisors can make when appraising employees. With the halo effect, a boss assumes that because an employee is outstanding in one particular field, the employee is outstanding in other ways too. Supervisors can let their own personal bias influence them. Another kind of error involves placing too much emphasis on recent behavior.

Tradition, laws, and the availability of company candidates influence whether a position is opened to the general public or someone is promoted from within the company. Some promotions are based on merit and ability; others are based on seniority.

Disciplinary action, demotions, and dismissals can usually be made only after oral and written warnings have been issued. Written warnings of substandard performance should be given before recommending a demotion or a dismissal. Before firing an employee, you must think of the employee, the department, the company, and yourself as a supervisor. If you don't release an incompetent worker, you are failing yourself, your department, and the company. Planning for layoffs and employing outplacement counselors can reduce the trauma associated with cutbacks for both those who are dismissed and the "survivors."

Rewards in the form of salaries and wages satisfy much more than simply the basic material needs of employees. They represent status, respect, and appreciation. In addition to ordinary wages of one sort or another, most companies offer their employees benefits that can amount to more than 35 percent of their base salaries. Most, but not all, of these provide employees with security in case of sickness, old age, or other emergencies. They include sick pay, group medical and dental plans, group life insurance, and vacations. Many large companies allow their employees to choose a benefits package from a list of benefits.

CASE STUDY 13-1 — WHAT REWARDS SHOULD BE GIVEN NOW?

Bruce Levin is the sales manager of the Amcox Corporation, which sells sewing notions to distribution and retail outlets. Bruce has twenty-three employees in his department, and all are paid on commission for their sales in their territories. For the past three years, the market for the company's goods has been growing steadily, and the majority of Bruce's men and women have met this growth with increased sales. However, one employee in particular, Jerry Lawson, has not kept up with the pace.

Jerry has been with Amcox for fifteen years and is now 59 years old. Jerry is a friendly man and is well liked by both his peers and those to whom he sells notions on a regular basis. The company has always considered Jerry dependable and loyal. Through the years Jerry has been counted as an asset to the company, but at the age of 59 he has gone into a state of semiretirement. Jerry's sales have not increased as the others have, and he doesn't have the determination to acquire a significant increase in sales.

Bruce wishes to change this situation. He wants to motivate Jerry into increasing his sales to match that of his younger peers. To accomplish this, Jerry must begin to do more than put in his time, but Bruce is not sure how to go about trying to motivate him. Unlike the majority of the new employees, Jerry is an older man, who within a few years will reach the age of retirement.

If you were Bruce, what would you do?

1. Would you threaten to fire Jerry?
2. Does your solution involve the feelings of others in your staff?
3. Would you increase his commissions?
4. Would you increase the retirement benefits for Jerry rather than offer him the increased commission rate?
5. Would you offer him more status in the way of a new title or new company car or place his desk in a better position in the office?
6. Is there some way in terms of appraisal and rewards that you can motivate Jerry?

CASE STUDY 13-2 — PROMOTION BASED ON SUPERVISORY CHARACTERISTICS

You are asked by your superior to recommend someone in your department to supervise the staff of ten salespersons. You think of three people in the department and you consider their backgrounds. Which person would you choose? What characteristics (either demonstrated or inferred) will help you make the choice?

John McVean has been a sales representative for five years and shows initiative and drive. He is friendly, loves to tell stories, and is basically easy to understand. He has exceeded his sales quota for the last four years. The major disadvantage is that he is overaggressive. Fellow salespeople have recently complained about his aggressiveness or rudeness in front of customers, and customers have complained about John's inability to deliver what he promises.

Kathy Crevier, a sales representative for three years, is very personable and outgoing and tends to be the life of the party when she is in a group. However, when discussing business with you, she tends to become quiet and reserved. Her contribution to the discussion is often limited and you wonder if you are doing something wrong. Kathy's sales record is outstanding, and her peers believe that she is a valuable member of the crew.

Bob Koyne has been with the company for seven years. The last six years have been outstanding sales years. Bob, in contrast to John and Kathy, is a steady, quiet producer. He is a "team man" in his conversations with you, and he feels uncomfortable when the discussion turns to him as an individual.

1. How do you feel the new supervisor should relate to the employees?
2. Is it important for a first-line supervisor to have technical competence?
3. Does the fact that a first-line supervisor has initiative and drive have any effect on subordinates?
4. Is emotional stability important for a supervisor? Why?

DISCUSSION AND STUDY QUESTIONS—TO KEEP YOU THINKING . . .

1. What are the purposes of performance appraisal? Can one instrument effectively serve more than one purpose?
2. Describe the various methods and types of performance appraisals.
3. Describe the types of frequent errors made in rating employees.
4. Explain why probationary employees should be evaluated frequently.
5. What are the best ways to be promoted in most organizations? Is it all right to outearn the boss?
6. What are effective ways to demote and dismiss individuals?
7. What are six types of employee benefits that can be provided by organizations?

NOTES

1. Tom Peters, *Thriving on Chaos: Handbook for a Management Revolution* (New York: Alfred A. Knopf, 1988), pp. 494–498.
2. Dennis M. Daley, "Performance Appraisal as an Aid in Personnel Decisions: Linkages between Techniques and Purposes in North Carolina Municipalities," *American Review of Public Administration,* September 1993, p. 211.
3. William Fitzgerald, "Forget the Form in Performance Appraisal," *HRMagazine,* December 1995, pp. 134, 136.
4. David P. Campbell, "Inklings," *Issues & Observations,* published by Center for Creative Leadership, Greensboro, North Carolina, Fourth Quarter 1993, p. 10.
5. David P. Campbell, "Inklings," *Issues & Observations,* published by Center for Creative Leadership, Greensboro, North Carolina, Fourth Quarter 1992, p. 8.
6. Richard J. Newman, "Job Reviews Go Full Circle: It's No Longer Just the Boss Who Gets to Judge How Well You're Performing," *U.S. News & World Report,* November 1, 1993, p. 97.
7. Clive Fletcher, "Appraisal: An Idea Whose Time Has Gone?" *Personnel Management,* September 1993, pp. 36–37.
8. John W. Lawrie, "Your Performance: Appraise It Yourself!" *Personnel,* January 1989, pp. 21–23.
9. G. Stephen Taylor, Carol Lehman, and Connie Forde, "How Employee Self-Appraisals Can Help," *Supervisory Management,* August 1989, pp. 32–41.
10. Nancy Day, "Can Performance Raters Be More Accurate?" *Journal of Managerial Issues,* Fall 1995, pp. 323–342.
11. Charles H. Gray, "Charting Your Employees' Potential," *Management World,* May–June 1988, pp. 11–12.
12. Walter F. Ulmer, Jr., "Inside View," *Issues & Observations,* published by Center for Creative Leadership, Greensboro, North Carolina, Fourth Quarter 1992, p. 8.
13. Gary Bielous, "The Five Worst Discipline Mistakes," *Supervisory Management,* January 1995, pp. 14–16.
14. Kenneth R. Gilberg, David McCarthy, and Jacqueline Shulman, "Disciplinary Guidelines," *Supervisory Management,* July 1989, pp. 16–17.
15. Robert A. Mamis, "Employees from Hell," *Inc.,* January 1995, pp. 50–57; and Cameron D. Reynolds and Morgan D. Reynolds, "State Court Restrictions on the Employment-at-Will Doctrine," *Regulation,* First Quarter 1995, pp. 57–66.
16. Harvey Gittler, "Free at Last, Free at Last," *The Wall Street Journal,* March 1, 1993, p. A14.
17. Andrall E. Pearson, "Muscle-Build Your Company," *Success,* July–August 1989, p. 10.

RECOMMENDED READING

Baker, Joe. *Causes of Failure in Performance Appraisal and Supervision.* Westport, Conn.: Greenwood Press, 1988.

Chappell, Tom. *The Soul of a Business: Managing for Profit and the Common Good.* New York: Bantam Books, 1993.

Cleveland, Jeanette N., and Kevin R. Murphy. "Analyzing Performance Appraisal as Goal Directed Behavior." *Research in Personnel and Human Resources Management,* Vol. 10. Greenwich, Conn.: JAI Press, 1992.

Drucker, Peter F. "We Need to Measure, Not Count." *The Wall Street Journal,* April 13, 1993, p. A14.

Eyres, Patricia S. "Legally Defensible Performance Appraisal Systems." *Personnel Journal,* July 1989, pp. 58–62.

Gerlin, Andrea. "Seminars Teach Managers Finer Points of Firing." *The Wall Street Journal,* May 26, 1995, p. B1.

Goodard, Robert W. "Is Your Appraisal System Headed for Court?" *Personnel Journal,* January 1989, pp. 114–119.

Kiechel, Walter, III. "When Subordinates Evaluate the Boss." *Fortune,* June 19, 1989, pp. 201–202.

Kohn, Alfie. "Punished by Rewards: The Trouble with Gold Stars, Incentive Plans, A's, Praise, and Other Bribes." *Personnel Psychology,* Winter 1995, pp. 941–945.

_____. "Why Incentive Plans Cannot Work." *Harvard Business Review,* September–October 1993, pp. 54–63.

Peters, Tom. *Thriving on Chaos: Handbook for a Management Revolution.* New York: Alfred A. Knopf, 1988.

Spruell, Geraldine. "Say So Long to Promotions." *Training and Development Journal,* May 1985, pp. 70–75.

Taylor, G. Stephen, Carol Lehman, and Connie Forde. "How Employee Self-Appraisals Can Help." *Supervisory Management,* August 1989, pp. 32–41.

Whitney, James L. "Pay Concepts for the 1990s." *Compensation & Benefits Review,* March–April 1988, pp. 33–44.

"Yeah, But What's My Raise? Why Money and Job Feedback Don't Mix." *Executive Female,* September–October 1993, pp. 15–16.

14

CREATIVITY AND
INNOVATION IN
DECISION MAKING

Look at these questions before reading the chapter. Perhaps you can use the questions to start a discussion after studying the chapter.

- Is creativity inherited or can it be developed?
- How critical is innovation to American industry?
- Do creative people perform better under rigid or relaxed managers?
- What makes a person an entrepreneur?
- What can be done in the workplace to make the environment more conducive to creativity?
- What are the benefits and variations of brainstorming?
- Do you ever make decisions based on intuition? Do you think people in responsible positions might make decisions based on intuition? Is there justification for such actions?
- Is an average person or a millionaire more likely to take risks or be fearful of failure when a decision is to be made? Is the difference long-term versus short-term decisions? dollar magnitude?

LEARNING GOALS

After studying this chapter, you should be able to:

1. Distinguish between creativity and innovation.
2. Discuss the relationship of innovation to decision making.
3. List the four P's of creativity and various concepts behind those ideas.
4. Describe the following four stages of the creative process:
   a. Perception
   b. Incubation
   c. Inspiration
   d. Verification
5. Explain the differences between unstructured, heuristic decisions and structured, logical decisions.
6. Explain the steps used in decision making.
7. Explain the differences between short-term and long-term decisions in relationship to risk and uncertainty.
8. Discuss the advantages and/or disadvantages of decisions made by
   a. Individuals
   b. A powerful few
   c. Groups

9. List the advantages and disadvantages of group decision making using the following methods:
   a. Brainstorming
   b. Statistical method
   c. Delphi technique
   d. Nominal group technique

10. Define and apply the following terms and concepts (in order of first occurrence):

- creativity
- innovation
- custodial person
- intelligence
- perception
- incubation
- invention
- entrepreneur
- intrapreneur
- brainstorming
- decision

- decision making
- heuristic
- program evaluation review technique (PERT)
- critical path
- intuition
- synergy
- Delphi technique
- nominal group technique (NGT)
- polarization
- crisis

WHAT IS CREATIVITY?

HOW IS CREATIVITY DEFINED?

Nothing new under the sun? Maybe not, but there are new ways of putting things together. Mark Twain said, "The man with a new idea is a crank until the idea succeeds."

As with justice, democracy, and liberty, "creativity" is a word with many different meanings for many different people. Basically, **creativity** is the ability to develop novel and useful ideas from diverse resources. The diverse resources are the sum total of our cultural heritage. What is new is the combination of these elements into new patterns of association. Einstein could never have postulated the theory of relativity if the patterns of Newtonian physics had not been established so firmly.

WHO HAS IT?

One viewpoint is that everyone has the potential for creativity. Some people develop that potential more than others. From childhood, people have vivid imaginations that, when cultivated and allowed to grow, become productive mechanisms for performing a job. "Creativeness often consists of merely turning around what is already there."

Can creativity be taught?   Can creativity be taught? Contrary to the preceding viewpoint, another view is that creativity cannot be taught. One of the most common criticisms of Japanese education is that too little time is spent in developing creativity and thought processes. The principal of a Japanese high school says that these talents cannot be taught.[1]

SELF-APPRAISAL

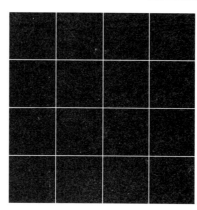

- How many squares are in the box?
- Now, count again.
- Only sixteen?
- Take away your preconception of how many squares there are.
- Now, how many do you find? You should find thirty!

If creativity is defined as the ability to combine already existing elements in new ways, we see clearly that a child's creative energies do not disappear with the onset of adulthood. They are simply expressed in different ways in many aspects of daily life: in homes, schools, offices, and factories. A secretary who designs a new, more efficient filing system, a factory worker who uses an unconventional tool to perform a familiar task more easily, a needy student who uses cement cinder blocks to build a bookcase—all are acting creatively.

Innovation is the end product of creative activity. It typically starts with a macro invention or change in procedure. There are incremental steps between macro inventions and a final product or process change, but innovations are typically driven by recognition of technical feasibility and/or potential or actual demand. Innovations can take place in policies, processes, and techniques as well as in people's activities and behaviors.

Management and organizations must innovate—or perish. Every organization—businesses, governments, educational institutions, churches, and other religious organizations—need one core competence: innovation. "Innovation is *the* core competence because it makes competitive advantage by any other strategy possible. Creating new products and product enhancements provides differentiation. Process innovation can lead to lower costs and improved customer satisfaction."[2]

The most innovative organizations possess common and achievable traits:

- **Strategy.** Knowing when and how to lead customers to new products and services.
- **Structure.** Using cross-functional and customer/supplier new-product teams.
- **Systems.** Creation and use of innovative management information systems.
- **Style.** Creating a vision or strategic intent focused on innovation.
- **Staff.** Providing time for reflection.
- **Shared values.** Encouraging risk taking and new ideas.
- **Skills.** Leveraging resources to achieve seemingly unobtainable objectives.[3]

Creative effort is more of a mental activity; innovation is more active. The "do-it, fix-it, try-it" mentality that authors Tom Peters and Robert Waterman, Jr., talk about is evidence of innovation. Peters writes that to get the constant innovation necessary for survival, managers must:

- Personally symbolize innovativeness in their daily affairs.
- Seek out opportunities to stand foursquare with innovators.

. . . It is essential that managers make a constant effort to recognize innovators (and applaud the details of their victories over organizational inertia), at all levels and in all functions.[4]

Tremendous pressures to innovate confront organizations. While pursuing their mission or corporate objectives in the mainstream, they must also generate "new streams." Mainstream businesses can quickly dry up or stagnate. Thus, companies must explore opportunities to pioneer in new directions, to seek innovations that will improve and even transform the mainstream.[5]

THE FOUR P'S OF CREATIVITY

Perhaps one of the best ways in which to approach the complex area of creativity is by looking at the four "P's" of creativity: the person, the process, the pressure, and the product. The following list provides a more complete breakdown of the four points:

1. Person   2. Process   3. Pressure   4. Product

    a. Approach   a. Perception   a. Social direction

    b. Intelligence   b. Incubation   b. Social pressure

    c. Education   c. Inspiration   and values

    d. Age   d. Verification

    e. Gender

    f. Behavior

    g. Inhibitors

First, let us study a creative person and compare the personality traits with those of a direct opposite—the custodial person. Table 14–1 contrasts the two types. The **custodial person** enjoys routine, is more satisfied with the status quo, and is less inclined to adopt creative change.

THE PERSON

Although all people have a creative spark, the potential is not always utilized fully. How does one recognize those who are developing their creative energies to the fullest? The essential traits of creativity are found among a wide variety of creative individuals: scientists, carpenters, social reformers, teachers, gardeners, businesspeople, politicians, doctors, parents—people in all walks of life, as well as the more traditional artists and poets. The potential for creativity resides within us all.

Potential for creativity resides within all.

APPROACH.   Highly creative people are apt to make "leaps of reasoning" from one fact to a seemingly unrelated fact and construct a bridge of logic across the chasm. The creative temperament distrusts pat answers and implicit assumptions. It has a tendency to break problems down into their most basic elements and then reconstruct them into whole new problems, thereby discovering new relationships and new solutions.

A creative person distrusts "pat" answers.

Highly creative people aren't afraid to ask what may seem to be naïve or silly questions. They ask such questions as: "Why don't spiders get tangled up in their own webs?" and "Why do dogs turn in circles before lying down?" Such questions may seem childlike, and in a way they are. Children have not yet had their innate creative energies channeled into culturally acceptable directions and can give full rein to their curiosity—the absolute prerequisite for full creative functioning, in both children and adults.

TABLE 14–1 Differences between the Custodial and the Creative Person

CUSTODIAL	CREATIVE
Enjoys routine and details	Enjoys variety
Works for simplification and streamlining	Speculates, guesses
Predictable personality	Unpredictable personality
Enjoys the status quo	Cannot understand people who are reluctant to try something new
Firm, fair, friendly	Enthusiastic
Micro-orientation (details)	Macro-orientation (the whole)

INTELLIGENCE AND EDUCATION.   According to many popular theories, great advances in creative thought are attributable to extraordinary intelligence, altered states of consciousness, and a "special" thought process that is available only to geniuses. Albert Einstein denied having any of these special talents or gifts.

One of the most common misconceptions about the highly creative personality is that there is a positive correlation between creativity and intelligence. The problem here is that *intelligence* is another word that means many different things to different people. If we mean by intelligence simply the ability to learn a lot of facts and relationships by rote memory and to put that knowledge into useful service, then there appears to be little correlation between intelligence and creativity. On the other hand, a high correlation exists if **intelligence** is defined as the ability to solve complex and unusual problems.

There has been some study and speculation as to which side of the brain houses the creative portion of one's personality. The right brain is believed to be the site of creativity, fantasy, and emotion, whereas the left side is the logical, analytic, and reasoning side.

AGE AND GENDER.   Contrary to popular myths that glorify youth, more creative achievements are likely to occur when people grow older. One researcher made a list of 1,000 ideas that have been important to the world and found that the average age of the innovators when they actually had those ideas was 74.[6] Genius may flare early and die young, but imagination generally grows by being used. Another researcher has found that mental ability grows until about age 60, then decreases—but so slowly that, at age 80, it is as if you are 30.[7] Although memory may falter with the senility that seems to come with age (but more likely is the result of a faulty diet), creativity seems to be ageless.

Dr. E. Paul Torrance has found no significant relationship between creativity and gender.[8] It does appear that less rigid male and female role identification increases the chances for creativity. For instance, a group of architects who were studied for intelligence were also given the Minnesota Multiphasic Personality Inventory (MMPI) to inquire into their psychological natures. The most striking aspect of the MMPI profiles was the tendency for creative males to score high on the femininity ratings.

BEHAVIOR.   Creative people are more concerned with the world of ideas and images than with the world of society. As a result, they tend to be somewhat antisocial. In their personal lives they may appear to be highly sensitive and self-centered. Their lifestyles may seem chaotic, but inner directed as they are, it doesn't matter to them what their lives look like to others. Their rewards are the joys of discovery, not the approval of society.

Table 14–2 outlines research on personality traits that often appear in creative personalities. Not all these traits must be present, however, for a person to be creative. All of them rarely appear together, and their presence does not always indicate creativity. The table is presented to familiarize you with possible indicators of creative ability.

INHIBITORS.   Early training and environmental influences can discourage natural curiosity and stifle impulses to explore and experiment. Schools still stress acquiring information rather than learning how to think. In many ways, the educational system tends to foster imitative rather than creative behavior.

There is little correlation between IQ and the creative quotient.

Creativity is housed on the right side of the brain.

Age does not seem to decrease creativity.

Neither males nor females are more creative.

Creative people are sometimes more interested in ideas than in people.

TABLE 14–2 Possible Personality Traits of a Creative Person

IN RELATION TO OTHERS	JOB ATTITUDES	ATTITUDES TO SELF
Not a joiner Few close friends Unconventional morality especially under pressure Independence of judgment	Preference for things and ideas to people High regard for intellectual interests Less emphasis on job security Less enjoyment in detail work and routine High level of resourcefulness Skeptical High tolerance for ambiguity Persistence, capacity to be puzzled	Introspective Open to new experiences Inner maturity Less emotionally stable Spontaneous, adventurous, compulsive, anxious

SOURCE: Adapted from John W. Haefele, *Creativity and Innovation* (New York: Reinhold, Publishing, 1962).

Finding fault and "labeling" are also inhibitors.

Some states of mind are less conducive to creativity than others. *Emotion-mindedness* is the habit of allowing feelings to distort reasoning and block objectivity. *Judicial-mindedness* is the tendency to find fault immediately with a new and different thought, thereby inhibiting further thoughts in that vein. *Label-mindedness* filters thought by finding the names for things rather than evaluating the facts about them.

Inhibitors to creativity include perceptual, cultural, and emotional blocks to creativity:

- One solution did not work, so I am having trouble finding another solution
- Making assumptions
- Going for a fast solution
- Not wanting to make errors
- I can't do it
- It is not my job
- I don't have time to let incubation take place or follow through
- I must not lose sight of long-term goals by taking a detour (sometimes the irrelevant is the most relevant!)

THE PROCESS

Deprivation breeds creativity, which is another way of saying "Necessity is the mother of invention." The unfolding of the creative process is still mysterious. Many attempts have been made to analyze it, but it remains little understood. However, certain obvious stages in the process can be identified. One practical innovation model incorporates the major parts of the creative thinking process:

1. **Discovery.** Identifies decisions that are accompanied by weak alternatives, uncovering dissatisfaction with the status quo, forcing a search for solutions, guiding the search for threat and opportunities.

FIGURE 14–1 Creativity Exercise. Can You Draw a Circle with a Dot in the Center without Lifting Your Pencil?

2. **Generation.** Requires the ability to move chameleon-like from logical to intuitive problem-solving modes.

3. **Definition.** Seeks clarification of the solution developed in step 2.

4. **Experimentation.** Achieved by a limited application of the idea, a pilot test, or the development of a prototype.

5. **Evaluation.** Now the idea is out in the open in the organization.

6. **Implementation.** Plans how the new idea will be launched.[9]

We will look at four steps in the process: *perception, incubation, inspiration,* and *verification.* Here is an exercise to test your creativity (see Figure 14–1). Using a piece of paper and a pencil, can you draw a circle with a dot in the center without lifting your pencil? It is possible. Once you have tried it and gone through the creativity stages, refer to page 439 for the answer—but no fair peeking!

PERCEPTION.   As introduced in Chapter 7, **perception** is a powerful individual factor that influences our views of facts, emotions, communication, and motivation. Likewise, it affects how creative we are. Because of differences in temperament and environment, everyone sees the world in a slightly different way. Some people perceive the world as orderly and just; others see only disorder and injustice.

A creative person brings together isolated ideas into a fused whole.

The creative person often sees problems where others see none and questions the validity of even the most widely accepted answers. Creative personalities are compulsive problem seekers, not so much because they thrive on problems, but because their senses are attuned to a world that demands to be put together, like a jigsaw puzzle scattered on a table.

The person with originality tends to view society from a different perspective than the custodial person. An analogy might be that the creative person sees the forest, whereas the custodial person sees the trees. A creative person is able to see problems that others are not able to see or do not want to see.

To "hatch an idea" may take an hour or months.

INCUBATION.   The mysterious part of the creative process that takes place subconsciously is called **incubation**. It is rather like a bird sitting quietly for days on end to hatch an egg. There appears to be no activity whatever occurring when, in fact, the creative action is actually astonishing. In the egg, the embryo of a chick is developing, and in the innovator's mind, a massive amount of data is being sorted, filed, classified, discarded, combined—in short, developed into a meaningful whole. During this stage the process continues, even in dreams. The second law of thermodynamics came to Johannes Kepler in a dream—after twenty years of conscious searching. This stage can last anywhere from a few hours to many years, depending on the complexity of the problem.

In the incubation stage, the mind creates remote associations leading to the formation of new ideas. Major concerns now in the incubation stage at many companies and in the minds of many individuals are "How to solve a food shortage," "How to find new fuel substitutes," "How to reorganize the transportation system," and "How to solve the water shortages that prevail in certain areas of the world."

INSPIRATION.   The payoff for all this conscious and subconscious mental activity is usually experienced as a flash, an instant insight, a slap on the forehead, and an astonished "Aha!" or "Eureka, I found it!" as the answer comes bursting through to consciousness. This stage is called *inspiration* or illumination (Figure 14–2), a moment representing the culmination of hours, days, or years of thought—although in actual time it lasts for just a few moments. It is a release of psychic tensions that have been building up all through the incubation period.

There is no way to predict when this moment of illumination will occur. Often it comes when least expected—say, in the middle of a conversation about

FIGURE 14–2 There Is No Way to Predict When the Moment of Inspiration Will Occur. Often It Comes When Least Expected.

a seemingly unrelated subject. A particular phrase or image or idea will ring a bell, provide the final link in the puzzle, and bring the parts together to create a new whole. It is the moment that cartoonists represent by a light bulb suddenly flashing on over the head of the character.

VERIFICATION. In a sense, illumination represents only the end of the beginning of the creative process. As Thomas Edison said, "Creation is one percent inspiration and ninety-nine percent perspiration." Now the innovator must elaborate on the idea. It must be tested, evaluated, reworked, retested, and reevaluated. The idea must be stacked up against the real, practical world—and it must be foolproof: no leaks, no loopholes, no weaknesses. If such problems do arise, then the idea must be transformed and the solution mended.

In verification the creative person needs the help of the custodial person.

It is during this stage that the innovator should, and often must, work closely with others of a more practical nature. Scientific discoveries must be tested thoroughly in the laboratory, and innovative ideas in business must be tested against all aspects of the enterprise, from production costs to marketability.

ACTION PROJECT 14-1 CREATIVE PROCESS TEST: PERCEPTION, INCUBATION, INSPIRATION (INDIVIDUAL EXERCISE)

This "test" does not measure your intelligence, nor your fluency with words, and certainly not your mathematical ability. It will, however, give some gauge of your mental flexibility and creativity.

Few people can solve more than half of the questions on the first try. Many, however, report getting answers after the test had been set aside—particularly at unexpected moments when their minds were relaxed. Some reported solving all the answers over a period of several days.

INSTRUCTIONS:

Each question below contains the initials of words that will make it correct. Find the missing words.

Example: 16-0. in a P.   16 ounces in a pound

1. 26-L. of the A. _____
2. 7-W. of the A.W. _____
3. 1001 - A.N. _____
4. 12-S. of the Z. _____
5. 54-C. in a D. (with the J.) _____
6. 9-P. in the S.S. _____
7. 88-P.K. _____
8. 90-D. in R.A. _____
9. 8-S. on a S.S. _____
10. 24 H. in a D. _____
11. 57-H.V. _____

12. 11-P. on a F.T. _____

13. 29-D. in F. in a L.Y. _____

14. 9-P. on a B.T. _____

15. 60-S. in a M. _____

16. 13 in a B.D. _____

17. 60-W. in a L.B. _____

18. L.M.M. sat on her T. _____

19. 4-S. and 7-Y.A. _____

20. 100-Y. in a C. _____

Your instructor should have the "key," but try to complete the exercise without help. It may take you several tries. Put it aside and come back when you have incubated over it and are inspired by an idea.

PRESSURE OF SOCIETY

SOCIAL DIRECTION AND NECESSITY. All children everywhere are born with some degree of innate creative energy, but the channels into which the energy will flow are determined by the values of a particular culture. In some parts of the world, such as the island of Bali, artistic ability is valued very highly, and almost every child grows up to be skilled in at least one art form. Most of us, if asked, would say, "I'm not a creative person: I don't paint or write poetry." But this is a very narrow view of the scope of the creative force.

In America, technological change is valued very highly, and in every new generation many children grow up to be skilled practitioners of at least one technological innovation. In the 1920s, if you wanted to own and drive a Model T Ford, and hundreds of thousands did, the odds were that it was necessary to repair it yourself. Thousands of patents for automobile improvements were granted in those years to self-taught, creative auto mechanics. Computer programming, software development, and applications are modern-day examples of the pressure for change.

Society can pressure us to find solutions to today's problems.

SOCIAL PRESSURE. Society often puts a great deal of pressure on creative people to channel their energies into specific areas to solve specific problems. Pollution, clean and abundant sources of fuel, and mass transportation, to name but three of the most pressing of today's social problems, require solutions as quickly as possible.

There is so much pressure to *be* creative, to *not* make mistakes, to be almost perfect. But being creative and successful in business sometimes means breaking the rules. Martine Costello says there are five mistakes every good manager should make—five commandments to *break:*

- Thou shalt be predictable.
- Thou shalt not fail.
- Thou shalt defer to experts.

- Thou shalt not pester the boss.
- Thou shalt honor the chain of command.[10]

THE PRODUCT

An invention is an idea, not an object.

As a rule, it is easy to identify the end product of artistic creative energy, although as modern life grows more difficult, identification is not always a simple task. Still, as a general rule, poems, plays, musical compositions, and sculpture leave little room for confusion as to what they are. Identifying the products of scientific or industrial creativity is not always as easy. Fortunately, the U.S. Supreme Court has helped to settle the issue. An **invention,** says the Court, is an idea. Inventions are not poems, or symphonies, or machines; they are the ideas behind things.

Product development is not the only way in which the innovator contributes to business success. Some businesses, for instance, don't deal with products at all. A management consulting firm would have little use for an inventor, but it would value the creative person who could devise a bold reorganization plan for a failing business.

One of the areas in which creativity makes a big difference is advertising. Anyone can see the difference in effectiveness between a competent, but dull, run-of-the-mill TV ad and one that excites comment and interest. Behind every successful advertisement there is at least one creator, someone who has sensed that there was a new and better way of presenting a product.

Creative personnel can contribute to better business office management or business systems analysis. An innovative office manager, for example, may discover new methods of operating the office for maximum efficiency. A creative systems analyst can take a fresh look at the accounting system used by a business for fifty years and in one swoop eliminate 75 percent of the busywork. In fact, there is virtually no aspect of business that can't be improved by a creative worker. Management itself must become more creative to see what is needed and where.

EXPRESS YOUR OPINION

Do you think that you are more creative than the average person? Many experts believe that creativity can be developed to a greater extent in each of us—if we try. Many feel that we clutter our way with too many inhibitors, which tends to hamper our creative ability.

Think of the times when you are the most creative. Do you tend to be more creative when you are with someone or when you are alone? Are you more creative early in the morning or late in the evening?

Do you write down your ideas, or do you only express them verbally, or do you only express them to yourself? Creative ideas need to be expressed orally, in written forms, and often, so that other individuals or groups can help in the verification.

Do you believe that creative people can develop more alternatives to problems but have a more difficult time deciding on a final selection? Would you rather be considered creative or practical? Why?

BUSINESS AND THE CREATIVE EMPLOYEE

MANAGEMENT ATTITUDES

While the creative temperament has much to offer to business and industry, it has special needs and does not always fit smoothly into an organization. Because of their sometimes unorthodox ways of doing things, creative people can create serious problems for organizations that aren't designed to accommodate them.

Disney is successful on the bottom line but does that by keeping new ideas coming. In fact, they treat their animators and other employees right and get "the best out of that often-prickly-but-you-can't-live-without-'em bunch of folks, 'the creatives.' "[11]

Management often prefers efficiency to unproven ideas.

An organization may encourage creative behavior while at the same time establishing policies that prevent the use of independent judgment, discretion, and innovation. Management tends to prefer the efficiency that results from using proven methods. It fears that the innovator will cause unrest in the organization, challenge the status quo, and generally disrupt what has been a successful company policy. At the same time, most managers give at least token recognition to the need for the creative employee.

This basic contradiction is often a reason why some small companies never quite get off the ground and some large companies stagnate and stop growing. Creativity, although acknowledged as being necessary, is continually stifled, and the company goes its merry way toward mediocrity, led by the boss and followed by legions of "yes men" and "yes women."

ENTREPRENEURIAL CHARACTERISTICS

An entrepreneur creates.

Traditionally, the entrepreneur has been defined as a risk taker who usually anticipates some type of profit. A more modern definition holds that the **entrepreneur** is a person who creates or perceives new kinds of demands and applies innovative techniques for meeting those demands. This definition includes individuals such as government officials, other public servants, and educators, who may not be anticipating monetary profit.

Regardless of whether entrepreneurs are economically motivated, they have certain strong needs. They need to (1) achieve, (2) accomplish or improve on something, (3) take responsibility, and (4) receive frequent feedback. Entrepreneurs are usually enthusiastic and persevering—maybe even abrasive to their work associates. They are probably better off self-employed than working for someone else.

For a large organization to be effective, it must include individuals with these characteristics. These individuals are referred to as **intrapreneurs** or entrepreneurs within large organizations. The key to their effectiveness is not to let them get lost in the bureaucracy. They need the freedom to function more autonomously and must be rewarded for their performance.

A recent study provides an international example of entrepreneurship, intrapreneurship, and transition from state-run to privately run enterprises. Respondents represent a growing body of businesspeople who are making transitions in the Estonian economy. Within recent years more than 20,000 enterprises have been registered in Estonia that fit into four categories:

ENTREPRENEURIAL TYPE	EXAMPLES
1. Self-motivated	*The baker.* Lack of good quality products supplied on a consistent basis prompted an entrepreneur to open his own bakery.
2. Joint-venture	*The T-shirt company.* This entrepreneur joined with a Swedish organization to produce advertising.
3. Take-over manager	*City- and state-owned brewery and pub.* Taken over by former employees: administrative, technical and production managers, brewmasters, and state's managers and waiters.
4. Intrapreneur	*The sewing factory and brush company.* Creative, innovative and resourceful workers in large, state-owned enterprises now sell their merchandise at free markets and have been thrust into customer-oriented situations.[12]

BRAINSTORMING

Various techniques that encourage creativity can and should be used in almost any business situation. One of the most successful and best known of these is called **brainstorming**—using the brain to storm a problem. Brainstorming sessions are designed to generate ideas to solve specific problems.

The following four rules provide the basis for a good brainstorming session.

1. **Criticism is ruled out.** Comments such as "That's stupid" are not allowed.

2. **"Freewheeling" is welcomed.** The more outlandish the idea, the better. It's always easier to tame down an idea than think it up.

3. **Quantity and variety are welcomed.** The greater the number of ideas expressed, the greater the likelihood of there being a winner.

4. **Combinations and improvements are welcomed.** Modifying, elaborating, and combining ideas is very productive, and combinations often generate totally new ideas. Hitchhiking on another person's ideas is encouraged.

Brainstorming can be done individually, but sessions seem to work best with about five to seven participants. Quality circles are classic examples of this type of group, which meets voluntarily, on company time, to brainstorm, solve problems, and receive training that will improve effectiveness.

"Hitchhiking" is fun and productive.

Group brainstorming has the further advantage of producing many ideas quickly. When ideas are shared in a group, they stimulate more ideas, just by the power of association. Pooling thoughts has a chain-reaction effect. Ideas that are triggered by the suggestions of others are called "hitchhikes." Just the atmosphere of acceptance and friendly rivalry has a way of reinforcing the desire to make suggestions, but remember rule 1 and the others listed earlier.

Chairpersons reject their own ideas too.

The chairperson should remind participants in brainstorming sessions that they should not feel badly about having their ideas rejected. The purpose of brainstorming is to generate alternative solutions to a problem. The chairperson will need to remind coparticipants that his or her own ideas are frequently rejected.

Once all the ideas are accumulated, the information can be reviewed, and the panel can evaluate the material with hopes that a couple of excellent ideas are available out of the more than twenty or thirty that were generated. The appraisal session can even come a day or two after the brainstorming session rather than immediately following. At this meeting, all the ideas should be reviewed in expectation that several usable ideas can be derived from them.

REWARDS

A serious problem in dealing with creative personnel is finding adequate ways in which to reward successful effort. Monetary rewards alone are not the answer. Organizations themselves should be more creative in their reward systems. This means knowing about your employees and their personal needs. This bit of extra effort nets larger gains. Creative people are often satisfied to receive a merely comfortable salary as long as the job offers the freedom and time that they feel they need to work well.

Perhaps the best reward for a good idea is recognition and immediate use of the idea.

Perhaps the best reward for a good idea is recognition and immediate use of the idea. Witnessing the application of an idea is often the highest form of reward. Other avenues may be explored, such as granting greater degrees of freedom or equipping the scientific researcher with his or her own private laboratory. More money is seldom frowned on. But what the true innovator responds to most is neither money nor status, but recognition—the enthusiastic "Hurrah" for the difficult problem that has been solved.

A major contribution that management can make to creative effort is bringing creative people together and providing them with the materials they require for their work. The ability to do this demands an unusually deep understanding of creative personalities and a degree of creativity in the manager. Introducing one innovator to another creates a new pattern of association of existing elements—in this case, people—and is thus itself a creative act.

PROFILE OF HUMAN BEHAVIOR

JANET SUGG

Janet Sugg is the creative director of the Gerber Life Insurance Company in White Plains, New York. She is a mother, homemaker, volunteer, and has many other civic responsibilities. Widowed, Janet continues to earn her living by "spending the day working with words." She recognizes that both creativity and innovation are essential to almost every aspect of her function as creative director. She states: "Without creativity there is no innovation."

Janet believes that creativity is widely dispersed in our society: "I don't believe it is unique to any population segment. As to the influence of 'age' on creativity, childhood is the most obvious population segment. Children can be extremely creative until they are inhibited by parent, teacher, or societal 'correct and incorrect' judgments."

In answer to the question, "What are important characteristics of creative and entrepreneurial people?" she replies: "Minimally, it would be the ability to use the established, obvious standard ideas in new combinations or from a new point of view. Maximally, the ability to conjure previously unimagined concepts—plus the ability to make profitable use of the creativity of others in addition to their own."

Employing "group techniques [like brainstorming] can provide stimuli for creative thinking. But I believe the ultimate creation/decision is best arrived at by one (maybe two) person(s) working and thinking alone. Group decisions frequently take more time than necessary—and can tend toward the safe but mediocre [because of groupthink]. When one person bears the full responsibility, the effort is often greater, the ideas more unique—unadulterated by group opinions."

Janet Sugg's assessment of the future of jobs and organizations like hers, as they pertain to creativity and innovation in decision making, is as follows:

- Use of more sophisticated software will continue to increase for both graphics and art—and for testing techniques that are at the heart of direct response advertising.
- Understanding of various ethnic cultures and languages will increase as the market mix becomes more and more diverse.
- The much-touted trend toward "interactive media" will certainly affect all areas of jobs like mine—but probably to a lesser extent than the more enthusiastic advocates predict.
- Database and modeling use will provide greater precision in identifying best prospects.
- The "privacy" issue will become more intense, especially as it applies to telemarketing.
- Computer use will continue to increase.
- As acquisition of new customers becomes more expensive, there will be more emphasis on the "lifetime value" of current customers.

WHAT IS DECISION MAKING?

Almost everything we do involves making decisions. A **decision** is a commitment—a resolution to do or stop doing an act, or to adopt or reject an attitude. Because attitudes often develop unconsciously, they are hard to see as part of the decision-making process until decisions are actually made. **Decision making** is a process of several steps, including choosing among alternatives, not a single step of deciding. The first step is correctly defining the problem. It is a discovery process.

The previous sections on innovation and creativity were designed to help you be better decision makers by creatively defining problems and seeking alternative solutions to problems. While creativity focuses on solving problems, decision making also implies a problem demanding a solution. Creativity requires an unstructured, heuristic approach, whereas decision making uses more structured, logical thinking. A **heuristic** approach to decision making and problem solving is intuitive, self-discovery oriented. Both the logical and heuristic approaches are necessary to solve problems, and they can be used together, alternating between the two kinds of thinking.

PROBLEM DEFINITION

All problems are opportunities—sometimes in disguise! Problems can be referred to as "challenges," "situations," or "discovering opportunities" but there is a stimulating, positive side to problem definition and solving.

Spend time defining the problem. A problem precisely defined is already half solved. Sometimes we have difficulty isolating the problem. The difficulty of isolating a problem is often due to spending the minimum amount of effort on problem definition, so we can get to work quickly on solving it. More time spent on correctly identifying a problem has a big payoff in the timeliness and quality of the ultimate solution.

Look to find the real problem first, not a symptom or the solution. You may find a solution to a symptom and ignore the real problem. Once the problem is defined, there are several "ACTION" steps to take.

Look for the "right" question before you look for the "right" answer.

STEPS IN DECISION MAKING AFTER PROBLEM DEFINITION

What steps must be taken to yield the highest probability of successful decisions? The acronym ACTION indicates six fundamental ones:

A   ANALYZE the problem and gather data.

C   CONSIDER the alternative solutions.

T   TAKE action—select a solution.

I   IMPLEMENT the solution.

O   ONGOING EVALUATION. Conduct an ongoing evaluation of the solution; encourage feedback from employees.

N   NEED for change. After you have tried the solution, consider the need for modifications of the original decision.

ANALYZE THE PROBLEM

Collecting accurate information for decision making is crucial[13] (see Figure 14–3). Using wrong or irrelevant data as the basis for a solution to a problem can be more detrimental than not solving the problem at all. Often the ability to collect useful information depends on how good the communication is within the firm. People sometimes hold back information to play it safe or to

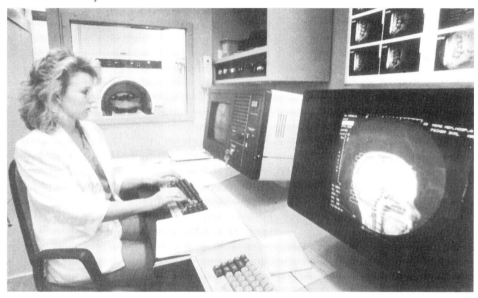

FIGURE 14–3 Collecting Accurate Information for Decision Making Is Crucial. Wrong Data Can Be More Detrimental Than Not Solving the Problem at All. Spencer Grant/Monkmeyer Press.

look good. Also, all information is filtered through individual perceptions, which are, by definition, subjective. Facts don't speak for themselves; people speak them.

Information related to a problem's solution is not always easy to acquire. A problem in real life is unlike a classroom case study in which many of the facts relevant to the case are available. In real life it is necessary to search thoroughly for the various facts that may illuminate a problem. Some of the ways of collecting these facts are (1) personal interviews, (2) review of records, (3) flowcharts, (4) organizational charts, (5) consultation of previous studies, and (6) outside information. Often a balanced combination of the appropriate methods will yield an objective and broad spectrum of data to use in assessing a problem.

CONSIDER THE ALTERNATIVE SOLUTIONS

Decision makers need to stretch their minds to develop all possible alternatives, even in the most discouraging situations. Even when one of the available alternatives is desirable, it is better to have choices than to be left with no choice at all. Doing nothing is also a decision—and can be worthwhile or it can be fatal.

There is always a tendency to be overly influenced by one alternative. Alfred Sloan, former chairman of General Motors, told the story of how there was board unanimity on a certain course of action. No one saw anything wrong with the alternatives including Mr. Sloan, so they postponed the decision until a later meeting where the alternative was rejected.

At Minnesota Mining and Manufacturing Company, the "Scotch tape" people, every division is expected to generate 25 percent of its sales each year from products that didn't exist five years earlier. The goal forces managers to use 3M's skills to come up with new products. The yellow "sticky" note pads (Post-its) for which 3M has been famous were the product of a failure from an adhesive standpoint because they did not adhere well. Developing alternatives—even from a failure—has made 3M millions of dollars.

People are happy when they have freedom of choice in making a decision, but choosing between negative alternatives seems like no choice at all. People tend to search for other, more positive, alternatives. Individuals prefer a number of alternatives, and they like hard choices between positive, closely similar alternatives. The law of diminishing returns applies to the number of alternatives, because too many can overwhelm people and make them feel trapped. When this happens, there is a higher possibility they will make an impulsive decision or no decision at all.

WE SEEK OUT POSITIVE ALTERNATIVES

NEGATIVE: The pipe under your kitchen sink springs a leak and you call in a plumber. A few days later you get a bill for $40. At the bottom is a note saying that if you do not pay within 30 days, then there will be a 10 percent service charge of $4. You feel trapped with no desirable alternatives. You pay $40 now or $44 later.

POSITIVE: The same case, but with two changes. The plumber sends you a bill for $44, but the note says that if you pay within 30 days you will get a special $4 discount. The difference is that you will save $4. You and the plumber are both better satisfied.

We need time to weigh our alternatives and arrive at decisions. In some Eastern cultures, the adaptation of man to time is seen as a viable alternative to rapid decision making. The Chinese are very conscious and considerate of others' time. The Japanese are meticulous in the way they segment time; they must experience an "unfolding" of the significant phases of an event such as decision making. Time is not linear but cyclic—repetitive rising and setting of the sun, birth and death, and succession in generations. "Cyclical time is not a scarce commodity. As they say in the East (cultures), 'when God made time, He made plenty of it.' "[14]

TAKE ACTION—A SOLUTION

After the alternative solutions have been developed, the probable desirable and undesirable consequences of each should be tested. The selection must be the best solution from the point of view of time and energy as well as money. The decision maker's selection will probably be based on a combination of factors, such as experience, intuition, advice, experimentation, and computer forecasts.

In the scientific world, many decisions are based on experimentation. When experimentation is not too costly, it is worth following. Even on a small scale, experimentation is almost always justified by good results. Moving machinery around in a factory to change the work flow, or changing the location of desks in a department to see if production rises or falls, are examples of small-scale experimentation, which can sometimes yield surprising results. Using a paper-and-pencil or computer simulation of the changes is also desirable and would be less costly.

When experimentation is not possible, the decision maker must select an alternative based on the most objective forecasting possible. The premise of strategic analysis, for example, is that decisions are different because the initial objectives, assumptions, and expectations are different.

IMPLEMENT THE SOLUTION

Good solutions must be backed up by good plans. Workable plans have four features in common: *unity, continuity, flexibility,* and *precision.* A plan may be divided into several parts, but those parts should be linked. The action of the plan should be continuous. Starting and stopping a new plan in the middle of the testing period can be disastrous for morale, but the plan should be flexible enough to bend to new pressures when necessary. When a plan has been accepted, it must be put into action carefully and monitored closely to ensure that it works.

General Foods Corporation provided a good example of planning for implementation when it decided to close down four plants in four states and combine operations in one new, larger plant in yet another state. About 1,800 employees were notified of the move by letter a year before the move was scheduled to take place. A few months later, a policy statement on transfer and termination was circulated to all employees, indicating the company's intention to transfer those employees who wished to move. Transferring employees were given job preferences over newly hired people. General Foods assisted those who did not wish to transfer in finding other employment. Such a carefully implemented, long-term approach not only eliminated many last-minute problems but kept employee motivation and morale high.

ONGOING EVALUATION

All the ramifications of a chosen solution cannot be seen readily until the plan is put into action. Even as the solution is being tried, you and your subordinates will see ways in which to improve the implementation plan. Ongoing evaluation is a necessity when developing a plan, and the key concept in this stage is feedback. You will need to solicit feedback openly from employees working on the project, from your peers, and from your superior.

PERT.
A system that is frequently used in monitoring and acquiring feedback is PERT. The **program evaluation review technique** evaluates a project at each step along the line in terms of new input and how it may affect the final result. The cost of the program up to that step is determined both financially and in terms of human adjustment.

PERT or a similar program, CPM (critical path method), is particularly well adapted to control of major one-time projects. The **critical path** is the sequence

FIGURE 14–4 A Simplified PERT Network Used to Introduce a New Product.

FIGURE 14–4 A Simplified PERT Network Used to Introduce a New Product.

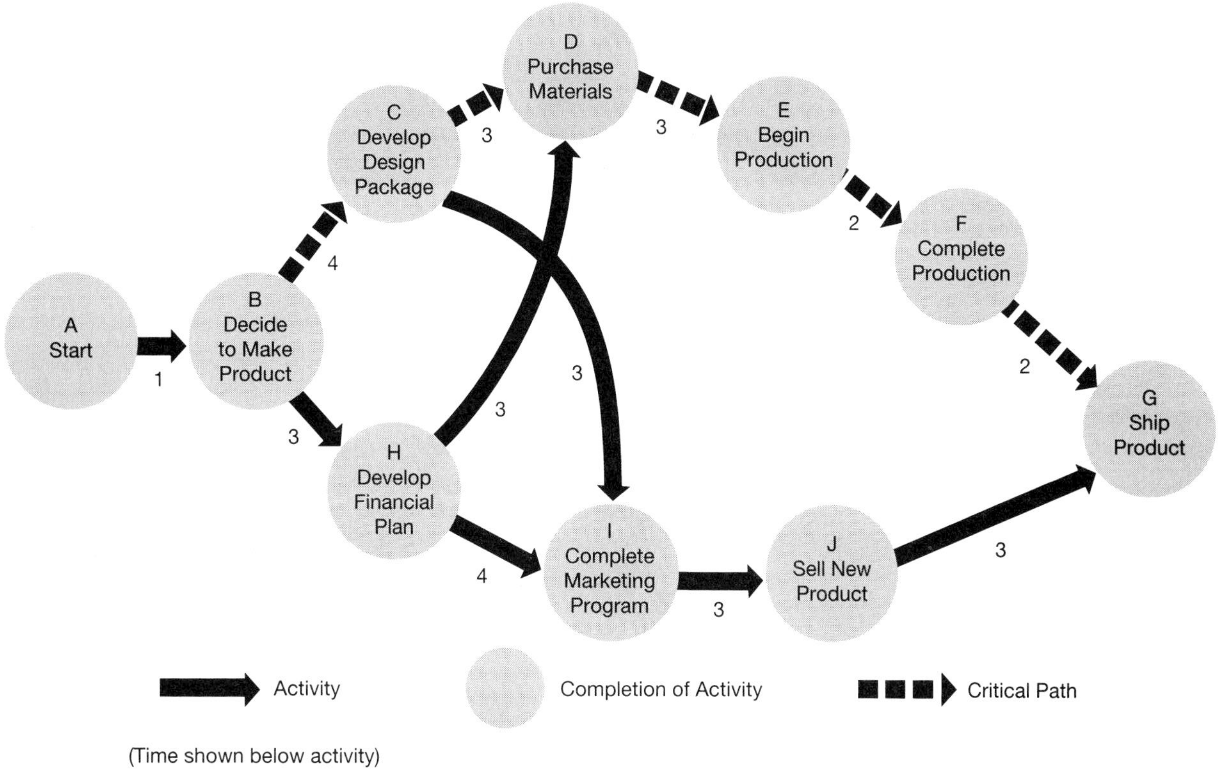

of in-series activities requiring the longest time for completion. The well-planned program shows how important timing is and that schedules must be constantly revised. Figure 14–4 shows how several departments are involved in a simplified PERT network to introduce a new product. The quality of a decision is influenced as much by the total process and acceptability of the decision as it is by quantitative measures.

NEED FOR CHANGE

A good decision maker must always be ready to consider new information and change a plan to satisfy new needs. If the solution is a good one, reevaluations and modifications will be concerned with details and will not affect the intention and general nature of the solution. How many times have you made a decision to go to the library to read a reserve book, only to find when you arrived that the book you wanted would be out for another two hours? You may have had to change certain details of your day so that you could return in two hours to read the book, but the essential plan remains unchanged.

The best solution, and the most careful planning for implementing, will not ensure against later flaws that almost always arise. When a particular solution is put into action, unthought-of difficulties will occur. As much time can be spent refining a decision as was spent analyzing the problem and collecting data. Whether it involves a professional goal or new methods of routing manufactured goods, a decision can have a long-lasting effect on us. The time spent on the refinement of the decision is often well worth it!

LONG- AND SHORT-RANGE DECISIONS

Short-range decisions involve little risk.

Long-range decisions involve more risk.

Short-range decisions are usually routine decisions that involve little risk or uncertainty. Many industries and business organizations try to create work environments in which as many decision-making functions as possible are standardized for greater production efficiency. The assembly line is the classic example of decisions made into a set of routine behaviors involving risks. In a short-range decision, the outcome can be seen readily, if not immediately. A long-range decision involves predicting and planning for the future. Whenever you plan for the future, you automatically encounter a certain amount of risk and uncertainty (see Figure 14–5).

Peter Drucker says that it's easier to define long-range decision making by what it is *not* than by what it is. First, it is not forecasting. People neither predict nor control the future. Long-range decisions do not deal with future decisions but, rather, with the probable results of present decisions. The long-range planner does not ask "What should we do tomorrow?" but instead asks "What do we do today to be ready for an uncertain tomorrow?" Organizations engaged in training programs for minorities and for women are preparing for the desirable working relationships of tomorrow.

FIGURE 14–5 Risk and Uncertainty in Decision Making Increase over Time.

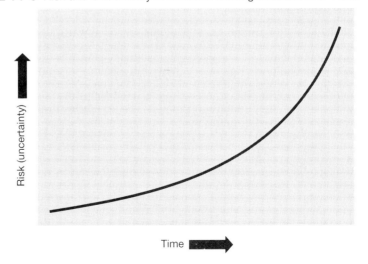

TRAITS THAT INFLUENCE DECISIONS

Decisions may be helped or hindered by the basic philosophies that decision makers have about life and how they interrelate with the people around them. Other traits affecting decision making include the following:

- Intelligence of management and other employees
- Level of personal commitment
- Tradition
- External environment
- Requirements of task at hand
- Power structure involved
- Openness of communication channels

People react to problems in many different ways; the solutions chosen reflect some of the assumptions that the person makes. Some of the personality traits that are particularly influential in the decision-making process are discussed next.

TAKING RISKS

There is no such thing as a riskless decision, but the degrees to risk vary. Many decision makers have an aversion to risk taking. Most people, when offered a 50:50 chance that a gamble will succeed, would choose not to gamble, even if winning would bring in many times what the risk is worth. Most people do not want to jeopardize the gains they have made in the past.

To risk all funds on a 50 percent gamble is poor decision making.

A graphic way in which to illustrate the degree of risk would be to offer a decision maker a high payoff on an even-chance gamble. A majority would turn down such a proposition even if the payoff were ten times as high as the sum at risk. If the sum at risk involved all or most of the corporate resources, this attitude would be entirely rational. Mature corporations are not in business to gamble their corporate existences on a 50 percent chance of high returns.

To risk a small fraction of total funds on 50 percent gambles for big returns is worthwhile.

Most decisions, however, involve only a small fraction of total corporate resources, and the opportunities for decisions to be made occur dozens of times every year. Taking several 50 percent chances every month to risk a small percentage of total resources for a tenfold return would appear to be very good business practice indeed and should pay off handsomely in the long run. Nevertheless, each decision maker tends to behave as though his or her own fate or that of the company is at stake with each decision.

DECISIVENESS

The failure to make decisions and to act is responsible for many of our national productivity problems, in both the private and public sectors. Some people are indecisive because they don't think they have adequate information. But we will never have enough information for most major decisions. Others just don't like to take the responsibility; the moment they see a problem, they become hopelessly confused.

To make a decision might be the first step to failure, so decisions may be delayed. Until a decision is made, judgments on individuals are often deferred. As a result of the lack of decisions, little growth or experience can be obtained concerning success or failure.

PERSONAL BIASES AND EXPERIENCE

Systems of reason are influenced by habits, reflexes, prejudices, appetites, and emotions. All logic is biased by personal feelings and affinities. Sometimes these feelings are appropriate to the situation; sometimes they are not. When making decisions, it helps to know your personal biases.

Knowledge gained by experience is a helpful guide to decision making. The greater the number of successful decisions, the greater the confidence one has when making decisions. On the other hand, it is dangerous to follow experience blindly. It is too easy for the person with "many years of experience" to fail to listen to innovative ideas from others.

Biases inhibit decision making.

Personal biases insulate the individual from anything new. For experience to be useful, a person must be flexible enough to see that it is just one of the many ingredients that goes into the decision-making process.

INTUITION

Intuition and hunches also help to determine decisions. **Intuition** is a way of knowing and recognizing the possible consequences of something without conscious reasoning. It is largely experiential; intuition and hunches are based on information or experience recorded in the subconscious.

Intuition is largely experiential.

Intuition can often provide the essential direction for solving a problem in a certain way, with the justification coming later. Decisions based on intuition gain much more credibility when they are also supported by logic and experience. Unfortunately, it is often difficult to tell the difference between intuition and bias.

Weston Agor encourages unlocking intuition and trusting instinct to help solve problems, make decisions, and increase productivity. Agor writes:

> There are a number of techniques that can be used to strengthen any manager's intuitive skills. A national survey of highly intuitive top managers indicates that these executives regularly use techniques—such as guided imagery, self-hypnosis, journal keeping and lateral styles of thinking—to strengthen their intuitive skills. [15]

Most executives will not admit to being clairvoyant, but they may see ways to solve business problems that defy computer logic. The bottom-line profit can be spectacular.

SITUATION

Your aunt, better known as "Mama Best," has made you a deal you cannot refuse. She has always wanted to spend a month's vacation in Italy, but her Italian sauce company has kept her too busy. She wants you to run the $150 million a year business. You will receive a million dollars for running the company for one month if you show good decision making during that time. "Mama" has given you only two guidelines to follow: first, "to risk all funds on a 50 percent gamble is poor decision making" and, second, "to risk a small fraction of total funds on a 50 percent gamble for big returns is worthwhile." Below are eleven questions for you to read and then decide on a yes or no response.

YES or NO   1. The spaghetti strainer breaks down, costing production $100,000 per day if something is not done immediately. You come up with some cheesecloth that can be used until the machine is fixed. Should you buy cheesecloth at $10,000 and continue production?

YES or NO   2. A salesman from Kerr jars comes to you and proposes that you switch from the Ball jars you now use. For an initial sum of $10,000 to start up the production line, he promises in writing to beat Ball's prices by $100,000 per month. Should you risk it?

YES or NO   3. A new machine for slicing pasta is now on the market and is available at a cost of $10,000. Your production supervisor tells you it could speed production and save $100,000 per month over the hand slicing process now used. Should you buy it?

YES or NO   4. Your production manager quits and you need a replacement immediately. Upon consulting personnel they find the best candidate in the business, but he will not work for less than $10,000 over the old manager's salary. His past performances have increased production at your competitor's 20 to 30 percent in a month. Do you make him an offer?

YES or NO   5. Beatrice wants to buy the entire company for $150,000,000. Do you sell the company?

YES or NO   6. Your supplier for tomato sauce is completely out of stock. Consulting with the purchasing department you find tomato paste can be obtained but must be mixed with water to obtain the right consistency. A mixer will cost $10,000, but each day production is down it will cost the company $100,000. Should you get the mixer and tomato paste?

YES or NO   7.   Advertising tells you that changing the colors and format of old labels could boost sales $100,000 per month, while the label change would cost $10,000. Should you change the label?

YES or NO   8.   Your Uncle Jeno is a line supervisor. His work record shows he consistently costs the company $100,000 per month more than any other supervisor. At age 63 he could retire early with nearly full benefits. Personnel suggests using a $10,000 early retirement inducement to get him to retire. Should you do it?

YES or NO   9.   Your premier sauce sales are down and marketing wants to use coupons to try and boost sales. Coupon cost and distribution will cost $10,000, but could boost sales $100,000 the first month. Should you go with the coupons?

YES or NO   10.   The spice company who supplies your company with all its spices wants to sell out to you for $100,000,000. Should you buy it?

YES or NO   11.   Sales is ready to market your new sauce. Safeway, one of the nation's largest grocery chains, will sell it for you with their best shelf space for a $10,000 initial fee. Other sauces have been shown to produce $100,000 per month income when introduced. Should you pay the fee?

RESULTS

When you are done, take out a coin and flip on all YES responses (heads = YES, tails = NO). After you have made your YES or NO decision there is still a 50:50 chance (in this exercise) of being "right" or "wrong." To figure your score, multiply $100,000 by the YES responses you flipped for, and $10,000 by the NO responses. Subtract the NO total from the YES total. If you have $300,000 or more, you get the $1,000,000 from Mama Best.

EXAMPLE

If nine questions were answered YES, then flip a coin for the final tabulation of YES responses. If 5 YES and 4 NO:

$$\begin{array}{ccc}
\$100,000 & & \$10,000 \\
\times \quad 5 & & \times \quad 4 \\
\hline
\$500,000 & - & \underline{\$40,000} = \$460,000
\end{array}$$

$460,000 > $300,000, so YOU win $1,000,000!!!

WHO MAKES THE DECISIONS?

The connection between individual decisions and organizational policy isn't always simple. A person who tries to shape an organization entirely to his or her way of thinking can expect to meet resistance. A strongly motivated person will form factions and cliques to work for the desired change. Those opposed will also band together. Adopting a policy is by no means the same thing as putting it into effect.

KEY PEOPLE IN DECISION MAKING

The people between the innovators and the major policy decision makers are often the key link in bringing about effective results. Key people share the following characteristics:

1. They derive a greater feeling of accomplishment from helping people to grow and develop than do nonkey personnel.
2. They enjoy working with others. They communicate more often with more people, in their own labs and outside their own units.
3. They place less importance on working with congenial workers and more emphasis on working with competent workers.
4. They enjoy a greater feeling of accomplishment from doing creative work than from exceeding expected standards of job performance. Practical problems and top management are the main sources of stimulation.
5. They use an environmental more than a humanistic approach, preferring to work with others on technical rather than social grounds.
6. They score no better and no worse than their colleagues on a test of creative ability, but they have more formal education.

Key people in decision making can be predicted with reasonable accuracy. They are apt to be concerned with the broad features of problems and with the innovative aspects of their work. Key people prefer to interact with other workers, but on a professional rather than on a social basis. Their performance record is usually good, and they probably have been influential in shaping their job goals.

INDIVIDUAL DECISIONS

The owner-manager may have difficulty delegating decision-making power to subordinates because of a belief that power and prestige are lost when authority is delegated. However, in actuality, more work can be gained by delegation and more experience can be learned by the subordinate. The supervisor who believes in more independent delegation spends less time checking up on the employees and thus has more time for more important work. Ideally, the employees get a chance to develop themselves by correcting their own errors. A climate of confidence results when the employees are allowed to check up on themselves, without the boss looking over their shoulders.

DECISIONS BY A POWERFUL FEW

Oligarchic decisions are made by a powerful few.

In decisions made by the few, or in oligarchic decision making, major decisions are made by a small group, usually at least three but no more than seven. In addition to participating in joint decisions, each person usually has an area in which he or she has the final say, such as in sales or production matters.

Oligarchic control can create delay, or even bring action to a standstill, if there is a deadlock and no one has the final power to decide. In one large corporation, three executives with equal power were deadlocked over several important labor matters. The production specialist wanted to settle with the union to keep the plant operating. The other two opposed agreement for various reasons. The deadlock was broken only when a competing firm signed with the union, thus forcing the two executives who opposed settlement to capitulate. Since that time the corporation has been moving steadily toward one-person control.

DECISIONS BY GROUPS

Decisions made by many people have been called *integrative* or *participative* decisions. These terms are preferable to democratic decision making because "democratic" implies an equality that usually does not exist—certainly not for income, or status, and usually not for the power to influence major decisions. Participatory action normally takes the form of informal consultation among top management and sometimes their subordinates.

Many firms use consultative decision making to bring those employees with technical backgrounds and know-how to the conference table. The technical staff is more likely to participate in making decisions when specific skills are involved than in those areas requiring long-range planning.

Few decisions have total group consensus.

Group decision making can be an exceedingly complex affair, but two facts hold true. First, majority decisions usually represent something less than total group commitment. Few groups operate with total group consensus. Second, the more abstract the matter being considered, the greater the chances of agreement. Put another way, the more concrete the matter, the less the chances for full agreement.

Group problem solving usually results in a synergistic relationship where $2 + 2 = 5$. **Synergy** means that the total outcome is greater than the sum of the individual parts. If too many parts are involved, the result may be $3 + 4 + 5 + 6 = 16$ instead of 18. Nevertheless, making decisions in groups can have the advantages previously noted. There are at least five group decision-making procedures: the ordinary group procedure, brainstorming, the statistical method, the Delphi technique, and the nominal group technique. Each is directed toward discovering the best solution for the problem. Each has particular advantages and disadvantages.

Ordinary group procedure.

The *ordinary group procedure* entails calling a group together, presenting the problem, and asking for comments. The meeting is open ended, with the discussion being free flowing and having few controls. The chairperson controls the speakers so that everyone does not talk at once. Finally, the consensus is stated by the leader once one is reached.

Brainstorming.

Brainstorming is a technique described earlier in this chapter. It deals with the development of many alternatives to problems and not the evaluation or selection of one of the ideas. The freewheeling, receptive atmosphere of a brainstorming session often produces workable solutions.

Statistical method.

The *statistical method* uses the ideas of a group of individuals, but does not ask these people to interact with one another in a group setting. The method is limited to quantitative problems. Simply, several people make individual estimates of the best answers to a problem. The estimates are collected, and one of a variety of aggregation procedures is used to determine the final solution.

The **Delphi technique,** dating back to the Greek oracles, extends the statistical method to include feedback and reestimates. The group does not need to meet face to face. In the Delphi procedure, the chairperson acts as the administrator of an estimate–feedback chain. The first of several questionnaires is constructed to state the problem as clearly as possible and is sent to the Delphi panel. Because the group never meets, there is no easy way to clear up any misunderstandings; thus, the problem statement must be particularly clear. Potential solutions are returned to the chairperson, who summarizes the solutions suggested and feeds them back to the panel via a second questionnaire. Preferences are again solicited in a third questionnaire–feedback report. By such a process, the supposed best solution is decided on by the panel of experts, without any one individual dominating the group. But many are not satisfied by a process without face-to-face interaction.[16]

The **nominal group technique** (NGT) is a fairly structured decision process with the interpersonal characteristics of face-to-face groups. After the problem is stated clearly, group members sit together but individually generate as many alternatives as they can. After about fifteen minutes, ideas are presented in round-robin fashion. Each individual presents a single idea, taking turns, until all the group's ideas have been presented. The leader records them in full view at the front of the room. As in group brainstorming, individuals are encouraged to piggyback or hitchhike on others' ideas.

A voting or rating process is used to reach a group decision. Each group member might vote for the five alternatives that he or she feels are best, rank ordering them from 1 to 5. Alternatively, each of the ideas can be rated on a ten-point scale, from good (1) to bad (10). Votes or ratings are done on private ballots. The chairperson tabulates the votes and announces them to the group. In most cases, the first ballot identifies a small set of possible solutions. If the vote should reveal a clear-cut winner, the group is finished. Also, this procedure provides backup alternatives should the initially chosen solution fail to produce a desired outcome. A comparison of various decision-making methods is given in Table 14–3.

TABLE 14–3 The Various Methods of Evaluating the Decision-Making Process

CRITERIA	ORDINARY	BRAINSTORMING	STATISTICAL	DELPHI	NGT
Number of ideas	Low	Moderate	NA	High	High
Quality of ideas	Low	Moderate	NA	High	High
Time and money costs	Moderate	Low	Low	High	Low
Task orientation	Low	High	High	High	High
Potential for interpersonal conflict	High	Low	Low	Low	Moderate
Feelings of accomplishment	High to low	High	Low	Moderate	High
Commitment to solution	High	NA	Low	Low	Moderate

NA—Not applicable.

MAKING DECISIONS DURING CONFLICT AND CRISES

When more than one person is involved in making a decision, it is often a challenge to arrive at a solution with a minimum of conflict. For example, suppose that the sales personnel of a cosmetics firm insist on a particular kind of packaging for a new product because of its eye-catching appeal. The production department, however, is firmly opposed to it on the grounds of expense and difficulty to manufacture. Both groups are right, at least within their respective areas of concern. This is the kind of situation that calls for alternatives to be developed and evaluated. Solutions to this kind of conflict are usually plentiful as soon as the parties involved agree to explore alternative choices together.

POLARIZATIONS

Polarization is strong opposing views.

Polarization is the establishment of two opposing views, with both parties unwilling to change their opinion. Decisions often involve disagreements, which sometimes can be resolved through discussing and understanding the different points of view. But deep-seated conflicts are not easily resolved. When terms such as "confrontation" and "nonnegotiable" are used in describing a situation, the resistance to argument may be so firm that effective decision making seems impossible.

Nonexistence.

One typical pattern in polarized conflict is called *nonexistence*. This occurs when one side refuses to listen to the arguments of the other side. Nonrecognition is often a ploy to force the antagonist to quiet down or to go away. You may recognize this tactic in such circumstances as the "freeze out" in a lovers' quarrel or the temporary banishment of a "difficult" child from the family.

The universal plot.

Universal plot theories can be used to explain just about anything. "It's a subversive plot" is a famous example of a conspiracy theory that can gain immediate support in some circles. It is a very human response to treat behavior we dislike as the work of our adversaries. By this tactic, the leaders of one group make the problem part of a larger, more sinister plot.

Win–lose approach.

The *win–lose approach* to conflicts implies a "go-for-broke" attitude where something is at stake. It assumes that a person's contributions to group effort will result in a *personal gain* or *loss* in esteem, prestige, or responsibility. It also discourages the possibility of free expression and change of ideas. Consciously or unconsciously, people will feel that they personally are being tested, not their ideas.

The idea of winning or losing is so ingrained in the American character that some management personnel accept it as a natural part of the human condition. This assumption rules out the easy use of such methods as group brainstorming and group decision making. Some advocates of competitive games such as win–lose maintain that without such games, employees may become more content but that they also become less productive and the quality of their work suffers.

Real Communication Leads to a Resolution

What can be done when two or more sides are polarized? How can a decision be reached that will prove effective and advantageous to all parties? As long as the hostile attitudes that frequently accompany conflict exist, it is difficult to arrive at a meaningful decision. Without real listening and a real desire to understand the other side's point of view, conflict cannot be resolved.

Bring in a mediator.

Two methods can help to promote a settlement. One is to bring in a neutral outsider. A mediator can often talk to both sides from a conciliatory point of view—one that is not emotionally charged. Emotions add fuel to a fire; calm facts extinguish the flames.

In another method, the bargainer empathizes by placing himself or herself in the shoes of the adversary so that the final outcome does not disgrace the bargainer or the opponent publicly. Humiliating the opponent may only give a temporary victory. To allow the opponent to "save face" may be in the best interest of the company, the union, or the nation.

Help your adversary "save face."

There is, of course, no simple solution to confrontation. Nevertheless, it is possible, through listening and through attending to the other communication techniques described in earlier chapters, to create an atmosphere in which, despite ongoing disagreement over details, the total process of decision making can continue. When this happens, solutions often emerge that neither side has envisioned.

Decision Making during Crises

Decision making during crises requires accelerated attention to all the foregoing factors. A **crisis** is a major, unpredictable event that has potentially negative results. The event and its aftermath may significantly damage an organization and its employees, products, services, financial condition, and reputation. There is a relationship between strategy and crisis. Crises are usually a surprise, threaten long-term values, and require decisions to be made in a short amount of time.[17]

Preparation and practice for decision making increase the quality of those quick decisions. To avert or handle crises well, strategy must be long term enough to anticipate a crisis and to manage its aftermath.

One crisis management expert says: "We expect problems—they are truly inevitable in the life of any person or organization. Some crises also share this characteristic—we know, for instance, that earthquakes and hurricanes occur and that these events are caused by natural forces that are largely out of our control."[18] That is what creative decision making is all about: being prepared to make decisions under uncertain conditions by having problems anticipated and defined correctly; having facts and alternatives available and taking a stand by making and evaluating a decision.

Creative decision making is anticipating inevitable problems.

Summary

The creative act combines old elements in new ways. Current concepts are the building blocks for new ideas. All people are born with the ability to create. This ability does not disappear with adulthood, but it takes many different forms.

Although timeliness, usefulness, and originality are not always applicable criteria for recognizing a creative idea, they are frequently reliable indications.

While creative people are necessary to successful organizations, creative behavior can definitely conflict with the smooth running of a business. The ambiguous feelings that many managers have toward creative people can be stated as the reasonable desire for a balance between creativity and practicality.

The creative person is valuable to employers because it is through creativity that companies develop new products. Products may be tangible or they may be ideas. An employee may not want status or more money as a result of a creative idea, as much as he or she wants recognition for it. The most direct rewards are acknowledgment of the creative act itself and encouragement for further creativity.

The creative process is still a mysterious one. Four stages have been recognized: perception, incubation, inspiration, and verification. The rewards for creativity and innovation include psychological fulfillment and social recognition. Creativity is an integral part of decision making, primarily in the selection of alternatives.

Long-range decisions require planning for contingencies, which automatically means that risk is involved. The future can only be predicted, whereas decisions are always based in the present. Decisions are often made as insurance against future events.

After problem definition, there are six ACTION steps to decision making: analyzing the problem; considering alternative solutions; taking action—selecting a solution; implementing it; making an ongoing evaluation of the solution as it is being implemented; and making necessary changes.

Decisions affecting groups are made by one person, by a few, or by many; and each method has its own rewards and drawbacks. Regardless of who has the final word, key people are always involved. Key people are go-betweens—they help to get an idea proposed by one party to be decided on by another.

Conflict situations have certain characteristics that indicate degrees of polarization. The only way in which to solve a polarized issue is through careful communication. Most of us like hard, positive choices. A choice between negative alternatives is really no choice at all. Too many choices can overwhelm us. When, as employees, we have an opportunity to participate in a decision, we are more likely to accept it.

Decision making during crises requires special attention and preparation. There is limited time for decision making, and practicing the process helps enhance creative decisions.

Figure 14–6 shows the solution to the creativity problem of Figure 14–1. In learning to be more creative, we learn to question the rules or facts implied or stated when attempting to solve a problem.

CASE STUDY 14–1

ACHIEVEMENT—ACCOMPLISHED BY INDIVIDUAL CREATIVITY OR BY "GROUPTHINK" TEAM EFFORT

In the United States today, individual achievement is highly valued. In our business setting, success or failure depends largely on individual capability, and the road toward success is an individual effort. This is pretty much the way it was for the first 200 years of our country's existence.

According to a poll of top corporate executives across the country, however, this characteristically American ideology is being replaced by an empha-

FIGURE 14–6 Solution to Creativity Exercise of Figure 14–1.

Step 1

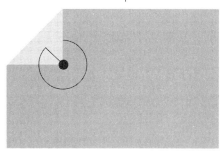

a. Fold corner of paper over.
b. Start dot at corner, making sure that part of dot is on both sides of paper.
c. Without lifting pencil, draw radius on back of paper to circumference of circle.
d. Start circle.

Step 2

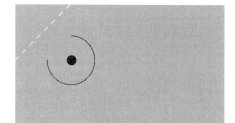

e. Unfold.

Step 3

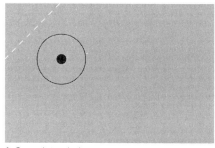

f. Complete circle.

sis on group achievement. Our ideology of the future will stress the use of teamwork in achieving goals. An effective team will be a group of people who work together noncompetitively to complete certain tasks.

The members of the team will support one another, be receptive to new ideas coming from both within and outside the team, and be able to communicate well. Individuals within the team will be recognized for individual efforts and achievements, but success will be credited to the group as a whole. When considering the creative individual, which ideology—our ideology of today or our ideology of the future—will best aid creative potential?

CASE STUDY 14–2

WHO MAKES THE DECISIONS IN THE BUSINESS?

Joe Sanchez and his partner, Wiley Othero, own a print shop that caters to customers in a regional shopping center. They employ two part-time press operators besides themselves. Joe's girlfriend handles the front desk and office bookkeeping. Joe wants to expand the business to do resumés, term reports, and other projects for a local college—its students, faculty, and staff.

1. Should they expand, or not?
2. What are important factors to consider in making this decision? (*Hints:* Remember that decision making is a process including identifying what you don't know as well as what you know.)
3. Can brainstorming help identify alternatives?

4. What are the pros and cons of each alternative? (*Additional hint:* Notice that there are more questions than there are facts—a frequent occurrence in decision making, and a good clue to effective decision making. Don't let yourself make decisions strictly on the basis of emotions and limited facts.)

CASE STUDY 14–3

MISSING COMPANY PROPERTY

One of the most difficult problems that a personnel department can face is how to track down company property that it suspects was "lifted" by light-fingered employees. No matter how careful management might be in searching for the culprits, its activities are likely to step on someone's toes.

Applied Computers was missing several things, from office supplies to small special hand tools. The office manager, Barbara Miller, was convinced that the pilferage was done by company employees. "Our clients don't have access to our supplies, but many of our employees do. One problem may be our checkout system in our warehouse and toolroom," said Miller one day.

Finally she was convinced that she should take a bold tack. She asked a representative of the local union, a shop steward, to meet her near the employees' locker room to discuss the pilferage problem and possibly open the employees' lockers. You have overheard the conversation. As the company's personnel director you are torn between telling Miller, your superior, something about her possible action, and reporting to her superior, Jim Sanford, the vice president of the firm. You know that there is nothing in the company policies about such action.

1. What will you do? If you talk to Barbara Miller, what will you say? If you talk to Jim Sanford, what will you recommend?
2. Does the employer have the right to invade its employees' private lockers, where personal belongings are kept, without the employees' permission?
3. If the company takes items from the lockers that belong to the company, is this an unwarranted invasion of privacy and an illegal search and seizure?
4. If the company had requested permission of the employees, then would the company still have the same opportunity to find the missing property?

DISCUSSION AND STUDY QUESTIONS—TO KEEP YOU THINKING . . . _____

1. Discuss the relationship of creativity to the following human factors: intelligence, education, age, and behavior.
2. Show the contrast between the custodial person and the creative person by listing different traits for each.
3. What is the role of intuition in making decisions?
4. Describe the differences between short-term and long-range decisions.
5. What are the pros and cons of group versus individual creativity and decision making?
6. What are entrepreneurial characteristics?
7. How is decision making during crises different from routine decision making?

NOTES

1. Byron R. Wien,"Japan's Nada High School: We've Nothing Like It," *The Wall Street Journal*, January 8, 1990, p. A10.

2. James M. Higgins, "Achieving the Core Competence—It's as Easy as 1, 2, 3,. . ., 47, 48, 49," *Business Horizons*, March–April 1996, pp. 27–32.

3. Ibid., pp. 29–31.

4. Tom Peters, *Thriving on Chaos: Handbook for a Management Revolution* (New York: Alfred A. Knopf, 1988), p. 252.

5. Rosabeth Moss Kanter, "Swimming in Newstreams: Mastering Innovation Dilemmas," *California Management Review*, Summer 1989, pp. 45–69.

6. Alex F. Osborn, *Applied Imagination* (New York: Scribner, 1963), p. 18.

7. Ibid.

8. Ibid., p. 22.

9. Michael McTague, "Tapping Creative Potential," *Training and Development Journal*, June 1989, pp. 36–41.

10. Martine Costello, "Five Mistakes Every Good Manager Should Make: How Screwing Up Can Make You a Star," *Working Woman*, May 1996, pp. 60–62.

11. Joe McGowan, "How Disney Keeps Ideas Coming," *Fortune*, April 1, 1996, p. 13.

12. K. R. Blawatt, "Entrepreneurship in Estonia: Profiles of Entrepreneurs," *Journal of Small Business Management*, April 1995, pp. 74–79.

13. William R. Pape, "Zeroing in on Data: A Guide to Getting the Right Information in the Most Efficient Way," *Inc.*, Technology Special Issue No. 1, 1996, pp. 23–24.

14. Richard D. Lewis, "Where Time Moves in Mysterious Ways," *Management Today*, January 1996, pp. 77–78.

15. Weston Agor, "Use Intuitive Intelligence to Increase Productivity," *HR Focus*, September 1993, p. 9.

16. Philip L. Roth, Lydia L. F. Schleifer, and Fred S. Switzer, "Nominal Group Technique: An Aid in Implementing TQM," *The CPA Journal*, May 1995, p. 68–69.

17. Laurence Barton, *Crisis in Organizations: Managing and Communicating in the Heat of Chaos* (Cincinnati: South-Western Publishing, 1993), pp. 2, 50.

18. Ibid., p. 3.

RECOMMENDED READING

Agor, Weston. *Intuitive Management: Integrating Left and Right Brain Management Skills.* Englewood Cliffs, N.J.: Prentice Hall, 1984.

———. "Use Intuitive Intelligence to Increase Productivity." *HR Focus*, September 1993, p. 9.

Amabile, Teresa M., and Regina Conti. "What Downsizing Does to Creativity." *Issues & Observations*, published by Center for Creative Leadership, Greensboro, N.C., Third Quarter 1995, pp. 1–6.

Buonocore, Anthony J. "Older & Wiser: Mature Employees and Career Guidance." *Management Review*, September 1992, pp. 54–57.

Creative Education Foundation. *Creatively Yours: A Catalog of Creative Resources.* Buffalo, N.Y.: The Creative Education Foundation, 1994.

Drucker, Peter. *Innovation and Entrepreneurship: Practice and Principles.* New York: Harper & Row, 1985.

Epstein, Seymour. *You're Smarter than You Think: How to Develop Your Practical Intelligence for Successful Living.* New York: Simon & Schuster, 1993.

Kanter, Rosabeth Moss. *The Change Masters: Innovation for Productivity in the American Corporation.* New York: Simon & Schuster, 1983.

———. *When Giants Learn to Dance.* New York: Simon & Schuster, 1989.

Mastenbrock, William F. G. *Conflict Management and Organization Development.* New York: John Wiley, 1987.

Peters, Tom. *Thriving on Chaos: Handbook for a Management Revolution.* New York: Alfred A. Knopf, 1988.

Postrel, Virginia L. "Pure Creative Joy: The Importance of Creative Thinking." *Forbes*, April 8, 1996, p. 114.

Saltzman, Amy, and Edward C. Baig. "Plugging in to 'Creativity.'" *U.S. News & World Report*, October 29, 1990, pp. 95–97.

Sebastian, Pamela. "Be Creative: Now! Companies Try to Inspire Creativity in a Leaner Workplace." *The Wall Street Journal*, June 13, 1996, p. A1.

Tanouye, Elyse. "Why Smart Managers Make Bad Decisions and How to Avoid Them." *Working Woman*, August 1989, pp. 55–57, 96–97.

PART 5

ORGANIZATIONAL DYNAMICS AND CULTURE

WE CHANGE AND GET TO KNOW OUR ORGANIZATIONS, SOCIETIES, AND CULTURE

15

Managing Change through Teamwork

Look at these questions before reading the chapter. Perhaps you can use the questions to start a discussion after studying the chapter.

- Is your first reaction "No!" when you are asked to change a procedure you are used to doing a certain way?
- Do certain kinds of change frighten you or threaten you?
- When it is clear that change must take place, do you try to hinder it or help it? Do you have any ideas about how to implement change?
- Is it right to change a person's personality? a person's behavior? When would it be ethical?
- Can change be mandated effectively? Can it be managed?
- What makes change successful in some cases, but unsuccessful in others?
- What are some of the work environment changes facing us today?
- What are some diagnostic techniques for studying organizations and their people?

After studying this chapter, you should be able to:

1. Discuss psychological resistance to change from the point of view of
   a. Occupational identity
   b. Fear of the unknown
   c. Status considerations
2. Explain in your own words why the idea of homeostasis is necessary to understanding how change takes place in groups.
3. List and understand the four basic economic reasons for fearing change.
4. Discuss the advantages and disadvantages of change through mandate as opposed to change through participation.
5. Describe the theory of behavior modification and how it can help supervisors to be more effective.
6. Describe the keys to a successful change.
7. Explain the characteristics of organization development and how it is related to group dynamics.
8. Discuss how to develop teamwork and trust.
9. Define and apply the following terms and concepts (in order of first occurrence):

- change
- equilibrium
- force-field analysis
- occupational identity
- homeostasis
- driving forces
- restraining forces
- high tech/high touch
- behavior modification
- positive reinforcement
- negative reinforcement
- mandated change
- organization development (OD)
- OD intervention
- teamwork
- sociometry
- sociogram
- trust
- Murphy's laws

POSITIVE CHANGE REQUIRES INNOVATIVE DECISIONS

Once a decision has been rendered, it must then be implemented. Implementation requires changing individual attitudes, procedures, and skills. This chapter focuses on the changing of individuals' behavior and then on organizational development.

Things change. Economic systems, technology, and social systems all change. But, as the old saying goes, "The more things change, the more they stay the same." Just when we think we have a situation under control, the variables change.

> At certain points in history, when we think we have political structures figured out and systems locked in, new winds begin to blow, changing what we thought was fixed. Ideologies surge and swirl, people and nations break out of boxes, attitudes change, our projections of what will and will not be are soon proven wrong, or at least incomplete.[1]

Change may be defined as a function of effort over time to learn new methods. The CET (Change equals Effort over Time) model makes it easier to consider change in a useful way. The abstract model separates change into four phases: (1) the *excitement* phase, the pizzazz, the crashing cymbals; (2) the *hard work* phase where existing habits, patterns, and the culture itself have to be fought; (3) the *turning-point* phase where it is getting easier; and (4) *institutionalized* change where it takes no more effort to do things the new way than it did the old.[2]

It is important to note that phase 1 is usually overemphasized and that the effort in phase 2 is underestimated. To make the CET model work, realistic analyses and more effective communication of needed change are required. Most programs of innovation do not succeed because the process of change is not managed properly. Key risk factors when developing innovative systems include the following:

Most innovation does not succeed because the change process is improperly managed.

- Novelty of the product or service to be supported
- Novelty of the system technology
- Need for speed in development
- Potential for gradual phase-in of the new system
- Contingency cushions
- Degree of user/system staff interface
- Commitment of the development team to the project[3]

Whenever several of these factors are present simultaneously, chances of success in the development project are greatly diminished.

PATTERNS OF CHANGE

The cliché that our technological society is rapidly changing expresses a truth that affects everyone. In the past, the progress of technology was measured by millennia, or at least by centuries. Today's technology has already outstripped the imaginations of the science fiction writers of a generation ago. Steel plants mass produce steel plates with the kind of minute precision that only computers can achieve. Freight trains are dispatched and rail car inventories are handled by computer banks. Instant credit checks are run in less than twenty seconds. Our increasingly sophisticated communication systems give us video and cellular telephones to carry in our pockets.

But some new technologies have not achieved their much acclaimed promise in the workplace. In the face of rapid change, many managers are preoccupied with the technical issues and neglect the equally important human resources element. Individuals who want to help achieve connections between people and technology should keep in mind eight key points:

1. Technological change is inevitable.
2. Resistance to change is natural.
3. Change must make sense to everyone involved.
4. Organizational settings vary.
5. Change takes time.
6. Change results in role overload.
7. Change requires ongoing technical support.
8. All change involves learning.[4]

Managers must take into account the inevitability of change and recognize that commitment to innovation, the environment, and technology—something over which they have little choice—is a commitment to ongoing change. To make them successful, we need the symbiosis of people and technology.

Need for a commitment to ongoing change.

Technological change has always been equated with progress, and who is against progress? Yet, when we examine the dynamics of change, we find that, although nearly everyone says that he or she is in favor of change, actual behavior patterns reveal contradictory and ambivalent feelings concerning its value.

FIGURE 15–1 A General Model for Change.

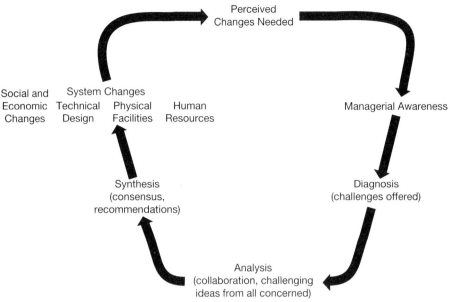

No matter how drastic our technological changes have been, are, or will be, social changes are even more dramatic. The power of information is great from a technological standpoint; it is even greater from a socioeconomic viewpoint. Peter Drucker notes that the social impacts of information may be greater than the technological impacts.[5]

Figure 15–1 describes a general model for change. The model begins with perceived changes needed, but is continuous and cyclical. Initiating changes in the work environment may cause the development of patterns of resistance. Hostility may be expressed openly or only implied. It may be directed against supervisors or against the work activities. The manner in which it is expressed depends on how much hostility can be expressed safely without endangering job security. It may take the form of sloppy efforts, slowdowns, lots of lip service, or a subtle combination of apathy and apple polishing, but no actual change in behavior.

WHEN TO EXPECT AND PREPARE FOR RESISTANCE

Expect resistance to vague or unclear changes.

We fear the unknown and the outcomes of change are unknown; so, in large part, we fear change. We all like to talk about the need for change, but there is tremendous resistance to doing it. If the elements of a proposed change are not made clear to the people who are going to be affected or influenced by it, resistance can be expected. People who dislike their jobs are particularly resistant to ambiguous or unclear orders to change. They want to know exactly what they have to do to minimize the unpleasant aspects of their jobs.

Various factors cause resistance to change: human nature, attitudes, anxiety, and insecurity, among many others. Human nature desires a change in status quo—whether humans are willing to effect or endure changes is another matter. Most people at all job levels in business and industry resist change for psychological, economic, and social reasons.

The amount of resistance can be related to the amount of participation that people have in the timing and direction of the innovation. Resistance will be least evident when workers *have the most to say about procedural matters and most evident when they have the least to say.* Much of the negative resistance can be avoided by preparation and involvement in "measured change," a term coined here for use in describing **equilibrium**—a balance between cautious resistance and blatant, constant change for the sake of change.

CHANGING THE INDIVIDUAL

A supervisor who seeks to change an individual in some way faces the fact that an individual may resist the change. When we want to change an individual, we are seeking to modify one or more of the forces that make the individual behave as he or she does. For a model of an individual, consider the one shown in Figure 15–2. To change this individual, we can add or subtract one or more of the forces affecting his or her behavior, thereby perhaps producing a fundamental change in the individual's behavior.

The more pressures are in harmony, the more predictable the outcome.

Naturally, pressure can evoke change, but the outcome cannot always be predicted. There are many forces on an individual, and the outcome of the various pressures can produce unexpected outbursts. Social adjustment to a new work environment can be difficult for those who belong to a tightly knit group. The process of breaking social ties with those at the old workstation and making new acquaintances can be threatening.

FIGURE 15–2 Various Influences on an Individual.

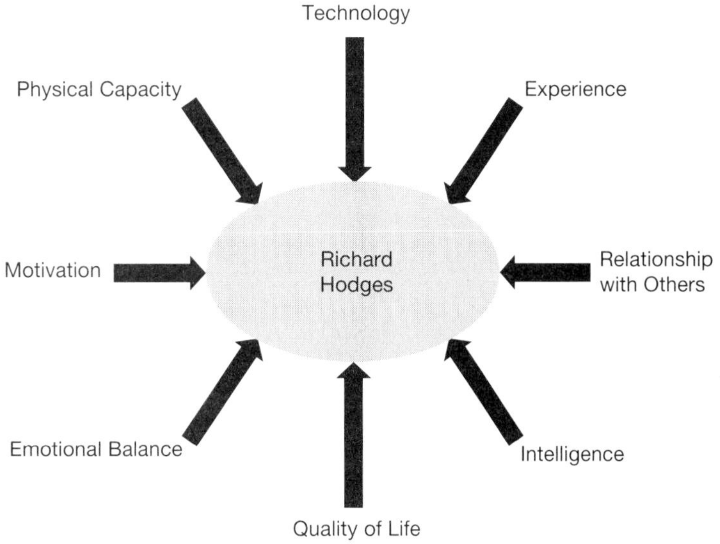

Technology

Physical Capacity

Experience

Motivation

Richard Hodges

Relationship with Others

Emotional Balance

Intelligence

Quality of Life

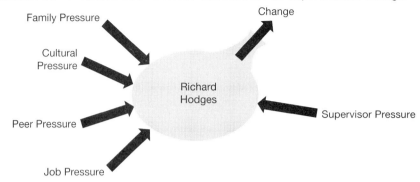

FIGURE 15–3 Various Counterforces Can Produce an Unpredictable Change.

Family Pressure

Change

Cultural Pressure

Richard Hodges

Supervisor Pressure

Peer Pressure

Job Pressure

Conflict between individual goals and group loyalties produce unpredictable results.

Studies have also shown that resistance to change often results from a conflict of individual and group loyalties (Figure 15–3). An individual may want to "please the boss," yet be restrained by group pressure to protect the slower members of the group who would be hurt most by a change. Group pressure may force a person to resist change even if that person believes in the innovation, because group acceptance is more important.

For every force of change there is a counterpressure. As shown by Figure 15–4 the group may exert pressure from above against the desires of the individual below. For example, an employee who would like to make a bonus by producing more parts may be dissuaded from doing so by the other workers:

> Hey, Charlie, we don't want a "rate-buster" in our shop. Sure, we can all produce more parts than is required, but why bust our butts? If we all did that, the guys in the head office would raise the standard and then where would we be? No bonuses, and we would have to produce more. Now, be a nice guy, Charlie, don't make waves. If you come in late, we will cover for you, so relax. Don't be an "eager beaver."

One of the important tools illustrated in Figure 15–4 is **force-field analysis,** a technique that assesses current state (the horizontal line), and the positive and

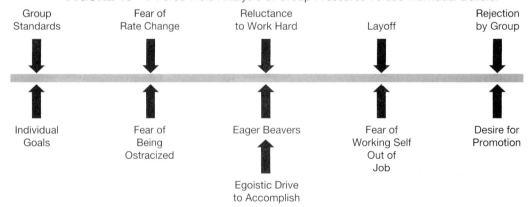

FIGURE 15–4 Force-Field Analysis of Group Pressures Versus Individual Beliefs.

Group Standards	Fear of Rate Change	Reluctance to Work Hard	Layoff	Rejection by Group
Individual Goals	Fear of Being Ostracized	Eager Beavers	Fear of Working Self Out of Job	Desire for Promotion

Egoistic Drive to Accomplish

negative forces working to change that equilibrium. The level of production can be raised either by increasing the forces below the line or by reducing the forces above the line. The greater the opportunity for a promotion for Charlie, the more likely he will become a "rate-buster." Likewise, the greater the turnover within the department, the less likely that group pressure will influence Charlie's production.

PSYCHOLOGICAL RESISTANCE

OCCUPATIONAL IDENTITY AND STATUS

The stronger the occupational identity, the greater the security.

Any change that affects an individual always involves some loss of security but also some degree of challenge and adventure. Change, by its very nature, forces confrontation with uncertainty. Familiar, predictable routines produce a sense of security that is psychologically both necessary and satisfying. When there is a strong sense of occupational identity, there is also a strong sense of psychological security. **Occupational identity** is the identity that one has by virtue of her or his job. The longer an occupation has been in society, the greater the likelihood of tradition and resistance to change.

Consider the case of skilled factory workers who have had to relearn their jobs using automated machinery. Work that used to require skilled hand, eye, and brain coordination is now done by automated methods. Unless those workers have learned new skills, their sense of occupational identity has probably been damaged severely.

Changes in nurses' occupational status provide another example. For years, registered nurses (RNs) and licensed practical nurses (LPNs) have co-existed and provided basic nursing care services. Registered nurses have been able to attain their status via three educational channels: a hospital school diploma (usually three years), an associate arts degree (usually two years), or a baccalaureate degree (usually four years). Considerable educational and status struggles have taken place within the RNs' ranks, in addition to the struggle surrounding the status differentials with LPNs. The resistance to job responsibility changes associated with the various levels of LPNs and RNs has been detrimental to the general advancement of nursing and health care provision.

When stable patterns are disturbed, the feelings of pressure and dissatisfaction that result may take the form of direct opposition or subtle resistance to change. Another psychological factor leading to resistance to change is the feeling many people have, often justified, that change threatens their status within the organization. Status always involves comparison, and major organizational changes usually bring in their wake the unintended side effect of lowering and raising the status of one or more individuals or work units. Naturally, the people who will be downgraded resist any such organizational change.

FEAR OF UNKNOWN FUTURE

Factory and even white-collar workers have no monopoly on resistance based on feelings of insecurity. Members of management and other professions are especially notorious for wanting a change—and then retrenching or retreating from their positions when implementation of the changes is imminent. Congress has passed laws, only to repeal them a year later when they found out the true impact of the legislation.

Individually or corporately, we set such unattainable standards for ourselves that worthwhile goals of change are never achieved. We may "talk a good game" in championing a new product, but the criteria for successful innovation are so high that it is impossible to meet them.

The NIH syndrome.

The difficulty of getting an idea through some systems suggests the NIH (Not-Invented-Here) syndrome: "If it's not my idea, it's probably no good." The insecurity demonstrated here is not as simple a matter as occupational identity, encompassing as it does complex financial, production, and sales aspects of the business. There can be no doubt, however, that fear of an uncertain future and possible failure play a large role in establishing rigid, impossible-to-meet criteria for change. The fear of the unknown is as potent a force in business as in any other realm of life.

Fear of the unknown is potent.

Change can be facilitated by recognizing and coping with these common barriers to change: (1) the surprise element, (2) fear of obsolescence, (3) inertia, (4) insecurity, and (5) personality conflicts. Knowing barriers exist and modifying their impact can lessen resistance and facilitate change.[6]

ECONOMIC RESISTANCE

Economic reasons for resistance to change are much easier to isolate than are psychological ones. How many blacksmiths are there in your community? Any steam locomotive engineers, stone cutters, or whale-bone corset manufacturers? In the past century, perhaps as many time-honored occupations have disappeared from the economic sector as new ones have been born.

Economic reasons to fear change usually focus on one or more of the following: (1) fear of technological unemployment; (2) fear of reduced work hours and, thus, less pay; (3) fear of demotion and, thus, reduced wages; and (4) fear of speed-up and reduced incentive wages.

Managers must assess organizational readiness for change.

According to two practicing change agents, as organizations continue to downsize, restructure, and make other transitions, managers must assess the organization's readiness for change. They use organizational diagnostic instruments to get the "lay of the land" including questions on mission and strategy, vision, culture, and systems that facilitate people's work. They advocate determining "strategic intent" or the organization's ability to use its core competencies, like intellectual assetsm to position itself for new challenges. "Developing strategic intent is crucial, not just for profitability and productivity but also for long-term viability and vitality."[7]

SOCIAL RESISTANCE

THE CONDITION OF HOMEOSTASIS

Recall that earlier we defined and discussed equilibrium as a desirable state of balance between cautious resistance and blatant change. That equilibrium is achieved through homeostasis. Whenever change threatens that equilibrium, the affected entity—an individual or group—acts to oppose it and to maintain the kind of balance it is used to. This balance-maintaining characteristic of groups is called **homeostasis,** that is, a state of stability or equilibrium.

Homeostasis helps to maintain a balance or stability.

For example, if management imposes new controls on a work group, the group may react with increased adherence to its own standards of group loyalty. Outside pressure will produce some changes in behavior, but it may also cause a reaction that resists change—moving in the direction of homeostasis, or the maintenance of familiar routines.

Another example: A clock is more than a collection of hands, cogs, and wheels because when it is assembled something new results—the registering and measuring of time. Similarly, a work group is more than a collection of individuals because when it is assembled something new results—important functions relating to establishing common standards, attitudes, goals, and leadership. Threatening or disrupting the equilibrium and homeostasis of that group can be very dysfunctional and take its toll on individuals and the total organization.

DRIVING FORCES AND RESTRAINING FORCES

In the change model, the forces that increase production (new machinery and specific instructions and supervision in its use) are called **driving forces.** The forces that keep production down to a level deemed safe for job security are called **restraining forces** (see Figure 15–5). Other driving forces to increase production in a work group might be the desire of some members to win promotions or higher salaries. These forces would be balanced by the group's fear of layoff—restraining forces that would make themselves known in the form of hostility to "eager beavers" or even ostracism of the offending group members.

Notice in Figure 15–5 that one category of forces acts against the other group of forces. Give and take must occur or, like an earthquake in the physical sciences, there is a cataclysmic event in the organization. Again there is a need for balance between constant change—with everything and everyone always up in the air and in a state of turmoil—and measured change where there is *unfreezing (thawing!), change effected,* then *refreezing* before the cycle begins again. There must be some stability in the organization.

I don't want to detract from the seriousness of the homeostasis process, including unfreezing, changing, and refreezing, but rather reinforce its validity by the following story where there is too much or constant change:

> A farmer was driving down the highway in his pickup truck with a camper shell on the back. Every mile or so, he pulled over, stopped, and got out of the truck to beat on the side of the camper shell with a baseball bat. Another

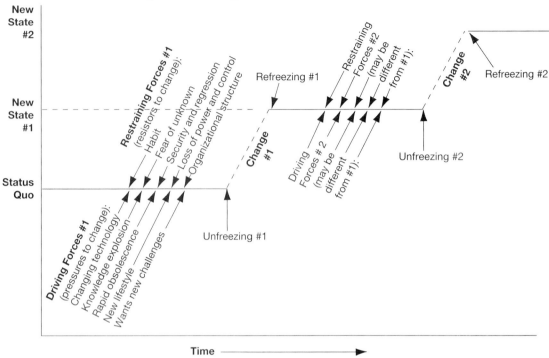

FIGURE 15–5 The Change Process from Status Quo to New State(s) of Equilibrium Via Driving and Restraining Forces.

driver had followed him and observed this behavior for several repetitions until his curiosity finally got the best of him and he pulled up behind the farmer's truck to ask him what he was doing. The farmer replied: "Well, you see, I only have a half-ton pickup truck, but I have a ton of canary birds inside the camper shell—and I have to keep over half of 'em in the air all of the time!"

The practice of keeping bodies up in the air—in a constant state of flux or turmoil—may be all right for canaries but it does not make for stability in an organization. Change occurs when an imbalance develops between the restraining and driving forces. Such imbalance "unfreezes" the pattern, and the group struggles to achieve a new balance of equilibrium.

An imbalance between forces "unfreezes" the pattern and permits a new homeostasis to develop.

Once found, the new equilibrium will be made up of different components; that is, the group refreezes at a new and different equilibrium level. These studies also show that, when efforts are made to change a work group by increasing the driving forces, the most common response of the group is to increase restraining forces to maintain the same balance. When a restraining force is weakened, the patterns are more easily unfrozen and the group experiences little difficulty moving on to new and different patterns of balance.

BALANCING THE FORCES

There is a good reason why it is difficult to bring about change through the increase of driving forces. When driving forces are increased, the tensions in the total system are likely to increase also. More tensions mean greater instability and a greater likelihood of irrational behavior on the part of group members.

Equilibrium is a balance of forces for and against change.

The equilibrium of any group at any time is a balance of the forces that work for and against change within the group. All groups are working simultaneously both for and against their ways of life. As noted earlier, resistance to change is a common and normal phenomenon. People have always objected to change when it threatens their accustomed ways of living. This applies to all groups: employees resisting change invoked by supervisors, companies opposing governmental regulations, and management objecting to union demands.

TECHNOLOGICAL RESISTANCE

CHANGE IN TECHNOLOGY AND "QUALITY OF LIFE"

Although it is true that technological innovation paved the way for the standard of living that we enjoy in the United States today, it is also true that the quality of our life has not always been enhanced by those changes. The environmental and ecology movements that have sprung up in the past decades are but one indication that growing numbers of people no longer believe that unchecked technological growth is the wisest course to follow.

Will the future be technology versus "quality of life?" Conflict between the person's and the company's " life-style."

Possibly, in the near future we may see the entire direction of change focus less on technological innovation and more on technological "containment" and on interpersonal, intergroup changes in human behavior. It is becoming increasingly obvious that the major issue in information technology is not technology based; it is management based.[8] Today, ideas being aired to preserve the environment call for changing our notions of the value of technological growth. Progressive social change may come to mean greater emphasis on the quality of life for the total population and less emphasis on the kinds and quantities of the goods we produce.

We can see that sometimes there is a conflict between personal and social values. For example, our lifestyle is seen as an outward evidence of our own values, beliefs, and perspectives. Certainly, our own lifestyles affect and are affected by company-related issues. Companies are aware of this influence, and many are careful to hire only those with compatible lifestyles, which can be contrary to equal opportunity principles. Large companies have installed "quality of work life" programs in an attempt to see to what degree members of the workforce are able to satisfy important personal needs through their experiences in the company. The more satisfying the quality of work life, the more similar the employee and the company lifestyles. The less similar the company's and the employee's lifestyles, the greater the chance of resistance to change.

WORK ENVIRONMENT CHANGE

As the information age develops, we recognize that it will never be possible to return to former industrial-based manufacturing, processes, and conditions.

That is not all bad. The information age brings with it a change in working conditions including working more at home than at the plant or in the office for some people.

Alvin Toffler predicts that work at home on a large scale could influence family structures and even redefine "love":

> Those who look ahead to working at home with a spouse, instead of spending the main part of their waking lives away, are likely to take more into consideration than simple sexual and psychological gratification—or social status, for that matter. They may begin to insist on Love Plus—sexual and psychological gratification plus brains (as their grandfathers once favored brawn), love plus conscientiousness, responsibility, self-discipline, or other work-related virtues. We may—who knows?—hear some John Denver of the future croon lyrics like:
>
>> I love your eyes, your cherry lips,
>> the love that always lingers,
>> your way with words and random blips,
>> your skilled computer fingers.[9]

The shift from an industrial to an information society is centered on five points:

1. The information society is an economic reality, not an intellectual abstraction.
2. Innovations in communications and computer technology will accelerate the pace of change by collapsing the information float (the amount of time information spends in the communication channel).
3. New information technologies will at first be applied to old industrial tasks, then, gradually give birth to new activities, processes, and products.
4. In this literacy-intensive society, when we need basic reading and writing skills more than ever before, our education system is turning out an increasingly inferior product.
5. The technology of the new information age is not absolute. It will succeed or fail according to the principle of high tech/high touch.[10]

"High tech/high touch" means that in the age of technological information, where individuals work alone at home or telecommute, there must be corresponding human responses. There is, as John Naisbitt says, "a need to be together."[11] How that need and the demands of the information age are to be reconciled remains to be seen.

There is a need to be together.

Work environment changes are not all based around information technology. There are changes in the type of work that people want and are capable of doing. Continual reassessment of both individual goals and organizational objectives results in a dynamic (changing), responsive work unit.

EXPRESS YOUR OPINION	Suppose your company is moving fifty miles away and you will probably need to be retrained to keep your job. What will bother you the most? Will you attempt to change employers? Will you move or commute? Will you resist being retrained? Why?

Because of budget cuts it is necessary to close one of two offices, and relocate the employees from the closed office to the remaining office. The question is, which office should be closed? The situation is this:

1. The offices are seventy miles apart.

2. Office A's characteristics are

    a. Fifteen employees

    b. Building is ten years old

    c. Located in a small town

    d. High cost of living

3. Office B's characteristics are

    a. Twenty employees

    b. Building is twenty-five years old

    c. Located in a large city

Go through the exercise twice: once as a member of office B, then as a member of office A.

WHICH SITUATION WOULD YOU RESIST THE LEAST?

1. The main office decides that the new location of the two offices should be office A. One reason was based on the age of the offices. Do you resist? _____

2. The main office asks for feedback from employees of both offices concerning which would be the best site. What would you suggest? _____ (pros and cons) _____

    _____

3. The main office sends you a copy of all the suggestions made by employees of both office sites. In looking over the material you see that seventeen people are in favor of office A and seventeen are in favor of office B. You cast the deciding vote. Which would you choose? _____

    _____Why?

Would your answer be different (especially to situation 3) if you were a member from office A? You, your instructor, and other class members may want to discuss your reactions to the three situations.

OVERCOMING RESISTANCE

PARTICIPATION

There is a greater chance for success when all involved participate.

Management theorists such as Kurt Lewin, Peter Drucker, and Leonard Sayles have created an impressive body of evidence indicating that, when all the parties to be affected by change participate in the planning of that change, the

FIGURE 15–6 Groups Everywhere Tend to Cooperate Rather Than to Resist When Presented with the Opportunity to Participate In Planning for the Change.

change has a real chance of succeeding. Groups everywhere tend to cooperate rather than to resist when presented with the opportunity to evaluate a situation and participate in planning for change (see Figure 15–6). Social psychology theory has established that the least effective way in which to motivate for change is through threat of punishment. In the past few decades, behavioral scientists have stressed the fact that force in human affairs, just as in physics, breeds counterforce.

Realistically, employees want to participate in change. Participation in the process of change motivates the individual by (1) fulfilling the developmental needs of a healthy personality, (2) promoting security through knowledge of the environment and exercising control over it, and (3) reducing basic fears of the unknown that cause resistance to change. The effectiveness of change is enhanced by participation. In fact, there is an inverse relationship between resistance to change and the degree of participation. As participation increases, resistance to change goes down.

There is a sizable gap, however, between social psychology theory and practice in the business world. The author knows of several companies where changes have been effected without any involvement or participation on the part of the employees other than doing the physical work. Changes were conducted in such a way as to discourage all participation below the level of top management. Management refused to solicit ideas from people who were most affected by the changes. Predictably, animosity and ill will erupted between management, supervisors, and employees. Changes in office arrangements and office moves are classic examples of these phenomena.

Another good reason for encouraging employees to take part in planning for change is that they usually have considerable useful information to contribute. Unfortunately, if they are not asked, they usually will not volunteer that information because they feel it will not be wanted or accepted.

BEHAVIOR MODIFICATION

Alternatives or changes should be made attractive. The more appealing the new approach appears to be, the more likely people are to change. **Behavior modification** is a technique used to bring about behavioral change by frequently praising and reinforcing positive behaviors and ignoring negative behavior. Accenting the positive is the behavior modification approach to a better and more permanent change. Performance on a task generally improves when the performer is positively reinforced.

Individuals want positive rewards for behaving certain ways.

Individuals want **positive reinforcement**—positive incentives and rewards for behaving in certain ways. They encourage repetition of that behavior so the reward will occur again. We resist **negative reinforcement,** which is the limitation or withdrawal of a variable. We all respond more positively to positive reinforcement.

As technological sophistication is introduced to the workplace, employees may resist the technology. This provides a starting point for a reward system to encourage acceptance of the new technology. That doesn't mean a whole new reward scheme but reinforced behavior modification.[12]

Behavior modification has worked well to change attitudes, but it does require people to keep records. Keeping records helps to clarify the behavior involved. Supervisors who note on paper every time they criticize an employee or point to some mistake will see how much criticism they issue during the day. Supervisors who keep a record of every time they commend the employee will see the extent of commending. If more commendations are issued, the supervisor will likely see improved employee performance (Figure 15–7).

FIGURE 15–7 Initiating Change Requires Certain Personality Traits.

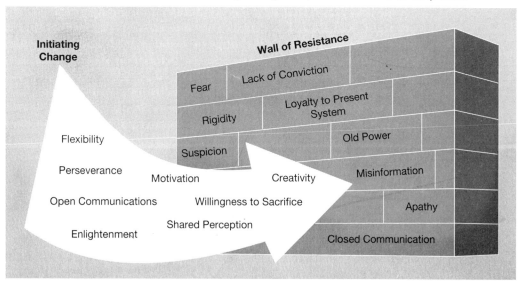

MANDATING CHANGE

Mandated change is change demanded by someone of authority. Some policies are mandated because laws, safety, or health seem to require it. Company economics may mandate a factory closing. The main advantage of mandating change from above is that change can take place quickly and efficiently. It took less than a decade for the white populations of southern cities to become accustomed to black salesclerks, a phenomenon that reversed 200 years of tradition.

Mandated change is fast but may be ineffective in long term.

Mandating change is a strictly authoritarian approach. The authoritarian is entirely responsible for major decisions. Resistance can be handled simply by firing or by transferring unruly employees. Resistance can be minimized because the authoritarian assumes the burden of risk. In fact, the authoritarian will often go to great lengths to protect employees from doubts or worries, fearing the resulting confusion. The authoritarian style of leadership appears to be strong because it appears to be able to overcome resistance. Nevertheless, resistance is to be expected when employees are pressured without a chance to contribute their own input.

We will examine several examples of mandated change in the next chapter: affirmative action, disabilities, legislation, and locally enforced no-smoking regulations.

EXPRESS YOUR OPINION

We have read about force-field analysis and how there are pressures to bring about change and pressures to resist change. The equilibrium or the balance of the two is a state of homeostasis.

Mandating appears to effect changes suddenly, swinging the homeostasis pendulum dramatically to the left or right. By contrast, behavior modification encourages making changes slowly, so that the pendulum moves more slowly to the left or right.

If situations change and a new direction is needed, which of the methods cited will encourage the fastest change? Do the laws of physics come into play? That is, if the pendulum is swinging quickly to the left or right, will a quick reversal cause it to move faster in the other direction? In other words, will change be faster in both directions under the mandating system as opposed to the behavioral modification system? Once behavioral modification has changed people's actions, will it work as a stronger pressure to resist change in the opposite direction?

Express your opinion with examples of changes that were mandated and changes that were effected by the behavioral modification method.

TIME ALLOWANCE

Even if there is no resistance to the change itself, it takes time to put the change into productive use. If the supervisor loses patience with the amount of time that a subordinate needs to learn how to handle a procedural change, the subordinate will begin to feel pushed. That feeling of being pushed can create a change in customary working relationships and breed resistance where there was none before.

Quantifying the need for changes into time tables may help effect and overcome resistance to change. Recall the use and explanation of PERT/CPM methods in the last chapter; these techniques may point out pitfalls and allow for modifications in the change process.

Managers and supervisors need to become much more aware of how human relationships affect the rate at which change can take place. Often, in the name of speed and efficiency, and without understanding the rhythms involved in creating the necessary atmosphere for change, management simply creates obstacles that later take much time and labor to overcome.

GROUP DYNAMICS OF CHANGE

Implementing change in individuals is a subtle process.

The process of implementing change in individuals requires subtle guidance. A slight change in words can cause certain actions to be interpreted as "enforced change." The influence of groups in bringing about change often yields equally amazing consequences. Recall that *group dynamics* refers to the effect that individuals collectively have on each other. The sense of belonging, prestige, and shared perceptions can dramatically affect one's individual behavior.

The term *group dynamics of change* refers to those forces operating in groups. Since change is an integral part of group life, it is desirable to study the group as a medium of change. You might want to review those properties of group dynamics studied in Chapter 9, namely, that groups are omnipresent, have power, and produce good and bad consequences.

ACTION PROJECT 15–2   MR. BLACK AND MR. BROWN (GROUP EXERCISE)

INSTRUCTIONS

This is an especially fun exercise that involves your instructor. We all, from time to time, hear stories and form opinions about some incident. We feel we might even produce a different outcome if we were in someone's place. Your instructor is going to read a story about two people and a horse. You are to listen carefully to the story and come to a conclusion.

Step 1: INSTRUCTOR—Read the following story to the class—ask them NOT to take notes—and see if they can determine what profit Mr. Brown or Mr. Black happens to make.

> Once upon a time, Mr. Brown went walking down the street and came across Mr. Black's house and saw one of his horses. "My, that's a fine horse," he thought and offered Mr. Black $60 for the horse. Mr. Brown took his new horse down to his farm. Later that afternoon, however, Mr. Black decided he really wanted to have his horse back. So he went to Mr. Brown and offered $70 for the horse. Mr. Brown accepted. However, the next day, as Mr. Brown went walking down the path, again he came across Mr. Black's horse and decided he certainly would like to have that horse and

offered Mr. Black $80. Mr. Black accepted the offer. Later again, however, that afternoon Mr. Black wanted to be sure to have his horse back and offered Mr. Brown $90 for the horse.

Now the question is, how much money was made by Mr. Brown or Mr. Black? Or was any profit made by either Mr. Brown or Mr. Black?

After you have formed your opinion, you will gather into groups. You will select the group that feels as you do.

Step 2: Who made a profit and, if any, how much—Mr. Brown or Mr. Black? Here are the four choices the students have:

1. No profit
2. $10 profit
3. $20 profit
4. $30 or more profit

Remember, the important point for purposes of this exercise is not who made profit, if any, or how much. The important lessons come from your answers to the following questions.

FOLLOW-UP DISCUSSION QUESTIONS

1. Were there opinion leaders in the class? Did they influence the group? _____
2. At what point in opinion forming are opinion leaders most effective? _____
3. Who are most resistant to change, the leaders or the followers? _____
4. Do the numbers in a group affect the resistance to change? _____ If so, how? _____
5. From this experiment, what can we learn about opinion forming? _____

_____

KEYS TO SUCCESSFUL CHANGE

To achieve change, there are several stages or key steps to follow. One is to make clear the *need* for change. This step involves communication and understanding. Other steps are also shown in Figure 15–8. We could add the needs for education and training, goals, and outcomes assessment to the list—and predict results with and without change.

The changes must be system-wide in any organization. To begin a program of planned change, Ralph Kilmann, author of *Managing Beyond the Quick Fix*, says:

> The first step in developing a completely integrated program for improving organizations entails identifying at least three sets of elements: (1) all the controllable variables—pinpointed via a systems' perspective—that determine organizational success, (2) all the multiple approaches—techniques, instruments, and procedures—that can alter these controllable variables, and (3) all the ongoing activities that drive organization-wide change.[13]

Various techniques and procedures for achieving organization change include team building, modifying the organizational culture, and reward systems. Implementation of a program must be flexible.

FIGURE 15–8 Keys to a Successful Change. Source: Goodwin Watson and Edward M. Glaser, "What We Have Learned About Planning for Change," *Management Review*, November 1965, pp. 34–36.

Need	1. Make clear the need for change.
Objectives	2. State the objectives clearly.
Participation	3. Encourage relevant group participation to clarify the needed changes.
Broad guidelines	4. Establish broad guidelines to achieve the objectives.
Details by group	5. Leave the details to the group that will be most affected by the change.
Benefits of change	6. State the benefits or rewards expected from the change.
Give rewards	7. Keep the promise of rewards to those who helped in the change.

ORGANIZATION DEVELOPMENT

Organization development (OD) can be defined as a long-term, systematic, and organization-wide change effort designed to increase an organization's total effectiveness. OD advocates maintain that the entire complex organization must be dealt with as a whole. This includes all the personalities and issues that continuously make the organization what it is.

Whole organization must change.

OD assumes that an entire organization, not just select individuals in it, must work for change. Organization development also recognizes the vulnerability of new employees who enter established work environments.

The OD process enjoyed very active usage in the 1980s and beyond. It was a viable concept before it was called OD, and it is still a useful approach to solving organizational problems—although it might not be called by that name.

Develop people's skills.

Organization development has two major objectives: (1) to develop people's specific skills that make it possible for them to do their jobs well and (2) to develop people's interpersonal and group membership skills. Capacities are developed in giving and receiving assistance, listening and communicating, and dealing with people and organizational problems. As implied, this method aims at developing the organization.

Organizational objectives may give way to individual goals.

OD is based on the belief that, although organizations begin with a purpose, as they grow in size and in age, organizational objectives give way to individual goals. When this happens, the organization begins to decay. OD also recognizes that people have needs and desires that must be considered part of organizational objectives. If all members of the organization participate in forming group goals, and in the process subscribe to them, then a great deal of energy is released for employees to move toward a common purpose.

CHARACTERISTICS OF ORGANIZATION DEVELOPMENT

Goal Setting	1.	OD subscribes to goal setting. It recognizes some purpose or direction for both the company and the individual.
Time and Money	2.	OD is a dynamic ongoing process. It takes time to develop and requires a considerable investment of time and money. There is a strong belief in training programs.
Psychology	3.	OD relies heavily on psychological ideas. If the company has a motivation problem, for example, management will investigate how other organizations have solved similar problems.
Mutual Trust	4.	OD encourages the development of mutual trust between management and the employees.
Team Building	5.	OD believes in team building and recognizes that one work group affects all others. One group cannot be changed without it affecting others. A development program must be a company-wide effort.
Experience Based	6.	It is experience based. If the design is to improve intragroup communications, the group activity will provide opportunities for the members to obtain insight into developing effective communication skills.

TYPES OF OD INTERVENTIONS

An **OD intervention** is a systematic attempt to correct an organizational deficiency. It may focus on individuals, groups or teams, a department, or the total organization. The overall objective remains to impact positively the entire organization. Interventions may be carried out using one or a combination of several approaches:

INTERVENTION	DESCRIPTION	FOCUS
Life/career planning	Self-analysis; planned development	Individual
Skill development	How to perform or improve performance on a job	Individual
Role analysis	Prescriptive—the jobs that people "ought to be doing"	Group
Team development	Building groups into effective teams	Group
Survey feedback	Using a questionnaire to gather data, analyzing those data, and feeding them back to employees so they can improve	Organization
Grid OD	A multiphased program that utilizes the Managerial Grid to change organizational leadership	Organization

Teamwork occurs when a cohesive group works to accomplish specific tasks in a supportive environment. One way of finding out how well a team functions is to observe communication and results patterns. One instrument that the author has used is shown in Figure 15–9. Knowing who is communicating with whom in an organization allows sociometric analysis of group interactions and provides evidence for later prescriptions. **Sociometry** is the physical measurement of activities and feelings of group members toward one another. The reporting relationships also offer surprises in some organizations.

A **sociogram** is a graphic illustration of who is communicating with whom, how often, and who is *not* communicating with whom (see Figure 15–10). Each time an individual communicates with others, an arrow connects those individuals. The point of the arrow indicates the direction of the message. Subsequent interactions are shown by cross marks on the arrow. If the communication is directed to the entire group, the arrow is drawn toward the center.

In the real example shown in Figure 15–10, notice that group members A and B have more communication than others; that is to be expected because A is the group leader—a director or chief administrator—and B is the first associate or deputy administrator. Others, such as F, are not communicated with as often as others within the group. If the communications of a manager or any

FIGURE 15–9 Diagnostic for Communications and Reporting Relationships. Source: Douglas A. Benton, "Team Development" Consulting for Federal Agencies, Other Public Agencies Including Hospitals, Large and Small Businesses.

To help in the *diagnosis* of your organization, please answer the following (the questions are *nonsensitive*, but please respond individually and CONFIDENTIALLY; your responses will be handled collectively and CONFIDENTIALLY):

1. Who are three people *to* whom you most frequently *send* communications—either verbally or written?

2. Who are three people *from* whom you most frequently *receive* communications—again, either verbally or written?

3. To whom *do* you report?

3a. To whom *should* you report?

4. How does your "boss" demonstrate concern for your job performance?

5. How does your "boss" demonstrate concern for you as a person?

6. Which work associates report to you?

6a. Which work associates *should* report directly to you?

7. What, on the management team, needs improving?

8. What are the barriers to your being a full participant on the management team?

FIGURE 15–10 An Abbreviated Sociogram Showing Who Does and Does Not Communicate with Whom, and How Frequently.

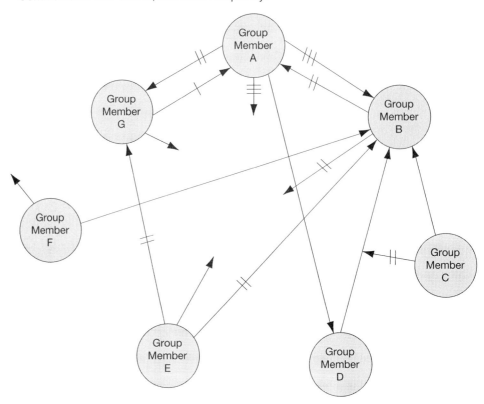

employee are all or predominantly one-way (either to or from), you may want to investigate further.

Another instrument that provides similar information is shown in Figure 15–11. Useful results are achieved by administering this instrument to various group members who are or have the potential to become team members. How do you test for and encourage team development in an organization? Before you can help an organization to be more successful, you must know the state of the organization now. The first step in organization development is diagnosis of the organization. Unfortunately, too many times, "quick-fix" consultants reach into their bags of tricks and prescribe "fixes" for an organization's ills before they know what, if anything, is wrong with the organization. Remember: "Prescription without diagnosis is malpractice in management as well as in medicine."

Diagnose an organization's ills, if any, before fixing them.

Teams cannot be formed by edict. An athletic coach, musical group leader, or project manager cannot just say "You are a team" and achieve instant commitment to accomplish organizational objectives. The group must grow into a team. How rapidly that growth occurs depends on several variables:

- Commitment to the organization
- Primacy of tasks
- Experience within the organization

FIGURE 15–11 Diagnostic for Objectives of a Team Development Program. Source: Douglas A. Benton, "Team Development" Consulting for Federal Agencies, Other Public Agencies Including Hospitals, Large and Small Businesses.

Please rank (1 = highest rank) the following potential OBJECTIVES OF A TEAM DEVELOPMENT PROGRAM:

(1 = HIGHEST RANK)	WHO HAS PRIMARY/SECONDARY RESPONSIBILITY FOR ACCOMPLISHING THESE OBJECTIVES	
_____ Create an open problem-solving climate throughout the organization.		
_____ Supplement the authority associated with rank or status with the authority, knowledge, and competence.	_____	_____
_____ Locate decision-making and problem-solving responsibilities as close to the information sources as possible.	_____	_____
_____ Build trust among individuals and groups throughout the organization.	_____	_____
_____ Make activity more relevant to work goals and maximize collaborative efforts.	_____	_____
_____ Develop a reward system that recognizes both the achievement of the organization mission (service?) and organization development (growth of people).	_____	_____
_____ Increase the sense of "ownership" of organization objectives throughout the work force.	_____	_____
_____ Help managers to manage according to relevant objectives rather than according to "past practices."	_____	_____
_____ Increase self-control and self-direction for people within the organization.	_____	_____

- Technical competence and skills of members
- Experience in working with fellow members
- Experience of appointed or potential leader
- Other factors

When teams are forced, they usually fail. Management assumes that a group should be more cohesive, more open in their communications, have higher morale, and so on. One group of management consultants and researchers learned that:

> . . . tough, specific performance challenges create teams, not "feel good" initiatives. . . . Teams that make or do things often need to develop new skills for managing themselves. Teams that recommend things often find their biggest challenge comes when they make the hand-off to those who must implement their findings. And, groups that run or manage things must overcome hierarchical obstacles and turf issues more often than groups that recommend, make, or do things. But notwithstanding such differences, any team will deliver results well beyond what individuals acting alone can achieve as long as it focuses on performance.[14]

The key to organization-wide change is a team effort. One or two individuals cannot change the organization appreciably, even from the top down, if there is not overall commitment to change. In turn, the key to a team effort is developing mutual trust and not misplacing that trust.

WHAT IS TRUST?

Trust means that an individual can rely on another with respect to a given situation. Specific manifestations of trust are status, self-esteem, mutual relationships, job, and career—even life itself. Walter Ulmer writes that trust includes the following leadership components:

- Competent in critical skills
- Fair and rational
- Committed to organizational values
- Willing to share in risks
- Open and direct
- Predictable or consistent[15]

Trust is earned and experienced, not something instantly installed externally (see Figure 15–12).

FIGURE 15–12 How to Develop Mutual TRUST in a Management Team. Source: Douglas A. Benton, "Team Development" Consulting for Federal Agencies, Other Public Agencies Including Hospitals, Large and Small Businesses.

DO:
- Assume trust initially (until proven otherwise).
- Communicate openly with one another.
- Share information—not evaluation.
- Display confidence in your own and others' abilities.
- Earn trust.
- Make and keep commitments.
- Respect one another.
- Operate with honesty and integrity toward one another.

DON'T:
- Take cheap shots.
- Knowingly hurt another.
- Talk out of both sides of your mouth.
- Talk behind backs.
- Scapegoat.
- Second guess.
- Doubt when listening.
- Play games with my career.
- Take organizational matters personally.

AL PARKER

"Persistence Pays Off"

Appropriately located on a street called Persistence Drive in Woodbridge, Virginia, the Polyfab Display Co. is a reflection of its president's values and work ethic.

Al Parker, 37, founded Polyfab, a manufacturer of point-of-purchase signs, displays, and graphics, with his 33-year-old partner, Steve Lawwill, in 1987. Both had been working for a waste-removal company in Northern Virginia but became disgruntled about their income potential and decided to form their own company.

Parker and Lawwill did not know each other very well, which made launching a business together difficult. Parker likens it to getting married. "You only see what you want to see, and then a lot of other things surface," he says.

One foundation they used to strengthen their relationship, Parker says, was the fact that they are both Christians. "Since we knew that we had our Christianity in common," Lawwill says, "we believed that we could trust each other, and we knew that we both had a good work ethic." Once that commonality was established, he says, "starting the business was just a matter of details."

Parker has a bachelor's degree in sales and marketing and an M.B.A., both from Miami University in Oxford, Ohio. Lawwill has extensive knowledge of the plastics industry. Together, their backgrounds and skills made the perfect combination for Polyfab.

Parker's willingness to learn a business that was somewhat unfamiliar to him while working with a partner he hardly knew helped to set the tone of dedication now pervasive throughout Polyfab. And the results are beginning to show. Parker estimates $1.2 million in sales for 1993, which would be more than double last year's outcome, and he expects $2.5 million in sales by three years from now. "Then," he says, "we'll have the capital to grow further." His goal: regional and national recognition.

The company's employees number from ten to sixty, depending on the number of projects the company has under way. Parker says that Polyfab's biggest asset is its staff, which he claims could hold its own against any other in the industry. "You have to start with quality people," he says, "people that innately want to excel and have a lot of personal pride in what they do."

In the beginning, Polyfab attempted to drum up business by going through the Yellow Pages and calling prospective clients. The first big break came shortly after the business opened, with a sizable order from *USA Today* for 8,000 plastic newspaper holders. Since that time, Polyfab has compiled an impressive list of customers, including McDonald's, Sony, Price Club, and Blockbuster Video.

Today, Polyfab engages in smart, low-cost marketing. One of its best vehicles for attracting customers has been the Virginia Regional Minority Supplier Development Council, an affiliate of the National Minority Supplier Development Council, which works to develop ties between big corporations and minority-owned businesses. "We've been able to network that very well," says Parker, who received a "Supplier of the Year" award from the national council in October.

Parker says the business has meant a lot of personal sacrifice: He has taken only one vacation in six years, and he describes his social life as "extremely limited." But the persistence at work on Persistence Drive is paying off. Says Parker: "We're very excited about the future."

SOURCE: Jesse H. Sweet, "Persistence Pays Off," *Nation's Business,* November 1993, p. 14. Reprinted by permission. Copyright © 1993, U.S. Chamber of Commerce.

MURPHY'S LAWS AND OTHER "THINGS" THAT CAN GO WRONG

In concluding this chapter, it is worthwhile to mention **Murphy's laws.** They have been written in a humorous fashion with several parts, yet there is a thread of truth in each:

1. If anything can go wrong, it will.
2. Everything takes longer than it should.
3. Nothing is as simple as it looks; among many others.

Take as an example a plan to change the date of monthly paychecks from the first of the month to the end of the month. Instead of receiving your check on the first of the next month, you would receive it at the end of the present month. Certainly everyone would like to be paid one day early. Surely there would be no resistance to such an administrative change. But the school board in one county found out differently after informing the school employees of its plan.

Immediately, the county school office was informed of the income tax problem. Instead of receiving twelve paychecks the first year, each employee would receive thirteen, thereby having to pay income tax on a larger income. The solution: The teachers would be paid on the first day of January and the last day of February. Every month after that they would be paid on the last day of the month, except for December at which time they would be paid on January 1. Yes, everything takes longer than it should. This plan took two-and-a-half years to implement, and a few things did go wrong, but ultimately they were fixed.

Planning for change and employing participative techniques allow the results to be more effective. Specific planning suggestions include (1) look deeper and ask questions, (2) allocate time for confusion and resistance, and (3) be prepared with action points and contingency plans.

Balance the change process with end results. Effectively planning for change and otherwise managing an organization requires leadership, but there is more to change, teamwork, and trust than the process itself. We need balance between process and results—too much bias in either direction is not helpful. Some bosses put too much emphasis on results; other team builders and team-building retreats put too much emphasis on process. One tongue-in-cheek trainer kiddingly suggests that to introduce major change in an organization you must focus on "employee alignment"—getting employees to think like the boss:

> You'll be needing a positive, can-do attitude (like mine), so I'll require you to participate in my favorite personal-growth experience, which happens to be a fire-walking seminar. Beckoning you onward from the far end of the glowing pit will be that big poster of . . . me. . . .
> And so on. You may think you resent some of this, but I know better. You're just "experiencing some natural discomfort with the change process." Pretty soon you'll be transformed. Happier. More productive. Brimming with team spirit. Aligned. Just like me. Sure you will.[16]

Another wag noted that a rousing game of softball or tag football can motivate a team just as well as a team-building retreat, and it costs a lot less, too!

Summary

Once a decision has been rendered, it must be implemented. The implementation process often requires changing people's attitudes to bring about lasting effects. We hear, "Study change, praise it, but don't do it; we may resist." You can expect resistance to vague or unclear changes. Resistance will be least evident when workers have the most to say about procedural matters and most evident when they have the least to say. Fear of the unknown is potent, but by encouraging participation in change, people can help to overcome this resistance monster.

When change is about to occur, the more the pressures are in harmony, the more predictable the outcome will be. If a striving worker is offered a promotion and transfer to another city and his family and friends are for it, then it is likely he will accept the move and promotion. The stronger a person's occupational identity happens to be, the greater the feeling of security. The greater the sense of security, the more likely there is to be resistance.

The concept of homeostasis is a balance between those who are attempting to bring about change and those who are opposing change. Studies show that change occurs when an imbalance develops between the restraining and the driving forces. Such imbalance "unfreezes" the pattern, and the group struggles to achieve a new balance of equilibrium. Once found, the new pattern will be made up of different components. That is, the group refreezes at a new and different equilibrium level.

Change can also be encouraged by behavioral modification. One premise of this method is that changes should be made attractive. People like to be commended on how well they are doing in achieving the new goal, and such actions should be done both orally and in writing.

Organization development is change throughout the entire organization. Concentrating on the whole organization allows many changes to occur at once rather than on a piecemeal basis, or putting-out-fires approach.

The keys to organization development and change in general are teamwork and trust. Both can be measured and developed internally. They are usually not successful when externally imposed by the boss or some fire-walking consultant.

GROUP PRESSURE–"RATE BUSTING"

Engineer Frank Gonzales came to set up a new piece of equipment in the plant. According to Mr. Krieger, the plant manager, the new machine would improve the production rate of the assembly crew. Leon Robbins, the informal group leader, doesn't like the idea of the new fancy machine. "What they're really after is a way to get more out of us without paying us any more than they have to. When they are done, you and I will be without a job. Just wait and see, one day this company won't need skilled people anymore; all they will need is a few button pushers."

When Frank completed the installation of the new machine, he asked for a volunteer to operate it. With the approval of the supervisor of the assembly department, John O'Neil began operating the machine under Frank's supervision. At the end of the day the machine and the operator far exceeded Frank's anticipated increase in production.

"What effect will these new machines really have on our jobs?" asked one worker.

"According to the plant manager, if the system works out well, we'll all be either running the machines or we'll have some other related task," replied O'Neil.

"Well, we know we don't have to worry about losing our jobs, that's one of the first things we were told," said another worker.

"I've been around a long time, friend—you haven't. Let's wait and see what happens," retorted Leon Robbins in a disgusted way.

During the second day of testing, Frank chose another person to operate the new machine. After giving the operator instructions on how to run the machine, Frank began to supervise the employee's performance. Throughout the day Frank felt that the man was performing at less than an appropriate speed. In fact, Frank got the feeling that the man was stalling. At the end of the day, the operator's rate was only marginally higher than the average production rate using the old machine.

Playing the role of Frank you are convinced that the machine is superior to those already in the plant. You also feel that some people do not want to learn the operation of a new machine and are quietly sabotaging any possibility of a really successful run on the machine. What would you do?

1. Go to the employee's supervisor?

2. Go to management and complain about your suspicions?

3. Spend more time with the employees through informal chats?

4. Call for a general meeting with the employees to explain the merits of the machine?

5. Keep trying in the same manner, but be sure that you are picking those employees to work on the machine who are willing to ignore the group pressure?

THE OVERQUALIFIED EMPLOYEE'S DILEMMA

Leslie Fisher has been employed as an administrative assistant in a large food service industry for nearly two years. Recently the chain suffered a serious financial crisis, and the Marketing Division where she works experienced an 80 percent layoff. Leslie was not laid off but was transferred involuntarily to the Corporate Planning and Development Division.

The new position has less responsibility and status, but her pay was not reduced. She has become bored by the new job, because the tasks involved offer less variety. She is also frustrated by the lack of opportunity for advancement within the division, and the company has a current "no-growth" policy.

To advance and stay within the corporation, Leslie applied and was selected for a promotional transfer into the Personnel Department. However, her supervisor was not aware of her request. Mr. Sullivan, the vice president of corporate planning and development, refused to allow her to transfer to Personnel. He claimed that he had a rush project in his department that Leslie was handling and would not be able to complete it within the next few weeks.

This week Leslie had her annual review and had hoped for a merit increase. Her immediate supervisor told her that, although her job performance has been up to standard, since she is overqualified and overpaid for her job, she will not receive an increase in pay.

1. What are Leslie's alternatives?
2. Should Leslie ask Mr. Sullivan why her transfer was denied?
3. How can a corporation best handle a situation of this type?
4. Do you feel that the corporation should have a policy regarding transfers? If so, how should it be worded?
5. What is the best solution for Leslie?

DISCUSSION AND STUDY QUESTIONS—TO KEEP YOU THINKING . . . _____

1. Describe how participation can help overcome resistance to change.
2. Describe the concept of behavior modification and how it can help supervisors to be more effective.
3. Differentiate between driving and restraining forces in making changes.
4. What are the key characteristics of organization development?
5. What are the necessary preconditions for teamwork to work effectively?
6. How do you develop mutual trust?
7. Prepare a sociogram of your work or social group. What does it tell you about communication, teamwork, and leadership?

NOTES_____

1. Roger C. Palms, "Change," *Decision*, October 1989, p. 22.
2. Clay Carr, "Following Through on Change," *Training*, January 1989, pp. 39–44.
3. Joseph T. Gilbert, "Reducing the Risks from Innovation," *Journal of Systems Management*, January–February 1996, pp. 12–15.
4. Lloyd P. Steier, "When Technology Meets People," *Training & Development Journal*, August 1989, pp. 27–29.
5. Peter Drucker, "Information and the Future of the City," *The Wall Street Journal*, April 4, 1989, p. A10.
6. Bryan W. Armentrout, "Have Your Plans for Change Had a Change of Plan?" *HR Focus*, January 1996, p. 19.
7. Bill Trachant and W. Warner Burke, "Traveling Through Transitions," *Training & Development Journal*, February 1996, p. 41.
8. Peter Wolfraim, "Creating Order from Chaos," *Management Review*, March 1996, p. 48.
9. Alvin Toffler, *The Third Wave* (New York: William A. Morrow, 1980), p. 235.

10. John Naisbitt, *Megatrends: Ten New Directions Transforming Our Lives* (New York: Warner Books, 1982), p. 19.

11. Ibid., p. 45.

12. Gerard George and Warren S. Stone, "Employee Technophobia: Understanding, Managing, and Rewarding Change," *Journal of Compensation & Benefits,* March–April 1996, pp. 37–41.

13. Ralph H. Kilmann, "A Completely Integrated Program for Creating and Maintaining Organizational Success," *Organizational Dynamics,* Summer 1989, pp. 5–6.

14. Jon Katzenbach, "The Right Kind of Teamwork," *The Wall Street Journal,* November 9, 1992, p. A14.

15. Walter F. Ulmer, Jr., "Inside View," *Issues & Observations,* published by the Center for Creative Leadership, Greensboro, North Carolina, First Quarter 1993, p. 6.

16. Jack Gordon, "Employee Alignment? Maybe Just a Brake Job Would Do," *The Wall Street Journal,* February 13, 1989, p. A10.

RECOMMENDED READING

George, Gerard, and Warren S. Stone. "Employee Technophobia: Understanding, Managing and Rewarding Change." *Journal of Compensation & Benefits,* March–April 1996, pp. 37–41.

Jellison, Jerald M. *Overcoming Resistance: A Practical Guide to Producing Change in the Workplace.* New York: Simon & Schuster, 1993.

Kanter, Rosabeth Moss, Barry Stein, and Todd Jick. *The Challenge of Organizational Change: How Companies Experience It and Leaders Guide It.* New York: The Free Press, 1992.

Katzenbach, Jon, and Douglas Smith. *The Wisdom of Teams: Creating the High-Performance Organization.* Boston: Harvard Business School Press, 1993.

Lynch, Dudley, and Paul L. Kordis. *Strategy of the Dolphin: Scoring a Win in a Chaotic World.* New York: William A. Morrow, 1988.

Martel, Leon. *Mastering Change: The Key to Business Success.* New York: Simon & Schuster, 1986.

Naisbitt, John. *Megatrends: Ten New Directions Transforming Our Lives.* New York: Warner Books, 1982.

Odiorne, George S. *The Change Resisters: How They Can Prevent Progress and What Management Can Do about Them.* Englewood Cliffs, N.J.: Prentice Hall, 1981.

Peters, Thomas J., and Robert H. Waterman, Jr. *In Search of Excellence: Lessons from America's Best-Run Companies.* New York: Harper & Row, 1982.

Spencer, Karen L. "Beyond the Wall of Resistance: Unconventional Strategies that Build Support for Change." *Academy of Management Executive,* February 1996, pp. 90–92.

Sweeney, Gerry. "Learning Efficiency, Technological Change and Economic Progress." *International Journal of Technology Management,* January–February 1996, pp. 5–27.

Trachant, Bill, and W. Warner Burke. "Traveling Through Transitions." *Training & Development Journal,* February 1996, pp. 37–41.

Wolfraim, Peter. "Creating Order from Chaos." *Management Review,* March 1996, pp. 44–48.

16

Job and Pay Discrimination

You may want to discuss some of these questions with others before you read the chapter. Maybe some different feelings will develop as a result.

- What is meant by prejudice?
- What is meant by discrimination?
- Do we inherit or learn prejudice, and how do we exhibit our discrimination in everyday life?
- What group is discriminated against most in your geographical area?
- Which social class exhibits the greatest discrimination? Does it seem to be a social class other than the one to which you belong?
- Is society giving more opportunities to minorities now as compared with five years ago?
- How do we discriminate against older workers? against workers with disabilities? (How do you define *older* and *disabled*?)

LEARNING GOALS

After studying this chapter, you should be able to:

1. Define and discuss the meaning of prejudice and discrimination.
2. Discuss the psychological and economic roots of prejudice.
3. Explain why women and minorities often have such poor self-images.
4. Discuss some of the ways in which it is possible to see and measure discrimination in the business world.
5. Describe and give examples of some of the ways in which discrimination can be overcome.
6. Discuss some of the ideas of affirmative action in relation to the following:
   a. Goals and objectives
   b. Hiring and promotion policies
   c. Recruitment
   d. Job restructuring
7. Appreciate why child care facilities make sense for both employers and employees.
8. Understand the protections for the aging, disabled, and other legally protected groups.
9. Define and apply the following terms and concepts (in order of first occurrence):

- **biases**
- **prejudice**
- **stereotypes**
- **cultural stereotypes**

- discrimination
- disparate treatment
- disparate impact
- Civil Rights Act of 1964
- Equal Employment Opportunity Commission (EEOC)
- Age Discrimination in Employment Act (ADEA)
- reasonable accommodation— religious preferences
- black pride
- older worker

- comparable worth
- glass ceiling
- sexism
- dual careers
- Americans with Disabilities Act (ADA)
- individual with disability
- reasonable accommodation— individual with disability
- affirmative action
- diversity training
- employment at will

BACKGROUND TO PREJUDICE AND DISCRIMINATION

Discrimination is by no means a dead or resolved issue. Progress has been made through better management practices and antidiscrimination laws, but there are still opportunities for better business and government practices with or without executive, legislative, or judicial intervention.

Discrimination is a continuing human relations problem for both management and workers. Most people are familiar with the overt, violent acts of political and racial discrimination that are reported by the media. Other kinds of discrimination, however, are often much less recognizable and, for this reason, difficult to overcome. Nevertheless, because it affects so many people in the job market, and because people need to work to live, even mild discrimination deserves serious attention.

PREJUDGMENTS AND BIASES

Making a prejudgment is normal, because we cannot handle every event freshly in its own right. If we did, what good would past experience be? Although prejudgments help to give order to our daily living, our mind has a habit of assimilating as much as it can into categories by which it prejudges a person or event. By overcategorizing, we tend to form irrational rather than rational categories, and this may lead us to biases, prejudices, and stereotyping.

Biases are predispositions to act and decide on preconceived notions rather than rational analysis. We know that all women are not incompetent at math, that all Chinese are not inscrutable and industrious, and that all African Americans are not suffering in exotic misery. People are more complicated, more varied, more interesting than that. They have more resiliency and survivability than we might think.

A person acts with prejudice because of his or her personality, which has been developed by socialization or learned behavior taught by family, school, and neighborhood environment. It is in one's environment that one's attitudes are shaped and can be reshaped.

WHAT IS PREJUDICE?

Prejudice is an attitude, not an act.

Prejudice has been defined as "being down on something you're not up on." **Prejudice** is an attitude, not an act; it is a habit of mind, an opinion based partially on observation and partially on ignorance, fear, and cultural patterns of group formation, none of which has a rational basis.

A prejudiced person tends to think of members of a group of people as being all the same, without considering individual differences. This kind of thinking gives rise to stereotypes. **Stereotypes,** like prejudices, are overgeneralized beliefs based partially on observation and partially on ignorance and tradition. **Cultural stereotypes** are general ideas or fixed opinions about groups of people that a society develops.

Stereotypes are hard to overcome.

Stereotyping on the basis of race, sex, or any other characteristic, even if unconscious, should not be part of the employment or promotion process. If it affects employment and promotion decisions, it is wrong and should be changed through education. Stereotypes are difficult to overcome because they have developed over long periods of time and because so many people share them, giving them an illusion of rationality. However, many people today are trying hard to rid themselves of stereotyped thinking about other people, and the effort shows in a general, growing consciousness that people are individuals and should be treated as such.

PREJUDICE WORKS BOTH WAYS

It is also important to point out that all people, not simply members of dominant cultural groups, are prejudiced. We all hold stereotypes about other groups. Furthermore, groups that are traditionally thought of as objects of prejudice and discrimination are usually also prejudiced themselves. African Americans, for example, may hold stereotypical views about whites, and women hold stereotypical views about men. The prejudices that people hold are usually met with equal prejudices from the other side, like reflections in a mirror.

> In an ideal workplace, people would accept co-workers on the basis of merit. Yet even among the most sincerely open-minded, stereotypes and subtle prejudices can create difficulties. Managers can't change others' opinions—but they can work to ensure that all workers are treated fairly.[1]

A person who holds a prejudice but who does not discriminate is tolerant and capable of allowing other people to live freely. Our society values freedom of thought highly, which is why most efforts to deal with discrimination are directed toward persuading people to be tolerant—to avoid harming other people—not at legislating ways of thinking.

PREJUDICE AND SELF-IMAGE

Minority groups also develop prejudices, not only against the in groups and other out groups, but also against themselves. They tend to accept the image that others hold of them, to be ambivalent about their own self-worth, to fulfill the stereotypes, and to suffer from lack of confidence. An employer who wishes to change the situation must be prepared not only to avoid discrimination completely but to encourage employees to overcome it.

People's action may arise more from situation than from skin color.

Employers and workers alike can become more sensitive to the problems of self-image that minority people and women face by "putting themselves in the other person's shoes." Role playing is a very useful technique for learning how discrimination affects people. A supervisor of any ethnic background who is an object of discrimination, if only for a short training session, can experience real changes in attitude and action as a result of experiencing the change in role.

A white man traveled as a black man.

One of the most interesting studies of such a role shift was made by a white sociologist, John Howard Griffin, who changed his skin color with a series of chemical and ultraviolet treatments. He passed himself off as a black man in the South and wrote a book about the experience called *Black Like Me.* His most vivid recollection of the adventure was that he found the rejections accumulating in his self-image, until he found himself fearful, clumsy, and self-rejecting.

How can one ethnic group know how any other ethnic group would feel? One reviewer of this book notes that "White writers/teachers cannot see the whole picture because we do not return to minority neighborhoods in the evening" and provides an article that quotes a young Harvard MBA, Karen, who works for an Atlanta-based telecommunications company:

> Each day, when I get into my car, I always begin the ride to work by turning on a black radio station so that it blares. . . . I boogey all the way down the highway. A few blocks from my job, I turn the music down and stop shaking my shoulders. When my building comes into view, I turn the music off, because I know the curtain is about to go up.[2]

The reviewer's comment was: "As a white, how would I ever have guessed this?"

WHAT IS DISCRIMINATION?

Discrimination is the actual behavior manifested by a prejudice. What kinds of discrimination are most common in the United States? Sometimes it is not easy to tell, because at any given moment the public media may be emphasizing one kind or another.

Discrimination is an act; prejudice is a feeling.

To understand job discrimination we must look at the prejudice that lies behind it. We are all likely to have some feelings of prejudice against those who are different from us and even display our prejudice through actions in the form of discrimination. Therefore, by definition, prejudice is an attitude, and discrimination is an overt act demonstrating our prejudice.

The way discrimination manifests itself takes two forms legally: disparate treatment and disparate impact. **Disparate treatment** occurs when different standards are used to treat different classes of employees. One group is protected

TABLE 16–1 Historical Events and Legislation Affecting Job Discrimination.

1863	Emancipation Proclamation frees slaves in rebel states.
1896	U.S. Supreme Court establishes "separate, but equal" doctrine.
1905–1910	Black Americans organize NAACP.
1938	Congress passes Fair Labor Standards Act, including Child Labor Laws, amended several times.
1954	Supreme Court rules that "separate education facilities are inherently unequal" and orders schools desegregated.
1963	Equal Pay Act passed.
1963–1965	Widespread civil rights demonstrations.
1964	Civil Rights Act of 1964 passed, establishing the Equal Employment Opportunity Commission (EEOC).
1967	Age Discrimination in Employment Act passed.
1968	Architectural Barriers Act (handicapped accessible) passed.
1973	Vocational Rehabilitation Act (for the handicapped) passed.
1974	Vietnam-Era Veterans Readjustment Act passed.
1974	Congress passes Employee Retirement Income Security Act.
1978	Amendment to the 1967 Age Discrimination Act banning mandatory retirement at 65 years of age.
1978	Pregnancy Discrimination Act passed.
1985	Consolidated Omnibus Reconciliation Act (COBRA).
1986	Age Discrimination in Employment amendments removing upper limit of any age to retirement.
1986	Immigration Reform and Control Act of 1986.
1987	Omnibus Budget Reconciliation Act affecting defined-benefits pension plans.
1990	Fair Labor Standards minimum wage amendments.
1990	Americans with Disabilities Act (ADA).
1991	Civil Rights Act of 1991 (punitive damages for victims of discrimination).
1993	Family and Medical Leave Act of 1993.

from rigorous standards that may be used for another class. **Disparate impact** occurs when standards appear to be neutral but there is an underrepresentation of a group in hiring, promotions, compensation, or other personnel decisions.

The brief review of historical events and legislation affecting discrimination in Table 16–1 shows that our society is moving to overcome discrimination. The **Civil Rights Act of 1964,** as amended, is the vanguard of civil rights legislation. It includes prohibitions against employment discrimination because of a person's race, color, religion, sex, or national origin. It established the **Equal Employment Opportunity Commission,** a federal government agency that establishes guidelines for hiring, recruiting, and promoting minority groups. The **Age Discrimination in Employment Acts** are the keystone laws protecting older workers.

RELIGIOUS DISCRIMINATION

Our founding fathers came to America to establish freedom of religion; however, some religions have had more difficulty than others in obtaining employment. Catholics, Jews, Mormons, and Buddhists have been subject to ridicule in various parts of the United States, more violently during certain times in history.

Religious fighting is more prevalent in other countries of the world than the United States. Riots and bombings in Ireland, India, and some Middle Eastern countries are just a few examples. Nevertheless, the United States does have religious discrimination problems.

The concept of reasonable accommodation for religious preferences has been the source of some confusion between the courts and the EEOC. **Reasonable accommodation—religious preferences** means employers are expected to consider religious beliefs in assigning work. The EEOC assigns the primary responsibility to the employer to reasonably accommodate religious preferences. Courts have put the primary responsibility on the individual. The challenge is to find a happy medium between the two extremes so that real reasonable accommodation of individual preferences and organization needs may take place. The number of religious discrimination cases is increasing dramatically.[3]

Conflicting signals on religious reasonable accommodation.

RACIAL DISCRIMINATION

The United States was divided from the beginning by racial tensions. White settlers drove out the native Americans and set up a system of labor based on black slavery. These two types of racism are still with us today. The native Americans were decimated, so that statistically the problem is not as great as with African Americans, who are the largest ethnic minority in the United States. However, the lot of today's native Americans is hardly better than that of many African Americans.

The United States also expanded into areas held by Spanish settlers and extended discrimination to the second largest ethnic minority, the Hispanic Americans. Asians, who first came here in large numbers to serve as cheap labor in the West, also suffer from discrimination. Originally, many other ethnic groups who immigrated here, such as the Irish, the Germans, and the Italians, were the objects of ethnic prejudice as well.

Almost 12 percent of the population is African American.

The subject of racial discrimination is an emotional issue and perhaps a few facts may help to give us all common ground for further discussions. African Americans number over 30 million, or almost 12 percent of the total U.S. population (see Figure 16–1). An additional 26,789,000 Americans, more than 9 percent of the total U.S. population, identify themselves as having an origin in a Spanish-speaking country. Those numbers are projected to reverse by the year 2005; that is, the numbers of Hispanic Americans are projected to grow more rapidly than the numbers of African Americans in the coming years.

Over nine percent of the population is Hispanic.

AFRICAN AMERICANS

Black pride is self-determination.

The term **black pride** (see Figure 16–2) was used to bring self-respect to some and fear to others. One store owner in Watts said, "Black pride means self-determination.

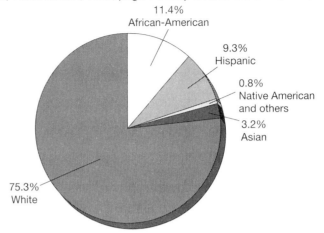

FIGURE 16–1 Distribution of Races Based on Adjusted 1990 Census in the United States According to the U.S. Bureau of the Census. Source: Statistical Abstract of the United States, 116th Edition, 1996, page 14. May Include More Than One Ethnic Origin.

That a black can determine his own destiny and his own future." This, in a way, is a great slogan for minorities but it may instill a fear in others.

Individuals need not necessarily see something good or bad when they perceive an object with color, but they are likely to see color. Bill Cosby, in films and lectures, has pointed out how our myths and fairy tales are filled with "white knights" and "black witches of the North." White attitudes about blacks have changed since the 1960s. Whites now see blacks in all sorts of settings they haven't seen them in before.

Integration has faded as a primary goal of many. The "here and now" issue of jobs is more important. There is a growing realization that integration won't put food on the table. And it is important to note that *hiring* minorities is not enough—they must be retained. That means effort on the part of employers, leaders, and peers. It is especially difficult for a minority employee who doesn't have very many, or even any, minority colleagues who share his or her cultural heritage and ethnic tastes in food, clothing, and entertainment.[4]

HISPANIC AMERICANS

Over 14 million Mexican Americans in four border states.

Of the more than 26 million Hispanics officially residing in the United States, 14 million are Mexican Americans. The four border states of California, Arizona, New Mexico, and Texas hold 90 percent of the Mexican Americans who live in the United States legally. Unless you live within this geographical area, you are not likely to know of the problems of discrimination that Mexican Americans may face.

Agriculture was the strongest agent in bringing together Hispanics. Mexican Americans may have ambivalent feelings about migratory workers in the farming community: Allowing people to come from Mexico to work as aliens, either legally or illegally, does put more people on the employment rolls, but a large supply of workers can keep the wages down for all of them. In addition, the Mexican Americans who are U.S. citizens often want to bring their relatives into the United States and also want to keep them out.

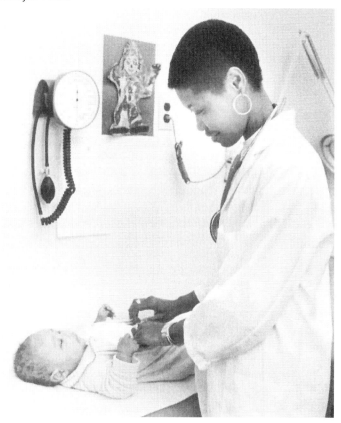

FIGURE 16–2 A New, Stronger Self-Pride Has Helped the Minority Cause in the Search for a Better Place in Society and for Job Opportunities. Spencer Grant/Monkmeyer Press

The Immigration Reform and Control Act passed in 1986 sought to deter illegal immigration so that the United States could continue our historically generous policy of legal immigration. The act requires employers to verify the eligibility of every new hire to work. Those who knowingly or negligently hire unauthorized workers are subject to stiff penalties.[5]

THE AMERICAN INDIAN NATIONS

A basic issue for many groups is how to integrate with the majority of society for the good of all but still maintain their unique individual cultures. A good illustration of the mobility of a member of the American Indian nations is U.S. Senator Ben Nighthorse Campbell from Colorado. Senator Campbell, elected in 1992, is also a successful businessman, entrepreneur, and rancher.

Many Indian leaders agree that unity of the native Americans or American Indians is in a large part the result of recent activism. Tribal officials indicate that there is a new determination among the nation's 1,500,000 Indians to "work within the system" through lawsuits to bring about legislation for their rights.

Three goals of native Americans. Their major goals include unity, respect, and results. Specifically, they want greater Indian control of the Bureau of Indian Affairs, federal lawyers to oversee Indian legal affairs, and direct supervision of federal funds by local tribes. The concept of Indian reservations is similar to government-sanctioned segregation.

ASIAN AMERICANS

Every major U.S. city has an Asian section that may be referred to as "Chinatown." However, the substantial Asian population is more evenly distributed throughout the United States than are the native Americans and Hispanic Americans. They can be found in rural areas as well as in the big cities.

Asian Americans appear as a race to experience less discrimination than any other racial minority. Why? Certainly the "coolies" of San Francisco and the railroad builders of the 1850s were treated much like slave labor. Can one reason be that as a group they are the most educated in America—even more educated than the Caucasians? The proportion of Japanese, Chinese, and Vietnamese men with college degrees is nearly 90 percent greater than it is for white men.

SOCIAL PROBLEMS OF RACE MIXING

The increase in Hispanic Americans has brought about rapid growth of bilingual and bicultural education in thousands of schools. A teacher in Los Angeles said that "English should be imposed only when the parents feel the child is ready for it, perhaps as late as the third grade. The child should learn in the language he thinks in. The child needs an approved emphasis on his own culture to feel good about himself." One minority member added, "I won't impose my culture on you, don't you impose your culture on me."

These conflicts could produce a backlash. Should an American taxpayer pay for bilingual education in schools, yet be denied a job because he or she is not bilingual? Further, should American taxpayers pay for welfare opportunities for illegal immigrants?

ACTION PROJECT 16–1 HOW LIKELY TO OCCUR? (INDIVIDUAL EXERCISE)

The following list is based on a sample from a military equal opportunity climate survey (National Guard version). You might complete the instrument for your own organization—military (if appropriate), company, school, or other organization. Use the following scale to make your judgments:

1. = There is a very high chance that the action occurred.
2. = There is a reasonably high chance that the action occurred.
3. = There is a moderate chance that the action occurred.
4. = There is a small chance that the action occurred.
5. = There is almost no chance that the action occurred.

In your unit during the past year:

1.	Unit special events (ath.etic programs, picnics, etc.) were attended by both majority and minority personnel.	1	2	3	4	5
2.	The commanding officer did not appoint a qualified white as executive officer, but instead appointed a less qualified minority.	1	2	3	4	5
3.	A race relations survey was taken, but no groups other than blacks and whites were used.	1	2	3	4	5
4.	During an intramural athletic event held during annual training, a white military member in the unit directed a racial slur at a member of another unit.	1	2	3	4	5
5.	A commander had lunch with a new black male officer (to make him feel welcome), but did not have lunch with a white male officer, who had joined his staff a few weeks earlier.	1	2	3	4	5
6.	A new minority person joined the unit and quickly developed close white friends from within the unit.	1	2	3	4	5
7.	A commanding officer discouraged cross-racial dating among personnel who would otherwise be free to date within the unit.	1	2	3	4	5
8.	When the commanding officer held staff meetings, females and minorities as well as white males were asked to contribute suggestions to solve problems.	1	2	3	4	5
9.	All equal opportunity staff were either females or minorities.	1	2	3	4	5
10.	A commanding officer giving a lecture took more time when answering questions from whites than when answering questions from minorities.	1	2	3	4	5
11.	When reprimanding a black enlisted person, the white noncommissioned officer used terms such as "boy."	1	2	3	4	5
12.	A reenlistment speech to a minority enlisted person focused on what a good deal the Guard is for part-time income; to a white enlisted, it focused on promotion.	1	2	3	4	5
13.	A commanding officer gave the same punishment to minority and white enlisted persons for the same offense.	1	2	3	4	5
14.	A commanding officer gave a minority subordinate a punishment for a minor infraction. A white who committed the same offense was given a less severe penalty.	1	2	3	4	5
15.	When a female complained of sexual harassment to her superior, he told her, "You're being too sensitive."	1	2	3	4	5
16.	The commanding officer assigned an attractive female to escort visiting male officials because, "We need someone nice looking to show them around."	1	2	3	4	5

1. You and other class members may want to compare responses with the instructor. Note that, unlike the original survey, this one does not ask for demographic data that could pinpoint you as the respondent (age, rank, ethnic origin, etc.).

2. What do you think of the appropriateness of this technique? of each question? Remember that this is just a sampling of a 100-question instrument.

THE OLDER WORKER

Older worker usually means those over 65 years of age but can mean those over 40 or 55, depending on the occupation; it may also mean 10 to 15 years from retirement. The troublesome truth is that the higher the age, the less dependable it is in revealing things about human beings. The aged may be more diverse and heterogeneous than any other group. One may be at different ages at the same time in terms of mental capacity, physical health, endurance, creativity, and emotions. Such overdone myths as senility, memory loss, dependence, and rigidity are still associated with aging.

Today more than 33 million Americans, or 12.7 percent of the total population, are over age 65 and the size of that age group is rising.[6] Certainly the number of older workers is increasing because of better health. Still the age of 40 arbitrarily seems to classify employees as older workers. And, whereas 35 is over the hill for many sports figures, age 60 can still be considered young for tool and die makers and some executives. The age of retirement minus ten or fifteen years usually marks the beginning of the "older worker cycle." The attitude of the individual, his or her skill, and company policies are all factors that tend to fix the age range for the older worker.

The "older worker" is age of retirement minus ten to fifteen years.

HOW OLD IS OLD?

"Middle age" is relative.

Have you ever thought how old an "older worker" really is? How old you are might determine how old you think an older employee might be. Age affects each person differently. Its effect depends on many factors, such as heredity, physical condition, working conditions, climate, use of alcohol or drugs, and emotional and psychological strain. However, supervisors should look for signs of change due to age in any employee over 50 years of age.

Psychologically, this period can be just as difficult for the older employee as the early years of employment are for the younger person. During this period the individual faces his or her last promotion. Individuals may be motivated to work harder, up to the point at which they know they probably will not reach another promotion. Thereafter motivation may operate to maintain the workers' status quo rather than to propel them toward self-realization.

SUPERVISING THE OLDER WORKER

In supervising an older worker, you have to consider the physical and psychological differences between the young and old. One study found that although older workers hold more positive beliefs about themselves than younger workers do, even younger workers tended to have generally positive beliefs.[7]

Quality often is more important than quantity to older workers.

How physical and psychological factors affect productivity and how technological change may affect the older worker must be considered. Errors are usually less acceptable to older workers than to younger ones. Efficiency and accuracy have become vital to them as evidence of their skill. The value of their contributions, too, is based more often on quality than on quantity. Figure 16–3 illustrates an example of an older worker productively employed.

HOW THE ORGANIZATION CAN HELP THE OLDER WORKER

The Age Discrimination in Employment Act (ADEA) protects employees aged 40 to 70 against employment discrimination because of their age. Historically, this legislation has been applied primarily to retirement, promotion, and lay-

FIGURE 16–3 Older Workers Are Usually Efficient, Accurate, and Team Players

off decisions but it applies to all human resource decisions and its use is increasing. Employers should be advised "that a blanket refusal to consider experienced or highly paid applicants for employment may operate to exclude older employees from job opportunities, in violation of the ADEA."[8]

Job engineering and job reassignment.

Job engineering and job reassignments are two other things that companies can accomplish to help the older worker. Job engineering is the process of redesigning the workstation so that work can be done in a way that is less taxing for the employee. It may be planning the work so that it can be done sitting down, providing different power equipment, reducing body movement, or changing the flow of work. Job reassignment is moving the person into a different position, in which the task does not demand so much in terms of dexterity or speed but is, it is hoped, just as rewarding. Older employees can become good trainers and setup workers and can rework rejects from the production line.

3. Do you have a clear idea of what you want from life five years from now? ___

4. Do you dress fashionably? _____

5. Do you read new books regularly? _____

6. Have you taken up a new hobby in the past year? _____

7. Have you made a new friend in the past year? _____

8. Does time seem to go fast for you? _____

9. Do you enjoy people who are younger than you are? _____

10. Do you enjoy traveling alone? _____

11. Are your friends a diverse group? _____

12. Would you consider a higher paying job that was less secure than your present one? _____

13. Are you flexible about your daily schedule? _____

14. Do you have romance in your life? _____

15. Have you bought something in the past six weeks that you knew you could not afford? _____

16. Can you laugh when you make an unimportant mistake? _____

17. Do you like change? _____

18. Are you so deeply involved in a job or a cause that you wake up in the morning eager to get at it? _____

19. Do you pamper your five senses every day: the taste of delicious food and drink? the smell of flowers or perfume? the sight of a sunset? the sound of music? the touch of a human hand? _____

20. Can you recall two new ideas or bits of philosophy you have learned or thought of in the last week? _____

The more "yes" answers you gave, the more youthful you are psychologically. Fewer than ten "yes" responses might indicate that you need to take a closer look at your attitudes, your society, and your feelings about your work.

THE EMPLOYMENT OF WOMEN

A working woman gains status.

The number of women professionals is growing significantly (see Figure 16–4). Today, of course, a good job is as much a status symbol for a middle-class woman as it is for a man, and even many affluent women now seek work for pay. More than 40 percent of working women are single, widowed, or divorced and are responsible for their own support and often that of others. Add to this figure another 10 to 25 percent of employed women who work because their mate's income is so low that the family cannot survive on one income. It is clear that few women go to work just for something to do or to buy luxuries.

Compared to other economies and cultures, women comprise a much larger portion of the workforce. Women make up 41 percent of the European workforce but they are not moving into middle and senior management jobs

FIGURE 16–4 More Than 50 Percent of the *Available* Workforce is Composed of Women.

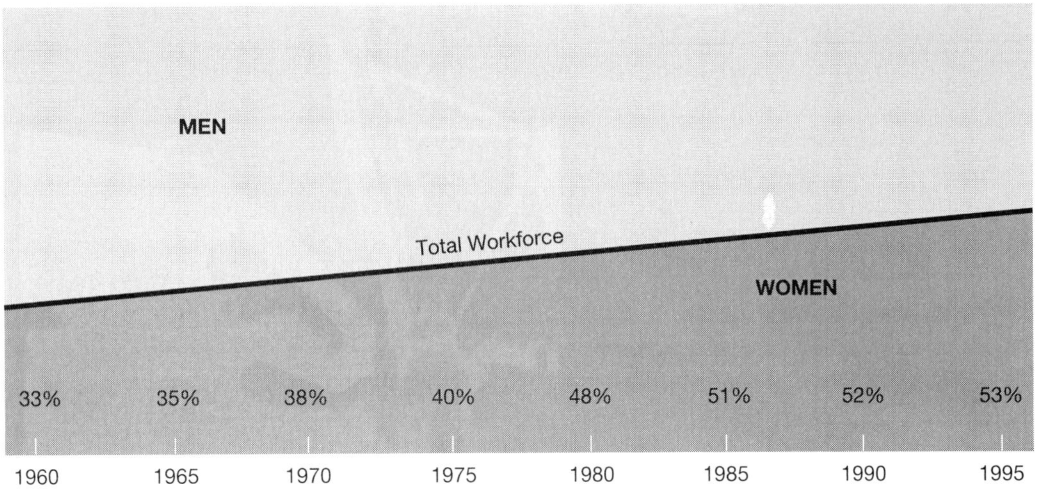

33%	35%	38%	40%	48%	51%	52%	53%
1960	1965	1970	1975	1980	1985	1990	1995

as fast as U.S. women.[9] Asian women comprise an even smaller percentage of the workforce, and ascend the corporate hierarchy much more slowly.

Possibly the new era for women started January 5, 1976, when *Time* magazine selected "Women of the Year" as having the most influence on history and everyday living for the year. The cover of the magazine pictured such people as Carla Hills, then head of the Department of Housing and Urban Development; Barbara Jordan, the black congresswoman from Texas; Billie Jean King of tennis fame; and Betty Ford, then first lady.

Women are advancing in responsible jobs.

Consider also Madeleine Albright, the first woman named to be U.S. Secretary of State, and the many Supreme Court justices and judges, women governors, U.S. senators, other politicians, and company presidents today. Many jobs are opening for women that were once taboo (see Figure 16–5). The greatest discrimination against women is most evident in industries such as steel, banking, finance, mining, and railroads. On the other hand, women have found less discrimination in advertising, high-fashion retailing, medicine, marine biology, dentistry, and physics.

Of course, there are some gender differences in jobs, training, turnover, and—unfortunately—pay. Significant differences are subject to interpretation:

> . . . the lower return to women's labor market experience may reflect employers' inability to accurately assess the amount of training obtained by the female worker in her previous employment. This lower return to experience could in turn induce women to choose jobs that offer lower training.[10]

AIMS OF WOMEN'S ACTION GROUPS

Some of the far-reaching attitudes of women that now influence business have been taken up by the women's action groups such as NOW (the National

FIGURE 16–5 As Yet No Woman Is Playing Halfback for the Los Angeles Rams, but Many Jobs Are Open for Women That Were Once Taboo, Such as Truck Driving, Telephone Line Work, and Auto Repair.

Organization for Women), the National Women's Political Caucus, and the Women's Progress Alliance, which was established in 1996 to improve the quality of lives for women and children.[11]

Demand for equal pay and promotion opportunities.

EQUAL PAY FOR EQUAL WORK AND COMPARABLE WORTH. The strongest demand is naturally equal pay for equal work, which is followed closely by equal opportunity for promotions. The reluctance to pass comparable worth legislation and adverse court decisions continue to hold back progress for equal pay made in recent years. Women's pay remains at about 70 percent of men's pay for comparable jobs, despite some slow movement to rectify the inequities.

Comparable worth is a belief that women performing jobs judged to be comparable on bases of knowledge, skills, and abilities should be paid the same as men. But the question is whether or not comparable worth should be legislated. One professor of government says "no":

> . . . We could help working women in ways costing far less than comparable worth by granting a fuller tax deduction for child-care costs, restoring the two-earner tax deduction, or punishing more severely noncustodial parents who ignore their legal obligations.
>
> Whether or not such measures are adopted, comparable worth should not be. Predictable and insurmountable problems have occurred wherever it has been tried. To adopt it as public policy would bring us more acrimonious politics and a much weaker economy. Women—and men—would both be losers.[12]

Another view is that equal pay for work of equal value has come to be inextricably associated with the application of job evaluations. Current trends towards performance-related pay systems may pose a threat to the pursuit of greater gender pay equality as discretion in pay determination increases, and there is no clear relationship between earnings and job grade.[13]

BREAKING THE GLASS CEILING.   Another objective of action groups is to break the "glass ceiling." The **glass ceiling** refers to a see-through barrier that prevents advancement for women and other protected groups to higher level jobs. They can see others in the jobs, but they cannot reach those jobs because of the barrier. Part of the Civil Rights Act of 1991 was a glass ceiling initiative to establish a commission to study and make recommendations on how to eliminate those barriers.

Some progress is being made in breaking the glass ceiling. According to one survey of marketing vice presidents, men were outearned by women who earned $127,000 to $129,000, respectively.[14] Another weakness of the glass ceiling is the high number of women executives in smaller companies. According to a Dun & Bradstreet survey, American women own 7.7 million businesses that employ 1.5 million Americans.[15] One other study concludes that long hours and exceeding performance standards are what it takes to break the glass ceiling for both men and women.[16]

CHILD CARE CENTERS.   There are almost 10 million working mothers whose children are under 5 years of age.[17] The demand for child care workers is among the fastest growing in the country, projected to be well over 1 million by 2005.[18] Companies are getting involved because they realize it is good business to take care of their employees. The president of one rapidly growing bank summarized many businesses' sentiments when "he helped open NationsBank's multimillion-dollar, state-of-the-art child care center for its employees in Charlotte, North Carolina. As local officials and bank employees sipped refreshments and admired the bank's first such center, Mr. McColl looked up at the cheery skylight and colorful mobiles and mused, 'I'd like to build about 60 of these.' "[19]

BIRTH CONTROL, PLANNED PARENTHOOD, AND FAMILY LEAVE.   The widespread use of birth control devices is only part of the issue of planned parenthood. Several companies are granting a day's leave for their male employees to have vasectomies. Some women and men are taking up the cause of family leave. They want to choose, without interference from the company, when they quit work to have a baby and when they will return. More men are taking paternity leave.

The family leave bill passed in 1993 provides up to twelve weeks of unpaid leave a year for birth or adoption of a child as well as to care for a family member with serious illness or to care for an employee's own health condition that makes him or her unable to perform the job.[20]

ABORTIONS.   Unwanted and unplanned childbirths have led to the acceptance of abortion by some women's groups. Note that the abortion and birth control issues have caused many women not to join the women's rights movement. There is some action to include abortion funds in national health care legislation. Although prevailing Supreme Court cases have found abortion to be a woman's constitutional right (*Roe v. Wade*, 1973), the Court has so far not recognized any constitutional right to use tax funds to implement that choice.

EDUCATION. Many women are encouraged to further their education beyond high school, not in the traditional areas of secretarial skills, but in fields pursued by males, such as accounting, law, and medicine. In high-risk or inner-city neighborhood areas, special courses are offered to mothers during the day, so they are not faced with walking to school at night. Short-term programs and televised courses are all attempts at meeting the demands of women for more education.

POLITICS. Although today there are several women senators, representatives, and judges, as well as women generals in the armed services, tension and conflict remain high between the sexes. Shari Caudron, frequent author and contributing editor for one of the nation's leading human resource journals, says: "The struggle for power, job insecurity and programs designed in the name of diversity, have all contributed to increased tension between the genders. Yet, few companies are doing much about it."[21] Based on her research, Caudron suggests how to deal with gender strife in the workplace:

- Admit that gender strife might be a problem at your company.
- Conduct employee surveys to learn how gender issues manifest themselves at your particular workplace.
- Start an ongoing dialogue between your male and female employees.
- Review HR programs such as sexual harassment prevention courses, diversity initiatives, and work–family programs.
- Address employee stress proactively by searching for ways to alleviate the sources of that stress, such as overwork, miscommunications, restructuring, etc.
- Be patient. Men and women working together is still a relatively new phenomenon.[22]

SEXISM. **Sexism,** job discrimination based on gender, is illegal. Recall that we discussed sexual harassment in Chapter 4. Courts are increasingly stringent about preventing sexual harassment and certainly sexual abuse, although these crackdowns may be freezing employer–employee as well as teacher–student relations.[23]

Nevertheless, there is reason to avoid stereotypical language, sexist job titles, and policies of exclusion. Terms like "gals," "girls," and "ladies" can all be offensive—just as "boys" or "you guys." People have names—use them! Sex bias also occurs in spoken and written words like "policemen" or "newsmen," demeaning terms to women who hold these jobs. They should be called "police officers" or "reporters."

DUAL CAREERS. **Dual careers** are career commitments for both husband and wife. For the dual-career couple, there is never enough time. Time is a precious resource. It requires an understanding of how the couple prefers to use it. And, as strange as it seems for the two people living together, it is often necessary to schedule pleasurable time together. Too often togetherness of a dual-career couple is dictated solely by their having to face and solve mutual problems.

Increased gender tension.

In 1980 a corporate scandal made the headlines of newspapers and the covers of business magazines. Mary Cunningham, an attractive Harvard MBA, and only 29 years old, was forced to resign from Bendix Corporation as a corporate officer.

The chairman of Bendix, William M. Agee, had elevated her in just fifteen months after graduating from Harvard Business School to his top assistant in charge of planning. At a meeting of Bendix employees, Agee, age 43, remarked that Cunningham's rapid advancement in the firm had nothing to do with the "personal relationship we have." Cunningham had insisted that she and Agee were never anything more than good friends. That caused a furor, and two weeks later Bendix's directors accepted Cunningham's resignation.

As a woman, what feelings would you have if you were in her place? What comments would you release to the press before the resignation? As William Agee, and after the board of directors and the public had expressed their concern about your "cozy relationship," what would your reaction be? What comments would you release to the press?

Who is more at fault, Mary Cunningham, William Agee, the board of directors, or the public?

EMPLOYMENT OF INDIVIDUALS WITH DISABILITIES

The **Americans with Disabilities Act** (ADA), passed into law in 1990, required employers to accommodate disabled individuals. As of July 1994 all employers with fifteen or more employees fell under the jurisdiction of the ADA. An **individual with disability** is someone who has a physical or mental condition that substantially impairs a "major life activity," has a history of, or is regarded by knowledgeable others as having such an impairment. Under the ADA, employers are expected to make **reasonable accommodation for an individual with disability,** any change in the work environment or in the way things are customarily done that enables an individual with a disability to enjoy employment opportunities.

Hiring individuals with disabilities does not increase insurance premiums.

Although thousands of firms are willing to hire individuals with disabilities, just as many are not. In the latter groups, reluctance to hire is based largely on the fear of extra expense. Here again there are fallacies about hiring people.

One insurance company stated that actuarial studies reinforced the belief that physically handicapped persons who are full-time employees not only do not increase group life, disability or medical care insurance cost, but actually exert a slight reduction in cost. An explanation offered for this is physically handicapped employees are aware of their condition, and are more careful in their work habits.

Individuals with disabilities may have special abilities. Illinois Bell financial strategist Dorsey Ruley has won national recognition as the skipper of his sailboat in major races on Lake Michigan. He also happens to be a quadriplegic. Ruley helped design a voice-controlled computer workstation that enables the user to dictate correspondence and execute computer programs. A modem and a series of voice commands enable the computer workstation to access electronic mail, dial, and answer the phone. Ruley says:

> The workstation makes it easier for companies to tap the disabled labor pool. It's a win–win situation, because there are lots of highly educated and trained people who are underemployed, or unemployed, because of a disability. It enables people with physical challenges to be part of today's high technology workplace, and provides employers with a solution in keeping with objectives of the Americans with Disabilities Act.[24]

AIDS

Acquired immunodeficiency syndrome (AIDS) is the final stage of an infection caused by the human immunodeficiency virus (HIV). HIV cripples the body's defenses, allowing cancers and life-threatening infections to develop. AIDS is covered against discrimination by the Americans with Disabilities Act. So is the rehabilitation of alcoholics and other drug users. Users of illegal drugs, those with sexual behavior disorders, and compulsive gamblers are not considered disabled.

Almost unheard of before 1981, more than 2 million people now have AIDS or are carrying the HIV virus.[25] But it is still difficult for most companies and other organizations to talk about employees with AIDS:

> . . . Current corporate mentality appears to consider that employing a person with AIDS is a "malady" worse than sexual harassment, computer fraud, employment discrimination, or insider trading. Our cultural, religious, moral, and ethical taboos typically exclude it from being discussed openly. Companies simply wish to ignore the reality that AIDS is an organizational problem that must be addressed.[26]

Develop an AIDS policy.

How should we address the organizational problems of AIDS? One of the important questions to be answered is "Who has organizational responsibility for decisions regarding employment of AIDS-affected individuals or HIV carriers?" Another is whether or not to have written policies regarding the infection. The preponderance of thought is that there should be comprehensive policies on the impact of AIDS to avoid fear and misunderstanding of the virus that can disrupt the workplace. A corporate AIDS/HIV policy should address the following issues:

- Loss of human potential
- Coverage and nondiscrimination of infected workers
- Equal treatment and workplace rights of HIV-positive employees
- Education and safety of coworkers
- Provision of health benefits
- Confidentiality for all employees

Levi Strauss is one organization that has a classic policy for AIDS awareness and treatment. Management believes that it is not enough for the personnel department to handle education with a flyer or announcement in a company manual. Levi Strauss Chairman Robert D. Haas says "there has to be support from the top." The goal is to create an atmosphere that makes HIV-positive employees "unafraid to disclose their illness. That involves a commitment not to ostracize the infected employee and an ongoing effort to sensitize coworkers and managers. 'You have to keep at it,' says Haas, 'but once people have HIV education, [AIDS] just settles down as an issue in the workplace. It's very moving, in fact, to see the way people respond to a coworker who has been afflicted by HIV.'"[27]

Treat all individuals with dignity and respect.

In summary, it is important that individuals with AIDS be treated with the respect and dignity accorded to every employee—just as we have discussed throughout this book.

OTHER TYPES OF DISCRIMINATION

There are other types of insidious discrimination—some labeled, some not. There is sometimes a harassment of individuals by management, and vice versa, irrespective of ethnic minorities, gender, and so on. Obesity and a generation gap are just two examples of more common discriminatory concerns.

OBESITY

Discrimination against obese workers also has won on-the-job protection. The EEOC has declared obesity to be a protected category under the federal disabilities law. But there is some resentment of that classification:

> "It's offensive," says Frances White [president of the National Association to Advance Fat Acceptance (NAAFA)]. "I am not disabled. I am an extremely healthy person." Instead, she and her group would like to see the civil-rights laws changed to address weight specifically.[28]

In 1994, obese workers did win protection under ADA. Nevertheless, the NAAFA believes that there is still discrimination against fat people. Ms. White relates that she applied for about 200 jobs and was asked to come in for interviews for more than 30 jobs:

> I would receive a call telling me I was exactly what they were looking for based on my resume. . . . I would be very encouraged, and I would show up for the interview, and there would be this shocked look on their faces— "You're Frances White?" Suddenly the job wasn't available.[29]

GENERATION GAPS

There have always been generation gaps. "Yuppies" were differentiated from other generations in the late 1980s and early 1990s. Another generation gap developed between employed "baby boomers" and more recent "twentysomethings" or "busters." The area of disagreement is that boomers seem "to get the best of everything" while today's young people get the dregs of society and low-status jobs. Several perce tions describe the differences:[30]

What "Busters" Dislike About "Boomers"	What "Boomers" Dislike About "Busters"
Brimming with energy and su erior technology	Threatened
You're blocking our way	Wait your turn
Too much politicking—not enough work	"Can you spell naive?"
You're stuck in old hierarchy	You have no respect for authority
You're not current on technology	You're right—stop rubbing it in
	Threatened by hotshots
	(The busters) are not loyal or committed

The most recent gap is that of "Generation X," the post baby-boom generation. According to Bruce Tulgan, CEO of a strategic think tank and author of *Managing Generation X,* "the label suggests that today's young people are unmotivated, apathetic, easily distracted and—to top it all off—arrogant and self-satisfied. In short, a human resources nightmare."[31] Fortunately, the behaviors described are still more the exception than the rule.

PSYCHOLOGICAL ROOTS OF PREJUDICE

Prejudice may be a projection of anger.

Sometimes prejudice is a projection onto other people of feelings we repress in ourselves. For example, if a person is angry and doesn't want to feel or show anger, he or she may suppress the anger into self and project it onto other people. That projection most often occurs when the person involved is dealing with the unconscious part of himself or herself.

We know that people's inner wars may be external to a common goal of anxiety, frustration, rationalization, and so on. Politicians know that one way to unite a constituency is to present the people with a common enemy. By providing oneself with an enemy to be feared, one can feel whole and not divided against oneself. In business, as in other aspects of life, we frequently meet individuals who blame their shortcomings on other people.

ECONOMIC ROOTS OF PREJUDICE

Prejudice and discrimination also have economic roots. Such fears are rational; obviously, if there are not enough jobs to go around, people will be competing for paying jobs, and people will compete for good wages. If one group of workers can be singled out, on the basis of some difference such as color, sex, ethnic background, or language, and if prejudice can be built up against such a group, then other workers will have a slightly better chance of getting the available jobs.

Competition for jobs feeds prejudice.

There is also a macroeconomic gain for employers in aiding and abetting discrimination in the workforce. Competition for jobs among workers can help employers to push down wages and working conditions. And there are always members of minority groups, having previously had little or no chance at jobs and needing to survive like everyone else, who are willing to take jobs that pay poorly or who will replace union workers to make a living. The situation is then ripe for social unrest.

Finally, as the United States becomes more involved in the international market, business managers are increasingly becoming aware that discrimination can make a disastrous impression on potential buyers and sellers abroad. When we practice discrimination and preach democracy, our credibility is lost.

PROFILE OF HUMAN BEHAVIOR

VALERIE J. MUNEI

Valerie Munei is the editorial manager for Quality Healthcare Resources, Inc. Her responsibilities include "managing the medical consultation report process; managing, training and mentoring of an editorial assistant; translating and uploading PC-based mainframe word processing; copyediting, rewriting, proofreading, and inputting consultation reports into the mainframe; developing, writing, editing, and producing the in-house style manual; managing and training freelance editors; providing orientation, continuing education, and ongoing feedback to in-house staff and independently contracted physician, nurse, hospital administrator, and engineering consultants; and serving as leader for a quality action team working on improving report turnaround time."

A tough "bill" to fill, but Valerie has taken advantage of her previous experience as a production editor, associate editor, and index editor at the Joint Commission on Accreditation of Healthcare Organizations, a bimonthly arts magazine, and Encyclopaedia Britannica, respectively. She has had many opportunities to interact with authors, other editors, and production staff.

Valerie's formal education includes undergraduate education in her native state of Hawaii, and a B.A. in Germanic languages and literature at the University of Chicago. As an Asian American, Valerie relates a number of concerns regarding job and pay discrimination: "It is a concern, although I have not experienced much racial discrimination in my career. I feel I have experienced pay discrimination in the field of work I have chosen. Publishing/editorial work tends to be demanding, yet does not compensate well.

"I think there is a link [between psychological, economic, and social roots of prejudice], but more that these roots affect educational opportunities, and therefore affect jobs and pay. For example, if you were raised with the idea that

(1) you are not smart enough, or (2) education is not important, you may not pursue education that could lead to a higher paying job. Or perhaps, you don't have enough money to do this, or your cultural group does not encourage education, or potential mentors will not help you pursue such goals.

"While I believe prejudice can affect self-image, I think more important to self-image development is the 'familial' environment you are raised in. I believe a caring, nurturing, ego-building environment can build a good self-image despite prejudice outside."

Valerie's response to the question: "How can the company help the older worker?" reveals a lot about her "get-up and go" and provides a good example of humility: "Do they need help? More likely, they can help the younger workers."

Valerie Munei concludes: "I never thought much about job and pay discrimination, although I believe I have felt their effects. In the past, I mostly thought about prejudice as a racial matter. Where I grew up (in Hawaii), prejudice is a fact of life and a minor one. Everyone had their prejudices, and yet people from all sorts of different ethnic backgrounds lived side by side as neighbors. I experienced much more racial prejudice when I moved to the mainland (as an Asian American, I had been part of the majority ethnic group before), but I did not experience it in my job life. I am well educated and really think that makes the difference. If you are lucky enough to be a skilled worker, racial discrimination diminishes."

FIGHTING DISCRIMINATION

Discrimination can be fought on the individual level, by reexamining prejudice and discrimination in the light of modern psychological theory. Self-knowledge is one of the most powerful weapons against prejudice. This sounds like such benign advice, yet any ideas listed here are only guidelines and constitute no magical solution.

EDUCATION

Discrimination can be fought through education. Much of the inertia that allows discrimination to exist is based on ignorance supported by tradition. Education is helping to break down old beliefs in the superiority of men over women, whites over nonwhites, one religion over another, and so on. Much of this battle against old patterns is taking place in the schools, but it is also affecting the public in the form of the public media, higher level training and research, and on-the-job training.

Unfortunately, there is some sliding backward as the rate of college-bound African Americans and Hispanic Americans declines. One source says that more than 50 percent of black high-school graduating seniors enrolled in college in 1976; that number shrunk to 36 percent in 1988.[32] The percentage of white college-bound students fluctuated between 50 and 55 percent over the same time period. According to an annual status report on minorities in higher education, blacks, Hispanics, and Native Americans continue to be underrepresented in four-year colleges and universities, and minority enrollments are either leveling off or declining.[33]

LEGAL AND LEGISLATIVE ACTION

The battle against discrimination is also being waged in the courts. Laws, of course, like education, do not substantially alter a society's general behavior—both systems reflect the trend of the majority and serve only to guide or coerce the minority into the general trend. It is important for business managers to understand the laws in order to avoid prosecution.

Civil Rights Act of 1964 prohibits discrimination.

The most important antidiscrimination bill of the many that have been passed in the last two decades is the Civil Rights Act of 1964, which made discrimination illegal if it was based on national origin, ethnic group, sex, creed, age, or race. Many discrimination cases have been brought to the courts by the Equal Employment Opportunity Commission, the federal agency established to enforce such laws. These cases define the areas in which the federal law applies and serve to rectify situations in which discrimination is being practiced.

EEOC enforces antidiscrimination laws.

Because the law is being clarified and modified continuously by the court decisions, employers need to be alert to changes in the laws at all levels of government.

One area clarified by the courts has been the testing of job applicants. The case of *Griggs v. Duke Power Company,* at Draper, North Carolina (1971), resulted in a decision that "(1) If any employment test or practice has a disparate effect on persons on the basis of race, sex, religion, or national origin, for example, a test with a higher percentage of black failures than white failures, and (2) that test has not been proven to be job-related and an accurate predictor of job performance, then that test constitutes an unlawful discrimination under Title VII of the Civil Rights Act of 1964."

In *Bakke v. University of California,* 1978, the U.S. Supreme Court agreed with Bakke and held that special college admissions procedures were unconstitutional. The school had accepted a lesser qualified minority applicant over a more qualified candidate. Bakke asserted that his rights had been violated because the school set aside 16 of 100 positions specifically for minorities. Thus, he was able to compete for only 84 of the 100 positions, whereas minorities could compete for all 100.

Reverse discrimination argument.

A classic case that cites reverse discrimination is *Firefighters Local Union No. 1784 v. Stotts* (1984). The U.S. Supreme Court held that the seniority rights of white firefighters could not be disregarded in protecting them from layoff. The decision reversed the lower court's findings in a class action suit filed under Title VII that charged the Memphis, Tennessee, fire department with engaging in a pattern or practice of racial discrimination in hiring and promotion practices.

The Supreme Court cut back on affirmative action programs in 1989 when, in *City of Richmond v. J. A. Croson,* it held that a plan to set aside 30 percent of construction contracts for minority business enterprises was constitutionally suspect. They said there is no such thing as benign racial classification—even if it is used as a tool to remedy past discrimination. Similarly, a dispute ensued regarding the University of Texas law school's affirmative action program. A circuit court of appeals declared the program unconstitutional, even rejecting the use of affirmative action for "the wholesome practice of correcting racial imbalance in the student body."[34] The ruling is on appeal to the U.S. Supreme Court.

In the summer of 1996, the U.S. Supreme Court did force formerly all-male military institutions like Virginia Military Institute or the Citadel to admit women, if they accepted government support.

WHAT IS AFFIRMATIVE ACTION?

Affirmative action is not neutrality but positive action.

Affirmative action is a federal mandate requiring an employer to make efforts to employ qualified members of minority groups. Affirmative action requires more than employment neutrality. An employer is required to make additional efforts to recruit, employ, and promote qualified members of groups formerly excluded. It recognizes the necessity for positive action to overcome the effects of systematic exclusion and discrimination, whereas neutrality in employment practices would tend to perpetuate the status quo.

In 1987 the Equal Employment Opportunity Commission directed government agencies to focus on removing barriers to the advancement of women and minorities. Managers were not required to meet quotas but they were directed that they should take race, national origin, and gender into account when choosing among qualified applicants.[35]

Many companies have affirmative action plans that contain specific procedures to ensure equal opportunity for employees in recruitment, selection, and hiring; training and promotion; termination and layoff; salary, benefits, leave; job classification; and nepotism.

There has been agitation to get rid of affirmative action goals and timetables, or at least to make them voluntary but many businesses prefer having at least flexible goals. Hewlett-Packard, General Electric, AT&T, IBM, and others have successfully used flexible goals and timetables in their affirmative action programs.

DIVERSITY

Capitalize on diverse strengths.

Many positive statements can be made for cultural, ethnic, and gender differences. Each group has special abilities, skills, and talents. It makes sense to capitalize on each group's strengths.

Diversity training (DT) is a business strategy to sensitize all employees to the unique culture and characteristics of its entire workforce. DT helps employees to increase their understanding and tolerance for people who are different. It helps management to develop more committed workers.

But in the wrong hands, training can disinter the very thing management is trying to accomplish. "Ineffective diversity training can raise the expectations of women and minorities, increase the fear and resistance among white males and harm an organization's diversity efforts."[36] Finger-pointing, white-male bashing, and language policing are just some of the ways to kill a good idea. In a very constructive article, H. B. Karp and Nancy Sutton describe seven symptoms shared by ineffective diversity training programs and their antidotes[37] (see Figure 16–6).

FIGURE 16–6 What's Wrong with Diversity Training?

WHERE DIVERSITY TRAINING GOES WRONG:	A MORE PRAGMATIC APPROACH:
1. Trainers are usually women or ethnic minorities.	No one can be entirely free of prejudice; trainers need to acknowledge their own prejudices.
2. Emphasis is on sensitizing the white male manager.	Audiences should be composed of mixed groups whenever possible; diversity training should be a priority for *all*.
3. Programs usually reflect a specific set of values.	Trainees have a right to state how they see things as long as the boundaries of good taste are reasonably observed.
4. Diversity awareness is the sole theme of the program.	Often more effective to deal with diversity as a component in a program focused on another need, such as team building.
5. Programs are frequently guilt-driven.	Acknowledge that past cultural injustices may have occurred; recognize that nobody has cornered the pain market; agree that each person must take full responsibility for his or her own actions, nothing else.
6. How something is said gains more importance than what is said or intended; training often centers on how misuse of words can create situations of chronic pain/loss of self-esteem.	Establish this guideline: "If anytime during the program someone says something that hurts you, interrupt with 'Ouch.'" That puts responsibility for taking care of oneself where it belongs—on the individual; gives the potential offender a chance to find out why; gives training itself credibility.
7. Time orientation is mostly past and future.	Deal with how people are, and make it safe to work now.

Others have been generally critical of diversity training and foresee its eventual demise.[38] More important than the diversity training programs is diversity itself. In large part, diversity is achieved better through education than training. Al Yates, featured in the Profile of Human Behavior in Chapter 11, says that

Diversity goes beyond the "melting pot."

> . . . higher education—like our society—will not survive if we rely on the myth of the "melting pot." Colleges and universities do not fulfill their obligation to students merely by enrolling them in classes. We are challenged to explore and realize the full measure of human potential—intellectually, culturally, socially and professionally. This cannot be accomplished through "disinterested benevolence." The issue of diversity is, and always has been, a question of balance and fairness. We cannot achieve our ideal by building artificial shelters—but we can build bridges.[39]

His sentiment is echoed by Donald Gerth, president of California State University at Sacramento and chair of the Accrediting Commission for Senior Colleges and Universities. Gerth says that diversity and educational quality are linked and are a

> . . . compelling condition of America today and tomorrow. Given our ethnically diverse society, what would you say of the quality of an education that provided no familiarity with the ways and histories of the groups to

which fellow students, citizens and coworkers will belong? We say that would represent a serious gap in educational quality and ultimately compromise America's future.[40]

The differences among people make our lives rich; it is important to remember that, as human beings, we have much in common but also significant diversity to contribute to our organizations and workplaces.

EXPRESS YOUR OPINION

1. Do you know persons (including yourself) who are underpaid because of an ethnic, religious, gender, or other discriminatory reason?

2. Do you know persons (including yourself) who have been sexually harassed at work?

3. Do you know persons (including yourself) who have been otherwise discriminated against on the job? in their living community? in social settings?

If you can answer "No" to questions 1–3, you are probably living in a protected, unique environment. On the other hand, if your answer is "Yes" to any of questions 1–3, then answer the following:

4. What is being done to diminish the effects of the acknowledged discrimination?

5. Are education and training playing any part in overcoming the specific discriminatory practices?

EMPLOYMENT AT WILL

An increasing concern in recent years has been the practice of employment at will. The **employment-at-will** doctrine holds that an employer can hire, promote, demote, or dismiss an employee at will for good cause, or for no particular cause, or even for morally wrong reasons. Employment at will is grounded in the free enterprise system, which leaves both the employer and employee free to enter into or terminate an employment relationship at will. Restrictions on that understanding have included laws that forbid firing based on discrimination or firing employees for organizing a union. Another major point to establish is whether an employee has been fired or quit willingly.[41]

The termination of poor performers is a particularly difficult problem in today's economic circumstances. Attention to employee rights discourages abuses and enhances employees' feelings of security, but it also can have a demoralizing effect on results-oriented managers. Thus it is important to get and keep our facts and records straight about who are good performers and who are not. Failure to follow a structured approach in dealing with problem employees can leave employers open to potential lawsuits and not allow them to salvage potentially good workers.

Loyalty is a two-way street.

Loyalty is a two-way street between employer and employee. Certainly there have been many examples in recent years of society granting more rights to individuals. It remains important for employers to respect the rights and human dignity of individuals with or without the law.

Prejudice is a feeling and discrimination is an action. In the last two decades, a social movement to combat discrimination has gathered force, especially in the area of employment. The prejudiced individual may be trying to project internal tensions and self-doubts onto another person or a group of people. He or she may also gain a sense of group solidarity or individual identity by following cultural patterns of prejudice against other groups or individuals. But the personal costs of prejudice are also high: guilt, tension, and the fear of retaliation.

According to the updated 1990 census, almost 12 percent of the population is African American, over 9 percent is Hispanic, and almost 3.5 percent is Asian. Discrimination is clear when we find that those percentages are not well represented in managerial and other professional areas.

Discrimination against the aged is common but often misunderstood. The aged may be more diverse; for instance, one person may be at different ages at the same time in terms of mental capacity, physical health, and endurance. There are overdone myths as to the dependence, rigidity, and senility of the aged; for example, less than 8 percent of "old people" suffer from senility.

About 53 percent of the total available workforce is composed of women. More than 40 percent of working women are single, widowed, or divorced and are responsible for their own support and often for that of others. It is clear that few women go to work just for something to do or to buy luxuries. Studies have shown that women's tardiness or absentee rates are in line with men's and that women are reliable workers.

Since the Civil Rights Act was passed in 1964, several laws have been enacted to aid in overcoming discrimination: primary emphases have been on antidiscrimination measures for the aging, individuals with disabilities, and family and medical leave provisions, as well as changes in minimum wage laws.

Affirmative action programs, some aspects of which are being phased out, still should be based on a thorough analysis of minority and female representation in various levels of the company. Disparities should be remedied by the achievement of a set of specific goals and objectives, not quotas, over a given period of time. Pay equity and comparable worth pay remain areas of blight on equal opportunity and affirmative action.

CASE STUDY 16–1

DISCRIMINATION AGAINST A WOMAN ACCOUNT EXECUTIVE

Diane Patterson is employed as a registered representative by Johnson and Hunt, a large metropolitan brokerage firm. Diane was promoted to this position five months ago when the company lost a few of its brokers to a competing firm. Diane had worked previously for a number of years as a secretary to Scott Pitts, one of the partners in the firm, and he recommended her for a promotion when a vacancy arose.

Although Diane assumed her duties with enthusiasm, Cliff Stevenson, the office manager, soon felt it necessary to question Diane on her deteriorating performance. Cliff suspected the reason for Diane's poor performance. When Diane assumed her duties as a registered rep, Cliff had heard some of the men speak against her, as if they resented her taking on the job. He also knew that Diane was losing customers for no apparent reason other than the fact that she was female.

When Cliff questioned Diane on this, she replied, "I don't like being the only female in the department. I feel as if everyone is against me here." And she added, "Many of my male clients seem to think that because I'm a woman, I'm not qualified to be an account executive." Diane also mentioned that perhaps a new start in another department would enable her to carry out her duties more effectively.

Cliff knows that Diane is capable of performing her duties, even though she has few clients, and with the shortage of account executives in Cliff's department, he does not want to lose her. Cliff decides to ask Scott's opinion on the problem.

"The men feel threatened by Diane," Scott replied. "They feel that being an account executive is a demanding job and should belong to men only. One of the men said that she has no right to fill a position that may be needed by a man to support his family."

"I find that a bit hard to believe," replied Cliff.

"Believe it, Cliff. Even Harry Morgan mentioned something about not only having to worry about younger men taking over his job, but now he'd have to worry about his secretary."

Now, understanding the problem that exists, Cliff must decide what course of action to take. If you were Cliff, what would you do?

1. Would you let Diane go?
2. Would you discuss the problem with the men separately?
3. Would you discuss the problem with Diane present?
4. How could you as a manager enhance Diane's status?
5. What is the best course of action for all concerned?

CASE STUDY 16–2

PROBLEMS IN PROMOTING A MINORITY

The executives of the Omega Computer Tape Company began to assemble for the bimonthly committee meeting. Wayne Baker, president of Omega Company, knew that this particular meeting would be a touchy one. The first item on the agenda, the one that he was concerned about, dealt with the proposed promotion of Jad Lloyd, a black resident of the community, to the position of supervisor of the shipping and receiving department.

For some time, the Omega Company has been without a minority member in a management position. Although the company has had minority members in management positions before, the last member left the company more than five years ago for a higher paying job in another city. When Brad Hall, the supervisor of the department under discussion, became eligible for promotion, this dispute began.

Bill Moore, head of the Personnel Department and former civil rights activist, feels that Jad Lloyd should be promoted to the supervisory position, because he is a minority member. He knows that Mr. Lloyd has been with the company for a good number of years, and from reports that he has received feels that Lloyd is qualified to handle a supervisory position.

Richard Speer, the administrative assistant of the shipping and receiving department, thinks otherwise. He feels that, regardless of the fact that the company needs minority members in management positions, the best qualified man should be promoted. It is his opinion that Mr. Lloyd is not the most qualified. He feels Mr. Manachek is more qualified and has more years with the company.

When the meeting begins and the discussion is opened on the topic, Bill Moore states, "If Mr. Lloyd is not promoted to this supervisory position, then we are failing in our obligation to ensure that minority members have an equal standing in this company."

"I'm all for giving minorities a fair shake," replies Mr. Speer, "but I won't stand for a man to be promoted over another just because of his color, black or white, as I feel you want done in this case."

"It's time that minority members were treated fairly around here, and it's high time we had one promoted to a management position!"

"Are you saying that regardless of ability, if it comes to promoting a black or a white, we should promote a black?"

"In this case, that is exactly what I am saying."

"That is reverse discrimination and I won't stand for it."

The meeting is obviously getting out of hand and Wayne Baker calls the discussion to a halt.

1. As president Wayne Baker, how would you handle the meeting?

2. Should he continue the meeting? If so, in what way?

3. Do you feel that Mr. Lloyd or Mr. Manachek should be promoted? Why?

DISCUSSION AND STUDY QUESTIONS—TO KEEP YOU THINKING . . . _____

1. Explain how discrimination is influenced by prejudice.

2. Explain why women and minorities often have poor self-images.

3. What are at least three ways in which discrimination can be overcome?

4. How old is old? What, if anything, should the organization do to help the older worker?

5. What are some of the actions that are being urged to lessen gender discrimination?

6. How do you define "individuals with disabilities" on the employment scene?

7. What is management's obligation to current and prospective employees regarding discrimination, irrespective of the law?

8. What role does "diversity training" play in overcoming workplace discrimination? Which is most important: "diversity" or "diversity training"?

9. How does "employment at will" affect both employers and employees? Explain how "loyalty" is a two-way street between employer and employee.

NOTES_____

1. "Diversity: Getting Past Stereotypes," *Supervisory Management,* August 1995, pp. 1, 6.

2. Bebe Moore Campbell, "To Be Black, Gifted, and Alone," *Savvy,* December 1984, p. 69.

3. Janine S. Pouliot, "Rising Complaints of Religious Bias," *Nation's Business,* February 1996, pp. 36–37.

4. E. K. Daugin, "Minority Faculty Retention: What It Takes—The Hire Is Only the Beginning," *Black Issues in Higher Education,* October 21, 1993, pp. 43–44.

5. Gillian Flynn, "The Immigration Reform and Control Act Demands a Closer Look," *Personnel Journal,* September 1995, pp. 151–153.

6. U.S. Bureau of the Census, Statistical Abstract of the United States, 116th ed., 1996, p. 21.

7. Barbara L. Hassell and Pamela L. Perrewe, "An Examination of Beliefs about Older Workers: Do Stereotypes Still Exist?" *Journal of Organizational Behavior,* September 1995, pp. 457–469.

8. Betty Southard Murphy, Wayne E. Barlow, and D. Diane Hatch, "Manager's Newsfront: Salary Test May Be a Proxy for Age Bias," *Personnel Journal,* October 1993, pp. 26–27.

9. Paula Dwyer, Marsha Johnston, and Karen Lowry Miller, "Out of the Typing Pool, into Career Limbo," *Business Week,* April 15, 1996, pp. 92–94.

10. John M. Barron, Dan A. Black, and Mark A. Loewenstein, "Gender Differences in Training, Capital and Wages," *The Journal of Human Resources,* Spring 1993, p. 361.

11. "New Alliance for Women," *Rocky Mountain News,* May 7, 1996, p. 34A.

12. Steven E. Rhoads, "Pay Equity Won't Go Away," *Across the Board,* July–August 1993, p. 41.

13. Jill Rubery, "Performance-Related Pay and the Prospects for Gender Pay Equity," *Journal of Management Studies,* September 1995, pp. 637–654.

14. R. Craig Endicott, "Crack Emerge in Gender Gap, Starting with the VP-Marketing," *Advertising Age,* December 11, 1995, pp. 26–27.

15. Sally C. Pipes, "Glass Ceiling? So What?" *Chief Executive,* April 1996, p. 16.

16. Bill Leonard, "Long Hours, Hard Work Can Break the Glass Ceiling," *HR Magazine,* April 1996, p. 4.

17. Statistical Abstract of the United States, 115th Edition, 1995, Table 615.

18. Statistical Abstract of the United States, 115th Edition, 1995, Table 651.

19. Martha Brannigan, "Coming on Strong: NationsBank Grows Rapidly via Innovation and a Slew of Mergers," *The Wall Street Journal,* December 28, 1992, p. A4.

20. Steven Olson, "Employees Dealing with Family Leave," *The Coloradoan* (Fort Collins), December 20, 1993, p. D8.

21. Shari Caudron, "Sexual Politics," *Personnel Journal,* May 1995, pp. 50–61.

22. Ibid., p. 52.

23. Jim Kennelly, "The Big Chill at School," *USA Weekend,* January 4–6, 1994, p. 18.

24. "Telecommunication: A Pathway to a Better Life," *Ameritech: Annual Report* 1992, p. 19.

25. Centers for Disease Control, Atlanta, Georgia quoted in Charles B. Clayman, M.D., *The American Medical Association: Home Medical Encyclopedia* (New York: Random House, 1989), p. 76.

26. Rose Knotts and J. Lynn Johnson, "AIDS in the Workplace: The Pandemic Firms Want to Ignore," *Business Horizons,* July–August 1993, p. 5.

27. Ron Stodghill II, "Managing AIDS: How One Boss Struggled to Cope," *Business Week,* February 1, 1993, p. 54.

28. Wade Lambert, "Obese Workers Win On-the-Job Protection against Bias," *The Wall Street Journal,* November 12, 1993, p. B5; also see, Robert L. Brady, "Obese Workers Win Protection under ADA," *HR Focus,* April 1994, p. 19.

29. Ibid.

30. Adapted from Suneel Ratan, "Generational Tension in the Office: Why Busters Hate Boomers," *Fortune,* October 4, 1993, pp. 57–70.

31. Bruce Tulgan, "Managing Generation X," *HR Focus,* November 1995, pp. 22–23.

32. "Colleges Enroll Fewer Blacks and Hispanics," *USA Today,* January 15, 1990, p. D1.

33. Ibid.

34. "Affirmative Action: Thumbs Down," *The Economist,* March 30, 1996, pp. 30–31.

35. "What is Affirmative Action?" *Government Executive,* April 1996, p. 14.

36. Shari Caudron, "Training Can Damage Diversity Efforts," *Personnel Journal,* April 1993, p. 1.

37. Adapted from H. B. Karp and Nancy Sutton, "Where Diversity Training Goes Wrong," *Training,* July 1993, pp. 30–34.

38. Jack Gordon, Marc Hequet, Chris Lee, and Michele Picard, "Is Diversity Training Heading South?" *Training,* February 1996, pp. 12–14; and William Beaver, "Let's Stop Diversity Training and Start Managing for Diversity," *Industrial Management,* July–August 1995, pp. 7–9.

39. Albert C. Yates, "Building Bridges: Diversity on Campus Demands New Responses," *Rocky Mountain News,* April 25, 1993, p. 95A.

40. Donald R. Gerth, "Letters to the Editor: Ethnic Diversity and Accreditation," *The Wall Street Journal,* January 26, 1994, p. A15.

41. William E. Lissy, "Fired or Quit?" *Supervision,* April 1996, pp. 20–21.

RECOMMENDED READING

Banas, Gary E. "Nothing Prepared Me to Manage AIDS." *Harvard Business Review,* July–August 1993, pp. 26–33.

Banta, William F. *AIDS in the Workplace: Legal Questions and Practical Answers.* Lexington, Mass.: Lexington Books, 1990.

Eichner, Maxine N. "Getting Women Work That Isn't Women's Work: Challenging Gender Biases in the Workplace under Title VII." *Yale Law Journal,* June 1988, pp. 1397–1417.

Fried, N. Elizabeth. *Sex, Laws & Stereotypes.* Dublin, Ohio: Intermediaries Press, 1994.

Hogler, Raymond L. *The Employment Relationship: Law and Policy.* New York: Ardsley House Publishers, Inc., 1989.

Howard, Cecil G. "Strategic Guidelines for Terminating Employees." *Personnel Administrator,* April 1988, pp. 106–109.

Hutchens, Robert M. "Do Job Opportunities Decline with Age?" *Industrial and Law Relations Review,* October 1988, pp. 89–99.

Karp, H. B., and Nancy Sutton. "Where Diversity Training Goes Wrong." *Training,* July 1993, pp. 30–34.

Knotts, Rose, and J. Lynn Johnson. "AIDS in the Workplace: The Pandemic Firms Want to Ignore." *Business Horizons,* July–August 1993, pp. 5–9.

Leo, John. "Our Hypersensitive Society." *U.S. News & World Report,* July 4, 1994, p. 21.

Lissy, William E. "Fired or Quit?" *Supervision,* April 1996, pp. 20–21.

McEvoy, Glenn M., and Wayne F. Cascio. "Cumulative Evidence of the Relationship between Employee Age and Job Performance." *Journal of Applied Psychology,* February 1989, pp. 11–17.

Solomon, Charlene Marmer. "The Corporate Response to Work Force Diversity." *Personnel Journal,* August 1989, pp. 43–53.

Susser, Peter A., and David A. Jett. "Accommodating Handicapped Workers: The Extent of the Employer's Obligation." *Employment Relations Today,* Summer 1988, pp. 113–120.

Waldholz, Michael. "Strong Medicine: New Drug 'Cocktails' Mark Exciting Turn in the War on AIDS." *The Wall Street Journal,* June 14, 1996, pp. A1, A4.

Williams, Christine. *Still a Man's World: Men Who Do 'Women's Work'.* Berkeley: University of California Press, 1995.

Wong, Diane Yen-Mei. "Why 'Model Minority' Doesn't Fit." *USA Weekend,* January 7–9, 1994, p. 24.

17

ORGANIZED
EMPLOYEE
RELATIONS

Again, here are some questions that you might think about as you read this chapter.

- Do you think that unions are as beneficial to society now as they were ten, twenty, or thirty years ago?
- Are there more strikes now than ten years ago? Why?
- What types of strikes are illegal?
- What is the difference between a mediator and an arbitrator?
- Do you think that public employees should be members of a union and be allowed to strike?
- What is the difference between a union shop and a closed shop?
- What is a yellow-dog contract? a boycott? a lockout?
- Why don't more people join unions?
- How does a gripe become a grievance?

LEARNING GOALS

After studying this chapter, you should be able to:

1. Appreciate the historical perspective and original needs for unions.
2. Explain the various attitudes that management can exhibit toward unions.
3. Give reasons why people join unions.
4. Relate the functions and difficulties of the shop steward and the company supervisor in the labor–management relationship.
5. Compare the basic negotiating procedures in collective bargaining from the union's and management's points of view.
6. Explain the various tactics that unions and management can use to achieve their goals.
7. Discuss "grievance procedures" and the types of arbitration that are used when no decision can be reached.
8. Describe the impact of internationalism on unions.
9. Define and apply the following terms and concepts (in order of first occurrence):

   - **organized employee representation**
   - **collective bargaining**
   - **National Labor Relations Act (the Wagner Act) of 1935**
   - **National Labor Relations Board**
   - **unfair labor practices (management)**
   - **Taft-Hartley Act of 1947**

- unfair labor practices (labor)
- right-to-work laws
- closed shop
- union shops
- Landrum-Griffin Act of 1959
- Fair Labor Standards Act
- labor union
- American Federation of Labor and Congress of Industrial Organizations (AFL-CIO)
- density
- containment
- cooperation
- dual loyalty
- certification
- shop steward
- grievance
- mediator
- arbitrator
- conciliation

A BRIEF HISTORICAL PERSPECTIVE

The history of organized employee representation is colorful—and sometimes violent. In short, **organized employee representation** means unions or other groups selected to represent employees to management. Much of the early part of this century was taken up in strike-breaking using Pinkerton guards and U.S. Army and National Guard units. At times, the "wars" became pretty ugly, bloody, and fatal, but eventually law prevailed. At first, most of the law to be enforced was common law, as determined by the courts.

Union membership increased until after World War I, when it leveled off during the "good times" of the Roaring Twenties. Then, with the coming of the Great Depression, Congress passed increasingly stringent legislation that encouraged and enforced collective bargaining.

Collective bargaining is the process by which representatives of employees and representative of management convene to negotiate a working agreement or other work rules. Collective bargaining first became part of statutory law with the passage of the **National Labor Relations Act (NLRA) of 1935.** The NLRA, commonly called the Wagner Act, guaranteed the workers' rights to form unions to represent them to management. It also set up the **National Labor Relations Board (NLRB)** to investigate cases of unfair labor practices committed by employers or unions. The NLRB is responsible for holding elec-

NLRA, as amended, controls organized employee relations.

tions to determine whether or not a firm's employees want a union or not and, if so, which one.

The act specifically listed **unfair labor practices (management)** on the part of the employer. It is an unfair labor practice for an employer:

- To interfere with, restrain, or coerce employees in exercising their legally sanctioned right of self-organization
- To dominate or interfere with either the formation or administration of a labor organization
- By discrimination in regard to hiring or tenure of employment to encourage or discourage membership in any labor organization
- To discharge or otherwise discriminate against employees simply because the latter had filed "unfair practice" charges against the company
- To refuse to bargain collectively with their employees' duly chosen representatives

Amendments to the NLRA include the Taft-Hartley Act of 1947 and the Landrum-Griffin Act of 1959. Essentially the **Taft-Hartley Act** amendments provided a list of "don'ts" or unfair labor practices on the part of labor (union). **Unfair labor practices (labor)** for an employee organization include

- Coercing or restraining employees in the exercise of the rights guaranteed to them for purposes of collective bargaining or processing of employee grievances
- Coercing or attempting to coerce an employer to discriminate in any way against an employee to encourage or discourage membership in a labor organization
- Refusing to bargain in "good faith" with an employer about wages, hours, and other employment conditions
- Engaging in certain strikes, boycotts, or other types of coercion
- Exacting excessive or discriminatory fees or dues from employees
- Causing or attempting to cause an employer to pay or deliver any money or other thing of value for services not performed ("featherbedding") and certain other discriminatory practices that will be defined later

A special part of the Taft-Hartley Act is the **right-to-work laws** provision outlawing the **closed shop,** under which only union members would be hired, and enabling the states to prohibit **union shops** requiring individuals to join a union before they can be hired. Right-to-work states include the following:

• Alabama	• Kansas	• South Dakota
• Arizona	• Louisiana	• Tennessee
• Arkansas	• Mississippi	• Texas
• Colorado (modified)	• Nebraska	• Utah
• Florida	• Nevada	• Virginia
• Georgia	• North Carolina	• Wyoming
• Idaho	• North Dakota	
• Iowa	• South Carolina	

The **Landrum-Griffin Act of 1959** was a bill of rights for union members designed to protect them from abuses of their own unions. Corruption and misuses of union funds, racketeering, and other practices prompted passage of the amendments. Rank-and-file union members continue to accuse their leadership of improprieties. In early 1994, a North Carolina teamster accused Teamster President Ron Carey of "excesses that drain the union's coffers."[1] Carey was proposing boosting dues by 25 percent to replenish depleted funds.

Executive Orders by Presidents Kennedy in 1961, Nixon in 1971, and others, brought to the public sector collective bargaining similar to that of the private sector. Many states as well as the federal government now authorize bargaining by government employees.[2] It seems that about every ten or twelve years, major legislation or executive action has been taken to bring about changes in labor laws.

The **Fair Labor Standards Act,** as amended, regulates the minimum wage, limits the number of hours that employees can work without being paid overtime, and discourages use of child labor. The law states the normal working week and requires time-and-a-half pay for all hours over forty worked by an employee during a week. There are some exceptions and exemptions, discussion of which is beyond the scope of this brief review.

WHERE ARE UNIONS GOING?

Some would argue that labor unions as we know them are quickly becoming a thing of the past. Indeed the rough-and-tumble, sometimes violent unions of the mid-twentieth century are, for the most part, changing. Of course, some violence remains in isolated strikes and other actions. But is the labor union movement dead or simply changing?

Some would mandate more union involvement and power. The Dunlop Commission, named for one of the members of the Commission on the Future of Worker–Management Relations, advocated active participation on the part of the government to increase the number of employees represented by unions. One of the fundamental principles of the NLRA, however, is that *employees*— not employers, not unions, not a government commission or agency—should decide whether they will be represented by a union.[3]

The strike has always been a major weapon of most unions. Some public employees, like police and firefighters in some jurisdictions, are prohibited from using the strike weapon. More fundamental than the right to strike, or otherwise get the attention of management, is the welfare of employees for which unions have fought. Many of the economic provisions employees desired have been obtained, and the unions must change their strategy and tactics to a more conciliatory and cooperative stance if they are to survive.

According to Peter Drucker, the single most important factor in the decline of labor unions is "the shift of gravity of the workforce from the blue-collar worker in manufacturing industry to the knowledge worker."[4] Drucker believes that unions have three choices: (1) do nothing and disappear, (2) maintain themselves by dominating the political power structure, or (3) rethink their function:

The union might reinvent itself as the organ of society—and of the employing institution—concerned with human potential and human achievement, and with optimizing the human resource altogether [emphasis added]. The union would still have a role as the representative of the employees against management stupidity, management arbitrariness, and management abuse of power. . . . The union would work with management on productivity and quality, on keeping the enterprise competitive, and thus maintaining the members' jobs and their incomes.[5]

No, unions and their influences are not dead but they must be restructured if they are to survive and serve a useful purpose. Certainly their impact and membership have declined but new horizons and opportunities for cooperative action remain and, in some sectors, are growing. Peter Seybold of Indiana University's Division of Labor Studies says:

The face of the labor movement is changing as women and minorities play an increasingly important role in the labor movement and in organizing drives. . . . Unions are focusing increasingly on issues that affect these newer members, such as child care, affirmative action, and sexual harassment. Other issues gaining prominence include national health-care reform, health and safety on the job, worker training, and education and rights of the disabled. [6]

ARE UNIONS PART OF A PROBLEM OR PART OF A SOLUTION?

Question: First, what problem? *Answer:* The productivity problem(s). Recall our discussion of productivity problems from Chapters 1 and 2. Are unions contributing to the productivity problems? In other words, are we better off with or without unions?

Unions can have positive influences.

Fortunately, a reevaluation of earlier research on the role of unions answers those questions. Richard Freeman, one of the outstanding authorities on unionization in the recent decades, confirms the following:[7]

1. Unionism reduces the probability that workers will quit their jobs and increases the tenure of workers with firms.
2. Unions alter the composition of the compensation package toward fringe benefits.
3. Unions reduce the inequality of wages among workers with measurably similar skills.
4. Union workplaces operate under more explicit rules than do nonunion workplaces.
5. Most unions are highly democratic, especially at the local level . . . far from being the corrupt institutions that union-baiters often allege.
6. The view that unions harm productivity is erroneous. In many sectors, unionism is associated with higher productivity. In only a few sectors is unionism associated with lower productivity.

7. It is erroneous to blame unionism for national macroeconomic problems, such as wage inflation or aggregate unemployment.

8. Union wage gains reduce the rate of profit of unionized firms, motivating considerable antiunion activity by employers.

9. The decline in union density is due in large part to employer opposition to union organizing in National Labor Relations Board representation election campaigns.

Unions can also have negative effects.

As positive as Freeman's analysis is, there are some negative aspects of union behavior today as well. Freeman concludes that the research and labor market developments of the 1980s clearly indicate that the unionism of the 1990s and into the twenty-first century will have to differ in major ways from the unionism that developed under the Wagner Act:[8]

And will have to change to survive.

> . . . To succeed, unions will have to enhance their voice role in defending workers, providing democracy at the workplace, and improving workplace conditions. . . . The evidence from the 1980s suggests that these changes are necessary, not only for society to obtain the greatest benefit from the union institution, but also for unions to rejuvenate themselves.

Recall the information on the change process and resistance to it described in Chapter 15:

1. People protect the status quo.
2. People resist making changes because of habit, fear of unknown, "security," and loss of power and control.

Union development today is a classic example of this resistance to change because of all the aforementioned reasons. Today's wage earners often fear that the company holds all the keys to their well-being and, rather than lose what they have, will accept what the company offers on any ground to protect what they have won for themselves in the past.

Employees don't own what they produce.

Laborers, craftsmen, and skilled workers no longer own what they make, as many of them did in the Middle Ages. Their labor and only their labor is contracted out to the factory. The factory or company is sole owner of everything produced by the workers. The only thing they can claim is ownership of their labor. If they sell their labor to a company, most laborers feel that they have the right to bargain over the price of their labor, just as the company has the right to haggle with the buyers of their product over its wholesale cost (see Figure 17–1).

This section includes a positive challenge: both employers (management) and employees (labor in general as perhaps represented by labor organizations) must be more flexible in the future. Flexibility here means attitude and "heart" as much as specific job assignment. Two authors summarize:

> The power to reassign work and workers, the flexibility so envied by managers in union companies, is not a productivity panacea because it sets in motion protective human behavior. Indeed in some nonunion settings, the company may choose to "buy" individual worker cooperation in ways that are ultimately counterproductive. . . .
>
>   The very fact that employee participation programs have been introduced so widely in the nonunion sector is evidence for our view in this regard. In part, nonunion employers are recognizing that the top-down exercise of managerial power may not maximize productivity, both *because*

FIGURE 17–1 Most Crafts People and Laborers Feel Their Wages Should Reflect Bargaining over the Price of Their Labor. Laima Druskis.

managers do not know everything [emphasis added] and because workers can react to "managerial flexibility" in ways inhibiting productivity.

WHO ARE UNION MEMBERS?

A **labor union** is an organization of employees formed for the purpose of furthering the interests of their members. Most people think of unions in terms of the "blue-collar" movement, because most union members have been in such fields. The **American Federation of Labor and Congress of Industrial Organizations (AFL-CIO)** is a national federation of many of the craft and industrial unions. One of the largest unions within the AFL-CIO today, however, is the American Federation of State, County, and Municipal Employees, which includes white-collar as well as blue-collar workers.

Other large unions include the Teamsters, the Food and Commercial Workers, and the National Education Association, an employee representation organization. The United Auto Workers is one of the largest unions affiliated with the AFL-CIO. It rejoined the AFL-CIO in June 1981 ending a thirteen-year separation. The Teamsters also affiliated with the AFL-CIO in the late 1980s. Another major merger was between United Steel Workers and United Rubber Workers on July 1, 1995.

Table 17–1 shows the percentage of union members in various employment sectors. Note that membership is declining in almost all sectors. The greatest potential for union development is in the retail, services, and financial sectors, and also among the medical and legal professions. Public employee

TABLE 17–1 Union Membership (as a Percentage of All Workers in an Employment Sector of the United States)

	1980	1985	1987	1992	1995
Transportation and public utilities	48.4%	37.0%	33.5%	31.2%	27.3%
Government	35.9	35.8	36.0	36.9	37.8
Manufacturing	32.3	24.8	23.2	20.3	17.6
Construction	30.9	22.3	21.0	21.1	17.7
Mining	32.0	17.3	18.3	15.0	13.8
Wholesale and retail trade	10.1	7.2	7.1	6.7	6.1
Services	8.9	6.6	6.3	5.7	5.7
Finance, insurance, and real estate	3.2	2.9	2.3	2.4	2.1

SOURCE: U.S. Department of Labor, Bureau of Labor Statistics, and Bureau of International Labor Affairs, *The American Workforce*, September 1992, p. 23; and U.S. Bureau of Census, *Statistical Abstract of the United States,* 116th ed., 1996, p. 438.

FIGURE 17–2 The Percentage of Union Members Relative to the Total Workforce. Source: *Statistical Abstract of the United States*, 116th ed., 1996, pp. 437–38.

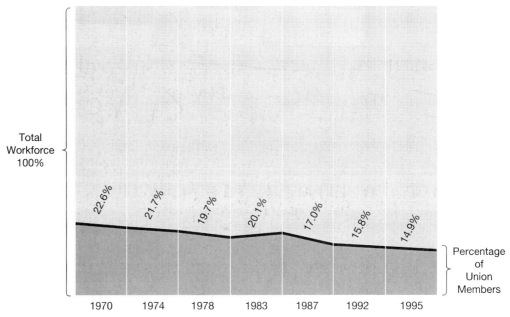

unions have been the fastest growing of any segment of unionism. This sector includes teachers, police officers, firefighters, and county employees.

Even middle-class workers have sought to join unions. More than 4 million white-collar workers are now represented by unions. Despite their growth, however, labor organizations have not kept up with the growth of the labor force (see Figure 17–2). This is due in part to management's decision to offer the same benefits to nonunion employees that union members would receive. Membership in unions has been steadily declining from more than 30 percent of the civilian labor force prior to 1960. **Density,** the percentage of civilians in the workforce who are union members or otherwise represented, is high in some sectors.

A CLASH OF GOALS

Management versus unions.

The relationship between labor and capital is hand in glove. One cannot survive without the other, but a struggle between the two has been going on for years. With few exceptions, every company in the United States, regardless of size, has been faced with the fact that attempts at union organizing are here to stay. There are no precise formulas to make dealing with unions easy and no directions on the back of union contracts to help management come to an understanding of how a union works or why it is necessary in the first place.

Too often, both the company management and the union forget that the other is made up of people and that working with and understanding people takes more time and effort than does mastering a complicated computer language. Computer languages are logical and always consistent; people rarely are. Management sees the union as a corporate body that is in opposition to management goals. Unions see management as a profit monster that will take no time or expense to attend to the needs of the workers who feed it. A good example of this clash of goals is in the major league baseball and football owners and players' associations.

MANAGEMENT'S ATTITUDES TOWARD UNIONS

The goals of management, which are varied, include profit making, market development, and corporate efficiency. By concentrating on efficiency and profit, the managements of many American companies have neglected personnel problems for a long time, leaving such problems to the supervisors and shop superintendents. Faced with unions challenging their authority, employers have in the past generally been opposed to unions.

Some U.S. employers have now come to accept unionism and forms of collective bargaining. But a few are bitterly opposed to the principles of unionism. The typical attitudes of employers can be classified from exclusion to *cooperation,* with intermediate steps of *containment, acceptance,* and *accommodation.*

Exclusion.

When the employer's policy is that of union exclusion, management tries to discourage workers from joining unions by coercion or by trying to provide the wage and fringe benefits that the competitors grant through collective bargaining.

Containment.

Faced with a law compelling them to deal with unions, many employers grudgingly act accordingly, but do everything possible to wean the loyalty of the workers away from the union. Under **containment,** all relations with the union are kept on a strictly "legal" basis, and the scope of collective bargaining is kept as narrow as possible. By doing so the company hopes to rid itself eventually of collective bargaining.

Acceptance, accommodation.

Another attitude toward unionism is that of acceptance and accommodation, in which the employer recognizes the union as part of the industrial scene and tries to use collective bargaining to improve its relations with its employees.

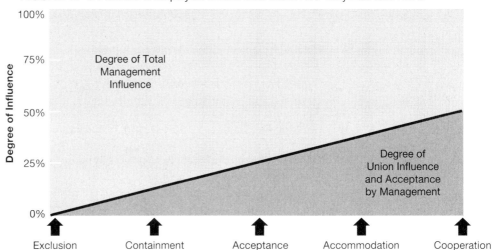

FIGURE 17–3 Attitudes of Employers toward Unions and How They Deal with Them.

Cooperation. Finally, there is the relationship of **cooperation,** in which management actually seeks the assistance of the union in production problems that are not usually the subject matter of collective bargaining. Acceptance and accommodation are more prevalent than are exclusion or cooperation (see Figure 17–3).

ACTION PROJECT 17–1 YOUR UNION ATTITUDE (INDIVIDUAL EXERCISE)

The following test will judge your attitude toward unions. Select one of three answers for each question. Your choices are as follows: "I agree with the statement" (Agree), "I am not sure how I feel" (?), or "I disagree with the statement" (Disagree).

	AGREE	?	DISAGREE
1. As an employee I would discourage other workers from joining a union by encouraging better wages without the union.	A	?	D
2. Collective bargaining is a strong tool of unions but not a good way to solve problems.	A	?	D
3. Union negotiations should be kept strictly to the letter of the law.	A	?	D
4. Employees would be better off without collective bargaining.	A	?	D
5. The unions are part of the American scene and must be accepted as an integral part of business today.	A	?	D
6. More people today accept the idea of unionism than they did ten years ago.	A	?	D
7. The employers today more readily recognize the unions and meet with them on a continuing basis.	A	?	D
8. Collective bargaining is a constructive way to improve relations between employees and employers.	A	?	D

9. Smart managers actually seek assistance from the unions   A   ?   D
   in production problems that are not the subject of
   collective bargaining.

10. The smart supervisor considers the shop steward as a help   A   ?   D
    rather than as an adversary (an enemy).

This test was constructed from the typical attitudes of employers toward unions. The first four questions relate to EXCLUSION and CONTAINMENT, and the remaining six questions relate to ACCEPTANCE, ACCOMMODATION, and COOPERATION.

If you answered "I agree" to the first four questions and "I disagree" to most of the last six, you are probably a strong management person. If you disagreed with the first four questions and agreed with most of the last six questions, you are probably a union person. Rate yourself based on the test:

MANAGEMENT PERSON _____ UNION PERSON _____ NOT SURE _____

DUAL LOYALTY

Dual loyalty or divided loyalty.

Dual loyalty is employee loyalty felt for both employer and union. Sometimes the employee must decide between the two just before a contract vote. With employment and union membership comes a problem unique to workers. Their wages come directly from their employer, but they perceive that the protection of their rights and privileges as employees comes from their union. Some personnel managers and union officials believe that employees will give their loyalties to the side that benefits the *individual* most, without considering the overall impact of their actions on society or on the economy.

Public reaction can give support to one side.

No longer can unions or management count on blind support from their members or employees. So many more aspects of labor problems have been brought to public attention that union employees cannot help but know the effects of their proposed actions even before they are taken. Workers are forced also to take public reaction into account now because the public, through television, may know about the strike or walk-out even before some of the workers do, and public reaction will be instantaneous. Public sympathy for a strike for higher wages or increased fringe benefits cannot be gained by simply making the facts known, no more than management can get the public on its side by claiming low profits and increased costs.

WHY DO PEOPLE JOIN UNIONS?

Poor morale rather than wages encourages employees to join unions.

On the surface, people join unions for economic advantage and security. In other settings, nonwork benefits, political ideology, and social values may be reasons for unionization.[9] They also gain some personal protection through the grievance procedures. But both unions and employers will often agree that it is not wages alone but inhumane treatment of employees that leads them to join unions.

Job satisfaction, job security, and positive attitudes toward unions are among major reasons why people join unions. If an individual does not receive job satisfaction on the job from management, then the union provides an attraction. Similarly, if an individual has no assurance of continued employment, he or she finds job security in belonging to a union.

Faced with the threat of unemployment in the 1990s, union members have shifted their priorities from compensation issues to job security issues.[10] It is more difficult for management to get rid of a union employee than a nonunion employee because of formalized grievance procedures and other mechanisms built into a collectively bargained agreement.

When a company becomes highly structured and bureaucratic, it can create a breeding ground for unions. When all the rules have been written by the employer with no representation on the part of the employees, look out nonunion companies! Many large industries such as banking, insurance, and finance cultivate bureaucratic systems, partly due to size. If there is no effective "open-door" or complaint and grievance policy, the firm is encouraging unionization.

WHAT CAN UNIONS PROMISE?

1. Unions can reveal working conditions that are not equal to those for other employees in similar situations, but they cannot promise better wages, working conditions, or benefits.
2. They can usually deliver a job posting system that provides employees with the opportunity for upward mobility. Every vacancy should be posted with a job description, salary range, and necessary qualifications.
3. They can usually develop a complaint system that can be monitored by the union to protect employees against jeopardy.
4. Most often, unions provide in their contracts for promotion by seniority where skills are equal, eliminating cutthroat competition and affording a feeling of regularity and justice.

EXPRESS YOUR OPINION

Analyze your own community in terms of union activity. Would you say that your community is becoming more union or more management oriented? For example, do you see evidence of union activity around the company plants, or on main street, or in the local newspaper? Have you seen pro- or antiunion activity on bulletin boards, on the local television, or at street rallies? What main points are used by union or management to gain supporters? Are the political issues really clear? Can you relate to a particular company in town and identify which attitude it is using with the unions? Is it exclusion, containment, acceptance, accommodation, or cooperation?

AN ELECTION CAN VOTE A UNION IN OR OUT

A **certification** is an election used by the NLRB to determine whether an identified union will represent the employees. They can also be decertified—

UNION ELECTION TERMINOLOGY

- **Recognition.** If the employees of a company wish to be represented by a union and more than 30 percent of the workers sign the recognition card, the cards will be submitted to the National Labor Relations Board. Once the NLRB certifies the list, an election will follow.

- **Certification (election).** Once an election is called, the union can request a list of all employees and their addresses. The union can contact them at home, but not on the company grounds. A simple majority, 50 percent plus one, of a substantial or representative number of eligible employees, can bring union representation into a company.

- **Decertification.** At the end of a union contract, if the union members wish to terminate their relationship with the union, more than 50 percent of the union members must vote for a decertification.

- **Deauthorization.** If union conditions are so bad during the time of the contract, a deauthorization vote can be called. To deauthorize a union, more than 50 percent of all the employees must vote to deauthorize a union. That includes employees who may be absent during the day of the vote.

---

removed as the representative of the employees. Both elections require a simple majority, 50 percent plus one, of those voting.

THE TWO PERSONALITIES IN THE MIDDLE

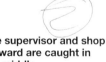

The supervisor and shop steward are caught in the middle.

There are two positions within the structure of the typical company whose occupants are answerable to more officials, managers, workers, and boards than any other positions, including company president (Figure 17–4). These two are the shop steward and the company supervisor. Although on opposing sides, their functions are similar, and each is situated in the hierarchy of either the union or the management so that each is one step above any worker on the line. Each has the unenviable position of being answerable to higher-ups who sometimes have no practical knowledge of the work.

SHOP STEWARD

The shop steward represents the employee.

The steward's attitude reflects the attitude of the employees.

On the union side, the **shop steward** is a representative for a specific group of workers and is generally elected by the workers in his or her department. The steward is an employee of the company and works by the side of the men and women represented. Provisions are usually made in the union contract that allow the shop steward time off to conduct union affairs. The steward's attitude toward management is a reflection of the attitude of the workers.

FIGURE 17–4 The Union Adds an Additional Formal Organization to the Employment Relationship.

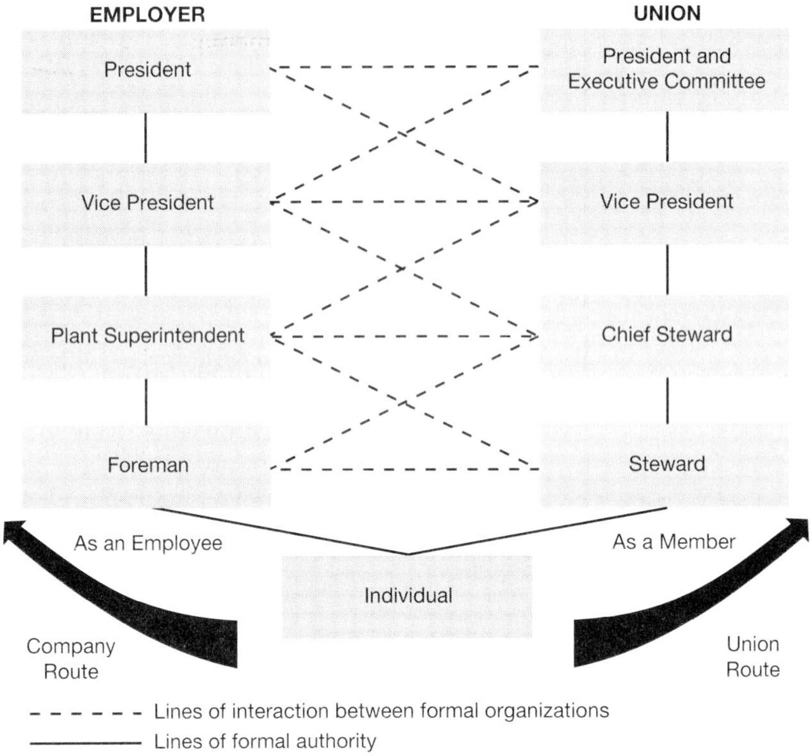

EMPLOYER		UNION
President		President and Executive Committee
Vice President		Vice President
Plant Superintendent		Chief Steward
Foreman		Steward

As an Employee   Individual   As a Member

Company Route   Union Route

- - - - - - Lines of interaction between formal organizations
——————— Lines of formal authority

If the union is new and the members are militant, they may elect a person whose main quality is expertise in rallying support against the company. This antagonism, if recognized by management, can be dealt with by establishing management credibility. Many of the problems coming from the growth of a new union are related to the workers' general suspicion of management.

The steward hears employee complaints.

The shop steward functions as a safety valve in most cases. He or she represents individual employees in grievance hearings with management. The steward listens to employee complaints and advises whether an employee is justified in taking the complaint to management. On occasion, the supervisor may bring a problem to the shop steward that the steward forwards to the individual involved. Generally, stewards are more satisfied with procedures that permit oral presentation of grievances at the first step and include screening by grievance committee or other union officials.[11]

COMPANY SUPERVISOR

A realization of the importance of the supervisor in labor–management relations has brought about critical changes in the selection and training of supervisors by American management. Some time ago, supervisors were selected primarily for their ability to produce and for their industrial skill. The emergence of the union as a force in business has caused a reduction in the power of the supervisor, forcing the qualities of leadership and ability in personal relationships to take precedence over manual skill in the selection of new supervisors.

Training programs for supervisors are needed.

An increasing number of companies have instituted training programs to teach their supervisors elemental psychology, leadership skills, and group dynamics. Even the most carefully designed training program sometimes fails to overcome the old system of unquestioned authority, and the supervisor must learn to satisfy the needs of management and to cope with the workers' new status as a bargaining force.

Union strength can undermine the supervisor's authority.

Union power is, in many cases, so strong—involving discipline, work assignments, seniority, transfers, and so on—that frequently supervisors feel they don't have the authority to deal properly with the people under them. As they become better acquainted with the union and its functions, the supervisors may realize that shop stewards, who were once regarded as the uncooperative antagonists, can be useful in maintaining discipline, screening unwarranted complaints, counseling employees on personal problems and work habits, and communicating with management about employee problems.

Developing mutually beneficial communications can result in a supervisor–steward relationship that would alleviate many of the difficulties inherent in the labor–management conflict. The shop steward is also a leader and is often influential in determining the opinions of the wage earner concerning management. A mutual understanding and open lines of communication between the steward and the supervisor are imperative.

COLLECTIVE BARGAINING AND GRIEVANCES

Bargaining agreement is legal, has time limits, and is complete.

Although considered by some to be a legal contract, the collective bargaining agreement is much more flexible than a contract. It does have some of the properties of a contract, however: (1) It can be enforced by law, (2) it has a time limit, and (3) it is complete in itself. But provisions for change that are built into the agreement allow one or the other of the parties to interpret and apply the clauses on a continuing basis. It is a working document of conflict resolution and, as such, is subject to renewed debate if conditions not covered by the agreement arise at a later date. Because the collective bargaining agreement is flexible, it is also interpreted in many different ways. In the opinion of some, it merely controls day-to-day union–management relations. This is a limited interpretation and covers only a small portion of the intended purpose of the agreement.

The collective agreement can be divided into three sections: (1) binding provisions, which include clauses in which little or no change is anticipated by either party (e.g., wages, union security, and the duration of the contract itself); (2) contingent clauses governing actions taken by union or management concerning new conditions not present at the time of agreement (e.g., promotion, transfer, change in operation techniques, governmental legislation); and (3) grievance procedures for use when disputes arise concerning interpretation of the agreement.

Understand the issues.

1. A clear understanding of the issues is necessary. The issues may be wages, severance, conditions of work, the criteria for promotion, seniority rules, discipline, delays in the settlement of grievances, or disputes over interpretation.

2. If the dispute involves procedures, it should be made clear that the disagreement concerns the ways of attaining goals. Formulating criteria and agreeing on how to evaluate procedures must be spelled out clearly in operational terms.

3. Management should be acquainted with the unions, their leaders, structure, policies, and style of negotiation. The basic attitudes of how union leaders or managers accept or reject ideas, and trust or suspect each other, will directly determine the degree of success at the bargaining table.

Negotiators must know what to obtain and what to concede.

4. Negotiators should estimate, as part of their preparation, what they want to get and what they are indifferent to getting. What they will concede, cannot concede, and could possibly concede are important tools of compromise. Negotiators should also be aware of the alternatives available to them in case agreement cannot be reached. They should be prepared to negotiate at a future time for employee benefits or changes that cannot be made at present. In effect the negotiating process should not be a zero-sum game—the more I win, the more you lose. However, the negotiation process seems to be ruled more by human nature than by logic.

A GRIPE CAN BECOME A GRIEVANCE

The company's handling of worker complaints is the same whether or not unions are involved. The essential difference in a unionized shop is that a dissatisfied worker may appeal the supervisor's decision by filing a formal charge, or grievance, against the company for a violation of one or more of the articles of the labor agreement. A **grievance** is a complaint about an alleged violation of a collective bargaining agreement or the law as it applies to a worker.

Consider each gripe a potential grievance.

A complaint handled improperly can and often does become a grievance.

The contract between union and management spells out precisely workers' rights involving wages, hours, and working conditions. The contract is a formal, written document that limits the union's authority, as well as management's in general, because all parties to the contract must operate within the restrictions spelled out in the contract.

HOW TO PREVENT GRIEVANCES

The only sound way to prevent grievances is to study the reasons behind complaints. Discontent among employees often stems from an accumulation of small, unresolved problems. Remember, supervisors get results through people.

1. Let each employee know how he or she is doing. Be honest and let people know what you expect. Help by pointing out how an employee can improve.

2. Give credit when credit is due. Look for the employee's extra performance and reward the person verbally during or shortly after the job.

3. If you think that a policy is unfair, express that opinion to your supervisor, not to your subordinates, and suggest changes to improve the policy.

4. Tell employees in advance about policy changes that will affect them and explain the reasons for each change. If possible get employees to participate in the change.

5. Make the best possible use of each person's ability. Instead of standing in a person's way, give him or her the opportunity for more responsibility and growth.

6. Solicit ideas from your employees. Employees often have great ideas for jobs or products that they should be encouraged to develop. Ask what can be done to eliminate bottlenecks and friction.

THE GRIEVANCE PROCEDURE

Where unions exist, a formal procedure for the processing of grievances will be spelled out in the union contract. A typical procedure follows. Some procedures may have more or fewer steps.

Step 1. If the supervisor cannot solve the complaint, it then becomes a grievance and the supervisor meets with the steward or grievance committee, while the employee files a written grievance. If the problem cannot be resolved at this level, it then moves to the second step (Figure 17–5).

Step 2. The supervisor's immediate superior and a representative from the labor relations department meet with the union grievance committee. At this point the problem usually involves more than one person and may relate to the individual rights of many. For example, a safety practice in the plant may have serious implications for all who work in the area. If the problem cannot be solved at this level, it moves to top management.

Step 3. Top management from both the company and the local union are now involved. The labor relations director and the plant or division manager meet with the union grievance committee. A representative from the local union may now represent the union's own grievance committee. Time and money begin to mount, and both sides usually want to solve the issue as quickly as possible.

Step 4. Members of top management discuss the issues with a group from the national union. If the local union has no affiliation with a national union, an attorney or business agent meets with management representatives. At this point, both parties could select a mediator. A **mediator** is a neutral third party who is called to review both sides of the issue. The mediator is often a public official—for example, an attorney or college professor—who is respected by both sides. After

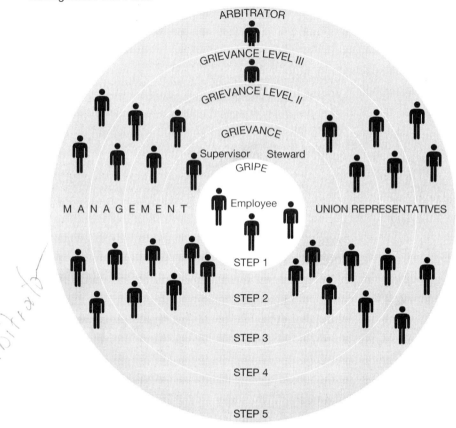

FIGURE 17–5 The Five Steps through Which a Complaint Involving Union and Management Can Pass.

ARBITRATOR

GRIEVANCE LEVEL III

GRIEVANCE LEVEL II

GRIEVANCE

Supervisor   Steward

GRIPE

MANAGEMENT   Employee   UNION REPRESENTATIVES

STEP 1

STEP 2

STEP 3

STEP 4

STEP 5

hearing both points of view, the mediator recommends a solution. However, his or her decision is not binding on either party.

Step 5. At this point an arbitrator is usually called in on the dispute. The **arbitrator** is a neutral third party who conducts fact-finding and mandates binding resolution. He or she is usually a professional arbitrator, recommended by the American Arbitration Association, the Federal Mediation and Conciliation Service, or one of the various state agencies. **Conciliation** means making peace among the parties by soothing anger and conflict. At this level, both sides have usually become polarized and the arbitrator often spends most of his or her time working with the disputing parties.

The arbitrator will conduct hearings that are similar to legal proceedings. Witnesses are called, and testimony is recorded. The hearing may be quite informal, however, depending on the arbitrator's style. The important difference between a mediator and arbitrator is that the decision announced by the arbitrator is *binding* on both the company and the union.[12]

The arbitrator's decision is binding on management and union.

ALTERNATIVE DISPUTE RESOLUTION

Alternative dispute resolution (ADR) is a concept that is becoming popular to avoid legal hassles over mandatory arbitration and government involvement. The Society for Human Resources Management encourages establishment of dispute resolution procedures that allow employers and employees to resolve disputes in a fair, balanced, and timely manner without expensive government administrative processes, or creating the need to resort to private litigation.

In 1995, McGraw-Hill announced its Fast and Impartial Resolution (FAIR) ADR program for its more than 15,000 employees in publishing. The three-step program is voluntary and starts with bringing in a supervisor or human resource representative to resolve a dispute. If that does not work, it moves to mediation with a neutral third party. If mediation is fruitless, the third step is binding arbitration with a written decision. The company pays the mediation and arbitration costs.[13]

Major advantages of ADR programs are that they can settle disputes more quickly than traditional methods involving detailed and outside intervention. Accordingly, morale is boosted—even when decisions go against the employees' wishes; quick closure is an asset so the employee doesn't boil, grumble, and experience lower morale and productivity.

ACTION PROJECT 17–2   A GRIEVANCE AT MERRILL ELECTRONICS (GROUP EXERCISE)

Consider a middle-sized electronics company of about 300 employees. About half the employees are members of a communications union, and most of the labor disputes have been solved by collective bargaining through this particular union.

John McIntyre works in a department that is completely dominated by the union. All fifteen employees of this department are members of the union. Gene Rosefeld, sharp, intelligent, and union trained, is the shop steward. Peter Longnecker, a reasonable and dependable veteran with the company, is John's supervisor.

John is the most experienced technician in the department and is responsible for setting up all new assembly runs and doing all the necessary experimental tests. There have been too many experimental test runs lately. That is the point of the dispute. John feels that he is always asked to work overtime with no consideration for his own personal life. The company business always comes first. He is tired of working fifty hours a week.

Peter, his supervisor, says that there is no one else who could do the experimental test runs and that by working on Saturday John has fewer interruptions by fellow employees. John has talked the problem over with his supervisor, but he is still asked to work eight to ten hours on Saturday. As a tired, frustrated employee, John McIntyre goes to the shop steward.

PROCEDURE

Form groups of five persons. If possible, have one person who scored as a management person in the "union attitude" project, given earlier in this chapter, act as the supervisor, Longnecker, and a person who scored as a union person act as the shop steward, Rosefeld. The part of the overworked employee, McIntyre, can be played by anyone. The other two persons will act as observers.

Role play the parts, with McIntyre and Rosefeld coming to the supervisor to discuss the grievance. See if a solution can be reached within ten minutes. If no solution can be reached, see if the situation could affect more than the one employee. Perhaps this may be a problem to take to a union representative or the department head. The two observers now become the union representative and the department head. The meeting may only be between the union representative and the department head; however, many times all five are involved in the discussion. Another ten minutes is allowed to establish some solution to the problem.

RESULTS AND FOLLOW-UP DISCUSSION

1. What is the final solution? _____

2. Was it a compromise solution? _____

3. How would the observers rate the supervisor's attitude? (Circle one)

   EXCLUSION   CONTAINMENT   ACCEPTANCE
        ACCOMMODATING   COOPERATIVE

4. How would the observers rate the shop steward's attitude? (Circle one)

   EXCLUSION   CONTAINMENT   ACCEPTANCE
        ACCOMMODATING   COOPERATIVE

5. When the two new people entered the situation, did the tone of the discussion change? How? _____

6. Was the second group more agreeable to a solution? _____

7. How would you rate the union representative? (Circle one)

   EXCLUSION   CONTAINMENT   ACCEPTANCE
        ACCOMMODATING   COOPERATIVE

8. How would you rate the department head? (Circle one)

   EXCLUSION   CONTAINMENT   ACCEPTANCE
        ACCOMMODATING   COOPERATIVE

9. Such meetings are often seen as a win-or-lose situation rather than the best solution to the problem. If asked, who would you say won? _____

   Whose side were you on? _____

   What was the group consensus? _____

10. Most important, was it worth the employee's time and effort to go through this grievance procedure? Why? _____

TACTICS OF THE UNION AND MANAGEMENT

If the union and management are unable to settle their grievances, one or both may resort to tactics that may be legal or illegal to force the other to come to a settlement. Such tactics are used when there appear to be no other alternatives.

UNION'S TACTICS

STRIKES

1. *Primary strike.* Workers fail to show up for work.

2. *Sympathy strike.* A strike is called by one union for the benefit of another union.

3. *Sitdown strike.* Workers sit down on the job but fail to perform their duties.

4. *Slowdown strike.* Workers simply perform their tasks at a slower rate.

5. *Wildcat strike.* Some union members go on strike without the authorization or knowledge of the international union.

6. *Jurisdictional strike.* Forcing the company to recognize one union over another. Sympathy, sitdown, wildcat, and jurisdictional strikes can be illegal.

PICKETS

1. *Primary picket.* Union members walk around the place of employment with placards to inform the public of unfair practices of the management.

2. *Mass picket.* So many union members are picketing around the company that it restricts entrance and exit of people into the company. Such activity is illegal.

BOYCOTTS

A union tries to get the public to refuse to buy products or do business with the boycotted firm.

MANAGEMENT'S TACTICS

1. *Lockout.* Employees are not allowed to come into the plant until they accept the employer's terms.

2. *Layoff.* Employees are released from employment for reason of lack of work. Employees are allowed to collect unemployment, but would not be able to if they were fired.

3. *Injunction.* A court order requiring certain action. A mandatory injunction requires performance of a specific act, such as requiring workers to return to work. A prohibitory injunction orders the other party to refrain from certain acts, such as ordering the union to stop mass picketing.

4. *Yellow-dog contract.* As a condition of employment a person agrees not to join a union. Outlawed by the Norris-LaGuardia Act, it is still practiced in some areas.

5. *Blacklisting.* A list of troublemakers that is available to other companies. Employment is not given to blacklisted union organizers. This activity is also illegal, but still used on occasion.

Other management weapons include inventory buildup for use during a strike, doing work at other plant locations, and subcontracting.

All of the tactics discussed here have been used by unions or management at some time in the history of the labor movement. Some are still being used and are "respectable" insofar as they are effective, if not always productive. The tactics used by unions today are generally aimed at production and, hence, the company's financial resources.

Management uses tactics aimed at the resources and solidarity of the union or the bank accounts of the workers. With very few exceptions, labor disagreements today are relatively mild compared with the bloody confrontations of fifty to seventy-five years ago. Nevertheless, these disagreements can have powerful economic repercussions if not dealt with promptly and effectively. If we don't end the national in-fighting, we cannot win globally.

GUIDELINES FOR PRESERVING OR RESTORING A UNION-FREE WORKPLACE

Steps that may discourage union organizing include the following:

1. Have supervisor push the company position and rebut the union talk on the plant floor.
2. Continue to manage fairly.
3. Hold frequent meetings with employees. Instead of telling or questioning employees, listen to them. Try to allay their hostility. You might just stand up and be honest by saying, "I blew it, help me." Ask what they think can be done to correct the problems.
4. Don't intimidate, interrogate, promise, or threaten. All these make the union seem like a good alternative.
5. Continue to inform employees with facts that favor your position.

Gary Dessler offers several guidelines for employers wishing to stay union free[14]:

- Practice preventive employee relations. Ensure fair discipline; open worker–management communications; offer fair salaries, wages, benefits.
- Recognize the importance of location. Unions have been weaker in the South and Southwest than in the North, Northeast, or far West.
- Seek early detection. Detect union-organizing activity as early as possible; remember that your best source is probably your first-line supervisors.
- Do not volunteer. Obviously, never voluntarily recognize a union without a secret election supervised by the NLRB.
- Beware the authorization cards. When confronted by a union official submitting authorization cards, get another manager as a witness and do not touch (or, worse, count or examine in any way) the cards; call your lawyer (and get ready for the NLRB to supervise your election).

- Consider your options. Consider the option of not staying union free; some employers do opt to let the union in.

"Union membership may make health benefits available at group rates that many employers could not afford, and industry- or association-wide wage agreements can remove the burden of having to negotiate salaries and raises with each of your employees. Some unions may be easier to get along with than others, if you have a choice. Therefore, consider your options."[15]

TODAY'S UNIONS

The worker of today is vastly different from the worker of even ten or fifteen years ago. American workers have opportunities for advancement and change that their parents couldn't have imagined. Today's workers are not particularly concerned with job permanence, are less inclined to conform to the decisions of higher authority, and are less likely to put up with uncomfortable working conditions. Workers' attitudes are in part responsible for current changes in unions, but there are other reasons.

WAGES AND BENEFITS

The part of the collective bargaining agreement of most concern to employees is wages. With few exceptions, the direction of wages has been upward, and the burden of the arguments for the change has been carried by the unions. The employers are not usually arguing against wage increases but against the amount of union demands.

Union members are the offensive team.

Leading unions set the trend for wages.

The general amount of wage increases for an industry is usually determined by settlements arrived at by the leading unions and large companies. Whatever settlement is made between the United Auto Workers and whichever employer of the Big Three automobile manufacturers they negotiate with first become the "pattern" for the industry. Sometimes one firm in a locality is recognized as the pace setter and other settlements follow it in much the same way.

Fringe benefits is a misnomer for the pension, hospitalization, supplementary unemployment, holidays, and vacation package, which now runs at least 30 to 33 percent of the per-employee wage cost paid by the employer. To make comparisons with what other employers and unions are doing, estimates of benefits are calculated as a per-hour expense, so that benefits have a dollar value.

MERGERS

The unions' power will continue to grow if they consolidate into fewer and larger unions, with more centralized control. The same difficulties that are involved in corporate mergers are evident in union mergers as well. Old rivalries and animosities often combine with ordinary merger problems to cause further delay. However, since the merger of the American Federation of Labor and the Congress of Industrial Organizations in 1955, the realization that union strength can be increased by a broad political base has impressed more and more union leaders.

SOCIAL AND TECHNOLOGICAL CHANGE

There has been an increase in "urban unions" composed of teachers, hospital workers, police personnel, firefighters, and sanitation workers. Trade unions and white-collar unions are becoming increasingly comprised of ethnic minorities adding a different social base and political outlook, which is considerably different from the "traditional" union of twenty years ago.

More minorities in unions.

Women are also finding recognition in unions. Working women are wielding more clout in the labor movement these days, both at the local level and the national level, because union women are more numerous and active than ever before. Of every ten union members at least four are women, meaning there are almost 6 million women union members.

Women are active in unions.

The issue of automation has been around for more than thirty years and, for the most part, unions have become begrudging converts to automation. They recognize that business must become more efficient to compete in today's market. They recognize that industry must automate or they will be out of business. The key is to ensure that employees with fifteen or twenty years of service are not let go. From this point of view the unions support Japan's Theory Z— paternalism and lifelong employment—discussed in an earlier chapter.

Unions are begrudgingly accepting automation.

Unions and theory Z.

QUALITY OF WORK LIFE

Cooperative efforts between union and management have led to several new programs. Depending on whom you talk with, union or management, both claim that they are responsible for many new programs. Few claim a shared responsibility for new ideas.

Unions and management have come to realize that they must work together for an enterprise to succeed competitively. Together, they have encouraged worker participation in business decisions and a greater emphasis on job security. The United Auto Workers, the Communications Workers of America, and many other unions, working with their counterparts in management, have reaffirmed their commitment to quality of work life (QWL). The Service Employees International Union (SEIU) wants a health care industry that is equitably funded, cost effective, and has a high degree of availability.[16]

The goal of QWL programs is to make work more fulfilling and productive. They are implemented by semiautonomous work teams or management committees. The tasks of QWL are to

1. Improve quality control
2. Improve work schedules
3. Improve compensation systems
4. Improve self-fulfillment

There seems to be an increased demand by workers for QWL programs. Companies such as GM, Procter & Gamble, Exxon, General Foods, TRW, Eastman Kodak, and Polaroid are all trying such programs. Another issue is whether QWL programs are unfair labor practices on the part of management under the NLRA, a topic discussed in the next section.

EMPLOYEE INVOLVEMENT PROGRAMS

Employee involvement (EI) teams allow workers and management to address issues jointly that impact workers' well-being, but they are sometimes considered illegal by the NLRB. Proposed legislation, the Teamwork for Employees and Management (TEAM) Act would make these involvement groups legal.[17]

Ninety-six percent of large employers have incorporated EI to some extent, yet many companies have had the NLRB attack them for violation of Section 8(a)(2) of the NLRA. The statute makes it an unfair labor practice for an employer to "dominate or interfere with the formation or administration of any labor organization or contribute financial or other support to it." When broadly defined, even two employees could be considered an illegal, employer-dominated work group if they discuss workplace issues with management in an effort to resolve problems.

Legalities of EI programs.

The TEAM Act would clean up the problem by removing restrictions on team-based employee involvement. The president of one labor policy organization asks: "Why shouldn't employees be allowed to work with management to improve the workplace?"[18]

SPIRIT OF COOPERATION

Although the element of conflict is ever-present between union and management, perhaps an equally omnipresent spirit of cooperation can be developed. Sensitive observers increasingly call our attention to the fact that human beings are not machines, that they have feelings and emotions that must be respected to get the highest degree of cooperation in the workplace and in labor management relations. The present emphasis on the study of individual and group relationships is a recognition that, along with the solution of technical problems, there must be increasing concern for human elements in production.

INTERNATIONALISM AND UNIONS

The new multinationalism has led American business managers to deal with foreign labor unions, and certainly they cannot be dealt with in the same way as American unions. By and large, foreign unions are more steeped in tradition, are more socialistically oriented, and lack strong centralized power. Workers have not always agreed with their union leaders on whether to stress collective bargaining or political action, but generally American unions have opted for collective bargaining, whereas unions in many other countries have relied more on political action.

Foreign unions are often more socialistic and lack strong central support.

Labor Relations in the 1990s? The Caterpillar–UAW strike. Courtesy of Professor Ray Hogler (drawing by Charles Hendershott). Reproduced by permission.

Strikes may be ineffective if local or global competition provides a market for labor resources. The United Auto Workers found that to be true in 1992 when they struck Caterpillar. The UAW was prepared to spend $800 million from its strike fund, but it did not work. Caterpillar told more than 12,000 employees with considerable seniority that they would be replaced—easy enough to do in a climate of global competition, high unemployment, and readily available replacement workers. Was the unchangeable dinosaur doomed unless it relinquished?

Union membership and density in several selected countries are shown in Figure 17–6. Notice that the United States has the lowest percentage of any country except France. But unions play quite different roles in other countries. Many of the unions in these countries have strong political action agendas and, in some cases, strong government ties. Even in the United States, there is sentiment that one of the major reasons for union decline is the passage of laws by governments, thus nullifying the need for unions.

The European and Asian (Japanese) models of labor–management cooperation have had a positive and profound effect on U.S. labor relations. New United Motor Manufacturing, Inc. (NUMMI), a joint venture of General Motors and Toyota, has adopted industrial relations practices emphasizing fewer job classifications, more teamwork and job rotation, and continuous improvement programs. These practices tend to replace direct supervision as the primary mechanism for obtaining high productivity and quality.

Labor relations have major effects on abilities to compete globally. Even in our own hemisphere, labor relations have major effects on our abilities to compete globally. Canada and Mexico both have relatively strong and fairly stable unions. Canadian employers have "neither the will nor the opportu-

FIGURE 17–6 Union Membership and Density (Percentage of Workforce Unionized) in 12 Countries.[1]

COUNTRY	EMPLOYED UNION MEMBERSHIP (THOUSANDS)		CIVILIAN WAGE AND SALARY WORKERS (THOUSANDS)		DENSITY RATIOS (%)	
	1980	1989	1980	1989	1980	1989
United States	20,095	16,960	89,950	106,924	22	16
Australia	2,568	2,536	6,415	7,398	40	34
Canada	—	4,028	—	12,089	—	33
Japan	12,369	12,227	39,470	46,550	31	26
Denmark	1,585	1,731	2,097	2,320	76	75
France	3,374	1,970	17,752	17,924	19	11
Germany	8,328	8,082	23,366	24,224	36	33
Italy	7,650	6,930	14,432	14,747	53	47
Netherlands	1,539	1,351	4,362	4,912	35	28
Sweden	3,115	3,415	3,877	4,071	80	84
Switzerland	849	782	2,578	2,764	33	28
United Kingdom	11,652	9,214	22,991	22,276	51	41

[1]Data are adjusted to cover employed wage and salary union members only. Pensioners, the unemployed, and self-employed union members are excluded.

SOURCE: Bureau of Labor Statistics, "Union Membership Statistics in 12 Countries," *Monthly Labor Review*, December 1991, p. 50.

nity to attack unions to the extent that they do in the United States."[19] In Mexico, there is a close relationship between the government and the labor movement.

Another, now-classic, example of union–management cooperation is the Saturn Corporation, featured in the following Profile of Human Behavior.

PROFILE OF HUMAN BEHAVIOR

SATURN CORPORATION

Unions and management *can* work together—and still produce highly competitive products. Witness the successes of the Saturn Corporation. While the history and current thrust of labor–management relations at the rest of General Motors, Ford, and Chrysler are adversarial, Saturn has a history of labor tranquility in Spring Hill, Tennessee. While the rest of GM and the UAW measure their operating relationship against a 597-page contract that expires every three years, Saturn and the union have used a 28-page contract that the company and union refer to as a *living constitution*. The contract, written in the early 1980s with no termination date, is open for either party to amend with 30-day notification.

The "Saturn culture" is quite different from traditional auto manufacturing, marketing, and human resource (HR) management. At the heart of the HR differences is a "Memorandum of Agreement" that contains basic principles including:

- Recognition of stakes and equities of everyone in the organization being represented

- Full participation by the representatives of the union
- Use of a consensus decision-making process, and
- Free flow of information.[20]

The Saturn approach was designed to be nonconfrontational, giving workers a voice in management and product decisions not usually afforded to the rank-and-file workers. The power of the HR/labor design is in its simplicity. Most businesses have a pyramidal hierarchy with a large base of front-line employees—supervisors, middle managers, vice presidents, and presidents above them. Saturn's structure is a series of concentric circles—each overlapping enough for all employees to have a say in consensus decision making.

Donald Ephlin, a retired UAW vice president, was the architect of the Saturn–UAW agreement and says: "What makes the agreement so unique is that it deals not only with wages, hours, and working conditions but how the plant will be managed and the role of the union in that management." Robert Boruff, vice president of Saturn's manufacturing operations, says "It [the agreement] is intentionally general to allow us all the flexibility needed to address specific issues when they come up. The more detailed that agreement becomes, the more controversy is stirred up over rules, how they are applied and how they are interpreted."[21]

There have been some rough spots in Saturn's labor history. Despite the good intentions of the company and union leadership there has been some dissent among rank-and-file workers:

- Recent hires who are less committed to Saturn's employee-participation ideals
- Burnout from 50-hours-and-up workweeks
- Growing distrust of the union's close ties with Saturn's management
- Anger at lack of elections for key union posts on the shop floor
- A scaling-back of training for new workers[22]

There is evidence that there may be future labor problems as well. General Motors has indicated that future Saturn factories will operate under traditional UAW contracts.[23] Nevertheless, the effects of Saturn's labor–management cooperation have been much more positive than negative in the long-term view.

The positive effects of Saturn are not confined to labor–management relations. They have been innovative in their production manufacturing and marketing techniques. There is speculation that in the future, they will even market a car under the name "Innovate"—and borrow the production technology from their foreign subsidiary, Opel.[24] Saturn's lasting impressions are in labor–management relations, design, production, marketing, and cross-cultural relationships—the topic of the next chapter.

SOURCES: "Saturn's Rings Replace Typical Management Pyramid," *Supervisory Management,* August 1994, pp. 8–9; Stephen N. Anderson, "Unions/Management Create Collaborative Culture," *Communication World,* April 1994, pp. 16–18; Liz Pinto, "Simplicity Is Key to Labor Tranquility at Saturn," *Automotive News,* September 7, 1992, p. 42.

Most people think of unions in terms of the blue-collar movements because most union members are in such fields. But, although many union members belong to the blue-collar unions, the white-collar and public employees sector has the greatest potential for organized employee representation. Today less than 16 percent of the workforce are members of unions.

Managements' attitudes toward unions can range from total exclusion to cooperation with them. Many people feel that having a union on company grounds develops a dual or divided loyalty on the part of the employee. Sometimes those loyalties are in conflict. Poor morale and perceived low wages encourage employees to join unions. Certainly when a company becomes highly structured, it can be a breeding ground for unions.

The shop steward is sometimes a powerful adversary on the floor and can have a direct effect on the attitudes of the workers. The supervisor also affects the attitudes of the workers. If a supervisor misinterprets the relationship with either the shop steward or the workers, it can mean a serious breakdown in working relationships.

Good supervisors understand their relationship with the workers as one in which they have the authority to ensure that the work that has to be done is done, but not the authority to decide arbitrarily that some of the workers are transferred to other areas or shifts. Nor do they have the power to discipline an employee without that disciplinary action being questioned by the shop steward.

Collective bargaining is probably the most complicated area of labor–management interaction. The tensions involved are frequently excessive on both sides of the table. Without a good understanding of the demands of the other, neither of the opponents will be able to come to terms with the issues. Cooperation on both sides may curtail a number of the problems.

The tactics used by both unions and management to express their dissatisfaction can be seen in many ways. Unions use strikes, such as the primary, sympathy, sitdown, slowdown, and wildcat strikes. They also use pickets and boycotts. Managements' methods are lockouts, layoffs, injunctions, yellow-dog contracts, and blacklisting. Many methods affecting both union and management are illegal, but it has not stopped some from using them.

International influences are being felt in bringing about more cooperative union–management relationships. Perhaps the element of conflict is always present between union and management, but a spirit of cooperation can be developed. Sensitive observers increasingly call attention to the fact that humans are not machines, that they have feelings and emotions that must be respected. Mutual respect must be brought about between union and management for higher production and mutual satisfaction.

CASE STUDY 17–1

FIREHOUSE UNION

Culver is a small and pleasant town with two modern and attractive fire stations. Most of the firefighters employed at these stations grew up together and now live within the city limits. They all get along well and frequently have family get-togethers. In spite of these conditions, the firefighters are far from happy.

For quite some time the firefighters have been in conflict with the city's board of administration over obtaining a wage increase. The men feel that their wages are too low and that the board is spending money unnecessarily. They feel that this money is being spent on fire equipment to impress the community instead of paying the men a reasonable salary in line with the amount being paid in neighboring communities.

Previous attempts to obtain a significant wage increase from the board have been futile. The only occasion when the firefighters managed to obtain an increase over 6 percent was when they hired a lawyer for an evening during negotiations at a cost of $400 of their own money. Tomorrow the firefighters will go into negotiations with the board. There is talk among the ranks that, if their request for a 9 percent wage increase is turned down, as it is expected to be, they will contact the local Teamsters Union and request an election for union representation.

Those who speak in favor of joining the union state that the union would have a great deal more leverage in dealing with the board. If the board refuses to cooperate with the union, the firefighters could go on strike with the financial support of the union. In addition, the union could stop all trucking in the town to support a firefighters' strike if need be.

The firefighters who are speaking against joining the union point out that the union requires what they consider high fees and that the firefighters might be called on to strike in support of other union members in the town. Additionally, a neighboring community fire station recently went on strike and, in that community, hostility was being expressed against the firefighters. If you were one of the firefighters, what would you do?

1. Recommend accepting the wage increase offered by the board?
2. Recommend hiring another lawyer?
3. Recommend joining the union?
4. Quit and find a better fire station in some other community?

CASE STUDY 17–2

UNIONS VERSUS MINORITY RIGHTS

Management decided that, due to a decline in business, the Rayon Furniture Plant would reduce the number of positions in the Finishing Department by twelve persons. After receiving the union's consent on the matter, the plant management gave the twelve workers with the least seniority their notice of termination.

Shortly after these events occurred, Tom Hale, head of the Personnel Department, contacted Bill Norton, the plant manager. Their discussion concerned the employees who received termination notices. Nine of these twelve were black, and they contacted the Fair Employment Practices Commission and filed a complaint against the company for discriminating against them. The complaint centered on the fact that only the Finishing Department was being forced to cut back and that only the Finishing Department was predominantly black. The workers saw this as discriminatory.

"I am aware that the majority of those to be laid off are black," stated Bill, "but we've been ordered to reduce that department, and we must follow the seniority provision of our union contract."

"Yes, I know," replied Tom, "but the seniority provision could well be contested. A few months ago, the Waltan Corporation laid off some workers based on seniority, and after a complaint of discrimination similar to our own, the FEPC won a case of discrimination in court."

"Well, what do you propose we do about it? Violate our union contract?"

"Can't we cut back in the Assembly Section and the Cutting Room too? That way, instead of laying off the twelve workers in one department, we could lay off four workers from each. Then it wouldn't seem discriminatory. There would be more whites laid off than blacks."

"But we don't need to cut back in the Assembly Section or the Cutting Room," Bill replied. "Besides, we have the workers with the greatest seniority of the entire company in the Assembly Section. Why, Fred has been with us for twelve years and he has the least seniority of anyone in the department."

"What do you think about transferring the majority of the twelve into other departments, then?"

"That doesn't solve the problem; the company is cutting back to save money, not to play musical chairs with the workers. As far as I'm concerned, the problem is out of our hands. Let's let the union handle it."

1. Whose solution to the problem do you think is best, Bill's or Tom's?
2. Should the union be asked for its views? Would this be a management attitude of exclusion, containment, acceptance, accommodation, or cooperation?
3. Should you accept the union's view as the right method? Then which attitude would management be accepting?
4. Are there other options to this problem?
5. Is there a compromise to this problem? Should there be a compromise?

DISCUSSION AND STUDY QUESTIONS—TO KEEP YOU THINKING . . . _____

1. What were the original needs for unions? Have they all been met?
2. Where are unions going? What are their options?
3. Why is labor union membership declining? Are there employment sectors that are exceptions to the trend?
4. What are the social changes affecting unions today?
5. Are unions part of a productivity problem? Or are they part of a productivity solution?
6. What are guidelines for preserving or restoring a union-free workplace? Is a union-free workplace always desirable? What are the exceptions, if any?

NOTES _____

1. Albert Karr, "Labor Letter: Raising Union Dues," *The Wall Street Journal*, February 1, 1994, p. A1.
2. Raymond L. Hogler, *Labor and Employment Relations* (St. Paul, Minn.: West Publishing Co., 1995), pp. 299, 306–308.
3. Edward Miller, "The Proposed New Role of the NLRB," *Journal of Labor Research*, Winter 1996, pp. 69–75.
4. Peter F. Drucker, "Reinventing Unions," *Across the Board*, September 1989, pp. 12, 14.
5. Ibid., p. 14.
6. "Trends in U.S. Labor Movement," *The Futurist*, January–February 1996, p. 44.

7. Richard Freeman, "Is Declining Unionization of the U.S. Good, Bad, or Irrelevant?" in Lawrence Hishel and Paula B. Voos, eds., *Unions and Economic Competitiveness* (Armonk, N.Y.: M. E. Sharpe, 1992), pp. 143–169.

8. Ibid., p. 167.

9. Yitchak Haberfield, "Why Do Workers Join Unions?" *Industrial & Labor Relations Review,* July 1995, pp. 656–670.

10. Bill Vlasic, "Bracing for the Big One," *Business Week,* March 25, 1996, pp. 34–35.

11. Brian Bremmels, "Shop Stewards' Satisfaction with Grievance Procedures," *Industrial Relations,* October 1995, pp. 578–592.

12. Michael B. Shane, "The Difference between Mediation and Conciliation," *Dispute Resolution Journal,* July–September 1995, pp. 31–33.

13. Dominic Bencivenga, "Fair Play in the ADR Arena," *HR Magazine,* January 1996, pp. 50–56.

14. Adapted from Gary Dessler, *Human Resource Management,* 6th ed. (Englewood Cliffs, N.J.: Prentice Hall, 1994), pp. 558–559.

15. Ibid., p. 559.

16. Betty Bednarczyk, "The SEIS: A Partner for Change in U.S. Healthcare," *Modern Healthcare,* February 19, 1996, p. 25.

17. Steve Bartlett, "Teamwork: The Illegal Management Tool," *Management Review,* April 1996, p. 7; see also Dwane Baumgardner, "There Ought to Be a Law," *Industry Week,* April 1, 1996, p. 16.

18. Gillian Flynn, "TEAM Act: What It Is and What It Can Do for You," *Personnel Journal,* February 1996, pp. 85, 87.

19. Hogler, *Labor and Employment Relations,* p. 34.

20. Stephen N. Anderson, "Unions/Management Create Collaborative Culture," *Communication World,* April 1994, pp. 16–18.

21. Liz Pinto, "Simplicity Is Key to Labor Tranquility at Saturn," *Automotive News,* September 7, 1992, p. 42.

22. David Woodruff, "Saturn: Labor's Love Lost?" *Business Week,* February 8, 1993, pp. 122, 124.

23. "General Motors Corporation: Future Saturn Factories Will Operate under Traditional UAW Contract," *The Wall Street Journal,* July 21, 1995, p. B5.

24. "Saturn Says Let's Innovate," *Ward's Auto World,* September 1995, p. 27.

RECOMMENDED READING

Applebaum, Eileen, and Rosemary Batt. *The New American Workplace: Transforming Work System in the United States.* Ithaca, N.Y.: ILR Press, School of Industrial Relations, Cornell University, 1994.

Beck, Al. "QWL and Unions in the 1990s." *Journal for Quality and Participation,* December 1988, pp. 20–24.

Caudron, Shari. "The Changing Union Agenda." *Personnel Journal,* March 1995, pp. 42–49.

Colosi, Thomas R., and Arthur Eliot Berkely. *Collective Bargaining: How It Works and Why.* 2nd ed. New York: American Arbitration Association, 1992.

Drucker, Peter F. "Reinventing Unions." *Across the Board,* September 1989, pp. 12, 14.

Eaton, Adrienne E., and Paula B. Voos. "Unions and Contemporary Innovations in Work Organization, Compensation, and Employee Participation." In Mishel, Lawrence, and Paula B. Voos, eds. *Unions and Economic Competitiveness.* Armonk, N.Y.: M. E. Sharpe, 1992.

Foegen, J. H. "Labor Unions: Don't Count Them Out Yet!" *Academy of Management Executive,* February 1989, pp. 67–69.

Goldfield, Michael. *The Decline of Organized Labor in the United States.* Chicago: University of Chicago Press, 1987.

Hogler, Raymond L. *Public Sector Strikes: Employee Rights, Union Responsibilities, and Employer Prerogatives.* Alexandria, Va.: International Personnel Management Association, 1988.

———. *The Employment Relationship: Law and Policy.* New York: Ardsley House, 1989.

———. *Labor and Employment Relations.* St. Paul, Minn.: West Publishing Co., 1995.

Milkman, Martin, and Merwin Mitchell. "Union Influence on Plant Size." *Journal of Labor Research,* Summer 1995, pp. 319–329.

Mishel, Lawrence, and Paula B. Voos, eds. *Unions and Economic Competitiveness.* Armonk, N.Y.: M. E. Sharpe, 1992.

Stone, Christopher D. *Where the Law Ends: The Social Control of Corporate Behavior.* Prospect Heights, Ill.: Waveland Press, 1992.

Warner, David. "A Bill to Outlaw Replacing Strikers." *Nation's Business,* June 1993, pp. 56–57.

Zachary, G. Paul. "Some Unions Step Up Organizing Campaigns and Get New Members: In a Major Shift in Strategy, They Now Woo Workers in the Bottom-Tier Jobs." *The Wall Street Journal,* September 1, 1995, pp. A1–A2.

18

Cross-Cultural Relations

Again it is time to ask ourselves questions. This time our topic is the field of cross-cultural relations—how do you feel about individuals from diverse ethnic groups and those with cultural backgrounds that differ from yours? How can we relate and work effectively with people in foreign lands?

- Why may we feel uncomfortable with foreign visitors in this country—even if they speak English? Why do we feel overly comfortable with individuals in their country when they speak English?
- Is time more important in American culture than it is to other cultures? Is physical space more important to us or to others?
- Since we are one of the most technologically advanced societies in the world, should we teach other countries to handle sales contracts as we do?
- What nonverbal actions have you observed about a particular foreign group that is different from your group of friends?
- What are some of the acceptable mores in our culture that are "off limits" elsewhere in the world?
- What impact has formation of the North American Free Trade Agreement (NAFTA) had on U.S. management and employee practices? the European Union formed and expanded since 1992? What impact will the Pacific Rim countries have on the United States?

LEARNING GOALS

After studying this chapter, you should be able to:

1. Discuss the importance of establishing good cross-cultural relations before embarking on an international business venture.
2. Describe the meaning of ethnocentrism, the pragmatic principle, cultural relativity, and reverse ethnocentrism as they relate to intercultural relations.
3. Discuss why cross-cultural relations are more important today in terms of imports and exports.
4. Discuss the importance of the following:
   a. Vertical and horizontal space in terms of cross-cultural business relationships.
   b. Hidden language of time difference between the United States and other cultures.
   c. The relationship of touch and friendship as it differs from one culture to another.
   d. Language of agreements in relation to each of the three basic types of rules that usually apply to business contracts.

5. Discuss what is meant by high- and low-context cultures and give an example of each.

6. Compare cross-cultural management differences, individual characteristics, and values.

7. What can individuals do to improve their effectiveness in global settings?

8. What can organizations do to improve their effectiveness in global settings?

9. Define and apply the following terms and concepts (in order of first occurrence):

- culture
- cross-cultural relations
- apartheid
- isolationism
- ethnocentrism
- enculturation
- parochialism
- principle of cultural relativity
- intercultural socialization

- pragmatic principle
- reverse ethnocentrism
- ugly American
- multinational corporations
- nationalization
- comparative management
- maquiladoras
- elasticity of time
- inner circle
- language of context
- repatriation

CROSS-CULTURAL RELATIONSHIPS IN A SHRINKING WORLD

This final chapter represents the culmination of the whole book—applied human relations not only in our microcosmic organizations and their cultures, but in the world at large. A **culture** is comprised of the values, beliefs, customs, and norms shared by people in a society. Cooperation with diverse cultures has now become imperative.

All cultures are tied together by information.

All cultures are now tied together by information. One futurist believes that "the hell on city streets is linked [by our common humanity] to the chaos in Bosnia and elsewhere," and that:

> This new information environment is leading to the basic psychological reorientation that is taking place throughout the world. It proceeds at a different pace in different cultures. There is both a leading edge and a lagging edge of this shift. Some people are more aware of it than others. It affects people differently. But taken in its totality, this psychological reorientation is the underlying reality of our time.[1]

As our world continues to shrink, the importance of cross-cultural relations increases. **Cross-cultural relations** require working with people who live and work in foreign cultures. Technology has made communication and travel not only easier, but essential for two reasons. First, technology has made it possible for nations to hold the threat of death over one another. Second, technology has made such demands on the world's material resources that scarcity of resources will result if the nations do not cooperate and share.

Unfortunately the peoples of this world have a history of not being able to share and cooperate. The problems of war and scarcity directly involve the business world in intercultural relations. Business is often one of the first links established between peoples that have previously been separate and even antagonistic. Business was one of the first links between the United States and Japan in the nineteenth century; business was one of the first links between the United States and Japan after World War II. It is one of the first links between the United States and China, after years of antagonism. We are establishing economic relationships with Vietnam and many other countries. These business ties have far-reaching effects on relations between American and other peoples by permitting the parties to offer each other material goods not available through other channels.

Business becomes one of the first links between countries.

COOPERATION OR CRISES?

The fuel and precious metals crises that have plagued the United States in recent years have reminded people in this country that we have needs that can only be met by cooperation with other countries. For this reason, if business is to fulfill its job of providing material needs, it must learn how to deal with other cultures in a way that satisfies the material and social needs of both parties.

We must learn how to deal with other cultures.

The fuel crisis of 1974 and the Persian Gulf war were object lessons in many ways. It became apparent very quickly that people were dependent on fuel and that the world would have to recognize the Arab culture to deal with the suppliers of this needed commodity.

Apartheid, the waning government-mandated economic and physical separation of races in South Africa and our government's economic interest in South Africa have presented a similar cultural dilemma. We object to apartheid on moral grounds but, so far, acknowledge the sovereignty of South Africa's government to deal with the problem. But risks remain in the transition of their government.[2]

The international business manager must be prepared in a special way to overcome the obstacles to peaceful trade that are set up in the form of political, linguistic, social, religious, economic, and human differences. This book cannot provide the kind of intensive training that a business executive seeking to trade with foreign countries will need, but it can suggest the areas with which he or she must be concerned and in which he or she must be educated to be successful.

HOW ARE WE DOING?

Americans have status, respect, and admiration in the global community. Our stances on ecological and environmental issues have strengthened our global position. Despite some gaffes and setbacks—Bhopal (an "accident" in India) and the *Exxon-Valdez* oil spill—Americans are recognized for their environmental efforts. If companies are to broaden their horizons in international markets, their supervisors' "repertoire of people-handling skills must expand to include employees of culturally diverse backgrounds. Supervisors are challenged to demonstrate greater finesse in communicating with people who speak English as a second language."[3]

The real bottom line.

In the discussion of cultural differences and intercultural relations that follows, the reader should not lose sight of the fact that we are all human; that beneath the external barriers to understanding; we are all people and there are more similarities than differences among us.

THE WAVE OF NEW AMERICANS

The annual surge of immigrants into the United States is about 1,000,000 a year. Asians and Latin Americans now represent 86 percent of the immigrants to this country; Europeans represent a little over 10 percent, down from the almost 40 percent in 1965.[4]

Since the 1970s, the United States has allowed more legal immigration than the rest of the world combined. The upshot is that in the 1990s, America's population is younger than that of any of its major competitors—particularly Europe and Japan. Such rapid immigration will inject a continuous dose of dynamism into the economic system according to Joel Kotkin and Yoriko Kishimoto.[5]

CULTURAL ATTITUDES TOWARD MULTICULTURAL DIVERSITY

Historically, some Americans may have adopted an attitude of **isolationism**— a policy of seclusion from international economics and politics. Events of this century have toppled our policy of isolationism, but they have not necessarily toppled our naïve **ethnocentrism,** that is, the feeling that our attitude is the only right attitude, the only way, the natural, normal way (Figure 18–1).

Ethnocentrism.

"The essence of the ethnocentric approach is the adoption of an international human resource management function that focuses solely on the overseas deployment of home-country expatriates."[6] The ethnocentric attitude is found all over the world, originating in the process of **enculturation**—learning cultural practices and values. As long as we are taught just one way, and know no other, we tend to accept that way as the right way.

Ethnocentric attitudes usually surface in the form of patronization, superiority, disrespect, or stereotyping. "If a manager adopts a sincere attitude by patiently accepting a subordinate from another culture, that empathy will normally be received in a trusting, positive manner."[7]

Parochialism is an attitude that the world is *always* like our own world. Parochial people are unable to appreciate cultural differences among others.

Cultural relativity.

Sometimes we develop a reaction against ethnocentrism—we discover the **principle of cultural relativity,** which holds that there are no absolute standards for judging customs, that a society's customs and ideas should be viewed in the

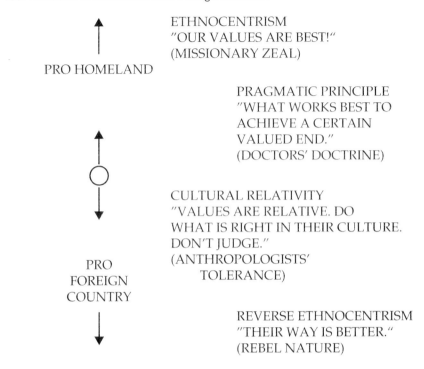

FIGURE 18–1 Attitudes toward Foreign Cultures. Where Do You Stand on Most of Your Attitudes to Individuals from Foreign Cultures?

ETHNOCENTRISM
"OUR VALUES ARE BEST!"
(MISSIONARY ZEAL)

PRO HOMELAND

PRAGMATIC PRINCIPLE
"WHAT WORKS BEST TO
ACHIEVE A CERTAIN
VALUED END."
(DOCTORS' DOCTRINE)

CULTURAL RELATIVITY
"VALUES ARE RELATIVE. DO
WHAT IS RIGHT IN THEIR CULTURE.
DON'T JUDGE."
(ANTHROPOLOGISTS'
  TOLERANCE)

PRO
FOREIGN
COUNTRY

REVERSE ETHNOCENTRISM
"THEIR WAY IS BETTER."
(REBEL NATURE)

context of that society's culture. A commonly drawn conclusion is that all cultures and cultural practices are equally valid, and therefore we should have tolerance and respect for other cultures and cultural practices, even if they happen to differ from ours.

Intercultural socialization involves becoming aware of another culture's habits, actions, and reasons behind behaviors. "Americans presume they are the safest, most sanitary culture in the world, but a large majority of the automobiles in the U.S. would not pass inspection in West Germany. The Japanese (and other cultures) think Americans are unhygienic for locating the toilet and bathing facility in the same area."[8]

The pragmatic principle.

The **pragmatic principle** states "That which works is better than that which doesn't work." More accurately, when people are given a choice between two ideas, the one that works better to achieve certain valued ends is what most people end up choosing most of the time. Such judging can be done in terms of the pragmatic *if . . . then. If* you value your children's lives, and don't want them to die of smallpox, *then* vaccination as prescribed by the doctor is better than animal sacrifice.

Sometimes a stage occurs called **reverse ethnocentrism.** It holds that our ways, rather than being better than others, are actually worse than others. The author recalls hosting the economic counselor of Iran during the celebration of the U.S. bicentennial. "I apologized for the 'fuss' we were making over our 200th birthday, compared to his country and culture (a classic case of reverse ethnocentrism). His response was: 'No need to apologize; look at what you have accomplished economically, politically, and socially in just 200 years!'"

Many Americans must learn to "go" international for employment. One of the major lessons to be learned is that "reaching a level of comfort with colleagues in a cross-cultural collaboration takes a long time. A necessary part of the process is allowing yourself the time you need to expose underlying assumptions that drive culturally determined behaviors you may not understand."[9] Americans must avoid making the mistakes of extremes—either ethnocentrism or being "the ugly American."

UGLY AMERICAN OR PROTECTIVE FATHER IMAGE?

Americans must modify their intolerance of others.

The image of the impolite, inarticulate, ill-mannered, patronizing **"ugly American"** barging through foreign countries like a barbarian at a tea party is legendary, and it contains some truth and some falsity. But the image does tell us something about the problems associated with attempting to establish good business and human relations with the people of other countries. The Japanese are relatively successful in the Third World because of their cooperative efforts. The author has personally observed striking contrasts between brash, arrogant American executives and humble Japanese executives. And the Japanese got the business! If we are to continue to gain economically, we must modify our intolerance of others.

Growth of multinational corporations.

Look at Table 18–1, which shows ten companies who derive more than 60 percent of their revenues from outside the United States. The recent growth of **multinational corporations,** companies that operate in several countries, points up the need to prepare the manager for dealing with foreign cultures and business practices. "Coca-Cola" is a word that has crept into almost every language spoken on earth, and the three initials "IBM" are understood in business conversation around the world.

TABLE 18–1 Selected Companies That Earn 60 Percent or More of Their Revenues from Foreign Operations

U.S. COMPANY	PERCENTAGE OF REVENUES FROM FOREIGN OPERATIONS
Exxon	76.8%
Gillette	69.2
Mobil	68.1
Coca-Cola	66.5
Colgate-Palmolive	64.2
CPC International	63.1
Digital Equipment	63.0
IBM	61.8
Citicorp	60.3
Motorola	60.3

SOURCE: "A Gloomy Picture with a Few Bright Spots," *Forbes,* July 19, 1993, pp. 182–183.

An alternative extreme of always being "ugly correct," is always being the protective, paternalistic father. To a degree, the United States enjoys a "respected society image" but it can backfire. Rose Knotts relates the following story:

> A man attending an international relations banquet was seated across from another man who possessed Asian physical characteristics. Wishing to advance international relations, he asked the Asian, "Likee foodee?" The man politely nodded his head. During the program, the Asian was introduced as an award-winning professor of economics at a prestigious university and was asked to make a few projections about world trade imbalances. After a brief discussion in perfect English, the Asian professor sat down, glanced across at his astonished neighbor, and asked, "Likee talkee?"

Knotts observes that "to avoid similar embarrassment situations, managers should not make assumptions from physical appearances, attributes, or superficial characteristics."[10] Good advice—domestically and internationally.

Additional good advice comes from Doug Ready, founder and CEO of the International Consortium for Executive Development Research:

> Don't believe your own press releases. It's too easy to think that you're a global company because you keep saying you're a global company. Search for measurable indicators that your organization is behaving more globally than it was last year and the year before. Believe in behaviors, not rhetoric. Celebrate your progress, but never allow yourself to become fully satisfied that you have made it.[11]

Don't be ugly; don't be arrogant.

What can American companies, other organizations, and individuals do to reverse the ugly American syndrome? The first and best answer is: "Don't be ugly; don't be arrogant portraying a 'we-are-better-than-you' attitude." If indeed we have a unique technology or skill, then we can export/market it, but remember our foreign host is our customer—deserving the respect any other customer, domestic or global, would receive.

SUBTLE DIFFERENCES

A gesture that is friendly in one culture may be interpreted as hostile in another; an innocent gesture can be an insult. These subtle cues to action complicate the problems of international business relations in a way that cannot be deduced from business experience in the United States.

Cultural differences go deep but are subtle.

The business manager who is faced with such subtle cultural differences as gestures and tone of voice is participating in a frame of reference that is different from his or her own. Because communication always takes place within a frame of reference, international business managers must make sure that they can communicate in one that is not their own. The broad outlines of a culture are marked by the political and economic frames of reference.

THE POLITICAL FRAME OF REFERENCE

When we watch the stock market fluctuate with every major or minor crisis in our political lives, we are aware of the close relationship between politics and business. The political climate of our nation is determined largely by its economic well-being. Major decisions in business and industry affect political movements and vice versa. This is also true on an international scale.

For example, with the fluctuating political détente with the communist world, American business managers have been establishing trade agreements with most of Eastern Europe, China, and some states of the former USSR. One lesson that we have learned is that the political structure of those nations is far more bureaucratic than is the organizational structure of American business. Trade agreements must be passed through dozens of government bureaus and may take three times as long to complete as similar transactions among private firms.

Another politically related problem facing the multinational corporation has been the risk of **nationalization,** the taking over of private companies, often under foreign control, by the host country. Some companies have sought to counter this problem by hiring managers from a third nation. The practice is augmented by hiring local managers from the country in which the corporation is operating, people who know the customs and the laws and who speak the language. When local nationals head up the branches of a multinational corporation, the company may be more immune from political expropriation or nationalization.

THE ECONOMIC FRAME OF REFERENCE

One of the first things that American business managers traveling abroad may recognize is the difference between the standard of living to which they were accustomed and those that exist in the host country. Americans still enjoy a higher standard of living and productivity than most of Europe, and the difference affects business relations there.

Workers in Europe are accustomed to working longer hours for less money than are American workers. According to the International Labor Organization, the U.S. worker averages 35 hours a week, whereas French and West German workers work more than Japan's 40 hours a week. Japanese workers are also accustomed to taking less time off from work, working night shifts, and generally working at a more hectic pace.

The low level of economic development in many of the emerging nations is aggravated by high birth rates and even higher rates of inflation. Both factors discourage saving, which is one of the prerequisites for capital accumulation necessary for investment and expansion. The workers of such countries are essentially trapped by the cycle of low income, large families, and inflation that encourages spending rather than saving.

The multinational corporation, however, has both the resources and the responsibility to help break the vicious circle in which such workers find themselves. In return for business profits realized from cheap labor and easy access to local natural resources, the multinational corporation can and should help develop the human resources of its host nation.

THE CULTURAL FRAME OF REFERENCE

When "the American way" of doing business is transplanted to foreign soil, it must bend and twist, give and take, absorb and develop, according to local expectations and traditions. In the process a third "way" to do business will be formed, one that borrows from both parties and aims at filling the needs of both. This process requires that the American business manager become versed not only in the economics and politics of a country but also in its culture and in its manners. We must learn to understand and respect its way of life.

Language is a major barrier.

Language is the foremost barrier to good international relations. Although English is still commonly accepted as the international business language, foreign business managers usually frown on the inability of Americans to converse in the native language. In fact, Americans have found it difficult to acquire other languages easily, which has made people of other countries feel that Americans do not make an effort to communicate.

Europeans, on the other hand, are in close and constant contact with people who speak other languages and sharply differentiated dialects. Switzerland, for example, has four national languages: French, Italian, German, and Romansch! In the future, American business managers will need to communicate in the language of their host countries, both by necessity and as a mark of goodwill.

Semester-at-Sea.

One aspect of international goodwill and a learning experience is the Institute for Shipboard Education's "Semester-at-Sea" program. Twice each year, approximately 600 college and university students, other adult passengers, faculty, and families go around the world on a ship, stopping for four to six days in ports of various countries. The formal classroom learning on the ship is supplemented by in-port field trips and other cross-cultural experiences (see Figure 18–2).

FIGURE 18–2 Young People Are Good Intercultural Communicators Despite Language Barriers. Mona Beame/Photo Researchers.

COMPARATIVE MANAGEMENT

Comparative management is the study of how management and leadership practices vary across different cultures. Two models provide good frames of reference for analyzing differences.

THE KLUCKHOHN-STRODTBECK MODEL

The Kluckhohn-Strodtbeck framework is a widely used model for analyzing differences among cultures. It is based on six cultural dimensions:[12]

1. **Relationship to the environment.** Are people dominating of, in harmony with, or dominated by the environment?
2. **Time orientation.** Does the culture focus on the past, present, or future?
3. **Nature of people.** Does the culture view people as good, evil, or a mix of the two?
4. **Activity orientation.** Does the culture emphasize being, doing, or controlling?
5. **Focus of responsibility.** Is the focus individualistic, hierarchical, or group oriented?
6. **Conception of space.** Does the culture conduct business in private, in public, or a mix of the two?

Table 18–2 shows the six dimensions and the combinations of variations within each.

THE HOFSTEDE MODEL

Geert Hofstede, at the University of Limburg in the Netherlands, is responsible for what is probably the best typology and assessment vehicle for cross-cultural differences among countries. His excellent article in the *Academy of Management Executive* is equally as provocative as some of his earlier works. He asserts:

The meaning of management differs around the world.

> Management as the word is presently used is an American invention. In other parts of the world not only the practices but the entire concept of management may differ, and the theories needed to understand it may deviate considerably from what is considered normal and desirable in the USA.[13]

TABLE 18–2 Variations in Value Dimensions.

VALUE DIMENSION		VARIATIONS	
Relationship to the environment	Domination	Harmony	Subjugation
Time orientation	Past	Present	Future
Nature of people	Good	Mixed	Evil
Activity orientation	Being	Controlling	Doing
Focus of responsibility	Individualistic	Group	Hierarchical
Conception of space	Private	Mixed	Public

Note: The jagged line identifies where the United States tends to fall along these dimensions.

SOURCE: Stephen P. Robbins, *Organizational Behavior: Concepts, Controversies, and Applications*, 6th ed. (Englewood Cliffs, N.J.: Prentice Hall, 1993), p. 75.

Another seed that he plants is that one of the shortcomings of American management research is that we concentrate our research on managers rather than workers: "Managers are much more involved in maintaining networks: if anything, it is the rank-and-file worker who can really make decisions on his or her own. . . . " Originally, Hofstede developed four dimensions for his assessments:

1. **Power distance.** The degree of inequality in power distribution among people in a national culture.
2. **Individualism/collectivism.** The degree to which people in a country prefer to act as individuals rather than collectively as members of groups in caring for themselves.
3. **Masculinity/femininity.** The degree to which tough values such as assertiveness, performance, success, and competition, which in most societies are associated with masculinity, dominate over tender values like the quality of life, maintaining warm personal relationships, service, care for others, and the environment.
4. **Uncertainty avoidance.** The degree to which people in a culture prefer structured over unstructured situations and feel threatened by uncertainties and ambiguities.

More recently, he has added a fifth dimension from a Chinese value survey:[14]

5. **Long-term versus short-term orientation.** On the long-term side are values oriented toward the future like thrift (saving) and persistence. On the short-term side are values like respect for tradition and fulfilling social obligations.

These dimensions serve as guides to effective leadership styles, control characteristics, and ways of delegating authority. Table 18–3 shows cultural value dimension scores for selected countries.

TABLE 18–3 Cultural Value Dimension Scores for Ten Selected Countries

COUNTRY:	PD	ID	MA	UA	LT
United States	40	91	62	46	29
Germany	35	67	66	65	31
Japan	54	46	95	92	80
France	68	71	43	86	30[a]
The Netherlands	38	80	14	53	44
Hong Kong	68	25	57	29	96
Indonesia	78	14	46	48	25[a]
West Africa	77	20	46	54	16
Russia	95[a]	50[a]	40[a]	90[a]	10[a]
China	80[a]	20[a]	50[a]	60[a]	118
Range	35–95	14–91	14–95	29–90	10–118[a]

[a]Estimated.

Key: PD = power distance, ID = individualism, MA = masculinity, UA = uncertainty avoidance, LT = long-term orientation.

SOURCE: Geert Hofstede, "Cultural Constraints in Management Theories," *Academy of Management Executive*, February 1993, p. 91.

THE CHANGING WORLD COMMUNITIES

In Chapter 16 we studied domestic discrimination against the Hispanic Americans, African Americans, and Asian Americans. Here we examine other cultures with whom we have had considerable cross-cultural relationships.

JAPAN, ANOTHER LOOK AT THEORY Z

In 1981 William Ouchi created a stir in the management field by writing *Theory Z: How American Business Can Meet the Japanese Challenge.* Theory Z was discussed in Chapter 11, but additional ideas are presented here:

1. Mutual trust and benefits among employer, worker, and union
2. The image of the company in the Japanese society
3. Team effort over individual drive
4. Maximization of profits

The qualities admired in American managers—ambition, risk taking, independence—are handicaps in Japanese companies where group cooperation and a strict decision-making hierarchy prevail.

> Japanese managers generally choose a company for life, and they move up the corporate ladder very slowly and according to seniority rather than ability. Regimented in a multi-layered management structure, they are known for working long hours and piling up years of unused vacation time. Japanese companies have been described as Machiavellian bureaucracies where absolute loyalty is demanded and where one wrong political move can ruin a career—dumping a promising manager into what the Japanese call the madogiwa-zoka (the by-the-window tribe).[15]

Because of the lifetime employment concept, great care is taken in the selection of a company for employment. And great care is taken among Japanese business concerns to maintain a strong company image. If the image is poor, it will be difficult for the company to attract good young people.

There are fundamental cultural differences between Japan and the United States. Americans are frequently described as social, "party animals," but our cultural and social values pale in comparison to the Japanese.

One practicing anthropologist, a vice president of a multinational pharmaceutical firm, examines several cultural databases, including social knowledge and cultural logic. One example of the importance of these databases can be seen in their drinking habits. Drinking (not always alcoholic drinking) provides the foreigner with a chance to mingle socially with Japanese hosts. The social knowledge (values) is that freedom of speech is acceptable, it is a place to get things "off the chest," and that everyone can be an "insider." The cultural logic (human values) is that this is an opportunity for *honne* (insider) talk, that feelings (reality) must be expressed, and understood (truth) by an insider group[16]:

> Business is usually not done at the bar, where drinking offers the Japanese an opportunity to express honne opinions about his relationships with colleagues, both foreign and Japanese. . . . Everyone is in the same social circle. For this reason, one must constantly be alert for signals that might indicate something is on a colleague's mind. [At one session, a manager] felt that something was bothering his Japanese counterpart, but as the evening wore on, nothing was said. Just before it ended, the Japanese manager put his face down on the table and muttered that he had something important to say. The American leaned forward and asked what it was. All the Japanese said was "Your Johns-san is an (expletive)." Nothing more was said and the subject was never raised again. The American assumed that just stating the opinion was enough to relieve the tension the Japanese had. The opinion was not reported to Johns. The next business day discussions with the Japanese gentleman were more relaxed than had been previously experienced.[17]

This scenario suggests a recollection of Paramount Communication's classic and hilarious but all-too-true film, *Gung Ho,* the story of a Japanese company's "friendly" takeover of an American automobile manufacturing facility!

ARABS INFLUENCE SO MUCH, YET WE KNOW SO LITTLE

We should not consider every country in the Arab world as having similar attitudes, philosophies, or political ambitions, just as foreigners should not think all Americans are the same. Certainly the attitudes of Canadians, Americans, and Mexicans are not always similar. However, all Middle Easterners are similar in one respect—they are all profoundly influenced by their religions.

In dealing with Middle Easterners, we must recognize the influence of their various religions. Because of a few basic religious beliefs, some Middle Easterners may view the world in a way totally alien to Americans. For example, the people of the Moslem world have strong feelings for the Koran, which says that society must come before the individual.

One of the first things you will notice when dealing with Arabs is their concentration on your eyes. Arabs generally watch the pupils of your eyes, although not for long, to judge your responses to different topics. If you are interested in something, your pupils tend to dilate; if you encounter something you don't like, they tend to contract. The Arabs have known about the pupil responses for centuries, and many, like Yasser Arafat, wear dark glasses even indoors to protect their thoughts from others. Arabs are reading the personal interaction on a second-to-second basis. By watching the pupils, they can respond rapidly to mood changes.

EUROPE

European Union represents a major economic market.

The European Union (EU) evolved from the European Economic Community, which was formed in 1992 to permit the free movement of goods and services, as well as human and financial capital. The now fifteen-nation group—with more potential members—makes up a single economic market, a commonwealth of nations without economic borders. There are more than 350 million consumers, capital, goods, and services moving freely as they do within the United States. But the national and regional differences in Europe are very sharp. A common economic community is the kind of issue that can be very emotional, deeply ingrained, and very difficult to reconcile.

A late 1996 summit meeting of the EU strengthened the organization's two main projects, establishing a single currency and expanding the EU eastward. Both France and Germany hope to begin the new currency in 1999. Other countries should be "on board" by 2002.

Perhaps the EU changes will not have a direct impact on human relations in the United States. But indirectly, we are influenced in our style of international management and ultimately in our domestic relationships as well. The EU will open many markets to U.S. business, and how we respond interpersonally to these opportunities will determine how successful we are.

Americans must "plan smart"—something that was not done when setting up Euro-Disney. Sufficient consideration was not given to European (especially French) eating and entertainment customs, labor unions, and even farming practices. Locals were not very happy with Disney's presence in the area, and there were other alternatives available.

CHINA, KOREA, AND OTHER PACIFIC RIM NATIONS

China and Korea as well as Japan are major markets.

Demographically, Asia is the greatest economic market for the United States. Many U.S. companies and other multinational conglomerates are charging into China: AT&T, Motorola, Asea-Brown-Boveri (Swiss–Swedish), Nissan (Japan), Volkswagen (Germany), and Total (France) are just a few. China has been described as the "emerging economic powerhouse of the twenty-first century," but there are problems (opportunities) both domestically and globally. For example, peasants searching for jobs far from their homes are creating growing social problems.[18] Truck transportation remains a significant problem, although their rail systems are quite good.

South Korea is already well on its way to becoming an economic power, not only in Asia, but globally. Again, they must solve some internal and neighboring country political problems if they are to be successful. Equally stimulating are the challenges of trading with the other Pacific Rim nations—some of which are referred to as the "Little Dragons" (Taiwan, Hong Kong, and Singapore, along with South Korea).

Beginning in 1997, Hong Kong will return to Chinese control. Other lesser, but still growing, players (Malaysia, Indonesia, and Thailand) may be referred to as "the kittens," but they are coming on strong.

NORTH AMERICA

Quality economic markets close to home.

Experience with the North American Free Trade Agreement (NAFTA) has led to many positive relationships with Canada and Mexico. Canada remains a major trading partner of the United States—in agriculture, automobiles, and other solid industries.

Even before NAFTA, we had good working relationships with Mexico because of the **maquiladoras,** domestic Mexican firms that manufacture or assemble products for a U.S. company. The author personally consulted on the high quality of some products from the maquiladoras: sterile packets for American Hospital Supply, toys for Mattel, and appliances and electronic products for Zenith and other manufacturers.

Major free-trade agreements are springing up all over the world: European Union, the Pacific Rim, and NAFTA are just a few. Like all cross-cultural relationships it takes some time to "work out the bugs" but they are here now and the competition is going to be tough.

HIDDEN LANGUAGES

Language and religion are only two of the more obvious frames of reference in which business takes place. A basic understanding of them allows American business managers to negotiate on roughly equal footing with their foreign associates. People communicate in hidden languages of time, space, agreements, touching, and friendship. These languages vary from culture to culture, are often incredibly complex, and are usually as important as the spoken language in establishing good communication and human relations abroad.

THE LANGUAGE OF TIME

In the United States a delay in answering a communication can mean to the person waiting that the decision is of low priority to the other person. In Ethiopia, the time required for a decision is directly proportional to its importance: The more money involved, the longer it will take to arrive at a decision.

> Northern Europeans, Americans, and Latins all share the belief that they can manage their time in the best possible way. In some Eastern cultures, however, the adaptation of man to time is seen as a viable alternative. Time is viewed neither as linear or subjective, but as cyclic. The evidence, they reason, is everywhere; each day the sun rises and sets, people grow old, die and are succeeded by their children. It has been this way for 100,000 years.

Cyclical time is not a scarce commodity. As they say in the East, when God made time, he made plenty of it.[19]

Business decisions in Asia are arrived at quite differently than in the West. An Asian thinks long term and does not see time wasting away but as coming around again in a circle, where the same opportunity will present itself again later—when the decision maker is several days, weeks, months, or even years wiser.

Deadlines can appear rude and pushy.

In the Arab world, close relatives take absolute priority in time; nonrelatives are kept waiting. Foreigners may be kept waiting for a long time. In the Middle East, assigning a deadline is a cultural trap, because a deadline in this part of the world is viewed as rude, pushy, and demanding.

In the language of time, most cultures other than ours may seem to be tied to antiquity. The Indians of South Asia have an elastic view of time; indefiniteness does not mean they are evasive—just deliberate. The **elasticity of time** is the length of time it takes to accomplish a task. The less important time is and the longer it takes to accomplish the task, the greater the elasticity of time.

THE LANGUAGE OF SPACE

Space speaks.

When business managers arrive in a foreign country, they must try to be sensitive to what space tells them. Some useful advice to a newcomer: Try to be aware of where people stand in relation to you and don't back up. This, in itself, can greatly enhance people's attitudes toward you. If employees are deemed more important, they are given more space and their offices are walled in completely. A person from another culture may wonder how managers can supervise when they are unable to see their subordinates.

In the United States the executive suites are usually on the top floor and the relative ranks of vice presidents are placed along "executive row." The top floor in Japan is frequently seen as the place for the average worker. Why must the executive spend his time going to the top floor? The privilege of class is for the first and second floors. Likewise, the top floor in a Japanese department store is not reserved for furniture, but the "bargain roof." Similarly, in Rio de Janeiro, Brazil, the higher one lives up on Sugarloaf Mountain, the poorer one is. The poverty stricken have the view, but the aristocrats have the conveniences of the beaches and living downtown.

Sociologists have also found that different cultures keep different social distances—the distances between people that correspond to the degree of comfort they feel in each other's presence. The distance we keep between ourselves and others is known as our **inner circle** or our personal space. Americans normally keep a distance of about four to six feet during business conversations, but other cultures are more inclined to reduce the distance, sometimes to three or four inches!

THE LANGUAGE OF TOUCH

We also communicate by the frequency and manner in which we touch each other, customs that differ radically from culture to culture. American men rarely go beyond a formal handshake. If they happen to be old friends, they may slap each other on the back. Infractions of these rules are fraught with tension: If someone refuses to shake a hand that is offered, he or she implies a serious insult or rejection. The person who is an indiscriminate back-slapper is usually viewed with either distaste or some fear, since the act implies intimacy without consent.

The relationships between men and women in other cultures are also sensitive to touching. The ease with which American women enter into touch may be interpreted as promiscuous by some cultures; in yet other cultures, American women may be seen as cold and unfriendly. Anything in the realm of sexuality is sensitive and even dangerous for all cultures.

THE LANGUAGE OF CONTEXT

Low context: you start business quickly.

The cultures of the world can be placed on a language-of-context continuum. The **language of context** is based on the amount of communication contained in the nonverbal context and "chit-chat" compared with the amount in the formal message. In a low-context culture you get down to business very quickly. The high-context culture requires considerably more time, simply because the people have developed a need to know more about you before a relationship can develop.

High context takes longer; learn to chit chat.

In India, for example, merchants and others are more comfortable doing business with you if they get to know you personally. In the Middle East, if you aren't willing to take the time to sit down and have coffee or tea with people, you will have a problem doing business with them.

The trouble with high-context cultures is that it's hard to get an American to take each step seriously and to be coached. In terms of high and low context, the United States tends toward the middle of the scale. The low-context Swiss around Zurich don't even know their neighbors. The Swiss value their privacy so much that they may not develop a large circle of friends. The privacy of Swiss bank accounts is legendary. Look at Figure 18–3. Where would you place other cultures on the context line of continuum?

FIGURE 18–3 Cultural Language of Context Placed on a Continuum.

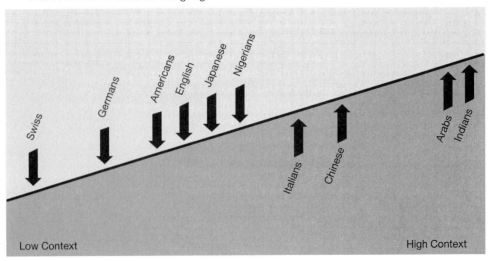

THE LANGUAGE OF FRIENDSHIP

Many Americans have offended others by refusing, or offering to pay for, items tendered as tokens of friendship. These types of encounters abroad have made some foreigners feel that Americans approach all human relations with the cynical and cold feeling that "everything has a price." The American abroad must be careful to distinguish between friendship and business relations and to find out what gestures are significant in matters of friendship and hospitality. The offering of food, for example, is a universal gesture of friendship—to protest that one is on a diet may be interpreted as an unwillingness to "break bread together," a rejection of friendships and good relations.

THE LANGUAGE OF AGREEMENTS

"Unwritten" rules for contracts.

For any society to produce goods and services on a commercial level, a set of rules must be developed and accepted on which agreements can be reached. The language of agreements may be absolute or flexible, sophisticated or informal; in any event it must be understood by both parties to the agreement.

In the Arab world, a man's word is considered as binding as his legal signature (a woman may not have certain legal rights in business). To require a Moslem to sign a formal contract runs the risk of violating his sense of honor.

A verbal contract may be more binding than a written contract.

On the other hand, to a Greek, a contract may only represent a sort of way station along the route of negotiations to be modified periodically until the work is completed. If an American complains about such a procedure, the Greek may exclaim, "Take me to court." But there is no court to settle international business disputes, and mutual satisfaction is reached only through mutual respect and understanding of the various meanings of the agreement.

Build good international human relations.

Americans must not only understand that the laws governing trade in the United States no longer apply on the world market, but that the laws of the host country may not protect them. The best guarantee, of course, is good international human relations—building up a relationship in which both parties willingly cooperate to reveal common goals of exchange.

ACTION PROJECT 18–1   THE INTERNATIONAL CULTURE QUIZ

How knowledgeable are you about customs, practices, and facts regarding different countries? The following multiple-choice quiz will provide you with some feedback on this question.

1. In which country would *Ramadan* (a month of fasting) be celebrated by the majority of people?
   - a. Saudi Arabia
   - b. India
   - c. Singapore
   - d. Korea
   - e. All of the above

2. On first meeting your prospective Korean business partner, Lo Kim Chee, it would be best to address him as
   - a. Mr. Kim
   - b. Mr. Lo
   - c. Mr. Chee
   - d. Bud
   - e. Any of the above are readily accepted

3. In Brazil, your promotional material should be translated into what language?
   a. French
   b. Italian
   c. Spanish
   d. No need to translate it
   e. None of the above

4. In Japan it is important to
   a. Present your business card only after you have developed a relationship with your Japanese host
   b. Present your business card with both hands
   c. Put your company name on the card, but never your position or title
   d. All of the above
   e. None of the above

5. Which one of the following sports is the most popular worldwide?
   a. Basketball
   b. Baseball
   c. Tennis
   d. Futbol
   e. Golf

6. For an American businessperson, touching a foreign businessperson would be least acceptable in which one of the following countries?
   a. Japan
   b. Italy
   c. Slovenia
   d. Venezuela
   e. France

7. Which of the following would be an appropriate gift?
   a. A clock in China
   b. A bottle of liquor in Egypt
   c. A set of knives in Argentina
   d. A banquet in China
   e. None of the above would be appropriate

8. Which one of the following countries has the most rigid social hierarchy?
   a. United Kingdom
   b. United States
   c. Japan
   d. India
   e. Germany

9. Traditional Western banking is difficult in which one of the following countries because their law forbids both the giving and taking of interest payments?
   a. Brazil
   b. Saudi Arabia
   c. Mongolia
   d. India
   e. Greece

10. As an American businessperson, in which of the following countries would you be expected to be on time for a business meeting?
   a. Peru
   b. Hong Kong
   c. Japan
   d. Morocco
   e. All of the above

Source: Prof. David M. Hopkins, University of Denver, 1991. Reprinted with permission.

THE INTERNATIONAL CULTURE QUIZ ANSWERS:

The correct answers are:

1. a	
2. b	
3. e (Portuguese)	
4. b	
5. d	
6. a	
7. d	
8. d	
9. b	
10. e	

TIPS FOR THE WORLD TRAVELER

First and foremost, "do your homework" before leaving for a foreign assignment. Know what to expect regarding social engagements, schools, if necessary, and living conditions. Study the culture, customs, religions, and taboos to avoid the cultural faux pas and embarrassments discussed earlier.

SPOUSES

Spouses must be considered—or their early return to their home country can be very expensive. Robin Pascoe writes that: "Corporations lose money when they post a family overseas and, after six months, the wife turns to her husband and says she is getting out. A wife who has been properly prepared for the experience is not as likely to want to run away."[20]

CULTURE SHOCK

Culture shock is "normal" and will occur! The author recalls his first exposure to traffic coming into Cairo from the airport. Not even Los Angeles, Mexico City, or New York City traffic prepared me for the hassles of "angry" drivers of donkeys and other animals, honking horns, pedestrians, injuries, and indifference to death all mixed into one Cairo intersection. I had a driver, but the trauma of that traffic gridlock was greater than any nonmilitary assignment before or since.

> Culture shock can go far deeper than the everyday hassles of learning how to use chopsticks, adjusting to hot weather, and getting locked in a traffic jam. Culture shock may also include an adjustment to loss of status and pay which normally comes with a job. The overseas assignment in a new culture may affect the state of a marriage; frustration with life in an overseas posting can definitely lead to anger and resentment toward the working partner.[21]

U.S. TELEVISION

All the world knows more about Americans than we do of any other country. That is because of all the U.S. television shows plus thousands of movies—not to mention magazines on every newsstand—that are distributed abroad. We have to spend some of our orientation and other working time overcoming misconceptions about our own cultures: *Not all Americans have three cars in their garages, sleep with everybody else, or carry guns for self-protection and violence.*

CROSS-CULTURAL TRAINING

Americans need to avail themselves of education and training opportunities to help in their enculturation. As noted earlier in this chapter and in Chapter 12, the U.S. Department of State, other government agencies, and universities set up elaborate education and training programs.

What should global training courses include? Sylvia Odenwald recommends that the menu of global training programs be arranged into six overlapping categories:

1. Cultural awareness
2. Multicultural communication
3. Country-specific training
4. Executive development
5. Language courses
6. Host-country workforce training[22]

It is wise for the individual to capitalize on these offerings. Several other good references appear in the Recommended Reading section at the end of this chapter.

REPATRIATION

One can, it is hoped, come home after assignment in a different culture. But will everything be the same? Of course not, depending on the length of stay, and so on. **Repatriation** is the process of transferring employees back to their home country—economically, socially, and organizationally.

> In addition to losing most or all of the generous company-provided benefits they enjoyed overseas, expatriates are likely to feel that their assignment had small value in the eyes of management, either because the company had no formal plans for repositioning them within the organization or because no one in the organization seems to care about what they learned while doing business overseas. Moreover, repatriates return home feeling personally changed by their overseas experiences, but find that everyone else has more or less stayed the same.[23]

Whether used for global orientation, training, financial planning, or ordinary communication, information technology can make expatriate administration a more efficient work experience.[24] Repatriates are vulnerable to being hired away by other organizations.

It is as important to concentrate on the repatriation process as it is on the initial orientation for foreign assignment. Too often, when repatriates return home "after a stint abroad (during which time they have typically been autonomous, well-compensated and celebrated as a big fish in a little pond), they face an organization that doesn't know what they've done for the past several years, doesn't know how to use their new knowledge and, worse yet, doesn't care."[25]

WHAT ORGANIZATIONS CAN DO TO IMPROVE IN GLOBAL SETTINGS

Remember that many small businesses benefit from cross-cultural relations and doing business abroad. Businesses and other organizations need to follow these suggestions:

1. Capitalize on our strengths as individuals; domestically, we advocate teamwork that is more prevalent in other cultures, but they also admire our individualism. *So, the key to effectiveness is putting the two dimensions together and using our individualism in a nonarrogant manner to work more closely with others—including other cultures—as a team.*

2. Tap one of our major resources: our higher education systems, including technical and community colleges. Our four-year institutions' abilities to deliver undergraduate, graduate, and continuing education, imperfect as they may be, are admired and unsurpassed as a group throughout the world. We need to work more closely with industry to provide even better fundamental education and tailor relevant training programs.

3. American and other countries' companies doing business abroad should capitalize on U.S.-educated, third-country nationals. The numbers of students—particularly graduate students—has increased dramatically in the last few decades, yet their newly acquired skills are not always captured by multinational companies.

4. Improve the political and social awareness of all Americans working in other cultures. The faux pas or social blunders of one unprepared representative can tear down many months—maybe even years—of preparation for cross-cultural commerce and other exchanges. Host countries may be very forgiving, but they also may not be; cross-cultural preparation is indispensable.

5. Learn the language. Again, this may vary from culture to culture. Some countries may not want you to understand their language in detail, but knowing the greetings and certain key phrases is essential. So is having an appropriate interpreter: if doing business, have an interpreter who understands economic terms and the language of business. Consulates and bank correspondents are good sources for interpreters.

6. Finally, coming full circle regarding our individualism, we need to maintain our identity but participate in other cultures. The advice of one wise sage operating in a different culture: "Mix with but don't get lost in them." This is not a matter of keeping social distance, although that too may be appropriate at times. But, if an individual's heritage is not important enough to preserve, then why should someone from another culture be interested in what that person is offering? I wish you happy continued discussion, thinking, learning, and living—forever.

PROFILE OF HUMAN BEHAVIOR

FORD MOTOR COMPANY

Ford goes global! Ford 2000! These are slogans that best describe major changes being made at Ford Motor Company in recent years. Ford 2000, as their new global concept is called, brings together many countries to produce cars for the twenty-first century.

The results of this global program are cars designed in Turin (Italy), Germany, England, and Dearborn (Michigan); engineered in Germany, England, and Dearborn; and assembled in Genk (Belgium), Cuaititian (Mexico), and Kansas City, Missouri! Soon the cars will be produced and marketed in Brazil and other parts of South America, and in the ever-increasing markets of Asia. The Fiesta, for example, is scheduled for production in Brazil and assembly in Asia.

Among the individuals behind the global-concept car is Alexander Trotman, chairman, CEO, and president of Ford. Trotman is a 41+ year veteran of Ford who started as a purchasing clerk at one of the company's European plants after his British/Scottish education and military duty as a flight officer-navigator for the Royal Air Force. As the guiding hand for Ford, he encourages use of computer networks and video links "to allow people around the world to work together on the same car. 'Such gizmos,' argues Mr. Trotman, 'will not only increase productivity by introducing something like a 24-hour day for particularly urgent projects; they will also raise creativity by allowing people from different continents to spark off each other as they stare at the same images on their computer screens.' "[26]

In writing about Ford and multinational teams, Tim Stevens urges us to forget preconceived notions and let "multinational teams serve as a classroom in human behavior":

> When it comes to working on multinational teams, "leave your paradigms at home," says Malcolm Thomas, vehicle-line director in Dunton, England. "If you judge people by what you have become used to in your environment, you can jump to totally wrong conclusions. For instance, if you're dealing with Spaniards, wearing a casual leather jacket to work is quite normal. But that could be construed as not taking the business seriously in some other circles.
>
> "Don't assume the man from Texas is slow just because he talks slow. Don't assume the foreigner who is good with English is good at everything else. Conversely, because a foreigner has difficulty communicating doesn't mean he's not extremely good at his job. . . ."In terms of body language, don't assume a person is nodding because he is understanding. The person is probably nodding to say, 'Keep communicating, I'm getting most of it.' "
>
> "There's a tendency to look at Europe as a whole," says Ford communication specialist John Gardiner of the UK, "but even with Europe managerial styles can be quite different. For instance, the British are more like Americans in that meetings can be brainstorming sessions where ideas flow. In Germany you'll often find that meetings are really to put a rubber stamp to things that have been discussed on a one-to-one or private basis beforehand."[27]

SOURCES: "The World That Changed the Machine," *The Economist,* March 30, 1996, pp. 63–64; Rob Cleveland, "Vive la Difference," *Ward's Auto World,* March 1996, p. 119; Tim Stevens, "Managing across Boundaries," *Industry Week,* March 6, 1995, pp. 24–30; David C. Smith, "Kansas City Here I Come. . . : Ford's 'Global Car' Team Gets Set for Job 1," *Ward's Auto World,* July 1994, p. 90.

SUMMARY

The first unofficial ambassadors to other countries are frequently business managers, and the multinational corporation is becoming so common on the international market that it bears the brunt of establishing good cross-cultural relations abroad. American business managers must learn how to relate successfully to people from other cultures to fulfill the role of business in our economy.

Our attitudes toward foreigners can vary from ethnocentrism to reverse ethnocentrism. Ethnocentricity is the view that our way of doing things is the only correct way. Another attitude is that of cultural relativity, which holds that a society's customs should be viewed in the context of that society's culture. Another attitude is that of the pragmatic principle, which means that the idea that works best is the one that should be used if it achieves the necessary valued end. We find that Americans have varying attitudes about foreigners and how to do business with them.

Theory Z tells us that Japanese culture reflects a great deal of mutual trust between the employee and employer, and after an appropriate breaking-in period, even foreigners. The company works hard at developing a strong company image, to attract the best workers for lifelong employment. Where Americans believe in individualism, the Japanese believe in group effort.

The Middle Eastern world is composed of countries that are principally of the Moslem faith. Arabs also have a strong belief in the power of society over the individual; therefore, individual status improvement is very difficult, if not impossible. Authority is not to be questioned, be it religious or governmental. Arabs can be strongly goal oriented and use a closer "inner circle" than Americans.

The European Union, based on an economic alliance formed in 1992, provides at once challenges and opportunities for U.S. human relationships. Job security and powerful European labor unions may dictate the relative success of the European economic community in world markets. Perhaps the greatest challenges are the Pacific Rim countries. The Chinese markets are developing rapidly, but different values—especially long-term orientation—make doing business in China and related cultures different from anywhere else.

The languages of time, space, touch, and context are sources of important cultural differences. They can be worked out if we keep in mind the fundamental concepts of human dignity, empathy, and individual differences, among others. Keep in mind also the basic common bond of humanity, understand that one's own values are not universal, but local to one's own culture, and make a serious effort to respect and understand cultural differences.

CASE STUDY 18–1	## INTERNATIONAL BRIBERY

Henry Cordero works for Maytax Industries, a large multinational corporation with production and research facilities in several foreign countries. Henry is in charge of one of the facilities in a South American country. Henry was recently informed by a member of the country's government that, if Maytax wished to remain operating in the country, it was strongly suggested that the corporation begin contributing to that country's medical research association.

Somewhat shocked, Henry asked if the order was official. He was told by the individual that, although the order did not come officially from the government, it could easily be enforced. Well aware that bribery payments were being demanded, Henry returned to the corporation's home office to discuss the matter with the corporation's vice president, Mr. Manoushek.

After filling in Mr. Manoushek on the details of the demand, Henry was asked what should be done concerning the matter. "It's my opinion," stated Henry, "that we shouldn't become involved in making bribery payments.

Aside from the fact that such payments are against our moral ethics and our system of free enterprise, the American public and our government take a pretty dim view of such matters."

"I agree with you there, Henry," stated Mr. Charles Manoushek, "but I don't think you understand the realities of the problem. In countries such as the one we're dealing with, bribery has been an accepted custom for years and years. Although our country is against this type of thing, many countries abroad are not. We are a corporation that does the majority of our business abroad and we must deal with these countries on their own terms. If we don't, some other company will."

"But if we begin paying these bribery payments every time someone suggests it, where will the demands end?" retorted Henry. "On the other hand, when we begin offering these payments on our own initiative, like Lockheed, Exxon, Gulf, or ITT, and the public finds out, we will be no better off for it. I know company images suffer when the American public finds out about their affairs. If it was my choice, I'd back out of the country if necessary."

"Our duty, Henry, is to our shareholders first, and that duty is protecting our investments abroad. If we must contribute to a country's medical research association to protect our investment, then that is what we must do."

1. Whose side do you favor—Henry Cordero's or Charles Manoushek's? Give reasons for your stand.

2. Is giving small gifts acceptable? When does it stop being a gift and become a bribery payment? At what point do you make the distinction? Is there a dollar value? *Hint:* Could the difference be that a gift is given freely, not solicited?

3. If codes should be established, who will say what is ethical?

4. Companies have stated that there will be no "unusual payments." What is considered unusual?

CASE STUDY 18-2

A PROBLEM OF CULTURAL COMMUNICATION

Harold Underhill walked into the office of the Latin American country's commercial attaché for help. Harold had arrived two weeks earlier from the United States for the purpose of securing a several-million-dollar production order. Harold is the sales manager of a corporation that produces communications systems. When Harold first arrived in the country he had been under the impression that his business would take no more than a few days, and then he could take a few days vacation before returning within his allotted seven-day period.

Upon arriving in the country Harold immediately contacted the minister of communications, whom he needed to have sign the production order. He was then instructed that Minister Muñoz would see him that afternoon. When Harold arrived he was forced to wait in the outer office for a considerable amount of time and then only to be greeted briefly, but politely, by the minister before being ushered out without any business being discussed. Harold was informed that the minister would see him next Wednesday for lunch. Although upset about the delay Harold accepted the invitation.

When Harold and Señor Muñoz did meet the following week for lunch, Harold soon realized that the minister had no intentions of talking business. Somewhat in a panic he tried pressing the fact that he needed the order signed.

As a result of this the minister politely cut short the business conversation and invited Harold to meet him again in a few days.

As a result of these events Harold asked the commercial attaché for his advice. "You must understand," stated the attaché, "that business relations are not the same here as they are in the United States. Things are not always done overnight here. Latin Americans feel a need to spend more time completing business transactions and to get to know who they are doing business with. You should not rush things—let them take the initiative. When you are in their country you must follow their rules of behavior."

When Harold met again with the minister of communications they took a walk in a memorial park near the minister's office. As Señor Muñoz commented on the beauties of the park, Harold failed to recognize the statue of Simon Bolivar, and then he compounded his error by stating that he had never heard of him. Insulted, the minister decided that the pushy, rude American was not the person with whom he wanted to do business and informed both Harold and his employer that he didn't wish to continue negotiations.

1. Identify the American's problem.
2. Name several errors in Underhill's approach.
3. How could Underhill's company have prepared him better for the business transaction?

DISCUSSION AND STUDY QUESTIONS—TO KEEP YOU THINKING . . .

1. What are the differences among ethnocentrism, the pragmatic principle, cultural relativity, and reverse ethnocentrism?

2. Discuss why individuals from other countries are so willing to invest in U.S. companies and real estate.

3. Relate the differences between space and touch in your culture and a culture of another country.

4. Relate the differences between context and friendship in your culture and a culture of another country.

5. Why is the Theory Z approach so successful in Japan? What are its advantages and pitfalls in both Japan and other countries including the United States?

6. Where are the greatest trading opportunities for the United States? What are the pitfalls of each?

7. Are Americans more similar or different than groups from other cultures?

8. What can organizations do to improve their effectiveness in global settings?

NOTES

1. William Van Dusen Wishard, "Humanity as a Single Entity?" *The Futurist*, March–April 1996, p. 60.

2. Steve H. Hanke and Alan Walters, "After Apartheid, What?" *Forbes*, July 18, 1994, p. 84.

3. Phil Van Auken, "International Business Realities That Affect Supervisors," *Supervision*, April 1996, p. 8.

4. *The World Almanac and Book of Facts, 1993* (New York: World Almanac, Scripps Howard, 1993), p. 397.

5. Joel Kotkin and Yoriko Kishimoto, quoted in David M. Smick, "A Guide to the Pacific Rim Phenomenon," *The Wall Street Journal,* December 5, 1988, p. A12.

6. Rochelle Kopp, "International Human Resource Policies and Practices in Japanese, European and United States Multinationals," *Human Resource Management,* Winter 1994, p. 594.

7. Rose Knotts, "Cross-Cultural Management: Transformations and Adaptations," *Business Horizons,* January–February 1989, pp. 32–33.

8. Ibid., p. 33.

9. Joan Tavares, "Building a Leadership Development Program: A Cross-Cultural Collaboration," *Issues & Observations,* published by Center for Creative Leadership, Greensboro, North Carolina, Fourth Quarter 1995, p. 9.

10. Knotts, "Cross-Cultural Management," p. 32.

11. "Don't Be an Ugly-American Manager," *Fortune,* October 16, 1995, p. 225.

12. F. Kluckhohn and F. L. Strodtbeck, *Variations in Value Orientations* (Evanston, Ill.: Row, Peterson, 1961).

13. Geert Hofstede, "Cultural Constraints in Management Theories," *Academy of Management Executive,* February 1993, p. 81.

14. Ibid., p. 90.

15. Leah Nathans, "A Matter of Control," *Business Month,* September 1988, p. 46.

16. Richard H. Reeves-Ellington, "Using Cultural Skills for Cooperative Advantage in Japan," *Human Organization,* Summer 1993, pp. 206–207, 212.

17. Ibid., p. 213.

18. Special Report, "China: The Making of an Economic Giant," *Business Week,* May 17, 1993, p. 58.

19. Richard D. Lewis, "Where Time Moves in Mysterious Ways," *Management Today,* January 1996, p. 77.

20. Robin Pascoe, "Employers Ignore Expatriate Wives at Their Own Peril," *The Wall Street Journal,* March 2, 1992, p. A10.

21. Ibid.

22. Sylvia Odenwald, "A Guide for Global Training," *Training & Development,* July 1993, pp. 24–29.

23. J. Paul Tom, "Abroad at Home," *Across the Board,* September 1992, p. 36.

24. Brian Croft, "Use Technology to Manage Your Expats," *Personnel Journal,* December 1995, pp. 113–117.

25. Charlene Marmer Solomon, "Repatriation: Up, Down or Out?" *Personnel Journal,* January 1995, p. 29.

26. "The World That Changed the Machine," *The Economist,* March 30, 1996, p. 63.

27. Tim Stevens, "Managing across Boundaries," *Industry Week,* March 6, 1995, p. 30.

RECOMMENDED READING

Derderian, Stephanie. "International Success Lies in Cross-Cultural Training." *HR Focus,* April 1993, p. 9.

Harris, Philip R., and Robert T. Moran. *Managing Cultural Differences: Leadership Strategies for a New World of Business.* 4th ed. Houston: Gulf, 1996.

Hofstede, Geert. "Cultural Constraints in Management Theories." *Academy of Management Executive,* February 1993, pp. 81–94.

———. *Uncommon Sense about Organizations: Case Studies and Field Observations.* Thousand Oaks, Calif.: Sage Publications, 1994.

Kaltenhauser, Skip. "China: Doing Business under an Immoral Government." *Business Ethics,* May–June 1995, pp. 20–23.

McRae, Hamish. *The World in 2020: Power, Culture and Prosperity.* Boston: Harvard Business School Press, 1995.

Munter, Mary. "Cross-Cultural Communication for Managers." *Business Horizons,* May–June 1993, pp. 69–78.

Odenwald, Sylvia. *Global Training: How to Design a Program for the Multinational Corporation.* Homewood, Ill.: Business One-Irwin, 1993.

Reeves-Ellington, Richard H. "Using Cultural Skills for Cooperative Advantage in Japan." *Human Organization,* Summer 1993, pp. 203–215.

Skelly, Joe. "Principles of Business: The Rise of International Ethics." *Business Ethics,* May–June 1995, pp. 24–27.

Solomon, Charlene Marmer. "Global Teams: The Ultimate Collaboration." *Personnel Journal,* September 1995, pp. 49–58.

Tu, Howard, and Sherry E. Sullivan. "Preparing Yourself for an International Assignment." *Business Horizons,* January–February 1994, pp. 67–70.

Wetlaufer, Suzy. "Foreign Subsidiaries: Determining Executive Compensation." *Harvard Business Review,* March–April 1996, pp. 11–12.

GLOSSARY

ability promotion A promotion based on the potential that an employee has to hold an advanced position.

action orientation A predisposition to take action as opposed to further time-consuming study and deliberation.

affirmative action A federal mandate requiring an employer to make efforts to employ qualified members of minority groups.

Age Discrimination in Employment Acts Laws protecting older workers.

alcoholic (industrial definition) Any employee whose repeated overindulgence in alcohol sharply reduces job effectiveness and dependability.

American Federation of Labor and Congress of Industrial Organizations (AFL-CIO) A national organization of many of the craft and industrial unions.

Americans with Disabilities Act Act requiring employers to accommodate disabled individuals.

anger An emotional feeling of distress, as opposed to a physical manifestation of anger, which is hostility.

apartheid The former government-mandated economic and physical separation of races in South Africa.

arbitrator A neutral third party who conducts fact-finding and mandates binding resolution of labor disputes.

assertiveness training Teaches people to stand up for their feelings in a straightforward, deliberate way of handling emotions.

attitudes Predispositions, mental states, emotions, or moods important to the well-being of both the individual and the organization.

A-type conflict Affective conflict that lowers team effectiveness by provoking hostility, distrust, cynicism, and apathy among team members.

autocratic leader Leader who is task oriented, quick to make decisions, looks after organizational goals, and probably believes in close supervision.

behavior modification A technique to bring about behavioral change by frequently rewarding positive behaviors and failing to reward improper responses.

behaviorally anchored rating scales Identify expectations of performance in specific behavioral terms.

belonging needs The social needs to be loved, accepted, and receive affection, or team spirit needs.

benefits Forms of tangible compensation given to employees other than direct pay.

benevolent autocrat An autocrat who uses reward power to manipulate or sell subordinates on the goals of the leader.

biases Predispositions to act and decide on preconceived notions rather than rational analysis.

biofeedback A system of electronic recording and feeding back of information about physiological responses.

black pride Determination by a black that he or she can determine his or her own destiny and own future.

blue-collar jobs Principally physical jobs, including construction, manufacturing, and some service industries.

body language The ability to observe the body movement of a person and interpret that person's attitudes and feelings.

brainstorming A conference technique of developing new alternatives by unrestrained discussions.

business ethics Taking into consideration the effects of one's decisions on many publics—employees, customers, even competitors.

career development All of the activities necessary to help individuals become aware of and acquire the knowledge, skills, and competencies to perform different jobs.

career paths Alternative progressions through jobs in an organization planned by both individuals and the organization.

catalytic leadership Stimulates involvement and thinking by subordinates, helping them to push the boundaries of their jobs.

central tendency bias The tendency of an evaluator to rate all of an employee's abilities and performance as average; it may also be the tendency to rate all the employees as average.

certification An election used by the NLRB to determine whether an identified union will represent employees.

change A function of effort over time to learn new methods.

Civil Rights Act of 1964 The vanguard of civil rights legislation. It includes prohibitions against employment discrimination because of a person's race, color, religion, sex, or national origin.

closed shop Shop in which only union members can be hired.

collective bargaining The process by which representatives of employees and management convene to negotiate a working agreement or other work rules.

commitment Allowing people to do things on their own willingly.

communication The process by which senders and receivers of messages transfer information and understanding.

comparable worth A belief that women performing jobs judged to be comparable on bases of knowledge, skills, and abilities should be paid the same as men.

comparative management The study of how management and leadership practices vary across different cultures.

compassion A feeling for and understanding of another person's difficult situation.

completed development work A corollary to compulsory advisory services, it means doing a thorough job of problem definition and solution.

compulsory advisory service This concept states that the advice and counsel of others must at least be heard by decision makers.

conciliation Making peace among the parties to a dispute by soothing anger and conflict.

connection power Based on the powerholder's ability to relate to influential people.

consensus An attempt to arrive at a solution acceptable to most group members.

containment All relations with a union are kept on a strictly legal basis, and the scope of collective bargaining is as narrow as possible.

contingency model A model developed by Fred Fiedler that attempts to identify a person's leadership style and then tries to analyze the job situation and determine the best possible combination of leader and job.

cooperation Management seeks the assistance of the union in production problems that are not usually the subject matter of collective bargaining.

cooperative conflict theory When people believe their goals are compatible, there is increased cooperation in reaching goals.

cooperative counseling A combination of some aspects of direct and nondirect counseling such as the advice and authority typical of directive methods, and the nonjudgmental and active listening of nondirective methods.

core job dimensions Key influences of skill variety, task identity and significance, autonomy, feedback, and interpersonal dimensions for the job characteristics model.

corporate/organizational values A composite of personal values and more, because of the synergistic (the sum of all parts is greater than the individual values) effect.

courtesy Goes beyond politeness or kindness; it means being civil to other people—customers, coworkers, subordinates, and others.

creativity The ability to produce original ideas, expressions, or products from diverse resources.

crisis A major, unpredictable event that has potentially negative results.

critical incident technique The written documentation of an employee's behavior, good or bad, which is put in his or her personnel file to be used later during the appraisal period.

critical path The sequence of in-series activities requiring the longest time for completion.

cross-cultural relations Requires working with people who live and work in foreign cultures.

C-type conflict Improves team effectiveness because team members participate in frank communication.

cultural relativity Principle that holds that there are no absolute standards for judging customs.

cultural stereotypes General ideas or fixed opinions about groups of people.

culture Comprised of the values, beliefs, customs, and norms shared by people in a society.

custodial person More satisfied with the status quo and less inclined to adopt creative change.

cyberspace Global systems interconnection whereby every computer and telecommunications network may have access to the same information space.

decibel A measure of noise; 50 decibels is the measure of a normal conversation.

decision A commitment—a resolution to do or stop doing an act, or to adopt or reject an attitude.

decision making A discovery process that includes several steps including choosing among alternatives; not a single step of deciding.

deductive method (of orientation/learning/training) The ability to learn the general concepts followed by more detailed aspects.

defense mechanisms Ways in which an individual may try to reduce the tensions caused by frustrations.

delegation Assignment of authority to another person to carry out a task and that person's acceptance of the task.

Delphi technique A group process of decision making that extends a statistical method to include feedback and reestimates.

density The percentage of civilians in the workforce who are union members or otherwise represented.

depressants Drugs designed to relax a person but that can become addicting.

designer drugs Tailor-made, synthetic drugs whose degree of potency and duration of effect can be laboratory controlled.

development Activity that puts emphasis on increasing the participant's abilities to perform effectively in other jobs as well as the current job.

developmental purpose (of performance appraisals) Allows individuals to know how they are doing so they can continue to improve on their strengths and alleviate their weaknesses.

disciplinary action One method of achieving discipline; usually more punitive than other methods.

discipline A state of order, positive morale, and readiness to achieve organizational objectives effectively.

discrimination An act of prejudice against a person or a group of people.

disparate impact Occurs when standards appear to be neutral, but there is an underrepresentation of a group in hiring, promotions, compensation, or other personnel decisions.

disparate treatment Occurs when different standards are used to treat different classes of employees.

distortion Any distractions to the communication process, such as stereotyping.

distress Negative stress that can have overpowering effects on individuals.

diversity training   A business strategy to sensitize all employees to the unique culture and characteristics of its entire workforce.

driving forces   Forces that encourage change.

drug abuse   Condition of individuals who are "hooked" on drugs of any type to the point that they cannot function without them.

dual careers   Career commitments for both husband and wife.

dual loyalty   Employee loyalty felt for both employer and union.

elasticity of time   The length of time it takes to accomplish a task.

empathy   The ability to put yourself in someone else's place and to understand that person's motives and points of view.

employee assistance programs   Provide counseling and other remedies to employees having substance abuse, emotional, or other personal problems.

employee empowerment   Means to give power or authority, to give ability, to enable or enfranchise employees to do their jobs.

employment at will   Doctrine that holds that an employer can hire, promote, demote, or dismiss an employee at will with or without good cause.

enculturation   Learning cultural practices and values.

entrepreneur   A person who creates or perceives new kinds of demands and applies innovative techniques for meeting those demands.

entrepreneurship   Creation of wealth or other utilitarian characteristics by adding value; may involve risks.

Equal Employment Opportunity Commission   A federal government agency that establishes guidelines for hiring, recruiting, and promoting minority groups.

equilibrium   A balance between cautious resistance and constant change.

equity   Fairness, which may manifest itself in internal, external, or individual consistency within an organization.

equity approach to motivation   Workers try to maintain balance between their own inputs and their rewards in comparison to other workers.

ERG approach to motivation   A hierarchical approach to motivation based on three sets of needs: (1) existence, (2) relatedness, and (3) growth.

ergonomics   The study of work, focusing on the dynamics of man/machine interfaces and the best design to accommodate humans.

ethnocentrism   A feeling that a culture's attitude is the only correct one.

eustress   Positive type of stress that has its foundations in meeting the challenges of a task or job.

expectancy approach to motivation   Based on the strength of an individual's belief that a course of action will result in a given performance and reward.

experiential methods   Any kind of training in which the participants interact and express their feelings.

expert power   Personal power based on skill and knowledge.

Fair Labor Standards Act   Regulates the minimum wage, limits the number of hours that employees can work without being paid overtime, and discourages child labor.

feedback   The process of reacting to a person's message, either verbally or nonverbally.

field review   A multiple appraisal or review of an employee's performance.

filtering   An example of distortion of the communication process where the receiver hears only what she or he wants to hear.

flat organizational structure   An organization that has fewer levels in its hierarchy than a tall structure. There are fewer supervisors, and each one has more people to supervise.

flextime   Allows employees to set their own work schedules within defined limits.

footcandle   A measure of light intensity.

force-field analysis   A technique that assesses current state, positive and negative forces working to change the equilibrium or status quo.

formal communications   Structured, stable methods of communicating between people and their superiors, subordinates, or peers.

free-rein leaders   Group-centered leaders who allow people to govern themselves and base decisions on "one person, one vote."

future shock   A reaction of human and other systems to rapid change.

glass ceiling   A see-through barrier that prevents advancement for women and other protected groups to higher level jobs.

goal congruency   Maximizing the overlap between organizational objectives and individuals' goals.

grapevine   The informal channel of communications between people.

graphic rating scale   An appraisal form that is checked to show how well an employee is doing in various aspects related to her or his job.

grievance   A complaint about an alleged violation of a collective bargaining agreement or the law as it applies to a worker.

group   A collection of people who either meet personally or in absentia for the purpose of accomplishing a social or work objective.

group cohesiveness   Both a cause and effect of group size and ability to reach consensus.

group dynamics   Social processes by which small groups interact; the effect that individuals collectively have on each other.

groupthink   The condition of everyone adopting the ideas and views of the group.

hallucinogens   Drugs that alter time and space perceptions and cause hallucinations.

halo effect   A supervisor or other rater assumes that, if an employee is above average in one area, the employee is above average in all areas.

Hawthorne studies   Conducted by Elton Mayo and his colleagues, this work began by studying the effects of illumination, ventilation, and fatigue on workers at the Hawthorne plant of Western Electric and revealed how human relations affected productivity.

heuristic   An approach to decision making that is intuitive, self-discovery oriented.

high tech/high touch   In the age of technological information, where individuals work alone at home, or "telecommute," there must be corresponding human responses.

homeostasis   The balance or equilibrium between two opposing forces: an effort to develop change within an organization or, conversely, to resist such a change.

homosexual   The most generally accepted designation for same-sex orientation.

honesty/integrity   Refraining from lying, cheating, or stealing; it is being truthful, trustworthy, and sincere, and being willing to accept responsibility even when things go wrong.

horizontal communications   Communications between people of equal status, at the same level in a hierarchy of authority.

hotelling   Workers who spend most of their time working at clients' locations and need no desk within their own company.

human goals   Influenced by many different kinds of social and psychological factors as well as by the organizational condition of the work environment. Examples: job satisfaction, recognition, and career advancement.

human relations   Refers to all the interactions that can occur among people, whether organizational or personal, conflicting or cooperating.

hygiene/motivation approach   Herzberg's approach that hygiene or maintenance factors only prompt us to keep from being dissatisfied and are not self-motivating; motivators take place on the job and help us to enjoy working.

in-basket technique   A technique of training designed to teach people to plan, organize, and delegate their responsibilities.

incentive   An inducement offered to influence future performance of an individual or team, or a total organizational unit.

incubation   The subconscious part of the creative process.

individual differences   For any given variable, such as mental ability, there are marked differences among people.

individual with disability   Someone who has a physical or mental condition that substantially impairs a "major life activity."

inductive method (of orientation/learning/training)   More general information is added to the learning pattern once some specifics are learned.

informal communication   Grows out of the social interactions among people who work together.

informal groups   More people-oriented than formal groups, they concentrate on sentiments derived from activities and interactions of the group members.

informal organization   Exerts tremendous influence over workers' behavior patterns.

inner circle   The personal space we keep between others and ourselves.

innovation   The action-oriented end product of creative activity; it can take place in processes as well as in people's activities and behaviors.

intelligence   The ability to solve complex and unusual problems.

intercultural socialization   Becoming aware of another culture's habits, actions, and reasons behind behaviors.

intrapreneur   An entrepreneur within a large organization who exhibits creative characteristics.

intrinsic motivators   Take place on the job and help us to enjoy working.

intuition   A way of knowing and recognizing the possible consequences of something without conscious reasoning.

invention   An idea; not necessarily an object or piece of work.

isolationism   A policy of seclusion from international commerce and politics.

job cycle   The length of time required to perform an operation before starting the task again.

job description   The beginning point in defining what is to be done on a job; should include responsibilities, relationships, duties (tasks), and performance elements.

job design   Includes all variables that will increase the quality and quantity of worker performance; a conscious effort to organize tasks, duties, and responsibilities into a work unit.

job enlargement   Enlargement of a position to include more duties.

job enrichment   The view that a job may include duties that are more complex and hence grant more responsibility and authority.

job performance   Determining the job to be done, the standards by which job completion is measured, and tying results to a reward system.

job rotation   Performance in several different jobs to learn a whole system and alleviate boredom.

job satisfaction   A personal matter based on each individual's value system and attitudes held about the job.

job sharing   Allows individuals, who might have time constraints because of other work, home, or school responsibilities, to be productive for their organizations by dividing a job, usually held by one individual, into jobs held by two or more employees.

kinesics   Another term for body language, the study of body movement.

labor union   An organization of employees formed for the purpose of furthering the interests of union members.

Landrum-Griffin Act of 1959   A bill of rights for union members designed to protect them from abuses of their own unions.

language of context   Based on the amount of communication contained in a nonverbal context compared with the amount in the formal message.

"leaderless" groups   *See* Substitutes for leadership.

leadership   The ability to influence the actions of others.

leadership continuum   Plots alternative ways for leaders to approach decision making, depending on how much participation is desired.

learning   Relatively permanent change in knowledge or skill produced by experience.

legitimate power   Organizational power based on position.

listening   An active, receiving half of the communication equation; involves hearing, understanding, remembering, and acting on information.

loyalty   Being aware, having the foresight to appreciate and involve employees, rewarding and being responsive to employee needs.

maintenance-related roles   Those behavioral expectations directly related to the well-being and development of the group.

management   An integrated hierarchy and team of people whose activities must be coordinated to achieve specific objectives.

management by objectives/results   A method of measuring achievement in which the supervisor and the employee determine specific goals and results for the employee to meet within a given time frame.

management games   Games played by teams of employees that simulate departments or companies and engage in competition.

Managerial Grid   A model based on a matrix of values 1 through 9 for two primary variables: a manager's concern for people and management's concern for productivity.

mandated change   A change demanded by someone in authority.

maquiladoras   Mexican firms that manufacture or assemble products for U.S. companies.

matrix organization   A team of people brought together from different departments to work on a product or project.

mediator   A neutral third party who is called to review both sides of a disputed issue.

meditation   A method of silent thinking used to learn how to be calm and alert through relaxing and concentrating on a thought.

merit promotion   A promotion based on past performance rather than on the ability to perform the duties of the advanced position.

morale   A composite state of mind and emotions that affects a group's mental condition and confidence.

motivation   An internal concept based on a person's needs and the fulfillment of those needs.

multinational corporations   Companies that operate in more than one country.

Murphy's laws   Among others: nothing is as simple as it looks; everything takes longer than it should; and if anything can go wrong, it will.

National Labor Relations Act of 1935   Commonly called the Wagner Act, it guarantees workers' rights to form unions to represent them.

National Labor Relations Board   An agency of the federal government set up to investigate cases of unfair labor practices by employers or unions.

nationalization   The taking over of private companies, often under foreign control, by the host country.

negative reinforcement   A limitation or withdrawal of a variable in the workplace.

neurolinguistic programming (NLP)   A model for understanding human behavior and a set of learning techniques based on the belief that people have a preferred mode of acquiring and processing information.

nominal group technique   A fairly structured decision process with the interpersonal characteristics of face-to-face groups.

nondirective counseling   A method that allows people to talk out their own problems, via catharsis. The counselor listens, helps in clarifying the problem, but gives no advice.

norm of reciprocity   An obligation to return consideration to another for continuance of a mutually beneficial relationship.

norms   Ideas or values that a group has regarding expected behaviors of individuals or group members.

occupational identity   The identity that one has by virtue of the job.

OD intervention   A systematic attempt by OD professionals to effect organizational change.

older worker   Usually means those over 65 but can mean those over 40 or 55, depending on the occupation; may also mean 10 to 15 years from retirement.

on-the-job training (OJT)   The burden is on the trainer—human or machine—to provide applied instruction.

open-door policy   In theory, this policy allows low-level workers to walk into the manager's office; in practice, the policy works better if the boss walks out to the workers.

organization chart   Shows an organization's structure in a kind of drawing indicating formal, official channels through which messages flow.

organization development (OD)   A long-term, systematic, and organizationwide change effort designed to increase an organization's total effectiveness.

organizational behavior   The study of how people, groups, and organizations behave.

organizational communication   Any communication that takes place within a total organization—usually formal and written messages, as opposed to informal, interpersonal communication.

organizational design   The macroscopic term that includes an organization's structure and its processes for decision making, communication, and performance management.

organizational engineering   A method of creating and maintaining effective leadership by frequent evaluation and changes in roles.

organizational power The capacity of managers to exert influence over others; derived from higher level management.

organizational structure Characterized by mechanisms including communication that are used to coordinate and control activities of organizational members.

organizational transformation A way of thinking and action, and commitment to change, required to create a new type of employee relationship and empowerment.

organized employee representation Unions or other groups selected to represent employees to management.

orientation Formal means by which employees learn about their new employer, their jobs, and coworkers.

parochialism An attitude that the world is always like our own world.

participative leader Leader who allows employees to express their feelings about situations but reserves the right to make the final decision.

path-goal approach Based on subordinate characteristics (ability, needs) and environmental factors (formal authority systems, primary work groups).

pay-for-knowledge Compensation plans that put emphasis on abilities to complete certifiable skills rather than points for subjective job evaluation.

pay-for-mastery Takes pay-for-knowledge one step further by requiring mastery of the work that employees perform.

peer appraisal Soliciting opinions and factual information from peers regarding an individual's performance.

perception A matter of individuals' beholding what others believe or see to be truly representative of a situation; it may be accurate or distorted.

performance appraisal Goes beyond performance evaluation by looking at potential for future development as well as past performance.

performance evaluation A method by which to measure a worker's performance on the job and let him or her know how they are doing.

performance measurement Determining how specific behaviors match pre-determined performance standards.

performance standards Criteria to be used for measuring job performance.

perseverance The resolution and determination to succeed in tasks regardless of temporary setbacks or failures.

personal power Obtained from the acceptance of followers, not usually derived from higher level management.

personal values Values that individuals hold and allow to guide their activities including work.

Peter Principle Named after Professor Lawrence Peter, this principle states that employees are promoted to their highest levels of incompetence.

playing politics A positive way of distributing power in offices and other organizations.

polarization The establishment of two opposing views, with both parties unwilling to change their opinion as to how a problem should be solved.

policy orientation (induction) Informing employees of company policies and benefits.

polydrug user A person who uses more than one drug in a given time, such as alcohol and depressants or alcohol and marijuana.

positive reinforcement Incentives and rewards for behaving in certain ways in the workplace.

positive sandwich technique Bad news between slices of good feelings.

power A person's ability to influence others, not just their behavior.

power plays Working behind the scenes to get what you want.

pragmatic principle The belief that the principle that works best is the one that should be used.

prejudice An attitude or habit of mind usually based on ignorance, fear, or cultural bias.

procedural orientation (process orientation) Making employees aware of locations and procedures that affect their abilities to do their jobs.

prodromal phase of alcohol addiction Warning or signaling disease; behavior that heralds the change to this phase is the occurrence of "blackouts" or amnesia-like periods during drinking.

professional A career type that is recognized by others as a profession.

Program Evaluation Review Technique (PERT) Evaluates projects at each step along a completion line to determine new input and how it will affect the final outcome.

programmed instruction A self-teaching method whereby small amounts of information are presented in logical sequence to the learner. After being presented with a small amount of information, the learner is tested.

project management A method for managing short-term, specific tasks.

proxemics The physical distance people put between themselves.

quality circles Voluntary groups of employees engaged in decision making at the lowest practical level of the organization.

quality of work life (QWL) Concept of making work meaningful for employees in an organizational environment where they are motivated to perform well and are satisfied with their work.

reasonable accommodation—individual with disability Any change in the work environment or in the way things are done that enables an individual with a disability to enjoy employment opportunities.

reasonable accommodation—religious preferences Employers are expected to consider religious beliefs in assigning work.

recency bias An employee may receive a higher or lower evaluation depending on his or her most recent performance.

referent others concept Individuals compare their rewards with others who have similar backgrounds, abilities, and responsibilities.

referent power   A following based on personal power, almost charismatic.

reinforcement   Repeated rewards that are timed to reward immediately following a desired behavior.

repatriation   The process of transferring employees back to their home country—economically, socially, and organizationally.

restraining forces   Forces that discourage change.

resumé   A summary of your educational and work accomplishments and goals.

reverse ethnocentrism   A belief that our ways, rather than being better than others, are actually worse than others.

right-to-work laws   State laws that prohibit closed and union shops.

role ambiguity   The condition that exists when a person is not too sure how to act or perform in a given situation.

role behaviors   Things that people actually do.

role conflict   Occurs when an individual lacks a clear understanding of expectations or when there is conflict about the expectations.

role playing   A simulation and experiential exercise in problem solving; participants are given descriptions of attitudes of the people they are to represent, which they develop and dramatize as best they can.

role prescriptions   Things that people are expected to do.

rumor   Information based on speculation, wishes, or imagination.

scientific management   This approach holds that greater productivity can be achieved by breaking down work into isolated, specialized tasks.

self-actualization   The realization of one's fullest potential; knowing the zenith of your ability and achieving it.

self-disclosure   The act of opening up your personality—your weaknesses as well as your strengths—to others.

self-fulfilling prophecy   What you expect of others determines the reactions of others.

semantics   The meaning given to individual words. Each of us may give different meanings to the same word at different times. Example: love.

sensitivity training   A technique used to teach individuals to understand how they function in a group setting and how a group functions.

sexism   Job discrimination based on gender.

sexual harassment   Unwanted attention of a sexual nature that occurs in the process of working or seeking work, and that interferes with a person's work ability.

shop steward   A representative for a specific group of workers who is generally elected by the workers in her or his department.

simulation   Replication of a real-life situation in a controlled environment.

situational leadership   Developed by Hersey and Blanchard, this approach suggests the leader match styles to subordinates' maturity levels.

social leaders   Concerned with the group working together and everyone understanding the others' points of view.

social stratification   Ranking of people within society, by others, into higher and lower social positions to produce a hierarchy of prestige.

sociogram   A graphic illustration of who is or is not communicating with whom and how frequently.

sociometry   The measurement of activities and feelings of group members toward one another.

span of management   The number of people that one person can supervise effectively and directly.

status   Ranking or ordering of people into relative positions of prestige and the social rewards offered with such positions.

status anxiety   Difficulty in changing role behavior to each of the status roles.

status inconsistency   Any discrepancy due to different status assignments awarded by society.

status symbols   External evidence of value that individuals attach to behaviors, people, and "things."

stereotypes   Overgeneralized beliefs based partially on ignorance.

stewardship   The willingness to be accountable for the well-being of the larger organization.

stimulants   Any drug that induces a feeling of excitement and energy and permits going without sleep for prolonged periods.

stress   Pressure, strain, or force on a system.

substitutes for leadership   A series of attributes that permit less direct leadership; these factors include subordinate ability, responsibility, routine tasks, and specific organizational plans.

synergy   The total outcome is greater than the sum of the individual parts.

Taft-Hartley Act of 1947   Amendments to the National Labor Relations Act, which provided a list of unfair labor practices on the part of labor (unions).

task leader   Contributes most to the achievement of the task; the task takes priority over the group's or the individual's concerns.

task-related roles   Those behavioral expectations that directly aid in the accomplishment of group objectives.

team   A cohesive group that works to accomplish specific tasks in a supportive environment.

teamwork   Working together to identify and solve group-related problems.

telecommuting   Allows employees to improve their productivity by working where they are at their peak or prime times of performance.

Theory Z   Founded in strong Japanese cultural tradition, uses ideas like consensus-building, mutual loyalty, a long-term perspective and cooperation.

360-degree feedback   A system that solicits appraisals of an employee's performance from many stakeholders including peers, customers, and suppliers.

total quality management (TQM) A comprehensive approach to quality that encourages everyone in the organization to provide customers with reliable products and services.

training Specific activity for improving the trainee's abilities to perform in particular jobs.

transactional analysis A method of studying communication by learning of the three ego states of child, adult, and parent.

transformational leaders Leaders capable of effecting major changes in their organizations because of their vision and willingness to give individual consideration to and empower employees through intellectual stimulation.

trust Reliance on another with respect to a given situation.

Type A behavior Highly competitive, pressured-for-time behavior that may result in reacting to frustration with hostility.

Type B behavior Behavior exhibited by people who have more interests in leisure activities than Type A persons; they may be more productive in the long run.

Type H behavior A subset of Type A behavior; the H refers to hostility.

ugly American The image of the impolite, inarticulate, and patronizing foreigner barging through foreign countries like a barbarian.

unfair labor practices (labor) Specific practices outlawed by federal law such as coercion, refusal to bargain, and certain strikes on the part of an employee organization (unions).

unfair labor practices (management) Specific practices outlawed by federal law such as coercion and interference on the part of employers.

union shops Requires individuals to join a union before they can be hired.

upward appraisal Obtaining feedback from subordinates on the supervisor's performance.

values Customs or qualities within a society that are regarded in a particular way as guiding principles for behavior and action.

vertical communications Communications that flow both up and down the organization.

virtual company Organizations that start a business with no physical office space.

visionary leadership Having the foresight to set a direction for a specific goal.

wellness programs Company-sponsored programs whose purpose is to improve and maintain employees' health and productivity.

white-collar jobs Principally office workers, managers, and some professionals.

whole person The interrelationships of the mind and the body, and their total effect on the individual.

whole-brain theories Based on a presumed preference for one of the two hemispheres of the brain.

whole-job concept The view that the employee is responsible for completing the entire task rather than a small portion of the task.

work Purposeful activity, as natural as other life relationships.

workaholic A person who takes great satisfaction in work but may carry that commitment to an extreme preoccupation that endangers health.

X leader Autocratic-type leader who is task oriented, is quick to make decisions, looks after organizational goals, and may believe in close supervision.

Y leader Democratic, participative leader who allows employees to express their feelings about situations but reserves the right to make the final decision.

zero-defects management A type of quality management that emphasizes products and services adhering to exact standards.

INDEX

Exercise, physical, 72
Expectancy approach, 140–41
Experiential training, 358–64

Facsimile (FAX) communication, 243
Fair Labor Standards Act, 512
Feedback, 197, 207–209, 395
Firing an employee, 394–96
Flexibility, 151
Flextime, 87
Followership, 309–10
Frustration, 146–48

Gender:
    and creativity, 412
    and job satisfaction, 170
Glass ceiling, 491
Goal congruency, 130–31
Goal setting, 143, 383–85, 464
Grapevine, 215, 217
Grievance, 523–28
Griggs (U.S. Supreme Court decision), 499
Group, 251
    behavior, 249–62, 274
    cohesiveness, 254–55
    consensus, 255–56 (see also
        Consensus)
    dynamics, 251–54, 461
    norms, 252, 472
    roles, 258–60
    size, 252–53
Groupthink, 261, 438–39
Growth needs, 138, 142

Halo effect, 388
Hawthorne Study, 11
Herzberg's hygiene/motivation approach, 138–140
Heuristic approach to decision making, 423
High context, 559
"High-tech" society, 456
Hispanic-Americans, 482–83
Hofstede model, 551–53
Homeostasis, 453
Honesty, 38–40
H-type behavior, 68–69
Human relations, 4–5, 27–28, 31–32
Human resource information systems (HRIS), 161, 166
Humor, 45–46
Hygiene/motivation approach, 138–40

In-basket method (of training), 354–57
Incentives, 143–44, 398–400
Indians, American, 482–84
Individual differences, 21, 31–32
Informal organization, 12, 133

Information society, 455–56
Innovation, 409–410, 422–25
Integrity, 38–40
Intelligence, 412
Internationalism, 533–34
Interview:
    appraisal, 377–79
    counseling, 113–16
Intrapreneurs, 419–20
Intuition, 430

Japan, 13, 319–20, 553–54
Job characteristics model, 152–53
Job cycle, 171
Job description, 161–62, 375–76
Job design, 148–52
Job discrimination, 475–507
Job enlargement, 150
Job enrichment, 150
Job loading, 148–50
Job performance, 161–68, 175–82
Job rotation, 150
Job satisfaction, 168–77
    blue-collar, 170–71
    white and pink-collar, 171
Job sharing, 87, 150
Job status, 295–300

Kluckhohn-Strodtbeck model, 551
Knowledge workers, 41–42

Labor unions, 11, 512–40
Landrum-Griffin Act of 1959, 512
Layoffs, 396–97
Leaderless groups, 333–34
Leaders, 306–38
    informal, 133, 336–37
    social, 261–62
    task, 261–62
Leadership, 24, 55, 306–38
    catalytic, 327
    democratic, 317–18
    free-rein, 319
    informal group, 333, 336–37
    participative, 317–18
    path-goal, 324–25
    situational, 323, 325–26
    style, 314–15, 335–36
    traits, 312–14
Learning, 41–42, 348
Least preferred co-worker, 322–23
Lighting, 185–86
Line and staff relationships, 226–28
Listening, 110–12, 197–98, 202–203
Low context, 559
Loyalty, 40, 400
    dual or divided (with unions), 519–20
    mutual trust and, 320

Magnanimity, 89
Management, 4, 26–27
    attitudes, 419
    and unions, 528–29
Management by objectives/results (MBO/R), 142–43, 384–85
Management by walking (or wandering) around (MBWA), 79, 166–67
Management development, 349–50
Managerial Grid, 321–22
Maslow's need hierarchy, 133–36
Massachusetts Institute of Technology (MIT), 9–10
Matrix organization, 229–30
Maturity, 89
Mediation, 525
Meditation, 364
Meetings, 79–80
Mentor, 85
Merit increases, 399–400
Mid-life crisis, 257
Mirroring, 115
Monotony, of work, 177
Morale, 168–87, 189
Motivation, 23–24, 127–58
Multinational corporations, 547–48 (see also Cross-cultural relations)
Murphy's laws, 470–71

National Labor Relations Act, 510
National Organization of Women (NOW), 489–90
Nationalization, 549
Needs, 129–30, 133–36
Neurolinguistic programming (NLP), 212–13
Noise, 183–84, 206
Nominal group technique (NGT), 435
Nonverbal communication, 210–13
Norm of reciprocity, 280
Not-Invented-Here (NIH) syndrome, 452

Occupational status, 451
Older workers, 485–88
On-the-job training (OJT), 352
Open-door policy, 236
Organization charts, 231
Organization development (OD), 463–64
Organizational design, 224
Organizational structure, 224–26
Organizational transformation, 18–19
Orientation, 341–45

Participation, 317–18, 457–58
Path-goal approach, 324–25
Patience, 44
Pay, 144, 165–66, 292
    discrimination, 488–93